Dic

Dictionary of English Spelling

MARTIN H. MANSER

Wordsworth Reference

Readers who are interested in other titles from
Wordsworth Editions are invited to visit out website at
www.wordsworth-editions.com

For our latest list and a full mail-order service contact
Bibliophile Books, 5 Thomas Road, London E14 7BN
Tel: +44 0207 515 9222 Fax: +44 0207 538 4115
e-mail: orders@bibliophilebooks.com

The edition published 1999 by Wordsworth Editions Limited
8B East Street, Ware, Hertfordshire SG12 9HJ
Reset in 2005

Copyright © Wordsworth Editions Limited 1999

ISBN 1 84022 314 6

Wordsworth® is a registered trademark of
Wordsworth Editions Limited

All rights reserved. This publication maynot be reproduced, stored in a retrieval system or transmitted in any form or by any means, electronic, mechanical, photocopying, recording or otherwise, without the prior permission of the publishers.

2 4 6 8 10 9 7 5 3 1

Typeset by Antony Gray
Printed and bound in Great Britain by
Mackays of Chatham plc, Chatham, Kent

INTRODUCTION

This dictionary has been designed as a simple guide to the spelling of English words. If you think you know how a word is spelled, then by looking it up in the dictionary you can find out whether you are right.

Some words have two or more spellings in common use, but only the most frequently used spellings are included in this dictionary. Where two spellings are included, the preferred form in standard English is given first.

Entries consist of the main entry word in bold type, definitions, and a list of undefined words. The definitions are brief statements of the word's meaning and are not meant to be exhaustive. They are designed to help you see that you are checking the word you want.

To allow for space for the greatest number of words, some words are included under their base forms – these are undefined words. There is an important rule to remember about the order of the undefined words. If the main entry word is a noun and its plural is irregular, or there might be doubt about what the plural form is, the plural is given first. All other undefined words are then listed in alphabetical order:

child young person; boy or girl
children child-bearing childbirth childhood childless child-minder childproof

Note that in the list of undefined words the spelling of noun forms is given, but where the noun comes from a verb, the verb – which is not shown – is written as two words:

check to examine or inspect; to slow or stop
check-in check-list check-out checkpoint checkup

Here, *check-in, check-out,* and *check-up* are the spelling of the nouns. The *verbs* are spelled as two words: *check in, check out,* and *check up.* Usage of the hyphen varies. There is an increasing trend to omit the hyphen in compound words, making the component elements into one single word. So such words as *book-end, sun-hat,* and *tea-bag* are increasingly being written as one word: *bookend, sunhat,* and *teabag.*

This revised edition contains many new words that have entered the language and also 150 panels which give spelling rules and tips on some words that may be confused.

Trademarks: This dictionary includes some words which are, or are asserted to be, proprietary names. However, the presence or absence of such assertions should not be regarded as affecting the legal status of any proprietary name or trademark.

Abbreviations

abbrev	abbreviation
Brit	British English
esp.	especially
fem.	feminine
masc.	masculine
pl.	plural
sing.	singular
US	American English

a indefinite article, used before consonant sounds

aardvark nocturnal burrowing mammal

abaca Philippine plant related to the banana

aback (**taken aback**) startled

abacus counting-frame
abacuses

abaft closer to the stern of a ship

abandon to give up; to forsake
abandoned abandonment

abase to humble oneself
abasement abasing

abate to decrease in intensity
abatement abating

abattoir slaughterhouse

abbacy rank or office of abbot
abbacies

abbess superior of a convent
abbesses

abbey building in which monks or nuns live
abbeys

abbot superior of a monastery
abbotship

abbreviate to make shorter
abbreviating abbreviation

abdicate to renounce power, a duty, etc.
abdicating abdication

abdomen part of the body containing the stomach and bowels
abdominal

abduct to remove forcefully
abduction abductor

abeam at right angles to the length of a ship or plane

aberration deviation from the normal
aberrance aberrant

abet to aid in doing wrong
abetted abetting abettor or *abetter*

abeyance temporary suspension

abhor to detest
abhorred abhorrence abhorrent abhorring

abide to tolerate; to live
abiding abode

ability skill or power to do something
abilities

abject wretched
abjection abjectly abjectness

abjure to renounce under oath
abjuration abjurer abjuring

ablative (*grammar*) case in Latin, etc.

ablaut variation in the vowel of a word

ablaze on fire

able with the skill or power to do something
able-bodied abler ablest ably

-able or -ible?
Both the suffixes *-able* and *-ible* are added to words to form adjectives. There is no hard-and-fast rule as to which suffix is used, but note:
- new words are formed by adding *-able*, e.g. *microwaveable*, *photocopiable*, not by adding *-ible*.
- the spelling *-able* is more common.

Commonly used words ending in *-ible* include:
accessible compatible convertible credible eligible flexible horrible incredible invisible irresistible possible responsible sensible terrible visible

Commonly used words ending in *-able* include:
acceptable accountable admirable available

capable charitable comfortable comparable considerable desirable enjoyable fashionable favourable formidable indispensable inevitable invaluable liable memorable miserable notable noticeable portable predictable probable profitable reasonable reliable remarkable respectable suitable unacceptable unbelievable uncomfortable valuable viable vulnerable

---

ablution ritual washing

abnegate to renounce
abnegating abnegation abnegator

abnormal different from the normal
abnormality abnormalities abnormally

aboard on a ship, aircraft, train, etc.

abode[1] dwelling-place

abode[2] past tense and past participle of **abide**

abolish to do away with
abolishes abolition abolitionist

abominable detestable; very bad
abominably

abominate to detest
abominating abomination

aborigine original inhabitant
aboriginal

abort to end or fail prematurely
abortive

abortion removal or expulsion of a foetus from the womb

aboulia or **abulia** loss of will-power

abound to exist in abundance

about concerning; near; around; approximately
about-face about-turn

above at a higher or greater point
above-board above-mentioned above-named

abracadabra conjuror's formula

abrade to rub away
abrading

abrasion rubbing away
abrasive

abreast alongside and facing in the same way

abridge to shorten
abridgement or *abridgment abridging*

abroad in or to a foreign country

abrogate to cancel formally
abrogating abrogation abrogator

abrupt sudden; unexpected
abruptly abruptness

abscess collection of pus
abscesses abscessed

abscond to run away secretly
absconder

abseil to descend a steep slope with a rope

absent not present; away from
absence absentee absenteeism absent-minded absent-mindedly

absinthe or **absinth** green liqueur made from herbs

absolute complete; perfect; unlimited
absolutely absolutism absolutist

absolve to release from blame or guilt
absolution absolving

absorb to take in; to suck up
absorbable absorbent absorption absorptive

abstain to hold back (from)
abstainer

abstemious sparing, esp. in eating and drinking
abstemiously

abstention holding back from voting

abstinence refraining, esp. from drinking alcohol
abstinent

abstract not material; summary; to consider theoretically
abstracted abstraction abstractive

abstruse difficult to understand

absurd ridiculous or incongruous
absurdity absurdities absurdly absurdness

Abu Dhabi sheikdom of United Arab Emirates

abulia see **aboulia**

abundance great supply
abundant

abuse to use wrongly or improperly; to treat cruelly; insulting language
abuser abusive
SEE PANEL

abuse or misuse?
Both words can be used as nouns and verbs to refer to wrong use or bad treatment.
Abuse is the stronger of the two in meaning, referring to cruel or violent treatment or to insults: *to abuse a child; hurl abuse at someone.*
Misuse means 'to use for an unsuitable purpose': *to misuse public funds.*

abut to border on
abutment abutted abutter abutting

abysmal very great; (*informal*) very bad
abysmally

abyss unfathomable hole
abysses abyssal

acacia kind of shrub or tree with yellow or white flowers

academic theoretical; scholarly
academically

academy institution; school
academies

accede to take up a position; to agree to
accedence acceding
SEE PANEL

accede or exceed?
Accede is a verb used in formal contexts to mean 'to agree': *accede to someone's requests/demands. To accede to the throne* means to become king or queen.
Exceed means 'to be greater than' or 'to go beyond': *Demand is exceeding supply; to exceed the speed limit.*

accelerando (*music*) becoming faster

accelerate to increase speed
accelerating acceleration accelerative accelerator

accent distinctive pronunciation; emphasis; written mark

accentuate to emphasize
accentuating accentuation

accept to receive; to agree to
acceptance acceptation accepted accepter or (*commerce, law, and science*) *acceptor*

acceptable satisfactory
acceptability acceptably

access right to approach or use
accesses

accessible able to be approached, used, etc. easily
accessibility accessibly

accession act of taking up a position; something added

accessory or (*law*) **accessary** useful additional part; person who incites another to commit a crime
accessories or (*law*) *accessaries*

accidence part of grammar dealing with inflections

accident unexpected chance event
accidental accidentally accident-prone

acclaim to greet or welcome with strong approval
acclaimer acclamation acclamatory

acclimatize or **acclimatise** to get used to a new climate
acclimatization or *acclimatisation*
acclimatizing or *acclimatising*

acclivity upward slope
acclivities

accolade award or praise; conferring of knighthood

accommodate to provide with lodging; to do a favour for
accommodating accommodation

accompany to go along with; to play a subsidiary or supporting musical part
accompanied accompanies accompaniment accompanist accompanying

accomplice helper in committing a crime

accomplish to achieve, complete, or manage
accomplishable accomplished accomplishes accomplishment

accord to be in harmony with
accordance according accordingly

accordion keyboard musical instrument with bellows
accordionist

accost to approach and speak to

account statement of finances; (to give a) description or explanation

accountable responsible
accountability accountably

accountant professional person concerned with business accounts
accountancy

accoutrements (US **accouterments**) equipment, esp. of soldiers

accredit to recognize officially
accredited

accretion increase by natural growth or external addition
accrete accreting accretive

accrue to come as an increase or addition
accrual accrued accrues accruing

accumulate to collect; to gather together; to increase
accumulating accumulation accumulative

accumulator storage battery

accurate correct; exact
accuracy accurately

accursed under a curse

accusative (*grammar*) case used to identify the direct object

accuse to charge someone with a particular crime
accusation accusatory accused accuser accusing accusingly

accustom to make used (to) or familiar (with)
accustomed

ace playing-card with one spot; (*informal*) expert

acerbate to make bitter
acerbating

acerbity bitterness
acerbities

acetate salt of acetic acid

acetic of or produced from acetic acid or vinegar

acetylene colourless gas used in welding metals

ache (to suffer from a) continuous dull pain
aching achy

achieve to succeed in doing
achievable achievement achiever achieving

Achilles heel point that is vulnerable to attack

Achilles tendon tendon joining calf muscles to heel-bone

acid sour; chemical compound
acidic acidity acidly acidness

acidify to change into or become an acid
acidification acidified acidifies acidifying

ack-ack (*informal*) anti-aircraft fire

acknowledge to admit; to recognize
acknowledgeable acknowledging acknowledgement or *acknowledgment*

acme highest point

acne skin disease of the face

acolyte assistant or follower

aconite kind of poisonous plant

acorn fruit of the oak tree

acoustic of sound or hearing
acoustical acoustically acoustics

acquaint to make familiar (with)
acquaintance acquaintanceship acquainted

acquiesce to agree to
acquiescence acquiescent acquiescing

acquire to gain possession of
acquirable acquirement acquiring acquisition acquisitive

acquit to declare not guilty
acquittal acquittance acquitted acquitter acquitting

acre unit of area, 4840 square yards
acreage

acrid unpleasantly bitter
acridity acridly acridness

acrimony bitterness in manner
acrimonious

acrobat performer of gymnastic feats
acrobatic acrobatically acrobatics

acronym word formed from the initial letters of other words

acrophobia fear of being at a great height
acrophobic

acropolis citadel of an ancient Greek city

across from one side to the other side (of); on the other side (of)
across the board

acrostic word-puzzle
acrostically

acrylic strong synthetic textile fibre

act deed; statute; main division of a play; to do something; to perform a part in a play, etc.
acting

actinide radioactive element

action process of doing something; lawsuit
actionable actionably

activate to make active
activated activating activation activator

active functioning; energetic
actively activeness activity activities

activism taking of direct action
activist

actor (*fem.* **actress**) person who acts in a play, film, etc.
actresses

actual real
actually

actuality reality
actualities

actualize or **actualise** to make real
actualization or *actualisation actualizing* or *actualising*

actuary statistician who calculates insurance risks and premiums
actuaries actuarial

actuate to put into action
actuating actuation

acuity sharpness; (*informal*) keen perception

acumen keen judgement
acuminous

acupuncture insertion of needles into the skin to relieve pain, etc.

acute severe; sharp; (*of an accent*) ´ (*of an angle*) less than 90°
acutely acuteness

ad (*informal*) short for **advertisement**

adage traditional saying

adagio (*music*) slow movement
adagios

adamant not yielding; determined
adamantine adamantly

adapt to make suitable; to modify to fit
adaptability adaptable adaptation adapter or *adaptor*

add to combine numbers into a total; to join

addendum something added, esp. at the end of a book
addenda

adder kind of small venomous snake

addict to cause to become dependent on a drug, etc.; person addicted, esp. to a drug
addicted addiction addictive

addition adding
additional additionally additive

addle to confuse someone's brain
addling

addled rotten; confused

address written description of where a building is; to speak to
addresses addressee addresser

adduce to offer as evidence
adducible adducing

adenoids mass of tissue at the back of the nose
adenoidal

adept skilled at

adequate sufficient; just satisfactory
adequacy adequately

adhere to stick to
adherence adherent adhering

adhesion sticking
adhesive

ad hoc (*Latin*) for a particular purpose

adieu goodbye
adieus or *adieux*

ad infinitum (*Latin*) without end

adipose fatty

adjacent having a common boundary; near
adjacency adjacently

adjective word used to describe a noun
adjectival adjectivally

adjoin to be next to
adjoining

adjourn to postpone temporarily
adjournment

adjudge to declare formally
adjudging

adjudicate to judge
adjudicating adjudication adjudicator

adjunct something joined on
adjunctive adjunctly

adjure to command or appeal
adjuration adjuratory adjuring

adjust to change slightly; to adapt
adjustable adjuster adjustment

adjutant assistant to a superior officer
adjutancy adjutant-general

ad lib to improvise in speaking or singing
ad libbed ad libbing

adman (*informal*) person who works in advertising
admen

admin short for **administration**

administer to direct, manage, or control; to dispense or give
administration administrative administrator

admiral chief navy commander
admiralty

admire to regard with great respect
admirable admirably admiration admirer admiring admiringly

admissible capable of being allowed
admissibility

admission (charge for) admitting; confession
SEE PANEL

---

admission or admittance?

Admittance means 'right to enter': *to gain admittance*. It is also used on signs: *No admittance.*

Admission is a less formal word used to refer to entering a place or the charge for entering, or, in a very different context, a confession: *apply for admission to the university; admission to the museum: £5; an admission of guilt.*

---

admit to allow to enter; to acknowledge
admissive admittable admitted admittedly admitting

admittance right to enter
SEE PANEL at **admission**

admixture mixture; ingredient

admonish to warn firmly but mildly
admonishes admonition admonitory

ad nauseam (*Latin*) to a tedious degree

ado fussy excitement; trouble

adobe sun-dried brick

adolescence period between puberty and maturity
adolescent

adopt to take, esp. a child, as one's own
adopter adoption adoptive

adore to love intensely; to worship
adorable adorably adoration adorer adoring

adorn to decorate
adornment

adrenal of or near the kidneys

adrenalin or **adrenaline** hormone secreted by the adrenal glands

adrift drifting

adroit skilful

adulation excessive flattery
adulate adulating adulator adulatory

adult fully-developed and mature person
adulthood

adulterate to make impure by adding something inferior
adulterant adulterating adulteration adulterator

adultery voluntary sexual intercourse between a married person and someone other than the spouse
adulterer adulteress adulterous

adumbrate to outline faintly; to foreshadow
adumbrating adumbration

advance to go forwards
advanced advancement advancer advancing

advantage favourable position, gain, or benefit
advantageous advantageously

advent coming or arrival

adventitious appearing or occurring accidentally
adventitiously

adventure exciting or risky event, undertaking, etc.
adventurer adventuresome adventuress adventurous

adverb word describing how, when, where, etc., something is done
adverbial adverbially

adversary enemy
adversaries

adverse unfavourable
adversely adverseness adversity
SEE PANEL

---

adverse or averse?

Adverse means 'unfavourable': *adverse weather conditions; drugs that have an adverse effect on the body.*

If you are not *averse* to something, you mean that you quite like it or want to do it: *I am not averse to spending more money.*

---

advert (*informal*) short for **advertisement**

advertise to present to the public in order to promote sales
advertisement advertiser advertising

advice recommendation on action or behaviour

advisable prudent
advisability advisably

advise to give advice to; to inform
advisedly adviser or *advisor advising advisory*

advocaat liqueur with a raw-egg base

advocate person who pleads for another; supporter; to recommend
advocacy advocacies advocating advocatory

adze (US **adz**) tool for cutting or shaping wood

Aegean of the sea between Greece and Turkey

aegis protection or sponsorship

aeon or **eon** immeasurably long period of time

aerate to charge with a gas
aerating aeration aerator

aerial of or in the air; rod or rods for transmitting or receiving radio waves

aerie see **eyrie**

aero- (*prefix*) of aircraft or aeronautics
aero-engine

aerobatics spectacular manoeuvres of aircraft

aerobics exercises designed to increase the intake of oxygen and to strengthen the heart and lungs
aerobic

aerodrome airfield

aerodynamics study of flow of air and motion of solid bodies
aerodynamic aerodynamically

aerofoil surface designed to produce lift in an aircraft

aerogram or **aerogramme** airmail letter

aeronautics study of flight
aeronautical

aeroplane (US **airplane**) aircraft

aerosol (suspension of) fine particles sprayed from a pressurized container

aerospace earth's atmosphere and space beyond it

Aertex (*trademark*) cellular cotton fabric

aesthetic (US **esthetic**) of or associated with the appreciation of beauty, taste, etc.
aesthetically (US *esthetically*) *aesthetics* (US *esthetics*)

aetiology (US **etiology**) study of the causes of a disease

afar at or from a distance

affable friendly; approachable
affability affably

affair matter or concern; event, extra-marital sexual relationship

affect[1] to influence; to move emotionally
affected
SEE PANEL

affect or effect?

Affect is a verb meaning 'to influence or cause to change in some way': *The housing market has been adversely affected by the recession.* In literary contexts, *affect* can also mean 'to pretend to have or feel': *He sat there, affecting an air of nonchalance.*

Effect is most commonly a noun meaning 'a result; something produced by a cause': *the effects of drugs on the body; The increases will take effect* (come into operation) *in January; Such a revolution would in effect* (essentially) *mean the end of life on this planet.*

Effect is also more rarely used as a verb in formal contexts meaning 'to bring about or produce': *the reforms effected by the previous government.*

affect[2] to pretend to have, feel, etc.
affectation affected
SEE PANEL at **affect**[1]

affection fondness
affectionate affectionately

afferent (*of nerves*) carrying towards the centre

affidavit written statement made on oath

affiliate to associate with, esp. as a member
affiliating affiliation

affinity natural liking; close similarity
affinities affinitive

affirm to declare positively

affirmable affirmant affirmation affirmatory affirmer

affirmative showing agreement
affirmatively

affix to attach; prefix or suffix
affixes

afflict to cause suffering to
affliction afflictive
SEE PANEL

---

afflict or inflict?
Afflict means 'to cause suffering to': *migraines that had afflicted her years earlier; a society afflicted by an all-pervading malaise of apathy.*
Inflict means 'to force something unpleasant on someone deliberately': *to inflict serious injuries; to inflict heavy casualties on the rebel troops.*

---

affluent wealthy; tributary stream
affluence affluently

afford to have enough to be able to do or spare something
affordable

afforest to plant trees on
afforestation

affray public brawl
affrays

affront (to) insult

Afghanistan country in Asia
Afghan

aficionado (*Spanish*) ardent supporter
aficionados

afield away from

afire on fire

aflame burning

afloat floating

afoot in progress

afore- (*prefix*) before
aforegoing aforementioned aforesaid aforethought

a fortiori (*Latin*) for a stronger reason

afraid frightened; sorry

afresh once more; again

Africa continent of the world
African

Africanize or **Africanise** to cause to gain African characteristics
Africanization or *Africanisation*
Africanizing or *Africanising*

Afrikaans South African Dutch language
Afrikaner

Afro hairstyle

Afro- (*perfix*) African
Afro-American

aft towards the stern of a ship

after following in time or space; in the same way as
afterbirth after-care after-effect afterglow afterlife afters aftershave after-taste afterthought afterwards

aftermath results of an event

afternoon period between noon and evening

again once more; further

against opposing; in contact with; in preparation for

agape[1] with the mouth open

agape[2] love feast; divine love

agate kind of precious stone

agave kind of spiny-leaved plant

age length of time a person or thing has existed; to grow old
aged ageing or *aging ageism ageist ageless agelong age-old age-stricken*

agency business providing a service; means
agencies

agenda list of items to be considered
agendas

agent person who acts for someone else; something that produces an effect

agent provocateur (*French*) person employed to incite suspects to commit illegal acts
agents provocateurs

agglomerate to form into a mass
agglomerating agglomeration

agglutinate to cause to stick or join
agglutinating agglutination agglutinative

aggrandize or **aggrandise** to increase the power of
aggrandizement or *aggrandisement*
aggrandizing or *aggrandising*

aggravate to make worse; (*informal*) to annoy
aggravating aggravation

aggregate to combine to form a whole; combined (mass); sand, etc. mixed with cement and water
aggregating aggregation aggregative

aggression unprovoked attack
aggressive aggressively aggressiveness aggressor

aggrieve to grieve
aggrievedly aggrieving

aggro (*slang*) aggression

aghast overcome with horror

agile quick; nimble
agilely agility

agitate to disturb or excite
agitatedly agitating agitation agitator

aglitter sparkling

aglow glowing

agnostic person who believes that it is impossible to know whether or not God exists
agnostically agnosticism

ago in the past

agog eager and curious

agonize or **agonise** to (cause to) suffer agony
agonizing or *agonising*

agony extreme pain
agonies

agoraphobia fear of open spaces
agoraphobic

agrarian concerning land

agree to share the same opinion; to assent (to); to suit the health of
agreeable agreeably agreed agreeing agreement

agribusiness businesses involved with the production and sale of farm products

agriculture science of farming
agricultural agriculturally agriculturist or *agriculturalist*

agronomy study of field-crop production and soil management
agronomist

aground on to the shore or the bottom of shallow water

ague malarial fever
agueish

ah exclamation, to express esp. delight

aha exclamation, to express esp. surprise

ahead in front; in the future

ahoy (*nautical*) call to attract attention

aid (to give) help

aide-de-camp military officer serving as personal assistant to a superior
aides-de-camp

aide-mémoire (*French*) aid to memory
aides-mémoire

Aids or **AIDS** acquired immune deficiency syndrome

aigrette tuft of feathers; spray of gems, etc.

ail to be unwell
ailing ailment

aileron movable surface of an aircraft wing

aim to point at; purpose
aimless aimlessly aimlessness

air mixture of gases; manner or quality; melody
airbase air-bed airborne airbus air-conditioned air-conditioning air-cooled aircraft aircraft-carrier aircraftman aircraftwoman airer airfield airflow airfreight airgun airily airiness airless airlift airline airliner airlock airmail airman airmanship airport airsea airship airsick airspace airstrip airtight air-to-air airway airwoman airworthy airy airy-fairy

Airedale large rough-haired terrier

aisle passageway between seats

aitchbone cut of beef containing hip-bone

ajar slightly open

akimbo with hands on hip and elbows turned out

akin similar (to)

alabaster fine-textured chalky stone

à la carte (*French*) from a menu with items priced separately

alacrity liveliness

à la mode (*French*) fashionable

alarm (to give a) warning signal; to frighten
alarmingly alarmist

alas exclamation of sorrow

alb long white linen vestment

Albania country in SE Europe
Albanian

albatross large sea-bird
albatrosses

albeit even though

albino person or animal with no natural colouring in skin and hair
albinos albinism albinotic

album book for collection of stamps, photographs, etc.; long-playing record

albumen white of an egg

albumin protein in blood plasma, egg-white, etc.
albuminous

alburnum sapwood

alchemy medieval kind of chemistry
alchemies alchemic alchemical alchemist

alcohol clear intoxicating liquid
alcoholic alcoholism

alcove recess in a wall

alder shrub or tree of the birch family

alderman civic official
aldermen aldermanic aldermanship

ale beer
alehouse

alert watchful; to warn

alexandrine 12-syllable verse line

alexia loss of the ability to read

alfalfa plant grown for animal fodder

alga kind of simple water-plant
algae algal algoid

algebra branch of mathematics
algebraic algebraical algebraically algebraist

Algeria country in NW Africa
Algerian

ALGOL computer language

algorithm systematic procedure for solving a mathematical problem
algorithmic

alias assumed name
aliases

alibi evidence of being elsewhere when a crime was committed; excuse
alibis

alien foreigner; opposed (to)

alienate to turn away from; to become unfriendly
alienating alienation alienator

alight[1] to come or get down from

alight[2] on fire

align to place in a line
alignment

alike similar

alimentary of or associated with nutrition
alimentation

alimony allowance made to a wife or former wife

alive living; aware of

alkali chemical base that dissolves in water
alkalis or *alkalies* *alkaline* *alkalinity*

alkaloid nitrogenous compound from plants, used as a drug

all whole amount of; wholly
all-clear *all-knowing* *all-purpose* *all-round* *all-rounder* *all-time* *all-up*

Allah Islamic word for God

allay to lessen
allayed *allaying*

allege to state without proof
allegation *allegedly* *alleging*

allegiance loyal support

allegorize or **allegorise** to compose as an allegory
allegorization or *allegorisation* *allegorizing* or *allegorising*

allegory story in which characters, etc. have a symbolic meaning
allegories *allegoric* *allegorical* *allegorically* *allegorist*

allegretto (*music*) fairly fast

allegro (*music*) brisk and lively

alleluia or **hallelujah** expression of praise to God

allergy abnormal reaction to a food or substance
allergies *allergenic* *allergic*

alleviate to relieve
alleviating *alleviation* *alleviative* *alleviator* *alleviatory*

alley narrow passage
alleys *alleyway*

alliance union or association

alligator kind of large reptile

alliteration repetition of the same consonant
alliterate *alliterating* *alliterative*

allocate to assign for a particular purpose
allocating *allocation*

allot to distribute; to apportion
allotment *allottable* *allotted* *allotting*

allotrope one of the different physical forms of a chemical element

allow to permit
allowable *allowably* *allowance* *allowedly*

alloy mixture of metals

allspice aromatic spice

allude to refer (to) indirectly
alluding

allure to entice
allurement *alluring*

allusion indirect reference
SEE PANEL

---

allusion, delusion, or illusion?
An *allusion* is an indirect reference: *literary allusions in a speech.*

A *delusion* is a false or mistaken idea or belief that is not based on evidence: *under a delusion that she is the Queen.*

An *illusion* is a misleading impression based on the senses: *an optical illusion; lighting that gives the illusion of extra space.*

---

allusive containing an indirect reference to
allusively *allusiveness*

alluvium material deposited by rivers
alluvia *alluvial*

ally to join with; country or ruler allied to another; supporter
allies *alliance* *allied* *allying*

almanac annual publication of reference information

almighty having all power

almond kind of tree; kernel of its fruit

almoner (*formerly*) official distributor of charity, hospital social worker

almost very nearly

alms charitable donations of money
almsgiving almshouse

aloe kind of plant with spiny-toothed leaves

aloft at a great height

alone apart from others

along over the length of; onwards; accompanying
alongshore alongside

aloof distant

alopecia baldness

aloud loud enough to be heard

alp high mountain
alpine alpinism alpinist

alpaca mammal related to the llama

alpenstock iron-pointed staff

alpha 1st letter of the Greek alphabet

alphabet set of letters in a writing system
alphabetical alphabetically

alphabetize or **alphabetise** to arrange into alphabetical order
alphabetization or *alphabetisation*
alphabetizing or *alphabetising*

alphanumeric consisting of both number and letter symbols

Alps mountain range in south central Europe

already by or before a particular time

Alsatian German shepherd dog

also besides
also-ran

altar place where sacrifices are made to a god; communion table
altar-piece

alter to change
alterable alterably alteration

altercation noisy argument
altercate altercating

alter ego (*Latin*) one's second self; very close friend

alternate (to occur) in turns; every other
alternately alternating alternation alternator
SEE PANEL

---

alternate or alternative?

The adjective *alternate* means 'every other; occurring in turns': *He sees his children on alternate weekends. Alternative* means 'of a choice; giving a choice': *an alternative plan* is one that can be tried in place of another: *an alternative solution to the problem. Alternative* also means 'unconventional': *alternative medicine; adopt an alternative lifestyle; alternative technology.*

Alternate is also a verb meaning 'to occur in turns': *His moods alternated between the heights of ecstasy and the troughs of despair. Alternative* is also a noun meaning 'a possible choice': *offer a viable alternative to unemployment.*

---

alternative giving or of a choice; possible choice
alternatively
SEE PANEL at **alternate**

although even though

altimeter instrument to measure altitudes

altitude height above sea-level

alto (singer with or music for) highest adult male voice
altos

altogether with everything considered; completely

altruism unselfish concern for others
altruist altruistic altruistically

aluminium (US **aluminum**) light malleable white metal

alumnus (*fem.* **alumna**) (*chiefly* US) graduate of a school, college, etc.
alumni (fem. *alumnae*)

always at all times

alyssum kind of garden plant

am 1st person singular of present tense of **be**

amalgam mercury alloy; blend

amalgamate to combine or unite
amalgamating amalgamation

amanuensis person employed to take dictation or copy manuscripts
amanuenses

amaranth kind of purple flower
amaranthine

amaryllis kind of lily-like plant

amass to collect or gather
amasser amasses

amateur not professional or expert
amateurish amateurism

amatory of or about love
amatorial

amaze to fill with wonder or surprise
amazement amazing

Amazon river in South America; legendary warlike woman
Amazonian

ambassador diplomatic representative to another country
ambassadorial ambassadorship ambassadress

amber yellowish fossil resin

ambergris waxy substance used in perfumes

ambidextrous able to use either hand equally well
ambidexterity ambidextrously ambidextrousness

ambient surrounding
ambience or *ambiance*

ambiguous having two or more possible meanings; doubtful
ambiguity ambiguities ambiguously ambiguousness

ambit range or scope

ambition strong desire for success
ambitious ambitiously

ambivalent with opposing feelings
ambivalence ambivalently

amble (to walk at a) leisurely relaxed pace
ambler ambling

ambrosia something pleasing to taste or smell
ambrosial ambrosian

ambulance vehicle for transporting the sick and injured

ambuscade (to lay an) ambush
ambuscading

ambush (to lie in wait for, in a) surprise attack
ambushes

ameba (US) see **amoeba**

ameliorate to make or become better
ameliorating amelioration

amen so be it; used at the end of a prayer

amenable likely to agree, etc.
amenably

amend to change formally; to improve
amendable amender amendment
SEE PANEL

---

amend or emend?

To *amend* something such as a law or contract is to improve it or formally to change it: *amend the constitution; The company may amend or vary the conditions of this contract at any time.*

Emend, a rarer word, means 'to correct; to remove mistakes from': *emend a text/manuscript.*

---

amends compensation or recompense

amenity useful facility
amenities

America continents of North and South America
American Americanism Amerindian

American and British English

Differences between British English and American English spelling include:

- Words ending *-our* in British English end *-or* in American English:
behaviour (US *behavior*) *colour* (US *color*) *favour* (US *favor*) *labour* (US *labor*) *neighbour* (US *neighbor*) *vigour* (US *vigor*)
- Words ending *-oul* in British English end *-ol* in American English:
mould (US *mold*) *smoulder* (US *smolder*)
- Words ending *-re* in British English end *-er* in American English:
centre (US *center*) *theatre* (US *theater*)
- Words ending *-ogue* in British English end *-og* in American English:
catalogue (US *catalog*) *dialogue* (US *dialog*)
- Words spelled with *ae* or *oe* in British English take *e* in American English:
aethetic (US *esthetic*) *diarrhoea* (US *diarrhea*) *oesophagus* (US *esophagus*)
- Doubling of consonants in British English in certain words, where in American English the consonants are not doubled: see DOUBLING OF CONSONANTS. A few verbs have a single consonant in British English but a double consonant in American English:
appal (US *appall*) *distil* (US *distill*) *enrol* (US *enroll*) *enthral* (US *enthrall*) *fulfil* (US *fulfill*) *instil* (US *instill*)
- *-ize* or *-ise* in verbs see -IZE OR -ISE?
- Individual words, e.g. *axe* (US *ax*) *cheque* (US *check*) *grey* (US *gray*) *plough* (US *plow*) *sceptic* (US *skeptic*) *tyre* (US *tire*)

Americanize or **Americanise** to cause to gain American characteristics
Americanization or *Americanisation Americanizing* or *Americanising*

amethyst purple or violet quartz used as a gemstone

amiable appearing pleasant and friendly
amiability or *amiableness amiably*
SEE PANEL

---

amiable or amicable?

Amiable means 'appearing pleasant and friendly': *an amiable expression on her face; He was an amiable, welcoming chap to be with.*

Amicable means 'showing friendly goodwill' and is used to refer to discussions, a relationship, etc.: *to part on amicable terms; to reach an amicable settlement.*

---

amicable showing friendly goodwill
amicability or *amicableness amicably*
SEE PANEL at **amiable**

amid in the middle of
amidships amidst

amino acid organic compound

amir Arabic title

amiss in a wrong way

amity friendship
amities

ammeter instrument measuring electric current in amperes

ammonia colourless strong-smelling gas
ammoniac ammoniacal ammonium

ammonite coiled fossil shell

ammunition bullets, bombs, grenades, etc.

amnesia loss of memory
amnesiac

amnesty general pardon
amnesties

amnion membrane enclosing an embryo
amnions or *amnia amniotic*

amoeba (US **ameba**) free-living, tiny, single-celled animal
amoebas or *amoebae* (US *amebas* or *amebae*) *amoebic* (US *amebic*)

amok or **amuck** in a murderous frenzy

among or **amongst** in the middle of; between

amontillado medium dry sherry

amoral non-moral

amorality amorally
SEE PANEL

amoral or immoral?
People who are *amoral* do not consider important whether their actions are right or wrong or they have no understanding of what is right or wrong: *an amoral attitude; amoral creatures such as animals.*

Immoral people or actions are those that are wrong, that is, contrary to accepted morals: *immoral behaviour; Many people believe it is immoral to perform medical experiments on live animals.*

amorous tending towards love
amorist amorously amorousness

amorphous having no definite shape or form
amorphism amorphously amorphousness

amortize or **amortise** to settle a mortgage or debt by instalments
amortization or *amortisation amortizing* or *amortising*

amount (to) total

amp (*informal*) ampere

ampere basic metric unit of electric current
amperage

ampersand symbol &, meaning 'and'

amphetamine kind of drug

amphibian animal that can live on land or in water
amphibious

amphitheatre (US **amphitheater**) building with an arena encircled by tiered seats

amphora ancient 2-handled narrow-necked jar
amphorae or *amphoras*

ample plentiful; large
amply

amplify to increase the strength of electric signals; to expand on
amplification amplified amplifier amplifies

amplitude extent or magnitude

ampoule (US **ampule**) sealed glass container for hypodermic dose

amputate to cut off by surgery
amputating amputation amputee

amuck see **amok**

amulet small object worn to protect from evil

amuse to entertain; to cause to laugh
amusement amusing amusingly

an indefinite article, used before vowel sounds

anachronism something placed in the wrong historical period
anachronistic

anacoluthon (*grammar*) inconsistency in syntactic construction
anacolutha or *anacoluthons anacoluthic*

anaconda kind of very large snake

anaemia (US **anemia**) deficiency in red cells, etc. in the blood
anaemic (US *anemic*)

anaerobic not requiring oxygen

anaesthesia (US **anesthesia**) loss of sensation, esp. of pain
anaesthetic (US *anesthetic*) *anaesthetist* (US *anesthetist*)

anaesthetize or **anaesthetise** (US **anesthetize**) to subject to anaesthesia
anaesthetization or *anaesthetisation* (US *anesthetization*) *anaesthetizing* or *anaesthetising* (US *anesthetizing*)

anaglypta thick wallpaper with a raised pattern

anagram word or phrase made by rearranging the letters of another

anal of the anus

analgesic pain-relieving substance
analgesia

analogy comparison; likeness or similarity
analogies analogical analogically analogist analogize or *analogise analogous analogue* (US *analog*)

analyse (US **analyze**) to examine in detail
analysing (US *analyzing*)

analysis act or result of analysing
analyses analyst analytic analytical analytically

anapaest (US **anapest**) metrical foot of 2 short syllables and 1 long syllable
anapaestic (US *anapestic*)

anarchy absence of government; lawlessness
anarchies anarchic anarchical anarchically anarchism anarchist anarchistic

anastigmatic (*of a lens*) not astigmatic

anathema something detested
anathemas anathematize or *anathematise*

anatomy study of the structure of organisms
anatomic anatomical anatomically anatomist anatomize or *anatomise*

ancestor (*fem.* **ancestress**) person from whom another is descended
ancestral ancestry

anchor device that holds a ship firmly to the sea-bed
anchorage anchorman

anchorite (*fem.* **anchoress**) hermit

anchovy kind of small herring
anchovy or *anchovies*

ancien régime (*French*) old order of things

ancient very old
anciently

ancillary subsidiary; supplementary
ancillaries

and in addition; also

andante (*music*) moving steadily

andiron support for logs in a hearth

Andorra country in SW Europe
Andorran

androgen male sex hormone
androgenic

androgynous having both male and female characteristics

android human-like robot

anecdote amusing story
anecdotal

anemia (US) see **anaemia**

anemometer instrument for measuring the speed of the wind

anemone kind of woodland plant

aneroid kind of barometer

anesthesia (US) see **anaesthesia**

anesthetize (US) see **anaesthetize**

aneurysm or **aneurism** abnormal dilation of an artery

anew again; afresh

angel divine messenger
angelic angelical angelically

angelica plant used in medicine and cookery

anger great annoyance

angina disease marked by spasmodic painful attacks

angle[1] space between lines extending from a common point

angle[2] to fish with hook and line
angler angling

Anglican of the Church of England
Anglicanism

Anglicize or **Anglicise** to make English
Anglicism Anglicizing or *Anglicising*

Anglo (*prefix*) English
Anglo-Saxon

Anglophile or **Anglophil** person who greatly admires England

Angola country in SW Africa
Angolan

angora long-haired goat or rabbit

angry very annoyed
angrier angriest angrily angriness

angst (*German*) feeling of anxiety and worry

anguish extreme suffering

angular having angles
angularity angularities

aniline colourless liquid used in making dyes, explosives, etc.

animadvert to criticize
animadversion

animal living creature able to feel and move

animalcule very tiny animal
animalcular

animate to give life to
animating animation animator

animism belief that natural objects have souls
animist animistic

animosity powerful active dislike
animosities

anion ion carrying negative electric charge

aniseed liquorice-flavoured seed of the anise plant

ankle joint connecting the foot and leg
anklet

annals historical, esp. yearly, records of events
annalist annalistic

anneal to toughen by heat treatment

annex to join to; to take possession of
annexation annexing

annexe additional subordinate building

annihilate to destroy completely
annihilating annihilation annihilator

anniversary date each year on which an event is celebrated
anniversaries

Anno Domini (*Latin*) in the year of our Lord

annotate to provide with explanatory notes
annotated annotating annotation annotator

announce to make known publicly
announcement announcer announcing

annoy to irritate or harass
annoyance annoyer

annual yearly
annually

annuity fixed yearly payment
annuities

annul to make void; to cancel
annullable annulled annulling annulment

annular ring-shaped

annunciate to announce
annunciating annunciation

anode positive electrode of an electrolytic cell
anodic

anodize or **anodise** to coat a metal with a protective oxide film
anodizing or *anodising*

anodyne something that relieves

anoint to apply oil, grease, etc. to
anointment

anomalous deviating from the normal
anomaly anomalies

anon (*archaic or literary*) soon; (*abbrev*) anonymous

anonymous by an unnamed or unknown author
anonymity

anopheles mosquito that transmits malaria
anopheline

anorak hooded waterproof jacket

anorexia (*medical*) loss of appetite

another additional or different (person or thing)

anschluss (*German*) union

anserine of the goose

answer (to) reply; to take responsibility (for)
answerable answerphone

ant kind of small insect

-ant or -ent?
Either suffix may be used to form nouns and adjectives.

Nouns ending in *-ant* include the following. (It may be helpful to note that many of these refer to people.)
accountant applicant assistant attendant commandant confidant consultant contestant defendant dependant descendant elephant giant immigrant infant informant instant lieutenant merchant migrant occupant participant peasant pheasant Protestant remnant sergeant servant tenant tyrant variant

Nouns ending in *-ent* include the following. (It may be helpful to note that many of these refer to actions.)
accident achievement acknowledgement adolescent advertisement agent agreement amusement apartment appointment argument assessment assignment basement commitment contentment correspondent department development disappointment document element employment environment equipment establishment excitement garment government improvement ingredient investment judgement management moment movement opponent parent parliament pavement predicament present president punishment refinement refreshment reinforcement statement student treatment unemployment

Adjectives ending in *-ant* include the following:
abundant adamant arrogant brilliant defiant distant dominant elegant exorbitant extravagant fragrant hesitant ignorant important incessant militant observant pleasant poignant predominant pregnant radiant redundant relevant reluctant resistant self-reliant significant tolerant vacant vigilant

Adjectives ending in *-ent* include the following:
absent confident consistent convenient current decent despondent different efficient eminent evident excellent frequent imminent impudent independent innocent intelligent magnificent patient permanent present prominent reverent silent sufficient transparent urgent violent

See also panels: CURRANT OR CURRENT? DEPENDANT OR DEPENDENT?

---

antacid medicine to neutralize acidity

antagonize or **antagonise** to arouse the hostility of
antagonism antagonist antagonistic antagonistically antagonizing or *antagonising*

Antarctica continent of the world
Antarctic

ante poker stake

ante- (*prefix*) before
antechamber ante-room

anteater kind of mammal feeding on ants

antecedent something that goes before

antedate to attach an earlier date to; to precede
antedating

antediluvian before the biblical Flood

antelope kind of fast-running mammal

ante meridiem (*Latin*) before noon

antenatal before birth

antenna one of a pair of feelers on the head of an insect, crustacean, etc. (pl. *antennae*); aerial (pl. *antennas*)

antenuptial before marriage

anterior situated or coming before

anthem church music; hymn of praise

anther pollen-bearing part of the end of stamen

anthology collection of poems, etc.
anthologies anthologist anthologize or *anthologise*

anthracite hard, slow-burning coal

anthrax disease of cattle and sheep

anthropoid like human beings

anthropology study of human beings
anthropological anthropologist

anthropomorphism attributing human behaviour, etc., to god or animal
anthropomorphic

anti- (*prefix*) against
anti-apartheid anti-depressant anti-lock anti-nuclear anti-perspirant anti-Semitic anti-theft anti-vivisection

anti-aircraft of defence against aircraft attack

antiballistic designed to destroy another ballistic missile

antibiotic (substance) used to treat infection caused by bacteria

antibody protein formed in the blood to counteract effects of harmful bacteria
antibodies

anticipate to expect; to see in advance and prepare for
anticipating anticipation anticipatory

anticlimax final event that is less exciting than expected
anticlimactic

anticline formation of stratified rock

anticlockwise moving in the opposite direction to a clock's hands

antics ludicrous acts or behaviour

anticyclone area of high atmospheric pressure
anticyclonic

antidote substance counteracting poison; remedy

antifreeze substance added to water to lower its freezing-point

antigen substance that stimulates antibodies

Antigua island in the West Indies
Antiguan

anti-hero main character who lacks usual heroic qualities
anti-heroes

antihistamine drug that neutralizes effects of histamines

antiknock compound added to petrol to reduce noise

antilogarithm or **antilog** number corresponding to a given logarithm

antimacassar cloth covering backs and seats of chairs

antimatter matter composed of antiparticles

antimony brittle metallic element

antinomy conflict of authority

antipathy strong dislike
antipathies antipathetic antipathize or *antipathise*

antiphon recited Bible verses; anthem or chant
antiphonal antiphony

antipodes places diametrically opposite; Australasia
antipodean

antiquarian concerning antiquities
antiquary antiquaries

antiquate to make out of date

antique very old; old sought-after object
antiquity antiquities

antirrhinum kind of brightly-coloured flower; snapdragon

antiseptic (substance) that stops growth of bacteria
antisepsis antiseptically

antisocial opposed to the interests of society; not sociable
antisocially

antithesis contrast or direct opposite
antitheses antithetic antithetical antithetically

antitoxin antibody that neutralizes a toxin
antitoxic

antitype person or thing that corresponds to a type or symbol

antler bony outgrowth on the head of a deer, etc.

antonym word meaning the opposite of another

antrum cavity in a bone
antra

anus opening in the body through which waste matter is discharged
anal

anvil block on which a metal is shaped

anxiety fear and worry
anxieties anxious anxiously

any some; every

anybody any person

anyhow in any case; carelessly

anyone anybody

anything any object, event, etc.

anyway in any case

anywhere in, at, or to any place

aorist verb tense

aorta large artery
aortas or *aortae aortic*

apace quickly

apart distant; separate

apartheid South African policy of racial segregation

apartment single room; set of rooms; (US) flat

apathy lack of interest
apathetic apathetically

ape tailless monkey; to imitate
aping apish

aperient laxative

aperitif alcoholic appetizer before a meal

aperture opening

apex highest point
apexes or *apices apical*

aphasia loss of power to use or understand words
aphasic

aphid greenfly or related insect
aphis aphid aphides

aphorism short pithy saying
aphoristic

aphrodisiac love potion

Aphrodite Greek goddess of love

apiary place where bees are kept
apiaries apiarist

apiculture keeping of bees
apicultural apiculturist

apiece for or to each one

apish like an ape; stupid

aplomb self-composure

apocalypse revelation
apocalyptic

Apocrypha books in the Septuagint and Vulgate but excluded from Protestant and Jewish Bible versions

apocryphal of questionable authorship

apogee point in its orbit at which the moon, a planet, or artificial satellite is furthest from the earth

apolitical politically neutral

Apollo Greek god of music, medicine and poetry

apologetic being sorry
apologetically

apologetics reasoned defence, esp. of Christianity
apologist

apologize or **apologise** to say one is sorry
apologizing or *apologising*

apology expression of regret
apologies

apophthegm or **apothegm** short instructive saying

apoplexy sudden loss of consciousness; stroke
apoplectic

apostasy abandonment of one's beliefs
apostate

a posteriori (*Latin*) reasoning from effects to causes

apostle 1 of the 12 disciples of Christ
apostleship *apostolic*

apostrophe[1] punctuation mark '

apostrophe[2] addressing of an absent or imaginary person
apostrophize or *apostrophise*

apothecary (*archaic* or US) pharmacist
apothecaries

apothegm see **apophthegm**

apotheosis deification
apotheoses

appal (US **appall**) to fill with horror, dismay, or shock
appalled *appalling*

Appalachians mountains in NE USA
Appalachian

apparatus set of equipment; machine or appliance
apparatuses

apparel clothing; to clothe or adorn
apparelled (US *appareled*) *apparelling* (US *appareling*)

apparent clearly seen or understood
apparently

apparition sudden or strange appearance; ghost

appeal (to) request; to be attractive (to)
appealable appealer appealing

appear to come into sight
appearance

appease to calm, esp. by making concessions to the demands of
appeasement *appeaser* *appeasing*

appellant person who appeals

appellation name or title

append to add as a supplement
appendage

appendicectomy (US **appendectomy**) surgical operation to remove the appendix
appendicectomies (US *appendectomies*)

appendicitis inflammation of the appendix

appendix additional material at the end of a book; short, closed tube extending from large intestine
appendices or *appendixes*

appertain to belong to

appetite desire, esp. for food
appetizer or *appetiser* *appetizing* or *appetising*

applaud to show approval of by clapping the hands
applause

apple round edible fruit

appliance machine or device

applicable appropriate or relevant
applicability *applicably*

appliqué cut-out material sewn or fixed onto another material
appliquéd

apply to put to use; to put into contact with; to request
applicable *applicant* *application* *applied* *applies* *applying*

appoint to choose, as for a task
appointee *appointer* *appointment*

apportion to divide and share
apportionment

apposite appropriate
appositely *appositeness*

apposition placing of a word or expression beside another which it describes

appraise to assess the worth or quality of
appraisal *appraiser* *appraising*
SEE PANEL

---

appraise or apprise?
To *appraise* something or someone means to assess their worth or quality: *to appraise someone's work; All procedures are regularly and rigorously appraised.*
To *apprise* means 'to inform or notify': *They were fully apprised of all the particulars.*

---

appreciable that can be noticed or measured
appreciably

appreciate to be grateful for; to recognize; to increase in value
appreciating *appreciation* *appreciative*

apprehend to understand; to arrest

apprehensible capable of being apprehended

apprehension anxious fear about what may happen
apprehensive

apprentice person learning a trade
apprenticeship

apprise to inform
apprising
SEE PANEL at **appraise**

apprize (*archaic*) to value
apprizing

approach to come near or nearer
approachability *approachable*

approbation approval or recognition

appropriate suitable; to take for one's own use
appropriately *appropriateness*
appropriating *appropriation*

approve to think favourably of; to authorize
approval *approver* *approving*

approximate nearly accurate or exact; to come very near to
approximately *approximation*

appurtenance accessory

après-ski (*French*) (of) time after a day's skiing

apricot round, orange-yellow fruit

April 4th month of the year

a priori (*Latin*) reasoning from causes to effects

apron protective garment; hard-surfaced area by an airport terminal

apropos concerning

apse semicircular recess at the east end of a church

apsis either of the 2 extreme points of the orbit of a planet, etc.
apsides

apt likely (to); suitable; clever
aptitude *aptly* *aptness*

apterous lacking wings

aqualung breathing apparatus for underwater swimmers

aquamarine greenish-blue

aquaplane (to ride on a) board towed by a motorboat
aquaplaning

aquarium tank or pool in which fish, plants, etc., are kept
aquariums or *aquaria*

Aquarius 11th sign of the zodiac

aquatic living or found in water

aquatics water-sports

aquatint etching technique

aqueduct man-made channel for water

aqueous of or like water

aquiline curved like an eagle's beak

arabesque decorative design; ballet posture

Arabia peninsula in SW Asia
Arab Arabian Arabic

arable (*of land*) fit for growing crops

arachnid member of the group comprising spiders, mites, scorpions, ticks, etc.

arachnoid web-like membrane covering the brain and spinal cord

Araldite (*trademark*) kind of epoxy resin

arbiter judge

arbitrary chosen randomly and without reason
arbitrarily arbitrariness

arbitrate to settle a dispute between two groups
arbitrating arbitration arbitrator

arboreal of trees

arboretum place where trees or shrubs are grown
arboreta or *arboretums*

arboriculture cultivation of trees or shrubs

arbour (US **arbor**) bower of trees, vines, etc.

arc curved line; to form an arc
arced arcing

arcade covered passage; line of arches

arcane secret or esoteric

arch[1] (to make into a) curved structure or shape
arches archway

arch[2] chief; mischievous

arch- (*prefix*) chief
arch-enemy

archaeology (US **archeology**) study of material remains of ancient human life
archaeological (US *archeological*)
archaeologically (US *archeologically*)
archaeologist (US *archeologist*)

archaic of a remote period; no longer used
archaism

archangel chief angel

archbishop highest rank of bishop
archbishopric

archdeacon clergyman next in rank below a bishop
archdeaconry

archdiocese archbishop's diocese
archdiocesan

archduke sovereign prince
archducal archduchess archdukedom

archeology (US) see **archaeology**

archer person who shoots with bow and arrow
archery

archetype perfect or typical example; original
archetypal

archiepiscopal of an archbishop
archiepiscopacy archiepiscopate

archipelago group of islands
archipelagos or *archipelagoes*

architecture science of designing buildings
architect architectural

architrave moulded frame round a door, etc.

archives (place for storing) official records
archival archivist

Arctic region north of Arctic Circle

ardent intensely felt
ardently

ardour (US **ardor**) enthusiasm and zeal

arduous needing great effort
arduously

are[1] plural of present tense of **be**

are[2] unit of area, 100 square metres

area extent or expanse; region or field

arena enclosed area for sports events
arenas

aren't (*informal*) are not

areola small area round something
areolae

arête mountain ridge

argent silver

Argentina country in South America
Argentine Argentinian

argon unreactive gas used in electric lights

argosy large merchant ship
argosies

argot jargon or slang

argue to quarrel; to present reasons for or against something
arguable arguably argued arguing

argument quarrel; reasons for or against something
argumentation argumentative

argy-bargy (*informal*) wrangle
argy-bargies

aria song for a single voice
arias

arid dry; lacking interest
aridity

Aries 1st sign of the zodiac

aright correctly or properly

arise to come into being
arisen arising arose

aristocracy (government by the) privileged noble class
aristocracies aristocrat aristocratic aristocratically

arithmetic branch of mathematics dealing with numbers
arithmetical arithmetically arithmetician

ark covered vessel in which Noah lived in the Flood

Arkansas US state

arm[1] upper human limb
armband armchair armful armhole armlet armpit armrest

arm[2] (to equip with a) weapon
armament armed

armada large number of ships
armadas

armadillo burrowing mammal covered with horny plates
armadillos

armature rotating part of electric motor

Armenia republic of Eastern Europe
Armenian

armistice temporary suspension of hostilities

armorial of heraldic arms

armour (US **armor**) defensive covering
armoured (US *armored*) *armourer* (US *armorer*) *armoury* (US *armory*) *armouries* (US *armories*)

arms weapons; heraldic symbols

army military land forces of a country
armies

aroma pleasant smell
aromatic

aromatherapy use of fragrant oils in massage

arose past tense of **arise**

around on all sides (of)

arouse to stimulate; to wake
arousal arouser arousing

arpeggio (*music*) notes of a chord played or sung in succession
arpeggios

arquebus see **harquebus**

arraign to charge before a court; to accuse
arraigner arraignment

arrange to put in order
arrangeable arrangement arranger arranging

arrant utter; notorious

arras wall hanging

array impressive display; to put in order; to decorate splendidly
arraying

arrears money owed; duty still to be dealt with

arrest to place in legal custody; to stop
arresting

arrière-pensée (*French*) mental reservation
arrière-pensées

arrive to come to a destination
arrival arriving

arrogant behaving in an aggressively proud way
arrogance arrogantly

arrogate to claim or take unjustifiably
arrogating arrogation

arrondissement division of a French department

arrow long slender pointed weapon
arrowhead

arrowroot kind of plant yielding edible starch

arsenal store for weapons and ammunition

arsenic steel-grey poisonous element
arsenical

arson act of maliciously setting on fire
arsonist

art skill; creative ability; painting, sculpture, etc.
artwork

artefact or **artifact** man-made object

arteriosclerosis abnormal hardening of the arteries
arteriosclerotic

artery thick-walled blood-vessel
arteries arterial

artesian well well by which water reaches the surface with little or no pumping

artful cunning
artfully artfulness

arthritis inflammation of the joints
arthritic

arthropod kind of invertebrate animal with a jointed body, limbs, and an outer skin made of chitin

artichoke kind of vegetable

article particular object; non-fiction writing in a newspaper

articulate (to speak) clearly; to be connected by joints
articulated articulately articulateness articulating articulation

artifact see **artefact**

artifice cunning; skill or cleverness

artificer skilled craftsman; mechanic

artificial not natural; made by human skill
artificiality artificially

artillery large mounted firearms
artilleryman

artisan skilled worker

artist person who creates paintings, etc.
artistic artistically artistry
SEE PANEL

---

artist or artiste?

An *artist* is someone who paints or draws pictures or produces sculptures, either as a job or as a hobby.

An *artiste* is a professional entertainer: *a circus artiste*. Less commonly, an *artist* is also a writer or a performer such as an actor, musician, or dancer.

---

artiste professional public entertainer
SEE PANEL at artist

artless simple; natural
artlessness

arty pretentiously artistic
artier artiest artily artiness arty-crafty (US *artsy-craftsy*)

arum kind of white lily

as in or to the same degree or manner; like; in the role of; because

asbestos fibrous, non-combustible mineral
asbestosis

ascend to go up
ascension ascent

ascendance or **ascendence** dominance
ascendancy or *ascendency ascendant* or *ascendent*

ascertain to discover or determine
ascertainable ascertainment

ascetic self-denying (person)
ascetically asceticism

ascorbic acid vitamin C

ascribe to assign
ascribable ascribing ascription

aseptic free from bacteria
asepsis

asexual lacking sex organs
asexuality asexually

ash[1] powder remaining after a fire
ashes ashen ashtray ashy

ash[2] tree of the olive family

ashamed feeling shame

ashore on or to land from water

Asia continent of the world
Asian Asiatic

aside on or to one side

asinine of asses; obstinate or stupid
asininity

ask to put a question (to)
asker

askance with distrust

askew not straight

aslant in a slanting position

asleep sleeping

asp kind of small viper

asparagus plant of the lily family; its shoots

aspect feature or appearance
aspectual

aspen kind of poplar tree

asperity roughness
asperities

asperse to spread false rumours about
aspersing aspersion

asphalt black sticky substance used in road-surfacing

asphodel kind of lily

asphyxiate to suffocate
asphyxia asphyxiating asphyxiation

aspic savoury jelly

aspidistra kind of long-leaved plant

aspirate (to pronounce with an) *h*-sound
aspirating

aspirator suction device
aspiratory

aspire to try to reach an aim
aspirant aspiration aspiring

aspirin pain-relieving drug or tablet

ass mammal related to the horse
asses

assail to attack violently
assailable assailant assailer

assassin someone who kills a famous person, esp. for political reasons

assassinate to kill a famous person, esp. for political reasons
assassinating assassination assassinator

assault (to make a) violent attack
assaulter assaultive

assay to evaluate; to test the purity of
assayable assayed assayer assaying

assegai or **assagai** light spear

assemble to bring, come or join together
assemblage assembler assembling assembly assemblies

assent (to express) agreement or acceptance
assenter or *assentor*

assert to declare
asserter or *assertor assertion assertive assertively assertiveness*

assess to estimate or determine a value or amount
assessable assesses assessment assessor

asset valuable thing, quality or person
asset-stripping

asseverate to declare solemnly
asseverating asseveration

assiduity diligent close attention
assiduities assiduous assiduously

assign to choose or designate
assignable assignation assignee assignment assignor

assimilate to absorb
assimilable assimilating assimilation assimilative

assist to help
assistance assistant assister

assize (*formerly*) court sessions
assizes assizer

associate to join or link; partner or colleague
associating association associative

assonance resemblance of sounds
assonant

assorted different; matched
assort assortment

assuage to moderate or soothe
assuagement assuager assuaging assuasive

assume to suppose; to undertake
assumable assuming assumption assumptive

assurance confidence; guarantee; kind of insurance

assure to make confident; to promise
assurable assured assurer assuring
SEE PANEL

---

assure, ensure, or insure?

You *assure* someone that something is true when you tell them that there is no doubt about it, especially in order to make them less worried or doubtful: *I assure you that the statistics quoted are entirely correct.*

Ensure is a formal word; if you *ensure* that something happens you make certain that it does happen: *An independent adjudicator has been appointed to ensure fair treatment of all cases.* In American English, *ensure* can also be spelled *insure*.

Insure is used to mean to guarantee or protect against risk or loss: *insure yourself against illness; insure your house and furnishings.*

---

aster kind of plant with daisy-like flowers

asterisk symbol *

astern in or to the stern; backwards

asteroid small planet orbiting the sun

asthma respiratory disorder
asthmatic asthmatically

astigmatism eye defect
astigmatic

astir out of bed; moving

astonish to surprise greatly
astonishes astonishingly astonishment

astound to shock with surprise and wonder
astoundingly

astraddle astride

astrakhan kind of curled lambskin

astral of the stars

astray off the correct path

astride with one leg each side (of)

astringent harsh; (substance causing) contraction of organic tissues
astringency

astrolabe early astronomical instrument

astrology study of the influence of planets, etc. on human affairs
astrologer astrological astrologist

astronaut traveller in space
astronautical astronautics

astronomy study of stars and planets
astronomer astronomical astronomically

astrophysics study of physical and chemical properties of stars, planets, etc.
astrophysical astrophysicist

Astroturf (*trademark*) artificial grass surface for sports fields

astute shrewd; perceptive
astutely astuteness

asunder apart

asylum place of safety or refuge
asylums

asymmetry lack of symmetry
asymmetric asymmetrical

at used to show position

atavism recurrence of earlier characteristics not present in intermediate generations
atavistic

ate past tense of **eat**

atelier workshop

atheism belief that there is no God
atheist atheistic atheistical atheistically

atherosclerosis degenerative disease of the arteries
atheroscleroses atherosclerotic

athirst eager

athlete person trained to compete in exercises or sports
athletic athletically athleticism athletics

at-home social gathering at one's house

athwart from one side to another (of)

Atlantic world's 2nd largest ocean

atlas book of maps
atlases

atmosphere air; environment or influence
atmospheric atmospherically atmospherics

atoll coral reef surrounding a lagoon

atom smallest particle of an element that takes part in chemical reactions
atomic atomize or *atomise*

atonal without reference to a musical key
atonality

atone to make amends for
atonable atonement atoning

atrium upper chamber of the heart
atria or *atriums*

atrocious very wicked; (*informal*) unpleasant
atrociously atrocity atrocities

atrophy wasting away; to waste away
atrophies atrophied atrophying

attach to join or fasten
attachable attacher attaches attachment

attaché diplomatic specialist; briefcase
attachés

attack to act forcefully against; to start energetically; strong, hostile attempt
attacker

attain to reach or achieve
attainable attainment

attar oil from rose-petals

attempt (to make an) effort
attemptable

attend to be present at; to take care of
attendance attendant

attention concentrated thought; awareness
attentive attentively

attenuate to make thin or weaker
attenuating attenuation

attest to declare to be true; to demonstrate
attestable attestation attester

attic space or room in the roof of a house

attire dress or clothing

attitude mental position
attitudinize or *attitudinise*

attorney person who has legal authority to act for another
attorney-general attorneys-general or *attorney-generals attorneyship*

attract to draw or pull to oneself; to arouse
attractable attraction

attractive pleasing to the senses
attractively attractiveness

attribute to regard as belonging to or produced by
attributable attributing attribution attributive

attrition wearing away by rubbing

attune to bring into harmony
attuning

atypical not typical

aubergine (kind of plant with) dark purple fruit

aubretia or **aubrietia** kind of trailing purple-flowered plant

auburn reddish-brown

auction public sale of goods or property to the highest bidder
auctioneer

audacious bold and daring
audaciously audacity

audible loud enough to be heard
audibility or *audibleness audibly*

audience group of people at a performance; formal interview

audio- (*prefix*) of hearing or sound
audiotape audiovisual

audit (to make an) official examination and verification of accounts
audited auditing auditor auditorial

audition test of a possible performer

auditorium part of a theatre, etc. in which the audience sits
auditoriums or *auditoria*

auditory of hearing

au fait (*French*) fully informed

auger tool for boring holes in wood

aught all; (*archaic*) anything

augment to make or become greater in strength, number, etc.
augmentation augmentative

augur to be a sign of
augural augury auguries

august dignified
augustly augustness

August 8th month of the year

auk kind of northern sea-bird

aunt sister of one's father or mother; uncle's wife;
(*informal*) *auntie* or *aunty aunties*

au pair foreign girl who does household duties in return for board and lodging and study opportunities

aura characteristic quality
auras

aural of the ear or hearing
SEE PANEL

---

aural or oral?

Aural means 'of the ear or hearing': *aural effects.*

Oral means 'spoken; verbal; of or through the mouth': *oral communication; oral hygiene.*

An *aural* comprehension is one that involves listening; an *oral* examination is one that is spoken.

---

aureola saint's halo

au revoir (*French*) goodbye

auricle upper chamber of the heart; external part of the ear
auricled auricular

auriferous containing or yielding gold

aurora dawn
auroras or *aurorae*

auspices patronage

auspicious favourable or propitious
auspiciously auspiciousness

austere stern or severe
austerely austerity austerities

Australasia Australia, New Zealand, and neighbouring South Pacific islands
Australasian

Australia continent of the world
Australian

Austria country in Europe
Austrian

autarchy absolute sovereignty
autarchies autarchic

autarky self-sufficiency, esp. economic
autarkies autarkic autarkist

authentic genuine or reliable
authentically authenticate authentication authenticity

author (*fem.* **authoress**) writer of a book, play, etc.
authorial authorship

authority power or right to influence or control
authorities authoritarian authoritative authoritatively authoritativeness

authorize or **authorise** to give authority to; to allow
authorization or *authorisation authorizing* or *authorising*

autism self-absorption
autistic

auto (US) short for **automobile**
autos

auto- (*prefix*) self
auto-suggestion

autobahn German motorway

autobiography account of a person's life, written by himself or herself
autobiographies autobiographer autobiographical

autocracy government by a ruler with unlimited power
autocracies autocrat autocratic

autocross motor sport

autocue television prompting device

auto-da-fé sentence of the Inquisition, esp. burning of a heretic
autos-da-fé

autogiro or **autogyro** kind of aircraft

autograph person's signature

automat coin-operated vending machine

automate to make a process, etc. automatic
automating automation

automatic working by itself; independent
automatically automatism

automaton mechanical device; robot
automatons or *automata*

automobile (US) car

autonomous self-governing
autonomously autonomy autonomies

autopsy medical examination of a dead body to determine the cause of death
autopsies

autoroute French motorway

autostrada Italian motorway

autumn season between summer and winter
autumnal

auxiliary additional; providing support
auxiliaries

avail to be of use to

available able to be obtained, used, or reached
availability availably

avalanche large mass of snow and ice falling down a mountain

avant-garde people with radically new ideas in the arts

avarice greed for riches
avaricious avariciously

avenge to take vengeance for
avenger avenging

avenue broad street, often tree-lined

aver to state positively
averment averred averring

average (to find the) result of adding quantities and dividing by the number of quantities
averaging

averse opposed; disinclined
averseness aversion
SEE PANEL at **adverse**

avert to turn away
avertible or *avertable*

aviary enclosure where birds are kept
aviaries

aviation science of flying aircraft
aviator aviatrix or *aviatress*

avid eager (for)
avidity

avocado kind of pear-shaped tropical fruit
avocados

avocation hobby

avoid to keep away from; to refrain from
avoidable avoidably avoidance

avoirdupois British system of weights

avow to state; to admit openly
avowable avowal avowedly

avuncular of or like an uncle

await to wait for; to expect

awake to wake; not sleeping
awaken awakening awaking awoke awoken

award to grant officially; prize

aware having knowledge (of)
awareness

awash washed over by waves

away from one place; in another direction; absent

awe wonder, deep respect, and fear
awe-inspiring awesome awe-stricken awe-struck

aweigh (*of an anchor*) raised clear of the bottom

awful very great; (*informal*) unpleasant; nasty
awfully awfulness

awhile for a short time

awkward clumsy; difficult

awl tool for making small holes

awning canvas cover

awoke past tense of **awake**

awoken past participle of **awake**

awry crooked(ly)

axe (US **ax**) tool for felling trees or chopping wood; to cut with an axe
axing

axiom self-evident truth
axiomatic axiomatically

axis line about which an object rotates
axes axial

axle bar or shaft on which a wheel rotates

ayatollah Iranian religious leader

aye or **ay** yes; ever or always

azalea kind of flowering shrub

Azerbaijan republic of Eastern Europe

azimuth angle on the earth's surface between a north-south line and the position of something

Azores islands in the North Atlantic

Aztec Mexican Indian people or language

azure sky-blue

B

babble to utter words, etc. incoherently
babbler babbling

babe baby

babel confused noises

baboon large monkey

baby very young child
babies babyhood babyish babysit baby-sitting

baccalaureate academic degree of bachelor

baccarat gambling card-game

bacchanalia drunken revelry
bacchanalian

bachelor unmarried man; holder of lowest academic degree
bachelorhood

bacillus rod-shaped bacterium
bacilli bacillary

back rear part, esp. of body; to move away or in a reverse direction; to support
backache back-bencher backbiting backbone back-breaking backchat backcloth backdate back-door backer backdrop backfire background backhanded backhander backing backlash backless backlist backlog back-pedal backrest back-scratcher backside backslide backspace backstage backstairs back-stitch backstroke backstreet backtrack back-up backward backwards backwash backwater backwoods

backgammon game played with dice

bacon meat from the cured side of a pig

bacterium single-celled microscopic organism
bacteria bacterial bactericide bacteriologist bacteriology

bad unpleasant; evil; decayed
badly badness bad-tempered

bade past tense of **bid**

badge distinguishing emblem or mark

badger burrowing animal; to pester

badminton game played with rackets and a shuttlecock

baffle to perplex; to frustrate
bafflement baffler baffling

bag (to put into a) flexible container
bagful bagged bagging

bagatelle trifle or triviality; board game

baggage luggage; equipment

baggy hanging loosely
baggier baggiest baggily bagginess

bagpipes reed-pipe musical instrument

baguette long thin French loaf

Bahamas group of islands in West Indies
Bahamian

Bahrain sheikdom on the Persian Gulf
Bahraini

bail[1] money guaranteeing the reappearance of a person in court
bailee bailor

SEE PANEL

---

bail or bale?

Bail is money paid as a security guaranteeing the reappearance of an arrested person in court: *He was released after an initial hearing on £500 bail.* In cricket, the *bails* are the crosspieces on the stumps.

A *bale* is a large bundle: *bales of hay/waste paper. Bale* can also be used as a verb: *to bale hay.*

In the senses of emptying water from a boat, making a parachute jump, or helping someone out of a difficult situation either *bail out* or *bale out* can be used: *bale out lameduck industries.*

bail[2] crosspiece on cricket stumps
SEE PANEL at **bail**[1]

bail[3] or **bale** to empty water from a boat
bailer or *baler*
SEE PANEL at **bail**[1]

bailey outer wall of a castle
baileys

bailiff official helping a sheriff; manager of a farm or estate

bait food to attract prey; to exasperate constantly

baize felt-like woollen fabric

bake to cook by dry heat in an oven
baker bakery bakeries baking

Bakelite (*trademark*) kind of synthetic resin and plastic

baksheesh money given as a tip

balaclava tight-fitting woollen hood

balalaika Russian stringed musical instrument

balance weighing device; (to bring or come into) equilibrium; difference between debits and credits
balanceable balancing

balcony platform extending from a wall; theatre upper gallery
balconies

bald without hair
bald-headed balding

balderdash rubbish

bale[1] (to make into a) large bundle
baling
SEE PANEL at **bail**[1]

bale[2] **(out)** to make a parachute jump, see also **bail**[3]
baling
SEE PANEL at **bail**[1]

baleful harmful or threatening
balefully balefulness

Bali island of Indonesia
Balinese

balk or **baulk** to stop short

ball[1] round mass
ball-bearing ballcock ball-point

ball[2] social gathering for dancing
ballroom

ballad simple song or poem

ballade kind of verse form; musical composition

ballast heavy material carried in a ship for stability

ballerina female ballet dancer

ballet artistic dancing and mime to music; group of dancers
balletic balletomane balletomania

ballistics study of motion of projectiles
ballistic ballistically

balloon bag of light material that is filled with gas or air and floats in the air
balloonist

ballot secret voting; to vote
balloted balloting

ballpark baseball park or stadium; approximate

ballyhoo noisy talk or publicity

balm soothing substance

balmy soothing; mild
balmier balmiest

baloney or **boloney** (*informal*) nonsense

balsa kind of (very light wood of a) tropical tree

balsam tree yielding balm; balm

baluster upright support for a rail

balustrade structure of balusters and rail

bamboo tall grass with hollow stems

bamboozle to confuse or trick
bamboozling

ban to prohibit

banned banning

banal trite; common
banality banalities banally

banana kind of crescent-shaped fruit

band[1] group of people, esp. musicians
bandmaster bandsman bandstand bandwagon bandwidth

band[2] thin strip of material

bandage (to cover with a) piece of material to dress a wound
bandaging

bandanna or **bandana** large handkerchief

bandeau band worn round the head
bandeaux

bandit robber; outlaw
bandits or *banditti banditry*

bandoleer or **bandolier** belt for cartridges

bandy (*of legs*) curving outwards at the knees; to pass about
bandied bandier bandiest bandying bandy-legged

bane cause of misery or trouble
baneful

bang (to make a) short loud explosive noise

banger (*informal*) firework; sausage; noisy old car

Bangladesh country in South Asia
Bangladeshi

bangle bracelet

banian see **banyan**

banish to expel
banishes banishment

banister or **bannister** handrail and upright supports

banjo kind of stringed musical instrument
banjos or *banjoes*

bank[1] establishment for keeping, lending, etc. of money
bank-book banker banknote

bank[2] (to form into a) slope or mound

bankrupt (a person who is) unable to pay his or her debts
bankruptcy bankruptcies

banner flag

bannister see **banister**

banns public announcement in church of a proposed marriage

banquet (to hold or take part in a) sumptuous meal
banqueted banqueting

banshee female wailing spirit

bantam small domestic fowl; small
bantamweight

banter to tease lightly; teasing

Bantu group of African languages

banyan or **banian** kind of Indian tree

baobab kind of tropical African tree

bap soft bread roll

baptism Christian ordinance of admission into the Church
baptismal Baptist baptistry or *baptistery*

baptize or **baptise** to administer baptism to
baptizing or *baptising*

bar long straight piece of something solid; (to obstruct with a) barrier; counter
barmaid barman barred barring bartender

barb sharp, backward pointing part of a hook, etc.

Barbados island in the West Indies
Barbadian

barbarian primitive or uncivilized (person)
barbaric barbarism

barbarous savage; inhuman
barbarity barbarities

barbecue (to cook on an) outdoor grill
barbecued barbecuing

barbel spine or bristle hanging from certain fish; kind of freshwater fish

barber men's hairdresser

barbican tower at a fortification

barbiturate kind of hypnotic or sedative drug

barcarole or **barcarolle** Venetian boat song

bard minstrel; poet
bardic

bare naked; exposed; mere; to expose
bareback barebacked barefaced barefoot barefooted barehanded bareheaded barelegged barely bareness barer barest baring

bargain (to make an) agreement, esp. about a price; something bought cheaply
bargainer bargaining

barge flat-bottomed vessel; to move awkwardly
bargee barge-pole barging

baritone (male singer with or music for) voice between tenor and bass

barium soft metallic element

bark[1] (*of a dog*) to make its typical cry

bark[2] protective layer on a tree

barley cereal grass
barleycorn

barm yeast

barmy (*slang*) crazy
barmier barmiest

barn large farm building
barnyard

barnacle kind of small clinging shellfish

barometer instrument for measuring atmospheric pressure
barometric barometrical barometry

baron lowest rank of nobility in Britain
baroness baronial barony

baronet member of the lowest hereditary titled British order
baroness baronetage baronetcy

baroque extravagantly decorative style of architecture, music, etc.

barouche 4-wheeled horse-drawn carriage

barque kind of sailing ship

barrack[1] to house soldiers in barracks

barrack[2] to jeer or scoff

barracks buildings accommodating soldiers

barracuda kind of predatory fish

barrage artillery fire; artificial construction

barrel (to put in a) cylindrical container; cylindrical part
barrelful barrelled (US *barreled*) *barrelling* (US *barreling*) *barrel-organ*

barren unable to produce crops or offspring
barrenness

barricade (to block with) a defensive barrier
barricading

barrier obstruction

barring unless

barrister lawyer who may plead in a higher court

barrow[1] handcart; wheelbarrow

barrow[2] prehistoric burial mound

barter to trade goods in exchange for other goods

basalt dark igneous rock

bascule kind of bridge

base[1] bottom or supporting part; to establish
basal baseboard baseless baseline basing

base[2] contemptible; inferior

baseball 9-a-side ball game

basement lowest part of a building

bash to strike violently; attempt

bashes basher bashing

bashful shy
bashfully bashfulness

basic fundamental
basically

BASIC computer language

basil kind of plant with aromatic leaves

basilica ancient Roman building with oblong nave; church like this

basilisk mythical reptile; small tropical lizard

basin round open container
basinful

basis foundation; main part
bases

bask to lie in pleasant warmth

basket container made from interwoven pieces of cane, etc.
basketful basketry basketwork

basketball 5-a-side ball game

Basque member of a people living in the West Pyrenees; their language

bas-relief sculpture in low relief

bass^1 (singer with or music for) lowest male voice

bass^2 kind of fish

bassinet wickerwork cradle

bassoon woodwind instrument
bassoonist

bast fibre used in making rope, etc.

bastard illegitimate child
bastardize or *bastardise bastardy*

baste to moisten meat with fat during cooking
basting

bastinado punishment of beating the soles of the feet with a stick

bastion (projecting part of) fortification

bat^1 (to hit with a) wooden implement used in certain games
batsman batted batter batting

bat^2 nocturnal flying mammal

bat^3 to wink
batted batting

batch (to put in a) group of similar things
batches batcher

bate to restrain
bated bating

bath (to wash in a) large container for washing the body
bathhouse bathrobe bathroom bath-tub
SEE PANEL

---

bath or bathe?

A *bath* is the large low container in which you wash yourself. To *bath* someone or to give them a *bath* means to wash them in a bath.

Bathe means 'to swim; to immerse in water': *bathe in the sea; bathe a wound with warm water.* In American English *bathe* means 'to have a bath'.

---

bathe to swim; to immerse in water
bather bathing bathing-suit
SEE PANEL at **bath**

bathos (*in writing*) sudden change from lofty to ordinary matters

bathysphere diving sphere for deep-sea observation

batik method of printing fabric

batiste fine plain-weave fabric

batman officer's personal servant
batmen

baton music conductor's small thin stick

bats (*informal*) crazy

battalion military unit

batten narrow strip of sawn timber

batter^1 to hit repeatedly and violently
battering-ram

batter^2 mixture of flour, eggs, and milk or water

battery electric cell or cells; group of guns
batteries

battle (to) fight or struggle
battleaxe battle-cry battledress battlefield battleground battle-scarred battleship battling

battlement parapet with open spaces for shooting from

batty (*informal*) crazy
battier battiest

bauble cheap showy ornament

baud unit used to measure the speed of data transmission

baulk see **balk**

bauxite mineral that is the principal ore of aluminium

bawdy coarse or indecent
bawdier bawdiest bawdily bawdiness

bawl to shout loudly

bay[1] wide inlet of sea, etc.

bay[2] alcove or recess

bay[3] (to make a) deep howling sound

bay[4] reddish-brown

bay[5] laurel-like shrub or tree

bayonet blade fixed to muzzle of a firearm; to stab with this
bayoneted bayoneting

bazaar eastern market; sale of miscellaneous goods

bazooka anti-tank rocket-firing weapon

be to exist
am are been being is was were

beach shore
beaches beachcomber beach-head beachwear

beacon signal fire or light

bead small pierced ball for threading on string, etc.

beading ornamental strip

beadle church or college official

beady small, round and bright
beadier beadiest

beagle small breed of hound; hunting with beagles
beagler beagling

beak projecting horny part of a bird's jaws

beaker tall wide-mouthed container for liquids

beam long thick piece of wood; narrow shaft of light
beam-ends beaming beamy

bean kind of pod-bearing plant; seed of this
beanbag beanfeast beanpole beanstalk

bear[1] to carry; to show; to support; to give birth to
bearable bearably bearer bore born borne

bear[2] kind of large animal with shaggy coat
bear-baiting bearish bearskin

beard hair growing on a man's face

bearing relevance; behaviour

beast animal
beastly

beat to hit repeatedly; to defeat; blow
beaten beater

beatify to declare blessed; to make very happy
beatific beatification beatified beatifies beatifying beatitude

beatnik unconventional person of 1950s and 1960s

beautician person who gives beauty treatments

beautify to make beautiful
beautification beautified beautifier beautifies beautifying

beauty qualities that delight the senses
beauties beauteous beautiful beautifully

beaver kind of large aquatic rodent

because for the reason that

beck[1] beckoning gesture

beck[2] mountain stream

beckon to summon with the hand or head

become to come to be; to suit
became becoming becomingly

becquerel SI unit of radiation activity

bed place on which to sleep or rest
bedbug bedclothes bed-cover bed-covering bedded bedding bedfellow bedpan bedpost bedridden bedroom bedside bedsit bedsitter bedsore bedspread bedstead bedtime bed-wetting

bedaub to smear

bedeck to adorn

bedevil to frustrate or harass
bedevilled (US *bedeviled*) *bedevilling* (US *bedeviling*) *bedevilment*

bedlam uproar

bedouin nomadic Arab

bedraggled wet or dirty from rain or mud

bedrock solid rock below surface; basic principles

bee 4-winged insect that produces honey
beehive beekeeper beeline beeswax

beech kind of hardwood deciduous tree
beechen beechnut beechy

beef meat from cow, bull, etc.
beefburger beefcake beefsteak beefy

beefeater yeoman of the guard at Tower of London

Beelzebub the Devil

been past participle of **be**

beep (to make a) short high-pitched sound
beeped beeper beeping

beer alcoholic drink
beerhouse beer-mat beershop beery

beet kind of plant with a thick fleshy root

beetle[1] insect with hard front wings; to scurry
beetling

beetle[2] heavy tool for beating

beetle[3] to overhang
beetle-browed beetling

beetroot beet with red root that is eaten in salads

befall (*formal*) to happen (to)
befallen befell

befit to be suitable for
befitted befitting

before at an earlier time (than); in front of

beforehand in advance

befoul to make dirty

befriend to make a friend of

befuddle to confuse, as if with drink
befuddlement befuddling

beg to ask for money; to ask humbly or earnestly
begged begging

beget to be the father of; to cause
begetter begot begotten

beggar person who lives by begging; to make poor
beggardom beggarly

begin to perform the first part of
began beginner beginning begun

begone go away!

begonia kind of plant with showy, waxy flowers

begrudge to concede reluctantly; to envy
begrudging

beguile to deceive; to charm
beguilement beguiler beguiling

begum Muslim lady of rank

begun past participle of **begin**

behalf interest or part

behave to act or function; to conduct oneself
behaving behaviour (US *behavior*) *behavioural* (US *behavioral*) *behaviourism* (US *behaviorism*) *behaviourist* (US *behaviorist*)

behead to cut off the head of

behest earnest request

behind at the back (of); later than

behindhand in arrears with; late

behold to observe
beheld beholder

beholden indebted or obliged

behove (US **behoove**) to be necessary
behoving (US *behooving*)

beige very light brown

being present participle of **be**; existence; living being

bejewelled (US **bejeweled**) decorated with jewels

belabour (US **belabor**) to beat severely

Belarus republic in Eastern Europe
Belarussian

belated coming later

belay to secure (with) a rope
belayed belaying

belch to expel gas through the mouth from the stomach; act of belching
belches belcher

beleaguer to besiege or harass
beleaguered

belfry steeple or tower in which bells are hung
belfries

Belgium country in Europe
Belgian

belie to give a false impression of
belied belies belying

believe to accept as true; to think; to trust
believable believer believing

belittle to cause to seem unimportant
belittling

Belize country in Central America
Belizean

bell device that makes a ringing sound
bell-bottomed bell-bottoms bell-ringer

belladonna deadly nightshade

belle attractive woman

belles-lettres (*French*) essays, poetry, etc.
belletrist

bellicose ready to fight

belligerent aggressive; at war
belligerence or *belligerency belligerently*

bellow to shout; to roar like a bull

bellows device that produces an air current

bell-wether male sheep leading a flock

belly abdomen; stomach; to swell
bellies bellyache belly-button belly-dance bellyflop bellyful

belong to be the property or possession (of)

belongings possessions

beloved dearly loved

below at a lower level (than)

belt band of leather, etc.
belted

belvedere raised building commanding a fine view

bemoan to mourn

bemused confused; preoccupied

bench long seat without a back; work-table
benches bencher benchmark

bend (to force or be forced into a) curve or turn
bent bentwood

beneath below

benediction blessing

benefaction act of kindness
benefactor benefactress

benefice church living

beneficent generous
beneficence beneficently

beneficial advantageous
beneficially

beneficiary person who benefits
beneficiaries

benefit advantage; payment; to be useful or profitable to
benefited benefiting

Benelux Belgium, the Netherlands, Luxembourg

benevolent kind
benevolence benevolently

Bengali of Bangladesh or Bengal; language of Bengal

benign kindly; not malignant
benignancy benignant benignity benignly

Benin country in West Africa
Beninese

bent not straight; past tense and past participle of **bend**

benumb to make numb

benzene flammable liquid obtained from oil and coal tar

benzine spirit obtained from distillation of petroleum

bequeath to leave property as a legacy
bequeathal bequeather bequest

berate to scold harshly
berating

bereave to deprive of a person or thing, esp. by death
bereavement bereaving bereft

beret soft flat round cap

beriberi tropical disease

Bermuda group of islands in NW Atlantic
Bermudan Bermudian

berry small edible fruit
berries

berserk frenziedly angry

berth bed or bunk on a ship or train; mooring-place

beryl precious stone

beryllium metallic element

beseech to ask earnestly
beseeched beseeches besought

beset to trouble constantly
besetting

beside by the side of (a person or thing)

besides in addition

besiege to surround with armed forces
besieger besieging

besmirch to make dirty

besom broom made of bundle of twigs

besotted infatuated; intoxicated

besought past tense and past participle of **beseech**

bespangled decorated with spangles

bespatter to splash with mud, etc.

bespeak (*formal*) to ask for in advance; to indicate
bespoke bespoken

bespectacled wearing spectacles

bespoke made-to-measure; made to order; dealing in such suits

best of the most excellent, etc. kind
best-seller

bestial like a beast; cruel
bestiality bestialize or *bestialise bestially*

bestiary medieval story about real or imaginary animals
bestiaries

bestir to rouse
bestirred bestirring

bestow to present a gift or honour
bestowal

bestrew to scatter or lie scattered about
bestrewn

bestride to stand or sit astride
bestridden bestriding bestrode

bet (to place) money risked, depending on a result
better or *bettor betting*

beta 2nd letter of the Greek alphabet

betake to cause (oneself) to go
betaken betaking betook

betel kind of climbing plant whose leaves are chewed
betel-nut

bête noire (*French*) particular dislike
bêtes noires

bethink to consider
bethought

betide to happen to
betiding

betoken to show

betray to expose to an enemy; to be disloyal to
betrayal betrayer

betroth to promise in marriage
betrothal

better of a more excellent, etc. kind; to make or become better
betterment better-off

between in the middle of (two things)

bevel (to shape to a) sloping edge
bevelled (US *beveled*) *bevelling* (US *beveling*)

beverage drink

bevy flock or group
bevies

bewail to express great sorrow over

beware to be cautious (of)

bewilder to confuse or puzzle
bewilderment

bewitch to cast a spell over; to charm
bewitched bewitches bewitching

beyond farther than

bezique kind of card-game

Bhutan country in central Asia
Bhutanese

bi- (*prefix*) 2, twice; appearing every 2 or twice
biaxial bimetallic bipolar biyearly

biannual twice a year
biannually
SEE PANEL

---

biannual or biennial?
Biannual means 'twice a year': *have a biannual medical examination.*

Biennial means 'occurring every two years; lasting for two years': *a biennial conference/festival.*

---

bias tendency; to prejudice
biased or *biassed biasing* or *biassing*

bib protective cloth used by a child when eating

Bible sacred writings of the Christian religion
biblical

bibliography list of writings on one subject or by one author
bibliographies bibliographer bibliographical

bibliophile person who collects or loves books

bibulous addicted to alcohol

bicameral having 2 legislative chambers

bicarbonate salt of carbonic acid

bicentenary 200th anniversary
bicentenaries bicentennial

biceps large muscle in upper arm

bicker to argue pettily

bicycle (to ride a) 2-wheeled vehicle
bicycling bicyclist

bid (to offer a) price at an auction; to order
bade biddable bidden bidder bidding

bide to wait for (an opportunity)
biding bode

bidet basin for washing the genitals

biennial occurring every 2 years; lasting 2 years
biennially
SEE PANEL at **biannual**

bier stand for a coffin

biff (*informal*) (to) whack or punch

bifocal having 2 different focuses

bifurcate to fork into 2
bifurcating bifurcation

big large in size; important or powerful
bigger biggest biggish big-headed big-hearted bigness bigwig

bigamy marrying someone while still married to someone else
bigamies bigamist bigamous

bight small bay; loop or slack middle part of rope

bigot intolerant person
bigoted bigotry

bijou small delicate item; jewel
bijoux or *bijous*

bike (*informal*) short for **bicycle**

bikini 2-piece swimming-costume

bilabial pronounced with closed lips

bilateral of or having 2 sides
bilateralism bilaterally

bilberry kind of edible fruit
bilberries

bile fluid secreted by the liver

bilge (*informal*) nonsense; lowest part of a ship's hull

bilharzia schistosomiasis

bilingual able to speak 2 languages fluently
bilingualism bilingually

bilious of the bile; with too much bile
biliousness

bilk to cheat out of what is due

bill[1] statement of money owed; notice; proposed law

bill[2] bird's beak

billboard hoarding

billet (to provide) accommodation for a soldier in a private home
billeted billeting

billet-doux love letter
billets-doux

billhook cutting tool

billiards game played on a cloth-covered table with cues and balls
billiard-ball billiard-cue

billion thousand million; (*formerly Brit*) million million
billionaire

billow large wave; to rise or swell

billy can used for cooking by campers
billies billycan

billy goat male goat

biltong strips of sun-dried meat

bimbo (*slang*) pretty but stupid young woman
bimbos

bimetallism use of 2 metals at fixed relative values as money standard

bimonthly every 2 months; twice a month

bin container

binary made up of 2 parts of digits

bind to fasten together with rope, etc.
binder bindery binding bound

bindweed kind of twining plant

binge (*informal*) excessive indulgence

bingo gambling game

binnacle housing for a ship's compass

binoculars instrument that makes distant objects appear nearer

binomial (*maths*) consisting of 2 terms
binomially

biochemistry study of chemistry of living organisms

biodegradable capable of being decomposed biologically

biography account of a person's life
biographies biographer biographical

biology study of living organisms
biological biologist

bionics application of living systems to man-made systems
bionic

biophysics application of physics to biology
biophysical biophysicist

biopsy examination of living tissue
biopsies

biorhythm pattern of biological processes in a person

bipartisan of or involving 2 parties

bipartite having 2 parts

biped 2-footed animal

biplane aircraft with 2 sets of wings

birch kind of smooth-barked tree
birches birchen birch-rod

bird feathered animal
bird-bath birdbrained birdcage bird-call birdlime bird's-eye view birdsong bird-table

birdie (*golf*) score of one stroke under par

biretta square cap worn by clergy

Biro (*trademark*) kind of ball-point pen

birth process of being born; origin
birth-control birthday birthmark birthplace birth-rate birthright birthstone

biscuit small flat dry cake

bisect to divide into 2 equal parts
bisection bisector

bisexual of or attracted to 2 sexes
bisexuality bisexually

bishop high-ranking clergyman; chess-piece
bishopric

bismuth brittle pinkish-white metal

bison large wild ox; buffalo

bistro small restaurant
bistros

bit[1] small piece
bitty

bit[2] mouthpiece on a horse's bridle; boring part of tool

bit[3] basic unit of computer information

bitch female dog, wolf, etc.; (*informal*) to be spiteful or unfair
bitches bitchy

bite to cut or seize with the teeth
bit biter biting bitten

bitter tasting sharp and unpleasant; resentful
bitterness bittersweet

bittern kind of wading-bird

bitumen black sticky substance used in road-making
bituminize or *bituminise bituminous*

bivalve shellfish with a shell consisting of 2 valves
bivalvular

bivouac (to make a) temporary camp
bivouacked bivouacking

bi-weekly every 2 weeks; twice a week

bizarre odd or unusual

blab to talk indiscreetly or thoughtlessly
blabbed blabber blabbermouth blabbing

black completely dark; without light
blackberry blackbird blackcurrant blackfly blackhead blackout blacksmith blackthorn

blackball to ostracize or vote against

blackboard board for writing on with chalk

blacken to make or become black; to defame

blackguard scoundrel
blackguardism blackguardly

blacking polish to make shoes black; boycotting

blackleg person who continues to work during a strike

blacklist (to put on a) list of suspicious or untrustworthy people or groups

blackmail to obtain money by threats; threatening or money extorted
blackmailer

bladder bag-like organ of the body that stores urine

blade cutting-part of a knife or weapon; flat wide part of an oar, etc.

blame to hold someone responsible (for); responsibility for a fault
blameable or *blamable blameless blamelessly blamelessness blameworthy blaming*

blanch to whiten; to scald or boil
blanches
SEE PANEL

---

blanch or blench?
Blanch means 'to whiten': *His face blanched with fear,* and 'to scald or boil': *to blanch vegetables; blanched almonds.*
If you *blench* (or more rarely, *blanch*) at something, you are very frightened of it: *blench at the sight of a spider.*

---

blancmange flavoured milk jelly-like dessert

bland mild; uninteresting
blandly blandness

blandishment coaxing or flattering

blank not written or printed on

blanket thick covering on a bed; to cover with this
blanketed blanketing

blare to sound loudly and harshly
blaring

blarney flattering talk

blasé indifferent, because overfamiliar

blaspheme to utter something irreverent or contemptuous
blasphemer blaspheming blasphemous blasphemously blasphemy blasphemies

blast explosion; rush of wind; to produce a loud harsh noise
blast-off

blatant obvious; conspicuous
blatancy blatantly

blather to speak foolishly

blaze[1] strong burning flame; to burn strongly
blazing

blaze[2] (to make a) mark on a tree
blazing

blaze[3] to make widely known
blazing

blazer lightweight jacket

blazon coat of arms
blazoner blazonry

bleach to whiten, esp. chemically; bleaching agent
bleaches bleacher

bleak cheerless; gloomy
bleakish bleakly bleakness

bleary dimmed by tiredness; blurred
bleariIy bleariness

bleat (to make the) cry of a sheep or goat

bleed to lose or emit blood
bled bleeding

bleep (to make a) high-pitched electronic signal
bleeper bleeping

blemish flaw; to spoil or tarnish
blemishes

blench to shy away in fear
blencher blenches
SEE PANEL at **blanch**

blend (to make) a mixture
blended blender

bless to wish happiness; to make happy; to make holy
blessed or *blest blessedly blessedness blesses blessing*

blew past tense of **blow**[1]

blight plant disease; (to exert an) impairing influence

blighter (*informal*) fellow

blind (to make) unable to see; cover for window; pretext
blindly blindness

blindfold to cover the eyes with a cloth

blink to close and open the eyes quickly; to shine intermittently

blinkers leather pieces attached to a horse's bridle
blinkered

blip bleep; spot of light on a radar screen

bliss perfect happiness
blissful blissfully

blister (to form a) swelling

blithe cheerful
blithely blitheness blither blithesome blithest

blithering (*informal*) foolish

blitz sudden violent attack
blitzkrieg

blizzard severe snowstorm

bloated swollen

bloater salted smoked herring

blob drop or spot of liquid

bloc group of people, countries, etc.

block large solid piece of wood, etc.; obstruction; to obstruct
blockage blockhead

blockade obstruction of access to an area; to obstruct access to
blockading

blockbuster powerful bomb; outstanding person or thing

bloke (*informal*) man

blond fair-haired

blonde blond girl or woman

blood red fluid circulating in the body
blood-bath blood-cell blood-curdling bloodhound bloodless blood-letting blood-poisoning blood-pressure bloodshed bloodshot bloodstained bloodstream bloodsucker bloodsucking bloodthirsty blood-vessel bloody

bloody-minded (*informal*) deliberately unhelpful

bloom (to produce a) flower
bloomed blooming

bloomer (*informal*) stupid blunder

bloomers variety of women's knickers

blossom (to produce) flowers on a plant, esp. a fruit tree
blossomed blossoming blossomy

blot (to make a) stain; to remove ink with blotting-paper
blotted blotter blotting

blotch (to make a) large discoloration
blotches blotchy

blouse women's shirt-like garment

blow[1] to force a current of air
blew blow-dry blower blowfly blowhole blowlamp blown blowout blowpipe blowtorch blow-up blowy

blow[2] powerful stroke; shock
blow-by-blow

blowzy dirty and untidy
blowzier blowziest

blubber whale fat; to sob noisily

bludgeon (to hit with a) short heavy stick

blue (to make or become the) colour of a clear sky
bluebell blueberry bluebird bluebottle blue-chip blue-collar blue-eyed bluing or *blueing bluish* or *blueishbluejacket blueprint bluestocking blue tit bluey*

bluff[1] to deceive
bluffer

bluff[2] high steep headland; hearty and frank

blunder (to make a) mistake; to move clumsily
blunderer blunderingly

blunderbuss kind of obsolete firearm

blunt not sharp; direct
bluntly bluntness

blur to make or become unclear or vague
blurred blurring

blurb short promotional description of a book

blurt to utter thoughtlessly

blush to become red from embarrassment, etc.
blushes

bluster to speak noisily and forcefully; to blow in gusts
blusterer blustery

boa kind of large snake

boar uncastrated male pig

board long flat piece of wood; food; group of people; to go on a ship, bus, etc.; (to be provided with) meals and lodging
boarder boarding-house boarding-school boardroom

boast to speak about oneself proudly
boaster boastful boastfully boastfulness

boat small open sailing vessel
boat-house boating boatload boatman boat-train boat-yard

boater stiff straw hat

boatswain senior ship's officer

bob[1] to move quickly up and down
bobbed bobbing

bob[2] hairstyle in which the hair is cut short

bobbin spool or reel

bobble small fluffy ball

bobby (*Brit informal*) policeman
bobbies

bobcat North American wild cat

bobsleigh kind of racing sledge

bobstay (*nautical*) rope to hold the bowsprit down

bobtail short tail

bod (*informal*) fellow

bode[1] to be a sign of
boding

bode[2] past tense of **bide**

bodice upper part of a dress

bodily of the body; as a whole

bodkin large blunt needle

body whole or main part of a human or animal
bodies bodied bodiless body-builder bodyguard bodysuit bodywork

Boer South African of Dutch descent

boffin (*informal*) scientist

bog marsh; to cause to sink as if in a bog
bogged bogging boggy

bogey golf score; see **bogy**
bogeys

boggle to be surprised or overwhelmed
boggling

bogie wheeled undercarriage of a railway coach
bogies

bogus not genuine
bogusness

bogy or **bogey** evil spirit
bogies or *bogeys*

Bohemian (person) living unconventionally

boil[1] to heat a liquid to a temperature at which it becomes vapour
boiler boilermaker boilerman boiler-room boiling-point

boil[2] inflamed swelling on the skin

boisterous noisy and rough
boisterously boisterousness

bold confident and courageous
boldly boldness

bole trunk of a tree

bolero kind of Spanish dance; kind of short jacket
boleros

Bolivia country in South America
Bolivian

boll seed pod of flax, cotton, etc.

bollard upright post

boloney see **baloney**

bolshie or **bolshy** (*informal*) rebellious
bolshiness

bolster long pillow; to support or reinforce

bolt (to lock with a) sliding bar to fasten a door; to move quickly
bolt-hole

bomb explosive device
bomber bombproof bombshell bomb-sight bomb-site

bombard to attack with artillery
bombardier bombardment

bombast pompous language
bombastic

bona fide (*Latin*) genuine

bonanza source of great wealth

bonbon kind of sweet

bond something that binds; promise
bondholder bondman or *bondsman bondswoman*

bondage slavery

bone hard tissue forming the skelton of an animal
bone-dry bonehead boneless bonemeal bone-shaker bony

bonfire large outdoor fire

bonhomie (*French*) friendliness

bonk (to) hit; (*slang*) (to have) sexual intercourse (with)

bonnet kind of hat; cover of a motor-vehicle engine

bonny looking healthy
bonnier bonniest bonnily

bonsai dwarf shrub or tree

bonus something extra that is given or paid
bonuses

bon vivant person with refined tastes in food
bon vivants

boo (to make a) sound of disapproval or contempt
booed booing

boob (*informal*) stupid mistake

booby foolish person
boobies

boogie-woogie style of jazz

book printed pages bound together; to reserve
bookable bookbinding bookcase book-endbookie booking booking-office bookish bookkeeper bookkeeping booklet bookmaker bookmark book-plate bookseller bookselling bookstall bookworm

boom[1] to make a deep hollow sound; period of increased economic activity

boom[2] long pole

boomerang curved wooden stick shaped so that it returns to the thrower

boon favour or benefit

boor rude or insensitive
boorish boorishly boorishness

boost (to) increase
booster

boot strong shoe; luggage compartment in a car
bootblack bootlace

bootee baby's soft knitted shoe

booth stall or small enclosure

bootleg to trade in illicit alcohol
bootlegged bootlegger bootlegging

booty plunder

booze (*slang*) (to drink) alcohol
boozer booze-up boozing boozy

borax kind of white mineral used as a cleaning agent

Bordeaux wine from Bordeaux region of France

border (to form the) edge or boundary
bordered borderer borderland borderline

bore[1] past tense of **bear**[1]

bore[2] to make a hole in wood, etc.
borer boring

bore[3] (to make tired by being) dull and tedious
boredom boring

boric of boron

born past participle of **bear**[1]; (brought into being) by birth; natural
born-again
SEE PANEL

born or borne?
Born is used to refer to coming into the world at birth: *She was born in 1947; to be born with a hole in the heart,* and also in the sense 'natural': *He is a born teacher.*

Borne is the past participle of the verb **bear**[1]: *She has borne him five girls; Responsibility must be borne by the individual; The additional costs must be borne by the customer; Recent research has not borne out earlier claims.*

borne past participle of **bear**[1]; carried
SEE PANEL at **born**

boron non-metallic element

borough town; administrative area

borrow to take temporarily on loan
borrower

Borstal training and rehabilitation centre for young offenders

bortsch Russian soup

bosh (*informal*) nonsense

bo's'n short for **boatswain**

Bosnia-Herzegovina republic of Eastern Europe, formerly part of Yugoslavia
Bosnian

bosom breast
bosomed

boss[1] (to behave as if the) person in charge of or employing others
bosses bossier bossiest bossily bossiness bossy

boss[2] round knob
bosses

botany study of plants
botanical botanist

botch to spoil ineptly; mess
botches botcher botchy

both the 2

bother to irritate; to care
botheration bothersome

Botswana country in Africa

bottle (to put into a) narrow-necked container for liquids
bottle-feed bottleneck bottler bottle-washer bottling

bottom lowest part of something
bottomless bottommost

botulism acute form of food poisoning

boudoir woman's private room

bouffant puffed out

bougainvillaea kind of climbing plant

bough main branch of a tree

bought past tense and past participle of **buy**

bouillon thin clear soup

boulder large smooth stone or rock

boulevard wide tree-lined road

bounce to spring back after hitting a surface suddenly
bounceable bouncer bouncily bouncing bouncy

bound[1] past tense and past participle of **bind**; sure; obliged

bound[2] (to) limit
boundless boundlessly

bound[3] going towards

bound[4] to leap

boundary dividing line
boundaries

bounteous give freely
bounteously bounteousness

bountiful generous; abundant
bountifully bountifulness

bounty generous gift; financial reward
bounties

bouquet bunch of flowers; perfume

bourbon type of whisky

bourgeois of the middle class
bourgeoisie

bourse European stock exchange, esp. one in Paris

bout period of activity

boutique small shop

bovine of oxen or cows

bow[1] strip of wood; ribbon knot
bow-legged bowman bowsaw bowstring bow-tie bow-window

bow[2] to lower one's head in respect; act of this

bow[3] forward part of a ship

bowdlerize or **bowdlerise** to remove vulgar words
bowdlerizing or *bowdlerising*

bowel intestine

bower leafy shelter

bowl[1] round hollow vessel
bowlful

bowl[2] ball used in bowls; (*cricket*) to throw the ball to the batsman
bowls bowler bowling bowling-alley bowling-green

bowler man's round hard hat

bowline kind of knot

bowsprit spar projecting from the bow of a ship

box[1] container
boxes boxful box-junction box-kite box-office box-room

box[2] to fight with gloved hands
boxer boxing boxing-glove

box[3] kind of small evergreen tree
boxwood

boxer breed of dog

Boxing Day (*Brit*) first weekday after Christmas Day

boy young unmarried human male
boyfriend boyhood boyish boyishly

boycott to refuse to deal with
boycotter boycotting

bra woman's undergarment for supporting the breasts

brace hand tool for drilling holes; clamping-device; pair; to support
bracing

bracelet wrist ornament

braces straps to hold up trousers

bracing invigorating

bracken large fern

bracket support from a wall; (to put in one of) marks () or []
bracketed bracketing

brackish (*of water*) slightly salty

bract small leaf near a flower

brad thin nail with slight projection at the head

bradawl tool for piercing holes in wood

brag to boast
bragged bragger bragging

braggadocio empty boasting

braggart person who boasts

Brahma creator god of Hinduism

Brahman member of highest or priestly Hindu caste
Brahmanism

braid (to) plait; decorative ribbon
braider braiding

Braille writing system for the blind in which letters are represented by raised dots

brain part of the body inside the skull; centre of thought
brain-child brainless brainpower brainstorm brain-teaser brainwash brainwave brainy

braise to cook slowly in a covered container
braising

brake[1] (to operate) a device for slowing down
braking

brake[2] overgrown land

bramble kind of prickly shrub; blackberry

bran husks of cereal grain

branch limb of a tree; subdivision; to divide
branches

brand particular make of goods; (to mark with an) identifying mark
brand-new

brandish to wave about; act of brandishing
brandishes brandisher

brandy strong alcoholic drink
brandies

brash tastelessly showy; rash
brashly brashness

brass alloy of copper and zinc

brasserie licensed restaurant

brassière (*formal*) bra

brassy like brass; rash
brassier brassiest brassily brassiness

brat child

bravado (display of) showy self-confidence
bravados or *bravadoes*

brave showing courage; to face courageously
braver bravery bravest braving

bravo well done!

brawl (to take part in a) noisy fight

brawn physical strength; jellied meat-loaf
brawny

bray (to make) the cry of a donkey
braying

braze to solder with an alloy
brazer

brazen made of brass; bold and shameless; to face boldly and shamelessly
brazen-faced

brazier[1] person who works with brass

brazier[2] container for holding burning coal

Brazil country in South America
Brazilian

breach crack; breaking of a promise, rule, etc.; to make a breach
breaches

bread food made of flour
bread-bin breadboard breadcrumb breadline bread-winner

breadth distance from side to side
breadthways breadthwise

break to (cause to) fall to pieces; gap or fracture
breakable breakage breakaway breakdown breaker break-in breakneck breakthrough breakup breakwater broke broken

breakfast first meal of the day

bream kind of freshwater fish

breast female milk-producing gland; front part of body between neck and stomach
breastbone breast-fed breastplate breast-stroke

breath air drawn in and expelled from the lungs
breathtaking breathy

breathalyser or **breathalyzer** device for measuring the amount of alcohol in the blood
breathalyse or *breathalyze breathalysing* or *breathalyzing*

breathe to take air into and expel from the lungs
breather breathing breathing-space

breech part of a gun behind the barrel; buttocks
breech-loader

breeches knee-length trousers
breeches-buoy

breed to give birth to young; to raise livestock; to produce
bred breeder breeding

breeze gentle wind
breezily breeziness breezy

breeze-block light building block

bren-gun kind of light machine-gun

brethren (*archaic*) brothers

Breton inhabitant of Brittany; Celtic language of the Bretons

breve longest musical note

breviary book containing Roman Catholic Church daily service
breviaries

brevity shortness

brew (to make or prepare) beer or tea
brewer brewery brew-up

briar see **brier**

bribe (to win over with a) gift offered to persuade or influence
bribable or *bribeable briber bribery bribing*

bric-à-brac assorted small ornaments

brick oblong building block of clay
brickbat brickfield bricklayer brickwork

bride woman at the time of her wedding
bridal

bridegroom man at the time of his wedding

bridesmaid bridal attendant

bridge[1] (to link by a) structure over a river, etc.
bridgehead bridging bridging-loan

bridge[2] kind of card-game

bridle headgear for a horse; to control
bridle-path bridling

brief short; summary
briefs briefcase briefly briefness

brier or **briar** kind of thorny shrub
brier-root brier-rose

brigade army unit
brigadier

brigand bandit
brigandage brigandry

brigantine 2-masted ship

bright giving out much light
brighten brightly brightness

brill kind of flat-fish

brilliant shining brightly; clever
brilliance or *brilliancy brilliantly*

brilliantine preparation to smooth hair

brim upper edge; rim of a hat; to fill
brimful brimmed brimming

brimstone (*archaic*) sulphur

brindled brown or grey with darker streaks

brine salt water
brinish briny

bring to carry; to cause
bringer brought

brink edge of a steep place
brinkmanship

brioche light slightly sweet roll

briquette or **briquet** block of compressed coal dust

brisk lively
briskly briskness

brisket meat from the breast of an animal

brisling Norwegian sprat

bristle short stiff hair; to stand on end
bristling bristly

Britain Great Britain
Briticism Briticize or *Briticise British*

Briton early inhabitant of Britain

brittle easily broken

broach to begin a discussion on
broaches

broad wide; full; general
broadcloth broaden broadly broad-minded broadness broadsheet broad-shouldered

broadcast to transmit on radio or television; to scatter
broadcasted broadcaster broadcasting

broadside side of a ship

broadsword broad-bladed cutting sword

brocade (to weave a) rich woven fabric
brocading

broccoli kind of vegetable related to the cauliflower

brochure pamphlet

brogue[1] stout walking shoe

brogue[2] Irish accent

broil to grill; to cook over a fire

broiler young chicken suitable for roasting

broke past tense of **break**

broken past participle of **break**
broken-down broken-hearted brokenly brokenness

broker agent; stockbroker
brokerage

brolly (*Brit informal*) umbrella
brollies

bromide compound of bromine; platitude

bromine non-metallic element

bronchitis inflammation of the bronchial tubes
bronchitic

bronchus branch of the windpipe
bronchi bronchial

bronco partially tamed horse
broncos

brontosaurus kind of large dinosaur

bronze alloy of copper and tin; to make brown
bronzing

brooch ornament fastened by a pin

brood group of young birds, etc. hatched together; to ponder gloomily
brooder broody

brook[1] small stream

brook[2] to tolerate

broom long-handled brush; kind of shrub
broomstick

broth soup or stock

brothel house of prostitution

brother son of the same parents; male belonging to a group
brotherhood brother-in-law brothers-in-law brotherly

brougham 4-wheeled carriage

brought past tense and past participle of **bring**

brouhaha commotion or uproar

brow forehead; top of a hill

browbeat to intimidate
browbeaten

brown dark colour between orange and black
browned-off brownish

brownie goblin

Brownie girl in junior section of Guides

browse to look through books casually and leisurely
browsing

bruise (to cause an) injury that discolours the skin
bruiser bruising

brunch late morning meal combining breakfast and lunch

Brunei country in NW Borneo
Bruneian

brunette woman with dark-brown hair

brunt main force or shock

brush[1] (to clean with a) device containing bristles, hairs, etc.
brushes brush-off brushstroke brushwork

brush[2] thick growth of shrubs and trees
brushwood

brusque offhand; abrupt
brusquely brusqueness

Brussels sprout kind of vegetable with small cabbage-like buds growing on the stem

brutal cruel
brutality brutalities brutally

brutalize or **brutalise** to make brutal
brutalization or *brutalisation brutalizing* or *brutalising*

brute beast; cruel person
brutish brutishly brutishness

bryony kind of climbing plant
bryonies

bubble thin spherical film of liquid inflated with air
bubble-and-squeak bubbling bubbly

bubo inflamed swelling of a lymph gland
buboes

bubonic plague plague marked by formation of buboes

buccaneer (to behave like a) pirate
buccaneering

buck male of certain animals; (*of horses*) to jump up with stiff legs and arched back
buckshot buckskin bucktooth

bucket open-topped container with handles for water, etc.
bucketful

buckle (to fasten with a) clasp for belts or straps
buckling

buckler small round shield

buckram stiff cotton or linen cloth

buckshee (*slang*) free

buckthorn kind of thorny small-flowered shrub

buckwheat kind of cereal plant

bucolic of country life, shepherds, or farming

bud (to produce a) small swelling on a tree that develops into a flower, etc.
budded budding

Buddha title of religious teacher Gautama Siddhartha
Buddhism Buddhist

buddleia kind of ornamental shrub

buddy (*chiefly* US) partner; mate
buddies

budge to move slightly
budging

budgerigar small Australian bird

budget (to make an) estimate of an amount of money needed
budgetary budgeted budgeting

budgie (*informal*) short for **budgerigar**

buff (to polish with a) strong yellow leather; enthusiast

buffalo kind of wild ox
buffaloes or *buffalo*

buffer something that reduces the effect of a shock or blow

buffet[1] to knock against sharply
buffeted buffeting

buffet[2] counter where food and drink are served

buffoon foolish person; clown
buffoonery

bug kind of insect; germ; (to install a) hidden listening device
bugged bugging

bugbear something that causes fear or anxiety

buggy light carriage
buggies

bugle (to play a) brass musical instrument
bugler bugling

build (to make a) structure
builder building build-up built built-in

bulb round plant-base; something shaped like this
bulbous

Bulgaria country in SE Europe
Bulgarian

bulge (to form a) swelling
bulging bulgy

bulimia (*medical*) compulsive overeating followed by self-induced vomiting

bulk large amount; larger part
bulkier bulkiest bulkily bulkiness bulky

bulkhead upright partition in a vessel

bull[1] adult male bovine animal
bulldog bullfight bullfighter bullfighting bullfrog bull-headed bullish bull-necked bull-nosed bullring bull-terrier

bull[2] formal document issued by the pope

bulldozer powerful vehicle for clearing land, etc.
bulldoze bulldozing

bullet small round missile
bulletproof

bulletin official statement of news

bullfinch common European finch

bullion gold or silver in mass

bullock young or castrated bull

bully person who uses his or her strength to intimidate others; to use one's strength to intimidate others
bullies bullied bullying

bulrush kind of large strong reed

bulwark defensive wall or structure

bum (*slang*) buttocks; tramp or loafer

bumbag (*slang*) pouch on a belt worn around the waist

bumble to speak or act in a stumbling faltering way
bumbling

bumble-bee large bee with a loud hum

bumf (*slang*) official papers

bump (to strike with a) heavy noise
bumpiness bumpy

bumper bar fixed to lessen the shock of a collision; extraordinarily large

bumpkin clumsy country person

bumptious offensively conceited
bumptiously bumptiousness

bun small round cake; hair gathered into the shape of a bun

bunch (to form into a) number of things growing or fastened together
bunches

bundle number of things loosely held together; to make a bundle
bundling

bung stopper
bunghole

bungalow one-storey house

bungee elastic cord used when jumping from a great height

bungle (to do a) clumsy or incompetent piece of work
bungler bungling

bunion inflamed swelling of the first joint on the big toe.

bunk nonsense

bunk-bed one of a pair of beds constructed one above the other

bunker large storage container for fuel

bunkum nonsense

bunny (*informal*) rabbit
bunnies

Bunsen burner kind of gas burner

bunting[1] kind of bird of the finch family

bunting[2] coarse cloth used for flags

buoy floating marker for ships

buoyant capable of floating; cheerful
buoyancy buoyantly

bur prickly seed-vessel

burble to make a gentle bubbling sound; to talk excitedly
burbler burbling

burbot kind of freshwater fish with barbels around its mouth

burden (to) load
burdensome

burdock kind of coarse plant

bureau writing-desk; office
bureaux or *bureaus*

bureaucracy government by officials
bureaucracies bureaucrat bureaucratic bureaucratically

burette graduated glass tube

burgeon to develop or grow

burger savoury flat cake of minced meat

burgess (*archaic*) citizen

burgh (*Scottish*) borough

burgher (*archaic*) citizen

burglar person who breaks into a building to steal
burglar-proof burglary burglaries burgle burgling

burgomaster mayor of Dutch, Flemish, or German town

burgundy kind of French red or white wine

burial burying

Burkina Faso country in West Africa
Burkinabe

burlesque (to imitate by) caricature
burlesqued burlesquing

burly strong and heavy

Burma country in SE Asia, officially called Myanmar
Burmese

burn[1] to be on fire; to set fire to
burner burned or *burnt burn-out*

burn[2] (*Scottish*) small stream

burnish to make shiny by rubbing
burnisher burnishes burnishing

burnous hooded Arab cloak

burp (*informal*) (to) belch

burr rough edge; whirring; pronunciation of *r* in country accents

burrow (to dig a) hole in the ground

bursar college treasurer; (*Scottish*) holder of a grant

bursary financial grant given to a student
bursaries

burst (to cause) to break open; rupture or outbreak

Burundi country in Central Africa
Burundian

bury to put in the ground
buried buries burying

bus (to travel or transport by a) large passenger vehicle
buses bused or *bussed busing* or *bussing*
bus-stop

busby tall fur hat
busbies

bush shrub; uncultivated area of land
bushes bushman bushranger bushy

bushel unit of volume

business trade; concern
businesses businesslike businessman businesswoman

busker street musician

bust[1] sculpture of head, neck and shoulders; woman's bosom

bust[2] (*informal*) to break; broken; bankrupt
bust-up

bustle (to hurry with) great activity
bustling

busy (to keep) fully occupied
busied busily busybody busying busyness

but however; except

butane flammable gas

butch (*slang*) with masculine appearance or qualities

butcher retailer of meat; brutal killer
butchery

butler head manservant

butt[1] large barrel

butt[2] thicker end of a weapon or stick
butt-end

butt[3] someone who is the object of ridicule; shooting-range; to push with the head
butted butting

butter (to spread with a) yellow fatty substance made from cream
butterbean butter-fingers buttermilk butterscotch

buttercup kind of plant with yellow cup-shaped flowers

butterfly kind of insect with large wings
butterflies

buttery like butter; room for storing provisions
butteries butteriness

buttocks round fleshy part of human or animal rear

button knob of plastic, wood, etc., used as a fastener; to fasten with buttons
buttoned button-through

buttonhole slit in a garment for a button; to detain in conversation
buttonholing

buttress (to) support (against a wall)
buttresses

buxom (*of a woman*) attractively plump

buy to obtain by payment of money
buyer buying buy-out bought

buzz (to make a) vibrating humming sound
buzzes buzzer

buzzard kind of large hawk

by near; beside; through the means or creation of
by-election bygone by-lane byline byname bypass bypath byplay by-road bystander byway byword by-your-leave

bye run made in cricket when ball passes batsman without striking the bat
byes

by-law or **bye-law** local law
by-laws or *bye-laws*

by-product something produced in addition to the main product

byre cow-shelter

byte (*computers*) sequence of binary digits processed as one unit

C

cab taxi; driver's compartment
cabby or *cabbie* *cabman*

cabal small group of political intriguers; secret plot

cabaret entertainment at a nightclub or restaurant

cabbage kind of leafy vegetable

caber tree trunk used in a Scottish sport

cabin ship or aircraft compartment; small simple dwelling

cabinet piece of furniture
cabinet-maker

Cabinet government executive and policy-making group

cable length of wire; (to send a) telegram
cablegram *cabling*

caboose ship's galley; (US) guard's van

cabriolet 2-wheeled horse-drawn carriage

cacao (seed of) the tropical American tree which is used in making cocoa and chocolate

cache hiding-place for weapons or provisions

cachet official seal; distinctive mark; capsule containing medicine

cachou lozenge eaten to sweeten the breath

cackle (to make the) noise of a hen
cackler *cackling*

cacophony harsh discordant sound
cacophonies *cacophonous*

cactus kind of spiny plant
cacti or *cactuses*

cad (*old-fashioned*) person who behaves in an ungentlemanly way
caddish

cadaver corpse
cadaverous *cadaverously*

caddie person who carries a golfer's clubs
caddies

caddy small container for tea
caddies

cadence rise and fall of sound; concluding musical phrase

cadenza technically showy solo passage near the end of a piece of music

cadet young person undergoing preliminary training

cadge to obtain by begging
cadger *cadging*

cadmium bluish-white metallic element

cadre nucleus of personnel, esp. military

caecum branch of an animal gut
caeca *caecal*

Caerphilly mild white moist cheese

caesarean (US **cesarean**) delivery of baby by cutting the mother's abdominal wall

caesura pause in the middle of a line of verse
caesuras or *caesurae*

café small or cheap restaurant

cafeteria self-service restaurant

caffeine alkaloid found in tea and coffee that acts as a stimulant

caftan or **kaftan** loose ankle-length long-sleeved tunic

cage enclosure of wires or bars
caging

cagey or **cagy** (*informal*) wary; secretive; shrewd
cagier *cagiest* *cagily* *caginess* or *cageyness*

cagoule light waterproof anorak

cahoots (*informal*) partnership

caiman see **cayman**

cairn mound of stones

cairngorm smoky-yellow or brown quartz

caisson watertight chamber; ammunition chest or wagon

cajole to persuade by flattery
cajolery cajoling

cake baked mixture of flour, sugar, eggs, butter, etc.; to form a hard or thick mass
caking

calabash gourd (tree)

calamine pink powder used in a soothing lotion

calamity great misfortune
calamities calamitous calamitously

calcareous of calcium carbonate

calcify to make or become hard by a deposit of calcium salts
calciferous calcification calcified calcifies calcifying

calcium white metallic element

calculate to solve mathematically; to estimate
calculable calculating calculation calculator

calculus branch of mathematics (pl. *calculuses*); stony concretion in the body (pl. *calculi*)

caldron see **cauldron**

calendar display chart showing the days, weeks and months of the year
SEE PANEL

---

calendar, calender, or colander?

A *calendar* is a chart that displays the days, weeks, and months of the year: *put holiday dates on the calendar; the year's sporting calendar; a rent of £450 per calendar month.*

A *calender* is a machine in which paper, cloth, or rubber is pressed to give a smooth, glossy finish.

A *colander* is a bowl with holes in it that is used to drain vegetables.

---

calender machine in which paper or cloth is smoothed
SEE PANEL at **calendar**

calf[1] young of cattle, elephant, seal, etc.
calves calf-leather calf-love calfskin

calf[2] thick fleshy part of the leg between the knee and the ankle

calibrate to determine the calibre of; to mark units of measurement on
calibrating calibration

calibre (US **caliber**) diameter of a cylinder, especially a gun-barrel; ability

calico plain white cotton cloth
calicoes

caliper (US) see **calliper**

caliph title of Muslim ruler
caliphate

calisthenics (US) see **callisthenics**

calix cup-like animal structure
calices

calk see **caulk**

call (to give a) loud cry; to name; to summon; to make a short visit; to telephone
caller calling call-up

calligraphy (the art of) beautiful handwriting
calligrapher calligraphic calligraphist

calliper (US **caliper**) instrument for measuring diameters; metal leg-supports

callisthenics (US **calisthenics**) exercises to develop general bodily fitness

callous insensitive; unfeeling
callously callousness
SEE PANEL

---

callous or callus?

Callous is an adjective that means 'insensitive; unfeeling': *a callous, cold-blooded murder; How could you be so callous?*

C*allus* is a noun that refers to an area of unnaturally hard or thick skin: *feet encrusted with calluses.*

callow immature; inexperienced

callus area of hard or thick skin
calluses
SEE PANEL at **callous**

calm (to make or become) still

calomel mercurous chloride

Calor gas (*trademark*) liquefied butane gas

calorie unit of heat; unit of measuring energy value of food
calories calorific calorimeter

calumny slander
calumnies calumnious

Calvary place where Jesus was crucified

calve to give birth to a calf
calving

Calvin French theologian
Calvinism Calvinist Calvinistic

calx residue left after a metal or mineral is heated
calces or *calxes*

calypso improvised West Indian ballad
calypsos or *calypsoes*

calyx outer part of a flower
calyces or *calyxes*

cam mechanical device that changes circular motion into vertical or horizontal motion
camshaft

camaraderie friendliness

camber slight upward curve on a road surface

cambium layer of cells in plants

Cambodia country in SE Asia

cambric fine white cloth

camcorder video camera that records sound and vision

came past tense of **come**

camel humped, long-necked desert animal
camel-hair

camellia kind of evergreen shrub

Camembert soft rich French cheese

cameo jewellery with a raised design; short piece of acting
cameos

camera device for taking photographs
cameras cameraman

Cameroon country in West Africa
Cameroonian

camisole women's short bodice undergarment

camomile or **chamomile** kind of medicinal plant

camouflage (to conceal by) disguising so that something blends with its surroundings
camouflaging

camp group of tents, huts, etc.; military quarters; to establish a camp
camp-bed camper camp-fire camping campsite

campaign series of planned activities or operations
campaigner

campanile bell-tower

campanology art of ringing bells
campanologer campanological campanologist

campanula kind of plant with bell-shaped flowers

camphor whitish fragrant compound
camphorate camphoric

campus college or university grounds
campuses

can¹ to be able or allowed to
cannot could

can² (to preserve food in a) container
canned cannery canneries canning

Canada country in North America
Canadian

canal man-made water-channel

canalize or **canalise** to provide with a canal
canalization or *canalisation* *canalizing* or *canalising*

canapé piece of bread or toast with savoury topping
canapés

canard false report; absurd story

canary kind of small yellow finch
canaries

canasta kind of card-game

cancan high-kicking dance

cancel to call off a meeting, etc.; to cross out
cancellation *cancelled* (US *canceled*) *canceller* (US *canceler*) *cancelling* (US *canceling*)

cancer malignant tumour
cancerous

Cancer 4th sign of the zodiac

candela the basic metric unit of luminous intensity

candelabrum branched candlestick
candelabra

candid frank and open
candidly

candidate person applying for a job etc., or taking an examination
candidacy *candidature*

candied encrusted or glazed with sugar

candle wax stick with a wick that gives light when burned
candleholder *candlelight* *candlepower* *candlestick* *candlewick*

candour (US **candor**) frankness and openness

candy (US) sweets
candies

candyfloss light fluffy spun sugar held on a stick

cane (to beat with the) long stem of certain plants
caning

canine of dogs; strong pointed tooth

canister small metal container

canker spreading sore or evil
cankerous *cankerworm*

cannabis hemp plant; preparation from this used as a drug

cannelloni pasta rolls

cannibal person who eats human flesh
cannibalism *cannibalistic* *cannibalize* or *cannibalise*

cannon kind of large heavy gun
cannonade *cannon-ball* *cannon-fodder* *cannonry*
SEE PANEL

---

cannon or canon?

A *cannon* is a kind of large, heavy gun: *the boom of a firing cannon.*

A *canon* is a clergyman who is on the staff of a cathedral; a standard, principle, or rule (*the time-honoured canons of duty and decorum*); a church decree that regulates practice (*canon law*); and the list of works (*the canon of Scripture*).

---

cannot can not

canny shrewd
cannier *canniest* *cannily* *canniness*

canoe (to travel by a) light narrow open boat
canoed *canoeing* *canoeist*

canon clergyman; church decree; standard, principle, or rule
canoness *canonical*
SEE PANEL at **cannon**

canonize or **canonise** to declare a person to be a saint
canonization or *canonisation* *canonizing* or *canonising*

canopy overhanging cloth covering
canopies

cant insincere talk; jargon; inclination from the vertical

can't (*informal*) cannot

cantaloup or **canteloupe** kind of melon

cantankerous bad-tempered
cantankerously cantankerousness

cantata short musical work

canteen restaurant at a factory, school, etc.; box for a set of cutlery

canter (to move at a) gentle gallop

canticle hymn

cantilever large framework that supports a bridge

canto division of a long poem
cantos

canton division of Switzerland

Cantonese Chinese language

cantonment large military station

cantor leader of singing in a choir; leading singer in a Jewish synagogue

canvas heavy coarse cloth
canvases
SEE PANEL

---

canvas or canvass?
Canvas, a noun, is heavy coarse cloth, on which, for example, a painting can be made: *an oil painting on canvas; a canvas travelling bag.* To live or sleep *under canvas* is to live or sleep in a *tent.*

To *canvass,* a very, means, 'to solicit votes or orders': *candidates canvassing support before an election; to canvass public opinion.*

---

canvass to solicit votes or orders
canvassed canvasser canvasses
SEE PANEL at **canvas**

canyon gorge or ravine

caoutchouc unvulcanized rubber

cap small soft hat; to cover
capped capping

capable able; competent
capability capabilities capably

capacious roomy

capacitance property of a system enabling electric storage

capacitor device for accumulating electric charge

capacity ability or power of containing or understanding something; amount that can be contained
capacities capacitate

caparison (to put a) decorative cover on a horse

cape sleeveless cloak; promontory

caper[1] shrub; its flower-bud

caper[2] to skip or leap playfully

capillary tiny hair-like tube
capillaries

capital main; punishable by death; place of government in a country; money to invest; large letter

capitalism economic system based on private ownership and profit
capitalist capitalistic

capitalize or **capitalise** to write in capital letters; to provide with capital; to profit by
capitalization or *capitalisation capitalizing* or *capitalising*

capitation tax or fee per head

capitulate to surrender
capitulating capitulation

capo device fitted across guitar strings to raise their pitch

capon castrated male chicken

cappuccino coffee made with hot frothy milk
cappuccinos

caprice sudden change of behaviour, attitude, etc.
capricious

Capricorn 10th sign of the zodiac

capsicum (rounded red or green fruit of) a kind of plant with pungent seeds

capsize (to cause) to overturn
capsizal capsizing

capstan rotating drum used for hauling

capstone copingstone

capsule seed-case; small soluble gelatin case for medicine; part of spacecraft for crew
capsular

captain officer in charge of a ship; army or navy officer; leader
captaincy captainship

caption short heading or description

captious inclined to find fault
captiously captiousness

captivate to fascinate or charm
captivating captivation

captive (held as) prisoner
captivity

capture to take prisoner; to gain possession of
captor capturing

car vehicle on wheels
car-ferry carload car-park carport carsick

carafe glass container for water or wine

caramel burnt sugar; toffee
caramelize or *caramelise*

carapace shell of a crab, tortoise, etc.

carat or **karat** measure of the purity of gold or weight of precious stones

caravan (to travel in a) large enclosed vehicle that can be pulled by a car and is equipped for living in
caravanned caravanner caravanning

caravanserai (US **caravansary**) inn with a courtyard that is used as a resting place for caravans

caravel small sailing-ship

caraway kind of plant with aromatic fruits

carbide compound of carbon

carbine short light rifle

carbohydrate organic compound that contains carbon, hydrogen and oxygen

carbolated containing carbolic acid

carbolic acid derivative of benzene used as a disinfectant

carbon non-metallic element occurring in all organic compounds
carbonize or *carbonise*

carbonated containing carbon dioxide

carbonic acid carbon dioxide combined with water

carboniferous producing coal or carbon

Carborundum (*trademark*) abrasive material

carboy large bottle

carbuncle gemstone; skin eruption
carbuncular

carburettor (US **carburetor**) device in a motor engine that mixes petrol with air

carcass or **carcase** dead body of an animal
carcasses or *carcases*

carcinogen substance that causes cancer
carcinogenic

carcinoma cancer
carcinomas or *carcinomata*

card[1] small stiff piece of paper/plastic
card-carrying card-game cardphone

card[2] (to process with a) machine that removes small fibres from cotton wool, etc.

cardamom aromatic seeds of a kind of tropical plant

cardboard stiff thick paper for making boxes, etc.

cardiac of the heart

cardigan knitted jacket

cardinal most important; number; member of the Sacred College of the Roman Catholic Church
cardinalship

care (to give) close attention; (to feel) worry; to like
carefree caretaker careworn caring

careen to sway

career one's life work; to rush uncontrollably
careering careerism careerist

careful taking great care; cautious
carefully carefulness

careless paying inadequate attention; negligent
carelessly carelessness

caress (to give a) loving touch
caresses

caret insertion mark

cargo goods carried
cargoes or *cargos*

Caribbean (of the) sea bounded by Central America, the West Indies and South America

caribou North American reindeer
caribous or *caribou*

caricature (to make an) amusing exaggerated representation of a person
caricaturing caricaturist

caries gradual decay, esp. of the teeth
carious

carillon set of bells

cariole see **carriole**

carmine rich red colour

carnage great slaughter

carnal of the body or physical appetites or pleasures
carnality carnally

carnation kind of sweet-smelling flower

carnelian see **cornelian**

carnet customs licence

carnival travelling fair; time of festivity

carnivore flesh-eating animal
carnivorous

carob kind of evergreen tree with edible pods

carol (to sing a) joyful Christmas song or hymn
carolled (US *caroled*) *caroller* (US *caroler*) *carolling* (US *caroling*)

carouse to drink heavily and merrily
carousal carousing

carousel (US **carrousel**) merry-go-round; turning conveyor system

carp[1] kind of freshwater fish

carp[2] to complain or nag
carper

carpel seed-bearing part of a flower

carpenter person skilled in woodwork
carpentry

carpet (to cover with a) heavy floor covering
carpet-bag carpet-bagger carpeted carpeting

carrel small individual study room in a library

carriage wheeled vehicle, esp. on a railway; act of conveying goods; body posture
carriageway

carrier person or thing that carries
carrier-bag

carriole or **cariole** 2-wheeled horse-drawn carriage

carrion dead and rotting flesh

carrot kind of orange-red root vegetable
carroty

carry to hold; to move or transport
carried carries carry-cot carrying

cart open vehicle
carter cart-horse cartload cartwheel cart-wright

carte blanche (*French*) full authority or discretion

cartel group of companies, etc. that combine to limit competition

cartilage tough elastic tissue in the body; gristle
cartilaginous

cartogram diagrammatic map

cartography map-making
cartographer cartographic

carton cardboard box

cartoon humorous drawing
cartoonist

cartridge casing for a bullet, film, or tape; part of the arm on a record-player

carve to shape or cut
carver carving

cascade (to flow or fall like a) waterfall
cascading

cascara dried bark of a shrub used as a laxative

case[1] example or instance; legal action; (*grammar*) form of a noun, pronoun, etc.
case-book casework

case[2] (to put into a) container; suitcase
casing

casein milk protein

casement kind of window or window-frame

cash (to exchange for) money
cash and carry cash-book cash-box cashcard

cashew kind of (tropical American tree with) nut

cashier[1] person responsible for receiving money in a shop; person who receives and pays out money in a bank

cashier[2] to dismiss with dishonour

cashmere fine soft wool

casing protective cover

casino room or building for gambling
casinos

cask barrel for alcoholic liquids

casket small box

Caspian Sea lake between SE Europe and Asia

cassava kind of tropical plant with edible starchy roots

casserole (food cooked in a) covered heatproof dish; to cook in a casserole
casseroling

cassette small sealed container for magnetic tape or photographic film

cassock long garment worn by clergymen

cassowary kind or large flightless bird
cassowaries

cast to throw; to vote; to shape an object; (to select the) performers in a play, etc.
castaway casting cast-off

castanets pieces of wood clicked together

caste social class or rank

castellated having turrets and battlements

castigate to rebuke or punish severely
castigating castigation castigator

castle large fortified building

castor or **caster** small swivelling wheel on furniture; small container for sprinkling sugar

castor oil medicinal or lubricating oil

castor sugar white finely ground sugar

castrate to remove the testicles of
castrating castration

castrato singer castrated in boyhood
castrati

casual happening by chance or accident; offhand; incidental
casually casualness

casualty person injured or killed in an accident
casualties

casuistry application of general ethics to moral problems; false but clever reasoning
casuist casuistic casuistical

cat kind of small furry domestic animal; any feline animal
catcall catfish catnap cat-o'-nine-tails cat's-eye cattish catwalk

cataclysm violent change or upheaval
cataclysmic

catacomb underground burial tunnel

catafalque ornamental coffin stand

catalepsy disturbance of consciousness marked by rigid body position
cataleptic

catalogue (US **catalog**) (to) list
catalogued (US *cataloged*) *cataloguer* (US *cataloger*) *cataloguing* (US *cataloging*)

catalyst substance that speeds a chemical reaction but itself remains unchanged
catalysis catalyse (US *catalyze*) *catalytic*

catamaran sailing vessel with twin hulls

catapult forked device for shooting stones, etc.

cataract large steep waterfall; opacity of the lens of the eye

catarrh inflammation of a mucous membrane, with production of mucus in the nose and throat
catarrhal

catastrophe sudden great disaster
catastrophic

catch to take hold of; act of this
catches catch-all catch-as-catch-can catchment catchpenny catch-phrase catch-22 catchword catchy caught

catechism instruction by questions and answers
catechist catechize or *catechise*

catechumen convert under instruction before baptism

categorical unqualified; absolute
categorically

category class or group
categories categorize or *categorise*

cater to supply what is required, esp. food
caterer

caterpillar wormlike larva of butterflies and moths

Caterpillar (*trademark*) tractor that is propelled by 2 endless tracks

caterwaul to cry noisily like a cat

catgut tough animal cord used in tennis rackets, musical instruments, etc.

catharsis purging; release of repressed emotions
catharses cathartic

cathedral principal church of a diocese

catheter long thin flexible tube to draw off body fluid
catheterize or *catheterise*

cathode negative electrode of an electrolytic cell
cathodic

catholic general; universal
catholicity

Catholic of the Roman Catholic Church

cation ion carrying positive electrical charge

catkin group of spiky soft flowers

cattle cows, bulls, etc.; bovine animals
cattle-grid

catty spiteful
cattiness

Caucasian of the Indo-European race

caucus (closed) political meeting
caucuses

caudal of the tail

caught past tense and past participle of **catch**

caul inner membrane covering the head of some infants at birth

cauldron or **caldron** large boiling pot

cauliflower kind of vegetable with a compact white flower-head

caulk or **calk** to make watertight

causality relation between cause and effect
causal causalities causation causative

cause that which produces an effect; to bring about; reason; charity
causeless causing

cause célèbre (*French*) famous law case
causes célèbres

causerie informal talk or writing

causeway raised path or road

caustic burning; sarcastic
caustically

cauterize or **cauterise** to destroy by burning
cauterization or *cauterisation cauterizing* or *cauterising*

caution care; (to give) warning
cautionary cautious cautiously cautiousness

cavalcade procession

cavalier[1] horseman; dismissive
cavalierly

cavalier[2] supporter of King Charles I in English Civil War

cavalry horse-mounted troops; troops in armoured vehicles
cavalries

cave underground hollow; to collapse
caveman caving

caveat caution or warning

cavern deep cave
cavernous

caviare or **caviar** salted roe of the sturgeon

cavil to raise trivial objections
cavilled (US *caviled*) *caviller* (US *caviler*) *cavilling* (US *caviling*)

cavity hollow space; decaying tooth hollow
cavities

cavort to prance
cavorter

caw (to make the) cry of a crow, rook, or raven

cayenne very hot red pepper

cayman or **caiman** kind of tropical American alligator

cease to come to an end
cease-fire ceaseless ceasing

cedar kind of tall evergreen tree

cede to surrender
ceder ceding

cedilla mark placed under a c: ç to show as *s*-sound

Ceefax (*trademark*) BBC teletext service

ceilidh informal social gathering with dancing and music

ceiling upper surface of a room

celandine kind of plant

celebrant priest officiating at esp. Eucharist

celebrate to observe a special occasion joyfully
celebrating celebration

celebrity famous person
celebrities

celerity rapidness

celery kind of plant with crisp edible stem

celestial of the sky; divine or spiritual

celibate unmarried (person)
celibacy

cell small simple room; smallest part of a plant or animal
cellular

cellar underground room esp. for storage
cellarage

cello kind of bowed stringed instrument
cellos cellist

Cellophane (*trademark*) thin transparent wrapping material

celluloid flammable plastic material

cellulose organic substance in plant tissue

Celsius or **centigrade** temperature scale

Celt member of one of a group of West European peoples

Celtic branch of Indo-European languages

cement binding substance for building
cementation

cemetery burial ground
cemeteries

cenotaph monument honouring person or people buried elsewhere

Cenozoic geological era

censer container for burning incense
SEE PANEL

---

censer, censor, or censure?

A *censer* is a container for burning incense.

If someone *censors* books or films, they have authority to examine them and remove parts which they think are objectionable: *to censor pornographic material.* The person with such authority is a *censor* : *the British Board of Film Censors.*

To *censure* someone is to criticize them strongly or to condemn or blame them: *to censure an official for failing to declare an interest.*

---

censor person with authority to remove objectionable parts from books, films, etc.
censorial censorious censorship
SEE PANEL at **censer**

censure to criticize strongly; to blame
censurable censuring
SEE PANEL at **censer**

census official counting
censuses

cent money unit of many countries

centaur mythical creature

centavo money unit of some Central or South American countries

centenary 100th anniversary
centenaries centenarian centennial

center (US) see **centre**

centigrade see **Celsius**

centigram or **centigramme** 100th part of a gram

centilitre (US **centiliter**) 100th part of a litre

centime money unit of many countries

centimetre (US **centimeter**) 100th part of a metre

centipede arthropod with many feet

centralize or **centralise** to bring under central control
centralization or centralisation
centralizing or centralising

centre (US **center**) (to put at the) exact middle point
central centralism centrally
centred (US centered) centrepiece (US centerpiece) centring (US centering)

centrifugal moving away from a centre
centrifugally centrifuge

centripetal moving towards a centre
centripetally

centurion officer commanding 100 Roman foot soldiers

century period of 100 years; 100 runs in cricket
centuries

cephalic of the head

ceramics art of making articles of clay, etc.
ceramic ceramist

cereal grass plant producing an edible grain

cerebral of the brain
cerebrally

cerebrum largest part of the brain
cerebra

ceremonial marked by ceremony or ritual
ceremonially
SEE PANEL

---

ceremonial or ceremonious?

Ceremonial means ´marked by ceremony or ritual´: *the costumes worn on ceremonial occasions.*

Ceremonious means ´excessively polite and formal´: *give a ceremonious bow upon entering the room.*

---

ceremonious excessively polite and formal
ceremoniously
SEE PANEL at **ceremonial**

ceremony formal act or occasion
ceremonies

cerise light purplish red

certain sure; determined; some
certainly certainty certainties

certificate official document

certify to confirm or declare formally
certifiable certified certifies certifying

certitude certainty

cerulean deep-blue

cervix neck; narrow outer end of the uterus
cervices cervical

cesarean (US) see **caesarean**

cessation ceasing

cession act of ceding

cesspit or **cesspool** underground pit or basin for disposal of sewage

Chablis dry white wine from northern Burgundy

chad country in Central Africa
Chadian

chafe to make or become sore or worn by rubbing
chafing

chafer kind of large beetle

chaff[1] husks separated from seeds; useless things

chaff[2] to tease

chaffer to haggle or bargain
chafferer

chaffinch kind of common European finch

chagrin feeling of annoyance and disappointment

chain length of metal links; unit of length, 22 yards; to confine
chain-gang chain-smoke

chair seat with a back for one person; to preside over a meeting
chair-lift chairman chairmanship chairperson chairwoman

chaise longue (*French*) long low seat
chaises longues

chalcedony form of quartz
chalcedonies chalcedonic

chalet hut or cottage, esp. in Switzerland

chalice drinking cup, esp. as used at the Eucharist

chalk soft whitish limestone; piece of this used for writing
chalky

challenge to call to justify oneself or compete; invitation to do this
challenged challenger challenging

chamber hall or room
chambermaid chamber-pot

chamberlain chief officer of a royal or noble household

chambers (*Brit*) judge's or barrister's offices

chameleon kind of lizard with the ability to change colour

chamois kind of small mountain antelope
chamois-leather

chamomile see **camomile**

champ to bite or chew noisily

champagne kind of white sparkling wine

champion winner; someone who pleads a cause
championship

chance (to take a) risk; fate or luck
chancy

chancel part of a church near the altar

chancellor head of government in any of certain European countries; high official; head of a university
chancellery chancellorship

chancery division of the High Court
chanceries

chandelier ornamental branched hanging light

chandler dealer in supplies, esp. candles
chandlery

change to make or become different; (to exchange) money in return for smaller units or foreign currency; alteration or modification
changeless changeling change-over change-round changing

changeable capable of changing; frequently changing
changeability changeably

channel narrow stretch of water; (to direct along a) course or passage; band of frequencies
channelled (US *channeled*) *channelling* (US *channeling*)

chant song or melody; to sing

chantey (US) see **shanty**

chaos utter confusion
chaotic chaotically

chap[1] to become raw and cracked
chapped chapping

chap[2] (*informal*) man

chapel place of worship

chaperon or **chaperone** person who accompanies a younger woman or girl on social occasions; to act as a chaperon to
chaperoning

chaplain clergyman
chaplaincy

chaplet wreath; short rosary

chaps leather overleggings

chapter division of a book, etc.; (meeting of) cathedral clergy

char to burn or scorch
charred charring

charabanc early kind of motor coach

character personal qualities; person in a play, story, etc.

characteristic typical (quality)

characterize or **characterise** to describe the character of; to distinguish
characterization or *characterisation*
characterizing or *characterising*

charades word-guessing game

charcoal wood burnt black

chard variety of beet

charge (to ask for as) payment; amount of electricity; (to make an) accusation
chargeable charge-cap charger charging

chargé d'affaires (*French*) deputy ambassador; government representative
chargés d'affaires

chariot 2-wheeled carriage used for fighting and racing
charioteer

charisma great appeal and charm that inspires loyalty and enthusiasm
charismatic

charitable generous or kind
charitably

charity kindness; organization that helps the needy
charities

charivari noisy medley of sounds

charlady see **charwoman**

charlatan pretender; fraud or quack
charlatanism or *charlatanry*

charleston kind of lively dance

charlock kind of wild mustard plant

charlotte kind of fruit dessert

charm quality of attraction; something thought to have magical powers
charmer charming

charnel-house building in which bodies are deposited

chart map; sheet or graph showing tables

charter formal document granting rights; to hire an aircraft
chartered

chartreuse liqueur; yellow or green colour

charwoman or **charlady** woman employed to clean a house, etc.
charwomen or *charladies*

chary cautious; wary
charily chariness

chase to follow quickly; to hunt
chaser chasing

chasm hole; great difference

chassis framework of a vehicle

chaste pure; virtuous
chastely chasteness chastity

chasten to discipline by punishing

chastise to scold severely
chastisement chastising

chastity purity or virginity

chasuble priest's vestment

chat (to have a) friendly informal talk
chatted chatting chatty

château castle or large country house in France
châteaux or *châteaus*

chatelaine mistress of a castle, etc.

chattel article of movable property

chatter to talk idly and quickly
chatterbox chatterer

chauffeur person employed to drive a car

chauvinism excessive patriotism or devotion to a cause
chauvinist chauvinistic

cheap low in price; tawdry; worthless; contemptible
cheapen cheapjack cheapskate

cheat to behave dishonestly; person who cheats
cheater

check to examine or inspect; to slow or stop
check-in check-list check-out checkpoint check-up

checker (US) see **chequer**

checkers (US) see **draughts**

checkmate complete defeat in chess

Cheddar kind of hard cheese

cheek side of the face below the eye; insolence

cheeky insolent; impudent
cheekier cheekiest cheekily cheekiness

cheep faint shrill cry of a young bird

cheer (to give) applause or shout of approval; (to give) encouragement
cheery

cheerful bright; in good spirits
cheerfully cheerfulness

cheerless miserable or dreary
cheerlessly cheerlessness

cheese solid food made from milk
cheeseburger cheesecake cheesecloth cheeseparing cheesy

cheetah animal of the cat family; swiftest mammal

chef skilled cook

chef-d'œuvre (*French*) masterpiece
chefs-d'œuvre

chemise woman's undergarment; straight-hanging dress

chemist someone trained in chemistry; dealer in medicines, etc.

chemistry science dealing with the nature of substances and their reactions
chemical chemically

chemotherapy treatment of disease by chemical agents

chenille (carpet or fabric of) velvety cord

cheque (US **check**) written order instructing a bank to pay money

chequer (US **checker**) (to mark with a) pattern of squares
chequered (US *checkered*)

cherish to show tenderness towards
cherishes

cheroot cigar with both ends squarely cut off

cherry kind of small fleshy round fruit
cherries cherry-pick

cherub kind of angel; sweet child
cherubim or *cherubs cherubic*

chervil kind of aromatic herb plant

chess board-game for two players
chessboard chessman chess-piece

chest upper front part of the body; large sturdy case
chesty

chesterfield heavily padded sofa

chestnut kind of tree with reddish-brown nuts

cheval-glass full length tilting mirror

chevalier member of certain orders of merit

chevron pattern or badge in a V-shape

chew to crush or grind food with the teeth
chewier chewiest chewing-gum chewy

chiaroscuro arrangement of light and dark in a picture
chiaroscuros

chic stylish; elegance

chicane series of tight turns in opposite directions on a road-racing course

chicanery verbal deception; dishonest trickery
chicaneries

chick young bird

chicken young domestic fowl
chicken-feed chicken-hearted chickenpox

chickpea chickweed

chicle gumlike substance; main ingredient of chewing-gum

chicory plant used in salads and coffee
chicories

chide to scold
chidden chided or *chid chider chiding*

chief most important; main; head or leader
chiefs chiefly chieftain chieftaincy chieftainship

chiffon fine transparent fabric

chiffonier tall chest of drawers; low cabinet

chignon roll or knot of hair

chihuahua breed of tiny dog

chilblain inflammation, esp. on the hands or feet, caused by cold

child young person; boy or girl
children child-bearing childbirth childhood childless child-minder childproof

childish immature
SEE PANEL

childish or childlike?
Childish means 'immature': *childish moods and outbursts of temper; Stop being so childish!*
Childlike is used to refer to the attractive qualities of childhood, such as enthusiasm and sincerity: *childlike simplicity.*

childlike like a child, having a child's attractive qualities
SEE PANEL at **childish**

Chile country in South America
Chilean

chill (to make or become) cold
chillier chilliest chilly

chilli pod of a hot pepper
chillies

chime (to ring a) series of notes struck on a bell
chiming

chimera mythical monster
chimerical

chimney vertical structure for carrying away smoke, etc.
chimneys

chimpanzee kind of African ape

chin front part of lower jaw
chinless chin-wag

china (articles made from) porcelain; crockery
chinaware

China country in Asia
Chinese

chinchilla kind of small South American rodent

chine[1] (to cut meat along) a backbone
chining

chine[2] (*Brit*) steep-sided ravine

chink[1] (to make a) light ringing sound, as of glasses striking together

chink[2] small narrow opening

chinook warm wind

chintz printed cotton, usually glazed
chintzes chintzy

chip (to break off a) small piece of something; strip of fried potato; gambling token; wafer of silicon crystal
chipboard chipped chipping

chipmunk small striped squirrel-like animal

chipolata small thin sausage

chiropody care and treatment of human feet
chiropodist

chiropractic manipulation of the spine and other parts to heal diseases
chiropractor

chirp (to make a) short sharp high-pitched sound
chirper chirpy

chirrup (to) chirp
chirruped chirruper chirruping chirrupy

chisel tool for working or shaping wood
chiselled (US *chiseled*) *chiseller* (US *chiseler*) *chiselling* (US *chiseling*)

chit note; voucher

chit-chat casual talk

chitin main part of the hard cover of insects and crustaceans
chitinous

chivalry courtesy and consideration
chivalric chivalrous

chive plant related to the onion

chivvy to tease persistently; to harass or nag
chivvied chivvying

chloride compound of chlorine

chlorine greenish-yellow poisonous gas
chlorinate chlorination

chloroform colourless liquid formerly used as an anaesthetic

chlorophyll (US **chlorophyl**) green pigment of plants

chock block or wedge of wood
chock-a-block chock-full

chocolate food prepared from cacao seeds
choc-ice chocolatey

choice choosing; selection; high-quality
choicely choicest

choir organized group of singers
choirboy choirmaster

choke to stop or hinder the breathing of; valve in petrol engine
choker choking choky

choler (*formal*) anger
choleric

cholera acute infectious disease

cholesterol fatty substance in animal and plant cells

choose to consider desirable
choosing chose chosen

choosy difficult to please; particular
choosier choosiest

chop to cut or hit; thick cut of meat
chopped chopping chopsticks

chopper chopping tool; (*informal*) helicopter

choppy (*of the sea*) fairly rough
choppier choppiest choppily choppiness

chopsuey Chinese dish

choral of a choir or chorus
chorally

chorale hymn or tune

chord[1] group of musical notes sounded together

chord[2] straight line joining two points on a curve; emotional response

chore routine domestic task

choreography art of arranging steps and movements in ballet and dancing
choreographer choreographic

chorister singer in a choir

chortle (to give a) gleeful chuckle
chortling

chorus group of singers; repeated part of a song; to sing or utter together
choruses choral chorused

chose past tense of **choose**

chosen past participle of **choose**

choux of a very light pastry used in éclairs, etc.

chow[1] (*informal*) food

chow[2] thick-coated breed of dog

chowder thick soup or stew

Christ title given to Jesus
Christendom Christian Christianity Christ-like Christology

christen to name and baptize
christening

Christmas yearly commemoration of the birthday of Christ
Christmassy

chromatic of colour; of the musical scale that consists of semitones
chromatically chromatism

chrome (pigment containing) chromium

chromium metallic element used in alloys and to coat other materials
chromium-plating

chromosome gene-carrying threadlike body in the nucleus of a cell

chronic constantly recurring
chronically

chronicle (to make a) record or register of events
chronicler chronicling

chronology arrangement of dates, events, etc., in order of occurrence
chronologies chronologer chronological chronologically chronologist

chronometer accurate instrument for measuring time
chronometric

chrysalis pupa of a butterfly or moth
chrysalides or *chrysalises*

chrysanthemum kind of flower with showy heads

chub kind of freshwater fish

chubby plump and round
chubbier chubbiest chubbily chubbiness

chuck[1] (*informal*) to throw; to tap gently under the chin

chuck[2] cut of beef; device for holding a tool or work-piece

chuckle to laugh quietly to oneself
chuckler chuckling

chuffed (*informal*) pleased

chug (to move with a) short heavy sound made by an engine running slowly
chugged chugging

chum close friend
chummy

chump thick block of wood; thick piece of meat; (*informal*) fool

chunk solid piece; lump
chunky

Chunnel (*informal*) the Channel Tunnel

church place for public, esp. Christian, worship
churches church-goer churchwarden churchyard

churl ill-mannered person
churlish

churn large container for milk; to make butter by beating milk

chute sloping channel for carrying things downwards

chutney condiment of fruit, spices, etc.

cicada kind of large winged insect
cicadas or *cicadae*

cicatrice or **cicatrix** scar
cicatrices

cider or **cyder** fermented apple juice

cigar roll of cured tobacco leaves for smoking

cigarette thin tube of paper filled with shredded tobacco

cilium tiny threadlike structure that grows from the surface of a cell
cilia ciliary

cinch (*informal*) easy task

cinchona tree whose bark contains *quinine*

cincture girdle or belt

cinder partly burnt coal or wood
cindery

cine- (*prefix*) of the cinema
cine-camera

cinema theatre where films are shown
cinematic

cinematograph film camera or projector
cinematographic

cinnamon yellowish-brown spice

cinque (*French*) 5 (on cards, dice, etc.)

cipher or **cypher** secret code; zero

circa (*Latin*) about

circle (to move round in a) closed plane curve
circler circlet circling circular

circuit (to make a) complete course; path of an electric current
circuitous circuitry

circular circle-shaped; leaflet, etc. for distribution

circularize or **circularise** to distribute circulars to
circularizing or *circularising*

circulate to move along a closed path; to spread widely
circulating circulation circulatory

circumcise to remove the male foreskin or female clitoris from
circumcising circumcision

circumference distance round the edge of a circle

circumflex mark ^ over a vowel in French, etc.

circumlocution indirect way of expressing something
circumlocutory

circumnavigate to sail completely round
circumnavigating circumnavigation circumnavigator

circumscribe to draw a line round; to restrict
circumscribing circumscription

circumspect cautious
circumspection circumspectly

circumstance factor, condition, or detail
circumstantial circumstantially

circumstantiate to supply detailed evidence
circumstantiating

circumvent to go round or evade; to outwit
circumvention

circus travelling group of performing animals, acrobats, etc.
circuses

cirrhosis disease of the liver

cirrus kind of cloud
cirri

cissy or **sissy** cowardly or effeminate boy or man
cissies or *sissies*

cistern water tank

citadel stronghold

cite to refer to; to give as an example
citable or *citeable citation citing*

citizen inhabitant of a town or city
citizenship

citric acid acid found in fruits such as lemon

citron kind of tree with lemon-like fruit

citrus group of trees including lemon, lime, and orange
citrous

city large and important town
cities city-state

civet fluid secreted by the civet cat, used for perfume

civic relating to a town, city, or citizens
civics
SEE PANEL

---

civic or civil?

Civic means 'of a town, city, or citizens': *a civic centre; a civic reception; fulfil one's civic responsibilities.*

Civil means 'of or relating to ordinary citizens': *civil war; civil disobedience; an erosion of civil liberties* or 'courteous, but not too friendly': *You might not like them, but do at least try to be civil to them.*

---

civil of citizens; courteous
civilian civility civilities civilly
SEE PANEL at **civic**

civilize or **civilise** to improve and educate; to refine
civilizable or *civilisable civilization* or *civilisation civilizer* or *civiliser civilizing* or *civilising*

civvies or **civies** (*slang*) civilian, not military, clothes

clack (to make a) sudden quick sound

clad covered or clothed

cladding protective covering

claim (to demand as a) right
claimant

clairvoyance alleged power of being aware of things beyond the natural range of senses
clairvoyant

clam kind of edible shellfish; to keep silent; to clog
clammed clamming

clamber to climb awkwardly with the hands and feet

clammy unpleasantly damp
clammier clammiest clammily clamminess

clamour (US **clamor**) loud noise or outcry
clamorous clamorousness

clamp (to hold or fasten with a) mechanical gripping device
clamp-down

clan group of families with a common ancestor
calnnish

clandestine secret; furtive

clang (to make a) loud resounding noise
clanger clangour (US *clangor*) *clangorous*

clank (to make a) short harsh metallic noise

clap to applaud by striking the hands together; sudden sharp sound
clapped clapper clapper-board clapping

claptrap insincere or foolish talk; empty words

claque group of people hired to applaud
claquer

claret red wine from Bordeaux

clarify to make clear
clarification clarified clarifier clarifies clarifying

clarinet kind of woodwind instrument
clarinetist or *clarinettist*

clarion (sound of a) medieval trumpet; clear and ringing

clarity clearness

clash (to make a) harsh noise; to come into conflict
clashes

clasp to hold or grasp firmly; (to join with a) fastening device

class (to put in a) group sharing a common characteristic; group of students taught together
classes class-conscious classless classmate classroom classwork

classic typical; excellent; distinguished
classics classicism classicist
SEE PANEL

---

classic or classical?

Something that is *classic* is typical or excellent: *a classic example of 1930s' Art Deco; the classic religious allegory 'Pilgrim's Progress'.* As a noun, a *classic* refers to an outstanding book, film, etc., that has become a standard work. *Classics* is the study of the language and literature of ancient Greece and Rome. *Classical* describes things that have a traditional form or style, in contrast to a modern one: *classical architecture.*

---

classical of ancient Greek and Roman cultures; of a kind of music of the 18th and 19th centuries
classically
SEE PANEL at **classic**

classify to arrange in different groups
classifiable classification classified classifies classifying

classy elegant; stylish
classier classiest classily classiness

clatter (to make a) rattling noise

clause part of a sentence; part of a legal document

claustrophobia fear of being in a confined space
claustrophobic

clavichord kind of keyboard instrument

clavicle collar-bone

claw nail on the foot of an animal
claw-back

clay soft earthy material that hardens when baked
clayey

claymore kind of large sword

clean (to make) free of dirt
clean-cut cleaner cleanliness cleanly cleanness clean-out clean-shaven clean-up

cleanse to purify
cleanser cleansing

clear (to make) bright; easy to see, hear, or understand; to empty
clearance clear-cut clear-eyed clear-headed clearing clearing-house clear-minded clearness clear-sighted clear-up clearway

cleat wedge-shaped support

cleavage separation between a woman's breasts; splitting

cleave[1] to split
cleaved or *cleft cleaver cleaving cloven*

cleave[2] to adhere loyally to
cleaved cleaver cleaving

clef (*music*) symbol to show pitch

clematis kind of climbing plant

clement merciful; mild
clemency clemently

clementine kind of citrus fruit

clench to close, squeeze, or grasp tightly
clenches

clerestory row of windows in upper part of a church wall
clerestories

clergy ordained group in a Christian church
clergies clergyman

cleric clergyman

clerical of clergy; of a clerk

clerihew satirical 4-line verse

clerk office-worker with general duties, esp. filing; (US) shop assistant

clever intelligent; skilful
cleverly cleverness

clew ball of thread; (to haul) lower corner of a sail

cliché hackneyed word or expression
clichéd cliché-ridden

click (to make a) brief sharp sound

client person seeking professional service or advice; customer
clientele

cliff very steep high face of a rock
cliff-hanger

climacteric critical or crucial period

climate normal general weather conditions of a place
climatic climatically

climatology study of climates
climatological climatologist

climax highest or most intense point
climaxes climactic

climp to go up
climbable climb-down climber

clinch to fasten or grasp tightly; to settle a deal, etc.; act of clinching
clinches clincher

cling to hold closely
clung

clinic centre for medical treatment and advice
clinical clinically

clink (to make a) sharp ringing sound

clinker stony matter left after coal has been burned

clinker-built (*of a boat*) made with the external planks overlapping

clip[1] (to fasten with a) clasping device
clipboard clipped clipping

clip[2] to cut or trim; to punch a hole
clipped clippers clipping

clique exclusive group of people
cliquey or *cliquy cliquish cliquishly cliquishness*

clitoris small female erectile organ
clitoral

cloak loose sleeveless outer garment
cloak-and-dagger cloakroom

clobber[1] (*informal*) clothes; equipment

clobber[2] (*informal*) to hit or defeat overwhelmingly

cloche cover for young plants; woman's close-fitting hat

clock device that measures and shows time
clock-face clocktower clock-watching clockwise clockwork

clod lump of earth or clay
cloddish clodhopper

clog to make or become blocked; wooden shoe
clogged clogging

cloister covered passage in a monastery, convent, etc.

clone individual produced asexually; to cause to grow as a clone
cloning

clonk (to make a) dull loud thud

close[1] near; enclosed precinct
close-cropped close-cut close-fisted close-fitting close-grained close-knit close-lipped closeness closer close-set closest

close[2] to shut; (to) finish
closed-circuit close-down

closet small cupboard or room

closure closing, esp. of a debate

clot (to form a) soft thick lump
clotted clotting

cloth woven fabric

clothe to supply clothes for
clothed or *clad clothier clothing*

clothes articles of dress
clothes-brush clothes-horse clothes-line clothes-peg

cloud mass of water vapour; to become overcast with clouds
cloudburst cloud-cuckoo-land cloudless cloudy

clout to hit; (*informal*) political influence

clove[1] past tense of **cleave**[1]

clove[2] dried flower buds of a kind of tropical tree

clove[3] segment of a bulb

cloven past participle of **cleave**[1]
cloven-footed cloven-hoofed

clover kind of plant with small three-part leaves

clown comic performer in circus
clownish

cloy to make weary because of an excess

club (to hit with a) heavy stick; group of people; society; playing-card suit
clubbable clubbed clubbing clubfoot clubhouse clubroom

cluck (to make the) gutteral noise of a hen

clue helpful information to solve a problem; to inform
clued clueing or *cluing*

clump cluster of trees or shrubs; to walk or tread heavily

clumsy awkward; unskilful; unwieldy
clumsier clumsiest clumsily clumsiness

clung past tense and past participle of **cling**

clunk (to make a) short dull metallic sound

cluster number of things growing or occurring together

clutch[1] to seize tightly; coupling mechanism
clutches

clutch[2] nest of eggs
clutches

clutter (objects in a) disordered state; to fill with clutter

Clwyd Welsh county

co- (*prefix*) together; with
co-author co-star co-worker

coach railway carriage; long-distance bus; tutor or instructor; to instruct
coaches coachman coachwork

coagulate to thicken or clot
coagulant coagulating coagulation coagulative

coal hard black mineral used as fuel
coal-dust coalface coalfield coalmine coalminer coal-pit

coalesce to combine or unite
coalescence coalescent coalescing

coalition alliance of political parties

coaming raised frame round a ship's hatchway

coarse rough; crude or vulgar
coarse-grained coarsely coarsen coarseness coarser coarsest

coast seashore; to move without using power
coastal coaster coastguard coastline

coat outer garment with sleeves; covering of an animal; layer of paint, etc.
coat-hanger coating coat-tails

coax to persuade by gentle urging
coaxer coaxes coaxingly

cob male swan; kind of horse; core of an ear of maize

cobalt hard silvery-white metallic element

cobble[1] stone used for paving
cobblestone

cobble[2] to make or repair shoes; to put together clumsily
cobbler cobbling

COBOL computer language

cobra kind of poisonous snake

cobweb fine web spun by spider
cobwebby

coca kind of South American shrub

cocaine drug used as a stimulant or as a local anaesthetic

coccus spherical bacterium
cocci coccal

coccyx bone at the end of the spine
coccyges or *coccyxes*

cochineal red colouring

cochlea spiral-shaped tube in the inner ear

cock male domestic fowl; valve or tap; to set upright or tilt; to set (a gun) ready for firing
cock-a-hoop cock-and-bull cock-crow cockfighting cock-robin cock-shot cock sparrow cock-up cocky

cockade ornamental badge on a hat

cockatoo kind of crested parrot
cockatoos

cockatrice legendary monster

cockchafer kind of beetle

cocker breed of spaniel

cockerel young domestic cock

cock-eyed squinting; absurd

cockle kind of edible shellfish; wrinkle; seat of deep feelings
cockleshell

cockney native or dialect of London, esp. East End

cockpit compartment in an aircraft

cockroach kind of dark-brown beetle-like insect
cockroaches

cockscomb kind of plant; cock's crest

cocktail mixture of alcoholic drinks; mixture of different foods

cocky over-confident

cocoa (drink made from) powdered cocoa beans

coconut large oval fruit of tropical tree

cocoon silky wrapping spun by larvae

cod kind of large sea-fish
codfish

coda concluding musical passage

coddle to pamper; to cook in water just below boiling-point
coddling

code secret system of letters or symbols; set of principles or rules

codeine drug used as a pain-killer

codex manuscript book
codices

codger (*informal*) eccentric old person

codicil supplement to a will
codicillary

codify to set out systematically; to arrange in a code
codification codified codifies codifying

codling[1] kind of long tapering apple

codling[2] young cod

codswallop (*slang*) nonsense

coeducation education of boys and girls together
coeducational

coefficient specified constant numerical factor

coerce to compel by force
coercer coercible coercing coercion coercive

coeval of the same age

coexist to exist together
coexistence coexistent

coextend to extend equally
coextension coextensive

coffee (kind of drink made from the roasted and ground seeds of) tropical shrub
coffee-bean coffee-cup coffee-house coffee-pot

coffer strong chest
coffer-dam

coffin box in which a corpse is buried

cog one of a set of teeth on the edge of a wheel
cogwheel

cogent strong and convincing
cogency cogently

cogitate to think deeply about
cogitating cogitation

cognac French brandy

cognate from the same source

cognition knowing; awareness and judgement
cognitive

cognizance or **cognisance** notice; awareness
cognizant or *cognisant*

cognomen surname; descriptive nickname
cognomens or *cognomina*

cognoscente well-informed person
cognoscenti

cohabit to live together as husband and wife
cohabitant cohabitation

cohere to hold or stick together

coherent well-planned; consistent; intelligible
coherence coherently
SEE PANEL

---

coherent or cohesive?
Something that is *coherent* is logical and well-thought-out; all its parts go well together: *a coherent argument/theory.* Someone who is *coherent* is able to express their thoughts in a calm, logical, and intelligible manner.

Something that is *cohesive* is made up of separate parts that stick together or, figuratively, fit together to form a unity: *the cohesive qualities of the glue; the different elements in the community that help it become a cohesive whole.*

---

cohesive sticking together; fitting together well
cohesion
SEE PANEL at **coherent**

cohort 10th part of a Roman legion

coif close-fitting cap

coiffeur hairdresser
coiffeuse coiffure

coil (to wind in a) spiral
coiled coiling

coin piece of metal money; to create
coinage

coincide to happen at the same time; to agree
coincidence coincident coincidental coincidentally coinciding

Cointreau (*trademark*) colourless liqueur with orange flavouring

coir fibre from coconut husks

coitus or **coition** sexual intercourse
coital

coke fuel remaining after gases, etc., have been extracted from coal

colander bowl with holes used to drain vegetables
SEE PANEL at **calendar**

cold having a low temperature, passive or indifferent; viral infection marked by sneezing, etc.
cold-blooded colder coldest cold-hearted coldly coldness

coleslaw salad of shredded white cabbage

colic severe abdominal pain
colicky

coliseum large building for public entertainment

colitis inflammation of the colon

collaborate to work in partnership
collaborating collaboration collaborator

collage art composition made by sticking pieces of paper, cloth, etc. on to a surface

collapse to break or give way; to cave in
collapsible or *collapsable collapsing*

collar part of a garment fitting round the neck
collar-bone

collate to collect and compare; to assemble in order
collating collation collator

collateral security pledge for the repayment of a loan; secondary
collaterally

collation collating; light meal

colleague fellow worker

collect[1] to bring or come together; to fetch
collectable or *collectible collection collective collectively collector*

collect[2] short prayer

collectivism collective control over production and distribution
collectivist collectivize or *collectivise*

colleen Irish girl

college institution of higher education
collegian collegiate

collide to come together forcibly
colliding

collie breed of sheepdog

collier coalminer; ship for transporting coal

colliery coalmine and its buildings
collieries

collision crash; impact; conflict

collocate to arrange in place
collocating collocation

colloid substance such as glue that is dispersed in a liquid

colloquial of informal conversation
colloquialism colloquially

colloquium conference or seminar
colloquiums or *colloquia*

colloquy formal conversation
colloquies

collude to conspire or plot
colluding

collusion secret agreement for fraudulent purposes

collywobbles (*informal*) stomach-ache; nervousness

cologne cooling scented liquid

Colombia country in South America
Colombian

colon[1] part of the large intestine
colons or *cola*

colon² punctuation mark:

colonel army officer

colonize or **colonise** to establish a colony in
colonization or *colonisation* *colonizing* or *colonising*

colonnade row of columns

colony settlement or settlers in a new territory
colonies *colonial* *colonialism* *colonialist* *colonist*

colophon inscription at the end of a book; publisher's identifying emblem

color (US) see **colour**

colossal huge; gigantic
colossally

colossus enormous statue
colossi or *colossuses*

colostomy surgical formation of a permanent opening into the colon
colostomies

colostrum first milk secreted for a few days after giving birth

colour (US **color**) visual sensation produced by light rays; paint; badge or flag
colour-blind (US *color-blind*) *coloured* (US *colored*) *colourful* (US *colorful*) *colouring* (US *coloring*) *colourist* (US *colorist*) *colourize* or *colourise* (US *colorize*) *colourless* (US *colorless*)

colporteur hawker of books, esp. Bibles

colt young male horse
coltish

colter (US) see **coulter**

coltsfoot wild plant with large leaves and yellow flowers

columbine plant of the buttercup family

column upright pillar; vertical printed section
columnar *columnist*

coma deep unconsciousness
comatose

comb toothed device for cleaning and arranging hair; crest of a fowl

combat (to) fight or struggle
combatant *combated* *combating* *combative*

combine to join together; union
combination *combining*

combustible capable of being set on fire easily
combustibility *combustion*

come to move towards the speaker
came *come-back* *come-down* *come-hither* *come-uppance* *coming*

Comecon former economic association of Communist countries

comedy light humorous play
comedies *comedian* *comedienne*

comely (*old-fashioned*) attractive
comelier *comeliest* *comeliness*

comestible food

comet celestial body

comfit sugar-coated sweet

comfort contentment; (to give) encouragement
comfortable *comfortably* *comforter* *comfortless*

comfrey kind of plant with hairy leaves

comfy (*informal*) comfortable
comfier *comfiest* *comfily* *comfiness*

comic intended to amuse; comedian; children's magazine
comical *comicality* *comically*

comity harmony; courtesy

comma punctuation mark,

command (to give an) authoritative direction or order
commandant *commander* *commander-in-chief* *commanders-in-chief* *commanding* *commandment*

commandeer to seize, esp. for military purposes

commando member of a specialized military attacking force
commandos

commedia dell'arte (*Italian*) 16th–18th century comedy

commemorate to honour the memory of
commemorating commemoration commemorative

commence to begin
commencement commencing

commend to praise or recommend; to entrust
commendable commendably commendation

commensurate equal in extent or duration; proportionate
commensurable commensurably

comment (to make a) remark or observation

commentary set of comments or description of something
commentaries

commentate to provide a broadcast commentary
commentating commentator

commerce business; trade
commercial commercialese commercialism commercially

commercialize or **commercialise** to make commercial
commercialization or *commercialisation commercializing* or *commercialising*

commingle to mix
commingling

commiserate to express sympathy for
commiserating commiseration

commissar Communist Party official

commissariat military department in charge of supplies
commissary commissaries

commission task; authority; rank; percentage paid to agent; to grant authority to

commissionaire uniformed attendant

commissioner head of a commission; government official

commit to entrust; to perform
commitment committable committal committed committing

committee group of people appointed to carry out a service or function

commode chest of drawers; chair containing chamber-pot

commodious spacious
commodiously commodiousness

commodity article of commerce
commodities

commodore rank in the navy and air force

common general; ordinary; open public land
commonality commonalty commoner commonly commonness commonplace common-room commonsensical

commonwealth group or association of states

commotion noisy confusion

commune[1] group of people living together; small administrative district
communal

commune[2] to communicate intimately (with)
communing

communicant person who receives Holy Communion; informant

communicate to convey; to transmit news
communicable communicating communication communicative

communion sharing of ideas; participation or fellowship

Communion Eucharist

communiqué official announcement
communiqués

communism social system in which the means of production are owned and controlled by the community
communist communistic

community group of people living in one area
communities

commutator device for reversing the direction of flow of an electric current

commute to travel regularly to work; to exchange or convert
commutable commutation commutative commuter commuting

compact[1] concise; packed together; case for face powder
compactly compactness

compact[2] agreement

companion someone accompanying another person
companionable companionship companion-way

company business organization
companies

comparative comparing; (*grammar*) (form of an) adjective or adverb expressing a higher degree of comparison
comparatively

compare to find out similarities and differences between
comparable comparableness comparing comparison

compartment divided section, esp. of an enclosed space
compartmentalize or *compartmentalise*

compass instrument used to show direction, having a needle that points to magnetic north; instrument for drawing circles
compasses

compassion sympathy or pity
compassionate compassionately

compatible capable of existing or working together harmoniously
compatibility compatibly

compatriot fellow countryman

compeer person of equal rank; equal

compel to force
compellable compelled compeller compelling

compendium summary; set of puzzles
compendiums or *compendia compendious*

compensate to make amends for loss or damage
compensating compensation compensatory

compère presenter of an entertainment; to present entertainment
compèring

compete to take part in a contest; to strive for
competing

competent capable; qualified
competence competently

competition contest involving rivalry
competitive competitor

compile to collect and arrange information
compilation compiler compiling

complacent self-satisfied
complacence or *complacency complacently*

complain to express discontent
complainant complainer complainingly complaint

complaisant polite; obliging
complaisance complaisantly

complement something that completes; to make complete
complementary
SEE PANEL

---

complement or compliment?
Both as a noun and a verb, *complement* describes something that completes, that is makes something complete or better. For example if one person or thing complements another, they go well together: *a richly coloured wallpaper that complements the traditional woodwork; the two lecturers' teaching styles complemented each other*. The *complement* of

things or people is the full amount or set that it usually has: *the ship's full complement of two hundred passengers and crew.*

To *compliment* a person, or to pay them a *compliment*, is to express admiration or praise to them: *She is to be complimented on her handling of the crisis.*

---

complete whole; thorough; finished; total; to make complete
completely completeness completing completion

complex difficult; made up of several different parts; set of feelings that affect behaviour
complexity complexities

complexion colouring and appearance of the facial skin

compliant willing to yield to others
compliance compliantly

complicate to make difficult to understand
complicating complication

complicity participation in a criminal act
complicities

compliment (to express) admiration or praise to
complimentary
SEE PANEL at **complement**

compline service of the day in the Roman Catholic Church

comply to do as person asks
compliance compliant complied complies complying

component part that makes up a whole

comport (*formal*) to behave
comportment

compose to create; to make up; to calm
composedly composer composing composition compositor composure

composite made up of different parts

compos mentis (*Latin*) of sound mind

compost mixture of decaying organic substances used as a fertilizer

compote fruit stewed in a syrup

compound[1] (something) made up of two or more parts; to combine to make a whole

compound[2] enclosed area

comprehend to understand; to include
comprehensibility comprehensible comprehensibly comprehension comprehensive comprehensiveness

compress[1] to press together
compresses compressibility compressible compression compressor

compress[2] cold pad to relieve pain or stop bleeding
compresses

comprise to be made up of
comprisable comprising

compromise (to reach a) settlement of a dispute by concessions made on both sides; to expose to disrepute
compromising

comptroller controller of public finance

compulsion compelling or being compelled

compulsive that one has to do and cannot give up
SEE PANEL

---

compulsive or compulsory?

Compulsive is used to describe a person with a habit that they find impossible to give up: *a compulsive gambler.* A book or film that is *compulsive* must, so the reader or viewer feels, be read or watched to the end: *the interview made compulsive viewing.*

Compulsory refers to something that is required by law: *The wearing of seat-belts is compulsory.*

---

compulsory required by laws, rules, etc.
compulsorily
SEE PANEL at **compulsive**

compunction feeling of guilt or remorse

compute to calculate
computable computation

computer electronic calculating machine that can store and process information
computer-literate

computerize or **computerise** to operate by means of computers; to equip with computers
computerization or *computerisation* *computerizing* or *computerising*

comrade friend or companion; fellow member
comradely comradeship

con (*slang*) (to) swindle
conned conning

concatenate to join or link in a series
concatenating concatenation

concave curved inwards
concavely concavity concavities

conceal to hide
concealer concealment

concede to admit; to yield
conceding

conceit exaggerated opinion of oneself
conceited conceitedly

conceive to imagine; to become pregnant
conceivable conceivably conceiving conception

concentrate to bring to a single aim; to make pure by removing certain parts
concentrating concentration

concentric having a common centre
concentrically concentricity

concept general idea; thought
conception conceptual conceptually

conceptualize or **conceptualise** to form a concept of
conceptualization or *conceptualisation* *conceptualizing* or *conceptualising*

concern to relate to; (to) worry; business
concerned concerning

concert musical performance; to plan with others
concerted concert-goer concert-hall concert-master

concertina (to collapse or fold like a) kind of accordion
concertinas concertinaed concertinaing concertinist

concerto composition for solo instrument and orchestra
concertos

concession something conceded, such as a demand or right
concessionaire concessionary concessive

conch kind of (spiral shell of a) large shellfish
conchs or *conches*

concierge (*French*) house-porter

conciliate to win over; to reconcile
conciliating conciliation conciliator conciliatory

concise brief
concisely conciseness

conclave secret meeting

conclude to end; to decide
concluding conclusion conclusive conclusively conclusiveness

concoct to make by combining; to invent
concoction

concomitant (person or thing) accompanying

concord agreement; harmony
concordant concordat

concordance index of words or pharses in a literary work

concourse large public open space; crowd

concrete (to set in a) building material; real; specific
concretely concreteness concreting concretion

concubine woman who lives with a man in addition to his wife

concupiscence sexual desire
concupiscent

concur to agree with; to happen together

concurred concurrence concurrent concurrently concurring

concuss to injure the brain by a violent blow
concussed concussion

condemn to disapprove of strongly; to pronounce a sentence on
condemnable condemnation condemnatory

condense to express in a shorter form; to change from gas to liquid
condensable condensation condenser condensing

condescend to behave in a way that one considers beneath one's dignity
condescending condescension

condign deserved; appropriate
condignly

condiment seasoning

condition a state or circumstance; necessary requirement; to train
conditional conditionally conditioner conditioning

condolence expression of sympathy
condolences

condom sheath worn over the penis during sexual intercourse to prevent conception

condominium (country under) joint rule; (US) unit in a block of flats
condominiums

condone to overlook or forgive
condonable condonation condoner condoning

condor kind of very large vulture

conduce to lead to
conducing conducive

conduct behaviour; to guide or direct
conductible conduction conductive conductivity conductor

conduit pipe or channel

cone solid that narrows to a point from a flat circular base; fruit of some evergreen trees
conic

coney see **cony**

confection sweet dish or cake
confectioner confectionery

confederate to join in a league; allied
confederacy confederacies confederating confederation

confer to bestow; to discuss
conferment conferrable conferral conferrer conferred conferring

conference formal discussion

confess to admit one's faults; to declare
confesses confession confessional confessor

confetti small pieces of coloured paper thrown at weddings

confide to tell secrets to
confidant confidante confiding confidingly

confidence trust; self-assurance
confident confidently

confidential private or secret
confidentiality confidentially

configuration arrangement or form

confine to restrict
confinable confinement confiner confines confining

confirm to prove to be true or valid; to admit to full membership of any Christian church
confirmation confirmative confirmatory

confiscate to seize as a penalty
confiscating confiscation confiscatory

conflagration large destructive fire

conflate to combine; to form a whole
conflation

conflict (to) fight; (to) clash

confluence flowing together
confluent

conform to comply with

conformable conformer conformist conformity

conformation general shape or structure

confound to put to shame; to refute; to bewilder; to curse
confounded

confront to bring face to face with
confrontation

Confucius Chinese wise man
Confucian Confucianism

confuse to muddle in the mind; to blur
confusedly confusing confusion

confute to prove to be mistaken
confutable confutation confuting

conga kind of dance

congé (*French*) permission to depart; abrupt dismissal

congeal to change from liquid to solid by cold
congealable congealment congelation

congenial pleasant; friendly
congeniality congenially

congenital existing from birth
congenitally

conger kind of large marine eel

congested crowded; clogged
congestion congestive

conglomerate company with widely diversified interests; (something) made up of many different parts
conglomerating conglomeration

Congo country in West Africa; river in Africa
Congolese

congratulate to speak to someone with praise and admiration for a success or happy event
congratulating congratulation congratulations congratulatory

congregate to gather together
congregating congregation congregational

congress meeting or conference
congresses congressional

Congress highest law-making body of a country such as the USA; Indian political party
congressman congresswoman

congruent having the same size and shape; agreeing
congruence congruity congruous congruously

conic cone-shaped
conical

conifer cone-bearing tree
coniferous

conjecture (to) guess
conjectural conjecturing

conjoin to join
conjoiner conjoint conjointly

conjugal of marriage
conjugally

conjugate (*grammar*) to give the main parts of a verb
conjugating conjugation

conjunction union; (*grammar*) word linking other words or phrases
conjunctive conjuncture

conjunctiva mucous membrane covering the eyeball and lining the eyelids
conjunctivas or *conjunctivae conjunctivitis*

conjure to perform magical tricks; to imagine or cause to appear
conjuration conjuring conjuror or *conjurer*

conk (*informal*) head or nose; (*of machines*) to break down

conker horse-chestnut

con-man (*informal*) swindler

connect to join or be joined
connection or *connexion connective connector*

Connecticut US state

connive to plot together
connivance conniving

connoisseur person with fine appreciation and taste

connote to imply or suggest
connotation connoting

connubial of marriage
connubiality connubially

conquer to overcome or defeat
conquerable conqueror conquest

consanguinity blood relationship
consanguineous consanguineously

conscience sense of right and wrong
conscience-smitten conscience-stricken

conscientious meticulous; hard-working
conscientiously conscientiousness
SEE PANEL

---

conscientious or conscious?
Someone who is *conscientious* works very hard and with meticulous care: *a very conscientious headteacher.*
Conscious means 'fully aware; aware': *remain conscious during the operation; I became conscious of someone standing behind me.*

---

conscious fully awake; aware
consciously consciousness
SEE PANEL at **conscientious**

conscript to call up for compulsory military service; person who is conscripted
conscription

consecrate to make or declare to be sacred
consecrating consecration

consecutive following on; successive
consecutively consecutiveness

consensus general agreement

consent (to give) agreement

consequence result; significance or importance
consequent consequential consequentially

conservation keeping from change, decay, etc.
conservational conservationist

conservative favouring traditional values and customs
conservatism

Conservative political party

conservatoire school of music

conservatory greenhouse for plants
conservatories

conserve to keep from change, decay, etc.; kind of jam
conservable conservancy conservancies conserving

consider to think carefully about
consideration considering

considerable large; significant
considerably

considerate thoughtful towards other people
considerately considerations

consign to entrust; to deliver
consignee consignor or *consigner consignment*

consist to be composed (of)

consistency degree of viscosity or firmness
consistencies

consistent conforming with previous behaviour, practice, etc.
consistently

consistory church tribunal
consistories consistorial

console[1] to comfort
consolable consolation consolatory consoling

console[2] control panel; supporting bracket

consolidate to strengthen; to unite
consolidating consolidation

consommé clear soup

consonance agreement or harmony

consonant speech sound or letter of the

alphabet that is not a vowel; in agreement with
consonantal

consort husband or wife of a ruler; to keep company with

consortium association of companies, etc.
consortia or *consortiums*

conspicuous clearly visible; attracting attention
conspicuously conspicuousness

conspire to plot
conspiracy conspiracies conspirator conspiratorial conspiratorially conspiring

constable police officer
constabulary constabularies

constant unchanging; happening continually; loyal
constancy

constellation pattern of stars in a group

consternation dismay

constipate to cause constipation in
constipating

constipation difficult evacuation of the bowels

constituency body of voters who elect a representative
constituencies

constituent making part of a whole; component; member of a constituency

constitute to form; to appoint
constituting constitutive

constitution set of principles by which a country, etc. is run; structure or condition
constitutional constitutionally

constrain to compel
constrained constraint

constrict to make narrow or tight
constriction constrictive constrictor

construct to build
construction constructional constructor

constructive suggesting improvement; positive
constructively constructiveness

construe to understand; to interpret
construing

consubstantiation doctrine of the Eucharist that the body and blood of Christ coexist with the bread and wine

consul government official
consular consulate consulship

consult to ask advice from
consultant consultation consultative consulting

consume to eat or drink; to use up
consumable consumer consumerism consuming

consummate to bring to completion; highly skilled; perfect or complete
consummately consummating consummation

consumption consuming; tuberculosis of the lungs
consumptive

contact (to) touch; to communicate with
contactual

contagion transmission of a disease by contact
contagious contagiously contagiousness

contain to hold or include; to limit
containable container containment

containerize or **containerise** to transport in standard-sized containers; to equip with such containers
containerization or *containerisation*
containerizing or *containerising*

contaminate to make impure
contaminating contamination

contemplate to think about intently for a long time
contemplating contemplation contemplative

contemporary modern; (person) living at the same time
contemporaries contemporaneous

contempt despising; scorn

contemptible deserving or arousing contempt
contemptibleness contemptibly
SEE PANEL

contemptible or contemptuous?
Something is *contemptible* when you have no respect for it and it deserves or arouses your contempt: *display a contemptible lack of common sense.*
Contemptuous means 'expressing or showing contempt': *be openly contemptuous of any authority; give a contemptuous little laugh.*

contemptuous expressing or showing contempt
contemptuously contemptuousness
SEE PANEL at **contemptible**

contend to struggle; to argue
contender contention

content[1] happy; satisfied; to satisfy
contented contentedly contentedness contentment

content[2] something that is contained; substance, not form

contentious controversial
contentiously contentiousness

contest (to) fight or struggle; test of skill
contestability contestably contestant

context particular setting or conditions of words or events
contextual contextually

contiguous touching; neighbouring
contiguity

continent[1] able to control urination and defecation; able to control oneself
continence continently

continent[2] one of the earth's large land masses
continental

Continent mainland Europe

contingency possible future event
contingencies

contingent depending on the occurrence of something else
contingently

continual regularly repeated
continually
SEE PANEL

continual or continuous?
Continual means 'regular or frequently repeated; constant': *our neighbours' continual complaints.*
Something that is *continuous* means 'without break or interruption; continuing to the end': *continuous gunfire; a continuous line; a continuous roll of paper.*

continue to go on; to carry on doing
continuance continuation continuing continuity

continuous in an uninterrupted or unbroken series or pattern; not ceasing
continuously continuousness
SEE PANEL at **continual**

continuum continuous whole; something made up of a succession of identical parts
continua or *continuums*

contort to twist out of shape
contortion contortionist

contour line on a map joining all points of equal height

contra- (*prefix*) against
contradistinction contraflow

contraband illegal or smuggled goods

contraception prevention of pregnancy
contraceptive

contract (to undertake by a) formal agreement; to reduce in size; to catch an infection
contracted contractible contractile contraction contractor contractual

contradict to state the opposite; to declare to be untrue
contradiction contradictor or *contradicter contradictory*

contralto (singer with or music for) lowest female singing voice

contraption complicated device

contrapuntal (*music*) of counterpoint

contrariwise conversely; vice versa

contrary (something) opposite or opposed; stubborn
contraries contrariety contrarily contrariness

contrast to distinguish by showing differences; such distinguishing features

contravene to go against a law
contravening contravention

contretemps (*French*) setback; mishap

contribute to give with others; to supply
contributing contribution contributive contributor contributory

contrite feeling deep regret or guilt
contritely contrition

contrive to plan or bring about; to think up
contrivance contriver contriving

control (to exercise) power, authority, or direction; to restrain
controllable controlled controller controlling

controversy matter for dispute
controversies controversial controversialist controversially

controvert to deny or dispute
controvertible

contumacious (*formal*) stubbornly disobedient
contumaciously contumacy

contumely scornful or humiliating insult
contumelies contumelious contumeliously

contuse to bruise
contusing contusion

conundrum riddle; puzzling problem
conundrums

conurbation large densely populated urban area

convalesce to recover from an illness
convalesced convalescence convalescent convalescing

convection transferring of heat
convector

convene to call together to a meeting
convenable convener or *convenor convening*

convenient suitable; easy to use
convenience conveniently

convent community of nuns; buildings in which they live

convention generally accepted principle; large formal meeting
conventional conventionalism conventionality conventionally

converge to move towards a point
convergence convergent converging

conversant familiar (with)

conversazione (*Italian*) meeting for discussion
conversaziones

converse[1] to talk (with)
conversable conversably conversation conversational conversationalist conversing

converse[2] opposite; reversed
conversely

convert to change or transform
conversion converter or *convertor convertibility convertible*

convex curved outwards
convexity convexities

convey to carry, transport, or communicate
conveyor or *conveyer*

conveyance transfer of legal rights to property
conveyancer conveyancing

convict to pronounce guilty; person found guilty and sentenced to imprisonment

conviction convicting; strongly held belief

convince to make someone believe
convincible convincing convincingly

convivial sociable; lively
conviviality convivialities convivially

convocation large formal assembly

convoke to call a meeting
convoking

convoluted twisted; involved
convolution

convolvulus kind of twining plant
convolvuluses or *convolvuli*

convoy group of ships, military vehicles, etc.; to escort
convoys convoyed convoying

convulse to shake violently
convulsing convulsion convulsive convulsively

cony or **coney** rabbit
conies or *coneys*

coo to make a low soft sound like a dove
cooed cooing

cook to prepare food by heating; person who does this
cookbook cook-chill cooker cookery cookhouse

cookie or **cooky** (*Scottish*) plain bun; (US) biscuit
cookies

cool moderately cold; to calm
coolant cooler coolest cool-headed coolish coolly coolness

coolie unskilled labourer

coop cage or enclosure
cooper

co-op (*informal*) short for **co-operative**

co-operate to work together for a common purpose
co-operating co-operation co-operative co-operator or *co-operater*

co-opt to vote an additional person on to a committee
co-opted co-option

co-ordinate to combine or harmonize; number specifying a location; one of a set of matching clothes
co-ordinately co-ordinating co-ordination co-ordinator

coot kind of black water-bird

co-partner partner or associate
co-partnership

cope[1] to deal successfully (with)
coping

cope[2] priest's long ceremonial cloak

copeck see **kopeck**

Copernican of Polish astronomer Copernicus

coping course of brick, stone, etc., at the top of a wall
copingstone

copious abundant
copiously copiousness

copper[1] reddish-brown metallic element
copper-bottomed copperhead copperplate coppersmith coppery

copper[2] (*informal*) policeman

coppice or **copse** thicket of small trees

copra dried kernel of coconut

copse see **coppice**

Copt member of a people descended from ancient Egyptians; member of Coptic Church
Coptic

copula verb that links a subject and complement
copulas or *copulae*

copulate to engage in sexual intercourse
copulating copulation copulative

copy (to make an) imitation or exact reproduction
copies copied copier copy-book copycat copying copyist copyright copy-typist copy-writer

coquetry flirting
coquetries

coquette woman who flirts
coquettish

coracle small round boat

coral hard deposit formed by skeletons of tiny sea-creatures
coralline

cor anglais kind of woodwind instrument
cors anglais

corbel projection from a wall to support something

cord string or rope made of twisted strands; part of the body, such as a nerve, resembling this; raised fabric, such as corduroy
cordage cordless

cordial warm; friendly; fruit drink
cordiality cordialities cordially

cordite smokeless explosive

cordon line of police, guards, etc.; ribbon

cordon bleu food prepared to a very high standard

corduroy ribbed cotton fabric
corduroys

core central part, esp. of an apple; to remove the core from
corer coring

co-respondent person alleged to have committed adultery with the respondent in a divorce case

Corfu island in the Ionian Sea

corgi breed of short-legged Welsh dog
corgis

coriander kind of plant, the seeds of which are used in flavouring food

Corinthian of Corinth; kind of pillar

cork (stopper made from the) thick light outer bark of the cork tree
corkage corked corkscrew

corm thick round underground plant stem

cormorant kind of sea-bird

corn[1] kind of cereal plant; (US) maize
corncob cornfield cornflakes

corn[2] hard thick skin area, esp. on a toe

corncrake kind of bird

cornea hard transparent covering of the front outer eye surface
corneas

cornelian or **carnelian** red quartz

corner angle or point where two lines or surfaces meet; to monopolize
cornerstone

cornet kind of brass musical instrument; cone-shaped ice-cream wafer

cornflour fine maize flour

cornflower kind of blue-flowered plant

cornice ornamental wall moulding just below the ceiling or at the top of a pillar

Cornish of Cornwall; ancient Celtic language

cornucopia great abundance
cornucopias

corny (*slang*) trite
cornier corniest

corolla set of petals on a flower

corollary natural or obvious consequence or result; inference
corollaries

corona circle of light seen round the sun or moon
coronas or *coronae*

coronary of arteries or veins of the heart; coronary thrombosis
coronaries

coronation ceremony of crowning a monarch

coroner public official appointed to investigate the cause of death

coronet small crown

corporal[1] of the body

corporal[2] non-commissioned officer

corporate shared; joint

corporation local authorities of a town or city

corporeal of the physical body; not spiritual
corporealize or *corporealise*

corps military formation; group

corpse dead body

corpulent bulky; fat
corpulence or *corpulency*

corpus body of writings or works
corpora

corpuscle particle; cell; blood-cell

corral (to drive into an) enclosure
corralled corralling

correct right, accurate, or approved; to show the faults in
correctable correction corrective correctly correctness corrector

correlate to connect in a mutual or reciprocal relationship
correlating correlation correlative

correspond to agree (with); to communicate (with) by letter
correspondence correspondent correspondingly

corridor passage

corrigendum error to be corrected
corrigenda

corrigible capable of being corrected
corrigibility corrigibly

corroborate to support or confirm
corroborating corroboration corroborative

corrode to wear away gradually by chemical action
corrodible corroding corrosion corrosive

corrugate to fold into furrows and ridges alternately
corrugating corrugation

corrupt (to make) dishonest or depraved
corrupted corrupter or *corruptor corruptible corruption corruptness*

corsage arrangement of flowers

corsair pirate; privateer

corset stiff supporting undergarment

Corsica island in the Mediterranean
Corsican

corslet piece of armour; one-piece undergarment

cortege or **cortège** procession, esp. at a funeral

cortex outer layer, esp. of grey matter of the brain
cortices cortical

cortisone steroid hormone produced by the cortex of the adrenal gland

corundum hard abrasive substance

coruscate to flash or sparkle
coruscating coruscation

corvette small fast warship

cos[1] kind of lettuce

cos[2] short for **cosine**

cosh (to hit with a) blunt weapon

co-signatory person that signs a document jointly with others
co-signatories

cosine trigonometric function

cosmetic prepared beautifying substance for the skin; superficial
cosmetically cosmetician

cosmic of the whole universe

cosmopolitan of the whole world

cosmos universe
cosmography comological cosmology cosmonaut

Cossack member of Russian people famous for their horsemanship

cosset to pamper
cosseted cosseting

cost (to) price
cost-effective

Costa Rica country in Central America
Costa Rican

costermonger seller of fruit, vegetables, etc. from a barrow

costive constipated

costly expensive
costlier costliest costliness

costume style of dressing; set of clothes
costumier

cosy (US **cozy**) snug; warm; intimate
cosier (US *cozier*) *cosiest* (US *coziest*) *cosily* (US *cozily*) *cosiness* (US *coziness*)

cot baby's small bed with high sides; (*chiefly* US) camp-bed
cot-death

cotangent trigonometric function

cote shelter for pigeons, sheep, etc.

Côte d'Ivoire country in West Africa

coterie small exclusive group of people

coterminous having the same boundary

cotillion or **cotillon** lively dance

cottage small simple house

cotter wedge, pin, etc., used to secure 2 pieces

cotton soft fibrous substance made from the seeds of the cotton plant
cotton-grass cotton-wool

cotyledon simple leaf that forms part of the embryo of a seed

couch bed, sofa, or long seat; to express in a particular way
couches

couchette sleeping berth in a railway compartment

cougar puma

cough to expel air from the lungs with a short sharp sound

could past tense of **can**[1]
couldn't

coulter (US **colter**) blade or disc in front of the ploughshare

council elected group or committee
councillor (US *councilor*)
SEE PANEL

---

council or counsel?

A *council* is an elected group or committee: *the County Council; the Arts Council.*

Counsel is a formal word meaning 'advice': *wise counsel given by one's elders* or 'to give advice': *a therapist who counsels people with eating disorders.* Someone's *counsel* is a lawyer who represents that person in court.

---

counsel (to give) advice; barristers
counselled (US *counseled*) *counselling* (US *counseling*) *counsellor* (US *counselor*)
SEE PANEL at **council**

count[1] to check, reckon, or add up with numbers
countable countdown

count[2] European nobleman
countess

countenance facial expression; to approve
countenancing

counter[1] raised level surface over which business is transacted; small disc used in games

counter[2] to oppose; (in a direction that is) opposite

counter- (*prefix*) against; opposite
counterattack

counteract to lessen or neutralize the effects of
counteraction

counterbalance (to act as a) weight or influence that offsets another

counter-espionage activities to oppose and thwart enemy espionage

counterfeit artificial; forged
counterfeiter

counterfoil detachable section of a receipt or cheque kept as a record

countermand to cancel or revoke an order already given

countermarch to march in the reverse direction
countermarches

countermeasure action designed to retaliate against or oppose another action

counterpane bedspread

counterpart person or thing that has the same function or qualities as another; copy or duplicate

counterpoint independent melody added to accompany another

counterpoise (to maintain a) balance of one thing with another

counter-productive tending to hinder the achievement of an aim

countersign to add another signature to

countersink to enlarge a hole so that the head of a screw can be set below the surface; to set the head of a screw below the surface
countersank countersunk

counter-tenor (singer with or music for a) male singing voice higher than a tenor

countervail to act against with equal force; to offset

countess wife or widow of an earl or a count; woman of the rank of an earl or count
countesses

countless too many to be counted
countlessly countlessness

country territory of a nation; land with open fields or woods
countries countrified country-and-western countryman countryside country-wide countrywoman

county administrative division of a country
counties

coup sudden successful action

coup de grâce (*French*) fatal blow; finishing stroke
coups de grâce

coup d'état (*French*) violent or unconstitutional overthrow of a government
coups d'état

coupé small 2-door car; horse-drawn carriage
coupés

couple (to) pair
coupling

couplet 2 successive lines of rhyming verse

coupling device connecting 2 things, esp. railway trucks or carriages

coupon form of ticket entitling the holder to obtain an article or service

courage bravery
courageous courageously

courgette small variety of vegetable marrow

courier tourist guide; messenger

course direction; procedure; series; to pursue
courser coursing

court enclosed area for games; sovereign and retinue; legal tribunal; to seek favour from; to woo
court-house courtier courtly courtship courtyard

courteous polite; respectful
courteously

courtesan prostitute

courtesy politeness; respect; favour
courtesies

court martial trial by a military court
courts martial court-martialled (US *court-martialed*) *court-martialling* (US *court-martialing*)

cousin child of one's aunt or uncle
cousin-german cousins-german cousinhood cousinly cousinship

couture designing and dressmaking
couturier

cove small bay

coven meeting of witches

covenant formal binding agreement
covenantor or *covenanter*

cover to spread over, esp. as a protection; to extend over; something that covers
coverage cover-up

coverlet bedspread

covert secret; shelter, esp. for animals
covertly

covet to eagerly desire something that belongs to another person
covetable coveted coveting covetous covetousness

cow[1] female of certain animals, esp. domesticated cattle
cowbell cowboy cowgirl cowhand cowherd cowhide cowhouse cowman cowpat cowpox cowshed cowskin

cow[2] to frighten with threats

coward person without courage or who shrinks from danger
cowardice cowardliness cowardly

cower to crouch or cringe with fear

cowl monk's hood; cover on a chimney for ventilation

cowling metal cover for an aircraft engine

cowrie kind of shiny tropical shell
cowries

cowslip small yellow primrose

cox (to act as) coxswain
coxes

coxcomb foolish and vain person

coxswain person who commands and steers a boat

coy shy; modest
coyer coyest coyly coyness

coyote small North American wolf

coypu kind of aquatic South American rodent

cozen to cheat
cozenage

cozy (US) see **cosy**

crab kind of shellfish

crabbed irritable; difficult to read

crabby bad-tempered

crack (to) break; (to make a) sudden sharp noise
crack-brained crack-down crackpot

cracker coloured paper tube that makes a bang when pulled apart; thin crisp biscuit; noisy firework

crackers (*informal*) crazy

crackle (to make a) series of slight cracking sounds
crackling crackly

crackling crisp brown skin on roast pork

cradle (to support as in a) baby's bed often on rockers
cradling

craft activity needing skill; skill or cunning; vessel, aircraft, etc.
craftsman craftsmanship craftswoman

crafty cunning
craftier craftiest craftily craftiness

crag steep rugged peak or rock
craggy

crake kind of bird

cram to pack too much into
cram-full crammed crammer cramming

cramp[1] painful involuntary contraction of muscles

cramp[2] metal clamp; to restrain or hamper

crampon metal spike fitted to climbing boots

cranberry kind of small red acid berry
cranberries

crane kind of large wading bird; device for lifting and moving heavy objects; to stretch out the neck
crane-fly craning

cranesbill kind of geranium

cranium skull
crania or *craniums cranial craniology*

crank device with a right-angled shaft for setting something into motion; eccentric person
crankcase crankpin crankshaft cranky

cranny small narrow opening
crannies crannied

crape crêpe, esp. when used for mourning clothes; see **crêpe**

crash[1] (to make or hit with a) sudden noisy smashing sound
crashes crash-dive crash-land

crash[2] coarse fabric
crashes

crass utter; stupid
crassly crassness or *crassitude*

crate (to pack in a) usually wooden framework or box
crating

crater bowl-shaped depression round the mouth of a volcano

cravat short light scarf worn loosely folded around the neck

crave to desire strongly
craving

craven cowardly (person)

crawfish kind of spiny lobster

crawl to move slowly with the body close to the ground; swimming stroke; to act in a servile way
crawler

crayfish kind of small freshwater lobster-like shellfish

crayon (to draw or colour with a) stick of coloured wax, etc.

craze exaggerated short-lived enthusiasm for something

crazy insane; (*of paving*) made up of irregular pieces
crazier craziest crazily craziness

creak (to make a) harsh squeaking or grating noise
creakier creakiest creakily creakiness creaky

cream (to remove the) fatty part of milk
cream-laid creamy

creamery establishment where dairy products are made or sold
creameries

crease (to make a) mark or line by pressing or folding
creaser crease-resistant creasing

create to cause to exist
creating creation creative creatively creativeness creativity creator

creature living being, esp. an animal

crèche nursery for young children

credence belief or acceptance

credentials document giving proof of identity or authority

credible believable; trustworthy
credibility credibly

credit money in a bank account; approval or acknowledgment; (to) trust; money lent by a bank
creditable creditably creditor

creditworthy qualifying for financial credit
creditworthiness

credo creed
credos

credulous believing too readily
credulity credulously

creed statement of beliefs, esp. religious one

creek narrow inlet of water; (*chiefly* US and Australia) small stream

creel wickerwork basket used to hold fish

creep to move slowly with the body close to the ground
creeper crept

creepy arousing shivery fear

creepy-crawly (*informal*) small creeping creature

cremate to burn a corpse to ashes
cremating cremation

crematorium building in which corpses are cremated
crematoria or *crematoriums*

crème de menthe peppermint liqueur

crenellate (US **crenelate**) to supply with battlements
crenellation (US *crenelation*)

creole language based on a European language and another language or other languages that has become the native language of its speakers

Creole descendant of European settlers in West Indies

creosote liquid derived from coal tar used as a wood preservative; to apply creosote to
creosoting

crêpe light wrinkled fabric; small thin pancake

crept past tense and past participle of **creep**

crepuscular active in or of the twilight

crescendo (*music*) with increasing loudness

crescent curved tapering shape, like a quarter-moon

cress any of various plants of the mustard family

crest showy tuft on a bird's head; top or ridge of a hill, wave, etc.
crestfallen

cretaceous of chalk

Crete island in the East Mediterranean

cretin someone born mentally retarded; idiot
cretinism cretinous

cretonne heavy cotton or linen fabric

crevasse deep crack

crevice narrow opening

crew[1] people working on a ship or aircraft; group working together

crew[2] past tense of **crow**[2]

crib baby's bed; cattle stall or manger; (*informal*) to steal another's writings
cribbed cribber cribbing

cribbage kind of card-game

crick painful muscle spasm in the neck or back

cricket[1] outdoor team-game played with bats and ball
cricketer

cricket[2] leaping insect that makes chirping sounds

cried past tense and past participle of **cry**

crier person who cries

crime offence prohibited and punishable by law

criminal person who is guilty of a crime; of crime
criminality criminally

criminology study of crime
criminologist

crimp curl or wave hair

Crimplene (*trademark*) synthetic material

crimson deep red

cringe to shrink or cower in fear or submission
cringer cringing

crinkle (to make a) small fold or wrinkle
crinkling crinkly

crinoline padded or hooped petticoat

cripple lame person; to make lame; to disable
crippling

crisis time of extreme trouble or danger; crucial point
crises

crisp brittle and dry; firm; thin slice of fried potato
crispbread crisply crispness crispy

criss-cross (to mark) with intersecting lines

criterion standard of judgement or decision
criteria

critic person who judges, evaluates, or finds fault

critical fault-finding; of or at a crisis; evaluating
critically

criticize or **criticise** to find fault with; to analyse
criticism criticizing or *criticising*

critique essay, etc., containing evaluative judgements

croak (to make a) hoarse throaty sound
croaker croakily croakiness croaky

Croatia republic in SE Europe, formerly part of Yugoslavia
Croat Croatian

crochet to loop thread in an interlocking pattern with a hooked needle; fabric made in this way
crocheted crocheter crocheting

crock[1] earthenware jar
crockery

crock[2] (*informal*) person or thing that is old or decrepit

crocodile kind of tropical reptile with massive jaws

crocus kind of small plant growing from bulb
crocuses

croft small enclosed field; small farm, esp. in Scotland
crofter

croissant (*French*) flaky crescent-shaped bread roll

cromlech prehistoric monument

crone withered old woman

crony (*informal*) close friend
cronies

crook staff with a hooked end; to bend; (*informal*) thief or swindler
crooked

croon to sing in a low soft tone
crooner

crop product that is grown and harvested; kind of whip; to cut short; to gather a crop
cropped cropper cropping

croquet lawn game played with mallets and wooden balls

croquette rissole of minced meat, etc.

crosier or **crozier** bishop's staff

cross structure or symbol of vertical post with beam across; to move across; angry
crosses crossbar cross-bench cross-bones crossbow cross-breed cross-check cross-country cross-cultural cross-current cross-cut cross-examine cross-eyed cross-fertilize or *cross-fertilise crossfire cross-grained cross-hatch cross-index crossing cross-legged cross-over crosspatch crosspiece cross-ply cross-pollination cross-purposes cross-question cross-reference crossroad crossroads cross-section cross-stitch crosstalk crossways crosswind crosswise crossword*

crosse long-handled netted stick used in lacrosse

crotch or **crutch** angle formed by the inner thighs where they join the human trunk
crotches or *crutches*

crotchet (*music*) note half the length of a minim

crotchety bad-tempered

crouch to bend low to the ground

croup[1] inflammation or spasm of the larynx

croup[2] or **croups** rump, esp. of a horse

croupier person who collects money and pays winners at gambling

croûton (*French*) small piece of fried or toasted bread

crow[1] kind of large black bird
crow's foot crow's feet crow's-nest

crow[2] (to make the) shrill loud cry of a cock; to gloat
crowed or *crew crower crowing*

crowbar heavy iron or steel bar used as a lever

crowd (to gather in a) large number of people
crowded

crown ornamental head-dress of a monarch; to place a crown on the head of; (to form the) top part

crozier see **crosier**

crucial decisive
crucially

crucible vessel in which substances are melted

crucifix model of (Christ on) the cross
crucifixes

cruciform shaped like a cross
cruciformly

crucify to put to death on a cross
crucified crucifies crucifixion crucifying

crude unrefined; rough; coarse
crudely crudeness cruder crudest crudity crudities

cruel taking pleasure in causing pain
crueller (US *crueler*) *cruellest* (US *cruelest*) *cruelly cruelty cruelties*

cruet small table container for salt, pepper, etc.

cruise to sail for pleasure from place to place; to travel at a moderate speed
cruiser cruising

crumb small fragment of bread
crumby

crumble to break info fragments
crumbling crumbly

crummy (*slang*) worthless; miserable; dirty
crumminess

crumpet round soft yeast cake

crumple to press or bend into creases
crumpling

crunch to bite or chew with a noisy crushing sound
crunches crunchy

crupper leather loop fastened to the back of a saddle

crusade (to be engaged in an) enthusiastic campaign for a good cause; medieval Christian military expedition
crusader crusading

cruse small earthenware container

crush to destroy by pressing down; large number of people
crushes crushable crusher

crust hard outer covering
crustily crustiness crusty

crustacean animal with a hard outer shell

crutch support for a disabled person; crotch
crutches

crux vital or decisive point
cruxes or *cruces*

cry (to) shout; (to) weep
cried cries crybaby crying

cryogenics study of production and effects of low temperatures
cryogenic cryogenically

crypt underground chamber, esp. in a church

cryptic hidden; mysterious
cryptically

cryptogram communication in cipher or code

cryptography secret writing
cryptographer cryptographic

crystal transparent kind of quartz; transparent colourless high-quality glass; regular shaped piece of substance
crystal-clear crystalline

crystallize or **crystallise** to form crystals; to take on a definite form
crystallization or *crystallisation crystallized* or *crystallised crystallizing* or *crystallising*

crystallography science of crystals

cub young of certain animals

Cub junior member of the Scout movement

Cuba country in the West Indies
Cuban

cubbyhole small enclosed space

cube solid body with 6 equal square faces; result obtained by multiplying a number by itself twice; to cut into cubes
cubic cubical cubically cubing cuboid

cubicle small enclosed division in a larger room

cubism art movement
cubist

cubit old unit of length

cuckold man whose wife is adulterous; to make a cuckold of
cuckoldry

cuckoo grey bird that lays its eggs in the nests of other birds

cucumber kind of long green fruit

cud food brought back for chewing again by cow, sheep, etc.

cuddle to hold closely and tenderly
cuddlesome cuddling cuddly

cudgel (to strike with a) short heavy stick
cudgelled (US *cudgeled*) *cudgelling* (US *cudgeling*)

cue[1] signal for an actor to speak; to give a cue to
cued cuing

cue[2] a long tapering rod used in billiards or snooker

cuff[1] end of a sleeve

cuff[2] to strike with the palm of the hand

cuirass piece of armour
cuirassier

cuisine style of cooking; cookery

cul-de-sac street closed at one end
culs-de-sac

culinary of cooking or a kitchen

cull to pick selectively

culminate to reach the highest point
culminating culmination

culottes women's trousers shaped to look like a skirt

culpable blameworthy
culpability or *culpableness culpably*

culprit someone who is guilty

cult system of worship; sect; intense devotion
cultic cultism cultist

cultivate to prepare land for crops; to grow
cultivable cultivating cultivation cultivator

culture traditions, customs, etc. of a people; appreciation of the arts; cultivation
cultural cultured

culvert drain or channel under a road, etc.

cumber to hamper or burden
cumbersome cumbrous cumbrousness

cumin kind of plant with aromatic seeds

cummerbund waist-belt

cumulate to heap up; to accumulate

cumulative increasing by successive additions

cumulus cloud in the form of mounded heap
cumuli

cuneiform wedge-shaped

cunning skilled at deceiving; deceit
cunningly cunningness

cup drinking bowl with a handle; to form into a cup shape
cupbearer cupful cupfuls cupped cupping

cupboard piece of furniture or recessed area of a room

Cupid Roman god of love

cupidity greed

cupola small dome

cupric containing copper

cupro-nickel copper and nickel alloy

cur mongrel or worthless dog
currish

curable that can be cured
curability

curaçao orange liqueur

curare extract from a South American plant used as a drug

curate clergyman who assists a vicar
curacy curacies curateship

curative (something) able to heal or cure

curator official in charge
curatorship

curb to restrain; strap or chain for restraining a horse

curd thick part of coagulated milk

curdle to turn into curds
curdler curdling

cure to restore to health; to preserve a food
cure-all cureless curing

curé French priest

curettage treatment by the use of curette

curette surgical instrument used for removing unhealthy tissue by scraping

curfew order to stay indoors between certain hours

curio small unusual article
curios

curious eager to learn; unusual
curiosity curiosities curiously

curl (to twist into a) spiral or wave
curler curly

curlew kind of large wading-bird

curling game played with stones on ice

curmudgeon surly or mean person
curmudgeonly

currant small seedless dried grape; small berry
SEE PANEL

---

currant or current?

A *currant* is a small seedless dried grape: *200 grams of currants.* The word *currant* is also used in the names of certain small soft berries: *blackcurrant.*

As a noun, *current* refers to a flow of water, air, or electricity: *be swept along by the strong current; 240 volts alternating current.*

---

currency money; general acceptance and use
currencies

current stream or flow of water, air, or electricity; contemporary; in general use
SEE PANEL at **currant**

curriculum course of study
curricula or *curriculums*

curriculum vitae (*Latin*) brief written summary of one's career
curricula vitae

curry[1] food flavoured with hot-tasting spices, etc.
curries

curry[2] to win favour by flattery; to rub down a horse

curried currier curries curry-comb currying

curse to call evil on; (to utter) profane swearing language
cursed or (*archaic*) *curst cursing*

cursive with the letters joined

cursor position indicator on a visual display unit; sliding part on a slide rule

cursory hasty and superficial
cursorily cursoriness

curt rudely brief
curtly curtness

curtail to make shorter
curtailment

curtain fabric hung as a screen, esp. at a window
curtain-call curtain-raiser

curtsy or **curtsey** (to make the) formal act of respect by women by bending the knees forward and bowing the head slightly
curtsies or *curtseys curtsied* or *curtseyed curtsying* or *curtseying*

curve (to form into a) continuously bending line
curvaceous curvature curvilinear curving

cushion bag made of fabric and filled with feathers, etc.; to reduce the impact of

cushy (*informal*) easy and pleasant
cushier cushiest

cusp point; apex

cussed (*informal*) cursed; obstinate

custard baked mixture of eggs and milk

custody imprisonment; keeping safe
custodial custodian

custom tradition; patronage
custom-built

customary usual
customarily

customer buyer

customs duty on imports or exports; government agency or area of a port for collection of such duties
customs-house

cut (to make a) slit or opening; to divide; wound; to shorten
cut-back cut-out cut-price cut-rate cutter cutthroat cutting

cutaneous of the skin

cute attractive; ingenious
cutely cuteness cuter cutest

cuticle layer of skin, esp. at the base of a fingernail or toenail

cutis skin; dermis

cutlass short sword with a curved blade
cutlasses

cutler maker of cutlery

cutlery knives, forks and spoons

cutlet slice of meat or fish

cuttlefish squid-like sea-animal

cutworm kind of nocturnal caterpillar

cyanide extremely poisonous compound

cybernetics science of control systems in humans and machines
cyberspace

cyclamen kind of flowering plant

cycle recurring series of events; complete set; bicycle or motor cycle; to ride a bicycle
cyclic cyclical cycling cyclist cyclo-cross

cyclone violent wind moving very rapidly round a calm centre
cyclonic cyclonically

cyclopedia or **cyclopaedia** encyclopedia

Cyclops mythical one-eyed giant
Cyclopes Cyclopean

cyclostyle (to use a) machine for making multiple copies from a stencil
cyclostyling

cyclotron kind of particle accelerator

cyder see **cider**

cygnet young swan

cylinder tube-shaped object
cylindrical

cymbal brass plate-like musical instrument beaten together in pairs
cymbalist

cynic someone who doubts others' sincerity
cynical cynically cynicism

cynosure centre of attraction

cypher see **cipher**

cypress kind of coniferous evergreen tree
cypresses

Cyprus island in the East Mediterranean
Cyprian Cypriot

Cyrillic alphabet used for Slavonic languages

cyst abnormal sac, often containing a watery liquid, that develops in the body
cystic cystitis

cytology (*biology*) study of cells

czar see **tsar**

Czechoslovakia country in Central Europe
Czech Czechoslovak Czechoslovakian

D

dab[1] to pat lightly; gentle touch
dabbed dabbing

dab[2] kind of flat-fish

dabble to wet slightly; to concern oneself with slightly
dabbler dabbling

dabchick kind of small water-bird

dace kind of freshwater fish of the carp family

dachshund breed of dog with a long body and short legs

Dacron (*trademark*) synthetic polyester textile fibre

dactyl metrical foot of 3 syllables
dactylic

dad (*informal*) father
daddy daddies

Dada unconventional artistic movement of the early 20th century
Dadaism Dadaist

daddy-long-legs crane-fly

dado contrasting lower part of an interior wall
dados or *dadoes*

daemon attendant spirit; Greek mythological supernatural being

daffodil kind of yellow-flowered plant

daft (*informal*) stupid or silly

dagger short sword

dago (*slang*) Italian, Spanish, or Portuguese Person
dagos or *dagoes*

daguerreotype (photograph made by an) early photographic process

dahlia kind of plant with showy flowers

Dáil Éireann lower chamber of parliament in the Republic of Ireland

daily (happening) every day
dailies

dainty small and delicate; delicacy
dainties daintier daintiest daintily daintiness

daiquiri kind of cocktail

dairy place where milk, butter, etc. are kept or sold
dairies dairying dairymaid dairyman

dais raised platform
daises

daisy kind of plant with petal-like rays in its flower-head
daisies daisywheel

Dalai Lama spiritual head of Tibetan Buddhism

dale valley
dalesman

dally to waste time idly; to play or flirt (with)
dalliance dallied dallies dallying

Dalmatian dog with a spotted coat

dam[1] (to restrict by a) barrier across a river, etc.
dammed damming

dam[2] mother of domestic animals

damage (to cause) harm, loss, or injury
damageable damaging

damages financial compensation for injury or loss

damascene (to mark with the) special pattern of Damascus steel

damask reversible patterned fabric; large fragrant pink rose

dame woman having the same rank as a knight

damn to condemn as bad; to condemn to the punishment of hell; to swear
damnable damnably damnation damnatory damned damnedest or *damndest*

damp (to make) slightly wet
dampen damper dampest dampish damp-proof

damsel (*archaic*) young woman

damson small purple plum

dance to move the body in time with music
danceable dancer dancing

dandelion kind of yellow-flowered wild plant

dander anger or temper

dandle to move a baby up and down in one's lap
dandling

dandruff loose flakes of dead skin from the scalp

dandy man who is too concerned with his dress and appearance
dandies dandified dandyish

Dane Danish person

danger risk; peril
dangerous dangerously dangerousness

dangle to hang loosely
dangler dangling

Danish (language) of Denmark

dank unpleasantly damp
dankly dankness

daphne kind of ornamental shrub

dapper neat and smart

dapple (to mark with) spots of a different colour or shade
dapple-grey dappling

Darby and Joan ideal devoted elderly married couple

dare to be brave enough; (to) challenge
dared daredevil daren't darer daring

dark with little or no light
darken dark-eyed dark-haired darkish darkly darkness darkroom

darling dearly loved (person)

darn to mend; darned patch

dart small narrow pointed missile; to move suddenly
darts dartboard

Darwinism theory of evolution based on natural selection
Darwinian Darwinist

dash to move quickly; punctuation mark –
dashes

dashboard instrument panel in a motor car

dashing lively; stylish

dastard (*archaic*) coward
dastardliness dastardly

data facts, observations, or information
database

date[1] (to mark the) day, month, and year of an event
datable or *dateable dateless date-line dating*

date[2] edible fruit of a tall palm

dative (*grammar*) case used to identify the indirect object

datum something known; single piece of information

daub to smear or spread
dauber

daughter female child of parents
daughter-in-law daughters-in-law daughterless daughterly

daunt to discourage or dishearten
dauntless

dauphin eldest son of a king of France

davenport (*Brit*) small ornamental writing-desk; (US) large sofa

davit one of 2 crane-like devices that lower a ship's boat

Davy Jones's locker bottom of the sea

dawdle to be slow; to waste time
dawdler dawdling

dawn daybreak; to begin to appear

day period of 24 hours; time of light
days daybreak day-dream daylight daylong day-room day-shift daytime

daze to stun or amaze
dazing

dazzle to overpower the sight of temporarily; to amaze with brilliance
dazzling

D-Day day on which the Allies began invasion of France in Second World War; day set for launching an operation

de- (*prefix*) to take away; reversal
demystify

deacon (*fem.* **deaconess**) officer in a Christian church
deaconesses deaconship

deactivate to render inactive or ineffective
deactivating

dead no longer alive; complete
deadbeat deaden deadhead deadpan

deadline time limit

deadlock complete standstill

deadly capable of causing death; (*informal*) boring
deadlier deadliest deadliness

deaf lacking a sense of hearing
deaf-aid deafen deafening deaf-mute

deal[1] to distribute; to be concerned with; to trade in; business transaction; large quantity
dealer dealings dealt

deal[2] fir or pine timber

dean college or university official; head clergyman of a cathedral chapter
deanery deaneries

dear well-loved; precious; expensive
dearly dearness

dearth scarcity

death ending of life
deathbed deathblow death-defying deathlike deathly death-rate death-trap death-warrant death-watch

débâcle sudden disaster

debar to exclude
debarred debarring

debase to lower the quality of
debasement debasing

debate (to take part in a) formal discussion
debatable debater debating

debauch to lead into depravity or self-indulgence
debauchee debaucher debauchery debaucheries debauches

debenture promise to pay a debt at a fixed rate of interest

debilitate to make weak
debilitating debility debilities

debit money owed; to charge in an account
debited debiting

debonair suave; elegant; carefree

debouch to move into an open space
debouches debouchment

debrief to interrogate after a mission, expedition, etc.

debris loose scattered fragments; ruins

debt something owed
debtor

debug (*informal*) to remove hidden microphones in; to remove defects in
debugged debugging

debunk to expose the falseness of

début or **debut** first public appearance
débutant or *debutant* *débutante* or *debutante*

deca- (*prefix*) 10

decade period of 10 years

decadence or **decadency** deterioration in moral standards, culture, etc.
decadent

decaffeinated (*of coffee*) having had most of the caffeine removed

decagon polygon with 10 sides
decagonal

decalitre (US **decaliter**) 10 litres

Decalogue the Ten Commandments

decametre (US **decameter**) 10 meters

decamp to go away suddenly and secretly
decampment

decant to pour liquid from one bottle into another container
decanter

decapitate to behead
decapitating *decapitation*

decarbonize or **decarbonise** to remove carbon from
decarbonization or *decarbonisation*
decarbonizing or *decarbonising*

decathlon athletic contest consisting of 10 events

decay (to) rot

decease (*formal*) death
deceased

deceive to mislead deliberately
deceit *deceitful* *deceitfully* *deceitfulness*
deceivable *deceiver* *deceiving*

decelerate to slow down
decelerating *deceleration*

December 12th month of the year

decent proper; respectable
decency *decently*

decentralize or **decentralise** to move from a central authority
decentralization or *decentralisation*
decentralizing or *decentralising*

deception act of deceiving; something that deceives
deceptive

decibel unit for measuring relative intensity of sound

decide to make up one's mind; to settle
decidedly *deciding*

deciduous tree having leaves that fall every autumn

decilitre (US **deciliter**) one-tenth of a litre

decimal of the number 10

decimalize or **decimalise** to change to a decimal system
decimalization or *decimalisation*
decimalizing or *decimalising*

decimate to kill a tenth; to destroy a large part of
decimating *decimation* *decimator*

decimetre (US **decimeter**) one-tenth of a metre

decipher to make out the meaning of
decipherable *decipherment*

decision act of deciding; conclusion
decisive *decisively* *decisiveness*

deck[1] floor of a ship or bus
deck-chair *deck-hand*

deck[2] to decorate

deckle-edged with rough untrimmed edges

declaim to speak loudly and rhetorically
declaimer *declamation* *declamatory*

declare to make known or announce; to state emphatically
declarable *declaration* *declaratory*
declaring

declassify to remove from a security list
declassification *declassified*
declassifies *declassifying*

declension (*grammar*) case ending

declination angular distance from true north

decline to refuse; to lose power; loss of power, strength, etc.; (*grammar*) to give case endings of a noun, etc.
declension declinable declination declining

declivity downward slope
declivities declivitous

declutch to disengage the clutch
declutches

decode to convert from code into intelligible language
decoder decoding

decoke to remove carbon from
decoking

décolleté (*French*) having or wearing a low-cut garment
décolletage

decolonize or **decolonise** to grant independence to a colony
decolonization or *decolonisation*
decolonizing or *decolonising*

decompose to separate into constituent parts; to rot
decomposable decomposing decomposition

decompress to release from pressure
decompresses decompression

decongestant drug that relieves congestion

decontaminate to free from contamination
decontaminating decontamination

décor style of decoration

decorate to ornament; to paint, wallpaper, etc.; to confer a medal on
decorating decoration decorative decorator

decorous proper; decent
decorously decorousness

decorum proper and correct behaviour

decoy something that leads a person into a trap; to lead into danger by a decoy
decoys decoyed decoying

decrease to lessen or diminish
decreasing

decree (to give an) official order or judgement
decreed decreeing

decrepit weakened by old age; worn out by long use
decrepitude

decry to express disapproval of
decried decrier decries decrying

dedicate to consecrate; to devote one's time to
dedicated dedicating dedication dedicator dedicatory

deduce to reach a conclusion; infer
deducible deducing deduction

deduct to take away or subtract
deductible deduction deductive

deed act or achievement; legal document

deem to consider or judge

deep extending far down
deep-dyed deepen deep-freeze deep-fry deep-laid deep-rooted deep-seated deep-set

deer kind of 4-footed animal, the male of which usually has antlers
deerskin deerstalker

de-escalate to reduce the intensity of
de-escalating de-escalation

deface to damage the appearance of
defacement defacing

de facto (*Latin*) in fact

defalcate (*formal*) to embezzle
defalcating defalcation defalcator

defame to attack the good name of
defamation defamatory defaming

default to fail to do what one is supposed to
defaulter

defeat to overcome
defeatism defeatist

defecate to discharge waste from the bowels
defecating defecation defecator

defect flaw or imperfection; to desert one's country, cause, etc.
defection defector

defective having a flaw or imperfection
defectively defectiveness
SEE PANEL

defective or deficient?
Something that is *defective* is faulty; it has a flaw or imperfection: *replace defective parts of the machine free of charge; born with defective hearing.*

Deficient means 'lacking a sufficient supply': *a diet deficient in essential vitamins.*

defence (US **defense**) protection or resistance against attack
defenceless (US *defenseless*)

defend to protect against attack
defendable defendant defender defensible defensive

defer[1] to postpone
deferment deferrable deferral deferred deferrer deferring

defer[2] to yield to
deference deferential deferentially deferred deferring

defiance open or bold resistance or disobedience
defiant defiantly

deficient lacking a sufficient supply
deficiency deficiencies deficiently
SEE PANEL at **defective**

deficit amount by which a sum of money is less than required or expected

defile[1] to make foul or dirty
defilement defiler defiling

defile[2] narrow pass; gorge

define to state the meaning of
definable definer defining definition

definite clear; certain; decided
definitely definiteness
SEE PANEL

definite or definitive?
Definite means 'clear; certain; decided': *give a definite answer; arrange a definite date for the meeting.*

Definitive means 'decisive; authoritative and comprehensive': *the definitive study of German post-war history; not be able to give a definitive ruling.*

definitive decisive; authoritative and comprehensive
definitively
SEE PANEL at **definite**

deflate to let air or gas escape from; to reduce the level of economic activity
deflating deflation deflationary

deflect to turn aside
deflection or *deflexion deflector*

defoliate to destroy the leaves of
defoliant defoliating defoliation

deforest to clear of forests
deforestation

deform to make misshapen
deformable deformation deformed deformity deformities

defraud to swindle

defray to provide the money required
defrayal defrayed defrayment

defrock to deprive of ecclesiastical office

defrost to make or become free of frost or ice
defroster

deft nimble
deftly deftness

defunct dead; no longer valid or functioning

defuse to remove the fuse from a bomb, etc.; to remove a cause of tension
defusing
SEE PANEL

defuse or diffuse?
To *defuse* a bomb means to remove its fuse so that it will not explode; to *defuse* a tense situation is to calm it down.
As a verb, *diffuse* means 'to scatter or spread out': *to diffuse light; diffuse information on alternative technologies.*

defy to disobey openly
defied defier defies defying

degenerate (to become) lower in character or quality
degeneracy degenerating degeneration

degrade to lower in rank or status
degradable degradation degrading

degree unit of measurement of temperature or angles; stage in scale; academic title

dehumanize or **dehumanise** to remove human qualities from
dehumanization or *dehumanisation*
dehumanizing or *dehumanising*

dehydrate to remove water from
dehydrating dehydration

de-ice to free from ice
de-icer de-icing

deify to make a god of
deification deified deifies deifying

deign to condescend

deism belief in the existence of a god, based on human reason, not revelation
deist deistic deistically

deity god; state of being a god
deities

déjà vu (*French*) sensation of having already experienced something

deject to dishearten
dejected dejection

de jure (*Latin*) by right

delay to put off to a later time
delayed delayer delaying

delectable delightful
delectability or *delectableness delectably*

delectation delight; enjoyment

delegate someone representing and acting on behalf of others; to appoint as a delegate
delegacy delegacies delegating delegation

delete to erase or strike out
deleting deletion

deleterious harmful or hurtful
deleteriously deleteriousness

delft or **delf** glazed Dutch earthernware

deliberate intentional; to consider carefully
deliberately deliberateness deliberating deliberation deliberative

delicacy being delicate; rare or choice food
delicacies

delicate fine or subtle; fragile; sensitive
delicately delicateness

delicatessen (shop or department selling) choice or foreign prepared foods

delicious pleasant to the senses, esp. taste
deliciously deliciousness

delight great pleasure; to please greatly
delightful delightfully

delimit or **delimitate** to fix the limits of
delimitating delimitation delimitative

delineate to show by drawing an outline of; to describe
delineable delineating delineation delineator

delinquent (person) guilty of doing wrong
delinquency

deliquesce to dissolve gradually in water absorbed from the air
deliquescence deliquescent deliquescing

delirium confused mental state during fever; wild excitement
delirious

deliver to hand over; to take; to set free; to help to bring to birth *deliverable deliverance deliverer delivery deliveries*

dell small hollow or valley

delouse to rid of lice
delousing

Delphic of Delphi or its oracle

delphinium plant of the buttercup family with spiky often blue flowers
delphiniums

delta area of land at river mouth; 4th letter of the Greek alphabet
delta-winged deltoid

delude to mislead or deceive
deluding delusive delusively delusory

deluge disastrous flood; overwhelming rush

delusion false or mistaken belief
SEE PANEL at **allusion**

de luxe luxurious

delve to search; to research intensively
delving

demagnetize or **demagnetise** to remove magnetic properties or a magnetic field from
demagnetization or *demagnetisation*
damagnetizing or *demagnetising*

demagogue leader who tries to gain power by appealing to feelings not reason
demagogic demagoguery demagogy

demand to ask for urgently; consumer's willingness and ability to buy something

demarcation marking the limits of different areas of work, etc.
demarcate demarcating

demean to lower (oneself) in rank, etc.

demeanour (US **demeanor**) behaviour

demented mad; insane
dementia

demerara brown crystallized cane sugar

demerit fault or defect
demeritorius

demesne landed estate; land

demi- (*prefix*) half; partly
demigod

demijohn large narrow-necked bottle

demilitarize or **demilitarise** to remove military forces, etc., from
demilitarization or *demilitarisation*
demilitarizing or *demilitarising*

demise cessation; death

demist to remove mist from
demister

demo (*informal*) short for **demonstration**

demob (*informal*) to demobilize
demobbed demobbing

demobilize or **demobilise** to discharge from military service
demobilization or *demobilisation*
demobilizing or *demobilising*

democracy government by the people, esp. through elected representatives
democracies democrat Democrat democratic democratically democratize or *democratise*

demodulation extraction of audio frequency waves from modulated carrier waves

demography study of population statistics
demographer demographic

demolish to pull down or destroy
demolishes demolition

demon evil spirit; devil; daemon
demoniac demoniacal demonic demonology

demonetize or **demonetise** to stop using a metal as a monetary standard
demonetization or *demonetisation*
demonetizing or *demonetising*

demonstrate to show or explain clearly with evidence
demonstrable demonstrably demonstrating demonstration demonstrative demonstrator

demoralize or **demoralise** to discourage
demoralization or *demoralisation*
demoralizing or *demoralising*

demote to lower in rank or position
demoting demotion

demotic of or by the common people

demur to object; objection
demurrable demurral demurred demurrer demurring

demure serious and reserved
demurely demureness

demystify to remove the mystery from
demystified demystifies demystifying

den wild animal's lair; secluded room or place

denarius small silver coin of ancient Rome
denarii

denary in 10s; decimal

denationalize or **denationalise** to transfer from public to private ownership
denationalization or *denationalisation*
denationalizing or *denationalising*

dendrochronology study of growth rings in trees to date past events

dendrology study of trees

denial declaration that something is untrue

denier unit of weight used to measure the fineness of nylon, silk, etc.

denigrate to belittle the reputation of
denigrating denigration

denim durable twilled cotton fabric
denims

denizen inhabitant

Denmark country in North Europe
Dane Danish

denominate (*formal*) to give a name to
denominating

denomination religious grouping

denominator part of a fraction below the line

denote to indicate
denotation denoting

denouement resolution or final outcome of a plot

denounce to condemn publicly
denouncer donouncing denunciation

dense thick; complicated; stupid
densely density

dent (to make a) hollow depression

dental of the teeth

dentifrice substance for cleaning the teeth

dentist someone qualified in the care of teeth
dentistry

dentition arrangement of teeth; teething

denture set of artificial teeth

denude to make bare
denudation denuding

denunciation public condemnation

deny to declare to be untrue
deniable denial denied denier denies denying

deodar East Indian cedar tree

deodorant substance that removes or masks unwanted smells

deodorize or **deodorise** to remove or mask odours
deodorization or *deodorisation deodorizer* or *deodoriser deodorizing* or *deodorising*

Deo volente (*Latin*) God willing

depart to leave; to go away
departed departure

department specialized division
departmental

depend to rely (on); to trust
dependable dependence dependency dependencies

dependant (US **dependent**) person who

relies on another for esp. financial support
SEE PANEL

dependant or dependent?
Your *dependants* (in American English, *dependents*) are the people that you support financially, especially your children: *In the event of your death, your dependants will be looked after.*

To be *dependent* on a person or thing means that you rely on them in order to survive or function: *dependent relatives; dependent on overseas trade.*

dependent relying on; subject to
SEE PANEL at **dependant**

depict to show by a drawing or picture; to describe
depiction

depilatory (substance for) removing hair
depilatories

deplete to use up; to exhaust
depleting depletion

deplore to disapprove of strongly
deplorable deplorably deploring

deploy to spread out; to use or arrange
deployment

deponent person who gives written evidence

depopulate to reduce the population
depopulating depopulation depopulator

deport to expel from a country; to conduct oneself
deportation deportee deportment

depose to remove from position or office or power
deposing deposition

deposit to put or set down, esp. for safekeeping; money paid in part payment; money paid into a bank; layer
deposition depositor

depositary person to whom something is entrusted
depositaries

depository place where something is deposited
depositories

depot storehouse; place where buses or railway engines are maintained

deprave to corrupt or pervert
depravation depraving depravity depravities

deprecate to show disapproval of
deprecating deprecation deprecative deprecator deprecatory
SEE PANEL

deprecate or depreciate?
Deprecate, a formal word, means ´to show disapproval of something´: *deprecate the increasing extent of violence on television.*

Depreciate means ´to become less in value´: *Since the completion of the new runway, local house prices have depreciated considerably.*

depreciate to become less in value
depreciating depreciation depreciative depreciatory
SEE PANEL at **deprecate**

depredation plundering; pillage
depredator

depress to discourage; to push down
depressant depressed depresses depressible depression depressive

deprive to take away from
deprivation depriving

depth distance downwards; deepness

depute to appoint as a representative
deputation deputing

deputize or **deputise** to act as a deputy
deputizing or *deputising*

deputy person chosen to act on behalf of another
deputies

derail to cause to go off the rails
derailed derailment

derange to make insane
derangement deranging

derelict abandoned and neglected
dereliction

derestrict to remove a speed limit from
derestricted derestriction

deride to scorn or mock
deriding derisible derision derisive derisory

de rigueur (*French*) according to etiquette

derive to originate from
derivable derivation derivative deriving

dermatitis kind of skin disease or inflammation

dermatology medical study of the skin and its diseases
dermatological dermatologist

derogate to make appear inferior; to detract
derogating derogation

derogatory belittling
derogatorily derogatoriness

derrick kind of large crane; framework over oil well

derring-do daring action

derringer short-barrelled pistol

derv fuel oil for diesel engines

dervish member of a Muslim religious order
dervishes

desalinate to remove salt from sea water
desalinating desalination

descant higher subordinate melody

descend to move or pass down
descendible or *descendable descent*

descendant person or animal descended from another
descendent descending

describe to give an account or representation of in words
describable describer describing description descriptive

descry to catch sight of; to detect
descried descries descrying

desecrate to violate the sacred character of
desecrating desecration desecrator

desegregate to eliminate racial segregation in
desegregating desegregation

desensitize or **desensitise** to make less sensitive or insensitive
desensitization or *desensitisation*
desensitizing or *desensitising*

desert[1] area of dry infertile land
desertification
SEE PANEL

---

desert or dessert?

A *desert* is a large area of dry infertile land: *the Sahara Desert.* As a verb *desert* means 'to abandon': *to desert his wife and children; to desert a job.* As a noun, *desert* is used in the expression *just deserts*, the unpleasant effects that deservedly happen to someone. *He's got his just deserts.*

Dessert is the sweet course of a meal: *eat bread-and-butter pudding for dessert.*

---

desert[2] to abandon
deserter desertion
SEE PANEL at **desert**[1]

deserts just reward or punishment

deserve to be worthy of
deserved deservedly deserving

déshabillé or **dishabille** (*French*) state of being partly or carelessly dressed

desiccate to remove moisture from; to dry
desiccant desiccated desiccating desiccation desiccator

desideratum (*formal*) something regarded as necessary
desiderata

design (to draw a) plan or sketch
designable designer designing

designate appointed to office but not yet taking office; to indicate, specify, or name
designating designation designator

desire to wish or long for; longing
desirability desirable desirableness desiring desirous

desist to cease; to abstain

desk piece of furniture used for reading and writing; table or counter
desktop

desolate barren; lonely
desolately desolation

despair to lose all hope; loss of all hope
despairingly

despatch see **dispatch**

desperado reckless or violent person, esp. a criminal
desperadoes or *desperados*

desperate despairing
desperately desperation

despicable contemptible; mean
despicableness despicably

despise to consider to be worthless or contemptible
despiser despising

despite in spite of

despoil to loot
despoiler despoilment despoliation

despondent downcast; gloomy
despondency

despot ruler who exercises absolute power; tyrant
despotic despotically despotism

dessert sweet course at a meal
dessertspoon dessertspoonful dessertspoonfuls
SEE PANEL at **desert**[1]

destination place at the end of a journey

destine to decide in advance; to direct for a certain purpose

destiny fate; predetermined course of events
destinies

destitute very poor; deprived (of)
destitution

destroy to ruin or demolish; to put an end to
destroyer destruction destructible destructive destructor

desuetude (*formal*) disuse

desultory passing aimlessly from one thing to another; unmethodical
desultorily desultoriness

detach to separate without damage
detachable detached detaches detachment

detail individual part or item
detailed

detain to hold back; to keep back
detainable detainee detainment

detect to discover; to find someone committing an offence
detectable or *detectible detection detective detector*

détente (*French*) easing of tension between countries

detention detaining or being detained

deter to discourage
determent deterred deterring

detergent cleansing agent

deteriorate to make or become worse
deteriorating deterioration

determine to decide; to be firm
determinable determinant determinate determination determined determiner determining

determinism belief that all human choices, acts, etc., are decided by earlier causes
determinist deterministic

deterrent something that can deter
deterrence

detest to hate

detestable detestably detestation detester

dethrone to remove from the throne
dethronement dethroner dethroning

detonate to (cause to) explode
detonating detonation detonator

detour deviation from a planned route

detract to remove something desirable from
detraction detractive detractor detractory
SEE PANEL

---

detract or distract?
If one thing *detracts* from another, it makes it less desirable or impressive: *The new skyscraper detracts from the pleasant view of the countryside.*
Distract means 'to draw attention away from': *Playing computer games may distract children from their homework; Do not distract the driver's attention while the vehicle is moving.*

---

detriment harm or disadvantage
detrimental detrimentally

detritus loose disintegrated material

deuce tennis score of 40 points each; playing-card with 2 spots; (*slang*) devil

deus ex machina (*Latin*) sudden, unexpected solution to a problem in drama, etc.

Deuteronomy 5th book of the Old Testament

devalue to reduce the exchange value
devaluation devaluing

devastate to lay waste; to ravage
devastating devastation

develop to (cause to) grow or mature; to appear or acquire gradually; to produce a photograph chemically
developable developer developing development developmental

deviate to turn away from
deviant deviating deviation deviator

device machine or scheme; design
SEE PANEL

---

device or devise?
A *device* is a machine, scheme, or design: *a new electronic device that can measure the flow of water; His pleasantness was merely a device used in order to gain her affection.*
Devise is a verb meaning to work out or plan in the mind: *to devise a new method for working out the school timetable.*

---

devil (supreme) evil spirit; to season food highly
devilish devilled (US *deviled*) *devilling* (US *deviling*) *devil-may-care devilment devilry*

devious deceitful; indirect
deviously deviousness

devise to work out or plan in the mind
deviser devising
SEE PANEL at **device**

devoid destitute (of); without

devolve to transfer power and duties to
devolution devolving

devote to apply or give (oneself) to
devoted devotee devoting devotion devotional

devour to eat up greedily

devout deeply religious; sincere
devoutly devoutness

dew moisture that condenses on cool surfaces at night
dewdrop dewy

dewlap fold of loose skin hanging from animal's throat

dexter (*heraldry*) on the right side from the bearer's point of view

dexterity skill
dextrous or *dexterous dextrously* or *dexterously*

dextrose glucose occurring in fruit

dhoti loincloth worn by Hindu men

dhow Arab lateen-rigged boat

diabetes disorder resulting in excess glucose in the blood
diabetic

diabolic like a devil; very difficult or cruel
diabolical diabolically

diabolism worship of or dealings with the Devil
diabolist

diaconate office of a deacon; group of deacons

diacritic mark above, below, or through a letter to show a different pronunciation

diadem royal crown or authority

diaeresis (US **dieresis**) mark ¨ to show that the second of two vowels is to be pronounced separately
diaereses (US *diereses*)

diagnosis identification of diseases by examining symptoms
diagnoses diagnose diagnosing diagnostic

diagonal from one corner to another
diagonally

diagram drawn plan or design
diagrammatic diagrammatical

dial numbered disc on a telephone, face of a clock, etc.; to operate a telephone dial
dialled dialling

dialect variety of language spoken in a particular region
dialectal

dialectic assessing the truth of a theory by systematic reasoning
dialectical dialectician

dialogue (US **dialog**) conversation between 2 people

dialysis purification of blood by removing waste products
dialyses dialyse

diameter line across the centre of a circle or sphere
diametric diametrical diametrically

diamond very hard precious stone; 4-sided figure

diaper kind or fabric; (US) nappy

diaphanous so fine as to be almost transparent

diaphragm membrane, esp. the one that separates chest from abdomen

diarchy rule by two authorities
diarchies

diarrhoea (US **diarrhea**) abnormally frequent and liquid bowel movement

diary personal record of daily events, appointments, etc.
diaries diarist

diatonic of a musical scale of 8 notes without chromatic deviation

diatribe bitter abusive attack

dibble or **dibber** small hand tool for making holes in the ground

dice (*singular* **die**) small cubes marked with spots; to cut into small cubes
dicing

dicey (*informal*) risky

dichotomy division into 2 parts
dichotomies dichotomous

dichromatic having 2 colours

Dickensian of or characteristic of (the writings of) Charles Dickens

dicky[1] or **dickey** false shirt or blouse front

dicky[2] or **dickie** (*informal*) weak; unsound

dicotyledon flowering plant with 2 seed-leaves

Dictaphone (*trademark*) tape recorder used for dictating

dictate to say aloud for a person to write down or for a machine to record; to give orders authoritatively
dictating dictation dictator dictatorial dictatorially dictatorship

diction clarity of speaking; choice of words

dictionary book consisting of an

alphabetical list of words and their meanings
dictionaries

dictum authoritative statement
dicta or *dictums*

did past tense of **do**

didactic intended to instruct
didactically didacticism

diddle (*informal*) to cheat or swindle
diddled diddling

didgeridoo long tubular Australian aborigine musical wind instrument

didn't (*informal*) did not

die[1] to stop living
died die-hard dies dying

die[2] pressing or cutting tool
dies die-cast die-stamping

dieresis (US) see **diaeresis**

diesel kind of combustion engine
diesel-electric

diet (to keep to a) special range of foods
dietary dietetics dietitian or *dietician*

differ to be unlike; to disagree
difference different differently

differentiate to show the difference; to distinguish
differential differentiating differentiation

difficult not easy; requiring skill or effort
difficulty difficulties

diffident lacking self-confidence
diffidence diffidently

diffraction breaking up of a light beam by passing through a small opening

diffuse to scatter or spread out
diffusely diffuseness diffusible diffusing diffusion
SEE PANEL at **defuse**

dig to break up or take away earth
digger digging dug

digest to break down food into easily absorbed substances; to absorb mentally; summary
digester digestible digestion digestive

digit numeral from 0 to 9; finger or toe
digital

digitalis foxglove plant; drug prepared from dried foxglove leaves

digitize to **digitise** to put data into digital form
digitization or *digitisation digitizing* or *digitising*

dignify to give dignity to
dignified dignifying

dignity being worthy of honour
dignitary dignitaries

digraph 2 letters to represent a single sound

digress to depart from the main theme
digresser digresses digression digressive

dike or **dyke** embankment built to prevent flooding; ditch

diktat harsh categorical statement by a ruler

dilapidated falling into ruin
dilapidation

dilate to make or become wider or larger
dilatable dilating dilation

dilatory tending to cause delay; slow
dilatorily dilatoriness

dilemma situation demanding a choice between 2 or more equally undesirable alternatives

dilettante person with superficial interest in something
dilettantes or *dilettanti dilettantism*

diligent hard-working; involving care and effort
diligence diligently

dill kind of plant whose seeds are used to flavour pickles

dilly-dally to waste time
dilly-dallied dilly-dallies dilly-dallying

dilute to add water to make less concentrated
diluting dilution

dim (to make or become) slightly dark or unclear; slow or stupid
dimly dimmed dimmer dimmest dimming dimness

dime coin worth one-tenth of a US dollar

dimension measurement in a particular direction
dimensional

diminish to reduce in size, value, or quantity
diminishable diminishes diminishingly

diminuendo (*music*) gradual decrease in loudness
diminuendos

diminution reduction or decrease

diminutive very small

dimple (to form a) small natural depression on the cheek or chin
dimpling

dim-wit (*informal*) silly or stupid person
dim-witted

din loud discordant noise; to instil (into)
dinned dinning

dinar money unit of certain Arab countries and Yugoslavia

dine to have dinner
diner dinette dining dining-car dining-room

dinette small area or room for use as a dining-room

ding-dong sound of a bell

dinghy small boat
dinghies

dingle small wooded valley

dingo Australian wild dog
dingoes

dingy drab; dirty
dingier dingiest dingily dinginess

dinky (*informal*) small; dainty

dinner main meal of the day
dinner-jacket

dinosaur large extinct reptile

dint (**by dint of**) by means of

diocese district under the jurisdiction of a bishop
dioceses diocesan

diode device that converts alternating current to direct current

dioxide oxide containing 2 oxygen atoms per molecule

dip to plunge or drop; to slope downwards; creamy mixture
dipped dipper dipping dipstick

diphtheria acute infectious disease

diphthong combined gliding sound made up of 2 vowels

diploma document conferring qualification or other honour
diplomas

diplomacy conduct of international relations; tact
diplomat diplomatic diplomatically diplomatist

dipsomania uncontrollable craving for alcohol
dipsomaniac

dipterous having 2 wings

diptych painting or carving on 2 hinged panels

dire awful; disastrous
direly direness direr direst

direct straightforward; to point out the way to; to order
directive directly

direction way to a place; supervising; instruction
directional

director board-member of a business firm; supervisor
directorate directorship

directory book listing names, addresses, and telephone numbers of people or businesses in an area
directories

dirge lament

dirigible able to be steered or directed; airship

dirk kind of dagger

dirndl kind of full-gathered skirt

dirt unclean substance
dirt-cheap

dirty (to make) unclean
dirtied dirtier dirties dirtiest dirtily dirtiness dirtying

dis- (*prefix*) opposite or reversal
disassemble disequilibrium disinfest

disable to deprive of an ability
disability disabilities disablement disabling

disabuse to free from a mistaken idea

disadvantage unfavourable person, thing, etc.; to handicap
disadvantaged disadvantageous

disaffected disloyal; resentful towards authority
disaffection

disagree to have a different point of view; to have unpleasant effects on
disagreeable disagreeableness disagreeably disagreed disagreeing disagreement

disallow to refuse to recognize

disappear to stop being visible
disappearance

disappoint to fail to come up to the expectations of
disappointed disappointingly disappointment

disapprobation (*formal*) disapproval

disapprove to consider wrong; to reject
disapproval disapproving

disarm to remove weapons from
disarmament disarmer

disarming allaying hostility, suspicion, etc.

disarrange to disturb the order of
disarrangement disarranging

disarray (to throw into) confusion
disarrayed disarraying

disassociate see **dissociate**

disaster event causing great destruction or misfortune
disastrous disastrously

disavow to deny knowledge of
disavowal disavowedly

disband to cease to exist as a group, unit, etc.
disbandment

disbar to deprive of the status of barrister
disbarment disbarred disbarring

disbelieve to reject as untrue; to refuse to believe
disbelief disbeliever disbelieving

disburse to pay out
disbursal disbursement disburser disbursing

disc (US **disk**) thin flat circular object; gramophone record

discard to throw away; to get rid of

discern to recognize or perceive clearly
discernible discerning discernment

discharge to dismiss or release; to emit; to fulfil
discharging

disciple follower

discipline to train to produce self-control and obedience; such training
disciplinable disciplinarian disciplinary discipliner disciplining

disclaim to deny or disown
disclaimer

disclose to make known; to reveal
disclosing disclosure

disco (*informal*) short for **discotheque**

discolour (US **discolor**) to cause to change colour
discoloration discoloured (US *discolored*) *discolouring* (US *discoloring*) *discolourment* (US *discolorment*)

discomfit to embarrass; to thwart
discomfited discomfiting discomfiture

discomfort lack of comfort; uneasiness; to make uneasy

discompose to disturb the composure of
discomposing discomposure

disconcert to disturb the composure of; to fluster

disconnect to separate
disconnected disconnection or *disconnexion*

disconsolate downcast

discontent dissatisfaction
discontented discontentedly discontentedness or *discontentment*

discontinue to bring or come to an end
discontinuance discontinuation discontinued discontinuing discontinuity discontinuous

discord lack of agreement or harmony; harsh sounds
discordant

discotheque or **discothèque** club for dancing to recorded music

discount reduction in price; to consider unimportant
discountable

discourage to depress or dishearten
discouragement discouraging

discourse talk or conversation; formal speech or writing; to express in speech or writing
discoursing

discourteous impolite
discourtesy

discover to find for the first time; to find out
discoverable discoverer discovery discoveries

discredit to harm the reputation of
discreditable discreditably

discreet cautious and tactful; modest
discreetly discretion discretionary
SEE PANEL

---

discreet or discrete?

Someone who is *discreet* is cautious and tactful: *make a few discreet inquiries; She was very discreet: she never told me anything about his private life.* Something that is modest because it is small and does not attract attention can also be described as *discreet*: *discreet jewellery; a discreet notice in the window.*

Discrete is a formal word meaning ´distinct; unconnected´: *analyse the responsibilities into discrete tasks.*

---

discrepancy conflict or variation
discrepancies discrepant discrepantly

discrete distinct; unconnected
discretely discreteness
SEE PANEL at **discreet**

discriminate to treat as different, esp. because of prejudice; to discern
discriminating discrimination discriminative discriminatory

discursive rambling in speech
discursively discursiveness

discus heavy disc thrown in sport
discuses or *disci*

discuss to have a conversation about
discussable or *discussible discusses discussion*

disdain to consider with contempt
disdainful disdainfully

disease illness
diseased

disembark to step down from a ship, aircraft, etc., onto land
disembarkation

disembody to free from the body
disembodied disembodiment

disembowel to remove the entrails of

disembowelled (US *disemboweled*) *disembowelling* (US *disemboweling*)

disenchant to destroy the illusions of
disenchantment

disencumber to free from a burden
disencumbrance

disendow to strip of endowments
disendowment

disenfranchise see **disfranchise**

disengage to release or withdraw from
disengaged disengagement disengaging

disentangle to free; to sort out; to untangle
disentanglement disentangling

disestablish to remove the established status of
disestablishes disestablishment

disfavour (US **disfavor**) disapproval or dislike

disfigure to spoil the appearance of
disfigurement disfiguring

disfranchise or **disenfranchise** to deprive of the right to vote
disfranchisement or *disenfranchisement* *disfranchising* or *disenfranchising*

disgorge to throw out; to discharge
disgorging

disgrace (to cause) shame, loss of reputation, and dishonour
disgraceful disgracefully disgracing

disgruntled dissatisfied and sulky

disguise to change the appearance of in order to hide identity
disguiser disguising

disgust (to cause) great loathing
disgusted disgustingly

dish (to serve in a) shallow open vessel
dishes dishcloth dishwasher dishwater

dishabille see **déshabillé**

disharmony discord
disharmonious

dishearten to weaken the hope, courage, etc., of

dishevelled (US **disheveled**) untidy; unkempt

dishonest not honest; deceitful
dishonestly dishonesty

dishonour (US **dishonor**) shame or disgrace; to discredit
dishonourable (US *dishonorable*) *dishonourably* (US *dishonorably*)

dishy (*slang*) attractive
dishier dishiest

disillusion to destroy the illusions of
disillusionment

disincentive deterrent; discouragement

disincline to make unwilling or reluctant
disinclination disinclining

disinfect to rid of infection
disinfectant disinfection disinfector

disinformation false information

disingenuous not sincere
disingenuously disingenuousness

disinherit to deprive of the right to inherit
disinheritance

disintegrate to break up into small fragments
disintegrating disintegration

disinter to remove from a grave; to unearth
disinterment disinterred disinterring

disinterested neutral; impartial
disinterestedly disinterestedness
SEE PANEL

---

disinterested or uninterested?

A person who is *disinterested* is neutral and gives an impartial opinion because they are not personally involved: *Let us hear what you, as a disinterested observer, have to say.*

A person who is *uninterested* has no interest in something or is bored with it: *be uninterested in politics.*

---

disinvestment reduction or withdrawal of investment

disjoin to make or become detached

disjoint to upset the order of
disjointed

disjunctive serving to separate or contrast

disk (*computers*) round flat plate with a magnetized coating for storing data; (US) disc

diskette (*computers*) floppy disk

dislike (to consider with) disapproval
disliking

dislocate to put out of place
dislocating dislocation

dislodge to remove forcibly from a fixed position
dislodging dislodgment or *dislodgement*

disloyal not loyal; unfaithful
disloyally disloyalty

dismal depressing; gloomy
dismally

dismantle to take apart
dismantling

dismay (to fill with) apprehension and discouragement

dismember to cut to pieces
dismemberment

dismiss to discharge from employment, etc.; to send away
dismissal dismisses dismissive

dismount to get off a horse, bicycle, etc.

disobey to refuse to obey
disobedience disobedient disobediently

disorder confusion; to disturb
disorderliness disorderly

disorganize or **disorganise** to disturb or confuse the arrangement of
disorganization or *disorganisation*
disorganizing or *disorganising*

disorientate or **disorient** to cause to lose one's bearings; to confuse
disorientating or *disorienting*
disorientation

disown to refuse to acknowledge

disparage to speak scornfully of
disparagement disparaging

disparate markedly different
disparately disparity disparities

dispassionate free from feeling or bias
dispassionately

dispatch or **despatch** to send away; message
dispatches or *despatches*

dispel to drive away
dispelled dispelling

dispense to give out; to manage without
dispensable dispensary dispensaries dispensation dispenser dispensing

disperse to scatter
dispersal disperser dispersing dispersion

dispirit to discourage
dispirited dispiriting

displace to move out of the usual position
displaceable displaced displacement displacing

display (to) show; to present
displayer

displease to annoy or upset
displeasing displeasure

dispose to get rid (of); to deal with; to place in order
disposable disposal disposing disposition

dispossess to take away from; to deprive
dispossesses dispossession dispossessor

disproportion lack of proportion
disproportional

disproportionate out of proportion
disproportionately

disprove to prove to be false
disproof disproving

dispute to quarrel or argue; quarrel or argument

disputable disputant disputation disputatious disputatiously disputer disputing

disqualify to exclude from a contest, etc., for violating rules
disqualification disqualified disqualifies disqualifying

disquiet (to cause) anxiety or concern
disquietude

disregard to consider unimportant; to ignore

disrepair condition of being worn out and requiring repair

disreputable having a bad reputation
disreputably disreputation

disrepute lack of respectability or good reputation

disrespect lack of respect; contempt or rudeness
disrespectful disrespectfully

disrobe to undress
disrobement disrobing

disrupt to throw into a disorganized state; to break up
disruption disruptive

dissatisfy to make discontented
dissatisfaction dissatisfied dissatisfies dissatisfying

dissect to cut up and examine
dissectible dissection dissector

dissemble to conceal one's feelings under pretence
dissembler dissembling

disseminate to distribute
disseminating dissemination disseminator

dissent to express disagreement
dissension dissenter dissentient dissenting

dissertation long written thesis

disservice unhelpful act; bad turn

dissident disagreeing (person)
dissidence dissidently

dissimilar not alike; not similar
dissimilarity dissimilarly dissimilitude

dissimulate to dissemble
dissimulating dissimulation dissimulator

dissipate to scatter; to squander; to indulge in the pursuit of pleasure
dissipating dissipation

dissociate or **disassociate** to break off associations with
dissociating or *disassociating dissociation* or *disassociation*

dissoluble capable of being dissolved
dissolubility

dissolute of loose morals
dissoluteness

dissolve to make or become liquid by soaking; to end officially
dissolution dissolvable dissolvent dissolving

dissonant discordant
dissonance

dissuade to defer from; to advise against
dissuading dissuasion dissuasive

dissymmetry lack of symmetry
dissymmetric

distaff rod on which wool is wound

distance space between two points; to keep at a distance
distanced distancing

distant remote
distantly

distaste dislike (for)
distasteful distastefully distastefulness

distemper[1] animal disease, esp. of dogs

distemper[2] paint of mixed pigments and size, etc.

distend to swell
distensible distension

distil (US **distill**) to purify by distillation; to heat a mixture, vaporize, condense, and collect a liquid
distillate distillation distilled distiller distillery distilleries distilling

distinct clear; noticeable
distinctly
SEE PANEL

---

distinct or distinctive?
Distinct means 'clear; noticeable': *detect a distinct change in his attitude.* Something that is *distinct* from something else is different and separate from it: *the increase in prices as distinct from the increase in the rate of increases in prices.*

Something is *distinctive* when it has a special quality that makes it easily recognizable: *He has a distinctive Welsh accent.*

---

distinctive characteristic
distinctively
SEE PANEL at **distinct**

distinguish to show the difference between; to bring honour to
distinction distinguishable distinguishes

distinguished noble; famous

distort to twist out of shape
distorted distortion

distract to draw attention away from
distracted distractedly distractible distraction
SEE PANEL at **detract**

distrain to seize goods as a pledge or for debt
distrainer distraint

distraught mentally agitated; frantic
distraughtly

distress (to cause) anguish or suffering
distresses distressed distressful distressing

distribute to share out; to circulate
distributable distributing distribution distributive distributively distributor

district area of land, esp. for administrative purposes

distrust (to regard with) suspicion
distrustful distrustfully distrustfulness

disturb to interrupt; to destroy the quietness or order of
disturbance disturbed disturbing

disunite to separate
disunion disuniting disunity

disuse being no longer in use
disused

disyllable word of 2 syllables
disyllabic

ditch long narrow channel dug in the ground; (*informal*) to discard
ditches

dither to be uncertain; to hesitate

ditto the same again

ditty short simple song or poem
ditties

diuresis increased flow of urine
diuretic

diurnal of the day or daytime

divan long low backless bed or couch

dive to plunge head first into water
dive-bomb dived (US *dove*) *diver diving*

diverge to separate at a point and go in different directions
divergence divergency divergent diverging

divers (*archaic*) various

diverse of different kinds
diversely diversity diversities

diversify to make different forms of; to vary products, etc.
diversifiable diversification diversified diversifies diversifying

divert to turn aside
diversion diversionary

divertimento piece of light music
divertimenti

divertissement (*French*) short ballet or interlude; light entertainment

divest to deprive (of); to strip (of clothes)
divestiture or *divestment*

divide to separate; to distribute
divider dividing divisibility divisible divisive divisor

dividend number to be divided; money payable to shareholders

dividers instrument with 2 pointed ends to measure lines, angles, etc.

divine of God or a god; to foretell intuitively
divination diviner divining

divinity nature of being a god; theology
divinities

division dividing; divided part; category
divisional

divorce legal ending of a marriage; to end a marriage by divorce
divorcee divorcing

divot piece to turf dug out by a golfer

divulge to make known
divulgence divulger divulging

dixie large metal pot for cooking by campers

dizzy giddy
dizzier dizziest dizzily dizziness

Djibouti country on NE coast of Africa
Djiboutian

do to carry out; to produce; function or gathering
doable do-gooder doing do-it-yourself

dobbin (*informal*) farm horse

docile easily disciplined or controlled
docilely docility

dock[1] area of water for ships to moor or be repaired; to join spacecraft in space
docker dockyard

dock[2] to cut off, esp. part of an animal's tail

dock[3] enclosure in lawcourt in which the accused stands

dock[4] kind of weedy plant with broad leaves

docket (to mark with a) document listing contents
docketed docketing

doctor qualified medical practitioner; higher academic degree; to treat or modify; to castrate
doctorate

doctrine set of principles, teachings, or beliefs
doctrinaire doctrinal doctrinarian

document written, esp. official, statement providing evidence or information
documentary documentation

dodder to move unsteadily
dodderer doddery

dodecahedron solid with 12 faces
dodecahedrons or *dodecahedra*

dodge to move position suddenly; to evade
dodger dodging dodgy

dodgem small electric car to be bumped into others at funfairs

dodo extinct flightless bird
dodos or *dodoes*

doe female deer, hare, or rabbit

doer person or thing that does something

does 3rd person singular or present tense of **do**

doesn't (*informal*) does not

doff to take off or lift one's hat

dog domesticated canine animal; to follow closely and persistently
dog days dog-eared dog-end dogfight dogfish dogging doggish doggy doghouse dogsbody dog-star dog-tried dog-tooth dogtrot dogwatch dogwood

dogged obstinately determined

doggerel comic irregular verse

doggo (*informal*) hiding without moving

dogleg sharp bend in a road, etc.

dogma authoritative priciples or beliefs
dogmas or *dogmata dogmatic dogmatically dogmatism dogmatist dogmatize* or *dogmatise*

doh (*music*) 1st note in a major scale

doily, **doyley**, or **doyly** small decorative openwork plate mat
doilies, doyleys, or *doylies*

dolce (*music*) sweetly

doldrums depressed state of mind

dole government unemployment benefit; to distribute in small portions
doling

doleful mournful; dreary
dolefully dolefulness

doll small toy model of human; to dress (up)

dollar money unit of USA, Canada, Australia, etc.

dollop mass or heap; to serve clumsily
dolloped dolloping

dolly child's word for doll; wheeled platform
dollies

dolour (US **dolor**) grief
dolorous

dolphin kind of sea mammal
dolphinarium

dolt slow-witted person
doltish

domain territory; area of study, etc.

dome roof shaped like a hemisphere

Domesday Book survey of English land made in 1086

domestic of the home or family
domestically domesticity

domesticate to bring under human control
domesticating domestication

domicile person's main home
domiciliary

dominate to control or influence; to overlook
dominance dominant dominating domination

domineer to behave overbearingly

Dominica island in the West Indies

Dominican order of friars founded by St Dominic

Dominican Republic country in the West Indies
Dominican

dominion power to govern; self-governing territory

domino flat oblong block of wood used in the game of dominoes; hooded cloak and mask
dominoes

don[1] to put on clothing
donned donning

don[2] university teacher; Spanish gentleman or nobleman
donnish

donate to give to charity
donating donation

done past participle of **do**

donjon strong inner tower of a medieval castle

donkey ass; stubborn person
donkeys

donor someone who gives something

don't (*informal*) do not

doodle to scribble aimlessly
doodling

doodle-bug flying bomb

doom (to destine or condemn to an) unhappy fate

doomsday day of Judgement

door barrier closing and opening entrance to a house or room
doorbell doorhandle door-keeper doorknob doorknocker doorman doormat doornail doorplate doorpost doorstep doorstop doorstopper doorway

dope thick liquid preparation; (to give a) drug (to)

doper dopey or *dopy doping*

doppelgänger (*German*) ghostly copy of a living person

Doric kind of architecture or column

dormant sleeping; inactive

dormer window projecting from a sloping roof

dormitory large room containing several beds
dormitories

Dormobile (*trademark*) small motorized caravan

dormouse kind of small rodent with a bushy tail
dormice

dorsal of the back

dory flat-bottomed boat with high sides
dories

dose (to give a) measured quantity of medicine
dosage dosing

doss (*slang*) to sleep
doss-house

dossier collection of papers containing detailed information

dot (to make a) small round mark
dotted dotting

dotage feebleness of mind in old age
dotard

dote to show great or excessive fondness towards
doting

dotty (*informal*) odd
dottier dottiest

Douay version of the Bible

double (to make) twice the amount
double-barrelled (US *double-barreled*) *double-bass double-breasted double-check double-cross double-dealing double-decker double-declutch double-edged double-faced double-jointed double-park double-quick double-take double-talk double-think doubling doubly*

double entendre (*French*) word or expression with a second meaning, often slightly obscene

doublet one of a pair of related things; (*formerly*) close-fitting jacket

---

doubling of consonants

Final consonants are sometimes doubled when adding a suffix that starts with a vowel.

With a word that has one syllable, this rule applies when there is a single vowel before the final consonant:

big, bigger fat, fatter hit, hitting sad, saddest stop, stopped win, winner

If the word has more than one syllable, this rule applies if:

- the last syllable is stressed and the final consonant is preceded by a single vowel:

begin, beginner equip, equipped permit, permitting

Exceptions:

- words with a final -l, which is doubled even though the syllable is unstressed:

quarrelled (US *quarreled*)
traveller (US *traveler*)

- individual words

handicap, handicapped kidnap, kidnapping (US usually *kidnaping*) *worship, worshipper* (US usually *worshiper*)

- final *-s* is sometimes doubled in:

bias, biased or *biassed focus, focused* or *focussed*

---

doubloon former Spanish gold coin

doubt (to have) disbelief and uncertainty
doubtful doubtfully doubtfulness doubtless doubtlessly doubtlessness

douche (to clean the body with a) stream of water

dough baking mixture of flour, water, etc.; (*slang*) money
doughnut doughy

doughty (*poetic*) bold

dour stern; sullen

douse or **dowse** to drench with water
dousing or *dowsing*

dove[1] kind of pigeon; symbol of peace
dove-coloured dovecot or *dovecote*

dove[2] (US) past tense of **dive**

dovetail (to join by a) wedge-shaped piece of wood; such a joint

dowager widow holding title or property from her late husband

dowdy shabby; old-fashioned
dowdier dowdiest dowdily dowdiness dowdyish

dowel pin for fixing the position of something by fitting into holes
dowelled (US *doweled*) *dowelling* (US *doweling*)

dower widow's life-interest in her late husband's property

down[1] from a higher to a lower position
down-and-out down-at-heel downbeat downcast downfall downgrade downhearted downhill down-market downpipe downpour downside downsize downsizing downstage downstairs downstream downstroke downtown down-train downtrodden downturn downward downwards downwind

down[2] covering of soft feathers
downy

Downing Street location of the official residence of the British prime minister

downright absolute; blunt; thoroughly

downs gently rolling uplands, esp. in South England

dowry money, property, etc., that a bride brings to her husband at marriage
dowries

dowse to search for hidden water with a divining rod; to douse
dowser dowsing

doxology expression of praise to God
doxologies

doyen (*fem.* **doyenne**) senior member of a group

doyley or **doyly** see **doily**

doze to sleep lightly
dozier doziest dozily doziness dozing

dozen 12

drab dull
drably drabness

drachm unit of weight; drachma

drachma money unit of Greece
drachmas or *drachmae*

draconian harsh; drastic

draft (to make a) rough sketch; order to pay money; (US) conscription or to conscript
draftee drafter draftsman or *draughtsman*

drafty (US) see **draughty**

drag to pull slowly and with difficulty; to trail along the ground
dragged dragging drag-net

draggle to make wet and dirty
draggled draggling

dragoman interpreter in some Middle East countries
dragomans or *dragomen*

dragon mythical monster

dragonfly kind of winged insect
dragonflies

dragoon to force; (*formerly*) heavily armed infantryman

drain (to remove liquid through a) pipe, channel, etc.
drainage draining-board drainpipe

drake male duck

dram unit of mass; small drink of spirits

drama theatrical play; highly emotional event
dramatic dramatically dramatics dramatist

dramatis personae list of characters in a play

dramatize or **dramatise** to present as a drama
dramatization or *dramatisation* *dramatizing* or *dramatising*

drank past tense of **drink**

drape to cover with cloth; to arrange or hand loosely
draper drapery draperies draping

drastic extreme or severe
drastically

draught (US **draft**) flow of air; depth of water; pulling a load; drawing beer, etc., from a barrel
draughtboard draughtsman or *draftsman*

draughts (US **checkers**) kind of board-game

draughty (US **drafty**) marked by or exposed to draughts of air
draughtier (US *draftier*) *draughtiest* (US *draftiest*) *draughtily* (US *draftily*) *draughtiness* (US *draftiness*)

Dravidian group of languages of South India, Sri Lanka, and Pakistan

draw to pull; to take out; to make a picture; to finish equal
drawbridge drawing drawing-board drawing-pin drawing-room drawn drawstring drew

drawback hindrance

drawer person or thing that draws; compartment that slides in and out of a piece of furniture

drawl to speak with drawn-out vowel sounds

dray[1] low delivery cart used by brewers

dray[2] see **drey**

dread (to feel) terror

dreadful very disagreeable or bad
dreadfully dreadfulness

dreadnought kind of battleship

dream (to have a) series of images, thoughts, etc., during sleep
dreamed or *dreamt dreamer dreamland dreamless dreamlike dreamworld dreamy*

dreary sad; bleak; dull
drearier dreariest drearily dreariness

dredge (to use a) machine that removes mud, etc. from the bottom of a river or sea
dredger dredging

dregs solid particles at the bottom of a liquid

drench to make completely wet
drenches

dress to put on clothes; woman's garment; to apply bandages to a wound
dresses dresser dressing-down dressing-gown dressing-room dressing-table dressmaker dressmaking dressy

dressage training of a horse

drew past tense of **draw**

drey or **dray** squirrel's nest

dribble to let saliva trickle from the mouth; to run slowly with a ball
dribbler dribblet dribbling

dried past tense and past participle of **dry**

drier comparative of **dry**; or **dryer** machine for drying

drift to be carried along by a current; something piled up; gist or general meaning
drifter drift-net driftwood

drill[1] (to use a) machine or tool for boring holes; (to instruct with) military training

drill[2] shallow furrow for sowing seeds

drill[3] strong twill-weave cotton cloth

drily or **dryly** in a dry manner

drink (to swallow) liquid
drank drinkable drink-driver drink-driving drinker drunk

drip (to allow) to fall in drops
drip-dry drip-feed dripped dripping

drive to operate a vehicle; to cause to move forcefully; journey; road
drivable or *driveable* *drive-in* *driven* *driver* *driveway* *drove*

drivel (to talk) nonsense
drivelled (US *driveled*) *driveller* (US *driveler*) *drivelling* (US *driveling*)

drizzle to rain lightly; light rain
drizzling *drizzly*

drogue sea anchor; small parachute

droll amusing in an odd way
drollery *drolleries*

dromedary 1-humped camel
dromedaries

drone male bee; (to make a) low humming noise
droning

drool to dribble; to show great enthusiasm (for)

droop to hand downwards; to sag
droopy

drop small quantity of liquid; (to allow) to fall
drop-kick *droplet* *drop-out* *dropped* *dropper* *dropping* *dropshot*

dropsy disease in which watery fluid accumulates in the body
dropsical

dross scum on molten metals; waste

drought long period of dry weather

drove[1] past tense of **drive**

drove[2] herd of animals
drover

drown to die or kill by submerging in water

drowse to be sleppy
drowsily *drowsiness* *drowsing* *drowsy*

drub to beat with a stick
drubbed *drubbing*

drudge (to do) hard, tedious, or menial work
drudgery *drudgeries* *drudging*

drug substance used in treating a disease; substance that causes addiction; to use a drug
drugged *drugging* *druggist* *drugstore*

drugget coarse fabric used as a carpet

Druid priest of an ancient Celtic order
Druidess *Druidic*

drum (to play a) musical instrument with a skin stretched over a hollow cylinder; eardrum
drumbeat *drumfire* *drumhead* *drummed* *drummer* *drumming* *drumstick*

drunk past participle of **drink**; intoxicated with alcohol
drunkard *drunken* *drunkenly* *drunkenness*

drupe fruit with a fleshy layer that encloses a stone around a seed

dry (to make or become) free from moisture
dried *drier* *dries* *driest* *drily* or *dryly* *dry-clean* *dryer* *drying* *dryness* *dry-shod* *drystone*

dryad wood nymph

dual double
dual-control *dualism* *duality* *dually* *dual-purpose*

dub[1] to knight by touching on the shoulder with a sword; to nickname
dubbed *dubber* *dubbing*

dub[2] to add or change a film soundtrack
dubbed *dubber* *dubbing*

Dubai sheikdom of United Arab Emirates

dubbin greasy dressing applied to leather

dubious doubtful; suspicious
dubiety *dubiously*

ducal of a duke or duchy

ducat former gold or silver coin

duchess wife or widow of a duke; woman ranking equally with a duke
duchesses

duchy territory of a duke or duchess
duchies

duck[1] kind of swimming-bird; batsman's score of nil in cricket
duckbilled duck-board duckling duckweed

duck[2] to lower the head or body quickly

duck[3] heavy cotton fabric

duct tube, pipe, or canal
ductless

ductile easily moulded; pliable
ductility

dud (*informal*) person or thing that is useless

dudgeon feeling of resentment or anger

due payable; owing; (something) deserved; expected
duly

duel (to) fight with weapons by 2 opponents
duelled (US *dueled*) *dueller* (US *dueler*) *duelling* (US *dueling*) *duellist* (US *duelist*)

duenna (in Spain, Portugal, etc.) older woman who acts as a chaperon

duet music for two performers

duffel or **duffle** coarse woollen cloth

dug[1] past tense and past participle of **dig**

dug[2] animal's udder

dugout boat made by hollowing out a log; underground shelter

duke nobleman of high rank
ducal dukedom

dulcet soothing; pleasant
dulcetly

dulcimer kind of stringed instrument

dull not bright; not sharp; slow or boring
duller dullest dullness dully

dullard stupid or dull person

duly in a proper manner

dumb lacking the power of speech; (*informal*) stupid
dumbly dumbness dumb waiter

dumb-bell short bar with adjustable weights, used to exercise muscles

dumbfound to startle or astonish
dumbfounded

dumdum bullet that expands on impact

dummy model or copy; baby's rubber teat
dummies

dump to put down carelessly; to throw away; place for depositing rubbish

dumpling ball of dough

dumps (*informal*) state of depression

dumpy short and plump
dumpier dumpiest dumpily dumpiness

dun[1] greyish-brown

dun[2] to demand payment
dunned dunning

dunce dull or stupid person

dunderhead foolish or slow person

dune mound or ridge of sand piled up by the wind

dung animal excrement
dunghill

dungarees overalls made of a coarse cotton cloth

dungeon underground cell or prison

dunk to dip into a liquid

duo pair of performers; piece written for 2 players
duos

duodecimal of or based on the number 12

duodenum first part of the small intestine
duodenal

duologue conversation between 2 people in a play

dupe to trick or deceive; someone who is easily deceived
dupable duper duping

duple double; (*music*) having 2 beats in a bar

duplex double; twofold
duplexity

duplicate (to make an) exact copy; identical
duplicating duplication duplicator

duplicity wilful deception

durable able to be used or lasting a long time
durability durableness durably

duration length of time that something lasts

duress threats or constraint

during throughout; at a point of time within

dusk darker part of twilight
duskily duskiness dusky

dust (to wipe or brush away) fine particles of earth or dirt
dustbin dust-bowl dustcart duster dustily dustiness dustman dustpan dustproof dust-sheet dust-up dusty

Dutch (people or language) of the Netherlands
Dutchman Dutchwoman

duty tax; obligation
duties duteous dutiable dutiful dutifully dutifulness duty-bound duty-free

duvet thick soft quilt

dwarf abnormally short person; short plant or animal
dwarfs or *dwarves dwarfish*

dwell (*formal*) to live; to think, write, or speak (about)
dwelling dwelling-place dwelt or *dwelled*

dwindle to become less in quantity
dwindling

dye (to change the colour of by applying) liquid colouring substance
dyed dyed-in-the-wool dyeing dye-line dyer dye-stuff

Dyfed Welsh county

dying present participle of **die**[1]

dyke see **dike**

dynamic active and energetic; of a motive force
dynamically dynamics dynamism

dynamite powerful explosive

dynamo machine that converts mechanical energy into electrical energy
dynamos

dynasty series of hereditary rulers
dynasties dynast dynastic

dysentery infectious disease marked by severe diarrhoea

dysfunction abnormal or impaired functioning
dysfunctional

dyslexia abnormal development in reading ability
dyslexic

dyspepsia chronic indigestion
dyspeptic

dystrophy impaired nourishment

E

final -e

When a suffix that begins with a vowel is added to a word ending with a silent final -e, the e is omitted:

amuse, amusing bake, baker believe, believed late, latest nice, nicer

There is a growing tendency to omit the -e- before the suffixes *-able* and *-age*:

lovable or *loveable* *movable* or *moveable* *unmistakable* or *unmistakeable*

If the word ends in *-ce* or *-ge*, the e is not omitted in front of *a* and *o*:

courageous outrageous peaceable replaceable

The following words can be spelled with or without the -e after *g*:

acknowledgement or *acknowledgment* *judgement* or *judgment*

In front of suffixes that begin with a consonant, the final -e is not usually omitted:

arrange, arrangement complete, completely

Exceptions:

argue, argument due, duly true, truly

each every (one)

eager keen; enthusiastic
eagerly eagerness

eagle large bird of prey
eagle-eyed eaglet

ear[1] organ of hearing
earache eardrum earful earmark earphone earpiece ear-piercing earplug earring earshot earsplitting

ear[2] part of cereal plant containing seed, grain, or kernel

earl title of a British nobleman
earldom

early at or near the start of a time; before the usual time
earlier earliest earliness

earn to receive money in return for work
earner earnings

earnest serious; determined; money given to seal a bargain; pledge

earth planet on which we live; land; not sea or air; soil; to connect an electrical device to earth
earthbound earthen earthenware earthly earthward earthwork earthworm earthy

earthquake violent upheaval of part of the earth's crust

earwig kind of small insect with forceps-like appendages

ease (to give) freedom or relief from pain
easement easing

easel frame for supporting a blackboard, artist's canvas, etc.

east 1 of the 4 compass points; direction of sunrise
eastbound easterly eastern easterner easternmost eastward eastwards

Easter festival commemorating the resurrection of Christ

easy not difficult
easier easiest easily easiness easygoing

eat to take into the mouth and swallow
ate eatable eaten eater eating

eau-de-Cologne perfumed toilet water

eaves overhanging lower edges of a roof

eavesdrop to listen secretly
eavesdropped eavesDropper eavesdropping

ebb to flow out to sea; to weaken
ebb-tide

ebonite black vulcanized rubber

ebony hard black wood

ebullient excited and enthusiastic

ebullience ebulliently ebullition

eccentric odd; having different centres
eccentrically eccentricity eccentricities

Ecclesiastes book in the Old Testament

ecclesiastic clergyman

ecclesiastical of a church

Ecclesiasticus book in the Apocrypha

echelon level of responsibility; steplike arrangement

echo (to resound as a) reflection of sound waves
echoes echoed echoic echoing echoless

éclair light finger-shaped pastry filled with cream

éclat showy display; renown

eclectic choosing from or using various sources
eclectically eclecticism

eclipse (to cause an) obscuring of one heavenly body by another
eclipsing ecliptic

ecology study of the relationship between living things and their environment
ecological ecologically ecologist

economic of a country's economy; profitable
economically
SEE PANEL

---

economic or economical?
Economic means 'relating to a country's economy': *changes in government economic policy*. An economic business is one that produces a profit: *to sell goods at an economic price*, i.e. one that gives a profit to the seller.
Something is *economical* if it does not cost a lot of money to operate: *What is the most economical fuel?* Someone who is *economical* spends money carefully and wisely: *tips for economical management*.

---

economical not needing a lot of money; prudent
SEE PANEL at **economic**

economize or **economise** to reduce expense and wastage
economizing or *economising*

economy system of making goods and using resources; thriftiness
economic economical economically economics economist

ecosystem ecological system that considers all the plants, people, etc. in one environment

ecru unbleached linen colour

ecstasy intense joy
ecstasies ecstatic ecstatically

ectopic (*medical*) in an abnormal position

ecu European Currency Unit

Ecuador country in South America
Ecuadorian

ecumenical or **oecumenical** of the universal Christian Church
ecumenically or *oecumenically*
ecumenism or *oecumenism*

eczema skin inflammation marked by inflamed itchy patches

eddy (to move round in a) circular movement of water, wind, dust, etc.
eddies eddied eddying

edelweiss small perennial alpine plant

edema (US) see **oedema**

Eden biblical garden where Adam and Eve lived

edge border; limit; side; to move gradually
edgeways edgewise edginess edging edgy

edible fit to be eaten
edibility or *edibleness*

edict decree or order

edifice large or imposing building

edify to improve intellectually, morally, or spiritually
edification edified edifier edifies edifying

edit to prepare for publication; to be in

charge of a newspaper, etc.; to arrange film, tape, etc. for broadcasting
edition editor editorial editorship

educate to teach and train; to develop the character, mind, etc., of
*educability educable educating education educational educationally educationist*or *educationalist educative educator*

Edwardian of or characteristic of the reign of King Edward VII

eel kind of snake-like fish

eerie or **eery** weird; frightening
eerier eeriest eerily eeriness

efface to obliterate; to make (oneself) modestly inconspicuous
effaceable effacement effacer effacing

effect something produced by a cause; impression; to bring about or produce
effective effectively effectiveness
SEE PANEL at **affect**

effectual capable of producing a desired effect
effectually effectualness

effeminate (*of a man*) having womanly qualities
effeminacy effeminately effeminateness

efferent (*of nerves*) carrying outwards from an organ

effervesce to produce many small bubbles of gas
effervescence effervescent effervescing

effete exhausted; weak
effetely effeteness

efficacious capable of producing the desired effect
efficacy efficacies efficaciousness

efficient working well; producing the desired effect with the least waste
efficiency efficiently

effigy sculpture or model of a person
effigies

effloresce to burst into flower
efflorescence efflorescent efflorescing

effluent something that flows out; industrial waste
effluence

effluvium offensive smell from decaying matter
effluvia

efflux effluence of liquid or gas

effort physical or mental exertion; attempt
effortful effortless effortlessly effortlessness

effrontery insolent boldness
effronteries

effulgent brilliant; radiant
effulgence

effuse to pour out; to gush
effusing effusion effusive effusively effusiveness

egalitarian of or supporting the belief in equality of all people
egalitarianism

egg[1] reproductive body produced by animals, birds, etc.
eggcup egghead eggnog egg-plant eggshell egg-timer egg-white egg-yolk

egg[2] to urge (on)

eglantine kind of rose; sweet-brier

ego person's inner self; self-esteem

egocentric self-centred
egocentricity

egoism self-centredness; self-interest
egoist egoistic egoistical egoistically

egotism too great concern with oneself
egotist egotistic egotistical egotistically

egregious (*formal*) conspicuously bad

egress means of going or coming out

egret kind of heron

Egypt country in NE Africa
Egyptian Eqyptologist Egyptology

eider sea-duck with fine soft down

eiderdown down of the eider; quilt filled with such down or other material

eight number 8
eighteen eighteenth eighth eighthly eightieth eightsome eighty eighties

Eire Gaelic name for (Republic of) Ireland

eisteddfod annual Welsh competitive festival of the arts

either 1 or the other (of 2); likewise

ejaculate to eject semen from the body; to utter suddenly
ejaculating ejaculation ejaculatory

eject to force out; to expel or evict
ejection ejector

eke (**eke out**) to make a supply last longer; to make a living with difficulty
eking

elaborate complicated; developed carefully; to describe in detail
elaborating elaboration

élan style and vigour

eland kind of antelope

elapse (*of time*) to pass by
elapsing

elastic springy; flexible rubber fabric
elasticate elasticity elasticize or *elasticise*

Elastoplast (*trademark*) elastic sticky plaster

elate to make high-spirited and exhilarated
elated elatedly elating elation

elbow joint where arm bends
elbow-room

elder[1] (person who is) older; church leader
elderly eldest

elder[2] kind of bush with berries
elderberry

El Dorado place of treasure or opportunity

elect to choose by vote; chosen, but not yet in office
election electioneer electioneering elective elector electoral electorate

electric of, worked by, or producing electricity
electrical electrically electrician

electricity power that gives heat and light and drives machines

electrify to equip for use with electric power
electrification electrified electrifies electrifying

electro- (*prefix*) electric
electrodynamics electromagnet electromagnetic electrometer electromotive electrostatic

electrocute to kill by electricity
electrocuting electrocution

electrode conductor through which electric current enters or leaves a device

electrolysis decomposition of a liquid by the passage of electricity; destruction of hair roots by electricity
electrolytic

electron very small particle with the smallest known negative electric charge
electronic electronically electronics

elegant graceful; tasteful
elegance elegantly

elegy mournful song or poem
elegies elegiac or *elegiacal*

element part that makes up a whole; basic chemical substance
elemental elementally

elementary of the first or basic principles
elementarily elementariness

elephant large mammal with trunk and long tusks
elephantiasis elephantine

elevate to move higher; to raise in status
elevating elevation elevator

eleven number 11
eleven-plus elevenses eleventh

elf mischievous fairy
elves elfin elfish or *elvish*

elicit to draw out a response

elicitable elicitation elicitor
SEE PANEL

elicit or illicit?
To *elicit* means 'to evoke or draw out': *to elicit a response; have difficulty eliciting information from the suspect.*
Illicit is an adjective meaning 'not allowed': *the use of illicit drugs; engage in an illicit relationship.*

elide to omit a vowel or syllable in pronunciation
eliding elision

eligible qualified or suitable for
eligibility or *eligibleness eligibly*

eliminate to remove or reject completely
eliminating elimination

élite small superior group
élitism élitist

elixir magic substance; cure-all

Elizabethan of or characteristic of the reign of Queen Elizabeth I

elk kind of large deer

ellipse closed plane curve; oval
ellipses ellipsoid ellipsoidal elliptic elliptical elliptically ellipticity

ellipsis omission of 1 or more words needed to complete a meaning
ellipses elliptical

elm kind of tall deciduous tree

elocution art of clear public speaking
elocutionary elocutionist

elongate to make or become longer
elongating elongation

elope to run away secretly with a lover in order to be married
elopement eloper eloping

eloquence fluent, expressive, and persuasive speech
eloquent eloquently

El Salvador country in Central America
Salvadorean

Elsan (*trademark*) kind of portable chemical toilet

else besides; apart from; otherwise
elsewhere

elucidate to make clear
elucidating elucidation elucidative elucidator elucidatory

elude to escape (from)
eluding elusion elusive elusively elusiveness

elver young eel

Elysium paradise; home of the blessed
Elysian

emaciate to make or become abnormally thin
emaciating emaciation

email electronic mail

emanate to issue or arise from
emanating emanation

emancipate to set free
emancipating emancipation emancipationist emancipator

emasculate to deprive of masculinity or strength
emasculating emasculation emasculator emasculatory

embalm to treat a dead body with preservatives
embalmer embalmment

embankment bank of earth or stone to restrain water or to carry a road or railway

embargo temporary ban on trade; to impose an embargo on
embargoes embargoed embargoing

embark to go on board; to begin
embarkation

embarrass to make self-conscious or awkward
embarrasses embarrassing embarrassment

embassy residence or mission of an ambassador
embassies

embattled prepared for battle

embed or **imbed** to place or fix firmly in
embedded or *imbedded* *embedding* or *imbedding*

embellish to make beautiful; to improve by adding details
embellisher *embellishes* *embellishment*

ember piece of glowing or smouldering coal or wood

embezzle to use fraudulently money that has been entrusted to one
embezzlement *embezzler* *embezzling*

embitter to make bitter
embittered *embitterment*

emblazon to decorate with a coat of arms; to make bright
emblazonment

emblem symbol or representation
emblematic *emblematical* *emblematically*

embody to incorporate; to give definite form to
embodied *embodier* *embodies* *embodiment* *embodying*

embolden to make bold

embolism obstruction of a blood-vessel by a particle or blood clot

embolus particle likely to cause an embolism
emboli

emboss to decorate with a raised design
embosser *embosses* *embossment*

embouchure shaping of the mouth and lips for playing a musical instrument

embrace to clasp in one's arms; to use
embraceable *embracer* *embracing*

embrasure door or window that widens inwards

embrocate to apply liquid to the skin to relieve pain
embrocating *embrocation*

embroider to decorate with needlework; to elaborate on
embroidery *embroideries*

embroil to involve in a conflict or confusion
embroiled *embroiling*

embryo animal in its earliest stage of development, before birth; something undeveloped
embryos *embryologist* *embryology* *embryonic*

emend to correct
emendable *emendation* *emendatory*
SEE PANEL at **amend**

emerald transparent green precious stone

emerge to come out; to come into view
emergence *emergent* *emerging*

emergency serious unexpected event demanding immediate action
emergencies

emeritus honourably retired

emery hard mineral used for polishing and grinding

emetic (drug or agent) causing vomiting

emigrate to leave one's country and settle in another
emigrant *emigrating* *emigration* *emigratory*

émigré (*fem.* **émigrée**) person leaving his or her native country for political reasons

eminent famous; notable, superior
eminence *eminency* *eminently*
SEE PANEL

---

eminent or imminent?

Someone who is *eminent* is famous because of their superior talents in their profession: *an eminent physician.*

Something is *imminent* if it is likely to occur soon: *The attack seemed imminent.*

---

emir ruler of any of several Muslim states
emirate

emissary person sent on a mission; representative
emissaries

emit to send out; to utter
emission emissive emitted emitting

Emmental kind of hard Swiss cheese that has holes in it

emollient softening or soothing (substance)

emolument fee or salary

emotion strong feeling of joy, sorrow, etc.

emotional of the emotions
emotionally
SEE PANEL

---

emotional or emotive?
Emotional means 'of the emotions': *his emotional needs; a purely emotional response; provide emotional support*. Someone who is *emotional* shows their feelings openly.

An *emotive* issue is one that arouses strong feelings, rather than reasoned opinions: *Euthanasia is one of the current emotive issues.*

---

emotive arousing strong feeling not reason
SEE PANEL at **emotional**

empanel or **impanel** to enter on a list; to enrol
empanelled or *impanelled* (US *empaneled* or *impaneled*) *empanelling* or *impanelling* (US *empaneling* or *impaneling*) *empanelment* or *impanelment*

empassioned see **impassioned**

empathy ability to understand and imaginatively enter into another person's feelings
empathic empathically empathize or *empathise*

emperor supreme ruler of an empire

emphasis special importance; stress
emphases

emphasize or **emphasise** to put emphasis on
emphasizing or *emphasising*

emphatic forceful; direct; with emphasis
emphatically

empire group of countries ruled by one supreme authority
empire-builder

empirical based on experiment
empirically empiricism empiricist

emplacement prepared position for guns; position

emplane or **enplane** to board or put on board an aeroplane
emplaning or *enplaning*

employ to provide with a paid job; (*formal*) to use
employable employment

employee person employed

employer person or firm that employs people

emporium large shop or market
emporiums or *emporia*

empower to give power or authority to

empress wife or widow of an emperor; female ruler of an empire
empresses

empty containing nothing; to make or become empty; something that is empty
empties emptied emptier emptiness empty-handed empty-headed emptying

empyrean highest heaven
empyreanal

emu large Australian flightless bird

emulate to imitate closely, esp. in order to equal or surpass
emulating emulation emulator emulous emulously emulousness

emulsify to convert into an emulsion
emulsification emulsified emulsifier emulsifies emulsifying

emulsion substance such as paint in which one liquid is dispersed in particles through another liquid

enable to make possible or practical
enabling

enact to perform; to make into a law
enactment enactor

enamel (to cover or decorate with an) opaque glassy coating
enamelled (US *enameled*) *enameller* (US *enameler*) *enamelling* (US *enameling*) *enamelware*

enamour (US **enamor**) to inspire with love
enamoured (US *enamored*)

en bloc (*French*) as a whole

encage or **incage** to put in a cage

encamp to set up a camp
encampment

encapsulate or **incapsulate** to enclose in a capsule; to express briefly and concisely
encapsulating or *incapsulating*
encapsulation or *incapsulation*

encase or **incase** to enclose in a case
encasement or *incasement* *encasing* or *incasing*

encash to exchange a cheque for cash
encashment

encaustic (process of) burning in colours

enceinte pregnant

encephalitis inflammation of the brain
encephalitic

encephalography X-ray of the brain ventricles

enchain to bind or hold fast

enchant to charm or bewitch
enchanter enchantingly enchantment enchantress

encircle to enclose in a circle; to surround
encirclement encircling

enclave small territory completely surrounded by a foreign territory

enclose to shut in; to surround; to insert
enclosing enclosure

encode to put into code
encoder encoding

encomium formal expression of praise
encomiums or *encomia*

encompass to surround
encompasses

encore (audience's call for an) additional performance
encoring

encounter to come upon; to meet

encourage to inspire with courage and confidence
encouragement encourager encouraging

encroach to intrude upon someone's rights; to go beyond certain limits
encroaches encroachment

encrust or **incrust** to cover with a crust
encrustation or *incrustation*

encumber or **incumber** to hinder the action or progress of
encumbrance or *incumbrance*

encyclical letter sent by the pope to all Roman Catholic bishops

encyclopedia or **encyclopaedia** book containing information on a wide range of subjects
encyclopedic or *encyclopaedic*
encyclopedist or *encyclopaedist*

end (to bring or come to the) final or extreme limit or point
ending endless endlessly endmost endpaper end-product endways

endanger to put in danger
endangerment

endear to cause to be loved
endearingly endearment

endeavour (US **endeavor**) to try

endemic native to a particular area

endive plant like a lettuce, with bitter leaves

endocrine secreting into the blood
endocrinal endocrinic endocrinology

endogenous produced within

endorse or **indorse** to approve; to

support; to sign on the back of; to record a driving conviction
endorsable or *indorsable* *endorsee* or *indorsee* *endorsement* or *indorsement* *endorser* or *indorser* *endorsing* or *indorsing*

endoscope (*medical*) long thin flexible instrument used for viewing internal parts of the body

endow to give money or property to so as to provide a source of permanent income
endower *endowment*

endue or **indue** to invest or provide
enduing or *induing*

endure to bear suffering or hardship; to tolerate; to last
endurable *endurance* *enduring*

enema (liquid for) injection into the rectum
enemas

enemy person or group that is hostile to another
enemies

energize or **energise** to give energy to
energizing or *energising*

energy power for activity or work
energies *energetic* *energetically*

enervate to weaken
enervating

enfant terrible (*French*) person given to making indiscreet remarks
enfants *terribles*

enfeeble to make weak
enfeeblement *enfeebler* *enfeebling*

enfold or **infold** to cover, enclose, or embrace

enforce to compel observance of
enforceable *enforcement* *enforcer* *enforcing*

enfranchise to grant the right to vote to
enfranchisement *enfranchising*

engage to gain the service of; to hold the attention of
engagement *engaging*

engagé (*fem.* **engagée**) (*French*) morally committed

engaged pledged to be married

engender to be the cause of

engine machine that converts energy into work or power
engine-room

engineer person skilled in the design, construction, and use of machines and structures
engineering

England largest division of Great Britain
English *Englishman* *Englishwoman*

engorge to congest with blood
engorging

engraft or **ingraft** to graft on to a stock; to implant

engrave to cut a design on to a hard surface
engraver *engraving*

engross to occupy fully the attention of; to prepare the final text of a legal document
engrosses *engrossment*

engulf or **ingulf** to swallow up

enhance to heighten an attractive quality of
enhancement *enhancing*

enigma person or thing that is mysterious or puzzling
enigmas *enigmatic* *enigmatically*

enjoin to order

enjoy to receive pleasure from
enjoyable *enjoyableness* *enjoyably* *enjoyment*

enkindle to arouse; to set on fire
enkindling

enlace to bind with laces; to intertwine
enlacement *enlacing*

enlarge to make or become larger
enlargement *enlarger* *enlarging*

enlighten to give information to
enlightenment

enlist to take into or enter the armed forces; to secure someone's help
enlistment

enliven to make active or lively
enlivenment

en masse (*French*) in a group

enmesh to surround (as if) in a net
enmeshes enmeshment

enmity feeling of hostility
enmities

ennoble to make noble or honourable
ennoblement ennobling

ennui boredom; listlessness

enormity extreme wickedness; (*informal*) something enormous
enormities

enormous unusually great in size, extent, or degree; vast
enormously enormousness

enough sufficient

en passant (*French*) in passing; by the way

enplane see **emplane**

enquire to ask
enquirer enquiring enquiry enquiries

enrage to make very angry
enraging

enrapture to fill with delight
enrapturing

enrich to make richer
enriches enrichment

enrol (US **enroll**) to record on a list; to become or cause to become a member
enrolled enroller enrolling enrolment (US *enrollment*)

en route (*French*) on the way

ensconce to establish firmly or comfortably
ensconcing

ensemble group of musicians performing together; complete outfit; whole

enshrine or **inshrine** to place in a shrine; to cherish or teasure
enshrining or *inshrining*

enshroud to cover (as if) with a shroud

ensign flag, sign, or banner

ensilage storing of green fodder

enslave to make a slave of
enslavement enslaver enslaving

ensnare or **insnare** to catch in a trap
ensnarement or *insnarement ensnaring* or *insnaring*

ensue to happen afterwards or as a consequence
ensuing

en suite (*French*) forming a unit

ensure (US **insure**) to make certain or sure
ensuring (US *insuring*)
SEE PANEL at **assure**

entablature part of classical temple above the columns

entail to have as a necessary consequence

entangle to catch or involve (as if) in a tangle
entanglement entangling

entente (*French*) friendly relationship between countries

enter to go or come into

enteritis inflammation of the intestines

enterprise project or undertaking; initiative
enterprising enterprisingly

entertain to hold the attention of; to show hospitality to
entertainer entertainment

enthral (US **enthrall**) to hold the complete attention of
enthralled enthralling enthralment (US *enthrallment*)

enthrone to place on a throne
enthronement enthroning

enthusiasm great liking and interest
enthusiast enthusiastic enthusiastically

enthuse to (cause to) show great enthusiasm
enthusing

entice to tempt or attract
enticeable enticement enticer enticing

entire complete; total
entirely entireness entirety

entitle to give the right to
entitlement entitling

entity something that has a separate existence
entities

entomb to put (as if) in a tomb
entombment

entomology study of insects
entomological entomologist

entourage group of attendants of an important person

entrails intestines

entrain to board or put aboard a train

entrance[1] act of entering; way in

entrance[2] to fill with intense delight; to enchant
entrancing

entrant person who enters

entrap to trap
entrapped entrapping

entreat to beseech
entreaty entreaties

entrechat dancing leap

entrecôte (*French*) steak cut from a boned sirloin

entrée (*French*) dish served before main courses
entrées

entremets (*French*) side dishes

entrench to dig; to construct a strong position; to establish firmly
entrenches entrenchment

entrepôt market or warehouse

entrepreneur controller of a business enterprise
entrepreneurial entrepreneurship

entresol storey between ground floor and first floor

entropy measure of disorder in a thermodynamic system

entrust or **intrust** to put into the care and protection of

entry entrance
entries

Entryphone (*trademark*) intercom telephone at the entrance of a building

entwine or **intwine** to twine around or together
entwining or *intwining*

E-number code number showing food additives

enumerate to count; to list by one
enumerating enumeration enumerator

enunciate to pronounce clearly and distinctly
enunciating enunciation enunciator

ensure see **insure**

envelop to wrap or cover; to obscure or hide
envelopment

envelope folded paper covering for a letter

envenom to put poison into; to make bitter

enviable arousing envy
enviably
SEE PANEL

---

enviable or envious?
Enviable means 'arousing envy': a particular advantage or quality is *enviable* when someone else has it and you wish that you had it also: *be*

in the enviable position of being able to turn down work.

Envious means 'showing or feeling envy': *be envious of her twin sister's successes.*

envious showing or feeling envy
enviously
SEE PANEL at **enviable**

environment surroundings; circumstances or external conditions
environmental environmentalist environmentally

environs surrounding areas of a city or town

envisage to visualize; to foresee
envisaging

envoi final stanza of a poem; postscript

envoy messenger, representative, or agent
envoys

envy (to have a) feeling of grudging discontent at the possessions or qualities of another
envied envies envying

enzyme organic substance produced by living cells

eon see **aeon**

epaulette or **epaulet** decorative material on the shoulder of a military uniform

épée sword used in fencing
épées

ephemera transient or short-lived things
ephemeral

epic long narrative poem describing legendary or heroic deeds

epicentre (US **epicenter**) place on the earth's surface at the point of origin of an earthquake

epicure person with discriminating tastes in food and drink
epicurean epicureanism

epidemic (disease) spreading rapidly through a community

epidermis protective outer layer of skin
epidermal epidermic

epidiascope kind of optical device that projects magnified images on to a screen

epidural (injection of anaesthetic) outside the dura mater

epiglottis flap of tissue that covers the larynx entrance during swallowing

epigram short witty comment
epigrammatic

epigraph quotation at the beginning of a book, etc.

epilepsy nervous disorder
epileptic

epilogue short final part of a play, etc.

Epiphany Christian festival commemorating the appearing of Christ to the wise men

episcopal of bishops
episcopacy episcopalian episcopate

episode complete event or incident, esp. one that is part of a series
episodic

epistemology study of knowledge
epistemological epistemologist

epistle (*formal*) letter
epistolary

epitaph commemorative words on a monument

epithet descriptive word or phrase

epitome typical example; embodiment

epitomize or **epitomise** to be an epitome of
epitomizing or *epitomising*

epoch period of time
epochal epoch-making

eponym word derived from the name of a person
eponymous

epoxy tough, resistant, flexible resin

epsilon 5th letter of the Greek alphabet

equable not varying; free from extremes
equability equably
SEE PANEL

equable or equitable?
Equable means 'not varying; free from extremes': *an equable climate; Her equable temperament means that she always stays calm.*
Equitable means 'fair; just': *Is democracy an equitable means of government?; distribute money in an equitable manner.*

equal (to have the) same amount, quality, value, etc.
equality equalled (US *equaled*) *equalling* (US *equaling*) *equally*

equalize or **equalise** to make equal
equalization or *equalisation equalizer* or *equaliser equalizing* or *equalising*

equanimity calmness of mind or temper

equate to regard as equal or similar
equating

equation mathematical statement that 2 expressions are equal

equator imaginary line round the earth through points that are equidistant from the North and South Poles
equatorial

equerry officer of the British royal household
equerries

equestrian of horse-riding; horse-rider

equidistant equally distant

equilateral (geometric figure having) all sides equal

equilibrium state of balance
equilibriums or *equilibria*

equine of horses

equinox either of the 2 times each year when the sun crosses the equator and day and night are equal
equinoxes equinoctial

equip to provide with what is necessary
equipment equipped equipping

equipage horse-drawn carriage and attendants

equipoise equilibrium; counterbalance

equitable fair; just
equitably
SEE PANEL at **equable**

equitation horsemanship

equities shares that do not bear fixed interest

equity fairness

equivalent equal in value or significance
equivalence

equivocal capable of receiving 2 or more interpretations; vague or doubtful
equivocally equivocalness

equivocate to use equivocal language
equivocating equivocation equivocator

era period in history

eradicate to put an end to
eradicable eradicating eradication

erase to rub out
erasable eraser erasing erasure

erect upright; to construct
erectile erection erector

eremite Christian hermit or recluse

erg unit of work or energy

ergo (*Latin*) therefore

ergonomics study of the relationship between workers and their environment
ergonomic ergonomically

Erie one of the Great Lakes, between USA and Canada

Erin old or poetic name for Ireland

Eritrea province in Ethiopia
Eritrean

ermine stoat and its white fur; this fur

Ernie (*Brit*) computer that randomly selects winning numbers of Premium Bonds

erode to wear away

eroding erosion erosive

erogenous sensitive to sexual stimulation

Eros Greek god of love

erotic of sexual desire
erotically eroticism

erotica erotic literature

err to make a mistake
errance errant

errand short journey to do something

erratic irregular or inconsistent
erratically

erratum error in writing or printing
errata

error mistake or inaccuracy
erroneous erroneously

ersatz artificial substitute

Erse Highland or Irish Gaelic language

erstwhile former; previous

eruct (*formal*) to belch
eructation

erudite learned
eruditely erudition

erupt (*of a volcano*) to shoot out lava, etc., suddenly
eruption eruptive

erysipelas acute infectious disease of the skin

escalate to make or become greater in size, extent, etc.
escalating escalation escalatory

escalator moving staircase

escalope thin slice of meat, esp. veal

escapade mischievous, daring act

escape to break free
escapable escapee escaper escaping escapism escapist escapologist escapology

escapement regulating mechanism in a clock

escarpment long steep slope

eschatology branch of theology dealing with the end of the world
eschatological eschatologist

escheat reversion of property to a government or feudal lord when there is no legal heir
escheator

eschew to avoid; to shun
eschewal eschewer

escort to accompany; person, etc. that escorts

escritoire writing-desk

escutcheon heraldic shield displaying a coat of arms

Esdras books in the Apocrypha

Eskimo or **Esquimau** member of a group of people living in North Canada, Greenland, etc.
Eskimos or *Esquimaux Eskimoan*

esophagus (US) see **oesophagus**

esoteric intended for a small group of initiated people

espalier ornamental trained fruit-tree

especial notable; exceptional
especially

Esperanto artificial universal language

espionage spying

esplanade level open way

espouse to support or adopt; (*archaic*) to marry
espousal espousing

espresso apparatus for making coffee
espressos

esprit wit; genius

espy to catch sight of
espied espies espying

Esquimau see **Eskimo**

essay written composition; (*formal*) to attempt
essays essayed essayist

essence basic intrinsic nature

essential necessary; basic
essentiality essentially

establish to set up; to settle
establisher establishes establishment

estate landed property

esteem to have a great respect for
estimable estimation

esthetic (US) see **aesthetic**

estimate (to make an) approximate calculation
estimable estimably estimating estimation estimator

Estonia republic in Eastern Europe, formerly in the Soviet Union
Estonian

estrange to lose the affection or friendship of; to alienate
estrangement estranging

estrogen (US) see **oestrogen**

estuary wide sea inlet at the mouth of a river
estuaries estuarial estuarine

et al. (*Latin*) and others

et cetera (*Latin*) and other things of the same kind

etch to make a picture, etc. on metal or glass by corrosive acid action
etcher etches etching

eternal lasting for ever
eternally eternity

ethane odourless colourless gas used as a fuel

ether colourless volatile flammable liquid used as a solvent; clear upper regions of the atmosphere

ethereal delicate; of (the) ether
etherealize or *etherealise*

ethics study of morality; moral principles
ethical ethically

Ethiopia country in East Africa
Ethiopian

ethnic of people grouped according to common features
ethnical ethnically

ethnography study of different human races and cultures
ethnographer ethnographic ethnographically

ethnology social anthropology, esp. dealing with preliterate cultures
ethnological ethnologically ethnologist

ethology study of animal behaviour

ethos distinctive character or attitudes of a people or culture

ethyl alcohol alcohol

etiolate to whiten a green plant through lack of sunlight
etiolating etiolation

etiology (US) see **aetiology**

etiquette conventionally accepted principles of social behaviour

étude short musical composition

etymology study of the origin and historical development of words
etymologies etymological etymologically etymologist

eucalyptus kind of evergreen tree grown for its gum, oil, and wood

Eucharist Holy Communion

Euclidean system of geometry

eugenics study dealing with the improvement of hereditary qualities, esp. by selective breeding
eugenic eugenicist

eulogize or **eulogise** to praise highly
eulogist eulogistic eulogizing or *eulogising*

eulogy formal speech or piece of writing that praises a person or thing

eunuch castrated man

euphemism mild expression used as a

substitute for something offensive or unpleasant
euphemistic euphemistically

euphonium brass musical instrument

euphony pleasant sound
euphonies euphonic euphonious

euphoria feeling of intense happiness
euphoric

euphuism artificial ornate Elizabethan prose style

Eurasia Europe and Asia
Eurasian

eureka exclamation to express triumph on discovering something

eurhythmics system of body training through movements in response to music

Euro European currency unit

Euro- (*prefix*) of Europe
Eurocrat Eurodollar

Europe continent of the world
European

euthanasia bringing about of the painless death of a person

evacuate to (cause to) withdraw; to make empty
evacuating evacuation evacuator evacuee

evade to avoid
evading evasion evasive evasively evasiveness

evaluate to determine the value, significance, etc. of
evaluating evaluation

evanescent fading away quickly
evanescence

evangelical of the Protestant group that emphasizes salvation by faith in the death of Christ
evangelicalism

evangelize or **evangelise** to preach the Christian gospel to
evangelism evangelist evangelistic evangelization or *evangelisation*

evaporate to turn into vapour; to expel water from
evaporable evaporating evaporation

eve evening or day before a day or event

even[1] flat; level; still
even-handed evenly evenness even-numbered even-tempered

even[2] (*archaic*) evening
evensong eventide

evening time of day from late afternoon to nightfall

Evensong daily Church of England evening service

event incident; happening; contest in a sports programme
eventful eventuality

eventual happening in the course of time
eventually

ever always; at any time
everlasting evermore

evergreen (*of some trees and shrubs*) having leaves that remain green throughout the year; evergreen tree or shrub

every each one; all
everybody everyday everyone everything everywhere

evict to remove a tenant from a house
eviction

evidence something that gives ground for belief or disbelief; sign or indication

evident obvious; clear
evidently

evil (something) bad or wicked
evildoer evilly evil-minded

evince (*formal*) to show clearly
evincible evincibly evincing

eviscerate to remove the internal organs of
eviscerating evisceration

evoke to bring a memory, etc. to the mind

evocation evocative evoking

evolve to develop gradually
evolution evolutionary evolutionist evolving

ewe female sheep

ewer large wide-mouth jug

ex without; former husband, wife, boyfriend, or girlfriend

ex- (*prefix*) former
ex-president ex-wife

exacerbate to make worse
exacerbating exacerbation

exact correct; precise; to demand or require money
exaction exactitude exactly

exaggerate to represent as greater, more important, more successful, etc. than is true
exaggerating exaggeration

exalt to raise in rank; to praise highly
exaltation

exam (*informal*) short for **examination**

examine to put questions to in order to test knowledge or skill; to look at closely
examinable examination examinee examiner examining

example something that is typical of its group or worthy of imitation

exasperate to annoy greatly
exasperating exasperation

Excalibur King Arthur's sword

ex cathedra (*Latin*) with authority

excavate to dig out a hole; to reveal by digging
excavating excavation excavator

exceed to be greater than; to go beyond
exceedingly
SEE PANEL at **accede**

excel to be better than others at doing something
excelled excelling

Excellency title of ambassador or governor
Excellencies

excellent extremely good
excellence excellently

except not including; apart from; to exclude
excepting exception

exceptionable objectionable
SEE PANEL

---

exceptionable or exceptional?
Exceptionable means 'objectionable', that is something to which exception might be taken: *What I find quite exceptionable is the manner of his personal attack on my character.*

Exceptional, which is far more common than *exceptionable*, means 'unusual; extremely good': *The committee will only consider late applications under exceptional circumstances; Well done; this is an exceptional essay!*

---

exceptional unusual; extremely good
exceptionally
SEE PANEL at **exceptionable**

excerpt extract from a book, speech, etc.

excess amount that is more than a certain, esp. normal or permitted, limit
excessive excessively

exchange to give or transfer in return for an equivalent
exchangeable exchanging

exchequer government department in charge of a country's revenue

excise[1] duty or tax on certain goods or services
excisable exciseman

excise[2] to remove (as if) by cutting
excising excision

excite to arouse the feelings of
excitability excitable excitation excitedly excitement exciting

exclaim to cry out suddenly and with strong feeling
exclamation exclamatory

exclude to reject; to shut out from
excluding exclusion

exclusive having the right to exclude; restricted; very fashionable; not including

excommunicate to exclude from membership of or participation in a group, esp. a church
excommunicating excommunication

excrement waste matter discharged from the body
excremental

excrescence abnormal outgrowth of tissue
excrescent

excrete to discharge waste matter from the body
excreta excretal excreting excretion excretive excretory

excruciating unbearably painful
excruciatingly

exculpate to free from blame or guilt
exculpating exculpation exculpatory

excursion short trip or outing
excursionist excursive

excuse to pardon; to free from blame; reason given for excusing a fault
excusable excusing

ex-directory intentionally not listed in a telephone directory

exeat temporary leave of absence from a school or other institution

execrable abhorrent
execrably

execrate to abhor
execrating execration execrative execratory

execute to carry out fully; to put to death as a legal punishment
executable executant executing execution executioner

executive part of government that administers a country's laws; person with managerial or administrative power

executor (*fem.* **executrix**) person appointed to carry out provisions of a will
executorship

exegesis exposition of the meaning of a text
exegetic exegetics exegetically

exemplar model, example, or copy

exemplary worthy of imitating; serving as a warning
exemplarily

exemplify to show by example; to be an example of
exemplification exemplified exemplifies exemplifying

exempt (to) free from an obligation or requirement
exemptible exemption

exequies ceremonies at a funeral

exercise set of questions designed to develop a skill; activity for training the body or mind; to make use of; to train
exercising

exert to apply (oneself); to bring to bear
exertion

exeunt (*Latin*) stage direction for everyone to leave the stage

ex gratia (*Latin*) voluntary

exhale to breathe out
exhalable exhalant exhalation exhaling

exhaust to tire out; to use up completely; waste gas or vapour ejected from an engine
exhaustible exhaustion

exhaustive thorough; detailed
exhaustively

exhibit to display to the public
exhibition exhibitioner exhibitor

exhibitionism desire to attract attention to oneself
exhibitionist

exhilarate to make lively
exhilarating exhilaration

exhort to urge strongly
exhortation exhortatory

exhume to dig up a corpse
exhumation exhuming

exigency urgency; emergency
exigencies exigent

exiguous scanty; small
exiguity

exile long enforced absence from one's country, etc.; to banish in this way; exiled person
exilic exiling

exist to be; to live
existence existent

existentialism philosophical movement
existential existentialist

exit way out; (*Latin*) stage direction for actor to leave the stage

ex libris (*Latin*) from the collection or library of

exocrine secreted through a duct

exodus departure of many people

ex officio (*Latin*) by virtue of one's official position

exonerate to free from blame
exonerating exoneration exonerative

exorbitant excessive
exorbitance exorbitantly

exorcize or **exorcise** to drive out evil spirits from a person or place; to drive out by prayer
exorcizer or *exorciser exorcizing* or *exorcising exorcism exorcist*

exordium introductory part of a discourse
exordiums or *exordia*

exotic not native; very unusual
exotica exotically

expand to make or become larger
expansibility expansible expansion expansionism expansionist expansive

expanse wide area over which something is spread out

expatiate to speak or write about at length
expatiating expatiation

expatriate person living abroad; to withdraw (oneself) to a foreign country
expatriating

expect to consider probable; to look forward to
expectancy expectation

expectant marked by expectation; pregnant
expectantly

expectorate (*formal*) to eject phlegm, etc. from the throat or lungs; to spit
expectorating expectoration

expedient useful; appropriate
expedience expediency

expedite to speed the progress of
expediting expeditious

expedition journey undertaken for a purpose such as exploration or war
expeditionary

expel to eject or drive out
expellable expelled expelling expulsion

expend to spend or use up
expendable expenditure

expense spending of money

expensive costing or charging a lot of money
expensively expensiveness

experience awareness or knowledge of something; to feel; skills and abilities learned
experienced experiencing

experiential based on experience
experientially

experiment (to conduct an) investigation; to test a hypothesis; trial arrangement
experimental experimentally experimentation experimenter

expert (someone) with great skill or knowledge
expertise expertly

expiate to remove the guilt incurred by a sin; to make amends for
expiable expiating expiation expiator expiatory

expire to breathe out air; to come to an end
expiration expiring expiry

explain to make plain or clear; to show the meaning of; to give reasons for
explanation explanatory explicable

expletive strong exclamation or oath

explicit clear; fully stated
explicitly

explode to burst noisily with force
exploding explosion explosive explosively

exploit to take unfair advantage of; notable deed
exploitation

explore to trail through unfamiliar areas for geographical discovery; to investigate
exploration explorative exploratory explorer exploring

exponent person or thing that explains or interprets
exponential exponentially

export to send goods or services to a foreign country; something exported
exportable exportation exporter

expose to uncover or reveal
exposing exposure

exposé exposure of scandal, etc.

exposition detailed explanation
expositor expository

expostulate to reason with, esp. in order to dissuade
expostulating expostulation expostulatory

expound to explain in detail

express to make known; to show; definitely stated; of or designed for quick travel or delivery
expressible expression expressionless expressive expressly

expressionism artistic and literary movement
expressionist

expressway (US) motorway

expropriate to dispossess
expropriating expropriation

expulsion act of expelling

expunge to delete; to blot out
expunging

expurgate to remove objectionable parts from a book, etc.
expurgating expurgation expurgator

exquisite delicately beautiful; keenly discriminating
exquisitely

ex-serviceman man who has formerly served in the armed forces

extant still in existence

extempore with little or no preparation
extemporaneous extemporarily extemporary extemporize or *extemporise*

extend to reach; to stretch out
extended extensible extensile extension extensive extensor

extent range, area, or length

extenuate to represent as being less serious
extenuating extenuation

exterior outer (surface or part)

exterminate to destroy completely
exterminating extermination exterminator

external of or for the outside; outward; of the foreign affairs of a country
externally

externalize or **externalise** to make external; to attribute to causes outside oneself
externalization or *externalisation externalizing* or *externalising*

exterritorial see **extraterritorial**

extinct no longer existing; (*of a volcano*) not liable to erupt
extinction

extinguish to put out a fire
extinguishable extinguisher

extirpate to destroy completely; to uproot
extirpating extirpation extirpator

extol (US **extoll**) to praise highly
extolled extoller extolling

extort to obtain by force or threats
extortion extortionate extortioner

extra additional

extra- (*prefix*) outside; beyond
extra-large extraterrestrial

extract to pull out; to remove
extraction extractor

extracurricular outside the regular course of studies

extradite to release for trial to another country
extraditing extradition

extramarital (*of sexual relations*) occurring outside marriage

extramural outside the normal course of a college, etc.

extraneous coming from the outside; not essential
extraneously

extraordinary unusual; remarkable
extraordinarily extraordinariness

extrapolate to estimate a future trend, etc. by using known data
extrapolating extrapolation

extrasensory (*of perception*) beyond the normal physical senses

extraterritorial or **exterritorial** not under the jurisdiction of the state in which one is resident

extravagant excessive; wasteful
extravagance extravagantly

extravaganza lavish spectacular show

extreme in a very high degree
extremely extremist extremity extremities

extricate to remove or free from
extricable extricating extrication

extrinsic not forming part of
extrinsicality extrinsically

extrovert person whose attention is directed towards interests outside himself or herself
extroversion extroverted

extrude to squeeze or force out
extruding extrusion

exuberant very lively
exuberance exuberantly

exude to ooze out
exudation exuding

exult to rejoice
exultant exultation exultingly

eye organ of sight; to watch closely
eyeball eyebath eyebrow eye-catching eyeful eyeglass eyehole eyeing or *eying eyelash eyeless eyelet eyelid eyelike eyeliner eye-opener eyepiece eyeshot eyesight eyesore eyespot eyestrain eyetooth eyewash eyewitness*

eyrie or **aerie** nest of an eagle

F

fa see **fah**

fable short moral story esp. about animals
fabled fabler

fabric cloth; structure

fabricate to make
fabricating fabrication fabricator

fabulous extraordinary; (*informal*) marvellous
fabulously

façade front of a building

face front of head; to be situated in the direction of
face-cloth faceless face-lift face-saving facial facing

facet any of many surfaces of a cut gem; aspect
faceted

facetiae humorous anecdotes

facetious joking; flippant
facetiously facetiousness

facia see **fascia**

facial of the face

facile easily done

facilitate to make easier
facilitating facilitation

facility ease; something facilitating an action
facilities

facsimile (to make an) exact copy
facsimileing

fact something known to have happened
fact-finding

faction splinter group
factional

factious trouble-making

factitious artificial; sham

factor (*maths*) one of the numbers that when multiplied together make a product; element or condition; agent
factorial factorize or *factorise*

factory place where goods are manufactured
factories

factotum servant employed to do all kinds of work
factotums

factual based on facts
factuality

faculty ability or power of the mind or body; university or college department
faculties

fad craze
faddish faddism faddist faddy

fade to (cause to) lose colour, freshness, or clarity
fade-in fadeless fade-out fading

faeces (US **feces**) waste discharged through the anus
faecal (US *fecal*)

faerie or **faery** (*archaic* or *poetic*) fairyland

Faeroes or **Faroes** Danish Islands in the North Atlantic
Faeroese or *Faroese*

fag (to do) boring work; (*Brit*) junior boy at some public schools; (*slang*) cigarette
fag-end fagged fagging

faggot[1] (*chiefly* US **fagot**) bundle of sticks; seasoned ball of minced meat

faggot[2] (*slang*) homosexual

fah or **fa** (*music*) 4th note in a major scale

Fahrenheit temperature scale

fail to (declare to) be unsuccessful; to break down; to disappoint
failing fail-safe failure

fain (*archaic*) rather; gladly

faint weak; to lose consciousness
faint-hearted faintly faintness

fair[1] light in colour; just; fine or beautiful
fair-haired fairish fair-minded fair-weather

fair[2] market; collection of entertainments; trade exhibition
fairground

fairly in a fair way; quite

fairway channel for ships; mown open part of golf-course

fairy small imaginary being
fairies fairyland fairy-tale

fait accompli (*French*) something done that cannot be reversed
faits accomplis

faith trust; belief
faithful faithfully faithfulness faith-healing faithless faithlessly faithlessness

fake (to make a) false copy
faker faking

fakir Muslim or Hindu holy man

falcon kind or bird of prey
falconer falconry

falderal see **folderol**

Falkland Islands group of islands in the South Atlantic

fall to drop down
fallen fallout fell

fallacy incorrect opinion or notion
fallacies fallacious fallaciously

fallible capable of being mistaken
fallibility fallibly

Fallopian tube either of the 2 tubes through which ova pass from the ovaries to the uterus

fallow[1] (*of land*) left unseeded after being ploughed

fallow[2] kind of small deer

false incorrect; untrue
falsehood falsely

falsetto artificially high-pitched voice
falsettos

falsify to make false
falsification falsified falsifies falsifying

falsity state of being false
falsities

falter to waver; to move unsteadily
falterer falteringly

fame reputation; renown

familiar well-known; acquainted (with)
familiarity familiarities familiarly

familiarize or **familiarise** to make familiar
familiarization or *familiarisation*
familiarizing or *familiarising*

family parents and their children; group of similar or closely related things
families

famine severe shortage of food

famished extremely hungry

famous very well-known
famously

fan[1] (device) to create a current of air
fanbelt fanlight fan-like fanned fanning fantail

fan[2] enthusiastic supporter
fanmail

fanatic too enthusiastic
fanatical fanatically fanaticism

fancy to imagine; to have a liking for; playful imagination; elaborate
fancies fancied fancier fanciest fanciful fancifully fancy-free fancying

fandango lively Spanish dance
fandangoes or *fandangos*

fanfare loud sounding of trumpets

fang long pointed tooth

fantasia free musical composition
fantasias

fantasize or **fantasise** to imagine wild ideas, etc.
fantasizing or *fantasising*

fantasmagoria see **phantasmagoria**

fantastic great; strange
fantastically

fantasy or **phantasy** something imagined, esp. wild or extravagant
fantasies or *phantasies*

fanzine magazine for fans

far distant; to a considerable extent
far-away far-fetched far-flung far-off far-reaching far-seeing far-sighted

farce humorous play
farcical farcically

fare money charged for a journey; food and drink; to get on
faring

farewell goodbye

farina flour or fine meal; starch
farinaceous

farm area of land for growing crops or raising animals
farm-bred farmer farm-hand farmhouse farmland farmstead farmyard

Faroes see **Faeroes**

farouche shy; sullen

farrago hotchpotch
farragos or *farragoes*

farrier person who shoes horses
farriery

farrow (to give birth to a) litter of piglets

farther more
farthermost farthest

farthing (*Brit*) quarter of an old penny

fascia or **facia** dashboard
fasciae or *faciae*

fascicle division of a book

fascinate to hold the interest of
fascinating fascination

Fascism nationalist authoritarian movement opposed to democracy and liberalism
Fascist

fashion style, esp. of clothes; way of doing something; to form
fashioner

fashionable stylish
fashionably

fast[1] quick; firmly fixed
fast-flowing fast-moving

fast[2] to go without food

fastback (car with) sloping roof

fasten to tie or attach
fastener fastening

fastidious too particular; difficult to please

fat soft greasy substance, esp. in animal bodies; overweight
fathead fatheaded fatness fatted fatter fattest fattish

fatal resulting in death
fatality fatalities fatally
SEE PANEL

---

fatal or fateful?

Fatal means 'resulting in death or ruin': *a fatal accident; a fatal illness; make a fatal mistake.*

If an event, action, or decision is *fateful* it has an important, often bad, effect on future events: *that fateful day; a fateful decision; a fateful meeting.*

---

fatalism belief that events are predetermined by fate
fatalist fatalistic

fate power predetermining events; destiny

fateful momentous
fatefully fatefulness
SEE PANEL at **fatal**

father (to be a) male parent; priest or leader
fatherhood father-in-law fathers-in-law fatherland fatherless fatherliness fatherly

fathom measure of water, 6 feet deep; to understand
fathomable fathomless

fatigue tiredness; weakness in metals; to make or become tired
fatiguing

fatten to (cause to) grow fatter
fattened

fatty fat (person)
fatties fattier fattiest fattily fattiness

fatuous foolish
fatuity fatuities fatuously

fatwa religious ruling by a Muslim leader

faucet (US) tap

fault mistake; flaw; break in earth's crust
fault-finder fault-finding faultless faultlessly

faulty defective
faultily faultiness

faun mythical rural god

fauna animals of an area or time
faunas or *faunae*

faux pas (*French*) social blunder

favour (US **favor**) to like or support; helpful act
favourable (US *favorable*) *favourably* (US *favorably*) *favourite* (US *favorite*) *favouritism* (US *favoritism*)

fawn[1] young deer

fawn[2] to try to gain attention by flattery, etc.

fax equipment used to send a document electronically by telephone; copy sent in this way; to send a copy in this way
faxed faxes faxing

fay (*poetic*) fairy

faze (*informal*) to disconcert or fluster
fazed

fealty loyalty
fealties

fear feeling caused by danger, pain, or evil; to be afraid of
fearful fearfully fearfulness fearless fearlessly fearlessness fearsome

feasible capable of being carried out; practicable
feasibility feasibly

feast (to eat a) large sumptuous meal

feat remarkable act

feather flat light structure from a bird's skin
feather-bed feather-brained feather-like featherweight feathery

feature prominent part, esp. of the face; special article in a magazine
featureless featuring

febrile feverish
febrility

February 2nd month of the year

feces (US) see **faeces**

feckless feeble; weak
fecklessly fecklessness

fecund fertile
fecundate fecundity

federal having power divided between central and regional government
federalism federalist

federalize or **federalise** to join in a federal union
federalization or *federalisation federalizing* or *federalising*

federate to join a federation
federating federation

fee payment

feeble weak
feeble-minded feebleness feebler feeblest feebly

feed to give food to
fed feedable feeder

feedback return of part of output to input; response

feel to examine by touch; to experience
feeler feeling feelingly felt

feet pl. of **foot**

feign to pretend
feigningly

feint[1] (to make) mock attack

feint[2] (*of lines*) faint

feldspar or **felspar** a rock-forming mineral
feldspathic

felicitate to congratulate
felicitating felicitation felicitator

felicity happiness
felicitous

feline of or like a cat
felinely felinity

fell[1] past tense of **fall**

fell[2] to cut down

fell[3] animal skin
fellmonger

fell[4] moorland in Northern England

fellatio oral stimulation of the penis

felloe wheel rim

fellow man or boy; boyfriend; person or comrade
fellow-feeling fellowship fellow-traveller (US *fellow-traveler*)

felony serious crime
felonies felon felonious

felspar see **feldspar**

felt[1] past tense and past participle of **feel**

felt[2] fabric made from compressing wool, hair, etc.
felt-tip

female (of the) sex that conceives and bears offspring
femaleness

feminine of women or qualities thought to be womanly
femininity

feminism movement supporting equality of women's rights with men
feminist

feminize or **feminise** to give a feminine quality to
feminization or *feminisation feminizing* or *feminising*

femme fatale (*French*) dangerously attractive woman

femur thigh-bone
femurs or *femora femoral*

fen area of low marshy land
fenny

fence (to surround with a) barrier; to fight with a sword or foil
fenceless fencer fencible fencing

fend to ward (off); to provide (for)

fender fireguard; protecting device

fenestration arrangement of windows

fennel kind of yellow-flowered herb with aromatic seeds

fenugreek kind of leguminous plant

feoff see **fief**

feral wild; savage

fermata (*music*) pause
fermatas or *fermatae*

ferment to (cause to) undergo a chemical change with effervescence
fermentable fermentation fermentative
SEE PANEL

---

ferment or foment?
Ferment is used as a verb to refer to the chemical changes with effervescence that produce alcohol: *fermented sugar; fermenting wine. Ferment* is also used as a noun to refer to

a state of trouble and uproar: *a state of political ferment.*

Foment is a verb meaning 'to incite': *foment a rebellion*, or, in medical contexts, 'to apply warmth or hear to'.

fern plant with feather-like leaves
ferny

ferocious fierce
ferociously ferocity

ferret small animal like a weasel; to search (out)
ferreter ferreting ferretry

ferric of iron

ferrous of iron

ferruginous containing iron

ferrule metal ring or cap on tip of stick

ferry (boat) to transport across a river or channel
ferries ferried ferryboat ferrying ferryman

fertile capable of producing offspring, crops, etc.; productive
fertility

fertilize or **fertilise** to make fertile
fertilization or *fertilisation fertilizing* or *fertilising*

ferule cane or rod for punishment

fervent passionate; ardent
fervency fervently fervour (US *fervor*)

fervid passionate; spirited

festal to a feast or festival
festally

fester to (cause to) form pus; to irritate

festival celebration; series of special events
festive festivity festivities

festoon to decorate with flowers, ribbons, etc.

fetch to go for and bring or take back; to bring in a price
fetcher fetches

fête or **fete** (to honour with a) festival
fêting or *feting*

fetid or **foetid** ill-smelling

fetish object believed to have magical power
fetishism

fetlock projection behind and above horse's hoof

fetter (to) chain or shackle

fettle condition or state

fetus see **foetus**

feud long-lasting quarrel
feudist

feudal of the medieval European land-holding system
feudalism feudalist feudalistic feudality feudalize or *feudalise*

fever disease marked by high body temperature
feverish

feverfew kind of bushy European plant

few not many

fey clairvoyant; visionary

fez brimless felt hat
fezzes or *fezes*

fiancé (*fem.* **fiancée**) person engaged to be married
fiancés (fem. *fiancées*)

fiasco complete failure
fiascos or *fiascoes*

fiat official order or decree

fib (to tell a) trivial lie
fibbed fibber fibbing

fibre (US **fiber**) fine thread; fabric made from such thread
fibreboard (US *fiberboard*) *fibreglass* (US *fiberglass*) *fibrous*

fibril small fibre
fibrillar fibrillose

fibrin fibrous protein in blood-clotting

fibrositis inflammation of fibrous tissue

fibula outer of 2 bones in lower part of leg
fibulae or *fibulas*

fiche microfiche

fickle constantly changing in affections, purposes, etc.

fiction something invented; invented story
fictional fictionalize or *fictionalise*
fictitious fictitiously

fiddle (*informal*) (to play a) violin; to fidget; (*slang*) to cheat
fiddler fiddlesticks fiddling

fiddle-faddle nonsense

fiddly needing close attention to detail
fiddlier fiddliest

fidelity faithfulness; loyalty

fidget to move about in a restless way
fidgeted fidgetiness fidgeting fidgety

fiduciary help or given in trust

fie (*archaic*) exclamation of disgust or dismay

fief or **feoff** feudal land

field open land; area; to stop and return a ball
fielder field-glasses fieldmouse
fieldsman fieldwork

fiend evil spirit; extremely wicked person
fiendish fiendishly

fierce violently cruel; intense
fiercely fierceness fiercer fiercest

fiery burning; passionate
fierier fieriest fierily fieriness

fiesta festival or celebration

fife small high-pitched flute
fifer

fifteen number 15
fifteenth

fifth coming next after fourth
fifthly

fifty number 50
fifties fiftieth fifty-fifty

fig kind of (tree with) soft pear-shaped fruit

fight (to) struggle
fighter fought

figment something imagined

figuration representation

figurative not literal
figuratively

figure symbol of a number; to reckon or consider
figurehead figurer figuring

figurine small statue

Fiji islands in SW Pacific
Fijian

filagree see **filigree**

filament very fine thread

filbert hazel-nut

filch to steal something of small value
filcher

file[1] (to place in a) folder for holding papers; line of people filing

file[2] steel tool used for smoothing

filial of a son or daughter

filibuster to use delaying tactics in a law-making body
filibusterer

filigree or **filagree** ornamental metallic lace-work

Filipino native of the Philippines
Filipinos

fill to make or become full; all that is needed to fill
filler fill-in filling-station fill-up

fillet strip of boneless fish or meat; to remove bones from
filleted filleting

fillip (to provide a) stimulus
filliped filliping

filly young female horse
fillies

film flexible material used in photography; (to make a) sequence of photographs
filmic filmsetting filmstrip filmy

Filofax (*trademark*) portable loose-leaf diary, personal organizer, etc.

filter (to purify with or use a) strainer
filterable filter-paper filter-tipped

filth dirt
filthier filthiest filthily filthiness filthy

filtrate filtered liquid or gas
filtrating filtration

fin organ of a fish
finless finned finning

final coming last; conclusive
finalist finality finally

finale last part of a performance

finalize or **finalise** to make final; to settle
finalization or *finalisation finalizing* or *finalising*

finance management of money; to provide money for
financier financing

financial of finance
financially

finch kind of small bird
finches

find to discover; to obtain; (*law*) to declare
finder found

fine[1] of very good quality; clear; delicate
fine-cut fine-drawn finely fineness finer finest fine-tune

fine[2] (to punish by imposing a) penalty
finable fining

finery showy clothes, etc.

finesse skilfulness

finger one of the parts extending from the hand
finger-board fingerless finger-mark fingernail fingerprint fingertip

finicky or **finicking** too fussy

finis the end

finish (to bring or come to an) end
finishes finisher

finite limited
finitely finiteness finitude

Finland country in North Europe
Finn Finnish

fiord or **fjord** narrow inlet between high cliffs

fir evergreen tree with cones and needle-like leaves

fire heat and light given off in burning; to shoot
fire-alarm firearm fire-ball fire-bomb fire-box firebrand fire-break fire-brick firecracker firedamp fire-drill fire-eater fire-engine fire-escape fire-extinguisher fire-fighter firefly fire-guard fire-hydrant fire-irons firelight fire-lighter fireman fireplace fire-power fireproof firer fire-raising fireside fire-stone firetrap firewood firework firing firing-line firing-squad

firkin small cask

firm[1] solid; steady
firmer firmest firmly firmness

firm[2] business company

firmament heavens

first (coming) at the beginning
first-born first-foot first-fruit firsthand first-rate

firth narrow inlet of the sea

fiscal of government finance
fiscally

fish (to try to catch) cold-blooded animal living in water
fish or *fishes fishbone fishbowl fisher fisherman fishery fish-eye lens fish-hook fishing-rod fish-meal fishmonger fishnet fish-paste fish-slice fishwife fishy*

fish-plate iron plate used to hold rails together

fissile able to undergo fission

fission splitting, as of an atomic nucleus
fissionable

fissure (to) crack or split

fist hand with fingers tightly closed in palm
fistfight fistful

fisticuffs fighting with the fists

fistula abnormal opening of internal organ
fistulae or *fistulas*

fit[1] suitable; ready; healthy; to make suitable for
fitted fitter fittest fitting

fit[2] sudden attack or convulsion
fitful fitfully fitfulness

fitment piece of equipment

five number 5
fivepins fiver

fives ball game played in walled court

fix to make firm; to direct; to repair
fixable fixedly fixer fixes fixture

fixation preoccupation

fixative something that hardens or fixes

fizz to make a hissing bubbling sound
fizzes fizzier fizziest fizziness fizzy

fizzle to make a spluttering sound
fizzling

fjord see **fiord**

flab soft flabby fat

flabbergast to be overwhelmed with surprise

flabby not strong or firm
flabbier flabbiest flabbily flabbiness

flaccid not firm; soft and limp
flaccidity

flag[1] banner with special design
flag-boat flag-day flagship flagstaff flag-waving

flag[2] to lose strength
flagged flagging

flag[3] paving-stone
flagstone

flag[4] plant of the iris family

flagellate to whip or flog
flagellant flagellating flagellation flagellator

flageolet kind of small flute

flagon large bottle for cider or wine

flagrant outrageous
flagrancy flagrantly

flail (to strike with a) threshing implement

flair natural ability

flak anti-aircraft gunfire; heavy criticism

flake to come off in thin loose layers or pieces; such a piece or layer
flaking flaky

flambé served in flaming brandy, etc.

flamboyant too showy
flamboyance flamboyantly

flame bright tongue-shaped part of a fire; to burn with flames
flameproof flame-thrower flaming

flamenco type of dance
flamencos

flamingo large pink and red wading-bird
flamingos or *flamingoes*

flammable capable of being easily set on fire
flammability

flan open pastry or tart for a sweet or savoury filling

flange projecting rim on a wheel edge

flank fleshy side of an animal between ribs and hip; side of anything

flannel kind of soft light woollen cloth;

small cloth to wash face and hands; to cover with a flannel
flannelled (US *flanneled*) *flannelling* (US *flanneling*)

flannelette cotton imitation of flannel

flap to move up and down or from side to side; material used to cover an opening
flapped flapper flapping

flapjack chewy biscuit made with oats and syrup

flare (to burn with an) unsteady bright flame; to widen towards the lower edge
flare-up flaring

flash (to give out a) sudden short blaze of light
flashes flashback flashboard flashbulb flashcube flasher flashgun flashing flashlight flashpoint flashy

flask narrow-necked bottle; vacuum flask

flat[1] level and smooth; (*of a musical note*) lower by a semitone
flat-bottomed flat-chested flat-fish flat-foot flat-footed flat-iron flatlet flatly flatness flatter flattest flattish flatworm

flat[2] self-contained set of rooms on one floor
flatlet flatmate

flatten to make or become flat
flattened flattener flattening

flatter to praise too much, esp. in order to win favour
flatterer flattery

flatulent suffering from excess gas in the alimentary canal
flatulence flatulently

flaunt to display in a showy manner
SEE PANEL

---

flaunt or flout?
Flaunt means 'to display in a showy manner': *flaunt one's wealth/success.*
Flout means 'to show scorn for; to disobey deliberately': *to flout laws/regulations.*

---

flautist flute player

flavour (US **flavor**) taste perceived in the mouth; (to add a) substance used to give a special taste
flavourful (US *flavorful*) *flavouring* (US *flavoring*) *flavourless* (US *flavorless*) *flavoursome* (US *flavorsome*)

flaw imperfection or blemish
flawless

flax kind of plant with blue flowers, grown for its fibre
flaxen

flay to strip off the outer covering of

flea small wingless bloodsucking jumping insect
flea-bite flea-bitten flea-pit

fleck small mark of colour; particle; to mark with flecks

fledge to rear a young bird until it is ready to fly

fledging or **fledgeling** young bird that has grown feathers; young inexperienced person

flee to run away from
fled fleeing

fleece sheep's wool; (*informal*) to deprive of money fraudulently
fleecing fleecy

fleet[1] group of warships under one command

fleet[2] swift
fleet-footed fleeting

Flemish 1 of the 2 official languages of Belgium

flesh soft substance of the body, esp. muscular parts
fleshiness flesh-pot fleshy

fleshly worldly; carnal
fleshliness

fleur-de-lis heraldic lily
fleurs-de-lis

flew past tense of **fly**[1]

flex flexible insulated electric wire; to bend
flexes flexor

flexible able to be bent easily without breaking; adaptable
flexibility flexibly

flexitime (*Brit*) system allowing flexibility of working hours

flibbertigibbet frivolous person

flick (to touch with a) light quick sharp movement
flick-knife

flicker (to burn or shine with an) unsteady or irregular light

flier see **flyer**

flight[1] movement through the air; set of stairs
flight-deck flightless

flight[2] fleeing; running away

flighty frivolous; wandering
flightily flightiness

flimsy not strong or substantial; light and thin
flimsier flimsiest flimsily flimsiness

flinch to draw back suddenly, as from fear
flinches flinchingly

fling to throw with great force; vigorous, esp. Scottish, dance
flinger flung

flint hard rock that makes sparks when struck with steel
flintlock flintstone flinty

flip to toss something sharply so that it turns over
flip-flop flipped flipping flip-side

flippant not showing proper respect; frivolous
flippancy flippantly

flipper flat broad limb of seals, etc. used in swimming; flat paddle-like device worn on the foot to help swimming

flirt to act amorously without serious intentions; to toy (with)
flirtation flirtatious

flit to move quickly and lightly
flitted flitter flitting

flitch side of pork

float to (cause to) rest on the surface of a liquid; something such as a cork that is designed to float; low flat lorry; sum of money
floatable floatage floater

floatation see **flotation**

flocculent like wool; fluffy
flocculence

flock[1] (to gather in a) group of animals or birds

flock[2] wool or cotton fibre or waste

floe sheet of floating ice

flog to beat severely; (*informal*) to sell
flogged flogger flogging

flood overflowing of water; overwhelming quantity; to cover with a flood
floodgate

floodlight (light providing a) broad beam of light to illuminate a building, stage, etc.
floodlit

floor lower surface of a room; bottom of the sea; storey of a building
floorboard floorcloth flooring

flop to fall in an awkward manner; (*informal*) to fail utterly
flopped flopping floppy

flora plants of an area or period of time

floral of flowers

florescent flowering
florescence

floret any of the small flowers forming a flower-head

florid ornate; ruddy

florin former British coin, equivalent to 10p

florist person who sells or grows flowers

floss fine silk thread

flotation or **floatation** launching or financing of a company or enterprise

flotilla small fleet of ships; fleet of small ships

flotsam floating wreckage from a ship

flounce[1] to move in an exaggerated manner
flouncing

flounce[2] wide ornamental ruffle on a garment

flounder[1] to move with difficulty

flounder[2] kind of small flat-fish

flour powdered grain of wheat, etc. used in baking
floury

flourish to prosper or thrive; to brandish or wave; act of flourishing
flourishes flourisher

flout to show scorn for
SEE PANEL at **flaunt**

flow to move freely and smoothly; steady movement

flower part of plant that produces seeds; (to) blossom
flower-bed flower-head flowerpot flowery

flown past tense of **fly**[1]

flu (*informal*) influenza

fluctuate to vary constantly and irregularly
fluctuating fluctuation

flue outlet in a chimney for smoke, gas, etc.

fluent able to speak a particular foreign language easily
fluency fluently

fluff soft light substance; to make or become fluffy
fluffy

fluid (liquid or gas) that can flow
fluidity

fluke accidental stroke of luck
fluky

flummery empty flattery; kind of cold sweet pudding

flummox to perplex or bewilder
flummoxed flummoxes flummoxing

flung past tense and past participle of **fling**

flunk (*informal*) to fail in an examination

fluorescence emission of light
fluorescent

fluoride compound of fluorine, used to combat tooth decay
fluoridate fluoridating fluoridation

fluorine chemical element; yellow toxic gas
fluorinate fluorinating fluorination

flurry light gust of wind; brief fall of snow; sudden commotion; to make or become agitated
flurries flurried flurrying

flush[1] to send water through a channel, toilet, etc.; level or even (with); to blush

flush[2] hand of playing-cards of the same suit

fluster (to put into a) xconfused nervous state

flute high-pitched keyed wind instrument; ornamental groove
flautist or *flutist fluted fluting*

flutter to wave or move rapidly; excited interest; (*informal*) bet

fluvial of rivers

flux continual change; soldering substance
fluxes

fly[1] to move through the air, esp. by wings; flap over an opening
flies flew flown fly-by-night flying flyleaf flyover fly-past flywheel

fly² 2-winged insect
flies fly-blown flycatcher fly-fishing fly-paper fly-trap flyweight

flyer or **flier** person, animal, or thing that flies

flyleaf blank leaf at the beginning or end of a book

flysheet short handbill; outer protective sheet covering a tent

foal (to give birth to a) young horse or related animal

foam (to make or produce a) mass of small bubbles on the surface of a liquid
foaminess foamy

fob¹ small pocket for watch

fob² (**fob off**) to trick someone into buying or accepting something of little or no value
fobbed fobbing

fo'c's'le see **forecastle**

focus point of convergence of light rays; point at which an object is seen most clearly; to bring or come into focus
focuses or *foci focal focalize* or *focalise focused* or *focussed focusing* or *focussing*

fodder food for animals, esp. hay and straw

foe enemy

foetid see **fetid**

foetus or **fetus** embryo of a mammal; developing human being from 8th week of pregnancy
foetuses or *fetuses foetal* or *fetal*

fog thick mist that is difficult to see through
fogbound fogged foggier foggiest fogginess fogging foggy foghorn fog-lamp fog-signal

fogy or **fogey** person with old-fashioned ideas
fogies or *fogeys*

foible minor weakness or peculiarity of character

foil¹ to baffle or frustrate

foil² very thin metal sheet; contrasting element

foil³ long thin flexible sword used in fencing

foist to force another to accept by deceit

fold¹ to bend so that one part covers another; folded part
foldaway

fold² enclosure for sheep

folder binder or file for papers

folderol or **falderal** showy trifle; nonsense

foliage leaves of a plant or plants

folio leaf of manuscript or book; sheet of paper folded once; large-sized book; folder
folios

folk people; (*informal*) family
folk-dance folklore folk-song folksy folk-tale

follicle very small sac or gland

follow to go or come after; to pursue; to understand
follower following follow-on follow-up

folly foolishness
follies

foment to apply moist heat; to incite
fomentation fomenter
SEE PANEL at **ferment**

fond having a liking for; affectionate

fondant soft flavoured sugar sweet

fondle to touch or stroke lovingly
fondling

fondue dish of melted cheese

font¹ bowl for baptismal water

font² see **fount²**

food substance taken into the body and used to provide energy
foodie foodstuff

fool¹ person without good sense

foolery foolhardiness foolhardy foolish foolproof

fool[2] kind of cold creamy dessert

foolscap large size of paper

foot lowest part of leg; lowest part of something; unit of length, 12 inches; basic unit in poetry
feet footage foot-and-mouth football footbrake footbridge footfall foothill foothold footing footlights footloose footman footnote footpad footpath footplate foot-pound footprint footrest footsore footstep footstool foot-warmer footway footwear footwork

footle to mess around; to waste time
footling

fop man who is too concerned with fashion
foppery foppish

for used to show purpose or direction; intended to be given to; considering; because (of); on behalf of

forage food for animals; to search for
foraging

forasmuch as (*archaic*) since

foray short sudden raid
forays

forbear[1] to abstain or refrain from
forbearance forbore forbrone
SEE PANEL

---

forbear or forebear?
To *forbear* to do something is to abstain or refrain from doing it: *forbear to describe all the details; forbear from answering.* To show *forbearance* is to show patience and self-control.

Your *forebears*, or, less commonly, *forbears* are your ancestors: *the endeavours of our illustrious forebears.*

---

forbear[2] see **forebear**
SEE PANEL at **forbear**[1]

forbid to prohibit
forbade or *forbad forbidden forbidding*

force strength, energy, or power; to compel
forced force-feed forceful forcefully forcefulness forcible forcibly forcing

force majeure (*French*) circumstances beyond one's control

forcemeat seasoned stuffing

forceps surgical pincers

ford shallow part of a river that can be crossed by car, etc.; to cross at a ford
fordable

fore (at or to the) front

forearm[1] part of the arm from the elbow to the wrist

forearm[2] to prepare in advance

forebear or **forbear** ancestor
SEE PANEL at **forbear**[1]

forebode to indicate in advance
foreboding

forecast to predict future events; such a prediction
forecasted forecasting

forecastle or **fo'c's'le** raised deck at the front of a ship

foreclose to deprive of the right to redeem a mortgage, esp. because of non-payment
foreclosing foreclosure

forecourt courtyard in front of building

forefather ancestor

forefinger finger next to the thumb

forefront extreme front; most prominent position

foregather see **forgather**

forego[1] to go before; to precede
foregoing foregone forewent
SEE PANEL

---

forego or forgo?
To *forgo* something means to do without it: *to forgo the temptation to gain profits in the short term.*

Forego means 'to go before' and is most commonly used in the derived form *foregoing,* meaning 'just mentioned or stated': *The conclusion from the foregoing is the company needs to dispense with the association's services as soon as is reasonably possible*; and in the expression *a foregone conclusion*, meaning 'a predictable or certain result': *Most of the electorate think that the outcome of the vote is a foregone conclusion.*

---

forego[2] see **forgo**
SEE PANEL at **forego**[1]

foreground part of a picture or view nearest the observer

forehand tennis stroke made with the palm of the hand turned in the direction of movement

forehead part of the face above the eyes

foreign from another country, esp. in or not of one's own country
foreigner

foreknow to know in advance
foreknew foreknowledge foreknown

foreland promontory

foreleg either of the front legs of a horse or other 4-footed animal

forelock lock of hair growing above the forehead

foreman (*fem.* **forewoman**) supervisory worker; principal juror
foremen (fem. *forewomen*)

foremast mast nearest the bow of a ship

foremost first in position or importance

forensic of or used in law-courts
forensics

foreordain to determine events in the future

foreplay erotic stimulation before intercourse

forerunner person or thing that goes before and prepares the way for another

foresee to see beforehand
foresaw foreseeable foreseeing foreseen

foreshadow to show or represent, esp. as a warning, beforehand

foreshore land bordering on a body of water; part of the shore beween limits of high and low tides

foreshorten to represent as shorter than in reality, to show perspective

foresight foreseeing; prudence

foreskin loose fold of skin covering the end of the penis

forest large wooded area with dense growth of trees
forester forestry

forestall to prevent by taking action first

foretaste limited experience of something in the future

foretell to predict
foretelling foretold

forethought careful thought and planning in advance

foretop platform at top of foremast

for ever for all time in the future; (**forever**) constantly

forewarn to warn beforehand

foreword introductory statement to a book

forfeit to lose the right to something as a penalty; something lost or removed as a penalty
forfeitable forfeiture

forgather or **foregather** to come together

forge[1] workshop with open furnace; to shape metal by heat; to counterfeit
forger forgery forgeries forging

forge[2] to move forward steadily
forging

forget to fail to remember; to disregard
forgetful forgetfully forgetfulness
forgettable forgetting forgot forgotten

forget-me-not kind of plant with small blue flowers
forget-me-nots

forgive to stop blaming; to pardon
forgave forgivable forgiven forgiveness forgiving

forgo or **forego** to do without; to give up
forgoing forgone forwent
SEE PANEL at **forego**

fork pronged implement; place where road, etc., separates into 2 or more parts

forlorn sad; forsaken
forlornly forlornness

form shape or appearance; paper with spaces to be filled in; school class; to shape
formation formative formless formlessness

formal polite; conventional
formalism formality formalities formally

formaldehyde colourless gas used as a disinfectant and preservative

formalin clear water solution of formaldehyde

formalize or **formalise** to make formal; to give formal status to
formalization or *formalisation*
formalizing or *formalising*

format size, shape, and appearance of a book

formative having an important influence

former of an earlier or previous time; first of 2 mentioned
formerly

Formica (*trademark*) kind of laminated plastic used for heat-resistant surfaces

formic acid pungent corrosive acid produced by ants

formidable arousing fear; very difficult
formidableness formidably

formula scientific rule made up of symbols; fixed set of words; statement of principle
formulas or *formulae formulary*

formulate to express in a formula or in a systematic way
formulating formulation

fornicate to have sexual intercourse voluntarily outside marriage
fornicating fornication fornicator

forsake to abandon; to give up
forsaken forsaker forsaking forsook

forsooth (*archaic*) in truth; indeed

forswear to give up doing or using; to deny absolutely
forswore forsworn

forsythia kind of yellow flowering shrub

fort fortified building or position

forte[1] something at which a person excels

forte[2] (*music*) loudly

forth onwards; out

forthcoming approaching; about to appear

forthright outspoken; direct
forthrightly forthrightness

forthwith immediately

fortify to make stronger
fortification fortified fortifier fortifies fortifying

fortitude patient courage and boldness

fortnight 2 weeks
fortnightly

FORTRAN computer language

fortress fortified place; fort
fortresses

fortuitous happening by chance
fortuitously fortuitousness
SEE PANEL

fortuitous or fortunate?

Something that is *fortuitous* happens by chance and turns out successfully: *A fortuitous meeting at a conference led me to an interview and my present job.*

A person or thing that is described as

fortunate is lucky. *You were fortunate to survive the accident; The college is fortunate in having so many halls of residence.*

fortunate lucky
fortunately fortunateness
SEE PANEL at **fortuitous**

fortune luck, esp. good luck; large sum of money
fortune-teller fortune-telling

forty number 40
forties fortieth

forum public place or meeting for discussion
forums or *fora*

forward for the future; to send on; eager; mainly attacking player in soccer, etc.
forward-looking forwardness forwards

fosse or **foss** ditch or moat

fossil remains or relic of an animal or plant of a past geological age

fossilize or **fossilise** to turn into a fossil; to make or become outmoded or fixed
fossilization or *fossilisation fossilizing* or *fossilising*

foster to bring up a child that is not one's own; to promote or encourage
foster-brother foster-child foster-father foster-mother foster-parent foster-sister

fought past tense and past participle of **fight**

foul disgusting to the senses; revolting; obscene; breaking of rules in a game
foully foul-mouthed foulness

found[1] past tense and past participle of **find**

found[2] to establish; to base
foundation founder

found[3] to melt and shape metal
founder

founder[1] person who establishes an institution, etc.

founder[2] to sink or collapse

foundling abandoned infant

foundry place where metal is cast
foundries

fount[1] source of fountain

fount[2] or **font** set of printing type of one style and size

fountain spring of water; jet of water

four number 4
fourfold four-ply four-poster fourscore foursome four-square four-stroke fourth

fourteen number 14
fourteenth

fowl bird; domestic bird used as food

fox wild flesh-eating animal; to perplex or puzzle
foxes foxhole foxhound fox-hunting fox-terrier foxy

foxglove kind of plant with thimble-like flowers

foxtrot (to perform a) kind of ballroom dance
foxtrotted foxtrotting

foyer entrance lobby of a theatre, etc.

fracas noisy quarrel

fraction part of a whole number; very small amount
fractional fractionally

fractious irritable; hard to control
fractiously fractiousness

fracture (to) break
fracturing

fragile easily broken; delicate
fragilely fragility

fragment broken-off part or piece; to break into fragments
fragmentary fragmentation

fragrant having a pleasant or sweet smell
fragrance fragrantly

frail weak; fragile
frailty frailties

frame structure that gives shape or

strength: outer structure; to put a frame round
frame-up framework framing

franc money unit of many countries

France country in West Europe
French

franchise right to vote in elections; right to sell particular goods or services or run a business, etc.

Franciscan member of religious order founded by St Francis of Assisi

Franco- (*prefix*) French
Franco-German Francophile

frank direct and honest; to mark a letter to cancel a stamp or instead of a stamp
franking-machine frankly

frankfurter kind of sausage

frankincense gum resin that is burnt as incense

frantic wildly excited; frenzied
frantically

fraternal of a brother; of a fraternity or society
fraternality

fraternity brotherliness; group of people with same interest, aims, etc.
fraternities

fraternize or **fraternise** to associate on friendly terms
fraternization or *fraternisation fraternizer* or *fraterniser fraternizing* or *fraternising*

fratricide killing of one's brother or sister

fraud deliberate deception; person who deceives
fraudulence fraudulent fraudulently

fraught filled (with)

fray[1] noisy quarrel
frays

fray[2] to wear away
frayed fraying

frazzle state of extreme fatigue

freak something abnormal
freakish freaky

freckle small brownish spot on skin
freckly

free not under the control of another; to release; costing or charging nothing
freebie freed freedman freedom free-for-all freehand freehold freeing freelance free-living freely freeman freer free-range free-spoken freest free-standing freestyle freethinking freeway freewheel

freebooter person living from plunder

freefone or **freephone** a telephone service in which the person dialling does not have to pay for the call

Freemason member of secret order
Freemasonry

Freepost a business postal service in which the person sending the letter does not have to pay the postage

freesia kind of plant with fragrant flowers

freeze to change from liquid into a solid because of a fall in temperature
freeze-dry freezer freeze-up freezing freezing-point froze frozen

freight transport of goods
freighter

French (language) of France
Frenchman Frenchwoman

frenetic or **phrenetic** frantic
frenetically or *phrenetically*

frenzy wild madness or excitement
frenzied

frequency rate of repetition of an event
frequencies

frequent occurring or appearing often; to visit often
frequenter frequenting

fresco watercolour picture painted on to damp plaster
frescoes or *frescos*

fresh new; original; most recent; not canned, frozen, or preserved; invigorating
freshen freshwater

fresher or **freshman** first-year student at college or university
freshmen

fret[1] to worry
fretful fretfully fretfulness fretted fretting

fret[2] ridge on finger-board of guitar, etc.

fretsaw saw with a long thin narrow blade

fretwork ornamental wood openwork

Freudian of or relating to Sigmund Freud
Freudianism

friable easily broken up; crumbly
friability

friar member of a religious monastic order
friary

fricassee stewed meat or poultry in a thick white sauce

fricative consonant such as *f* pronounced by friction of breath in narrow opening

friction rubbing of one thing against another; conflict

Friday 6th day of the week

fridge (*informal*) short for **refrigerator**

fried past tense and past participle of **fry**[1]

friend person whom one knows and likes
friendless friendlier friendliest friendliness friendly friendship

frier see **fryer**

Friesian breed of black and white dairy cattle

frieze ornamental band along a wall

frigate kind of warship

fright sudden fear or shock

frighten to make suddenly afraid

frightful causing fear; (*informal*) very great; disagreeable
frightfully frightfulness

frigid extremely cold; unfeeling in manner; (*of a woman*) lacking sexual desire
frigidity frigidly

frill gathered strip of cloth
frilly

fringe outer edge; decorative border of hanging threads, etc.; hair cut short over the forehead

frippery tawdry ornamentation
fripperies

Frisbee (*trademark*) light plastic disc thrown by flicking the wrist

Frisian (language of the) people living in Friesland and the Frisian islands

frisk to leap about playfully; to search a person for hidden weapons
frisky

fritter[1] to waste or squander

fritter[2] piece of fried batter containing an apple, etc.

frivolous not serious; irresponsible
frivolity frivolities

frizz (to form into a) mass of tight curls; to roughen
frizzy

frizzle[1] to frizz the hair
frizzling

frizzle[2] to fry until crisp; to scorch; to sizzle
frizzling

fro back

frock dress

frog kind of small jumping amphibian
froggy

frogman swimmer equipped for underwater swimming
frogmen

frogmarch to force someone to move against his or her will

frolic to play about in a lively happy way; lively happy activity
frolicked frolicking frolicsome

from used to show an original location; out of; because of

fromage frais (*French*) smooth soft cheese like thick yoghurt

frond leaf of a palm or fern

front forward part; promenade by a seashore
frontage frontal front-bencher front-runner

frontier border between 2 countries
frontiersman

frontispiece illustration facing title-page of book

frost weather when temperature falls below freezing-point; white deposit of ice particles
frostbite frostbitten frostily frostiness frosty

froth mass of small bubbles of air or gas in a liquid
frothy

froward obstinate; contrary
frowardly frowardness

frown to wrinkle the brows

frowsty stuffy; stale

frowzy untidy; unkempt

froze past tense of **freeze**

frozen past participle of **freeze**
frozenness

fructify to make or become fruitful
fructification fructified fructifies fructifying

frugal not wasteful; thrifty
frugality frugally

fruit part of plant containing seed; product or result
fruiterer fruitful fruitfully fruitfulness fruitier fruitiest fruitiness fruitless fruitlessly fruitlessness fruity

fruition fulfilment or realization

frump dowdy unattractive woman
frumpish

frustrate to prevent or hinder; to discourage
frustrating frustration

fry[1] to cook in hot fat
fried fries frying frying-pan

fry[2] young of fish or other animals

fryer or **frier** container for frying food

fuchsia shrub with drooping showy flowers

fuddle to make muddled or drunk
fuddling

fuddy-duddy dull fussy old-fashioned person
fuddy-duddies

fudge[1] soft flavoured sweet

fudge[2] to avoid commitment on; to fake

fuel (to provide with) material burnt to produce light, heat, or energy
fuelled (US *fueled*) *fuelling* (US *fueling*)

fug hot stale atmosphere
fugginess fuggy

fugitive person who flees fleeing; transient

fugue musical composition with theme that is repeated and developed

fulcrum pivot about which a lever turns
fulcrums or *fulcra*

fulfil (US **fulfill**) to carry out; to perform
fulfilled fulfilling fulfilment (US *fulfillment*)

fulgent (*formal*) dazzling
fulgently

full[1] completely filled; completely satisfied
full-blooded full-blown fuller fullest full-frontal full-length fullness or *fulness full-scale fully fully-fashioned fully-fledged*

full[2] to cleanse and thicken cloth
fuller

fulmar kind of sea bird related to the petrel

fulminate to utter strong condemnation
fulminant fulminating fulmination

fulsome exaggerated or insincere
fulsomely fulsomeness

fumble to handle awkwardly
fumbler fumbling

fume offensive smoke, gas, etc.; to be very angry
fuming fumy

fumigate to treat with smoke, vapour, etc. in order to disinfect
fumingating fumigative fumigator

fun amusement, entertainment, or sport
funfair

function to operate; purpose of activity; ceremony
functional functionalism functionally

functionary official
functionaries

fund supply of money for a purpose; store or supply; to provide money for
fundholder fundholding

fundamental basic or primary (fact or principle)
fundamentally

fundamentalism belief in the literal truth of the Bible
fundamentalist

funeral formal ceremony at which a dead person is buried or cremated
funereal

fungus plant that lacks chlorophyll and reproduces by spores
fungi or *funguses fungicide fungoid fungous*

funicular (*of a railway*) operated by means of a cable

funk (*informal*) fear; coward; to avoid because of fear

funnel wide-mouthed hollow utensil; shaft for smoke, etc. to escape
funnelled (US *funneled*) *funnelling* (US *funneling*)

funny amusing; peculiar
funnier funniest funnily funniness funny-bone

fur soft thick hair of many animals
furred furring furry

furbelow flounce on women's clothing

furbish to polish; to restore
furbishes

furious extremely angry; wild
furiously furiousness

furl to roll up

furlong unit of length, 220 yards

furlough leave of absence from duty

furnace enclosed chamber for a great fire

furnish to provide with furniture; to provide or equip
furnisher furnishes furnishings

furniture movable articles such as chairs that equip a house

furore (US **furor**) great outburst of protest

furrier dealer in furs
furriery

furrow (to make a) long narrow trench in the ground

furry of or like fur

further to a greater distance or degree; in addition; to promote
furtherance furthermore furthermost furthest

furtive sly and secretive
furtively furtiveness

fury violent anger
furies furious

furze gorse

fuse[1] length of wire in an electric circuit; to unite (as if) by melting together
fusible fusing fusion

fuse[2] length of material for setting off an explosive charge

fuselage main body of an aircraft

fusilier member of certain regiments

fusillade firing of guns simultaneously or in rapid succession

fuss excessive or unnecessary excitement or agitation; display of great affection; to show excessive concern or worry for
fussier fussiest fussily fussiness fusspot fussy

fustian hard-wearing cloth; pompous talk

fusty stale or musty
fustier fustiest fustily fustiness

futile worthless or useless
futilely futility

futon Japanese quilted mattress used as a bed

future (of or in the) time to come
futurism futurist futuristic futurity futurology

fuzz[1] mass of fine light fibres

fuzz[2] (*slang*) police

fuzzy like fuzz; unclear or blurred
fuzzier fuzziest fuzzily fuzziness

G

gab (*informal*) idle talk

gabardine durable fabric

gabble to speak or utter quickly and indistinctly
gabbler gabbling

gaberdine medieval loose cloak

gable triangular upper part of an outside wall between sloping roofs
gabled gabling

Gabon country in West Africa
Gabonese

gad to travel about aimlessly
gadded gadding

gadfly kind of bloodsucking fly
gadflies

gadget small mechanical device
gadgetry

Gaelic Celtic language

gaff stiff pole with a hook

gaffe social blunder; indiscreet remark

gaffer old man; boss

gag something put in or over the mouth; joke; to put a gag in or over the mouth of
gagged gagging

gaga (*slang*) senile; slightly mad

gage (to) pledge

gaggle flock of geese; to cackle
gaggling

gaiety cheerfulness; light-heartedness; merrymaking

gaily in a gay manner

gain to acquire; to profit; (to) increase
gainful gainfully

gainsay (*formal*) to deny
gainsaid gainsaying

gait manner of walking; leg movement of a horse

gaiter covering for the ankle or leg

gala festive occasion; sports competition

galantine meat served cold in jelly

galaxy system of starts, gas, and dust; Milky Way
galaxies galactic

gale very strong wind

gall[1] impudence; bitterness; bile
gall-bladder gallstone

gall[2] to annoy; sore on the skin
galling

gall[3] abnormal growth on plants caused by insects

gallant brave; attentive to women
gallantly gallantry gallantries

galleon large Spanish sailing-ship

galleria group of small shops under one roof

gallery covered passage; balcony; upper floor in a theatre, etc.; room or building for displaying works of art
galleries

galley kitchen in a ship or aeroplane; ancient long low ship
galleys

Gallic of Gaul or France

gallimaufry medley

gallivant to gad about

gallon unit of liquid measurement, 4 quarts

gallop (*of a horse*) (to ride at the) fastest speed
galloped galloper galloping

gallows frame used for hanging criminals

Gallup Poll method of sampling of opinions of a representative group of people

galore in abundance

galosh or **golosh** waterproof overshoe

galumph to leap about

galvanize or **galvanise** to cover with zinc; to stimulate into sudden activity
galvanizing or *galvanising* *galvanometer*

Gambia country in West Africa
Gambian

gambit opening move, esp. in chess

gamble to risk money on the outcome of an event; to play games for money
gambler *gambling*

gambol to skip or jump about
gambolled (US *gamboled*) *gambolling* (US *gamboling*)

game form of amusement or sport; scheme; wild animals hunted for sport or food; to gamble; brave
gamebird *gamekeeper* *gamesmanship*

gamete sexual reproductive cell

gamma 3rd letter of the Greek alphabet

gammon kind of cured ham

gammy lame

gamut entire range

gamy or **gamey** having the scent or flavour of game

gander male goose

gang group of criminals; group of workmen

gangling tall and awkward

ganglion collection of nerve cells and fibres; cyst
ganglia

gangplank movable plank for boarding and leaving a ship at a quay

gangrene death of body tissues, esp. due to loss of blood supply
gangrenous

gangster member of a gang of criminals

gangway passage between rows of seats; gangplank

gannet kind of large sea bird

gantry bridgelike framework to support a crane, motorway signs, etc.
gantries

gaol see **jail**

gap break, opening, or interruption

gape to open the mouth wide; to stare
gaping

garage building for a motor vehicle; commercial establishment where cars are repaired or sold or where petrol, etc. is sold
garaging

garb clothes; to clothe
garbed

garbage nonsense; (US) rubbish

garble to distort a story
garbling

garden area of land where trees, flowers, vegetables, etc. are growing; to cultivate a garden
gardener

gardenia kind of tree or shrub with white showy flowers

gargantuan huge

gargle to rinse the throat with a medicinal fluid by gurgling
gargling

gargoyle carved waterspout

garish gaudy; showy
garishly *garishness*

garland (to decorate with a) wreath of flowers

garlic onion-like plant
garlicky

garment article of clothing

garner to gather or store, esp. grain

garnet deep-red precious stone

garnish to decorate esp. food; something used as a garnish
garnishes garnisher

garret attic

garrison (troops who guard a) fortified place; to station troops in a garrison
garrisoned

garrotte or **garotte** (device for) strangulation; to execute in this way
garrotter or *garotter garrotting* or *garotting*

garrulous very talkative
garrulity garrulously

garter band to hold up a sock or stocking

Garter highest order of the British knighthood

gas airlike substance; to poison or affect with gas
gases gasbag gaseous gas-fired gasholder gaslight gasmask gasometer gassed gassing gassy gasworks

gash (to make a) long deep cut
gashes

gasify to make into or become a gas
gasification gasified gasifies gasifying

gasket sealing material put between 2 surfaces

gasoline (US) petrol

gasp to catch one's breath sharply; act of gasping

gastric of the stomach
gastritis gastroenteritis

gastronomy art of good eating
gastronome gastronomic gastronomically

gastropod mollusc with a head that has sensory organs

gate movable barrier for closing an opening in a wall or fence
gatehouse gatekeeper gateman gatepost gateway

gâteau rich cream cake
gâteaux

gatecrash to go to a party uninvited
gatecrasher

gather to bring or come together

gauche awkward
gaucherie

gaucho South American cowboy
gauchos

gaudy showy; too bright or colourful
gaudier gaudiest gaudily gaudiness

gauge (device or instrument with which) to measure, test, or estimate
gaugeable gauging

Gaul (native of) ancient region of Europe

gaunt very thin and haggard
gauntly gauntness

gauntlet protective glove; challenge to fight

gauze kind of transparent cloth

gave past tense of **give**

gavel small mallet used by auctioneer, chairman, etc.

gavotte kind of dance or music

gawky awkward; ungainly
gawkier gawkiest gawkily gawkiness

gawp to stare stupidly

gay cheerful; bright; (*informal*) homosexual
gaiety gaily gayer gayest gayness

gaze to look at long and steadily; act of gazing
gazing

gazebo summer-house
gazebos

gazelle kind of small slender antelope

gazette newspaper or official journal

gazetteer section of a book listing places

gazump to thwart a prospective house-buyer by raising the price after agreeing a price

gear toothed wheel in a mechanism; mechanism or equipment
gearbox gearing gear-lever gearwheel

gecko kind of small lizard
geckos or *geckoes*

gee[1] call to a horse to go faster
gee-gee gee-up

gee[2] mild exclamation

geese pl. of **goose**

geezer (*informal*) old or eccentric man

Geiger counter instrument for measuring radioactivity

geisha Japanese female entertainer
geishas

gel (to set into) semi-solid solution
gelation gelled gelling

gelatin or **gelatine** colourless jelly-like substance
gelatinize or *gelatinise gelatinous*

geld to castrate, esp. horses
gelding

gelignite kind of dynamite

gem precious stone; treasure
gemlike gemmed gemming gemstone

Gemini 3rd sign of the zodiac

gen (*informal*) information; to give information to
genned genning

gendarme (*French*) policeman
gendarmes gendarmerie

gender grammatical category of nouns, esp. masculine, feminine, and neuter

gene unit of heredity in a chromosome

genealogy descent of a person or group from an ancestor
genealogies genealogical genealogist

general of the whole; not limited; chief army officer
generality generalities generally generalship
SEE PANEL

general or generic?

The adjective *general* has several meanings: 'of the whole; as a whole; overall': *describe the political situation in general terms*; 'not limited or specific': *general knowledge; The general secretary has wide responsibilities for the union's organization.*

A *generic* drug is one that does not have a particular brand name and so is cheaper than one with a trademark. A *generic* term is one that relates to a whole class or group of similar things: *different kinds of play falling under the generic category 'tragedy'.*

generalissimo supreme commander of armed forces
generalissimos

generalize or **generalise** to make a broad general statement
generalization or *generalisation generalizing* or *generalising*

generate to produce or create
generating generative generator

generation generating; group of people born at about the same time

generic of a whole class or group
generically
SEE PANEL at **general**

generous giving readily and liberally
generosity generosities

genesis beginning or origin

genetics study of heredity
genetic genetically geneticist

genial friendly; cheerful
geniality genially

genie spirit who fulfils wishes
genies or *genii*

genital of sexual organs or reproduction
genitals

genitive (*grammar*) case used to show possession or source

genius (person with) exceptional intelligence or ability
geniuses

genocide murder of a race of people
genocidal

genre style, esp. of art

genteel of the gentry; refined; very fashionable
genteelly

gentian kind of mountain plant with blue flowers

Gentile anyone not a Jew

gentility gentry; respectability

gentle not severe; mild or kind
gentlefolk gentleness gently

gentleman man
gentlemen gentleman-at-arms gentlemanly

gentry people just below nobility

genuflect to bend the knee
genuflexion or *genuflection*

genuine not artificial; sincere or real
genuinely genuineness

genus biological group that contains one or more species
genera

geography study of the natural features of the earth's surface
geographer geographical geographically

geology study of the structure, composition, etc. of the earth
geological geologically geologist

geometry branch of mathematics dealing with measurements and properties of angles, lines, and surfaces
geometric geometrical geometrically

georgette thin crêpe fabric

Georgia republic by the Black Sea

Georgian of or characteristic of the reign of any of the kings of England called George

geostationary (*of a satellite, etc.*) travelling at the same speed as the earth, so remaining above the same place

geranium kind of plant with showy flowers
geraniums

gerbil kind of small burrowing rodent

geriatrics branch of medicine dealing with diseases and problems of elderly people
geriatric geriatrician

germ micro-organism that can cause disease
germicide germinal

german having the same parents or grandparents

germane relevant (to)

Germany country in central Europe
German

germinate to cause to grow or develop
germinating germination

gerontology study of growing old
gerontological gerontologist

gerrymander to divide a voting area unfairly

gerund noun ending in *-ing* formed from a verb
gerundial gerundive

gestate to carry in the womb during pregnancy
gestation

gesticulate to express with movements of the hands or arms
gesticulating gesticulation gesticulator

gesture movement, esp. of the hands or arms to express a feeling or for emphasis

get to obtain or receive; to become; to move
get-at-able getaway getting get-together get-up got (US *gotten*)

geyser natural spring of heated water; gas water-heater

Ghana country in West Africa
Ghanaian

ghastly horrific; unpleasant; very pale
ghastlier ghastliest ghastliness

gherkin small cucumber used for pickling

ghetto part of city in which a minority group lives
ghettos

ghost disembodied spirit of a dead person
ghostlike ghostliness ghostly ghost-writer

ghoul evil spirit
ghoulish

giant (*fem*. **giantess**) mythical superhuman being
giantesses

gibber to utter quickly and unintelligibly
gibberish

gibbet gallows-like structure

gibbon long-armed Asian ape

gibe or **jibe** to jeer or taunt
gibing or *jibing*

giblets edible internal organs of a fowl

Gibraltar British crown colony at southern tip of Spain
Gibraltarian

giddy feeling unbalanced; dizzy
giddier giddiest giddily giddiness

gift something given; talent
gifted

gift-wrap to wrap a gift attractively
gift-wrapped gift-wrapping

gig[1] light 2-wheeled carriage

gig[2] musician's booking for 1 performance

giga- (*prefix*) 10^9

gigantic enormous
gigantically

giggle to laugh foolishly; such a laugh
giggler giggling

gigolo male escort or partner
gigolos

gild to cover with gold
gilded or *gilt*

gill[1] respiratory organ of a fish

gill[2] unit of measurement, quarter of a pint

gilt covered with gold; gold
gilt-edged

gimbals device that provides free suspension for a compass, etc.

gimcrack showy trifle

gimlet small hand tool for boring holes in wood

gimmick something designed to attract attention or publicity
gimmickry gimmicky

gin[1] alcoholic drink distilled from grain

gin[2] tool or device; to snare; to separate seeds from raw cotton
ginned ginning

ginger plant with pungent stem; reddish-brown
gingery

gingerly (in a way that is) cautious or reluctant

gingham striped or checked cotton fabric

ginkgo or **gingko** kind of ornamental Chinese tree
ginkgoes or *gingkoes*

gipsy see **gypsy**

giraffe long-necked African animal

gird to fasten with a belt; to surround
girded or *girt*

girder large main supporting beam

girdle belt or cord that goes round the waist

girl young unmarried human female
girlfriend girlhood girlie girlish girlishly

Giro Post Office or bank system of money transfer
Giros

girth distance round something

gist essential points of a speech, argument, etc.

give to hand over; to make a present of; to yield under pressure
gave give-and-take give-away given giver giving

gizmo or **gismo** (*slang*) gadget
gizmos or *gismos*

gizzard enlargement of the alimentary canal of a bird

glacé glazed or candied

glacier mass of slowly moving ice and snow
glacial glaciate glaciation

glad pleased; happy
gladden gladder gladdest gladly gladness

glade open place in a forest

gladiator trained fighter in ancient Rome
gladiatorial

gladiolus kind of plant with sword-shaped leaves and coloured flower spikes
gladioli or *gladioluses*

gladsome (*archaic*) glad

glamorize or **glamorise** to make glamorous
glamorization or *glamorisation*
glamorizing or *glamorising*

glamour (US **glamor**) alluring attractiveness
glamorous glamorously

glance to look at quickly; to strike lightly and obliquely; quick look
glancing

gland organ or set of cells producing a chemical substance
glandular

glare to shine in a dazzling harsh manner; to stare angrily; dazzling harsh light; angry stare
glaring

glaring conspicuous
glaringly

glasnost (*Russian*) (in former USSR) policy of greater openness in government

glass hard brittle transparent substance; something made of this such as a drinking container
glasses glass-blower glass-cutter glassful glassfuls glasshouse glassily glass-paper glassware glass wool glass-works glassy

glaucoma kind of eye disease
glaucomatous

glaucous greenish

glaze to fit or cover with glass; (to cover with a) glassy non-porous coating
glazier glazing

gleam (to shine with a) small soft beam of light

glean to gather gradually, esp. grain after reaping
gleaner gleaning

glee joy
gleeful gleefully gleefulness

glen deep narrow valley

glengarry Scottish cap with ribbons at the back
glengarries

glib superficial; fluent but in an insincere way
glibly glibness

glide to move along smoothly
glider gliding

glimmer to shine or appear faintly; glimmering light; trace

glimpse to look at briefly; brief look
glimpsing

glint to flash brightly; bright flash or gleam

glissade to slide down a slope

glissando (*music*) in a gliding manner

glisten to shine with a reflected light

glitter to sparkle brightly; bright sparkling light

glitterati (*slang*) rich and famous people

glitz (*slang*) showy superficial display
glitzy

gloaming twilight or dusk

gloat to think about with malicious happiness

globe sphere on which a map of the world is drawn
global globe-trotter globoid

globule tiny ball or drop
globular

glockenspiel tuned metal plates hit with hammers
glockenspiels

gloom darkness; sadness
gloomier gloomiest gloomily gloominess gloomy

glorify to make glorious; to praise
glorification glorified glorifies glorifying

glory praise or honour
glories glorious gloriously

gloss[1] brightness of a polished surface; to try to hide
glosses glossy

gloss[2] short note of explanation
glosser

glossary alphabetical list of technical or special words
glossaries

glottis space between vocal cords
glottal

glove hand covering with parts for each finger

glow (to shine with a) bright steady light
glow-worm

glower to scowl

glucose crystalline form of sugar

glue (to join with a) strong adhesive
glued glue-pot glue-sniffer glue-sniffing gluey gluing

glum gloomy
glumly glummer glummest glumness

glut (to supply with an) excessive amount
glutted glutting

glutamate kind of salt used to make food taste better

gluten protein of wheat flour
glutinous

glutton person who eats too much
gluttonous gluttony

glycerine or **glycerin** colourless sweet liquid

gnarled twisted or rough

gnash to grind teeth together
gnashes

gnat kind of small 2-winged biting fly

gnaw to bite constantly

gneiss laminated rock

gnome legendary dwarf
gnomish

gnomon arm that casts the shadow on a sundial

gnu kind of antelope

go to move or travel; to operate; to become
goes go-ahead go-between go-by goer go-getter going going-over goings-on gone go-slow went

goad (to urge forward with) pointed stick; to stimulate

goal aim; structure into which players put a ball, etc. to score
goalie goalkeeper goalpost

goat kind of horned ruminant mammal
goatee goatherd goatish goatskin

gob (*slang*) mouth
gobsmacked

gobble[1] to eat greedily and noisily
gobbling

gobble[2] (*of turkeys*) (to make a) loud gurgling sound
gobbling

gobbledegook or **gobbledygook** pretentious pompous jargon

goblet stemmed drinking vessel

goblin mischievous elf

goby kind of small fish
gobies

god (*fem.* **goddess**) (**God**) supreme being; image or idol that is worshipped
godchild god-daughter godfather God-fearing God-forsaken Godhead or *godhead godless godlessness godlier godliest godlike godliness godly godmother godparent godsend godsent godson Godspeed*

goggle to stare at
goggle-eyed goggling

goggles protective glasses

goitre (US **goiter**) enlargement of thyroid gland causing swelling

go-kart miniature racing car

gold valuable yellow metal
gold-dust gold-field goldfish goldmine

golden of gold; favourable

goldfinch kind of finch

golf game played with ball and clubs on a large open course
golf-course golfer

golliwog soft doll with a black face

golly exclamation of mild surprise

golosh see **galosh**

gondola long narrow boat in Venice; cabin suspended from a balloon
gondolas gondolier

gone past participle of **go**
goner

gong metal plate-like disc that produces a resounding tone when struck

gonorrhoea (US **gonorrhea**) kind of venereal disease with discharge

goo (*informal*) sticky substance; sentimentality
gooey gooier gooiest

good favourable; pleasing; well-behaved; virtuous; benefit
good-for-nothing good-humoured good-looking goodly good-natured goodness good-tempered

goodbye (US **goodby**) farewell

goods movable or manufactured articles

goodwill kindly feeling; favour that a business has gained

goody child's expression of delight; something good to eat; hero
goodies goody-goody

goof (*informal*) foolish error
goofy

googly (*cricket*) ball bowled so that it breaks in the opposite direction from that which the batsman expected
googlies

goon stupid person

goose kind of large long-necked web-footed bird
geese goose-flesh goose-pimples goose-skin goosey

gooseberry shrub with green edible berries
gooseberries

gopher kind of American burrowing rodent

Gordian knot complicated problem

gore[1] blood shed from a wound

gore[2] to pierce or stab with horns, etc.
goring

gore[3] tapering piece of material used to shape something

gorge narrow steep-sided valley; to stuff (oneself) with food
gorging

gorgeous magnificent and beautiful
gorgeously gorgeousness

Gorgonzola blue-veined strong Italian cheese

gorilla largest manlike ape

gormless (*informal*) stupid

gorse evergreen yellow-flowered spiny shrub

gory bloody; bloodthirsty
gorier goriest

gosh exclamation of surprise or wonder

goshawk kind of long-tailed short-winged hawk

gosling young goose

gospel teaching of Jesus and the Apostles; truth; teachings
gospeller

Gospel (reading from) one of the first 4 books of the New Testament

gossamer very fine delicate fabric

gossip person who talks idly and maliciously about other people's affairs; (to engage in) such talk
gossiped gossiper gossiping gossipy

got past tense and past participle of **get**

Gothic style, esp. of architecture

gotten (US) past participle of **get**

gouache technique of water-colour painting

Gouda kind of mild Dutch cheese

gouge (to scoop out with a) kind of chisel
gouging

goulash meat stew seasoned with paprika

gourd fleshy fruit with a hard rind that is dried and used as an ornament, etc.

gourmand glutton
gourmandise
SEE PANEL

---

gourmand or gourmet?

A *gourmand* is someone who enjoys eating large amounts of food, without taking into account its quality.

A *gourmet* is a person who is a connoisseur of fine food and drink. *Gourmet* is also used to describe food that is more sophisticated and often more expensive than ordinary food: *a gourmet dinner; Discover a discriminating gourmet's culinary tips in this exciting new book.*

---

gourmet connoisseur of fine food and drink
SEE PANEL at **gourmand**

gout disease marked by painful inflammation of joints
goutiness gouty

govern to direct and control
governable governance governess governor

government executive policy-making body of a country

gown outer garment

grab to grasp hastily or roughly
grabbed grabber grabbing

grace elegance or beauty in movement or expression; kindness or favour; to add elegance or beauty to
graceful gracefully gracefulness graceless gracelessly gracelessness gracing gracious graciously graciousness

grade (to arrange in a) scale of qualities, value, or ranks; mark given to students' work
gradation grading

gradient degree of slope of a road, railway, etc.

gradual proceeding by steps; not abrupt
gradually gradualness

graduate to receive an academic degree; someone who has graduated; to mark with units of measurement
graduating graduation

graffiti words or drawings scribbled on a wall

graft[1] small piece of a plant or living tissue joined to another; to join by grafting

graft[2] (*informal*) work; taking unfair advantage of one's position

Grail (**Holy Grail**) platter used by Jesus at the Last Supper

grain (small seed or fruit of) cereal grass; tiny particle; general pattern of texture in wood, etc.

gram or **gramme** metric unit of weight

grammar study of structure of sentences, esp. regarding conformity to stated rules
grammarian grammatical grammatically

gramophone record-player

granary building for storing grain
granaries

grand large and impressive; splendid; most important; (*of relationships*) in the second degree of ascent or descent
grandchild granddaughter grandfather or *grandad* or *grandpa grandmaster grandmother* or *grandma* or *granny grandson*

grandeur magnificence

grandiloquent using pompous language
grandiloquence grandiloquently

grandiose (pretending to be) grand

grandstand roofed stand for spectators

grange farm and outbuildings

granite hard coarse-grained rock

grant to allow or give; something given
grantee granter or *grantor*

granulate to make into grains
granulator

granule small grain
granular

grape juicy skinned berry of the vine
grape-juice grapevine

grapefruit kind of large yellow citrus fruit

graph diagram showing relationship between quantities or numbers

graphic of writing or drawing; vivid
graphically graphics

graphite soft form of carbon used in pencils

graphology study of handwriting
graphological graphologist

grapnel device with clawed hook at end

grapple (to) gripe; to struggle with
grappling

grasp (to) grip; to understand; understanding
grasping

grass plant with long narrow green leaves
grasses grassland grass-snake grassy

grasshopper kind of jumping insect

grate[1] to rub against
grater grating

grate[2] metal frame holding fuel in a fireplace
grating

grateful feeling or showing thanks
gratefully gratefulness

gratify to be a source of pleasure; to satisfy
gratification gratified gratifier gratifies gratifying

gratis free of charge; without payment

gratitude thankfulness

gratuitous given free; unjustified
gratuitously

gratuity tip; gift of money
gratuities

gravamen substantial grounds of a complaint
gravamens or *gravamina*

grave[1] place for burying a corpse
gravestone graveyard

grave[2] serious; earnest
gravely graveness graver gravest

grave[3] accent mark `

gravel (to cover with) small stones and coarse sand
gravelled (US *graveled*) *gravelling* (US *graveling*) *gravelly*

graven carved; engraved

gravitas seriousness

gravitate to move by gravity; to be attracted to
gravitating gravitation

gravity seriousness, importance, or solemnity; natural force moving objects towards the centre of the earth

gravure intaglio printing process

gravy juice from cooked meat

gray (US) see **grey**

graze[1] to feed on grass
grazier grazing

graze[2] to touch lightly in passing; to scrape the skin from
grazing

grease (to apply an) oily substance
greasepaint greaseproof greasing greasy

great relatively large; eminent; (*of relationships*) one generation removed in ascent or descent
great-aunt Great Britain great-grandchild great-granddaughter great-grandfather great-grandmother great-grandparent great-grandson greatly great-uncle

grebe kind of short-winged water bird with lobed toes

Greece country in SE Europe
Grecian Greek

greed having a great desire, esp. for food
greedier greediest greedily greediness greedy

green colour between blue and yellow; immature and inexperienced; protecting the environment
greenery greenish greenness

greenfly kind of small green plant pest

greengage small green plum

greengrocer retailer of fresh vegetables and fruit
greengrocery

greenhorn inexperienced person

greenhouse building with glass walls and roof for growing plants in

Greenland largest island in the world
Greenlander Greenlandic

greenmail business strategy of buying many shares in another company; to practise greenmail on
greenmailer

greet to address with words of welcome
greeting

gregarious fond of the company of other people

gremlin mischievous spirit allegedly causing mechanical faults

Grenada island in the West Indies
Grenadian

grenade small container filled with explosive
grenadier

grew past tense of **grow**

grey (US **gray**) colour between black and white
greyish

greyhound fast slender long-legged dog

grid network of horizontal and vertical lines; network for distributing electricity, etc.; grating

griddle metal surface on which food is cooked

gridiron framework of bars used to grill meat, fish, etc.

grief deep sorrow
grievous grievously

grievance cause for complaint

grieve to feel great sorrow
grieving

griffin fabulous creature

griffon large vulture; small breed of dog

grill to cook under direct heat; framework for cooking on; (*informal*) to question intensely

grille framework of metal bars, used as a screen; grating

grim stern; harsh
grimly grimmer grimmest grimness

grimace distorted face; to contort the face
grimacing

grime dirt or filth
griminess grimy

grin (to give a) broad smile
grinned grinning

grind to crush into fine particles
grinder grindstone ground

grip to hold firmly
gripped gripping

gripe sharp pain in the stomach; to complain

grippe (*French*) influenza

grisly terrible

grist grain for grinding; something beneficial

gristle tough elastic animal tissue
gristly

grit small hard particles of sand, earth, etc.; to clench the teeth; to cover with grit
gritstone gritted gritting gritty

grizzle (*informal*) (*of a child*) to whine or fret
grizzling

grizzly grey; grey-haired; large grey bear

groan (to utter a) deep sound of pain, disapproval, etc.

groat obsolete English coin worth 4 old pennies

groats hulled crushed grain of oats

grocer retailer of food and household provisions
grocery groceries

grog alcoholic drink; diluted rum

groggy weak; shaky
groggier groggiest groggily grogginess

groin fold where the legs join the abdomen

grommet firm eyelet designed to line a hole

groom bridegroom; person employed to look after horses; to clean and tend

groove (to form or cut a) long narrow channel
grooving

groovy (*informal*) exciting; very good

grope to search by feeling with the hands
groping

gross outrageous; bulky; whole amount, not net; coarse; 144
grossly

grotesque odd; ugly and strange
grotesquely grotesqueness grotesquerie

grotto cave
grottoes or *grottos*

grotty (*informal*) nasty; unpleasant
grottier grottiest grottily grottiness

grouch (*informal*) (to) grumble
grouches grouchy

ground[1] surface of the earth; soil; area; reason
groundless groundsheet groundsman groundwork

ground[2] past tense and past participle of **grind**

groundnut kind of plant with edible tuberous root; peanut

groundsel kind of small weed with yellow flower-heads

group number of people or things together or having a common feature
groupie

grouse[1] kind of game bird

grouse[2] (*informal*) (to) grumble
grousing

grout thin mortar for filling spaces
grouter grouting

grove small wooded area

grovel to humble oneself
grovelled (US *groveled*) *groveller* (US *groveler*) *grovelling* (US *groveling*)

grow to increase in size, etc.; to become mature; to become; to raise
grew grower grown grown-up growth

growl (to make a) low rumbling sound

groyne breakwater

grub to dig or uproot larva; (*informal*) food
grubbed grubber grubbing

grubby dirty
grubbier grubbiest grubbily grubbiness

grudge (to have a) feeling of resentment
grudging

gruel thin oatmeal porridge

gruelling (US **grueling**) exhausting

gruesome horrific
gruesomely gruesomeness

gruff deep and harsh; surly
gruffly gruffness

grumble to complain in a nagging manner
grumbler grumbling

grumpy bad-tempered
grumpier grumpiest grumpily grumpiness

grunt (to make the) short low snorting sound of a pig or a sound like this

Gruyère kind of Swiss cheese

guano excrement from sea birds used as fertilizer

guarantee (to give a) formal promise or undertaking
guaranteed guaranteeing guarantor guaranty guaranties

guard to watch over and protect or look after; person that guards
guardedly guardhouse guardroom guardsman

guardian person legally entrusted with the care of another
guardianship

Guatemala country in Central America
Guatemalan

guava tropical tree with fruit; such fruit

gubernatorial of a governor

gudgeon kind of small freshwater fish

guerrilla or **guerilla** member of small independent armed force

guess (to form or express an) opinion or estimate without full knowledge or calculation
guesses guesswork guestimate

guest visitor
guest-house guest-room

guffaw (to give a) crude boisterous laugh

guide person who leads the way; to lead; member of girls' movement
guidance guidebook guide-dog guideline guiding

guild association formed to further members' interests
guildhall

guilder money unit of the Netherlands

guile cunning
guileful guileless guilelessly guilelessness

guillemot kind of diving sea bird

guillotine device for beheading people; device for cutting paper

guilt feeling that one is to blame; fact of having done wrong
guiltier guiltiest guiltily guiltiness guiltless guilty

guinea former British gold coin

Guinea country in West Africa
Guinean

Guinea-Bissau country in West Africa

guise outward appearance; pretence

guitar kind of plucked stringed instrument
guitarist

Gulag central administration of former USSR security service

gulf large deep bay

gull kind of sea bird

gullet throat; oesophagus

gullible easily deceived
gullibility gullibly

gully channel cut by water
gullies

gulp to swallow quickly, esp. in large mouthfuls

gum[1] sticky substance exuded by certain plants; to stick
gummed gumming gummy gum-tree

gum[2] fleshy tissue covering base of the teeth
gumboil

gumboots strong waterproof rubber boots

gumption common sense

gun kind of firearm
gunboat gunfire gunman gunmetal gunnage gunner gunnery gunpoint gunpowder gunroom gun-running gunship gunshot gunsmith

gunge (*informal*) sticky matter; to clog
gunging

gunnel[1] kind of eel-like fish

gunwale or **gunnel**[2] top of side of boat

guppy kind of small brightly coloured fish
guppies

gurgle (to make a) low bubbling sound
gurgling

Gurkha Nepalese soldier serving in Indian of British army

guru personal religious teacher, esp. in Hinduism

gush to pour out profusely; sudden great flow
gushes

gusset material inserted into a garment; piece for strengthening an angle in a framework
gusseted

gust sudden rush of wind, etc.
gustier gustiest gustiness gusty

gusto lively enjoyment

gut (lower part of) alimentary canal; to remove entrails from; to destroy the inside of a building
gutted gutting

guts (*informal*) courage
gutless gutsy

gutta-percha hard rubber-like substance

gutter channel to carry off rainwater
guttering guttersnipe

guttural (*of a sound*) made in the throat

guy[1] (*informal*) man; effigy of Guy Fawkes
guys

guy[2] rope, etc. used to secure something in position
guys

Guyana country in South America
Guyanese

guzzle to consume food or drink greedily
guzzler guzzling

Gwent county in Wales

Gwynedd county in Wales

gym gymnasium; gymnastics
gymslip

gymkhana public display of horse-riding

gymnasium room or building for physical exercises
gymnasiums or *gymnasia*

gymnastics exercises to develop bodily strength
gymnast gymnastic

gynaecology (US **gynecology**) branch of medicine dealing with diseases of women
gynaecological (US *gynecological*)
gynaecologist (US *gynecologist*)

gypsum mineral used in making plaster of Paris

gypsy or **gipsy** person who moves from one place to another
gypsies or *gipsies*

gyrate to move in circles or spirals
gyrating gyration gyratory

gyroscope device containing a disc that can turn freely on an axis in any direction

Habakkuk prophet and book in the Old Testament

habeas corpus legal order requiring that a person be brought before a court

haberdasher shopkeeper who sells articles used in sewing
haberdashery

habit usual manner or behaviour; costume of a nun or monk
habitude

habitable fit for living in
habitability

habitat natural environment of animal or plant

habitation dwelling-place
habitability habitable

habitual regular; usual
habitually habitualness

habituate to make used to
habituating habituation

habitué frequent visitor to a place

hachures shading on a map to show gradients

hacienda large estate; ranch

hack[1] to chop or cut roughly; to clear by cutting; to gain unauthorized access to a computer system
hacker hacking hack-saw

hack[2] riding horse; horse kept for hire; writer who does tedious or hard work
hackwork hack-writer

hackles long neck feathers on a pheasant, etc.

hackney breed of horse; cab, carriage, etc. for hire

hackneyed trite because used too often

had past tense and past participle of **have**
hadn't

haddock kind of sea fish, smaller than cod

Hades (*Greek mythology*) underworld

haematite (US **hematite**) iron oxide

haematology (US **hematology**) branch of medicine dealing with diseases of the blood

haemoglobin (US **hemoglobin**) substance within red blood cells

haemophilia (US **hemophilia**) hereditary disease in which the blood does not clot normally
haemophiliac (US *hemophiliac*)

haemorrhage (US **hemorrhage**) great loss of blood from blood-vessels

haemorrhoids (US **hemorrhoids**) swollen veins in the area of the anus

haft handle of an axe, knife, etc.

hag unpleasant ugly old woman; witch
haggish

Haggai prophet and book in the Old Testament

haggard looking worn out and worried

haggis Scottish dish of an animal's stomach lining stuffed with sheep's offal, minced meat, etc., and boiled

haggle to argue about terms of an agreement, prices, etc.
haggler haggling

hagiography biography of saints
hagiographer

ha-ha sunken fence
ha-has

hail[1] small pellets of ice
hailstone hailstorm

hail[2] to great enthusiastically; to have come (from)
hail-fellow-well-met

hair thread-like structure growing from the skin
hairbrush haircloth haircut hair-do hairdresser hairdressing hairdrier hairgrip hairless hairline hairnet hairpiece hairpin hair-raising hairslide hair-splitting hairspring hairstyle hairy

Haiti country in the Caribbean Sea
Haitian

hake fish related to cod

halal meat from animals that have been killed according to Muslim law

halberd ancient weapon consisting of spear and battleaxe
halberdier

halcyon peaceful and calm

hale healthy and strong

half either of two equal parts
halves half-and-half half-back half-baked half-blood half-breed half-brother half-caste half-cock half-dozen half-hearted half holiday half-hour half-hourly half-jokingly half-length half-mast half moon half-past half pay halfpenny half-price half-sister half-term half-timbered half-time half-tone half-truth half-volley halfway halfwit half-witted half-yearly

halibut kind of large flat-fish

halitosis state of having bad breath

hall passage at entrance of a house or building; large room for public meetings
hallway

hallelujah see **alleluia**

halliard see **halyard**

hallmark (to stamp with an) official mark on gold or silver articles

hallo, **hello**, or **hullo** exclamation used in greeting, attracting attention, etc.
hallos, hellos, or *hullos*

hallow to make holy
hallower

Hallowe'en 31 October

hallucination vivid perception of something that does not really exist
hallucinate hallucinating hallucinatory

hallucinogen drug that causes hallucinations
hallucinogenic

halm see **haulm**

halo ring of light round the head of a saint, etc. in a painting or round the moon
haloes or *halos*

halogen non-metallic chemical element
halogenous

halt (to bring or come to a) stop

halter rope or strap for a horse

halting hesitant
haltingly

halve to divide into two equal parts
halving

halyard or **halliard** line used to raise or lower a sail, flag, etc.

ham (meat from) hind leg of a pig; (*informal*) amateur radio operator; (*informal*) to overact
ham-fisted hammed hamming

hamburger round flat minced beef cake

hamlet small village

hammer tool with a heavy head for driving in nails, etc.

hammock hanging bed

hamper[1] to hinder the progress or movement of

hamper[2] large covered basket and food inside it

hamster kind of rodent with cheek pouches

hamstring (to cripple by cutting the) tendon at the back of the knee
hamstrung or *hamstringed*

hand part of the arm at the end of the wrist; pointer on a clock; manual worker; cards dealt to a player; to give with the hand
handbag handball handbill handbook handbrake handcart handcuffs handful handgrip handloom handmade handmaiden hand-me-down hand-out hand-over hand-picked handrail handset handshake hands-off hands-on handstand hand-to-hand handwork handwriting handy handyman

handicap disability; (to put at a) disadvantage so that all competitors have an equal chance of winning
handicapped handicapper handicapping

handicraft skilled work done with the hands

handiwork something done with the hands

handkerchief small piece of cloth for wiping the nose
handkerchiefs or *handkerchieves*

handle part of an object designed to be held in order to move, lift, etc. the object; to touch with the hands; to deal with
handlebars handler handling

handsome good-looking; generous
handsomely

handy convenient; skilful with the hands
handily handiness

hang to fix to a point so that the lower part is free (past tense and past participle *hung*); to put to death by suspending from a rope (past tense and past participle *hanged*)
hanger hanger-on hangers-on hang-gliding hangman hang-out hang-up
SEE PANEL

---

hanged or hung?

Hung is the past tense and past participle for most senses of the verb **hang**: bunting hung in the town's main square; The walls were hung with enormous oil paintings.

Hanged is limited to the sense 'to put to death by suspending from a rope': *They were hanged at first light on Monday; He hanged himself the night before his court appearance.*

---

hangar large shed for housing aircraft

hangnail loose skin near a fingernail

hangover severe headache, etc. that occurs after heavy drinking

hank coil of rope

hanker to have a strong desire

hanky or **hankie** (*informal*) handkerchief
hankies

hanky-panky (*informal*) improper behaviour

Hansard official report of the proceedings of the British Parliament

hansom horse-drawn 2-wheeled carriage

haphazard random; careless
haphazardly haphazardness

hapless unfortunate
haplessly haplessness

happen to occur
happening

happy glad or pleased; fortunate
happier happiest happily happiness happy-go-lucky

hara-kiri suicide by ritual disembowelment

harangue (to address in a) long critical speech
harangued haranguer haranguing

harass to trouble by persistent attacks, questions, etc.
harasser harasses harassingly harassment

harbinger sign of something approaching

harbour (US **harbor**) port for ships; to protest; to keep in the mind

hard firm or tough; difficult; requiring great energy; harsh *hard-and-fast hardback hard-baked hard-bitten hardboard hard-boiled hard-core hardcover harden hardener harder hardest hard-headed hard-hearted hardline hardness hard-pressed hard-sell hardship hardware hard-wearing hardwood hard-working hardy*

hardly scarcely; in a hard manner

hare fast animal larger than a rabbit
hare-brained harelip

harebell plant with pale-blue bell-shaped flowers

harem women's part of a Muslim household

haricot kind of French bean

hark to listen

harlequin clown, usually masked
harlequinade

harlot prostitute

harm to injure or damage; damage or injury
harmful harmfully harmfulness harmless harmlessly harmlessness

harmonica mouth-organ

harmonium kind of keyboard instrument like an organ

harmonize or **harmonise** to make or become harmonious
harmonization or *harmonisation*
harmonizing or *harmonising*

harmony agreement; pleasant combining of sounds
harmonies harmonic harmonious

harness (to put on an) arrangement of straps, etc. to attach to a horse; to control
harnesses harnesser harnessing

harp kind of musical instrument; to talk about constantly
harpist

harpoon (to strike with a) spear with a rope attached
harpooned harpooner

harpsichord kind of musical instrument like a piano
harpsichordist

harquebus or **arquebus** kind of portable gun

harridan ill-tempered old woman

harrier[1] kind of bird of prey

harrier[2] kind of hound; cross-country runner

harrow implement used to break up soil; to distress greatly
harrowing

harry to ravage or annoy
harried harries harrying

harsh rough, severe, or cruel
harshly harshness

hart adult male deer

harum-scarum reckless (person)

harvest (to gather in) ripened crops; season when this is done; result of effort
harvester harvesting

has 3rd person sing. of present tense of **have**
has-been hasn't

hash meal of reheated cut cooked meat; mess

hashish resin obtained from certain species of hemp

haslet cooked pig's offal

hasp metal fastening for a lock, etc.

hassle (*informal*) (to) trouble or fight
hassling

hassock firm cushion for kneeling on in a church

haste speed; hurry
hastily hastiness hasty

hasten to rush or hurry

hat head covering, esp. with brim and crown
hatband hatbox hatless hatpin hatstand

hatch[1] to bring out young from an egg; to come out from an egg; to contrive a plan
hatchery hatcheries hatches

hatch[2] door in an aircraft; covering in a ship, etc.
hatches hatchback hatchway

hatch[3] to draw fine parallel lines on
hatching

hatchet short axe

hate (to feel an) intense dislike
hatable or *hateable hateful hatefully hatefulness hater hating hatred*

hatter maker and seller of hats

haughty arrogant and proud
haughtier haughtiest haughtily haughtiness

haul to pull with effort; to transport; amount obtained
haulage haulier

haulm or **halm** stalks or stems

haunch human hips or hindquarters; leg and loin of an animal
haunches

haunt (*of ghosts*) to frequent

haute couture (*French*) exclusive elegant fashion

have to possess or obtain; to hold
had has have-nots haven't

haven harbour; place of refuge

haversack canvas bag carried on the back

havoc widespread destruction; chaos

haw fruit of the hawthorn

Hawaii US state in central Pacific
Hawaiian

hawk[1] kind of bird of prey
hawk-eyed

hawk[2] to offer goods from house to house
hawker

hawse-hole hole in bows of a ship for anchor rope

hawser larger heavy rope

hawthorn kind of thorny shrub with red berries

hay cut and dried grass or clover used to feed animals
haybox haycock hayfork hayloft haymaker haymaking hayrick haystack

haywire out of control

hazard (source of) risk or danger; to risk
hazardous

haze thin mist
hazily haziness hazy

hazel kind of shrub with rounded edible nuts
hazelnut

he subject pronoun referring to a male person or animal
he-man

head part of the body containing eyes, ears, brain, etc.; upper or front part; leader or director
headache headband headboard head-butt headcount head-covering head-dress header headfirst headgear head-hunter heading headlamp headland headless headlight headline headlong headman headmaster headmistress head-on headphones headquarters headres headroom headscarf headship headsman headstall headstone headstrong headteacher headway headwind headword heady

heal to make or become healthy
healer

health condition of body or mind; being well
healthful healthy

heap (to put in a) pile of things lying on top of one another

hear to perceive sound with the ear; to pay attention to
heard hearer hearing hearing-aid hearsay

hearken (*archaic*) to listen to

hearse vehicle used to carry a coffin

heart organ that pumps blood round the body; love; central part of something
heartache heartbeat heartbreak heartbreaking heartbroken heartburn hearten heartfelt heartland heartless heart-rending heart-searching heartstrings heartthrob heart-to-heart heart-warming hearty

hearth floor of fireplace; fireside
hearthrug hearthstone

heat being hot; to make or become hot; preliminary stage in a competition
heated heatedly heater heat-resistant heatspot heatstroke

heath large area of open uncultivated land

heathen person who does not believe in any of the main world religions
heathendom heathenish

heather kind of evergreen shrub found on moors

Heath Robinson (*of a mechanical device*) absurdly complicated

heave to lift or move with great effort; to rise and fall heavily
heaved heaving hove

heaven dwelling-place of God; place of greatest happiness; sky
heavenly heaven-sent heavenward heavenwards

heavy weighty; difficult; hard
heavier heaviest heavily heaviness heavy-duty heavy-handed heavy-hearted heavyweight

hebdomadal weekly
hebdomadally

Hebrew Israelite; Semitic language
Hebraic

Hebrides group of islands off Scotland
Hebridean

heck (*informal*) euphemism for hell

heckle to interrupt a public speaker with comments, taunts, etc.
heckler heckling

hectare unit of area, 10,000 square metres

hectic marked by busy activity
hectically

hector to bully

he'd (*informal*) he would; he had

hedge row of densely growing bushes; to avoid giving a straight answer
hedger hedgerow hedging

hedgehog kind of small nocturnal spine-covered mammal

hedonism belief that pleasure is the greatest good in life
hedonist hedonistic

heed to pay close attention to
heedful heedfully heedfulness heedless heedlessly heedlessness

hee-haw sound of a donkey's bray

heel[1] back part of the foot below the ankle
heel-bone

heel[2] (*of a ship*) to lean over

hefty large and strong
heftier heftiest heftily heftiness

hegemony domination of one state, group, etc. over others
hegemonies

hegira or **hejira** start of the Muslim era

heifer young cow, esp. one that has not yet given birth to a calf

height distance measured from the bottom to top of something; high area

heighten to make or become higher or more intense
heightened

heinous evil
heinously heinousness

heir (*fem.* **heiress**) person who inherits or is entitled to inherit
heiresses heirdom heirloom heirship

heist (*slang*) robbery

hejira see **hegira**

held past tense and past participle of **hold**[1]

helicopter aircraft with horizontally rotating blades

heliocentric having the sun as its centre

heliograph signalling instrument that uses the sun's rays reflected from a mirror

heliotrope kind of plant with small purple flowers

heliport airport for helicopters

helium light gas used for filling balloons

helix spiral; spiral curve
helices

hell dwelling-place of the Devil; place of punishment or extreme misery; (*informal*) exclamation of anger, etc.
hell-bent hell-cat hell-fire hellish

he'll (*informal*) he will

Hellenism principles, etc. of Greek civilization
Hellenistic

hello see **hallo**

helm steering-control apparatus of a ship
helmsman

helmet defensive or protective head-covering
helmeted

help (to) aid or support
helper helpful helpfully helpfulness helpless helplessly helplessness helpline helpmate

helter-skelter high spiral slide at a fair; (in a way that is) careless

helve handle of an axe or pick

Helvetian Swiss

hem turned-back and sewn-down edge of a garment; to provide with a hem; to surround
hemline hemmed hemmer hemming hemstitch

hematite (US) see **haematite**

hematology (US) see **haematology**

hemisphere half of a sphere; half of the earth
hemispherical

hemlock poisonous plant

hemoglobin (US) see **haemoglobin**

hemophilia (US) see **haemophilia**

hemorrhage (US) see **haemorrhage**

hemorrhoids (US) see **haemorrhoids**

hemp plant whose fibres are used to make rope and whose flowers yield a narcotic drug
hempen

hen female bird; chicken
hen-coop hen-house hennery hen-party henpeck henpecked hen-roost

hence for this reason; from this time or place
henceforth henceforward

henchman faithful supporter
henchmen

hendiadys expression of an idea by 2 words joined by a conjunction

henna (reddish dye obtained from) tropical shrub

hepatitis inflammation of the liver

heptagon polygon with 7 sides
heptagonal

heptahedron solid with 7 faces
heptahedrons or *heptahedra*

her object or possessive form of **she**
hers herself

herald official announcer of news; forerunner

heraldry study and use of coats of arms
heraldic

herb plant used in cooking and medicine
herbage herbal herbalist herbarium herbicide

herbaceous of fleshy, not woody plants

herbivore plant-eating animal
herbivorous

herculean requiring enormous strength

herd large group of animals, esp. cattle
herder herdsman

here in or to this place; in or to this point
hereabouts hereafter hereby herein hereinafter hereof hereon here's hereto heretofore hereunder hereupon herewith

heredity transmission of genetic factors from one generation to the next
hereditable hereditary

heresy opinion, esp. religious, that is contrary to orthodox beliefs
heresies heretic heretical heretically

heritage something inherited or handed down by tradition
heritable

hermaphrodite animal or plant with male and female reproductive organs
hermaphroditic

hermeneutics interpretation of the Bible
hermeneutic

Hermes (*Greek mythology*) messenger and herald of the gods

hermetic airtight
hermetically

hermit person who has chosen to live alone
hermitage

hernia projection of part of internal organ through an enclosing structure
hernias

hero (*fem.* **heroine**) very courageous person; main person in a play, etc.
heroes heroic heroically heroism

heroin pain-killing drug made from morphine

heron kind of long-legged wading bird
heronry heronries

herpes inflammatory virus disease of the skin

herpetology zoology concerned with reptiles
herpetologist

herring kind of important food-fish
herring-bone

hers (the one or ones) belonging to her

hertz (*physics*) unit of frequency

he's (*informal*) he is; he has

hesitate to be slow or reluctant in speech or action
hesitance or *hesitancy hesitant hesitating hesitation*

Hesperus evening star, esp. Venus

hessian kind of coarse fabric

heterodox not orthodox
heterodoxy

heterogeneous composed of dissimilar parts

heterosexual sexually attracted to people of the opposite sex
heterosexuality heterosexually

het up (*informal*) excited or angry

heuristic of the methodology that a learner should find out things for himself of herself
heuristically

hew to strike, cut, or carve
hewed or *hewn hewer hewing*

hexagon polygon with 6 sides
hexagonal

hexahedron solid with 6 faces
hexahedrons or *hexahedra*

hexameter line of verse with 6 metrical feet

hey exclamation used to show discovery, surprise, etc.

heyday time of greatest popularity

hiatus break or gap in continuity
hiatuses

hibernate to spend the winter in a dormant state
hibernating hibernation

Hibernian (*poetic*) of Ireland

hibiscus kind of herbaceous shrub
hibiscuses

hiccup or **hiccough** (to make a) sudden sharp gasping noise

hickory kind of North American hardwood tree that bears edible nuts
hickories

hide[1] to put or keep out of sight; hidden place for observing animals and birds
hid hidden hide-and-seek hideaway hiding

hide[2] animal's skin

hidebound narrow-minded

hideous very ugly
hideously hideousness

hiding flogging or beating

hierarchy system arranged in ranks
hierarchies hierarchical

hieroglyphics ancient Egyptian pictorial writing

hi-fi (*informal*) high-fidelity

higgledy-piggledy muddled; jumbled

high reaching far from bottom to top; far above the ground; above normal; raised in pitch
highbrow high chair high-class higher highest highfalutin high-flown high-flyer high-flying high-handed high-heeled highland high-level highly highly-strung high-minded high-necked high-pitched high-powered high-rise high road high-sounding high-speed high-spirited high-tech

highlight to emphasize
highlighter

highness title used to address a royal person
Highnesses

highway main road
highwayman

hijack to seize control of an aircraft, esp. to divert it
hijacked hijacker hijacking

hike (to take a) long walk for pleasure
hiker hiking

hilarious very funny
hilariously hilariousness or *hilarity*

Hilary spring term at some universities

hill natural rise in ground
hill-fort hillock hillside hilltop hilly

hill-billy unsophisticated person from the mountains of SE USA
hill-billies

hilt handle of a sword

him object form of **he**
himself

Himalayas mountain range in Asia
Himalayan

hind[1] at the back
hindermost hindmost hindquarters

hind[2] female deer

hinder to get in the way of
hindrance

Hindi language of North India

hindsight wise understanding after the event

Hinduism main religious system in India
Hindu

Hindustani dialect of Hindi spoken in Delhi

hinge on which a door, etc. turns
hinging

hinny sterile offspring of a male horse and female ass

hint (to give a) brief suggestion

hinterland land lying inland from a coast

hip[1] side of the body where legs join the trunk

hip-bath hip-bone hip-flask hip-joint hip-pocket hipster

hip[2] fruit of a rose

hippie or **hippy** young person with unconventional lifestyle
hippies

hippodrome music-hall or theatre

hippopotamus very large African river mammal
hippopotamuses or *hippopotami*

hipster (*of trousers*) worn from the hips

hire to pay for the temporary use of a person or thing; such payment
hireable hire-car hireling hire-purchase hiring

hirsute hairy

his possessive form of **he**; (the one or ones) belonging to him

hiss (to make an) *s*-sound, expressing disapproval
hisses hissing

histamine chemical compound released from body tissues

historic famous; memorable; significant
SEE PANEL

historic or historical?
A *historic* event is one that is memorable or significant: *This is a historic moment: the birth of a new nation; gain a historic victory in the World Cup.*

Historical means relating to the study of history more generally: *artefacts of historical interest; historical events* are those that really happened.

historical of or based on history
SEE PANEL at **historic**

history (study of) past events
histories historian historicity historiographer historiography

histrionic artificially dramatic
histrionically histrionics

hit (to deal a) blow; successful record, etc.
hit-and-run hit-or-miss hitter hitting

hitch to fasten with a hook, etc.; slight difficulty; to hitchhike
hitches

hitchhike to travel by asking for free lifts
hitchhiker hitchhiking

hither to this place
hitherto

hive shelter for bees; busy place

hoar deposit of ice-crystals on the ground
hoar-frost

hoard (to) store for future use

hoarding large board for advertisements

hoarse harsh-sounding
hoarsely hoarseness

hoary having grey or white hair

hoax to deceive as a trick or joke; such a deception
hoaxes hoaxer

hob flat top part of stove

hobble to walk lamely or awkwardly
hobbler hobbling

hobby activity pursued in spare time
hobbies hobby-horse

hobgoblin mischievous spirit

hobnail short heavy nail for soles of boots
hobnailed

hobnob to associate
hobnobbed hobnobbing

hobo (*chiefly* US) tramp; migratory worker

Hobson's choice no choice at all

hock[1] middle joint of an animal's back leg

hock[2] German white wine

hock[3] to pawn

hockey game played with long curved sticks and ball

hocus-pocus trickery; conjuror's spell

hod open wooden box for carrying bricks
hodman

hoe (to use an) implement to till the soil
hoed hoeing

hog castrated male pig; to take more than one's fair share of
hogged hogging hoggish hogback hogwash

hogmanay (*Scottish*) New Year's Eve

hogshead unit of liquid measure; large cask

hoi polloi common people

hoist (to raise by using an) apparatus of ropes and pulleys

hoity-toity assuming importance; haughty

hold[1] to keep in the hands or arms; to contain
held holdall holding hold-up

hold[2] space for cargo in a ship or aircraft

hole (to make a) hollow space or opening in something
hole-and-corner holey holing

holiday period of rest from work
holiday-maker

holism philosophy that the whole is greater than the sum of its parts
holistic

holland coarse linen cloth

Holland the Netherlands

hollandaise rich sauce made with butter, egg-yolks, etc.

holler (*informal*) to shout or yell

hollow having a space within; sunken (area)
hollowly hollowness

holly kind of shrub with prickly and shiny evergreen leaves

hollyhock tall plant of the mallow family

holmium metallic element

holm-oak kind of evergreen oak tree

holocaust great destruction or loss of life, esp. mass murder of Jews in 1939–45

hologram pattern of light partly caused by a laser
holography

holograph document handwritten by its author

holster leather case for a pistol

holy sacred; godly
holier holiest holiness

homage show of respect, honour, or allegiance

homburg man's hat

home place where one lives
homebird home-brewed home-coming home-grown homeland homeless homelessness home-made homesick homesickness homespun homestead homewards homework

homely unpretentious; kind; (US) plain or ugly
homeliness

homeopathy see **homoeopathy**

homicide killing of one person by another
homicidal homicidally

homily sermon or moralizing talk
homilies

homing able to return home

hominid family of primates, including man

hominoid of or like man; manlike animal

homoeopathy or **homeopathy** treatment of an illness by prescribing drugs in small doses
homoeopathic or *homeopathic*

homogeneous of the same kind or nature
homogeneity

homogenize or **homogenise** to break up fat globules in milk
homogenization or *homogenisation*
homogenizing or *homogenising*

homograph word spelt in the same way as another but having a different meaning

homologous having a similar or corresponding shape or structure

homonym word spelled and pronounced in the same way
homograph or *homophone*

homophobia strong dislike or fear of homosexuals

homophone word pronounced in the same way as another but having a different spelling, meaning, or derivation

Homo sapiens mankind

homosexual sexually attracted to people of one's own sex
homosexuality homosexually

Honduras country in Central America
Honduran

hone (to sharpen or polish on a) whetstone
honing

honest truthful or trustworthy; fair
honestly honesty

honey syrup made by bees from nectar
honey-bee honeycomb honeydew honeyed

honeymoon holiday taken by a newly-married couple

honeysuckle kind of climbing shrub with sweet-smelling flowers

honk (to make the) loud harsh sound of a goose

honky-tonk style of ragtime music

honorarium fee for professional services
honorariums or *honoraria*

honorary conferred as an honour
SEE PANEL

---

honorary or honourable?

An *honorary* degree or title is one that is given as an honour to a person, because of their public achievements rather than because they have gained the required qualifications: *receive an honorary doctorate. Honorary* is also used to describe a post that is unpaid: *the honorary secretary of the society.*

People are described as *honourable* if they behave fairly and morally and act with integrity; an *honourable act/achievement* is one that can be admired: *The only honourable thing under the circumstances is to resign. Honourable* is also used as a title of respect: *the Right Honourable Raymond Lee-Smith.*

---

honorific (expression) indicating respect

honour (US **honor**) (to) respect; reputation; privilege

honourable (US **honorable**) moral and just; that can be admired
honourably (US *honorably*)
SEE PANEL at **honorary**

hood loose covering for head and neck; (waterproof) cover for a pram, etc.

hoodlum gangster; lawless youth

hoodwink to trick

hoof horny covering at the end of the foot of a horse, deer, etc.
hooves or *hoofs*

hoo-ha noisy fuss

hook (to fasten with a) curved piece of metal, etc. used to hang, catch, or pull something
hooked hook-up hookworm

hookah oriental pipe

hooligan rough lawless young person
hooliganism

hoop rigid circular band
hoopla

hoopoe kind of bird with pinkish-brown plumage and fan-like crest

hooray or **hoorah** see **hurrah**

hoot (to make the) sound of an owl or horn, etc. of a vehicle
hooter hooting

Hoover (*trademark*) vacuum cleaner; to clean with a vacuum cleaner

hop[1] (to) jump, esp. on one foot
hopped hopping hopscotch

hop[2] climbing plant with flowers used to give a bitter flavour to beer
hop-picker hop-pole

hope (to feel) expectant desire for something
hopeful hopefully hopefulness hopeless hopelessly hopelessness hoping

hopper funnel-shaped container

horde crowd or throng

horehound kind of plant whose juice was formerly used as a medicine for coughs

horizon line at which earth and sky appear to meet

horizontal parallel to the horizon
horizontally

hormone substance that circulates in the blood to cause a particular response
hormonal

horn pointed bony growth on the head of some animals; musical instrument; warning device on a vehicle, etc.
horn-rimmed horny

hornbeam kind of tree with hard white wood

hornbill kind of bird with very large bill

hornblende dark mineral

hornet kind of large stinging wasp

hornpipe lively dance traditionally performed by sailors

horology science of time measurement; art of clock-making

horoscope prediction of a person's future based on position of starts at birth

horrendous horrible
horrendously horrendousness

horrible very unpleasant
horribleness horribly

horrid unpleasant; repulsive
horridly horridness

horrific to fill with terror
horrified horrifies horrifying

horror feeling of terror
horror-stricken horror-struck

hors de combat (*French*) disabled

hors d'œuvre (*French*) light appetizer at the beginning of a meal
hors d'œuvres

horse 4-footed animal with mane and tail, used for riding, etc.; to play (around)
horseback horsebox horse-chestsnut horse-drawn horse-flesh horsefly horsehair horselaugh horseman horsemanship horsemeat horseplay horsepower horse-race horse-racing horse-radish horseshoe horsewoman horsy

hortatory or **hortative** encouraging

horticulture art and science of growing fruit, vegetables, and flowers
horticultural horticulturist

hosanna expression of acclamation and praise to God

hose flexible pipe for carrying water, etc.; stockings, socks, etc.
hosepipe hosier hosiery hosing

hospice home for caring for the terminally ill

hospitable given to hospitality
hospitably

hospital place where the ill and injured are treated

hospitality generous and kind welcoming of guests

hospitalize or **hospitalise** to send into hospital
hospitalization or *hospitalisation*
hospitalizing or *hospitalising*

hospitaller (US **hospitaler**) member of a charitable brotherhood

host[1] person who welcomes guests into his or her home
hostess

host[2] great number

Host bread in the Eucharist

hostage person held as a security that particular terms will be met

hostel building providing accommodation
hosteller

hostelry inn or hotel

hostile opposed; unfriendly; antagonistic
hostilely hostility hostilities

hot having a high temperature
hotbed hot-blooded hotfoot hothead hotheaded hothouse hotline hotplate hotpot hot-tempered hotter hottest

hotchpotch jumbled mixture

hotel commercial establishment providing food and rooms for travellers
hotelier

houmous see **hummus**

hound dog used for hunting; to pursue or harass

hour 24th part of a day
hourglass hourly

house building for people to live in; to provide accommodation for
house-agent houseboat housebound housebreaker housebreaking housecoat housedog housefather house-flag housefly houseful household householder housekeeper housekeeping houseless houselights housemaid houseman housemaster housemistress housemother houseparent house-proud house-to-house housetop house-trained house-warming housewife housework housing

hove past tense of **heave**

hovel small ramshackle dwelling-place

hover to remain in the air in one place

hovercraft vehicle supported on a cushion of air
hoverport

how in what way; to what extent
howbeit how-do-you-do how's

howdah seat on an elephant's back

however to whatever extent; nevertheless
howsoever

howitzer short-barrelled cannon

howl (to utter a) long loud cry

howler obvious mistake

hoyden tomboy

hub central part of a wheel

hubbub confused noise; uproar

hubby (*informal*) husband
hubbies

hubris pride or arrogance

huckaback coarse absorbent cloth

huckleberry (dark blue berry or black berry of an) American heath shrub
huckleberries

huckster hawker

huddle to crowd together; crowded mass
huddler huddling

hue[1] shade of colour

hue[2] (**hue and cry**) general outcry

huff mood of anger; to blow
huffish huffy

hug (to) embrace
hugged hugging

huge very large
hugely hugeness huger hugest

hugger-mugger secrecy; confusion; in secret

Huguenot French Protestant of 16th and 17th centuries

hula Hawaiian dance

hulk body of an abandoned ship; bulky person or thing
hulking

hull main body of a ship; outer covering of a fruit

hullabaloo commotion

hullo see **hallo**

hum (to make a) low continuous vibrating sound
hummed humming humming-bird

human person; of people
humanity humanities humankind
SEE PANEL

human or humane?
The adjective *human* mean 'of or relating to people': *human relationships; human nature; human rights. Human* is also used to describe certain qualities, such as a concern for others and a tendency to make mistakes, that are thought to be typical of people: *You needn't be afraid of the boss – he's quite human really; I'm sorry ... it was a mistake, after all I'm only human.*

Humane is used to describe a person or someone's behaviour that is kind and sympathetic and wants to cause as little suffering as possible to people and animals: *humane techniques in the treatment of animals.*

humane kind; sympathetic
humanely humaneness
SEE PANEL at **human**

humanism philosophy emphasizing human worth, skills, etc.
humanist

humanitarian (person) advocating human welfare

humanize or **humanise** to make or become human
humanization or *humanisation*
humanizing or *humanising*

humanoid being having a human appearance

humble not proud; submissive; to cause to feel humble
humbler humblest humbling humbly

humbug nonsense; hard peppermint sweet; to deceive
humbugged humbugging

humdrum ordinary; routine

humerus long bone of the upper arm
humeri

humid moist
humidity

humidify to make air humid
humidification humidified humidifier humidifies humidifying

humiliate to hurt someone's pride
humiliating humiliation

humility being humble

hummock hillock; mound

hummus or **houmous** dip made from chickpeas

humour (US **humor**) funniness; temper; to indulge
humoresque humorist humorous

hump round projection
humpback humpbacked

humus soil of decomposing organic matter

Hun member of ravaging Asiatic race of 4th and 5th centuries

hunch intuitive guess; (to bend into a) hump
hunches hunchback hunchbacked

hundred number 100
hundredfold hundredth

hundredweight unit of weight

hung past tense and past participle of **hang**
hung-over
SEE PANEL at **hang**

Hungary country in Central Europe
Hungarian

hunger (to have a) feeling caused by lack of food

hungrier hungriest hungrily hungry

hunk large piece; strong sexually attractive man
hunky

hunt to search for; to pursue and kill
hunter huntsman huntswoman

hurdle (to jump over a) light barrier
hurdler hurdling

hurdy-gurdy barrel-organ
hurdy-gurdies

hurl to throw forcefully

hurly-burly confusion or commotion
hurly-burlies

hurrah, **hooray**, or **hoorah** cheer of joy, approval, etc.

hurricane violent storm; tropical cyclone

hurry to (cause to) go with haste
hurried hurries hurrying

hurt to injure; to feel pain; harm
hurtful hurtfully hurtfulness

hurtle to rush forcefully
hurtling

husband married man in relation to his wife; to use economically

husbandry management; farming
husbandman

hush to make or become quiet; silence
hushes hush-hush

husk dry external covering of fruit or seed

husky[1] hoarse and rasping; (*informal*) big and strong
huskier huskiest huskily huskiness

husky[2] Eskimo dog
huskies

hussar member of cavalry regiment

hussy cheeky or promiscuous woman
hussies

hustings proceedings at a parliamentary election

hustle to push roughly
hustler hustling

hut small rough house or shelter

hutch small cage for rabbits, etc.
hutches

hyacinth kind of plant with fragrant flowers

hybrid offspring from 2 unrelated animals, plants, etc.
hybridism

hybridize or **hybridise** to cross-breed
hybridizing or *hybridising*

hydra persistent trouble

hydrangea kind of a shrub with large clusters of flowers

hydrant pipe from water-main to which a hose can be attached

hydrate compound of water and another substance; to combine with water
hydrating hydration

hydraulic operated or caused by water
hydraulics

hydride compound of hydrogen and another element

hydrocarbon organic compound of hydrogen and carbon

hydrocephalus excess of fluid on the brain

hydrochloric acid solution of hydrogen chloride

hydrodynamics study of mechanical properties of liquids in motion

hydroelectric generated by water-pressure
hydroelectricity

hydrofoil ship whose hull is raised out of the water by foils; such a foil

hydrogen gas that is the simplest, lightest, and most abundant element in the universe
hydrogenous

hydrolysis reaction of a chemical compound with water

hydrometer instrument for measuring the relative density of a liquid

hydrophobia aversion to water; rabies
hydrophobic

hydroplane speedboat fitted with hydrofoils

hydroponics cultivation of plants in water rather than soil

hydrostatics study of mechanical properties of liquids not in motion

hydrotherapy treatment of certain illnesses by applying water externally

hydrous containing water

hyena kind of flesh-eating animal

hygiene maintenance of health; cleanliness
hygienic hygienically hygienist

hygrometer instrument that measures humidity

hymen mucous membrane covering the opening to the vagina

hymn song of praise, esp. to God
hymnal hymn-book hymnist hymnody hymnology

hype (*slang*) (to promote in) intensive or exaggerated publicity
hyped hyping

hyperactive unusually active
hyperactively

hyperbola curve formed by a conic section
hyperbolic

hyperbole deliberate exaggeration
hyperbolic

hypercritical too critical
hypercritically

hypermarket very large supermarket

hypersensitive too sensitive
hypersensitivity

hypertension excessively high blood-pressure

hypertext method that enables the user to move round different topics in computer documents

hyperventilation abnormally fast breathing
hyperventilate

hyphen punctuation mark - used to join or separate words

hyphenate to join or separate with a hyphen
hyphenation hyphenating

hypnosis state like deep sleep when a person may be influenced by another
hypnotic hypnotism hypnotist

hypnotize or **hypnotise** to induce hypnosis in; to charm
hypnotizing or *hypnotising*

hypochondria great but unnecessary anxiety about one's health
hypochondriac hypochondriacal

hypocrisy pretence of good standards or beliefs
hypocrite hypocritical hypocritically

hypodermic (syringe) for injecting beneath the skin

hypostasis essential nature of something
hypostases hypostatic

hypotenuse side in a right-angled triangle opposite the right angle

hypothermia abnormally low body temperature

hypothesis provisional suggested explanation
hypotheses hypothetical

hypothesize or **hypothesise** to form or take as a hypothesis
hypothesizing hypothesising

hyrax kind of rodent-like mammal

hyssop kind of aromatic herb plant

hysterectomy surgical removal of the uterus
hysterectomies

hysteria intense uncontrollable emotion or excitement
hysterical hysterically hysterics

I

I subject pronoun referring to the person who is speaking or writing

iambus metrical foot of 1 short syllable followed by 1 long syllable
iambuses or *iambi* *iambic* *iambics*

Iberian member of Caucasian people who in ancient times inhabited South and East Spain; native or inhabitant of Spain or Portugal

ibex kind of wild goat
ibexes or *ibex*

ibis kind of wading bird of warm regions
ibises or *ibis*

Ibiza island in the West Mediterranean

ice frozen water; to form ice
iceberg *icebound* *icebox* *icebreaker* *ice-cap* *ice-cold* *ice-cream* *ice-free* *ice-pick* *icing* *icy*

Iceland country in North Atlantic
Icelander *Icelandic*

I Ching ancient Chinese book of Confucian and Taoist philosophy

ichthyology study of fishes
ichthyological *ichthyologist*

icicle hanging spike of ice

icing sweet decorative coating for cakes

icon sacred painting or image of Christ or a saint

iconoclast person who attacks established principles
iconoclasm *iconoclastic*

I'd (*informal*) I had; I would; I should

idea conception or notion

ideal (something considered) perfect; existing only in the mind
idealism *idealist* *idealistic* *idealistically*

idealize or **idealise** to represent or consider as ideal
idealization or *idealisation* *idealizing* or *idealising*

idée fixe (*French*) obsession
idées fixes

identical being the same; exactly alike
identically

identity to determine or show the identity of; to associate oneself (with)
identification *identified* *identifies* *identifying*

Identikit (*trademark*) set of different facial features composed to make a picture of a person wanted by the police

identify being identical; features of someone's personality, etc.
identities

ideogram or **ideograph** sign used to represent a thing or idea

ideology set of ideas or beliefs
ideologies *ideological* *ideologically* *ideologist*

idiocy stupidity
idiocies *idiot*

idiolect linguistic system of one individual

idiom expression that cannot be understood from the meaning of its constituent parts
idiomatic *idiomatically*

idiosyncrasy personal, esp. eccentric, manner of behaving or temperament
idiosyncrasies *idiosyncratic* *idiosyncratically*

idiot stupid person
idiot *idiotically*

idle lazy; not used

idleness idler idlest idling idly

idol object of worship
idolater idolatress idolatrous idolatry idolatries

idolize or **idolise** to admire devotedly
idolization or *idolisation idolizing* or *idolising*

idyll (description of a) peaceful pastoral country scene
idyllic idyllically

---

ie or ei?

The well-known rule '*i* before *e* except after *c*' applies to most words in which these letters represent the sound *ee*. Examples include:

i before e ...
achieve belief believe brief chief diesel field frieze grief grieve hygiene niece piece priest relief relieve reprieve shield shriek siege thief yield

... except after *c*
ceiling conceit conceive deceit deceive perceive receipt receive

Exceptions include:
caffeine Keith Neil protein seize Sheila species weir weird

The spelling *ei* is used when the sound represented is *ay*:
beige deign eight feign feint freight heinous neighbour reign rein reindeer sleigh sleight (of hand) *veil vein weigh weight*

---

if in the event that; whether

iffy (*informal*) uncertain or questionable

igloo dome-shaped Eskimo house made of snow
igloos

igneous consisting of solidified molten rock

ignite to set fire to; to catch fire
ignitable igniting ignition

ignoble dishonourable
ignobility ignobly

ignominy disgrace
ignominies ignominious

ignoramus ignorant person
ignoramuses

ignorance lack of knowledge
ignorant ignorantly

ignore to refuse to notice; to fail to notice
ignoring

iguana kind of large tropical tree-climbing lizard
iguanian

ileum last part of the small intestine
ileal

ilk sort of kind

I'll (*informal*) I will; I shall

ill unwell; bad
ill-advised ill-bred ill-considered ill-defined ill-disposed ill-equipped ill-fated ill-favoured (US *ill-favored*) *ill-founded ill-gotten ill-humoured* (US *ill-humored*) *ill-informed ill-mannered ill-natured ill-starred ill-timed ill-treat ill-use*

illegal forbidden by law
illegality illegalities illegally

illegible not legible
illegibility illegibly

illegitimate born of parents not married to each other; against the law
illegitimacy illegitimately

illicit not allowed
illicitly illicitness
SEE PANEL at **elicit**

illimitable limitless
illimitably

Illinois US state

illiterate not literate
illiteracy illiterately

illness disease or sickness; bad health

illogical not logical
illogicality illogically

illuminate to light up; to make clear
illuminant illuminating illumination illuminative illuminator

illusion misleading impression

illusionist illusive illusorily illusory
SEE PANEL at **allusion**

illustrate to provide with pictures or drawings; to explain by examples
illustrating illustration illustrative illustrator

illustrious distinguished and famous
illustriously illustriousness

I'm (*informal*) I am

image representation; optical appearance; mental picture
imagery

imaginary not real; existing in the imagination
SEE PANEL

---

imaginary or imaginative?
A person or thing that is *imaginary* is not real and exists only in the imagination or in a story: *an imaginary danger; a six-year-old talking to his imaginary friend.*
To describe a person or someone's ideas as *imaginative* means that they show creative imagination and an ability to think of exciting new things: *an imaginative designer; imaginative writing; an imaginative scheme for a new concert hall.*

---

imaginative showing creative imagination
imaginatively
SEE PANEL at **imaginary**

imagine to form a picture in the mind
imaginable imagination

imam Muslim priest

imbalance lack of balance

imbecile very stupid person
imbecilic imbecility

imbed see **embed**

imbibe to drink in; to assimilate
imbibing

imbroglio confused or complicated situation; tangle
imbroglios

imbue to instil or inspire
imbued imbuing

imitate to copy or mimic
imitable imitating imitation imitative imitator

immaculate completely clean; flawless
immaculately

immanent indwelling; inherent
immanence immanently

immaterial not important or relevant; having no physical substance
immaterially

immature not mature
immaturity

immeasurable not capable of measurement because of great size
immeasurability immeasurably

immediate without delay; direct
immediacy immediately

immemorial originating before what can be remembered
immemorially

immense extremely large
immensely immensity

immerse to plunge into a liquid, esp. water
immersing immersion

immigrate to come into and settle in a foreign country
immigrant immigrating immigration

imminent likely to occur soon; impending
imminence
SEE PANEL at **eminent**

immiscible incapable of being mixed

immobile unable to move; motionless; fixed
immobility

immobilize or **immobilise** to make immobile
immobilization or *immobilisation*
immobilizing or *immobilising*

immoderate excessive
immoderately immoderation

immodest indecent; shameless
immodestly immodesty

immolate to kill as a sacrifice
immolating immolation

immoral contrary to accepted morals
immorality immorally
SEE PANEL at **amoral**

immortal living for ever
immortality immortally

immortalize or **immortalise** to give eternal fame to
immortalization or *immortalisation*
immortalizing or *immortalising*

immovable not movable
immovability immovably

immune not susceptible to something such as infection
immunity immunodeficiency immunology

immunize or **immunise** to render immune to infection, etc.
immunization or *immunisation*
immunizing or *immunising*

immure to enclose with walls; to build into a wall
immuring

immutable unchanging
immutability immutably

imp small devil; mischievous child
impish

impact (force of) collision of 2 things; impression; to fix firmly

impair to weaken or damage
impairment

impala kind of African antelope

impale to pierce with a sharp pointed instrument
impalement impaling

impalpable intangible
impalpability impalpably

impanel see **empanel**

impart to communicate or convey

impartial fair; not biased
impartiality impartially

impassable not capable of being travelled through or over
impassability impassably

impasse difficult situation from which there does not appear to be a way of escape; deadlock

impassioned or **empassioned** stirred with great emotion

impassive not affected by emotion
impassively impassiveness or *impassivity*

impatient not patient or tolerant
impatiently impatientness

impeach to accuse of serious crime
impeachable impeaches impeachment

impeccable flawless
impeccability impeccably

impecunious having little or no money
impecuniously impecuniosity

impede to restrict the progress of
impediment impeding

impedimenta baggage, equipment, or encumbrances

impel to urge or constrain
impelled impellent impeller impelling

impend to be imminent
impending

impenetrable incapable of being penetrated
impenetrability impenetrably

impenitent not sorry; unrepentant
impenitence impenitently

imperative essential; urgent
imperatively

imperceptible too small, slight, etc. to be perceived
imperceptibility imperceptibly

imperfect marked by faults
imperfection imperfectly

imperial of an empire, emperor, or empress; sovereign; of British non-metric weights and measures

imperialism imperialist imperially
SEE PANEL

imperial or imperious?
Imperial means 'of an empire, emperor, or empress': *the imperial palace; his imperial powers.* The *imperial* system of weights and measures is the system that uses feet and inches to measure distance, pounds and ounces to measure weight, and gallons and pints to measure volume, which is being replaced by the metric system.

To describe someone as *imperious* means that they are dominant and commanding: *I do not wish to sound imperious but such behaviour is unacceptable; a proud imperious look.*

imperil to place in danger
imperilled imperilling

imperious dominant or commanding
SEE PANEL at **imperial**

impermanent not permanent; transitory

impermeable not allowing the passage of a liquid
impermeability

impersonal objective; not showing feelings
impersonally

impersonate to pretend to be another person
impersonating impersonation impersonator

impertinent cheeky; rude
impertinence impertinently

imperturbable not easily excited
imperturbability imperturbably

impervious impermeable; not able to be influenced
imperviously imperviousness

impetigo kind of contagious skin disease

impetuous marked by rash hasty action
impetuosity impetuously

impetus stimulus or incentive
impetuses

impiety lack of reverence
impieties

impinge to infringe or encroach
impingement impinging

impious not pious or reverent
impiously

impish of or like an imp

implacable not capable of being appeased
implacability implacably

implant to fix or insert
implantation

implausible not plausible; unlikely
implausibility implausibly

implement tool; to carry out; to put into action
implementation

implicate to imply; to involve in a crime
implicating implication

implicit not expressed plainly; complete and unquestioning
implicitly

implode to collapse inwards

implore to beg earnestly
imploring

imply to hint at indirectly
implication implied implies implying
SEE PANEL

imply or infer?
To *imply* something is to hint at it directly: *implied criticism; Are you implying that I was responsible for his death?*

Infer means 'to conclude by reasoning from facts': *I inferred from what she said that she had been married before; to infer long-term tendencies from brief historical data.*

impolite not polite
impolitely impoliteness

impolitic unwise
impoliticly

imponderable that cannot be assessed or evaluated
imponderability imponderably

import to bring in goods or services from a foreign country; something imported; significance
importable importation importer

important significant; authoritative
importance importantly

importunate making persistent demands
importunately importunity

impose to apply or enforce
imposing imposition

imposing impressive

impossible not possible
impossibility impossibly

impostor or **imposter** person who deceives others

impotent powerless; (*of males*) unable to engage in sexual intercourse
impotence impotently

impound to confine legally

impoverish to make poor
impoverishes impoverishment

impracticable incapable of being accomplished
impracticability impracticably
SEE PANEL

---

impracticable or impractical?

Something is *impracticable* if it is impossible to do: *It is impracticable to use the television when there is a power cut; Your suggestion is imaginative but I'm afraid it's impracticable.*

An idea or action is described as *impractical* if it is not sensible, reasonable, or realistic: *It is impractical to use the tumble-drier to dry only one or two garments; a vast, impractical kitchen.* Someone can be described as *impractical* if they are not skilled at undertaking practical work such as making or repairing things.

---

impractical not practical; not workable
impracticality impractically
SEE PANEL at **impracticable**

imprecate to curse or swear
imprecating

imprecation curse
imprecatory

imprecise inexact; inaccurate
imprecision

impregnable incapable of being captured or taken by force
impregnability impregnably

impregnate to fertilize; to fill
impregnating impregnation impregnator

impresario manager or director of an opera, concert company, etc.
impresarios

impress to produce a deep effect (on); to produce an imprint
impressible impression impressionable

impressionism 19th-century French art movement
impressionist

impressive striking; making a strong impression
impressively

imprimatur official license to print

imprint (to) mark or print

imprison to confine in prison
imprisonment

improbable not likely; doubtful
improbably

impromptu something, esp. a speech, that is undertaken spontaneously and without preparation
impromptus

improper indecent; inappropriate
improperly

impropriety indecent; being improper
improprieties

improve to make or become better
improvable improvement improving

improvident not thrifty; imprudent or rash
improvidence improvidently

improvise to make quickly with available

materials and no previous planning; to perform impromptu
improvisation improviser improvising

imprudent not prudent
imprudence imprudently

impudent cheeky; disrespectful; rude
impudence impudently

impugn to challenge or attack
impugnable impugnment impugner

impulse sudden urging drive or desire
impulsion impulsive

impunity exemption or freedom from punishment

impure not pure
impurely impurity impurities

impute to attribute
imputable imputation imputing

in used to show a position in space; inside; (*informal*) fashionable

in- (*prefix*) not; lack of
inability inaccessible inaccuracy inaccurate inaction inactive inactivity inadmissible inadvisable inapplicable inapposite inappropriate inapt inaptitude inattentive inaudible inauspicious incapable incoherent incombustible incommunicable incompatible incompetence incompetent incomplete incomprehensible inconsistency inconsistent inconspicuous inconsolable inconstant incorrect incorruptible incurable indecent indecipherable indecisive indeclinable indefensible indefinable indestructible indigestible indirect indiscernible indiscipline indisputable indistinct indistinguishable indivisible ineffective ineffectual inefficiency inefficient inelastic inelegant ineligible inequitable inequity ineradicable inessential inexact inexactitude inexpedient inexplicable inexpressible inextinguishable infertile infrequent ingratitude inhospitable injudicious inopportune insensitive inseparable insignificant insincere instability insufficiency insufficient insurmountable insusceptible intangible intolerable intolerance invisible invulnerable

inadequate not adequate; unable to cope
inadequacy inadequately

inadvertent careless; unintentional; negligent
inadvertence inadvertently

inalienable not able to be taken away or transferred to another
inalienability inalienably

inane meaningless; silly
inanity inanities

inanimate without life

inanition being empty; loss of energy

inarticulate not articulate; not coherent
inarticulately

inasmuch as in view of the fact that; since

inaugural marking a beginning

inaugurate to begin or open formally
inaugurating inauguration

inboard situated within the hull of a boat

inborn existing from birth; natural

inbred produced from inbreeding; deeply ingrained

inbreeding breeding of closely related individuals

in-built built in; inherent

incage see **encage**

incalculable too great to be calculated

in camera (*Latin*) not in open court

incandescent emitting light as a result of being heated
incandescence

incantation ritual magic spell

incapacitate to disable; to make ineligible
incapacitating

incapacity lack of power or abilities

incapsulate see **encapsulate**

incarcerate to imprison

incarcerating incarceration

incarnate possessing human bodily form
incarnation

incase see **encase**

incendiary designed to start fires
incendiaries

incense[1] substance burnt for its sweet smell

incense[2] to make very angry
incensing

incentive motivating or urging influence; stimulus

inception beginning
inceptive

incertitude doubt; uncertainty

incessant continual
incessancy incessantly

incest sexual intercourse between people too closely related to marry
incestuous

inch unit of length; one-twelfth of a foot
inches

inchoate just beginning; undeveloped

incidence degree or rate of occurrence

incident occurrence or event

incidental happening as a result of something more important
incidentally

incinerate to burn to ashes
incinerating incineration incinerator

incipient beginning
incipience incipiently

incise to cut a design or lines in
incising incision

incisive penetrating
incisively

incisor sharp front cutting tooth

incite to stir up; to provoke
incitement inciting

incivility impoliteness; rude act
incivilities

inclement (*of weather*) stormy or cold

incline (to cause) to lean or slope; slope; to tend
inclination inclining

include to put as part of a large group; to contain
including inclusion inclusive

incognito person living under an assumed name or in disguise
incognitos

incognizant unaware (of)

income amount of money gained, esp. from work

incoming coming in

incommensurable incapable of being measured
incommensurability incommensurably

incommensurate not commensurate; disproportionate

incommode to bother
incommoding incommodious

incommunicado deprived of communication with others

incomparable that cannot be compared; unequalled or matchless
incomparably

inconceivable incapable of being conceived or imagined
inconceivability inconceivably

inconclusive not resulting in a definite conclusion
inconclusiveness

incongruous out of place
incongruity incongruities

inconsequent or **inconsequential** illogical or irrelevant
inconsequently or *inconsequentially*

inconsiderable small; trivial
inconsiderably

inconsiderate thoughtless
inconsiderately

incontinent not able to control the discharge of the bladder or bowels
incontinence

incontrovertible incapable of being contradicted or disputed
incontrovertibility incontrovertibly

inconvenience something that causes slight discomfort, etc.; to cause inconvenience to
inconveniencing inconvenient inconveniently

incorporate to include as a part of a whole; to form a legal corporation
incorporating incorporation

incorporeal not having material form or substance

incorrigible incapable of correction
incorrigibly

increase to make or become greater; act of increasing
increasing

incredible unbelievable; (*informal*) amazing
SEE PANEL

---

incredible or incredulous?
Incredible means 'unbelievable', and, in informal contexts, 'amazing': *Incredible though it may seem, on average someone buys one of our products every three seconds; an incredible holiday round the Great Barrier Reef; a most incredible acrobatic display.*

Someone who is described as *incredulous* cannot believe something because it seems shocking, very surprising, or very unlikely: *'That's impossible … how did you manage it?' she gasped incredulously.*

---

incredulous disbelieving
incredulity incredulously
SEE PANEL at **incredible**

increment increase, esp. one of a series
incremental

incriminate to involve in or suggest involvement in a crime, etc.
incriminating incrimination incriminatory

incrust see **encrust**

incubate to hatch eggs
incubating incubation incubator

incubus evil male spirit; nightmare
incubuses or *incubi*

inculcate to instil the mind by constant repetition
inculcating inculcation

inculpate to incriminate or blame
inculcating inculpation

incumbent resting or imposed as a duty; clergyman
incumbency

incumber see **encumber**

incur to bring upon oneself
incurrable incurred incurring

incursion sudden attack or raid
incursive

indebted owing money or gratitude
indebtedness

indecorum impropriety
indecorous

indeed really; in fact

indefatigable unable to be tried out
indefatigability indefatigably

indefinite not defined exactly
indefinitely indefiniteness

indelible incapable of being erased
indelibility indelibly

indelicate embarrassing to good taste; crude
indelicacy indelicacies

indemnify to compensate for injury or loss
indemnification indemnified indemnifies indemnifying indemnity indemnities

indent to set a line in from the margin; to notch; (to make out as) official order
indentation indention

indenture contract or agreement, esp. between a master and apprentice

independency country that has gained independence
independencies

independent self-governing; objective; not dependent on others
independence independently

in-depth detailed; thorough

indescribable too extreme to be described
indescribably

indeterminable incapable of being determined

indeterminate not definite in extent or amount
indeterminacy

index alphabetical list at the back of a book; pointer; number indicating changes in value
indexes or *indices indexation indexer index-linked*

India country in South Asia
Indian Indic

indiarubber piece of rubber used for rubbing out pencil marks

indicate to point or show
indicating indication indicator

indicative indicating; (*grammar*) (*of a mood*) used to make statements

indict to charge with an offence
indictable indictment

indifferent showing no concern; of only moderate quality
indifference indifferently

indigenous originating naturally in

indigent poor; needy
indigence

indigestion (pain associated with) difficulty in digesting food

indignant angry because of something unjust
indignation

indignity humiliation
indignities

indigo deep-blue colour or dye

indiscreet not discreet; tactless
indiscreetly indiscretion

indiscrete not divided into parts; not discrete

indiscriminate random or reckless
indiscriminately

indispensable essential
indispensability indispensably

indisposed slightly unwell; unwilling
indisposition

indite to write
inditing

individual one person or thing; separate
individuality individualities individually

individualism assertion of one's independence
individualist individualistic

individualize or **individualise** to make individual; to treat individually
individualizing or *individualising*

indoctrinate to fill the mind with a set of teachings
indoctrinating indoctrination

indolent lazy
indolence indolently

indomitable incapable of being subdued
indomitably

Indonesia country in SE Asia
Indonesian

indoor (taking place) inside of a building
indoors

indorse see **endorse**

indubitable incapable of being doubted
indubitably

induce to cause, persuade, or influence; to cause labour to begin; to draw a conclusion
inducement inducing induction inductive

induct to bring formally into office

indue see **endue**

indulge yield to the wishes of
indulgence indulgent indulging

indulgence indulging; (*in Roman Catholic Church*) remission of punishment due to sin

industrialize or **industrialise** to develop industry in
industrialization or *industrialisation*
industrializing or *industrialising*

industrious hard-working; diligent
industriously industriousness

industry branch of esp. manufacturing industry; hard work
industries industrial industrialism industrialist industrially

inebriate to make drunk
inebriating inebriation inebriety

inedible not fit to be eaten
inedibility

ineducable incapable of being educated

ineffable too great to be expressed; indescribable
ineffably

inept inappropriate; awkward
ineptitude ineptly

inequality lack of equality
inequalities

inert not having the power to move; (*of a gas*) unreactive
inertly inertness

inertia state of being inert; property of matter by which it remains at rest

inescapable that cannot be avoided
inescapably

inestimable incapable of being estimated
inestimably

inevitable that cannot be avoided
inevitability inevitably

inexcusable that cannot be excused or justified

inexhaustible incapable of being used up completely

inexorable relentless; not able to be moved by persuasion
inexorability inexorably

inexpensive not expensive; cheap
inexpensively inexpensiveness

inexperience lack of experience
inexperienced

inexpert not expert
inexpertly

in extremis (*Latin*) in great difficulties; at the point of death

inextricable that cannot be escaped from
inextricably

infallible not fallible; not liable to fall
infallibility infallibly

infamous having a bad reputation
infamously infamy infamies

infant child in the earliest stage of its life
infancy infanticide infantile

infantry soldiers who fight on foot
infantryman

infatuated filled with strong but shallow love
infatuation

infect to affect with a disease
infection infectious infectiously

infelicitous not apt
infelicitously infelicity

infer to conclude by reasoning from facts
inferable inference inferential inferred inferrer inferring
SEE PANEL at **imply**

inferior (person who is) lower in rank or worth
inferiority

infernal of hell; (*informal*) outrageous
infernally

inferno hell; extremely hot fire

infest to overrun in large numbers and have an unpleasant effect on
infestation

infidel unbelieving (person)

infidelity lack of loyalty or faith
infidelities

infield area near the wicket in cricket or enclosed by the bases in baseball

infighting intense conflict within an organization; boxing at close quarters

infiltrate to permeate; to pass undetected and gradually
infiltration

infinite endless; innumerable
infinitely infinitude infinity

infinitesimal extremely small
infinitesimally

infinitive form of a verb not indicating person or tense

infirm weak, esp. from old age
infirmity infirmities

infirmary hospital
infirmaries

infix to fix in; affix inserted into the middle of a word

inflame to arouse very strong feeling
inflaming inflammatory

inflammable liable to catch fire easily; not flammable

inflammation red painful swelling on the body

inflate to fill with air or gas
inflatable inflater inflating

inflation general rise in prices
inflationary

inflect (*grammar*) to change the ending of a word; to change the pitch or loudness of voice
inflection or *inflexion inflectional inflective*

inflexible not flexible; stubborn
inflexibility inflexibly

inflict to force something unpleasant
infliction
SEE PANEL at **afflict**

in-flight provided during the flight

inflorescence arrangement of flowers on stalks

inflow flowing in

influence (ability or power to produce an) effect; to affect
influencing influential influentially

influenza virus disease marked by fever, aches, pains, etc.

influx flowing in or entry
influxes

infold see **enfold**

inform to tell or communicate
informable informant information informative informer

informal not formal
informally

infraction violation

infra dig (*informal*) below one's dignity

infrangible incapable of being broken

infrared (*of radiation*) having a wavelength between the red end of visible light and microwaves

infrastructure basic structure of a system

infringe to violate a law
infringement infringing

infuriate to anger greatly
infuriating

infuse to soak in order to extract flavour; to instil or inspire
infuser infusible infusing infusion

ingenious clever or skilful
ingeniously ingenuity
SEE PANEL

---

ingenious or ingenuous?

Ingenious means 'clever or skilful': *an ingenious high-tech device that folds away to a quarter of its original size; come up with an ingenious way of selling our products.*

To describe someone as *ingenuous* means that they are innocent or simple: *give an ingenuous smile; You're far too ingenuous to make it to the top of your organization.*

---

ingenuous innocent; simple
ingenuously ingenuousness
SEE PANEL at **ingenious**

ingest to take into the body

inglenook chimney corner

inglorious shameful; dishonourable
ingloriously

ingoing entering

ingot piece of cast metal

ingraft see **engraft**

ingrained firmly and deeply fixed

ingratiate to put (oneself) into someone's favour
ingratiating

ingredient one of the parts of a mixture, esp. in cooking

ingress going in
ingresser

in-group small exclusive group of people

ingrowing growing abnormally inwards
ingrown ingrowth

ingulf see **engulf**

inhabit to live in; to occupy
inhabitable inhabitant

inhale to breathe in
inhalant inhalation inhaler inhaling

inherent being part of the essential nature of
inherence inherently

inherit to receive by legal right after someone's death
inheritable inheritance inheritor

inhibit to restrain; to forbid or prevent
inhibition inhibitor inhibitory

in-house within a company or institution

inhuman unkind; cruel
inhumanity inhumanities inhumanly

inhumane without compassion
inhumanely

inimical unfavourable; hostile
inimically inimicalness

inimitable incapable of being imitated
inimitability inimitably

iniquity wickedness
iniquities iniquitous

initial of the beginning; (to write the) first letter of a name or word
initialled (US *initialed*) *initialling* (US *initialing*) *initially*

initiate to begin; to accept into a society with special ceremonies
initiating initiation initiator initiatory

initiative first action; resourceful enterprise

inject to introduce liquid into the body using a syringe; to introduce
injectable injection injector

injunction legal instruction or order

injure to hurt, damage, or offend
injuring injurious injuriously

injury physical damage or hurt
injuries

injustice lack of justice

ink coloured liquid for writing
inkpot inkstand ink-well inky

inkling slight suggestion

inland (concerning the) interior of a country

in-law relative by marriage

inlay to set into a surface as a decoration; dental cavity filling
inlaid inlaying

inlet narrow inland opening of the coastline

in loco parentis (*Latin*) in the place of a parent

inmate person confined to an institution such as a prison

inmost deepest; innermost

inn public house or small hotel providing accommodation and food
innkeeper

innards (*informal*) internal organs

innate inborn
innately innateness

inner situated inside
innermost

innings (*cricket*) batting turn

innocent not guilty; simple or naïve
innocence innocently

innocuous harmless
innocuously innocuousness

innovate to introduce something new
innovating innovation innovator

innuendo indirect reference, esp. malicious
innuendoes

innumerable too many to be counted
innumerably

inoculate to introduce a microorganism into; to vaccinate
inoculating inoculation inoculator

inoffensive harmless
inoffensively inoffensiveness

inoperable not suitable for surgery
inoperably

inoperative not functioning

inordinate immoderate
inordinately

inorganic not organic
inorganically

in-patient person who receives accommodation and food while being treated in hospital

input something put in, esp. supplied to a computer; to put in
inputting

inquest investigation into the cause of death

inquietude restlessness

inquire to ask; to investigate
inquirer inquiring inquiry inquiries

inquisition searching, esp. ruthless investigation
inquisitor inquisitorial

inquisitive eager to learn; prying
inquisitively inquisitiveness

inroad raid or invasion

inrush rush or influx

insane mad or crazy; irresponsible
insanely insanity

insatiable that cannot be satisfied
insatiability insatiably

inscribe to write or mark on a surface
inscribing inscription

inscrutable mysterious
inscrutability inscrutably

insect small invertebrate animal with 6 legs and 2 pairs of wings
insecticide insectivore

insecure not confident
insecurely insecurity

inseminate to impregnate with semen
inseminating insemination

insensate unfeeling

insensible unconscious; unaware or callous
insensibility insensibly

insert to put in; something inserted
insertion

in-service undertaken during service

inset to put in; something put in
insetting

inshore near to the shore

inshrine see **enshrine**

inside (or, in, or to the) inner part
insider

inside out with the inner surface on the outside; thoroughly

insidious working in a secret harmful manner
insidiously

insight ability to perceive deeply

insignia symbols of office

insinuate to suggest something unpleasant indirectly
insinuating insinuation

insipid lacking flavour or interest
insipidity insipidly

insist to demand strongly
insistence insistent insistently

in situ (*Latin*) in position

insnare see **ensnare**

insobriety intemperance

insole inner sole of shoe

insolent impudent; disrespectful
insolence insolently

insoluble that cannot be dissolved or solved
insolubility insolubly

insolvent unable to pay one's debts; bankrupt
insolvency

insomnia sleeplessness
insomniac

insomuch to such a degree (that)

insouciant carefree; showing no concern
insouciance insouciantly

inspect to examine very carefully, esp. for official purposes
inspection inspectorate inspectorship inspectress

inspire to act as a creative stimulus to; to arouse
inspiration inspirational inspiring

install or **instal** to place in position and make ready for use
installation installed installer installing

instalment (US **installment**) part of a repayment; part of a series

instance case or example

instant moment; immediate; of the present month
instantly

instantaneous immediate
instantaneously instantaneousness

instead as an alternative or substitute

instep arch between ankle and toes

instigate to bring about
instigating instigation instigator

instil (US **instill**) to introduce gradually
instillation instilled instilling

instinct inborn capacity or power
instinctive instinctively

institute to establish or organize; organization for particular purposes
instituting institution institutional institutionalism

institutionalize or **institutionalise** to make or put into an institution
institutionalizing or *institutionalising*

instruct to teach, direct, or order
instruction instructional instructor instructorship instructress

instructive conveying information
instructively instructiveness

instrument implement or tool; device that produces musical sounds
instrumentalist instrumentation

instrumental of musical instruments; serving as a means for doing something
instrumentality instrumentally

insubordinate not willing to submit to authority
insubordination

insubstantial not substantial; weak
insubstantiality insubstantially

insufferable unbearable; intolerable
insufferably

insular of an island; narrow-minded
insularism insularity insularly

insulate to cover, etc. with a material that reduces transmission of heat, electricity, etc.
insulating insulation insulator

insulin a protein hormone

insult to speak to rudely and offensively; insulting utterance or action
insultingly

insuperable incapable of being overcome
insuperably

insupportable that cannot be supported or tolerated

insure to guarantee or protect against risk, loss, etc.; (US) to ensure
insurable insurance insured insuring
SEE PANEL at **assure**

insurgent rebellious
insurgence insurgency

insurrection rebellion against government, etc.
insurrectionary insurrectionist

intact undamaged; complete

intaglio incised design
intaglios

intake taking in; people, things, etc., taken in

integer whole number

integral essential to the whole
integrality integrally

integrate to form into a whole; to end esp. racial segregation
integrated integrating integration

integrity honesty; soundness

integument layer or covering

intellect capacity to think, reason, and understand
intellectual intellectually

intellectualize or **intellectualise** to treat intellectually
intellectualization or *intellectualisation*

intelligence mental ability; information about an enemy
intelligent intelligently

intelligentsia intellectual group in a society

intelligible easily understood
intelligibility intelligibly

intemperate immoderate, esp. in drinking
intemperance intemperately

intend to propose; to design
intended

intense extreme; deep
intensely intensity
SEE PANEL

---

intense or intensive?

Intense means ´extreme or deep´: *the intense heat of the furnace; a period of intense activity; Intense interest has already been shown in the proposal.*

Intensive means ´concentrated or thorough´: *an intensive two-week training course; intensive methods of farming; the hospital´s intensive-care unit.*

---

intensify to make or become more intense
intensification intensified intensifier intensifies intensifying

intensive marked by intensity; concentrated; thorough
intensively intensiveness
SEE PANEL at **intense**

intent something intended; determined

intention purpose or aim
intentional intentionally

inter to bury
interment interred interring

inter- (*prefix*) between or among; together
intercity interdenominational interdepartmental interdisciplinary

intergalactic interpersonal interplanetary intertribal intertwine

interact to act on each other
interaction interactive

inter alia (*Latin*) among other things

interbreed to cross-breed
interbred

intercede to plead on behalf of another; to intervence
interceding intercession intercessional intercessor

intercept to stop, seize, or interrupt on the way
interception interceptor

interchange to exchange or alternate
interchangeable interchanging

intercom internal telephone system in a building or aeroplane

intercommunicate to communicate mutually; to interconnect
intercommunicating intercommunication

interconnect to connect with one another
interconnection

intercontinental between continents

intercourse communication between 2 people, groups, etc.; insertion of the penis into the vagina

interdependent depending on each other
interdependence interdependently

interdict prohibition
interdiction

interest (to arouse a) sense of curiosity or concern; charge for borrowed money
interested interesting interestingly

interface common point or boundary between 2 things or systems

interfere to meddle or obstruct
interference interfering

interim intervening period; temporary or provisional

interior inner (surface or part); inland region

interject to interpose a remark suddenly
interjection

interlace to join by lacing together
interlacing

interlard to intersperse

interleave to put in an extra leaf of paper between regular leaves
interleaving

interlinear inserted between printed lines

interlining material used as an additional lining

interlock to join together

interlocutor person who takes part in a conversation
interlocutory

interloper intruder

interlude interval

intermarry to marry someone from the same or another group
intermarriage intermarried intermarries intermarrying

intermediary mediator; intermediate
intermediaries

intermediate between 2 points

intermezzo short musical composition
intermezzi or *intermezzos*

interminable endless or seemingly endless
interminably

intermingle to mix together
intermingling

intermission interval or pause

intermittent occurring at intervals; periodic
intermittence intermittently

intern to detain or confine, esp. during war; (US) houseman
internee internment

internal of or for the inside; inner; of the domestic affairs of a country
internally

internalize or **internalise** to make internal; to incorporate within oneself
internalization or *internalisation*
internalizing or *internalising*

international of 2 or more nations
internationalism internationalist

internationalize or **internationalise** to make or become international
internationalization or *internationalisation*
internationalizing or *internationalising*

internecine mutually destructive

Internet international network of computers

internuncio papal ambassador
internuncios

interpellate to question in parliament, often by interruption
interpellating

interpenetrate to penetrate thoroughly
interpenetration

interplay mutual action and reaction

Interpol International Criminal Police Commission

interpolate to insert, esp. to give a false impression
interpolating interpolation

interpose to introduce
interposal interposing interposition

interpret to explain the meaning of
interpretable interpretation interpretative interpreted interpreter

interregnum period between 2 reigns or holders of office
interregnums or *interregna*

interrelate to be in a relationship where one relates well to another
interrelating interrelation interrelationship

interrogate to ask questions closely
interrogating interrogation interrogator interrogatory

interrogative expressing a question

interrupt to break in on; to break the flow of
interrupter interruptible interruption

intersect to cut through or across
intersection

interspace to separate by spaces
interspacing

intersperse to scatter among
interspersing

interstate between 2 or more states, as in the US or Australia

interstellar among the stars

interstice tiny opening or gap
interstitial

interval time or space between 2 events, etc.; (*music*) difference in pitch between 2 notes

intervene to be or come between; to enter in order to stop a disagreement
intervening intervention interventionist

interview formal discussion to assess an applicant for a job; questioning of a person for newspaper, television, etc.; to conduct an interview with
interviewee interviewer interviewing

intestate not having made a will
intestacy

intestine part of the alimentary canal between the stomach and the anus
intestinal

intimate[1] marked by close association; personal or private
intimacy intimately

intimate[2] to suggest
intimating intimation

intimidate to frighten by threatening
intimidating intimidation intimidator

into to the inside of; to a different state, etc.

intonation pitch of the voice in speech

intone to recite in a chanting tone
intoning

in toto (*Latin*) entirely

intoxicate to make drunk or stimulate to the point of excitement
intoxicant intoxicating intoxication

intractable difficult to influence or cure
intractability intractably

intramural within an institution

intransigent refusing to compromise
intransigence intransigently

intransitive (*of verbs*) not having a direct object

intra-uterine within the uterus

intravenous into or within a vein

in-tray tray for incoming documents needing attention

intrepid daring; fearless
intrepidity intrepidly

intricate very complicated; complex
intricacy intricacies intricately

intrigue to fascinate; to arouse the curiosity of; (to) plot
intrigued intriguer intriguing

intrinsic belonging to the essential nature of something
intrinsicality intrinsically

introduce to bring into use; to make (oneself or another person) known by name
introducing introduction introductory

introit music sung or played at the beginning of a church service

introspection examination of one's own thoughts, feelings, etc.
introspective introspectively

introvert person whose attention is concentrated on himself or herself
introversion introverted

intrude to force oneself on to without invitation
intruding intrusion intrusive

intrust see **entrust**

intuition knowledge not derived by reasoning or intelligence
intuitional intuitive intuitively

intwine see **entwine**

inundate to flood or swamp
inundating inundation

inure or **enure** to accustom
inurement or *enurement inuring* or *enuring*

invade to enter a country, etc. by military force
invader invading invasion invasive

invalid[1] sick or disabled person

invalid[2] not valid

invalidate to render invalid
invalidating invalidation invalidity

invaluable priceless
invaluableness invaluably

invariable unchanging
invariability invariably

invective very strong abusive denunciation

inveigh to attack with vehement language

inveigle to persuade to do something by trickery
inveiglement inveigler inveigling

invent to create or originate; to produce
invention inventor

inventive resourceful; skilled at making new things
inventiveness

inventory list of goods
inventories

inverse (thing that is) opposite (to another)
inversely

invert to reverse in position, order, etc.
inversion inverter

invertebrate (animal) lacking a backbone

invest to commit money to a business

expecting a profit; to clothe or adorn (in official robes, etc.)
investiture investment investor

investigate to examine closely
investigating investigation investigative investigator investigatory

inveterate long-established
inveteracy inveterately

invidious tending to arouse resentment or unpopularity
invidiously invidiousness

invigilate to supervise candidates in an examination
invigilating invigilation invigilator

invigorate to refresh
invigorating invigoration

invincible incapable of being conquered
invincibility invincibly

inviolable that must not be violated
inviolability inviolably

inviolate not violated

invite to ask politely to come; to request
invitation inviting

invoice list of goods or services supplied and money due; to present a customer with an invoice
invoicing

invoke to call upon (God); to appeal to
invocation invocatory invoking

involuntary unintentional; performed without conscious control
involuntarily involuntariness

involute complex or involved
involution

involve to include or entail; to associate; to make complicated
involvement involving

inward in or to the middle
inwardly inwards

inwrought worked into material

iodine purple-black non-metallic element

iodize or **iodise** to treat with iodine
iodization or *iodisation iodizing* or *iodising*

ion electrically charged atom
ionic

Ionic of a kind of classical architecture

ionize or **ionise** to change into ions
ionization or *ionisation ionizing* or *ionising*

ionosphere part of the earth's atmosphere containing ions

iota 9th letter of the Greek alphabet; tiny amount

IOU written promise to pay a debt

ipso facto (*Latin*) by that very fact

Iran country in SW Asia
Iranian

Iraq country in SW Asia
Iraqi

irascible easily angered
irascibility irascibly

irate very angry
irately

ire anger

Ireland island in NW Europe
Irish Irishman Irishwoman

Irian Jaya province in East Indonesia

iridescent displaying rainbow-like colours
iridescence

iridium silver-white hard element

iris muscular tissue in the eye surrounding the pupil; kind of plant with showy flowers
irises or *irides*

irk irritate or annoy
irksome

iron metallic element that can be magnetized; (metal implement) to smooth or press clothes
ironclad iron-mould ironware ironwork

ironmonger dealer in hardware, locks, etc.
ironmongery

irony using words to express the opposite of the literal meaning
ironies ironic ironical ironically

irradiate to shine upon; to illumine
irradiating irradiation

irrational illogical
irrationality irrationally

irreconcilable incompatible
irreconcilability irreconcilably

irrecoverable not able to be recovered

irredeemable that cannot be redeemed or rectified
irredeemably

irredentist person supporting restoration of territories to the countries to which they are related
irredentism

irreducible not able to be reduced
irreducibility irreducibly

irrefutable that cannot be proved wrong
irrefutability irrefutably

irregular not regular
irregularity irregularities irregularly

irrelevant not relevant
irrelevance or *irrelevancy irrelevancies irrelevantly*

irreligion lack of or opposition to religion
irreligious irreligiously

irremovable not able to be removed

irreparable beyond repair
irreparably

irreplaceable that cannot be replaced

irrepressible not capable of being repressed

irreproachable blameless of faultless

irresistible very attractive; not able to be resisted
irresistibility irresistibly

irresolute hesitating
irresolutely irresolution

irrespective not taking account of

irresponsible not responsible
irresponsibility irresponsibly

irretrievable that cannot be retrieved or recovered
irretrievably

irreverent not reverent
irreverence irreverently

irreversible not able to be reversed
irreversibility irreversibly

irrevocable not able to be revoked

irrigate to supply water to, esp. by artificial channels
irrigable irrigating irrigation irrigative irrigator

irritable easily annoyed
irritability irritably

irritate to annoy; to make inflamed
irritant irritating irritation

irrupt to rush in
irruption

is 3rd person singular of present tense of **be**

isinglass gelatin made from air bladders of sturgeon

Islam Muslim religion; Muslims; Muslim civilization; countries in which Islam is main religion
Islamic

island land surrounded by water
islander

isle (small) island
islet

isn't (*informal*) is not

isobar line on map linking places with the same atmospheric pressure

isolate to place alone
isolating isolation isolationism isolationist

isometrics physical exercises to increase muscle strength
isometric

isosceles (*of a triangle*) having 2 sides of equal length

isotherm line on map linking places with the same temperature

isotope 1 of 2 or more atoms that have the same atomic number but have a different atomic mass or physical properties

Israel country in SW Asia
Israeli Israelite

issue flowing or sending out; edition of a magazine; offspring; topic; to bring or come out
issuable issued issuer issueless issuing

isthmus narrow strip of land
isthmuses isthmian

it subject or object pronoun referring to a thing or animal

italic (of a) style of printing in which the letters slope to the right

italicize or **italicise** to print in italics
italicization or *italicisation italicizing* or *italicising*

Italy country in South Europe
Italian

itch (to have an) irritating skin sensation
itches itchy

item a single unit

itemize or **itemise** to list
itemization or *itemisation itemizer* or *itemiser itemizing* or *itemising*

iterate to repeat
iterant iterating iteration

itinerant travelling from place to place
itinerantly

itinerary planned route for journey
itineraries

it'll (*informal*) it will

its of it
SEE PANEL

---

its or it's?
Its is used to describe something that belongs to or relates to a thing, animal, or place that has already been mentioned: *The wood is at its most beautiful in autumn; The cat has hurt its leg; I like Sydney for its cosmopolitan qualities.*

It's is the spoken and informal written form of *it is* and *it has: For what it's worth, here's what I think; It's been very interesting hearing your news again.*

---

it's (*informal*) it is; it has
SEE PANEL **at its**

I've (*informal*) I have

ivory hard tissue of elephant tusks
ivories

ivy kind of evergreen climbing plant
ivies

-ize or -ise?
Many verbs can end in either *-ize* or *-ise*. For example:
authorize or *authorise civilize* or *civilise criticize* or *criticise realize* or *realise*

The *-ise* ending is more common in British English than American English. In British English, the *-ize* ending is being used increasingly. For the following verbs only the *-ise* spelling is used:
advertise advise apprise arise chastise circumcise comprise compromise despise devise disguise excise exercise franchise improvise incise merchandise premise promise revise rise supervise surmise surprise televise

Note also:
analyse (*US analyze*)
breathalyse or *breathalyze*
capsize not-*ise*
paralyse (*US paralyze*)
prise or *prize* as in *prise open*

J

jab to poke or thrust
jabbed jabbing

jabber to speak quickly and incoherently; such talk
jabberer

jabot decorative frill on woman's bodice

jacaranda kind of tropical American tree with blue flowers

jack device for raising heavy objects; playing-card ranking just below a queen; electrical plug-in device; to raise with a jack
jack-in-the-box

jackal wild member of the dog family

jackanapes conceited or impudent person

jackass male donkey

jackboot heavy military boot that reaches to the knee

jackdaw bird related to the crow

jacket short outer garment

jackknife pocket knife with a blade that folds back; to turn to form a sharp angle
jackknives jackknifing

jackpot large money prize

Jacobean of or characteristic of the reign of King James I of England

Jacuzzi (*trademark*) bath with underwater massaging jets of water

jade hard semi-precious stone, usually green

jaded worn out

Jaffa variety of orange

jag to cut unevenly; jagged point or notch
jagged jagging

jaguar kind of large cat with dark spots on a yellow coat

jail or **gaol** prison
jailbird or *gaolbird jailbreak* or *gaolbreak jailer* or *gaoler*

jalopy dilapidated old car
jalopies

jalousie outside window shutter

jam[1] preserve containing sweetened thickened fruit

jam[2] (to) squeeze; to crowd; blockage
jammed jamming jam-packed

Jamaica country in the West Indies
Jamaican

jamb vertical side post of a frame of a door or window

jamboree large gathering or celebration

jangle (to make a) harsh discordant sound
jangling

janitor (*chiefly* US) caretaker

January 1st month of the year

japan (to cover with a) hard glossy black lacquer
japanned japanning

Japan country in East Asia
Japanese

japonica Japanese quince shrub

jar[1] wide-mouthed cylindrical glass or earthenware container
jarful

jar[2] (to make a) harsh discordant sound
jarred jarring

jardinière ornamental flowerpot

jargon specialized language; pretentious talk

jasmine kind of shrub with fragrant flowers

jasper opaque quartz

jaundice yellowing of the skin; resentment
jaundiced

jaunt (to go on a) short trip for pleasure

jaunty sprightly; cheerful
jauntier jauntiest jauntily jauntiness

Java island of Indonesia
Javanese

javelin light spear thrown in sport

jaw bony part holding the teeth
jawbone

jay kind of bird related to the crow

jaywalk to cross a street carelessly
jaywalker

jazz kind of music with syncopated rhythm; to make more lively
jazziness jazzy

jealous showing resentful suspicion of a rival; watchful and protecting
jealously jealousy jealousies

jeans close-fitting casual trousers

jeep small robust motor vehicle

jeer to scoff; jeering remark

Jehovah or **Yahweh** personal name of God in the Old Testament

jejune meagre; dull

jejunum section of the small intestine between the duodenum and the ileum
jejunal

Jekyll and Hyde person with 2 different personalities, good and evil

jell to change into a jelly-like substance; to take on a definite form

jellify to convert into jelly
jellification jellified jellifies jellifying

jelly soft firm sweet made from gelatine
jellies jellied jellyfish

jemmy (US **jimmy**) crowbar used by burglars
jemmies (US *jimmies*)

jenny female donkey; spinning frame
jennies

jeopardize or **jeopardise** to risk
jeopardizing or *jeopardising jeopardy*

jerboa kind of nocturnal rodent

jeremiad long lamentation or complaint

jerk (to move with a) sudden uneven motion; (*slang*) stupid person
jerky

jerkin short sleeveless jacket

jerry-build to build houses, etc. badly and with cheap materials
jerry-builder jerry-building jerry-built

jersey knitted garment for the upper part of the body
jerseys

Jersey largest of the Channel Islands

jest (to make a) joke
jester jestful jesting

Jesuit member of Roman Catholic Society of Jesus
Jesuitical

Jesus founder of Christianity

jet[1] stream of liquid, gas, etc. forced through a narrow opening; aeroplane powered by a jet engine; to rush out in a jet; to travel by jet
jet-propelled jetted jetting

jet[2] hard black mineral

jetsam goods thrown overboard from a ship

jettison to abandon; to throw overboard
jettisoned jettisoning

jetty pier or breakwater
jetties

Jew (*fem.* **Jewess**) person of Semitic race or religion of Judaism
Jewish Jewry

jewel precious stone
jewelled (US *jeweled*) *jeweller* (US *jeweler*) *jewellery* (*chiefly* US *jewelry*)

jib[1] triangular sail

jib[2] to be reluctant to go; (*of a horse*) to refuse to go further
jibbed jibbing

jib[3] projecting arm of a crane

jibe see **gibe**

jiffy (*informal*) short period of time
jiffies

jig (music for) lively dance; to dance; device for holding something in position
jigged jigging jigsaw

jiggered (*informal*) surprised

jiggery-pokery (*informal*) trickery

jiggle to move with a short jerky action
jiggling

jilt suddenly reject or leave a lover

jim-jams (*slang*) nervous anxiety

jimmy (US) see **jemmy**

jingle (to ring repeatedly with a) light metallic sound; short catchy verse
jingling jingly

jingoism aggressive patriotism
jingo jingoist jingoistic

jinks boisterous play

jinnee spirit in Muslim mythology
jinn

jinx force, thing, or person that brings bad luck

jitter to be nervous
jittery

jitters nervous anxiety

jive (to dance a) lively jerky dance
jiving

job occupation; work or task; to do occasional pieces of work
jobbed jobbing jobcentre jobless job-share job-sharing

jobber stockjobber

jockey rider in horse-races; to manoeuvre deviously
jockeys jockeyed jockeying

jockstrap genital support for male athletes

jocose humorous
jocosely jocosity

jocular jolly
jocularity jocularly

jocund merry
jocundity jocundly

jodhpurs long riding breeches

jog to nudge slightly; to run slowly and steadily
jogged jogger jogging

joggle to shake slightly
joggler joggling

joie de vivre (*French*) joy of living; enjoyment of life

join to bring or come together; to become a member of

joinder joining in legal action

joiner skilled woodworker
joinery

joint shared; place where two things join; large piece of cut meat
jointly

jointure property settled upon a wife as a provision for widowhood

joist supporting beam of timber or metal

joke funny anecdote; ridiculous circumstance
joker joking joky

jollify to cause to be jolly
jollification jollified jollifies jollifying

jolly (to make) merry or cheerful; (*informal*) very
jollied jollier jollies jollity jollying

jolt to push with a sudden jerky action

jonquil kind of narcissus

Jordan country in SW Asia
Jordanian

joss-stick thin stick of incense

jostle to push roughly
jostler jostling

jot to write down quickly; little bit
jotted jotter jotting

joule unit of work or energy

journal periodical or magazine; diary; record of book-keeping transactions

journalese superficial style of writing thought to be typical of newspapers

journalism profession of reporting stories for the news media
journalist journalistic

journey (to make a) trip
journeys journeyed journeying

journeyman qualified worker employed by another
journeymen

joust (*esp. of knights*) (to) fight on horseback with lances

Jove Jupiter

jovial cheerful; good-humoured
joviality jovialities jovially

jowl (lower) jaw; cheek

joy deep happiness
joyful joyfully joyfulness joyless joylessly joylessness joyous joyously

joyride (to go for a) ride in a stolen car
joyrider joyriding

joystick hand-operated control lever

jubilant showing or feeling great joy
jubilance jubilantly jubilation

jubilee 50th anniversary

Judaism religion of the Jews
Judaic Judaist

Judaize or **Judaise** to bring into conformity with Judaism
Judaizer or *Judaiser Judaizing* or *Judaising*

judder to shake jerkily

judge public official with authority to decide legal cases; to hear and decide a legal case; to examine critically
judgement or *judgment judgemental* or *judgmental judging*

judicature administration of justice

judicial of justice or law-courts
judicially
SEE PANEL

judicial or judicious?
judicial is used to refer to a country's legal system or to law-courts: *hold an independent judicial inquiry; go through the proper judicial procedures.*

If you describe behaviour or a decision as *judicious* it is wise and sensible: *give judicious advice; make a judicious choice.*

judiciary judges collectively
judiciaries

judicious having wise judgement
judiciously
SEE PANEL at **judicial**

judo kind of unarmed wrestling
judoist

jug container for pouring liquids; to stew hare, etc. in an earthenware container
jugful jugged jugging

juggernaut large articulated lorry; overwhelming force

juggle to throw and catch several objects at one time
juggler juggling

jugular of the throat or neck

juice natural liquid of a fruit, etc.
juicier juiciest juicily juiciness juicy

ju-jitsu traditional form of Japanese self-defence

jukebox automatic coin-operated record-player

julienne clear soup containing vegetables cut into thin shreds

July 7th month of the year

jumble (to mix in a) confused disorder
jumbling

jumbo (*informal*) very large; elephant
jumbos

jump to leap or spring clear of the ground; space or obstacle to be jumped
jumped-up jump-start jumpy

jumper knitted garment for the upper part of the body

junction place where several roads, etc. meet or cross

juncture point in time

June 6th month of the year

jungle tropical forest with dense mass of vegetation
jungly

junior (person) younger or lower in rank

juniper kind of coniferous tree or shrub

junk[1] discarded articles; rubbish
junk-shop

junk[2] Chinese sailing vessel

junket sweet of flavoured curdled milk; (*informal*) to feast
junketed junketing

junkie or **junky** (*informal*) drug addict
junkies

junta group holding power in a country after a revolution

Jupiter principal Roman god; planet 5th from the sun

Jurassic of a geological period

juridical of law or justice

jurisdiction right to administer justice; (extent of) legal authority

jurisprudence science or philosophy of law
jurisprudential

jurist person well versed in law; (US) judge or lawyer

jury people chosen to decide whether the accused is guilty or not
juries juror jury-box juryman jurywoman

just fair; deserved; righteous; only; not long since

justice being just; administration of the law; title of a judge
justiceship

justify to prove or show to be right or just
justifiable justifiably justification justified justifies justifying

jut to project
jutted jutting

jute plant whose fibres are used in making sacks, ropes, etc.

juvenile immature; young person
juvenility

juvenilia artistic or literary works produced in an artist's or writer's youth

juxtapose to place side by side
juxtaposing juxtaposition

K

kaftan see **caftan**

kaiser Emperor of Germany (1871–1918)

kale kind of cabbage

kaleidoscope tube in which loose coloured chips are placed between mirrors producing changing patterns
kaleidoscopic

kamikaze suicide pilot

kangaroo large Australian leaping marsupial

kaolin fine white clay used in ceramics

kapok mass of silky fibres of a tropical tree, used for stuffing pillows, etc.

kaput (*informal*) broken; exhausted; ruined

karaoke form of entertainment in which people sing to prerecorded music

karat see **carat**

karate oriental form of unarmed combat

karma (*Hinduism and Buddhism*) moral force influencing person's destiny in next existence

kart go-cart

Kashmir region of NW India
Kashmiri Kashmirian

kayak Eskimo canoe

Kazakhstan republic in Central Asia

kazoo musical instrument in which a membrane is vibrated by singing or humming
kazoos

kebab small pieces of meat, etc. cooked on a skewer

kedge (cable of a light anchor used) to draw a ship along

kedgeree dish of rice, fish, and eggs

keel main structural member extending along the centre of the bottom of a vessel; to turn over

keen eager; astute
keenly keenness keen-sighted keen-witted

keep to retain possession of; to remain; to look after; fort or castle
keeper keepsake kept

keg small barrel

kelp kind of large brown seaweed

kelvin basic metric unit of temperature

ken range of knowledge

kennel shelter for a dog; to keep in a kennel
kennelled (US *kenneled*) *kennelling* (US *kenneling*)

Kenya country in East Africa
Kenyan

kepi military cap

kept past tense and past participle of **keep**

kerb (US **curb**) stone, etc. edging of pavement
kerbing kerbstone (US *curbstone*)

kerchief cloth worn over the head

kerfuffle (*informal*) fuss

kernel edible seed of a nut or fruit in a shell or stone; central essential part

kerosine or **kerosene** paraffin

kestrel kind of small falcon

ketch small 2-masted sailing vessel

ketchup seasoned sause made with vinegar, etc.

kettle metal container for boiling water

kettledrum large bowl-shaped drum

key shaped instrument used to turn a lock or wind a mechanism; system of related musical notes; most important
keyboard keyhole keynote keypad keyring keystone keystroke keyword

khaki dull yellowish-brown (cloth used for military uniforms)

kibbutz Israeli collective settlement
kibbutzim kibbutznik

kick to hit or propel with the foot; act of kicking
kickback kick-off kick-start

kid[1] young of a goat, etc.; leather from goatskin; young person
kiddie or *kiddy*

kid[2] to tease; to deceive (oneself)
kidded kidder kidding

kidnap to seize and hold someone, esp. for ransom
kidnapped (US *kidnaped*) *kidnapper* (US *kidnaper*) *kidnapping* (US *kidnaping*)

kidney urine-secreting organ
kidneys

kill to cause the death of; to put an end to
killer killjoy

killing (*informal*) very funny; very tiring; sudden gain
killingly

kiln oven for drying, baking, etc., bricks or pottery

kilo short for **kilogram**
kilos

kilo- (*prefix*) 1000

kilobyte 1024 bytes

kilogram or **kilogramme** basic metric unit of mass; 1000 grams

kilohertz unit of frequency, 1000 hertz

kilometre (US **kilometer**) 1000 metres

kilowatt 1000 watts

kilt knee-length pleated skirt
kilted

kimono loose sashed wide-sleeved outer garment
kimonos kimonoed

kin person's relatives
kinsfolk kinship kinsman kinswoman

kind[1] friendly; helpful; generous
kind-hearted kindlier kindliest kindliness kindly kindness kindnesses

kind[2] group with common characteristics; type or sort

kindergarten school for very young children

kindle to set alight; to arouse
kindling

kindred person's relatives; similar

kinematics study of motion of bodies without considering mass or force
kinematic

kinetics study of motion of bodies
kinetic

king male sovereign ruler
kingdom kinglike kingly kingship king-size king-sized

kingfisher kind of brightly coloured fish-eating bird

kingpin pivot pin; most important person

kink sharp twist; eccentricity
kinky

kiosk small booth

kip (*informal*) (to) sleep
kipped kipping

kipper smoked salted herring

Kirghizia republic in Asia, on the border with China

Kiribati group of islands in the Pacific Ocean

kirk (*Scottish*) church

kirschwasser cherry liqueur

kismet fate

kiss (to) touch with the lips
kisses kissing

kissogram novelty greetings message delivered with a kiss

kit (to provide with a) set of equipment or parts
kitbag kitted kitting

kitchen room where food is cooked
kitchenette

kite light covered frame flown in the wind; bird of the hawk family
kitemark

kith (**kith and kin**) friends and relations

kitsch tawdry or pretentious articles

kitten young cat

kitty shared fund of money
kitties

kiwi nocturnal flightless New Zealand bird
kiwis

klaxon powerful horn or warning signal

kleptomania strong irresistible desire to steal
kleptomaniac

knack talent or skill; resourceful way of doing something

knacker person who buys and slaughters old horses

knackered (*slang*) exhausted

knapsack bag strapped on the back

knave rogue; (*in playing-cards*) jack
knavery knavish

knead to work and press into a mass with the hands

knee joint between the thigh and lower leg
kneecap knee-deep knee-high knee-jerk knee-pad

kneel to rest or fall on the knees
kneeler knelt

knell sound of a church bell rung at a funeral

Knesset Israeli parliament

knew past tense of **know**

knickerbockers baggy breeches gathered at the knee

knickers woman's or girl's underpants

knick-knack small trivial ornament

knife cutting instrument consisting of a sharp blade with handle
knives

knight man with title 'Sir'; chess-piece
knighthood knightly

knit to loop yarn or thread using long needles; to join closely
knitted knitting knitting-machine knitting-needle knitwear

knob rounded handle
knobbly

knobble small round lump
knobbly

knock (to hit with a) sharp blow; (to) rap
knock-about knock-down knocker knock-kneed knock-on knock-out knock-up

knoll small rounded hill

knot fastening made by tying a piece of rope in a particular way; to tie or fasten in a knot; protuberance on a tree; speed of 1 nautical mile per hour
knotted knotting knotty

know to be aware of; to understand or recognize
knew know-how knowingly known

knowledge information known
knowledgeable knowledgeably

knuckle finger-joint
knuckleduster

knurl or **nurl** small projection or ridge

KO knock-out
KO's KO'd KO'ing

koala Australian tree-dwelling marsupial

kohl cosmetic powder

kohlrabi turnip cabbage

kookaburra kind of Australian bird; laughing jackass

kopeck or **copeck** Russian money unit

Koran or **Qur'an** sacred book of Islam
Koranic

Korea either of 2 countries in NE Asia, Democratic People's Republic of Korea or Rupublic of Korea
Korean

kosher prepared according to Jewish dietary laws

kowtow to behave with servile respect towards

kraal village of South African tribesmen

Kremlin the Russian government

krona money unit of Sweden (pl. *kronor*); money unit of Iceland (pl. *kronur*)

krone money unit in Denmark and Norway
kroner

krugerrand South African gold coin

krypton gaseous chemical element

kudos honour; prestige

kung fu Chinese martial art

Kuwait country on NW coast of Persian Gulf
Kuwaiti

Kyrie eleison formal liturgical prayer

L

la (*music*) 6th note in a major scale

lab short for **laboratory**

label piece of material attached to an object to give information about it; to fix a label on
labelled (US *labeled*) *labelling* (US *labeling*)

labium lip or lip-like structure of the body
labia *labial*

laboratory place equipped for scientific experiments or research
laboratories

laborious marked by or needing great effort
laboriously *laboriousness*

labour (US **labor**) work or exertion; process of childbirth; to work; workers
laboured (US *labored*) *labourer* (US *laborer*) *labour-intensive* (US *labor-intensive*) *labourite* (US *laborite*) *labouring* (US *laboring*) *labour-saving* (US *labor-saving*)

Labour political party

Labrador retriever dog

laburnum kind of shrub or tree with bright yellow flowers

labyrinth complex network of tunnels, paths, etc.
labyrinthine

lace silk, linen, etc. fabric woven in a decorative open design; cord or string used to fasten a garment or shoe; to fasten with a lace; to add spirits to
lace-up *lace-work* *lacing* *lacy*

lacerate to tear or wound
lacerating *laceration*

lachrymal of tears

lachrymose tearful

lack insufficiency or shortage; to be short of

lackadaisical lacking vitality
lackadaisically

lackey servile follower; male servant
lackeys

lacklustre (US **lackluster**) not lively or bright

laconic concise or terse
laconically

lacquer (to coat with a) clear or coloured varnish
lacquerer

lacrosse field-game played with a ball and long-handled netted rackets

lactate to secrete milk
lactating *lactation*

lacteal of milk

lactic of milk

lactose white crystalline sugar in milk

lacuna blank space
lacunae or *lacunas*

lad boy

ladder framework of 2 sidepieces joined by rungs used for climbing up and down; (to develop a) line of undone stitches

lade to load or weigh down
laden *lading*

la-di-da (*informal*) affectedly genteel

lading cargo or freight

ladle long-handled spoon with a deep bowl for serving liquids; to serve with a ladle
ladling

lady woman; refined woman or woman of high social class; titled woman
ladies lady-in-waiting ladies-in-waiting lady-killer ladylike ladyship

ladybird kind of small beetle, usually red with black spots

lag[1] to fall behind
laggard lagged lagging

lag[2] to cover with insulating material
lagged lagging

lager light beer

lagoon shallow pool separated from a larger pool by coral reefs, etc.

laid past tense and past participle of **lay**[1]
laid-back

lain past participle of **lie**[2]

lair den of a wild animal

laird (*Scottish*) landowner

laissez-faire (*French*) non-interference in others' affairs

laity lay people, as distinct from clergy

lake[1] large inland body of water
lakeland

lake[2] deep purplish-red pigment

lam[1] (*informal*) to thrash
lammed lamming

lam[2] (*chiefly* US *slang*) sudden flight from the law

lama Buddhist monk in Tibet
lamasery lamaseries Lamaism

lamb (meat of) young sheep
lambkin lambskin lambswool

lambaste or **lambast** to beat or censure
lambasting

lambent flickering softly
lambency

lame (to make) crippled in the legs or feet; unconvincing
lamely lameness lamer lamest laming

lamé fabric in which silver or gold threads are interwoven

lament (to express) deep grief
lamentation lamenter lamentingly

lamentable deplorable
lamentably

lamina thin layer or plate
laminae or *laminas*

laminate to separate into thin sheets; to cover with a thin sheet of material; laminated material
laminated laminating

lamp device that produces light
lamp-holder lamppost lampshade

lampoon (to ridicule in a) satirical attack

lamprey bloodsucking eel-like vertebrate
lampreys

lance long pointed weapon; to pierce with a lancet
lancing

lancet pointed surgical knife; window or arch with an acutely pointed head

land solid part of earth's surface; to come on to the shore or down from the air; country
landed landfall landfill landholder landlady land-locked landlord landlubber landmass land-mine landowner landship landsman landward landwards

landau 4-wheeled horse-drawn carriage
landaus

landing coming to land; floor area at top of a flight of stairs

landmark prominent object or feature of a landscape

landscape (picture of an) area of scenery; to improve the natural features of a garden, etc.
landscaping

landslide fast movement of rock, etc. down a slope; overwhelming victory in an election

lane narrow road or way

language speech of a particular people; human speech

languid without energy; sluggish
languidly

languish to lose strength or energy

languor tiredness; dreaminess
languorous languorously

lank thin and tall; (*of hair*) straight and limp
lankier lankiest lankiness lanky

lanolin wool grease used in ointments

lantern light in a transparent protective case

lanthanum white soft metallic element

lanyard short rope for fastening something

Laos country in SE Asia
Lao Laotian

lap[1] upper surface of the thighs of a seated person

lap[2] one circuit of a racecourse; stage; to fold or wrap over
lapped lapping

lap[3] to take in liquids with the tongue, as a cat does
lapped lapping

lapel folded-back front edge of a jacket or coat
lapelled

lapidary person who cuts, shapes, and polishes stones; engraved on stones
lapidaries

lapis lazuli rich blue precious stone; its colour

Lapland region of North Europe
Laplander Lapp Lappish

lapse slight error; moral decline; to become worse; passage of time
lapsing

lapwing kind of plover

larceny theft
larcenies larcenist

larch kind of coniferous tree with short deciduous leaves

lard (to cover with) rendered fat from a pig

larder room or cupboard for storing food

large relatively great in size, area, scope, etc.
largely largeness larger large-scale largest largish

largess or **largesse** generous gift

largo (*music*) (passage) to be performed slowly
largos

lariat (US) lasso

lark[1] kind of brown singing bird

lark[2] (to engage in) playful fun

larkspur kind of delphinium

larva immature form that develops into a different adult form
larvae larval

larynx upper part of the windpipe containing vocal cords
larynges or *larynxes laryngeal laryngitis*

lasagne or **lasagna** pasta in wide ribbons

lascivious lustful
lasciviously lasciviouness

laser device generating a beam of high-intensity light

lash[1] cutting blow from a whip; eyelash; to whip
lashes lasher

lash[2] to secure with a rope
lasher lashes

lass girl or young woman
lasses lassie

lassitude weariness

lasso (to catch with a) long rope with a noose
lassos or *lassoes lassoed lassoing*

last[1] coming to the end, after all the others, or most recently
last-ditch lastly

last[2] to continue for a period of time
lasting

last[3] form shaped like a foot

latch (to fasten with a) device consisting of a bar that falls into a groove, etc.
latches latchkey

late coming after the expected or normal time; far on in the day or night; recently deceased
latecomer lately lateness later latest latish

lateen of a kind of rig with a triangular sail
lateen-rigged

lately recently

latent potential but not active
latency latently

lateral of or on the sides
laterally

latex milky liquid produced by rubber trees, etc.
latexes or *latices*

lath narrow strip of wood
laths

lathe machine for shaping metal or wood

lather (to coat with) foam

Latin (of the) language of ancient Rome; of the peoples whose languages are derived from Latin
Latinate Latinist

latitude distance north or south of equator measured in degrees; freedom of action
latitudinal latitudinally latitudinarian

latrine (small pit used as a) toilet

latter second of 2 mentioned; nearer to the end
latter-day latterly

lattice open framework of crossing strips
latticed

Latvia republic in Eastern Europe, formerly in NW Soviet Union
Latvian

laud (*literary*) to praise
laudable laudably laudatory

laudanum tincture of opium

laugh (to make the) sound expressing amusement
laughable laughably laughing-gas laughing-stock laughter

launch[1] to move a vessel into the water; to propel with force
launcher launches

launch[2] large motor boat
launches

launder to wash and iron
launderette laundress laundry laundries

laureate crowned with laurel leaves

laurel tree with glossy leaves; sign of victory

lava molten rock discharged from volcano

lavatory toilet
lavatories

lavender kind of shrub with purple flowers that are used in perfumes

lavish generous or abundant; to give generously
lavishes lavishly lavishness

law authoritative rule of behaviour; legal profession
law-abiding law-court lawful lawfully lawfulness lawgiver lawless lawlessly lawlessness lawsuit lawyer

lawn area of mown grass

lax not firm; loose
laxity laxly

laxative agent stimulating emptying of the bowels

lay[1] to put in a horizontal position; to produce eggs

laid layabout lay-by lay-bys laying
SEE PANEL

lay or lie?
To *lay* something somewhere means to put it there: *lay the newspaper down on the table; lay out all the cutlery neatly.* When a hen *lays* eggs, it produces eggs.

Lie means 'to be in a horizontal position; to rest'; it is not used with a grammatical object: *to lie completely still; to lie down and go to sleep.*

Confusion between the two words may arise because *lay* is also the past tense of *lie: Broken glass lay scattered all over the ground.*

lay[2] of people who are not clergymen or not experts
layman laywoman

lay[3] past tense of **lie**[2]
SEE PANEL at **lay**[1]

lay[4] ballad or song

layer thickness or covering
layered

layette set of articles including clothing for a new-born baby

layout arrangement of something

laze to behave lazily
lazing

lazy not wanting to work
lazier laziest lazily laziness lazy-bones

lea (*poetic*) meadow; grassland

lead[1] to guide; to show the way to
leader leadership lead-in led

lead[2] soft heavy metal; graphite in pencil
leaden

leading first; principal

leaf outgrowth from plant stem; sheet of paper
leaves leaf-mould leafy

leaflet folded printed pamphlet giving information; to distribute leaflets in an area
leafleted leafleting

league[1] association or union; to form a league
leagued leaguing

league[2] unit of distance, 3 miles

leak (hole or crack for a liquid) to escape or enter
leakage leaky

lean[1] to (cause to) rest against a support
leaned or *leant leaning lean-to lean-tos*

lean[2] not fat; meagre
leanness

leap (to) jump
leaped or *leapt leaping*

leap-frog children's game in which one person leaps over another who is bending over
leap-frogged leap-frogging

learn to gain knowledge of or a skill in
learnable learned or *learnt learner*

learned having a great knowledge

lease contract for the use of something, esp. property, usually for rent
leasable leaseback leasehold leaseholder leaser

leash cord or strap fixed to a dog's collar
leashes

least smallest or slightest
leastways

leather tanned animal skin
leathery

leave[1] to go away from; to cause to remain; to bequeath
leaving left

leave[2] permission to do something; permission to be absent

leaven substance producing fermentation in a dough
leavened

Lebanon country in SW Asia
Lebanese

lecher promiscuous man
lecherous lechery lecheries

lectern reading desk in a church

lecture (to give a) formal talk for instruction
lecturer lectureship lecturing

led past tense and past participle of **lead**[1]

ledge shelf

ledger account book

lee side away from the wind; sheltered side
leeward

leech bloodsucking worm-like animal

leek kind of plant with thick edible stem

leer (to give a) sly or suggestive look

lees sediment of a liquor

leeway freedom of action within certain limits

left[1] past tense and past participle of **leave**[1]
left-overs

left[2] opposite of right; having radical or socialist political views
left-handed leftist leftward leftwards left-winger

leg lower limb of animal on which it moves; stage in a journey or competition
leg-bye leg-pull leg-rest leg-room leggy

legacy gift of money or property by will
legacies

legal of the law; allowed by law
legalese legalism legalist legalistic legality legally

legalize or **legalise** to make legal
legalization or *legalisation legalizing* or *legalising*

legate delegate or messenger

legatee person to whom a legacy is bequeathed

legation diplomatic mission; official residence of a diplomatic mission

legato (*music*) smoothly

legend old traditional story; inscription or title; explanation
legendary

legerdemain trickery; sleight of hand

leggings additional outer covering for the lower legs

leghorn fine plaited straw (hat)

legible capable of being read
legibility legibly

legion unit in ancient Roman army; large military force; very large number
legionary legionaries

legionnaire member of a military force

legislate to make laws
legislating legislation legislative legislator legislature

legitimate reasonable; lawful
legitimacy legitimately

legitimize or **legitimise** to make legitimate
legitimization or *legitimisation legitimizing* or *legitimising*

legume edible pod or seed

leguminous pod-bearing

leisure time for relaxation
leisurewear

leisurely relaxed
leisureliness

leitmotiv or **leitmotif** recurring musical phrase; recurring theme

lemming kind of northern vole-like rodent

lemon kind of yellow citrus fruit

lemonade drink of lemon juice, water, and sugar

lemur kind of tree-dwelling mammal

lend to give for temporary use
lender lent

length measure of how long something is
lengthways lengthwise lengthy

lengthen to make or become longer
lengthener

lenient tolerant; merciful
lenience or *leniency* *leniently*

lens curved piece of glass in optical instruments; part of the eye
lenses

Lent 40 weekdays from Ash Wednesday to the Saturday before Easter
Lenten

lentil seed of leguminous plant

lento (*music*) slowly

Leo 5th sign of the zodiac

leonine of a lion

leopard (*fem.* **leopardess**) large member of the cat family with dark spots on a yellow skin
leopardesses

leotard close-fitting garment for dancers or acrobats

lepidopteran butterfly or moth
lepidopterist

leprechaun mischievous elf of Irish folklore

leprosy chronic skin and nerve disease
leper *leprous*

lesbian female homosexual
lesbianism

lèse-majesté (*French*) treason

lesion change in the structure of an organ or tissue; injury or wound

Lesotho country in Southern Africa

less smaller; not so much
lesser

lessee person to whom a lease is granted

lessen to make or become less
lessened *lessening*

lesson period of instruction

lessor person who grants a lease

lest so that not; for fear that

let[1] to allow; to cause to; to allow the use of property for payment
let-down *let-out* *letting* *let-up*

let[2] obstruction

lethal (capable of) causing death

lethargy lack of energy; slowness
lethargic *lethargically*

let's (*informal*) let us

letter symbol of alphabet; written message
letter-bomb *letter-box* *lettered* *letterhead* *lettering* *letterpress*

lettuce kind of plant with large edible green leaves

leucocyte white blood cell

leukaemia (US **leukemia**) disease in which the blood contains too many white blood cells

levee[1] river embankment

levee[2] reception or assembly

level on a flat horizontal plane; amount; to make or become level
level-headed *levelled* (US *leveled*) *leveller* (US *leveler*) *levelling* (US *leveling*)

lever (to move or open with a) rigid bar turning on a fixed point
leverage

leveret young hare

leviathan something huge or powerful; sea-monster

Levi's (*trademark*) denim jeans

levitate to rise and float in the air
levitating *levitation*

Leviticus 3rd book of the Old Testament

levity lack of seriousness; frivolity

levy (to impose and collect a) tax, etc.
levies *leviable* *levied* *levying*

lewd obscene or indecent

lexical of words or the vocabulary of a language

lexicography (art of) writing dictionaries
lexicographer lexicographic lexicographical

lexicon dictionary

ley arable and temporarily under grass

liable likely or subject (to); legally responsible
liability liabilities

liaise to maintain contact with
liaising

liaison communication and co-operation; love affair

liana kind of tropical climbing plant

liar person who tells lies

libation liquid use in a sacrifice to a god; drink

libel publication of defamatory matter in permanent form
libelled (US *libeled*) *libeller* (US *libeler*) *libelling* (US *libeling*) *libellous* (US *libelous*)

liberal generous; tolerant
liberalism liberality liberally

Liberal political party
Liberal Democrat

liberalize or **liberalise** to make more liberal
liberalization or *liberalisation liberalizing* or *liberalising*

liberate to set free
liberating liberation liberator

Liberia country in West Africa
Liberian

libertine person with loose morals

liberty freedom from restraints or control
liberties libertarian

libido sexual desire
libidos libidinous

Libra 7th sign of the zodiac

library (building or room with) book collection
libraries librarian librarianship

libretto text of an opera, etc.
librettos or *libretti librettist*

Libya country in North Africa
Libyan

lice pl. of **louse**

licence (US **license**) official or legal permission; irresponsible use of freedom
SEE PANEL

---

licence or license?

In British English, the noun used to refer to a document that gives official permission to do something is spelled *licence: a driving licence; an import licence.* In American English the noun is spelled *license.*

License is the spelling of the verb meaning ′to give official permission to′: *licensed to sell alcohol; license a gun.*

---

license to give a licence to; to authorize
licensee licenser licensing
SEE PANEL at **licence**

licentious behaving in a sexually irresponsible manner
licentiously licentiousness

lichee see **lychee**

lichen moss-like plant growing on rocks

lich-gate or **lych-gate** roofed gate to a churchyard

licit permissible
licitly licitness

lick to pass the tongue over

licorice see **liquorice**

lid cover for a box, etc.; eyelid
lidded lidless

lido public outdoor recreation area and swimming pool
lidos

lie[1] to speak falsely intending to deceive
lied lying

lie[2] to be in a horizontal position; to rest
lain lay lie-down lie-in lying
SEE PANEL at **lay**[1]

Liebfraumilch dry white German wine

Liechtenstein principality in Central Europe

lied (*German*) ballad or romantic poem
lieder

liege owing or owed feudal allegiance
liegeman

lien legal right to the property of another until a claim is met

lieu (**in lieu of**) instead of

lieutenant military officer
lieutenancy

life state of being alive; period between birth and death
lives lifebelt lifeblood lifeboat lifebuoy lifeguard life-jacket lifeless lifelike lifeline lifelong lifer life-sized lifestyle lifetime

lift to raise; apparatus for transporting people or goods to a different level
lift-off

ligament tough tissue joining bones

ligature thread used in surgical operations

light[1] something that makes things visible; not dark; to ignite or illuminate
lighted or *lit lighter lighthouse lightness lightship light-year*

light[2] having little weight; soft; to find accidentally
lighted or *lit lighter lightest light-fingered light-footed light-headed light-hearted lightweight*

lighten[1] to make or become brighter

lighten[2] to make or become less in weight
lightening

lighter[1] device for providing a flame to light cigarettes

lighter[2] flat-bottomed barge

lightning electrical discharge between clouds or between clouds and the ground

lights lungs of sheep, etc. as food

ligneous woody

lignite brown woody rock

like[1] similar (to); in the same way as
like-minded likeness likewise

like[2] to find enjoyable or agreeable
likeable or *likable liking*

likely probable; suitable
likelier likeliest likelihood

liken to compare

lilac kind of shrub with large fragrant flowers

lilliputian tiny

lilt (to have a) regular flowing rhythm

lily plant grown from bulb and having showy flowers
lilies

limb arm or leg; branch of a tree

limber flexible; to loosen the muscles

limbo[1] state of uncertainty; intermediate state
limbos

limbo[2] kind of West Indian dance
Limbos

lime[1] white substance; calcium oxide; to treat with or spread lime
lime-kiln limestone liming

lime[2] kind or round greenish-yellow citrus fruit
lime-juice

lime[3] kind of ornamental tree

limelight position of receiving a great deal or public attention

limerick 5-line comic verse

limey (US *slang*) British person, esp. a sailor
limeys

limit ultimate boundary; furthest degree; to restrict
limitation limited limitless

limousine large and luxurious car

limp[1] to walk unevenly because of a weak leg; uneven walk
limper limpingly

limp[2] not firm or stiff
limply limpness

limpet kind of small clinging shellfish

limpid clear or transparent
limpidity limpidly

linchpin locking pin inserted transversely; crucial person or thing

linctus syrupy medicine to relieve coughs

linden lime tree

line[1] narrow continuous mark made by a pen, etc.; length of cord or rope; row; route or course
lineal linear line-out linesman line-up lining

line[2] to add an extra layer to the inside of a garment
linable lining

lineage line of descent

lineament feature, esp. of the face

linen cloth made from flax; clothes, sheets, etc. of linen or cotton

liner passenger ship

ling[1] kind of food fish

ling[2] heather

linger to delay leaving; to go slowly

lingerie women's underwear and nightclothes

lingua franca language used for communication by people of different mother tongues
lingua francas or *linguae francae*

lingual of the tongue; of language or languages

linguist person who speaks many foreign languages; person skilled in linguistics

linguistics study of language
linguistic linguistically

liniment oily liquid applied to the skin to relieve stiffness

link one of the rings or loops forming a chain; to connect
linkage linkman link-up

links golf-course

linnet kind of small finch

lino short for **linoleum**
linocut

linoleum waterproof floor-covering with a canvas backing

linseed seed of flax

linsey-woolsey thin coarse fabric of linen and wool

lint absorbent linen-based material used to dress wounds

lintel horizontal beam over a door, window, etc.

lion (*fem.* **lioness**) large flesh-eating member of the cat family
lionesses lion-hearted

lionize or **lionise** to treat as very important
lionization or *lionisation lionizer* or *lioniser lionizing* or *lionising*

lip fleshy edge of the mouth; edge or rim
lipped lipsalve lip-service

lip-read to understand someone's speech by watching his or her lip movements
lip-reader lip-reading

lipstick cosmetic for colouring the lips

liquefy to make liquid
liquefaction liquefiable liquefied liquefies liquefying

liqueur highly flavoured sweetened alcoholic drink

liquid fluid; easily convertible into cash
liquidity

liquidate to pay a debt, to close a business because of bankruptcy; to eliminate
liquidating liquidation liquidator

liquidize or **liquidise** to make or become liquid
liquidizer or *liquidiser* *liquidizing* or *liquidising*

liquor drink, esp. spirits

liquorice or **licorice** kind of shrub whose root is used as a sweet

lira money unit of Italy and Turkey
lire or *liras*

lisle strong fine cotton thread

lisp saying of a *th*-sound instead of an *s*-sound; to speak like this

lissom or **lissome** supple
lissomness or *lissomeness*

list[1] series of names, things, etc., one under the other
listable

list[2] (*of a ship*) to lean over to one side

listen to pay attention to; to concentrate on hearing
listener

listless lacking energy or enthusiasm
listlessly *listlessness*

lit past tense and past participle of **light**[1] and **light**[2]

litany form of prayer
litanies

litchi see **lychee**

liter (US) see **litre**

literal of the primary, explicit, or exact meaning of an expression
literalism *literally*
SEE PANEL

---

literal, literary, or literate?

Literal is used to refer to the primary, explicit, or exact meaning of an expression: *a literal translation; decimate, in the literal sense of the word, meaning 'destroy one in ten'.*

Literary means 'concerned with literature; formal': *the literary editor of the magazine; 'vale' is a literary word for 'valley'.*

A person who is *literate* is able to read and write: *a surprisingly high number of school-leavers are not literate. Literate* also means 'well-educated': *highly literate students;* a person who is *literate* in a particular field of knowledge or with particular things: *computer literate.*

---

literary of or fond of literature; formal
SEE PANEL at **literal**

literate able to read and write
literacy *literately*
SEE PANEL at **literal**

literati literary or learned people

literature artistic writings; printed matter

lithe flexible
lithely *litheness*

lithium soft silvery lightest-known metallic element

lithography printing in which printing areas are ink-receptive
lithograph *lithographic*

lithosphere solid rocky crust of the earth

Lithuania republic in Eastern Europe, formerly in West Soviet Union
Lithuanian

litigate to contest an issue at law
litigable *litigant* *litigating* *litigation*

litmus colouring from lichens that turns red in acid and blue in alkaline solutions
litmus-paper

litotes understatement in which an affirmative is expressed by the negation of its opposite

litre (US **liter**) metric unit of capacity, cubic decimetre

litter rubbish, esp. when left in a public place; offspring of an animal
litterbug

little small; in a small amount

littoral of the seashore; area by the coast

liturgy form of public worship
liturgies *liturgical*

live[1] to have life; to reside

liveable or *livable* *liver* *living*

live² not dead; having power; broadcast simultaneously

livelihood occupation or employment

livelong (*poetic*) long or whole

lively full of vigour or action
livelier *liveliest* *liveliness*

liven to make or become lively

liver organ that secretes bile and causes changes in the blood
liverish

liverwort moss-like plant

livery identifying uniform of guild or servants
liveries *liveried* *liveryman*

livestock farm animals

livid very angry; greyish-blue
lividly *lividness* or *livity*

living alive or existing; means of support; benefice

lizard small reptile with 4 legs

llama kind of South American ruminant mammal

lo (*archaic*) look

load something carried; burden or worry; to put a load on

loadstar see **lodestar**

loadstone or **lodestone** magnetic odixe of iron

loaf¹ shaped mass of bread
loaves

loaf² to spend time idly
loafer

loam rich soil of clay, sand, etc.
loaminess *loamy*

loan lending; something lent; to lend

loath or **loth** unwilling or reluctant
SEE PANEL

---

loath, loth, or loathe?

If you are *loath* (less commonly spelled *loth*) to do something, you are unwilling or reluctant to do it: *Having only just moved into this house I'd be loath to move house for a few years.*

Loathe is a verb meaning 'to detest; to hate very much': *I simply loathe Mondays!; I loathe commuting to and from word every day.*

---

loathe to detest
loathing *loathsome* *loathsomeness*
SEE PANEL at **loath**

lob to hit, kick, or toss a ball so that it travels in a high arc
lobbed *lobber* *lobbing*

lobby entrance room; vestibule; to try to influence public officials
lobbies *lobbied* *lobbying* *lobbyist*

lobe lower soft part of the ear; rounded projection
lobate *lobed*

lobelia kind of plant with clusters of small showy flowers

lobotomy removal of a lobe; kind of brain operation
lobotomies

lobster kind of shellfish with large claws and 4 pairs of walking legs

local of a particular place or district; not general
localism *locality* *localities*

locale place; scene of operations

localize or **localise** to make or become local; to confine to an area
localization or *localisation* *localizing* or *localising*

locate to position; to find the situation of something
locating *location*

locative (*grammar*) of the case indicating direction or place

loch (*Scottish*) lake

lock¹ (to operate a) fastening mechanism for a door, gate, etc.; enclosed section of a

canal where the water-level can be changed
lockout locksmith lock-up

lock[2] strand or curl of hair

locker small compartment or cupboard

locket small decorative case, usually worn round the neck, holding a memento

lockjaw (early symptom of) tetanus

loco short for **locomotive**
locos

locomotion moving from place to place

locomotive self-propelled engine used to draw carriages, etc. along a track

locum short for **locum tenens**

locum tenens temporary substitute doctor
locum tenentes

locus place or point
loci

locust crop-devouring insect related to the grasshopper

locution manner of speaking or expression

lode vein of mineral deposit

lodestar or **loadstar** guiding star, esp. pole star

lodestone see **loadstone**

lodge small house at entrance to a country estate; to occupy temporarily; to fix in place
lodgement or *lodgment lodger lodging lodging-house*

loess loamy deposit

loft attic; roof space

lofty majestic or exalted; of great height
loftily loftiness

log length of tree-trunk; record of movements of a ship or aircraft; (to record details in a) logbook
logbook logged logging

loganberry kind of dark red fruit
loganberries

logarithm exponent indicating the power to which a number is raised to produce a particular number

loggerheads (**at loggerheads**) disagreeing

loggia roofed open area; gallery

logic (science of) reasoning
logician

logical of logic; marked by clear reasoning
logically

logistics science of movement of troops; practical details of an operation

logo device used as a sign or emblem for an organization
logos

loin lower part of the back between the hip-bone and the lower ribs
loincloth

loiter to stand idly
loiterer

loll to rest lazily; to hang down loosely

lollipop boiled sweet on a stick

lollop to move with an awkward leaping action
lolloped lolloping

lolly (*informal*) lollipop; (*slang*) money
lollies

lone solitary; single
lonesome

lonely unhappy to be alone; solitary; desolate
lonelier loneliest loneliness

loner person who avoids the company of others

long[1] not short in measurement or time
longboat longbow long-distance longhand long-playing long-range longship long-sighted long-standing long-suffering long-term longways long-winded

long[2] to feel a strong persistent desire
longing

longevity length of life

longitude distance east or west of meridian measured in degrees
longitudinal longitudinally

loo (*informal*) toilet
loos

loofah (US **loofa**) dried seed pod of a plant used as a sponge

look to direct the eyes; to appear
look-alike looker-on look-in looking-glass look-out look-over look-through

loom[1] weaving apparatus

loom[2] to come into view, esp. threateningly

loon kind of large fish-eating diving bird

loony or **looney** (*informal*) crazy

loop doubled-over piece of string, etc.; to make a loop in

loophole means of evasion or escape, such as an ambiguity in a law

loopy full of loops; (*informal*) slightly crazy

loose not confined or restrained; not compact or tight; to release or unfasten
loose-leaf loosely looseness loosing
SEE PANEL

---

loose or lose?

Loose is primarily an adjective meaning 'not confined or restrained; not compact or tight': *a loose belt; loose floorboards; a loose tooth; loose clothes; loose soil.*

As a verb *loose* means 'to release or unfasten': *loose the tiger from its cage.*

Lose is used to describe mislaying, or not keeping or winning something: *lose one's keys; lose a fight; lose weight; lose your balance.*

---

loosen to make loose
loosener

loot stolen money or valuables; to pillage or plunder
looter

lop[1] to cut off
lopped lopping

lop[2] to hang loosely
lop-eared lop-sided

lope to move with long bounding strides
loping

loquacious talkative
loquaciously loquacity

lord ruler or master; nobleman; to act in a superior manner
lordly lordship

lore traditional knowledge or wisdom

lorgnette spectacles mounted on a handle

lorry large motor vehicle for carrying heavy loads
lorries lorryload

lose to mislay; to fail to keep or win
losable or *loseable loser losing lost*
SEE PANEL at **loose**

loss losing; something lost
losses loss-leader loss-making

lot great number or quantity; fate; items for sale at an auction; plot of land

loth see **loath**

lotion medicinal or cosmetic preparation for the skin, etc.

lottery system for raising money by distributing numbered tickets some of which entitle the holder to a prize
lotteries

lotto children's game; bingo

lotus water-lily; (*Greek mythology*) fruit inducing forgetfulness
lotuses lotus-eater

loud noisy; (*of colours*) striking
loudly loudness

loudspeaker device that turns electrical signals into sound waves

lough (*Irish*) loch

Louisiana US state

lounge sitting-room; to sit around lazily
lounger lounging

lour or **lower** to frown

louse small wingless parasitic insect
lice

lousy (*informal*) very bad
lousily lousiness

lout rough ill-mannered person
loutish

louvre or **louver** one of a set of overlapping slats in a door
louvred or *louvered*

love (to feel a) strong affection or devotion; score of nil in sports
lovable or *loveable love-affair love-bird love-hate loveless love-letter lovemaking lover lovesick love-song love-story loving*

lovelorn sad because of unrequited love

lovely attractive
lovelier loveliest loveliness

low[1] not high or tall; not loud; inferior
lowbrow low-down lower lowest low-key lowland low-level low-minded low-necked low-pitched low-spirited

low[2] (to make the) sound characteristic of cattle

lower[1] (to make) less high

lower[2] see **lour**

lowly humble
lowlier lowliest lowliness

loyal faithful
loyalist loyally loyalty loyalties

lozenge small medicated tablet that is dissolved in the mouth; rhombus

lubber big clumsy fellow

lubricant lubricating substance

lubricate to treat with oil in order to lessen friction
lubricating lubrication lubricator

lucerne kind of plant grown for fodder, alfalfa

lucid clear
lucidity lucidly

Lucifer Satan before being expelled from Heaven

luck (good) fortune; chance
luckier luckiest luckily luckiness luckless lucky

lucrative profitable

lucre money; wealth

ludicrous absurd
ludicrously ludicrousness

ludo simple board-game with counters

luff to sail nearer the wind

lug[1] to pull or drag with effort
lugged lugging

lug[2] small projection by which something is connected, supported, etc.

luggage suitcases, etc.

lugger small boat with a lugsail

lugsail 4-sided sail

lugubrious mournful
lugubriously lugubriousness

lukewarm tepid; lacking enthusiasm
lukewarmly lukewarmness

lull to calm or soothe; short pause

lullaby quiet song to help children to sleep
lullabies

lumbago pain in the lower back

lumbar of the part of the body between the lower ribs and the hip-bones

lumber[1] unwanted furniture, household articles, etc.; to burden with something unwanted; (US) timber
lumberjack lumberyard

lumber[2] to move awkwardly
lumbering

lumen basic metric unit of luminous flux; space or cavity inside a tube
lumina or *lumens*

luminary body, such as the sun or moon,

that gives off light; person who enlightens others
luminaries

luminescent of the emission of light
luminescence

luminous shining or glowing
luminosity luminously

lump shapeless mass; swelling; to put together, esp. indiscriminately
lumpy

lumpish like a lump; awkward
lumpishly lumpishness

lunacy foolishness or madness
lunatic

lunar of the moon

lunch (to eat a) meal at the middle of the day
lunch-box

luncheon formal lunch

lung one of a pair of breathing organs in the chest

lunge (to make a) forward thrust
lunging

lupin kind of leguminous spiky flowering plant

lupine of or like a wolf

lurch[1] to pitch or sway to one side; such action
lurches

lurch[2] difficult position

lure to tempt or entice; something that attracts; bait
luring

lurid gaudy or vivid; sensational
luridly luridness

lurk to lie hidden, esp. for bad purposes

luscious very attractive; appealing to the taste or smell
lusciously lusciousness

lush luxurious; profuse
lushly lushness

lust (to feel a) strong desire, esp. sexual
lustful lustfully lustfulness

lustre (US **luster**) brilliance; splendour
lustrous

lusty strong and healthy
lustily

lute kind of stringed musical instrument
lutenist or *lutanist*

Lutheran of a Lutheran church or teachings derived from Martin Luther

Luxembourg grand duchy in West Europe
Luxembourger

luxuriant growing profusely
luxuriance luxuriantly
SEE PANEL

---

luxuriant or luxurious?

Luxuriant plants or trees are ones that are growing profusely: *luxuriant foliage; luxuriant vegetation.*

Something that is *luxurious* is very enjoyable, comfortable, and expensive: *stay at a luxurious hotel; luxurious furnishings.*

---

luxuriate to revel
luxuriating

luxurious very enjoyable, comfortable, and expensive
SEE PANEL at **luxuriant**

luxury something very enjoyable and pleasant but unnecessary
luxuries

-ly

When the suffix *-ly* is added to a word the base form stays the same except for the ending *-ll*, which changes to *-lly*, and *-le* which changes to *-ly*:

able, ably ample, amply full, fully idle, idly late, lately nice, nicely terrible, terribly

Exceptions:

due, duly true, truly whole, wholly

For the change of the final *-y* to *-i-* (e.g. *happy, happily*) see panel at Y.

---

lychee, **litchi** or **lichee** kind of Chinese tree grown for its edible fruit; this fruit

lych-gate see **lich-gate**

lye strong alkaline solution

lying present participle of **lie**[1] and **lie**[2]

lymph body fluid containing white blood cells
lymphatic

lynch to kill or hang without lawful trial
lynches

lynx short-tailed wildcat with tufted ears
lynxes or *lynx*

lyre ancient Greek stringed instrument

lyric short poem; of poetry or songs
lyricist

lyrical lyric; enthusiastic

M

ma'am short for **madam**

Maastricht city in the Netherlands; name of European treaty

mac short for **mackintosh**

macabre gruesome

macadam road surface made of compressed layers of small crushed stones
macadamize or *macadamise*
macadamizing or *macadamising*

macaque kind of short-tailed Old World monkey

macaroni pasta tubes

macaroon sweet biscuit made of ground almonds

macaw kind of large tropical American parrot

mace[1] ceremonial staff; medieval club
macebearer

mace[2] spice made from the dried covering of nutmeg

Macedonia former Yugoslavian republic

macerate to soften or be softened by soaking
macerating maceration

machete large heavy knife

machiavellian cunning or unscrupulous

machinate to contrive or plot
machination machinating machinator

machine assembly of connected working parts to perform a certain task; to shape with a machine
machinable or *machineable machine-gun machine-readable machinery machining machinist*

machismo exaggerated or assertive masculinity

Mach number ratio of speed of a body to the speed of sound in the surrounding atmosphere

macho exaggeratedly or assertively masculine (man)
machos

mack short for **mackintosh**

mackerel kind of edible sea fish

mackintosh waterproof raincoat

macramé loose kind of decorative lacework

macrobiotics dietary system consisting mainly of whole grains and vegetables

macrocosm universe; large-scale complex

macron sign placed over a vowel or syllable

macroscopic visible to the naked eye

macula or **macule** small patch of skin of a changed colour
maculae, maculas, or *macules*

mad insane or very foolish; (*informal*) very enthusiastic (about); very angry
madcap madder maddest madhouse madly madman madness madwoman

Madagascar island in the Indian Ocean
Madagascan

madam polite term of address to a woman

madden to make or become very angry

made past tense and past participle of **make**
make-up

Madeira fortified wine from Madeira; group of islands west of Morocco

madonna representation of the Virgin Mary

madrigal unaccompanied part-song

maelstrom powerful whirlpool

maestro distinguished musician
maestri or *maestros*

Mafia Sicilian secret society prevalent in US

magazine periodic publication; case containing cartridges for weapons

magenta deep purplish-red

maggot larva of a fly
maggoty

Magi three wise men from the East who paid homage to the baby Jesus

magic (of the) art of calling upon supernatural powers to produce wonders; conjuring tricks
magical magically magician

magistrate officer who administers the law
magisterial magisterially magistracy or *magistrature*

magma molten rock material; pasty suspension
magmata or *magmas*

Magna Carta or **Magna Charta** charter of liberties, 1215

magnanimous showing noble generosity
magnanimity magnanimously

magnate influential person

magnesia white tasteless powder; magnesium oxide

magnesium light silver-white metal

magnet body of iron, steel, etc. that attracts iron
magnetic magnetically magnetism

magnetize or **magnetise** to provide with magnetic properties
magnetization or *magnetisation*
magnetizing or *magnetising*

magneto kind of electric generator
magnetos

magnificat song of Virgin Mary

magnificent splendid; very fine
magnificence magnificently

magnify to make appear larger
magnification magnified magnifier magnifies magnifying

magniloquence grand in style
magniloquent

magnitude importance, size, or extent

magnolia kind of flowering tree or shrub

magnum wine bottle holding twice the usual amount

magnum opus (*Latin*) author's chief work
magna opera

magpie chattering crow-like bird

Magyar of main Hungarian race; Hungarian language

maharaja or **maharajah** Indian prince

maharanee or **maharani** wife of maharaja

maharishi Hindu wise man

mahatma revered person

mah-jong or **mah-jongg** Chinese game played with tiles

mahogany kind of (tropical tree with) reddish-brown wood

mahout elephant keeper and driver

maid female servant; (*archaic*) unmarried girl or woman
maiden maidenhead maidenhood maidservant

maidenhair kind of delicate tropical fern

mail[1] (to) post
mailbag mailsack mailshot

mail[2] flexible body armour

maim to mutilate or cripple

main principal; chief
mainland mainly mainmast mainsail mainspring mainstay mainstream

mainframe large computer

maintain to keep or continue; to keep in good condition; to assert
maintainable maintenance

maisonette self-contained dwelling on 2 floors

maître d'hôtel (*French*) house steward
maîtres d'hôtel

maize sweet corn

majesty sovereign power; title used to address a king or queen
majesties majestic majestically

major important; of a musical scale or key; army rank; to specialize in

Majorca island in the Mediterranean

majority greater or greatest part; full legal age

make to produce, perform, or create; to cause to take place; to gain or earn; brand
made make-believe makeshift make-up making

maladjustment poor adjustment to one's environment or living conditions
maladjusted

maladministration bad or inefficient administration

maladroit clumsy; tactless

malady disease or illness
maladies

malaise feeling of unease

malapropism unintentional confusion of words

malaria disease and fever transmitted by mosquitoes
malarial

Malawi country in East Africa
Malawian

Malaysia federation in SE Asia
Malay Malaysian

malcontent discontented (person)

male of the sex that does not bear offspring
maleness

malediction curse
maledictory

malefactor wrongdoer
malefaction

malevolent wishing harm or evil to others
malevolence malevolently

malfeasance misconduct; illegal act

malformation being abnormal in shape or structure
malformed

malfunction to fail to operate in the normal way; instance of this

Mali country in West Africa
Malian

malice desire to harm
malicious

malign to speak ill of

malignant harmful; injurious; (*of a tumour*) growing uncontrollably
malignancy malignantly malignity

malinger to pretend illness, esp. to avoid work
malingerer

mall public walkway; shopping precinct

mallard kind of wild duck

malleable able to be shaped or influenced
malleability malleably

mallet hammer with wooden head

mallow kind of plant with hairy lobed leaves and showy flowers

malmsey sweet Madeira wine

malnutrition lack of adequate nutrition

malodorous having a bad smell

malpractice negligent or improper behaviour

malt germinated grain used in brewing

Malta island in the Mediterranean
Maltese

maltreat to treat badly
maltreatment

mamba kind of poisonous African snake

mamilla nipple
mamillae mamillary

mamma child's name for mother

mammal animal which suckles its young

mammary of the breasts
mammography

Mammon wealth considered as an evil

mammoth large extinct hairy elephant; gigantic

man human being; adult human male; to supply with people to enable operation, service, etc.
men man-at-arms men-at-arms man-eater manhole man-hour manhunt manliness manly man-made manned manning mannish man-of-war men-of-war manpower manservant mantrap

manacle (to) shackle
manacling

manage to be in charge of or direct; to succeed
manageability manageable management manager manageress managerial managing

mandarin former Chinese official; high-ranking official; small sweet orange

Mandarin official Chinese language

mandate official authorization or commission
mandating

mandatory of a mandate; compulsory

mandible lower jaw-bone; upper or lower part of a bird's bill
mandibular mandibulate

mandolin or **mandoline** stringed instrument

mandrake kind of plant with a forked root

mandrel spindle

mandrill kind of large African baboon

mane long thick hair on the neck of a horse, lion, etc.

maneuver (US) see **manoeuvre**

manful strong
manfully manfulness

manganese brittle greyish-white metal

mange skin disease affecting domestic animals
mangy

mangel-wurzel large beet grown as cattle food

manger open box from which cattle feed

mangle[1] machine with two rollers through which clothes are smoothed
mangler mangling

mangle[2] to disfigure or mutilate
mangling

mango kind of (tree bearing) yellowish-red fruit with succulent flesh
mangoes or *mangos*

mangrove kind of tropical tree with tangled roots

manhandle to handle roughly; to move or manage by human force
manhandling

manhood state of being a man

mania excited (violent) state; great enthusiasm
maniac maniacal maniacally manic-depressive

manicure care of the hands and finger-nails; to care for these
manicuring manicurist

manifest clear; to show clearly; list
manifestation manifestly

manifesto public declaration of policy
manifestos or *manifestoes*

manifold of many different kinds

manikin little man; dwarf; anatomical model

Manila hemp or **Manilla hemp** fibre obtained from the abaca plant used for rope, paper, etc.

manipulate to handle skilfully, esp. to one's own advantage
manipulating manipulation manipulator

mankind human beings collectively

manna food miraculously supplied to the Israelites in the wilderness

mannequin dressmaker's model

manner way of being, doing, or speaking
mannered manners

mannerism individual distinctive habit

manoeuvre (US **maneuver**) cerefully developed plan, esp. of troop movement; to move carefully
manoeuvrability (US *maneuverability*)
manoeuvrable (US *maneuverable*)
manoeuvrer (US *maneuverer*)
manoeuvring (US *maneuvering*)

manor large country house; landed estate
manorial

mansard kind of roof

manse clergyman's house

mansion large imposing house

manslaughter unintentional killing of a person

mantelpiece shelf forming part of an ornamental frame for a fireplace

mantilla Spanish lace or silk scarf

mantis kind of tropical insect like a grasshopper

mantissa part of a logarithm

mantle loose sleeveless cloak; cover

mantra chart used by Buddhists and Hindus in meditation

manual performed with the hands; handbook; organ keyboard
manually

manufacture to produce goods on a large scale, esp. with machinery; to make or invent
manufacturer manufacturing

manure animal excrement used as a fertilizer
manuring

manuscript written or typed document

Manx of the Isle of Man

many large number of
many-coloured

Maoism theories developed by Mao Tse-tung
Maoist

Maori Polynesian people of New Zealand; language of this people

map plan or representation of part of the earth's surface; to make a detailed map or plan of
mapped mapping

maple kind of tree; hardwood of this used in making furniture

mar to spoil or harm
marred marring

marabou kind of large African stork

maraca dried gourd, etc. used as one of a pair of percussion instruments

maraschino sweet liqueur made from cherries
maraschinos

marathon long-distance running race

maraud to wander in search of plunder
marauder

marble form of hard limestone; small ball of glass

march to walk with regular steps, as soldiers do; musical composition
marches march-past

March 3rd month of the year

marchioness wife or widow of a marquis; woman of the rank of marquis

Mardi Gras festival of Shrove Tuesday

mare female horse, zebra, etc.

margarine substitute for butter made from vegetable oils, etc.

marge (*informal*) margarine

margin border or edge; difference between cost price and selling price; small amount
marginal *marginalize* or *marginalise* *marginally*

marguerite kind of daisy-like flower

marigold kind of plant with bright yellow or orange flowers

marijuana or **marihuana** dried leaves and flowers of the hemp plant, used as a drug

marimba percussion instrument like a xylophone

marina dock or basin for yachts and pleasure boats

marinade spiced liquid in which food is soaked to enrich its flavour

marinate to soak in a marinade
marinating

marine of the sea or shipping; soldier trained for service on land or at sea
mariner

marionette puppet whose jointed limbs are moved by strings

marital of marriage
maritally

maritime of navigation or shipping

marjoram kind of plant with aromatic sweet-scented leaves

mark[1] (to make a) visible impression on a surface; token; (to) grade
markedly *mark-up*

mark[2] money unit of Germany

market public place where goods are sold; to deal in a commodity
marketable *market-day* *marketing* *market-place*

marksman (*fem.* **markswoman**) person skilled in shooting
marksmanship *marksmen* (fem. *markswomen*)

marl fine-grained rock used as a fertilizer

marlinspike or **marlinespike** pointed tool for separating strands of rope in splicing

marmalade preserve made from citrus fruit, esp. oranges

marmoset kind of small South American monkey

marmot kind of small burrowing rodent

maroon[1] brownish-red

maroon[2] to abandon on an island; to isolate
marooned

marquee large tent

marquetry or **marqueterie** inlaid work used as a decoration for furniture

marquis or **marquess** nobleman next in rank below a duke

marriage state of being husband and wife; ceremony in which a man and woman become husband and wife
marriageable

marrow fatty tissue in bones; kind of large cucumber
marrowbone *marrowfat*

marry to join or take in marriage
married *marries* *marrying*

Mars 4th planet from the sun; Roman god of war
Martian

Marsala sweet wine

marsh low soft wet land
marshy

marshal highest-ranking officer; official; to arrange
marshalled (US *marshaled*) *marshaller*

(US *marshaler*) *marshalling* (US *marshaling*)

marshmallow soft spongy sweet

marsupial of a mammal that carries its young in a pouch
marsupium

mart trading centre

Martello tower small circular fort for coastal defence

marten kind of small weasel-like mammal

martial of war
martially

martin swallow-like bird

martinet strict disciplinarian

martingale strap to restrain upward movement of horse's head

martini gin and vermouth cocktail

martyr person who undergoes death or great suffering rather than give up a belief or cause
martyrdom

marvel to be very surprised at; to wonder at; something that causes wonder
marvelled (US *marveled*) *marvelling* (US *marveling*)

marvellous (US **marvelous**) extraordinary; excellent
marvellously (US *marvelously*)

Marxism economic and political theories of Karl Marx
Marxian Marxist

marzipan paste made from ground almonds, sugar, and egg-whites

mascara cosmetic for darkening the eyelashes

mascot person or thing thought to bring good luck

masculine of men or qualities thought to be manly
masculinity

maser device for amplifying microwaves

mash (to crush into a) soft pulpy mass

mask (to put on a) cover worn over the face for disguise or protection

masochism pleasure derived from suffering pain or humiliation
masochist masochistic

mason person skilled in building with stone
masonic masonry

Mason short for **Freemason**
Masonic Masonry

masque 16th–17th-century dramatic entertainment

masquerade party at which guests wear masks and costumes; to disguise
masquerading

mass large quantity; large body; to form into a mass
mass-produced

Mass (esp. Roman Catholic) service of the Eucharist

Massachusetts US state

massacre slaughter of a great number of people or animals; to kill indiscriminately
massacres massacring

massage rubbing, etc. of parts of the body; to give a massage to
massaging

masseur (*fem.* **masseuse**) person who gives massages

massif mountain mass

massive large and heavy; bulky
massively massiveness

mast tall upright spar to support a ship's sail
masthead

mastectomy surgical removal of a breast
mastectomies

master teacher; employer; expert; skilled craftsman; to overcome; to acquire skill in or knowledge of *master-at-arms masterclass masterpiece master-stroke mastery*

masterful showing mastery; domineering
masterfully masterfulness
SEE PANEL

masterful or masterly?
If you describe a person or their behaviour as *masterful,* you mean they are able to exert their authority in situations: *the manager's confident, masterful approach to his staff.*
Something that is *masterly* shows that it has been undertaken with great skill: *exhibit a masterly display of tact.*

masterly showing great skill
masterliness
SEE PANEL at **masterful**

mastermind to plan and direct a complex project

mastic gum-resin

masticate to chew food
masticating mastication

mastiff large powerful dog

mastoid nipple-shaped; of the part of the bone behind the ear
mastoiditis

masturbate to stimulate the sexual organs by hand
masturbating masturbation

mat[1] fabric used as a floor covering; to tangle
matted matting

mat[2] see **matt**

matador bullfighter

match[1] short wooden stick with a tip that ignites by friction on a rough surface
matches matchbox matchstick matchwood

match[2] contest; person of equal skill, etc.; to equal in skill, etc.; to be harmonious
matches matchless

mate breeding partner; friend; to pair for breeding
matey mating

material substance from which a thing is made; cloth; of matter; important
materialism materialist materialistic materially

materialize or **materialise** to assume a bodily form; to actually happen
materialization or *materialisation*
materializing or *materialising*

maternal of or like a mother; related through the mother
maternally

maternity motherhood; (of) pregnancy

mathematics science of numbers, quantities, etc.
mathematical mathematically mathematician

maths (US **math**) short for **mathematics**

matinée afternoon performance at a cinema, theatre, etc.

matins or **mattins** morning prayer

matriarch woman who is the head of a family or tribe
matriarchal matriarchy matriarchies

matricide killing of one's own mother
matricidal

matriculate to enter or admit to a university
matriculating matriculation matriculator

matrimony marriage
matrimonies matrimonial

matrix substance in which something originates; mould; regular mathematical array
matrices or *matrixes*

matron older married woman; woman housekeeper in a school, etc.; head of nursing staff in a hospital

matt or **mat** dull; not glossy

matter physical substance; subject or material; to be of importance
matter-of-fact

matting coarsely woven fabric

mattins see **matins**

mattock tool that is a kind of large pick

mattress strong cover filled with straw or foam rubber, used to lie on
mattresses

maturate to mature
maturating maturation

mature fully grown or developed; adult; to make or become mature
maturely maturing maturity

matutinal of the morning

matzo unleavened bread
matzos or *motzoth*

maudlin tearful and sentimental

maul to injure by treating roughly
mauler

Maundy Thursday Thursday before Easter

Mauritania country in NE Africa
Mauritanian

Mauritius island in the Indian Ocean
Mauritian

mausoleum large elaborate tomb
mausoleums

mauve pale purple colour

maverick (US) unbranded animal, esp. a calf; independent person of unorthodox views

mavis song thrush

maw stomach, mouth, or crop of an animal

mawkish falsely sentimental
mawkishly mawkishness

maxi- (*prefix*) very long or large
maxi-skirt

maxilla upper or lower jaw-bone
maxillae

maxim general truth or principle

maximize or **maximise** to increase to a maximum
maximization or *maximisation*
maximizing or *maximising*

maximum greatest possible (amount, etc.)
maximums or *maxima maximal*

may[1] auxiliary verb used to express possibility, permission, or a wish
maybe mayn't might

may[2] hawthorn

May 5th month of the year
maypole

mayday international radio distress signal

mayfly kind of insect
mayflies

mayhem violent destruction or confusion

mayonnaise thick creamy egg-based dressing, esp. for salads

mayor (*fem.* **mayoress**) chief executive or head of a city or borough
mayoral mayoralty mayorship

maze complex and confusing network of paths

mazurka lively Polish dance

me object pronoun referring to the speaker or writer

mead fermented alcoholic drink

meadow area of grassland

meagre (US **meager**) deficient; thin
meagrely (US *meagerly*) *meagreness* (US *meagerness*)

meal[1] regular occasion of eating
mealtime

meal[2] coarsely ground seeds of a cereal grass
mealy

mealy-mouthed reluctant to speak frankly

mean[1] not generous; poor
meanly meanness

mean[2] to intend; to be a sign of
meaning meaningful meaningfully

meaningless meaninglessly meaninglessness meant

mean[3] equally distant from 2 extreme points

meander to wander or wind

means method or way; resources; income

meantime or **meanwhile** intervening time

measles infectious disease with red spots

measure quantity or size; standard or unit; step, action, or proposed law; to determine the size, etc., of
measurable measureless measurement measuring measuring-jug

meat flesh of animals as food
meatball meaty

mechanic workman skilled in using, repairing, etc. machines

mechanical of machines
mechanically

mechanics study of motion and force

mechanism machinery; action
mechanistic

mechanize or **mechanise** to equip with machinery
mechanization or *mechanisation*
mechanizing or *mechanising*

medal small commemorative piece of metal
medallist (US *medalist*)

medallion large medal

meddle to interfere
meddler meddlesome meddling

media pl. of **medium**

medial of or in the middle
medially

median of or in the middle
medianly

mediate to act as a go-between or negotiator
mediating mediation mediator

medicament medicine

medicate to treat with medicine
medicating medication

medicine study or prevention and cure of disease; substance used in treatment of disease
medical medically medicinal

medieval or **mediaeval** of the Middle Ages
medievalist or *mediaevalist*

mediocre neither good nor bad; indifferent; rather bad
mediocrity

meditate to think deeply
meditating meditation meditative meditatively

Mediterranean sea between Europe, Africa, and Asia

medium agency or intermediate state (pl. *media*); method of transmitting information (pl. *media*); person claiming to be a spiritual intermediary between the dead and the living (pl. *mediums*)

medlar kind of small tree with fruit that is eaten when it has begun to decay

medley mixture of different elements
medleys

medulla marrow
medullae

meek mild; patient and humble
meekly meekness

meerschaum (tobacco pipe with a bowl made of a) white clay mineral

meet to come together with; to satisfy a need or requirement
meeting met

mega (*slang*) great; extremely

mega- (*prefix*) 10^6; extremely large
megahertz megamillionaire megasized megastar megavolt megawatt

megabyte (*computers*) measure of data capacity, 1,048, 576 bytes

megalith huge stone, esp. part of a monument
megalithic

megalomania mental illness marked by delusions of grandeur, power, etc.
megalomaniac

megalopolis very large city

megaphone voice-amplifier

megaton explosive force equivalent to 1,000,000 tons of TNT

meiosis understatement; biological cell division
meioses

melamine strong resilient plastic material

melancholy gloominess; gloomy
melancholia melancholic

Melanesia group of Pacific islands

mélange mixture

Melba toast thin crisp toast

mêlée fray
mêlées

meliorate to improve
meliorating melioration meliorative

mellifluous smooth
mellifluence mellifluously

mellow mature and rich; not harsh; to become mellow
mellowed mellowly mellowness

melodrama romantic or exaggerated drama
melodramatic melodramatically

melody tune; pleasant sequence of sounds
melodies melodic melodious

melon kind of large round fruit with juicy flesh

melt to make or become liquid by heating
meltdown melted melting-point melting-pot molten

member person belonging to a club, society, etc.; part of the body
membership

membrane thin skin-like tissue of material
membranous membraneous

memento something by which a past event is remembered
mementoes or *mementos*

memo short for **memorandum**
memos

memoir biography or autobiography; historical description
memoirs

memorable worth remembering; easily remembered
memorabilia

memorandum written reminder; business communication
memorandums or *memoranda*

memorial (something) serving as a commemoration

memorize or **memorise** to commit to memory
memorizing or *memorising*

memory ability to remember; something remembered
memories memorable memorably

men pl. of **man**

menace to threaten; threat
menacing menacingly

ménage household

menagerie collection of wild animals

menarche first menstrual period

mend to repair or rectify
mendable mender

mendacity untruthfulness; falsehood
mendacious

mendicant begging; beggar
mendicancy or *mendicity*

menfolk men

menial of servants; lowly or degrading
menially

meninges membranes covering the brain and spinal cord

meningitis inflammation of the meninges

menopause period when a woman's menstrual cycle stops

menses monthly discharge of blood from the uterus during menstruation

menstruate to discharge menses
menstrual menstruating menstruation

mensuration study of measurement
mensurable

menswear clothes for men

mental of or in the mind
mentally

mentality extent of mental power; mental attitude
mentalities

menthol extract of peppermint oil
mentholated

mention brief reference; to refer to briefly
mentionable

mentor wise or trusted adviser

menu list of dishes available in a restaurant; list of computer options

meow see **miaow**

mercantile of or associated with trade
mercantilism

mercenary motivated by greed or gain; hired foreign soldier
mercenaries

mercer (*Brit*) dealer in textiles
mercery

merchandise commercial goods

merchant person engaged in buying and selling goods

mercury heavy silver metal
mercurial

Mercury planet nearest the sun; (*Roman mythology*) messenger of the gods

mercy compassion; restraint; pity
merciful mercifully mercifulness merciless mercilessly mercilessness

mere[1] nothing more than
merely

mere[2] lake

meretricious superficially attractive; insincere

merganser kind of large marine diving duck

merge to write, join, or blend
merger merging

meridian imaginary line joining the North and South Poles and at right angles to the equator

meridional of a meridian of the south

meringue baked mixture of sugar and egg-whites

merino fine-woolled sheep
merinos

merit deserving quality; to deserve
merited meriting

meritocracy rule by people with skills and talents
meritocracies

meritorious showing merit; deserving a reward

mermaid (*masc.* **merman**) imaginary sea creature with an upper human body and the tail of a fish

merry jolly; funny; (*informal*) slightly intoxicated
merrier merriest merrily merriment merriness merry-making

merry-go-round fairground revolving circular platform with wooden model horses

mescal kind of small cactus
mescaline

mesentery fold of the peritoneum
mesenteries

mesh net; gap in netting; to interlock
meshes meshing

mesmerize or **mesmerise** to hypnotize
mesmerism mesmerist mesmerizing or *mesmerising*

Mesolithic division of the Stone Age

Mesozoic geological era

mess state of untidy confusion; place where group of servicemen eat
mess-room mess-up messy

message communication

messenger person who takes messages

Messiah expected king and deliverer of the Jews; Jesus Christ
Messianic

Messrs pl. of **Mr**

met past tense and past participle of **meet**

metabolism set of chemical processes that occur in a living body to maintain life
metabolic metabolize or *metabolise*

metacarpus 5 bones of the hand
metacarpal

metal one of a group of mineral substances such as iron or copper; to fit or cover with metal
metalled (US *metaled*) *metallic metalling* (US *metaling*) *metalwork*

metalloid element having properties of metals and non-metals

metallurgy study of the properties of metals and their extraction, etc.
metallurgical metallurgist

metamorphose to (cause to) undergo metamorphosis
metamorphosing

metamorphosis complete change in form, substance, or character
metamorphoses metamorphic

metaphor use of a literal expression in which an idea is applied to another to suggest a likeness
metaphorical metaphorically

metaphysics study of being and knowing
metaphysical metaphysically

metastasis transfer of a disease from one part of the body to another

metatarsus 5 bones of the foot
metatarsal

mete (**mete out**) to allot or distribute
meting

meteor streak of light seen in the night sky when a meteoroid enters the earth's atmosphere
meteoric

meteorite large piece of a meteoroid that has fallen to earth

meteoroid small body in orbit round the sun

meteorology study of the atmosphere and weather
meteorological meteorologist

meter[1] device that measures and records an amount

meter[2] (US) see **metre**

methane odourless colourless flammable gas

methanol wood alcohol

method way of doing something
methodical methodically methodology

Methodism Christian denomination founded by John Wesley
Methodist

meths (*informal*) methylated spirit

methylated spirit form of alcohol

meticulous precise; painstaking
meticulously meticulousness

métier profession or trade

metonymy substitution of a word referring to an attribute for the thing that is intended

metre (US **meter**) basic metric unit of length; rhythmical pattern in verse
metric metrical

metricate to convert to a metric system of measurement

metricating metrication

metronome device that indicates the tempo in music

metropolis main city of a country
metropolises metropolitan

mettle courage or spirit

mew (to make the) cry of a cat

mews street of buildings once used as stables but now adapted for living accommodation

Mexico country in North America
Mexican

mezzanine low intermediate storey between ground and first floor

mezzo (*music*) moderately

mezzo-soprano woman's voice between a soprano and a contralto
mezzo-sopranos

mezzotint method of engraving a copper plate

miaow or **meow** (to make the) cry of a cat

miasma ill-smelling mist or vapour
miasmata miasmal

mica silicate substance

mice pl. of **mouse**

Michaelmas autumn term at some universities

Michaelmas daisy kind of aster

micro- (*prefix*) tiny; one-millionth
microsecond

microbe micro-organism; germ

microbiology study of micro-organisms
microbiological microbiologist

microchip tiny wafer of silicon, etc. as part of an integrated circuit

microcircuit miniature electronic circuit

microcomputer small computer whose central processing unit is held on one or more silicon chips

microcosm miniature representation

microdot photographic reproduction reduced to the size of a dot

microelectronics branch of electronics concerned with microcircuits

microfiche sheet of film containing rows of miniature images of printed matter

microfilm strip of film on which documents are recorded in reduced form

microlight small light low-speed aircraft

micrometer device for measuring small distances

micron one millionth part of a metre

Micronesia group of Pacific islands

micro-organism tiny organism

microphone device that converts sound into electrical energy

microprocessor single integrated circuit that performs basic computer functions

microscope instrument with lenses that produce magnified images of tiny objects
microscopic microscopist microscopy

microwave electromagnetic wave between 0.3 and 0.001 metres; oven in which food is cooked by microwaves; to cook in such an oven
microwaveable or *microwavable*

micturate to urinate
micturating micturition

mid in the middle of; among
midfield midmost mid-off mid-on midpoint midsummer midterm midway midweek midwicket midwinter

midday noon

middle (at a) point equally distant from 2 extremes
middle-aged middleman middle-of-the-road middleweight middling

midge kind of small gnat or fly

midget abnormally small person or thing

midi woman's garment extending to the mid-calf

midland central part of a country

midnight 12 o'clock at night

midriff diaphragm; abdomen

midshipman young naval officer
midshipmen

midst middle

midwife nurse qualified to assist women in childbirth
midwives midwifery

mien person's manner or bearing

miffed (*informal*) slightly annoyed and hurt

might[1] past tense of **may**[1]
mightn't

might[2] strength or power
mightily mightiness mighty

migraine severe headache often associated with visual disturbances

migrate to move from 1 country or area to another
migrant migrating migration migratory

mike (*informal*) short for **microphone**

milch (*of cattle*) kept for milk production

mild gentle; moderate; not strong or extreme
mildly mildness

mildew (fungus producing a) whitish growth on organic matter

mile unit of length, 1760 yards
mileage miler milestone milometer

milieu surroundings or environment
milieux

militant aggressive (person)
militancy militantly

militarize or **militarise** to equip with military forces, etc.
militarization or *militarisation militarized* or *militarised militarizing* or *militarising*

military (of the) armed forces
militarily militarism militarist militaristic

militate to have an effect
militating
SEE PANEL

---

militate or mitigate?

If something *militates* against something, it has a powerful adverse effect on it, making something less likely to happen: *At 50, his age militates against his appointment.*

Mitigate means to make something less severe, harsh, or unpleasant: *attempt to mitigate the problems of unemployment; mitigating circumstances.*

---

militia supplementary armed force of citizens

milk whitish fluid secreted by female mammals to feed their young; to draw milk from
milk-float milkiness milkmaid milkman milksop milky

mill building with machinery that grinds grain into flour; factory; to grind
miller milling millpond millstone millwright

millennium period of 1000 years; time of universal happiness
millenniums or *millennia millennial*

millepede or **millipede** small creature with many segments, most of which bear 2 pairs of legs

millet cereal grass

milli- (*prefix*) one thousandth
milligram or *milligramme millilitre* (US *milliliter*) *millimetre* (US *millimeter*) *millisecond*

milliard (*Brit*) thousand million

millibar unit of atmospheric pressure

milliner person who makes or sells women's hats
millinery

million 1,000,000
millionaire millionairess millionth

millipede see **millepede**

milt male fish sperm

mime acting with gestures and without speaking; to express in this way
miming

Mimeograph (*trademark*) machine for producing multiple copies from a stencil; to produce copies on a Mimeograph

mimic to imitate, esp. for comic effect
mimicked mimicking mimicry

mimosa kind of shrub that bears ball-like clusters of flowers

mina see **myna**

minaret thin tower on a mosque

mince to chop; to moderate; minced meat
mincer mincing

mincemeat mixture of fruit, spices, etc.

mind intellect; intelligence or understanding; to look after; to object to
mind-bending mind-blowing mind-boggling minder mindful mindless mindlessly mindlessness

mine[1] (the one or ones) belonging to me

mine[2] excavation from which coal, etc. is dug; metal case containing explosive; to extract in a mine
mine-detector minefield minelayer miner minesweeper mining

mineral natural substance obtained by mining, etc.
mineralogist mineralogy

minestrone rich thick vegetable soup

mingle to mix
mingler mingling

mini- (*prefix*) very small or short
minibus minicab minicomputer miniskirt

miniature small-scale, small painting
miniaturist

minim (*music*) note lasting half a semibreve

minimal smallest possible size, number, etc.
minimally

minimize or **minimise** to reduce to a minimum
minimization or *minimisation minimizing* or *minimising*

minimum lowest possible (amount, etc.)
minima or *minimums*

minion (servile) assistant

minipill contraceptive pill

minister government official; clergyman; to provide help (to)
ministerial ministerially ministration

ministry government department; duties of a clergyman

mink (fur of) small slender stoat-like animal

Minnesota US state

minnow kind of small freshwater fish

minor less; of a musical scale or key; person not legally of age
minority minorities

Minorca island in the Mediterranean

minster cathedral or large church

minstrel medieval musician or performer

mint[1] place where money is made; to make coins by stamping metal
minter

mint[2] kind of fragrant plant used for flavouring; sweet
minty

minuet slow graceful dance

minus subtracting

minuscule very small

minute[1] one-sixtieth of an hour; one-sixtieth of a degree

minute[2] tiny
minutely

minutes official record of the proceedings of a meeting

minutiae minor details

minx flirtatious woman

Miocene geological epoch of the Tertiary period

miracle extraordinary event, esp. with a supernatural cause
miraculous miraculously

mirage illusory image

mire deep mud

mirror piece of glass that reflects images; to reflect
mirrored mirroring

mirth laughter; merriness
mirthful mirthless

mis- (*prefix*) badly or wrongly
misapply miscount misdirect misjudge misread misrule misspend

misadventure unlucky event

misalliance unsuitable alliance or marriage

misanthrope person who dislikes other people
misanthropic misanthropist misanthropy

misapprehend to misunderstand
misapprehension

misappropriate to take dishonestly
misappropriating misappropriation

misbehave to behave badly
misbehaver misbehaving misbehaviour (US *misbehavior*)

miscalculate to calculate wrongly
miscalculating miscalculation

miscarry to suffer the spontaneous expulsion of a foetus from the womb before it can live independently
miscarriage miscarried miscarries miscarrying

miscast to cast badly

miscegenation interbreeding of races

miscellaneous of a variety of kinds
miscellanea miscellany miscellanies

mischance bad luck

mischief foolish or playful behaviour, esp. by children
mischievous mischievously mischievousness

miscible capable of being mixed

misconception misunderstanding
misconceive misconceiving

misconduct immoral or bad behaviour

misconstrue to interpret wrongly
misconstruction misconstruing

miscreant villain or wrongdoer

misdeed wrongful action

misdemeanour (US **misdemeanor**)
misdeed

miser person who hoards money
miserliness miserly

miserable very unhappy
miserably

misericord projection underneath a hinged seat in a church choir stall

misery great unhappiness
miseries

misfeasance wrongful exercise of lawful act

misfire to fail to fire properly
misfiring

misfit person who is not well adjusted to his or her circumstances; ill-fitting garment

misfortune bad luck

misgiving feeling of apprehension or doubt

misguided ill-advised

mishandle to treat or handle badly
mishandling

mishap unfortunate accident

mishmash mixture

misinform to give wrong information to

misinterpret to interpret wrongly
misinterpretation

mislay to lose temporarily
mislaid mislaying

mislead to lead in a wrong direction; to give false information to
misleading misled

mismanage to manage badly
mismanagement mismanaging

misnomer wrong use of a name

misogamy hatred of marriage
misogamist

misogyny hatred of women
misogynist misogynous

misplace to put in the wrong place
misplacing

misprint (to make an) error in printing

mispronounce to pronounce wrongly
mispronouncing mispronunciation

misquote to quote incorrectly
misquotation misquoting

misrepresent to represent inaccurately
misrepresentation

miss to fail to hit, catch, achieve, etc.; to discover the absence of; failure to hit, etc.
misses missed missing

Miss title of unmarried woman or girl
Misses

missal Roman Catholic prayer book

missel-thrush kind of large thrush

misshape to deform

missile thrown or projected object or weapon

mission group of envoys, task, duty, or vocation
missionary missionaries

missis or **missus** (*informal*) wife; married woman

Mississippi US state; US river

missive (*formal*) letter

Missouri US state; US river

misspell to spell wrongly
misspelled or *misspelt misspelling*

mist (to cover with a) thin fog
misty

mistake error; to misunderstand or confuse
mistakable or *mistakeable mistaken mistakenly mistaking mistook*

Mister full form of **Mr**

mistime to time wrongly
mistiming

mistletoe parasitic shrub used as Christmas decoration

mistral strong cold dry wind of South France

mistress woman in authoritative position; woman teacher; man's lover
mistresses

mistrial trial declared void because of an error

mistrust to lack trust in

misunderstand to understand wrongly
misunderstanding misunderstood

misusage wrong use

misuse to use wrongly; to treat badly; wrong use; bad treatment
misusing
SEE PANEL at **abuse**

mite tiny infesting creature; tiny child or object

mitigate to make or become less severe or harsh
mitigating mitigation mitigative
SEE PANEL at **militate**

mitre (US **miter**) tall head-dress of bishop or abbot; joint of 2 pieces of wood
mitre-box

mitt glove leaving the ends of the fingers uncovered; mitten

mitten glove having 1 wide covering for the fingers and another part for the thumb

mix to combine or blend; to be sociable; something mixed
mixes mixed-up mixer mixture mix-up

mizen-mast or **mizzen-mast** mast behind the mainmast

mnemonic aid to one's memory
mnemonics mnemonist

moan (to utter a) long mournful sound; (to) grumble

moat water-filled trench round castle

mob disorderly crowd; to attack or acclaim in a large crowd
mobbed mobbing

mobcap woman's cap

mobile easily movable; hanging structure with moving parts
mobility

mobilize or **mobilise** to prepare for service or war
mobilization or *mobilisation* *mobilizing* or *mobilising*

moccasin soft leather shoe

mocha good-quality coffee; coffee and chocolate flavouring

mock to ridicule; sham or imitation
mockery mockeries mockingbird mockingly mock-up

modal of a mode or manner; (*grammar*) of a verbal mood
modality modally

mode manner or way something is done; fashion

model small-scale representation; pattern; exemplary; to shape
modelled (US *modeled*) *modeller* (US *modeler*) *modelling* (US *modeling*)

modem electronic device that connects 2 computers by telephone line

moderate not extreme or excessive; to make or become moderate
moderately moderating moderation

moderato (*music*) in moderate time

moderator mediator; presiding officer

modern of the present time
modernism modernist modernity

modernize or **modernise** to make or become modern
modernization or *modernisation*
modernizing or *modernising*

modest not vain or boastful
modestly modesty

modicum small amount

modify to adapt, change, or qualify
modification modified modifies modifying

modish fashionable

modiste fashionable dressmaker or milliner

modulate to change the tone, amplitude, etc. of; to regulate
modulating modulation modulator

module standard unit in measurement; independent component or unit
modular

modus operandi (*Latin*) method of working
modi operandi

modus vivendi (*Latin*) practical compromise; manner of living
modi vivendi

mogul rich powerful person

mohair hair of the angora goat

Mohammed see **Muhammad**

moiety half
moieties

moiré having a watered or wavy pattern

moist slightly wet
moisten moistness

moisture liquid diffused through a substance or present in the air *moisturize* or *moisturise* *moisturizer* or *moisturiser*

molar grinding tooth

molasses think brown syrup drained from raw sugar

mold (US) see **mould**[1] and **mould**[2]

Moldavia country in Eastern Europe bordering Romania and Ukraine

molder (US) see **moulder**

mole[1] small dark pigment on human skin

mole[2] kind of small burrowing mammal
molehill *moleskin*

mole[3] breakwater

mole[4] basic metric unit of the amount of a substance

molecule smallest particle of a substance that still retains its chemical properties
molecular

molest to annoy or accost harmfully
molestation

mollify to soothe or moderate
mollification mollified mollifies mollifying

mollusc invertebrate with a soft unsegmented body

mollycoddle to pamper
mollycoddling

molt (US) see **moult**

molten past participle of **melt**

molto (*music*) very

molybdenum a hard metallic element

moment very short time; importance

momentary lasting for a very short time
momentarily
SEE PANEL

momentary or momentous?
Momentary means 'lasting for a very short time': *a momentary lapse in concentration; a momentary loss of consciousness.*

Momentous means 'of great significance or importance': *a momentous decision/occasion.*

momentous of great significance or importance
momentously
SEE PANEL at **momentary**

momentum force of moving body; impetus
momenta

Monaco principality in SW Europe
Monégasque

monad unit; atom

monarch king or queen
monarchal monarchial monarchic monarchical monarchism monarchist monarchistic monarchy monarchies

monastery building where monks live
monasteries monastic monasticism

monaural (*of sound reproduction or broadcasting*) using only 1 channel

Monday 2nd day of the week

monetarism theory of regulating supply of money to control a country's economy
monetarist

monetary of money or currency

money coins and banknotes; wealth
moneys or *monies* *moneybags* *money-changer* *moneyed* *moneylender* *moneymaker*

Mongolia region of central Asia
Mongolian

mongolism Down's syndrome
mongol *mongoloid*

Mongoloid of a racial grouping consisting of the peoples of East Asia and the Arctic region of North America

mongoose kind of small predatory mammal
mongooses

mongrel dog or animal of mixed or unknown breeding

monitor senior pupil; device that checks or controls; to check

monk male member of a religious community living in a monastery
monkish

monkey long-tailed primate
monkeys

mono short for **monophonic**

mono- (*prefix*) single; 1
monolingual

monochrome having only 1 colour
monochromatic

monocle lens for 1 eye
monocular

monogamy practice or state of being married to only 1 person at a time
monogamist monogamous

monogram design of a person's initials

monograph treatise dealing with 1 subject

monogyny practice or state of having only 1 wife at a time
monogynous

monolith large block of stone
monolithic

monologue long speech made by 1 person in a play, etc.

monomania obsession with 1 idea or topic
monomaniac

monophonic (*of sound reproduction or broadcasting*) using only 1 channel

monoplane aeroplane with only 1 pair of wings

monopoly (person or group having) exclusive control of something
monopolist monopolistic monopolize or *monopolise*

monorail railway with a single track

monosodium glutamate crystalline substance used to season foods

monosyllable word of 1 syllable
monosyllabic

monotheism belief in only 1 God
monotheist monotheistic

monotone single unvarying tone
monotonous monotonously monotony

Monotype typesetting machine that casts each character separately

monoxide oxide containing 1 oxygen atom per molecule

Monsignor Roman Catholic title

monsoon seasonal wind of South Asia

monster imaginary beast; wicked person
monstrosity monstrosities monstrous

montage picture made of many different pictures or photographs

Montenegro republic of former Yugoslavia

month 1 of 12 divisions of the year
monthly monthlies

monument thing built to commemorate a person or event

monumental like a monument; very important
monumentally

moo (to make the) long deep sound of a cow

mooch (*informal*) to wander aimlessly

mood[1] state of mind or spirit
moody

mood[2] (*grammer*) form of a verb

moon natural satellite of the earth
moonbeam moonscape moonshine moonshot moonstone moonstruck moony

moonlight light from the moon; to have two paid jobs
moonlighter moonlit

moor[1] expanse of open land, esp. covered with gorse or heather
moorhen moorland

moor[2] to secure a vessel with a rope or cable
moorage moorings

moose kind of large North American deer

moot subject to debate; to suggest for discussion

mop (to clean with a) bundle or rags, etc. fixed to long stick
mopped *mopping* *mop-up*

mope to be gloomy
moped *moper* *moping* *mopish*

moped light motor cycle

moquette thick velvety fabric

moraine mass of earth, stones, etc. deposited by a glacier

moral concerned with right and wrong; moral lesson or principle
moralist *moralistic* *morality* *moralities*
SEE PANEL

---

moral or morale?
Moral means ´concerned with right or wrong´: *moral responsibilities; moral values/standards.* The *moral* of a story is a lesson or principle that you can learn from a situation: *The moral of the story is simple – look before you leap.*

Morale is the confidence felt by people: *Threats of redundancy meant that morale was low; efforts to boost the soldiers´ morale.*

---

morale confidence of a group
SEE PANEL at **moral**

moralize or **moralise** to make pronouncements about morals
moralization or *moralisation* *moralizer* or *moraliser* *moralizing* or *moralising*

morass marshy area

moratorium authorized postponement
moratoriums or *moratoria*

morbid having an unnatural preoccupation with death or unpleasant things; diseased
morbidity *morbidly*

mordant biting; caustic or sarcastic

more (to a) greater number, degree, etc.; additional
moreish

morello dark, sour cherry
morellos

moreover in addition

mores conventional or customary social standards

morganatic of a marriage between people of different social rank

morgue mortuary

moribund near death

Mormon member of Church of Jesus Christ of Latter-day Saints
Mormonism

morn (*poetic*) morning

mornay rich cheese sauce

morning period of the day until noon

morocco soft goatskin leather

Morocco country in NW Africa
Moroccan

moron person with stupid or weak mind
moronic

morose gloomy

morpheme meaningful linguistic element that cannot be subdivided into further such elements

morphine or **morphia** opium alkaloid used as a painkiller

morphology study of form and structure, esp. in biology
morphological

morris dance old English traditional folk dance

morrow (*formal*) next day

Morse code signalling code consisting of dots and dashes

morsel small bit or piece, esp. of food

mortal subject to death; causing death; human being
mortality *mortally*

mortar building material of lime, cement, water, etc.; short-barrelled cannon
mortarboard

mortgage (to give a) claim on property as security for payment of a loan
mortgagee mortgaging mortgagor

mortify to subdue by discipline, etc.; to humiliate
mortification mortified mortifies mortifying

mortise or **mortice** hole made to receive a protruding piece, as on a lock or joint
mortising

mortuary building where dead bodies are kept before burial or cremation
mortuaries

mosaic design made up of small coloured pieces of stone or glass

Moselle light white German wine

Moslem see **Muslim**

mosque Muslim place of worship

mosquito kind of insect, the female of which sucks blood
mosquitoes

moss plant that grows densely on trees, rocks, and in moist areas
mosses mossy

most (to the) greatest number, degree, etc.
mostly

mote tiny particle or speck

motel roadside hotel for motorists

moth butterfly-like night-flying insect
mothball moth-eaten mothproof mothy

mother female parent; woman leader of a convent; to give birth to or look after in a motherly way
motherhood mother-in-law mothers-in-law motherland motherless motherliness motherly mother-of-pearl

motherboard (*computers*) printed circuit board

motif idea or dominant theme

motion movement; proposal suggested to a meeting; to signal by gesturing
motionless

motivate to give an incentive to; to inspire
motivating motivation

motive incentive; reason; causing motion

motley made up of elements of varying quality; multicoloured

motor engine that causes motion; motor car; to drive
motorboat motorist motorman motorway

motorcade parade or procession of cars

motorize or **motorise** to equip with a motor
motorization or *motorisation motorizing* or *motorising*

mottled marked with streaks or blotches of different shades or colours
mottling

motto short pithy saying that expresses the guiding principles of a group, organization, etc.
mottoes or *mottos*

mould[1] (US **mold**) shaped hollow used to give a definite form to something; to give shape or form to
moulding (US *molding*)

mould[2] (US **mold**) fungus that forms on damp or decaying matter
mouldy (US *moldy*)

moulder (US **molder**) to crumble

moult (US **molt**) to shed feathers or hair
moulter (US *molter*) *moulting* (US *molting*)

mound raised mass of earth

mount[1] mountain

mount[2] to climb; to increase; to climb up on; support

mountain high landmass

mountaineer mountaineering mountainous

mountebank charlatan

mourn to feel or express sorrow over the death of someone or a loss
mourner mournful mournfully mournfulness mourning

mousaka or **moussaka** dish of meat and aubergines with a cheese topping

mouse small long-tailed rodent; small cursor-moving device connected to a computer
mice mousetrap mousy

mousse light creamy dessert

moustache (US **mustache**) hair that is allowed to grow on the upper lip

mouth opening through which food is taken into body; opening or outlet
mouthful mouth-organ mouthpiece mouthwash mouth-watering

move to change in position; to proceed; to arouse an emotion; to propose
movable or *moveable movement mover moving*

movie (*informal*) cinema film

mow to cut down grass
mowed mower mowing mown

Mozambique country in SE Africa
Mozambican

much (to a) great extent or amount
muchness

mucilage sticky substance

muck farmyard dung; dirt; (*informal*) rubbish; to spread manure on
muckraking mucky

mucus slimy secretion from the nose, etc.
mucosity mucous

mud soft wet earth or clay
mudguard mud-slinging

muddle to mix or confuse; confusion
muddle-headed muddling

muddy covered with mud; to make or become muddy
muddied muddier muddies muddiest muddiness muddying

muesli mixture of cereals, nuts, dried fruit, etc.

muezzin mosque official who calls the faithful to prayer

muff[1] open cylindrical wrap of fur or cloth to keep the hands warm

muff[2] to bungle

muffin light round yeast bun

muffle to cover for warmth or to deaden sound
muffler muffling

mufti civilian dress, not military uniform

mug[1] drinking container with a handle; to attack and rob
mugful mugged; *mugger mugging*

mug[2] (*informal*) to study hard
mugged mugging

muggy unpleasantly warm and humid
muggier muggiest mugginess

Muhammad or **Mohammed** prophet and founder of Islam
Muhammadan or *Mohammedan*

mulatto person with one black and one white parent
mulattos or *mulattoes*

mulberry (tree of the fig family with a) purple fruit
mulberries

mulch (to spread a) compost covering to protect plants and enrich soil

mule[1] sterile offspring of a horse and donkey
muleteer mulish mulishly mulishness

mule[2] backless slipper

mull[1] to ponder

mull[2] to heat wine, etc. with spices

mullah person learned in or teaching Muslim sacred law

mullet kind of food-fish

mulligatawny curry-flavoured soup

mullion vertical bar between panes or panels of a window, etc.
mullioned

multi- (*prefix*) many or much
multicoloured multicultural multidirectional multilingual multimedia multinational multiracial multi-storey multitasking multi-user

multifarious having many different kinds
multifariously multifariousness

multilateral involving 2 or more parties; having many sides

multimillionaire person with several million pounds or dollars, etc.

multiple having many parts; quantity that contains another quantity an exact number of times
multiple-choice

multiplex of a system that allows several messages to be transmitted by a single communication channel; cinema with many screens

multiply to add a quantity to itself a given number of times
multiplicand multiplication multiplicity multiplied multiplier multiplies multiplying

multitude large number of people
multitudinous

mum[1] (*informal*) mother

mum[2] (*informal*) silent

mumble to utter unclearly; unclear utterance
mumbling

mumbo-jumbo meaningless ritual or language
mumbo-jumbos

mummer masked actor in a traditional play
mummery mummeries

mummify to embalm a body
mummification mummified mummifies mummifying

mummy[1] (*informal*) mother
mummies

mummy[2] preserved embalmed body
mummies

mumps virus infection causing neck swellings

munch to chew steadily and noisily; munching action
munches muncher

mundane ordinary or routine; earthly
mundanely mundaneness

municipal of a town, city, or borough or its local government
municipally

municipality self-governing city, town, or borough

munificent generous
munificence munificently

munitions military armaments and ammunition

mural large painting on a wall; of a wall

murder killing of another person with intent; to kill in this way
murderer murderess murderous murderously

murk darkness

murky dark or gloomy
murkier murkiest murkily murkiness

murmur (to make a) low indistinct noise
murmurer murmuringly

muscatel wine made from the muscat grape

muscle tissue of elongated cells that expand and contract
muscleman muscular muscularity muscularly musculature

muse[1] to reflect on
musing

muse[2] source of inspiration

museum place where interesting objects are exhibited

mush soft pulpy mass
mushiness mushy

mushroom fungus with a slender stalk and cap

music art of combining and ordering sounds
musical musicality musically music-hall musician musicianship musicology

musk strong-smelling substance secreted by male musk deer, used in perfumes
musky

musket long-barrelled shoulder gun
musketeer musketry

muskrat kind of North American aquatic rodent

Muslim or **Moslem** follower of Islam

muslin fine plain cotton cloth

musquash (fur of) muskrat

mussel kind of bivalve shellfish

must auxiliary verb to express obligation, etc.
mustn't

mustache (US) see **moustache**

mustang wild horse

mustard kind of yellow-flowered plant, whose pods are grown for their pungent seeds; paste made from these

musty (smelling) stale or mouldy
mustier mustiest mustily mustiness

mutable tending or likely to change
mutability mutant

mutate to change in form
mutating mutation

mute dumb (person); speechless; to reduce the volume of
mutely muteness muting mutism

mutilate to maim; to spoil by cutting off the essential part of
mutilating mutilation

mutiny open rebellion against authority; to rebel in this way
mutinies mutineer mutinied mutinous mutinying

mutter to utter in a low unclear way; such an utterance

mutton flesh of sheep used as food

mutual felt or directed by each towards or to the other
mutualism mutually

Muzak (*trademark*) recorded light music

muzzle projecting jaws and nose of an animal; guard or strap fitted over this; to fit a guard or strap; open end of a gun barrel
muzzling

muzzy hazy or confused

my possessive form of **I**
myself

Myanmar official name of Burma, country in SE Asia

mycology study of fungi

myna, **mynah**, or **mina** kind of tropical starling

myopia short-sightedness
myopic myopically

myriad large indefinite number

myrrh kind of (tree exuding an) aromatic resin

myrtle kind of evergreen shrub

myself form of **I** used reflexively or for emphasis

mystery thing that cannot be or has not been explained
mysteries mysterious mysteriously

mystic of hidden or symbolic religious

meaning; person who seeks God inwardly
mystical mysticism

mystify to puzzle or confuse
mystification mystified mystifies mystifying

mystique atmosphere of mystery

myth traditional fictitious story; something imaginary
mythical mythological mythologist mythology mythologies

myxomatosis infectious viral disease in rabbits

N

nab (*informal*) to arrest; to grab
nabbed nabbing

nacelle housing for an aircraft engine

nacre mother-of-pearl

nadir lowest point, esp. that opposite the zenith

naevus (US **nevus**) birthmark

naff (*slang*) unfashionable

nag[1] (*informal*) old or worn-out horse

nag[2] to find fault with constantly
nagged nagger nagging

naiad river-nymph
naiads or *naiades*

nail horny layer at end of fingers or toes; to join with small thin metal spike
nail-brush nail-file

naïve or **naive** unsophisticated; innocent; artless
naïvely or *naively naïveté* or *naïvety*

naked wearing no clothes
nakedly nakedness

namby-pamby insipidly sentimental (person)

name word by which a person or thing is known or identified; reputation; to give a name to
nameable or *namable name-dropping nameless namely name-plate namesake naming*

Namibia territory in Africa
Namibian

nancy homosexual or effeminate boy or man
nancies

nanny children's nurse; child's name for grandmother
nannies

nanny-goat female goat

nano- (*prefix*) one thousand millionth part of

nap[1] (to have a) short sleep
napped napping

nap[2] raised surface on cloth

nap[3] card-game

napalm thick highly flammable liquid used in bombs

nape back of the neck

naphthalene kind of hydrocarbon

napkin piece of cloth or paper used to protect the clothes while eating; nappy

nappy piece of cloth or paper worn by babies to absorb their excrement
nappies

narcissism obsessive love of oneself
narcissist narcissistic

narcissus kind of bulbous plant
narcissuses or *narcissi*

narcosis drug-induced stupor or unconsciousness

narcotic pain-relieving (drug)

nark (*slang*) police informer; to annoy

narrate to tell a story
narrating narration narrative narrator

narrow (to make or become) small in breadth
narrowly narrow-minded narrowness

narwhal kind of small arctic whale

nasal of the nose; sounded in the nose
nasally

nasalize or **nasalise** to pronounce nasally
nasalization or *nasalisation nasalizing* or *nasalising*

nascent starting to develop

nasturtium kind of trailing plant with showy flowers
nasturtiums

nasty unpleasant; mean or spiteful
nastier nastiest nastily nastiness

natal of birth

nation people living in the same country or under the same government; race of people
national nationalism nationalist nationality nationalities nation-state nationwide

nationalize or **nationalise** to put under state control
nationalization or *nationalisation*
nationalizing or *nationalising*

native person born in a particular place; belonging to a particular place

nativity birth, esp. of Jesus Christ
nativities

natter (*informal*) to chatter

natty (*informal*) smart; neat
nattier nattiest nattily nattiness

natural of nature; not artificial; simple
naturally

naturalize or **naturalise** to give full rights of citizenship to; to (cause to) be adopted fully
naturalization or *naturalisation*
naturalizing or *naturalising*

nature set of essential qualities; system of existence and forces; plants and animals
naturalism naturalist naturalistic

naturism nudism
naturist

naught nothing

naughty mischievous; disobedient
naughtier naughtiest naughtily naughtiness

Nauru island country in SW Pacific

nausea feeling of sickness
nauseate nauseating nauseous

nautical of ships, seamen, or navigation

nautilus kind of small mollusc related to the octopus or squid
nautiluses or *nautili*

naval of a navy

nave central part of a church

navel small depression in the middle of the abdomen

navigate to direct the course of a ship, aeroplane, etc; to travel
navigability navigable navigating navigation navigator

navvy labourer
navvies

navy country's warships; branch of armed services comprising such ships
navies

nay (*archaic*) no

Nazism racist and totalitarian principles of the National Socialist German Workers' Party, founded by Adolf Hitler
Nazi Nazis

Neanderthal Middle Palaeolithic man

neap of a tide of the smallest range
neap-tide

Neapolitan of Naples; of an ice-cream with layers of different colours

near (to come or go) close to
nearby nearly nearside near-sighted

neat tidy and clean
neaten neatly neatness

nebula body of gas or dust in space
nebulae or *nebulas nebular*

nebulous without definite form
nebulously

necessary (something) essential
necessaries necessarily

necessitate to make necessary
necessitating necessity necessities

neck part of an animal connecting the head to the rest of the body
neckband neckcloth neckerchief necklace neckline necktie neckwear

necromancy communicating with the dead; sorcery
necromancer

necrophilia (erotic) obsession with corpses
necrophile necrophilic

necropolis large cemetery
necropolises

necropsy examination of a dead body

necrosis death of part of a tissue

nectar sweet fluid produced in some flowers

nectarine kind of peach

née used to show the maiden name of a married woman

need to require; to be necessary; reason; distress
needful needfully needfulness needless needlessly needlessness needn't needy

needle thin pointed piece of metal used in sewing or knitting; to irritate
needlecase needlecord needlecraft needlepoint needlewoman needlework needling

ne'er (*poetic*) never
ne'er-do-well

nefarious wicked
nefariously nefariousness

negate to nullify; to contradict
negating negation

negative indicating a refusal or denial; type of electric charge; photographic image with the positive dark and light parts reversed; less than zero
negatively negativeness

neglect to fail to look after; to omit to do something
neglectful neglectfulness

négligé or **negligee** woman's light dressing-gown

negligent careless
negligence negligently
SEE PANEL

---

negligent or negligible?
Someone who is *negligent* is careless: *The disciplinary tribunal decided that the council's officers had been negligent in not checking the procedures to ensure adequate care in its homes.*

Something that is *negligible* is too small to consider: *Once increased taxes have been taken into account, the pay increase will have a negligible effect on workers' take-home pay.*

---

negligible too small to consider
negligibly
SEE PANEL at **negligent**

negotiate to discuss in order to reach an agreement
negotiable negotiating negotiation nogotiator

Negro member of black-skinned race
Negroes Negritude Negress Negresses Negroid

negus hot drink made of wine, etc.

neigh (to make the) noise of a horse

neighbour (US **neighbor**) person who lives near to another
neighbourhood (US *neighborhood*) *neighbouring* (US *neighboring*) *neighbourliness* (US *neighborliness*) *neighbourly* (US *neighborly*)

neither not 1 nor the other (of 2); not either; nor

nekton free-swimming aquatic animals

nelson wrestling hold

nemesis vengeance
nemeses

neo- (*prefix*) new; revival of
neoclassical neo-colonialism

Neolithic last division of the Stone Age

neologism newly-coined word
neologist

neon inert gas used in lighting

neophyte new convert; beginner

Nepal country in South Asia
Nepalese Nepali

nephew son of one's sister or brother

nephritis inflammation of the kidneys

nepotism favouritism shown towards one's relations, esp. in appointing them to jobs
nepotist

Neptune 8th planet from the sun; Roman god of the sea

neptunium radioactive metallic element

nerve fibre that transmits impulses between part of the body and a nerve-centre; courage; (*informal*) impudence
nerve-cell nerve-centre nerveless nerve-racking nervous nervously nervousness nervy

nerves anxiety

nescience ignorance
nescient

ness headland

nest structure in which birds rear their young
nest-egg

nestle to settle comfortably
nestling

net[1] (to cover with an) openwork fabric of string, wire, etc.
netball netted netting

net[2] or **nett** remaining after all deductions have been made; to gain by profit
netted netting

nether underground
nethermost

Netherlands country in NW Europe

nettle plant with leaves that are covered with stinging hairs
nettle-rash nettling

network system of crossing lines; interconnecting system
networking

neural of the nerves
neuritis neurological neurologist neurology neurosurgery

neuralgia sharp spasmodic nerve pains
neuralgic

neurosis nervous disorder of phobias, depression, etc.
neuroses neurotic neurotically

neuter (*grammar*) neither masculine nor feminine; to castrate

neutral not belonging to either side in a conflict; with no special features
neutrality neutrally

neutralize or **neutralise** to make or become neutral
neutralization or *neutralisation*
neutralizing or *neutralising*

neutron particle without an electric charge

névé kind of snow on a glacier

never at no time
never-ending never-failing nevermore never-never nevertheless

nevus (US) see **naevus**

new recently made; additional
new-blown new-born newcomer newfangled newly newlyweds New Zealand New Zealander

newel central upright pillar of a spiral staircase

Newfoundland breed of large dog

news description of recent interesting events
newsagent newsboy newscast newscaster newsdesk newsflash newsletter newspaper newspaperman newsprint newsreader

newsreel news-sheet news-stand newsvendor newsworthy newsy

newt kind of small semi-aquatic amphibian

next following immediately; closest

nexus connection
nexuses or *nexus*

nib writing point of a pen

nibble to take small bites
nibbler nibbling

Nicaragua country in Central America
Nicaraguan

nice pleasant; fine
nicely niceness nicer nicest nicety niceties

niche recess in a wall for a vase, etc.

nick small cut or groove; moment; (*slang*) prison; (*slang*) to steal

nickel (to plate with) hard silver-white metallic element; (US) 5-cent piece
nickelled (US *nickeled*) *nickelling* (US *nickeling*) *nickel-plate*

nickname (to give a) humorous additional name to
nicknaming

nicotine drug found in tabacco
nicotine

niece daughter of one's sister or brother

nifty (*informal*) clever; very good
niftily niftiness

Niger country in West Africa
Nigerian

Nigeria country in West Africa
Nigerian

niggard stingy person
niggardliness niggardly

nigger (*offensive*) Negro

niggle to complain about trivial matters; to irritate
niggling

nigh (*archaic* or *poetic*) near

night period of darkness between sunset and sunrise
nightcap nightclothes nightclub nightdress nightfall nightgown nightie or *nighty night-life night-light night-long nightly nightshade nightspot*

nightingale kind of brownish songbird

nightjar kind of nocturnal bird

nightmare frightening dream
nightmarish

nihilism total rejection of all beliefs and values
nihilist nihilistic

nil nothing

nilgai kind of large Indian antelope

nimble agile
nimbleness nimbly

nimbus dark rain-bearing cloud; halo
nimbi or *nimbuses*

nincompoop stupid person

nine number 9
ninepins nineteen nineteenth ninetieth ninety nineties ninth ninthly

ninny (*informal*) foolish person
ninnies

nip[1] to squeeze or pinch; (*informal*) to hurry
nipped nipping

nip[2] small drink of spirits

nipper small child; claw of a crab, etc.

nippers instrument for pinching or clipping

nipple teat of breast

nippy chilly; agile

nirvana (*Buddhism and Hinduism*) release from the cycle of reincarnation

Nissen hut kind of prefabricated hut

nit (egg of an) insect such as a louse; (*informal*) fool
nit-picking

nitrate salt of nitric acid

nitre (US **niter**) potassium nitrate

nitrogen colourless odourless gas present in the air
nitric nitrogenous nitrous

nitroglycerine highly explosive liquid

nitty-gritty (*informal*) basic detailed facts

nitwit foolish person

no used to deny, refuse, etc.; not any
noes no-ball no-go

nob[1] (*slang*) head

nob[2] (*slang*) wealthy or influential person

nobble (*slang*) to disable a racehorse by drugging; to gain dishonestly; to cheat
nobbling

Nobel Prize prize awarded for outstanding achievements in the service of humanity

noble aristocratic; honourable
nobility nobleman nobleness nobler noblest noblewoman nobly

noblesse oblige (*French*) nobility necessitates honourable behaviour

nobody no one; insignificant person
nobodies

nocturnal of the night; (*of animals*) active at night

nocturne short piece of music; painting of a night scene

nod to move the head down and up to show agreement, etc.
nodded nodder nodding

node point on a stem from which leaves or buds grow; swelling

nodule small rounded lump
nodular nodulated

Noel or **Noël** Christmas

noggin small measure of spirits

noise sound, esp. a harsh and loud one
noiseless noiselessly noiselessness noisier noisiest noisily noisiness noisy

noisome offensive or harmful
noisomely noisomeness

nomad member of a tribe that wanders to find food
nomadic

nom de plume (*French*) pen-name; pseudonym
noms de plume

nomenclature terminology; naming

nominal in name only; token
nominalism nominally

nominate to propose for office; to specify
nominating nomination nominator nominee

nominative (*grammar*) case used to identify the subject

non- (*prefix*) not
non-aligned non-commissioned noncommittal non-contributory non-existent non-fiction non-metallic non-proliferation non-resident non-smoker non-starter non-stick non-stop

nonagenarian (person) aged between 90 and 99 years

nonagon polygon with 9 sides
nonagonal

nonce occasion
nonce-word

nonchalant indifferent
nonchalance nonchalantly

non compos mentis (*Latin*) of unsound mind

nonconformist (person) who does not conform to established patterns of behaviour
nonconformity

nondescript with no outstanding features

none not any; not at all; to no extent

nonentity insignificant person or thing
nonentities

nonesuch or **nonsuch** unrivalled person or thing

nonetheless nevertheless

non-event disappointing event

nonpareil unmatched person or thing

nonplus to perplex
nonplussed (US *nonplused*) *nonplussing* (US *nonplusing*)

nonsense something that is unintelligible, meaningless, or absurd
nonsensical

non sequitur (*Latin*) statement that does not follow logically from what has preceded it

noodle narrow strip of pasta

nook corner or recess

noon 12 o'clock midday
noonday noontide

noose loop at the end of a rope with a slip-knot

nor and not

norm standard or average

normal usual or ordinary
normalcy normality normally normative

normalize or **normalise** to make or become normal
normalization or *normalisation* *normalizing* or *normalising*

Norman (native of) Normandy; style of architecture

Norse of ancient Scandinavia; older language of Norway
Norseman

north one of the 4 compass points, opposite of south
North America North American northbound north-east northeaster north-easterly north-eastern northerly northern northerner Northern Ireland northernmost northwards north-west northwester north-westerly north-western

Norway country in North Europe
Norwegian

nose organ of smell and breathing; sense of smell; to find out by smelling
nosebag noseband nosebleed nose-cone nosedive nosegay nose-piece nose-wheel nosing

nosh (*slang*) (to eat) food
nosh-up

nostalgia sentimental longing for the past
nostalgic nostalgically

nostril 1 of the 2 openings of the nose

nostrum questionable medicine

nosy or **nosey** (*informal*) inquisitive
nosier nosiest nosily nosiness

not used to express negation

nota bene (*Latin*) note well

notable distinguished; remarkable
notability notabilities notably

notary public law official
notaries

notation specialized system of signs or symbols

notch (to make a) V-shaped cut
notches

note (to write a) brief comment; to notice; musical sound
notebook notecase notelet notepad notepaper noting

noteworthy worthy of notice
noteworthiness

nothing not anything
nothingness

notice to become aware of; public announcement; attention
noticeable noticeably notice-board

notify to inform or announce
notifiable notification notified notifies notifying

notion concept, idea, or whim
notional notionally

notorious well-known; infamous
notoriety notoriously

notwithstanding in spite of

nougat hard chewy sweet containing nuts

nought zero

noun word referring to a person, place, or thing

nourish to nurture, foster, or feed
nourishes nourishment

nous mind or reason; (*informal*) common sense

nouveau riche (*French*) someone who has recently become rich
nouveaux riches

nova star that suddenly increases in brightness and then gradually fades
novae or *novas*

novel[1] long work of narrative fiction
novelette novelist

novel[2] new; original
novelty

November 11th month of the year

novice beginner; new member, esp. of a religious community
noviciate or *novitiate*

now at the present time
nowadays

nowhere not anywhere

noxious harmful or poisonous
noxiously noxiousness

nozzle spout on a pipe, etc. from which a liquid is discharged

nuance subtle difference in colour, meaning, etc.

nub lump; central point

nubile (*of a girl*) of marriageable age

nucleus central part; positively charged core of an atom
nuclei nuclear nucleate nucleic

nude naked; not wearing any clothes
nudely nudism nudist nudity

nudge to push gently, esp. with the elbow; (to) jog
nudging

nugget solid lump of precious metal

nuisance annoying person or thing

null not valid; worthless
nullity

nullify to make ineffective
nullification nullified nullifies nullifying

numb deprived of sense or feeling; to make numb
numbly numbness

number symbol used in counting; to count; to total
numberless number-plate numerable

numeral number or figure
numerical numerically

numerate understanding numbers and arithmetic
numeracy numeration numerator

numerous many; having many parts

numismatics study or collection of coins or medals
numismatist

numskull stupid person

nun female member of a religious community
nunnery nunneries

nuncio papal ambassador
nuncios

nuptial of marriage
nuptially nuptials

nurl see **knurl**

nurse person skilled in looking after the ill or young children; to look after; to suckle
nurseling nursemaid nursing

nursery place where young children are looked after; playroom; place where young plants are grown
nurseries nurseryman

nurture to grow or rear; nourishment or development
nurturing

nut dry fruit or seed with a hard shell and an edible kernel; piece of metal used with a bolt to fasten or tighten
nut-brown nutcrackers nutshell nutty

nuthatch small tree-climbing bird

nutmeg kind of aromatic seed used as a spice

nutria (fur of the) coypu

nutrition process of taking in food; study of this
nutrient nutriment nutritional nutritious nutritive

nuzzle to push gently with the nose
nuzzling

nylon synthetic fibre

nymph (*mythology*) minor female goddess of nature; larva of certain insects

nymphomania abnormally intense sexual desire in women
nymphomaniac

O

o see **oh**

oaf clumsy or loutish person
oafish

oak tree of the beech family producing acorns
oaken

oakum loose hemp or jute fibre

oar pole with a blade used to propel and steer a boat
oarsman oarsmanship

oasis fertile area in a desert
oases

oast kiln of drying hops
oasthouse

oat cereal grass
oatcake oatmeal

oath solemn vow; curse

obbligato (*music*) essential accompaniment
obbligatos or *obbligati*

obdurate hard-hearted, stubborn
obduracy obdurately

obedient willing to do as one is told
obedience obediently

obeisance sign of deference, homage, or respect

obelisk tall upright pillar

obese very fat; corpulent
obesity

obey to do as one is told; to comply with rules

obfuscate to darken or obscure
obfuscating obfuscation obfuscatory

obituary public announcement of death with a short biography
obituaries

object[1] solid thing; purpose or aim; (*grammar*) noun, etc. that is acted on by a verb
object-lesson

object[2] to argue against
objection objectionable

objective independent; purpose or aim
objectively

objet d'art (*French*) work of artistic value
objets d'art

oblate flattened or depressed at the poles

oblation offering to God

obligate to compel
obligating obligation

obligatory compulsory
obligatorily

oblige to require by law; to help
obliging

oblique slanting; indirect or evasive
obliquely obliquity

obliterate to wipe out
obliterating obliteration

oblivion being or having forgotten
oblivious obliviously

oblong 4-sided figure with adjacent sides unequal

obnoxious very unpleasant
obnoxiously obnoxiousness

oboe kind of woodwind instrument
oboist

obscene offensive; indecent
obscenely obscenity obscenities

obscure (to make) unclear or dim; not well known
obscuration obscurely obscureness obscuring obscurity

obsequies funeral rites

obsequious showing great servile respect
obsequiously obsequiousness

observe to watch; to conform to; to commemorate
observable observance observant observation observatory observatories observer observing

obsess to preoccupy the mind
obsesses obsession obsessional obsessive

obsidian dark glassy volcanic rock

obsolescent becoming out of date
obsolescence

obsolete not current
obsoletely obsoleteness

obstacle hindrance to progress

obstetric concerned with childbirth
obstetrical obstetrician obstetrics

obstinate holding firmly to an opinion
obstinacy obstinately

obstreperous noisy and rough

obstruct to block with an obstacle
obstruction obstructional obstructive obstructor

obtain to acquire; (*formal*) to be valid
obtainable

obtrude to push forward, esp. when this is not desired
obtrusing obtrusion obtrusive

obtuse (*of an angle*) between 90° and 180°; blunt or slow

obverse side of coin bearing the main design; turned towards the observer
obversely

obviate to do away with
obviating obviation

obvious clear or evident
obviously obviousness

ocarina kind of wind instrument with an oval body

occasion time or opportunity; reason

occasional happening from time to time
occasionally

Occident the West
occidental

occlude to block or obstruct
occluding occlusion occlusive

occult magical or supernatural
occultism occultist

occupy to stay in; to take up; to keep busy
occupancy occupancies occupant occupation occupational occupied occupier occupies occupying

occur to happen; to come to mind
occurred occurrence occurring

ocean one of the earth's 5 great seas
ocean-going oceanic oceanographic oceanography

ocelot kind of American wildcat

ochre (US **ocher**) red or yellow mineral
ochreous ochry

o'clock used to show the hour of the day or night

octagon polygon with 8 sides
octagonal

octahedron solid with 8 faces
octahedrons or *octahedra*

octane liquid hydrocarbon found in petroleum

octave series of 8 notes

octavo page or book size
octavos

octet (musical composition for) 8 instruments or voices; 8 lines of verse

October 10th month of the year

octogenarian (person) aged between 80 and 89 years

octopus sea animal with 8 tentacles
octopuses or *octopi*

ocular of the eyes

oculist ophthalmologist or optician; eye-doctor

odd unusual or peculiar; not even; incidental
oddball oddity oddities oddly oddment odd-numbered

odds probability; sometimes expressed as a ratio
odds-on

ode lyric poem

odious offensive
odiously odiousness

odium hatred or dislike

odometer instrument for measuring the distance travelled

odontology study of (disease of the) teeth
odontological odontologist

odoriferous producing a scent or odour

odour (US **odor**) smell, esp. an unpleasant one
odorous odourless (US *odorless*)

odyssey long wandering journey

oecumenical see **ecumenical**

oedema (US **edema**) swelling
oedematous (US *edematous*)

Oedipus complex child's attraction to the parent of the opposite sex and jealousy of parent of the same sex

o'er (*poetic*) over

oesophagus (US **esophagus**) gullet
oesophagi (US *esophagi*)

oestrogen (US **estrogen**) hormone that stimulates growth of female sex characteristics

oestrus regularly occurring period of mammal's sexual excitability
oestrous

of belonging to; containing; concerning; from; made from

off away; not on; completed
off-beat off-centre offcut off-day offhand offhandedly offish off-key off-licence off-line off-load off-peak offprint off-putting off-season offshore offside off-stage offstreet off-the-peg off-white

offal edible internal parts of an animal

offence (US **offense**) breaking of a law

offend to break a law; to displease

offensive unpleasant; rude; attack
offensively offensiveness

offer to present; to be willing; something offered
offered offerer offering

offertory offering of bread and wine in Eucharist; money collected in church service
offertories

office room where business is carried out; position of authority or responsibility
office-block office-boy office-girl

officer holder of position of authority or responsibility

official person who holds an office; of an office; authorized
officialdom officialese officialism officially
SEE PANEL

---

official or officious?

The adjective *official* means 'of an office; authorized': *an official visit; The official statistics show an increase; Let's stick to the official explanation.*

If you describe a person or their behaviour as *officious,* you mean that they are self-important: *an officious clerk who likes to tell people what they can and can't do.*

---

officiate to act as an official; to supervise or direct
officiating

officious self-important; too zealous in carrying out one's duties
officiously officiousness
SEE PANEL at **official**

offing part of the sea that can be seen from the shore

offset to make up for; printing process
offset-litho offsetting

offshoot shoot growing from the main stem

offspring children, or young of animals

oft (*poetic*) often
oft-recurring oft-repeated oft-times

often frequently

ogee moulding in architecture

ogle to look at with amorous interest
ogling

ogre (*fem*. **ogress**) ugly man-eating giant in folklore
ogrish

oh or **o** expression of surprise

ohm metric unit of electrical resistance

oil smooth greasy liquid; petroleum; to lubricate
oilcake oilcan oilcloth oil-colour oilfield oil-fired oil-gauge oil-painting oilskin oil-slick oil well oily

ointment oily cream preparation applied to the skin

OK expression of approval; to approve
OK's OK'd OK'ing

okapi kind of ruminant African animal

Oklahoma US state

okra kind of plant with pods used to thicken soup

old aged; known for a long time; former
olden older oldest old-fashioned oldish oldness old-time

oleaginous of oil

oleander kind of poisonous evergreen shrub

oleiferous oil-producing

olfactory of the sense of smell
olfaction olfactive

oligarchy government by a small group of people
oligarchies oligarch oligarchic

olive kind of (evergreen tree bearing) small bitter stone fruit; dull green
olive-branch olive oil

Olympiad celebration of Olympic Games

Olympic (of) international athletic games

Oman sultanate in SE Arabia
Omani

ombudsman official who investigates individuals' complaints against government or public bodies
ombudsmen

omega last letter of the Greek alphabet

omelette (US **omelet**) dish of beaten eggs

omen sign of something good or evil in the future

ominous threatening
ominously ominousness

omit to leave out; to neglect
omission omitted omitting

omnibus (*formal*) bus; collection of separate books or parts
omnibuses

omnidirectional capable of moving, or receiving or transmitting signals in all directions

omnipotent having unlimited power
omnipotence omnipotently

omnipresent present everywhere all the time
omnipresence

omniscient having infinite knowledge
omniscience

omnivorous eating animal and vegetable substances

on touching or attached to; covering; supported by; concerning
oncoming ongoing on-line onlooker on-screen onshore onside onto onward onwards

once one time; in the past
once-over

one number 1; individual; people generally
oneness one-off oneself one-sided one-time one-to-one one-track one-up one-upmanship one-way

onerous burdensome
onerously onerousness

onion kind of plant grown for its rounded bulb

only single; merely; exclusive(ly); however

onomatopoeia formation of words whose sound imitates the thing represented
onomatopoeic

onrush forceful rush

onset attack; beginning

onslaught violent attack

ontology study of the nature of being
ontological

onus responsibility
onuses

onyx translucent quartz with layers of different colours

oolite rock, esp. limestone with small concentric grains

oolong kind of dark China tea

ooze[1] to flow or trickle out slowly
oozing

ooze[2] muddy deposit
oozy

opal semi-transparent silica mineral

opalescent showing an iridescent shimmer of colours
opalescence

opaque not transparent; unintelligible
opacity opacities

open not closed; to make or become open; to begin
open-and-shut opencast open-ended opener open-eyed open-handed open-hearted opening open-minded open-mouthed openness open-plan openwork

opera dramatic production set to music
opera-glasses opera-house operatic

operate to work or function; to perform surgery
operable operating operation operational operative operator

operculum flap, esp. one covering the gills of a fish
opercula or *operculums*

operetta light opera
operettas operettist

ophthalmia inflammation of the eye

ophthalmic of the eye

ophthalmology study of the eye and its diseases
ophthalmological ophthalmologist

opiate narcotic drug

opine to state as an opinion
opining

opinion judgement or view
opinionated

opium narcotic drug from the seed capsules of the opium poppy

opossum kind of New World marsupial

opponent someone who opposes

opportune at a suitable or advantageous time

opportunist person who takes advantage of opportunities
opportunism

opportunity favourable circumstance or chance
opportunities

oppose to fight against
opposable opposing opposition

opposite facing; contrary; corresponding

oppress to rule unjustly
oppression oppressive oppressor

opprobrious (*formal*) scornful; shameful

opprobrium (*formal*) reproach, blame, or disgrace

oppugn to dispute
oppugner

opt to choose

optative showing choice or wish

optical of the eye or vision
optic optically optician optics

optimism inclination to expect the best
optimist optimistic optimistically

optimize or **optimise** to make the most effective use of
optimization or *optimisation* *optimizing* or *optimising*

optimum most favourable or best (condition, amount, etc.)
optima or *optimums*

option choice; thing chosen

optional left to individual choice
optionally

opulent wealthy
opulence opulently

opus artistic, esp. musical, composition
opera

or used in front of an alternative

oracle reply given by a god; advice or prophecy
oracular

oral spoken; verbal; of or through the mouth
orally
SEE PANEL at **aural**

orange kind of round juicy citrus fruit; yellowish-red
orangeade orangery orangeries

orang-utan or **orang-outang** kind of large tree-dwelling ape

oration long formal speech
orator oratorical

oratorio long religious musical composition
oratorios

oratory[1] art of speaking
oratories

oratory[2] small room for private prayer
oratories

orb sphere or globe
orbicular orbiculate orbiculated

orbit curved path of a planet or satellite; to revolve in an orbit
orbital orbited orbiting

orchard area where fruit trees are grown

orchestra large group of musicians playing different instruments

orchestrate to arrange a piece of music for an orchestra
orchestrating orchestration

orchid plant with striking 3-petalled flowers

ordain to consecrate as a priest; to decree or appoint

ordeal severe trial

order manner in which things are arranged; request to supply goods; to arrange; to command; to request goods

orderly arranged neatly; disciplined; male hospital attendant; soldier
orderlies orderliness

ordinal (number) showing the position in a sequence

ordinance authoritative rule, law, or practice

ordinand candidate for ordination

ordinary usual; familiar; commonplace; unexceptional
ordinarily ordinariness

ordination conferring of holy orders

ordnance military supplies or munitions

ordure excrement

ore mineral from which metals can be extracted

oregano wild marjoram whose leaves are used to season food

organ musical keyboard instrument with

pipes; part of the body with a particular function

organdie (US **organdy**) fine transparent muslin

organic of bodily organs or living organisms
organically

organism living animal or plant

organist person who plays the organ

organize or **organise** to arrange systematically
organization or *organisation* *organizing* or *organising*

organza thin fabric of silk, nylon, rayon, etc.

orgasm most intense point of sexual excitement
orgasmic *orgastic*

orgy wild party
orgies *orgiastic*

Orient the East
oriental

orientate or **orient** to find one's position; to adjust to circumstances
orientating or *orienting* *orientation*

orienteering finding one's way using a map and compass

orifice opening or aperture

origami paper folding

origin source or beginning

original first; (being the) source
originality *originally*

originate to bring or come into existence
originating *origination* *originator*

oriole kind of songbird

Orkney Islands islands off NE Scotland

ormolu gilded brass or bronze used to decorate furniture

ornament thing that adds decoration or enhances appearance; to decorate
ornamental *ornamentation*

ornate elaborately decorated

ornithology study of birds
ornithological *ornithologist*

orography study of mountains
orographic *orographical*

orotund sonorous; pompous

orphan child, one or both of whose parents are dead
orphanage *orphanhood*

orris kind of fragrant rootstock

orthodontics dentistry concerned with the correction of irregularities of the teeth
orthodontic *orthodontist*

orthodox of generally established views
orthodoxy

orthography writing system
orthographic

orthopaedics (US **orthopedics**) surgery concerned with correcting or preventing bone and muscle deformities
orthopaedic (US *orthopedic*) *orthopaedist* (US *orthopedist*)

ortolan kind of brownish European bunting

oryx kind of large African antelope
oryxes or *oryx*

oscillate to swing to and fro; to move between extremes
oscillating oscillation oscillator oscilloscope

osculate to kiss
osculating *osculation* *osculatory*

osier willow, used for making baskets

osmosis diffusion of a liquid through a membrane
osmotic

osprey kind of large fish-eating bird of prey
ospreys

osseous of bone

ossify to change into bone; to harden
ossification *ossified* *ossifier* *ossifies* *ossifying*

ostensible apparent; pretended
ostensibly

ostensive showing; demonstrative
ostensively

ostentation showy display
ostentatious ostentatiously

osteoarthritis degenerative arthritis

osteopathy treatment of illness by manipulating bones and muscles
osteopath osteopathic

ostler stableman

ostracize or **ostracise** to banish from a group, society, etc.
ostracism ostracizing or *ostracising*

ostrich kind of large swift-footed flightless bird

other remaining; different
otherwise otherworldly

otiose futile
otiosely otioseness

otter kind of (dark-brown fur of an) aquatic fish-eating mammal

ottoman long backless padded seat

ought auxiliary verb used to express obligation, etc.
oughtn't

Ouija (*trademark*) board used in spiritist seances

ounce unit of weight

our possessive form of **we**
ours ourself ourselves

ousel see **ouzel**

oust to remove or expel

out away from; exhausted; revealed
out-and-out out-of-doors

out- (*prefix*) going beyond; to excess
outbid outdistance outlast outmatch outpace outpouring outrank outrun outsell outsmart outstare out-talk outvote

outback remote interior of Australia

outboard (attached to the) outside of the stern of a boat

outbreak sudden breaking out

outbuilding building separate from a main building

outburst sudden expression

outcast person excluded or rejected from a social group

outclass to surpass or excel

outcome consequence or result

outcrop part of rock that appears above the surface

outcry loud cry; protest
outcries

outdated old-fashioned

outdo to surpass in quality
outdid outdoes outdoing outdone

outdoor (taking place) in the open air
outdoors

outer external
outermost

outfall outlet of a river, sewer, etc.

outfield part of cricket field far from the pitch or part of baseball field furthest from the bases

outfit set of clothing or equipment for a particular task

outflank to go round the flank of an enemy

outflow flowing out

outgoing departing or retiring; sociable

outgoings expenditure

outgrow to grow too large for
outgrew outgrown outgrowth

out-herod to surpass in evil

outhouse small building separate from a main building

outing trip or journey for pleasure

outlandish very unusual or unconventional
outlandishly

outlaw fugitive; to make illegal
outlawry

outlay expenditure of money, etc.

outlet vent or opening

outline (to present a) preliminary plan or summary
outlining

outlive to live longer than
outliving

outlook (point of) view

outlying distant or remote

outmanoeuvre (US **outmaneuver**) to defeat by skilful manoeuvring
outmanoeuvring (US *outmaneuvering*)

outmoded out of date; unfashionable

outnumber to exceed in number

out-patient non-resident hospital patient

outplacement finding new employment for redundant executives

outpost outlying settlement; remote military position

output amount produced; production; to produce or supply
outputting

outrage offensive or violent act; to shock greatly
outraging

outrageous shocking; offensive
outrageously outrageousness

outrider attendant, escort, or scout

outrigger projecting spar or framework on a boat

outright absolute; absolutely

outset start

outside (at or to the) exterior

outsider person who is not a member of a group; horse with little chance of winning

outsize larger than normal

outskirts outlying area of a city

outspoken candid or frank
outspokenly outspokenness

outstanding excellent; unresolved or unpaid
outstandingly

outstation remote position or station

outstay to stay longer than

outstretched extended

outstrip to surpass
outstripped outstripping

out-tray tray for completed outgoing documents

outward on or to the outside
outwardly outwards

outweigh to surpass in weight, value, or importance

outwit to get the better of by cunning
outwitted outwitting

outwork work done away from the business where it was commissioned and undertaken, esp. at home

ouzel or **ousel** kind of diving bird

ouzo Greek aniseed-flavoured drink

oval egg-shaped
ovally ovalness

ovary female organ that produces eggs
ovaries ovarian

ovate egg-shaped
ovately

ovation enthusiastic applause

oven enclosed compartment in which food is baked or roasted
ovenware

over above; more than; across; remaining
overly overmuch

over- (*prefix*) to excess; above

overbid overbook overburden overcapitalize or *overcapitalise overcloud overconfident overcook overcritical overcrowd overdevelop overeat overemphasize* or *overemphasise overexpose overindulgent overinquisitive overload overpopulate overqualified overrated overripe oversell oversensitive oversimplify overstretch overuse*

overact to act in an exaggerated manner
overactive

overall loose-fitting protective garment; including everything

overarm thrown or bowled with the arm raised above the shoulder

overawe to overcome with awe
overawing

overbalance to (cause to) lose balance
overbalancing

overbearing domineering
overbearingly

overblown (*of a flower*) past its fullness of bloom

overboard over the side of a boat or ship and into the water

overcast (*of the sky*) covered with cloud

overcharge to charge too much
overcharging

overcoat warm heavy outdoor coat

overcome to defeat; to succeed in dealing with
overcame overcoming

overdo to do, work, etc. to excess; to exaggerate
overdid overdoes overdoing overdone

overdose too large a dose
overdosage

overdraw to draw a cheque for more than the credit balance in a bank account
overdraft overdrawn overdrew

overdress to dress too elaborately

overdrive mechanism providing an extra gear above the normal top gear in a vehicle

overdue delayed; unpaid

overestimate to value too greatly
overestimating overestimation

overflow to flow over the limits of;
overflowing

overgrown grown over with weeds, etc.

overhang to extend over
overhung

overhaul to examine very closely; to overtake

overhead above

overh eads general business expenses

overhear to hear without the knowledge or intention of the speaker
overheard

overjoyed delighted

overkill ability to destroy an enemy with excess nuclear force

overland across land

overlap to cover or coincide partly
overlapped overlapping

overlay to lay over or across; something laid over something else
overlays overlaid overlaying

overleaf on the other side of a page

overlook to have as a view from above; to fail to see

overnight during or for the night

overpass flyover

overpay to pay too much
overpaid overpaying

overplay to exaggerate or overestimate

overpower to conquer by greater force

overprint to print additional matter on

overrate to value too highly
overrating

overreach to try to reach too far

overreact to show an excessive reaction

override to set aside (as if) with superior authority; to dominate
overridden overriding overrode

overrule to rule against
overruling

overrun to swarm over; to go beyond
overran overrunning

overseas across the sea; abroad

oversee to supervise
oversaw overseen overseer

oversexed having a great sexual desire or urge

overshadow to cast darkness over; to be more important than

overshoe protective outer shoe

overshoot to go beyond
overshot

oversight omission; supervision

oversleep to sleep beyond the intended time
overslept

overspend to spend more than one can afford
overspent

overspill surplus, esp. excess population

overstate to exaggerate
overstatement overstating

overstay to stay too long

overstep to go beyond a limit
overstepped overstepping

overstrung very sensitive

oversubscribe to apply for more shares than are available
oversubscribing oversubscription

overt open
overtly

overtake to move past another vehicle by travelling faster; to come upon suddenly
overtaken overtook overtaking

overtax to tax too heavily; to put too great a burden on

overthrow to defeat; to upset
overthrew overthrown

overtime (work undertaken) in addition to normal hours

overtone additional meaning or quality

overture musical introduction; approach

overturn to turn or overthrow

overview survey

overweight weighing more than is normal or healthy

overwhelm to engulf or overcome

overwork to work too hard

overwrought tense; excited

oviduct tube through which ova pass from an ovary

oviparous producing young that hatch outside the mother's body
oviparity oviparously

ovoid egg-shaped

ovulate to produce eggs; to discharge eggs from the ovary
ovulating ovulation

ovule small structure in a flower's ovary

ovum female egg-cell in animals
ova ovoid

owe to be in debt to
owing

owl nocturnal bird of prey
owlet owlish

own individual; to possess; to acknowledge
owner owner-occupier ownership

ox kind of bovine mammal; adult castrated male of species of cattle
oxen oxtail

ox-eye kind of plant having flowers with yellow rays and dark centres

oxide compound of oxygen and another element

oxidize or **oxidise** to combine with oxygen
oxidation oxidization or *oxidisation*
oxidizing or *oxidising*

oxyacetylene mixture of oxygen and acetylene

oxygen colourless odourless gas

oxygenate to combine or enrich with oxygen
oxygenating oxygenation

oyez town crier's call to win attention

oyster kind of edible shellfish

ozone form of oxygen; pure sea air
ozone-friendly ozone layer

P

pace single walking step; speed or rate; to walk slowly
pacemaker pacesetter pacing

pachyderm thick-skinned mammal

Pacific world's largest ocean

pacifism belief opposing war
pacifist

pacify to calm; to restore to order
pacific pacifically pacification pacified pacifies pacifying

pack (to put into a) container or bundle; group of dogs or wolves; set of playing-cards; to crowd or fill
pack-drill packer packhorse pack-ice packing-case

package parcel; to put in a parcel
packaging

packet (to wrap up in a) small pack
packeted packeting

pact agreement or alliance

pad (to fill with a) soft cushioning material; set of blank paper; launching area for helicopters or spacecraft
padded padding

paddle (to propel a boat with a) short oar; to walk about barefooted in shallow water
paddle-boat paddle-steamer paddle-wheel paddling

paddock small enclosed field for horses

paddy riceplant; rice field
paddy-field

padlock (to fasten with a) detachable lock with a movable shackle

padre chaplain in the armed services

paean hymn or song of praise

paederasty see **pederasty**

paediatrics (US **pediatrics**) medicine concerned with children and their diseases
paediatric (US *pediatric*) *paediatrician* (US *pediatrician*)

paedophilia sexual desire towards children
paedophile

paella Spanish dish of rice, fish, and meat

paeon metrical foot of 1 long and 3 short syllables

pagan heathen
paganism

page[1] leaf of paper in a book; one side of this

page[2] young boy-servant; to summon by name over a public-address system
pageboy paging

pageant colourful public display
pageantry

pager electronic device for contacting a person

paginate to number pages in sequence
paginating pagination

pagoda eastern temple or memorial

paid past tense and past participle of **pay**

pail bucket
pailful

pain bodily suffering; anguish in the mind
painful painfully painfulness pain-killer painless painlessly painlessness pain-relieving

pains trouble or care
painstaking

paint (to cover with a) liquid colouring substance

paintbox paintbrush painter painting paintwork

pair set of 2 things that go together; to put together in twos

paisley pattern of small curved shapes

pajamas (US) see **pyjamas**

Pakistan country in South Asia
Pakistani

pal (*informal*) friend; to become friendly with
palled palliness palling pally

palace official residence of a monarch or high official such as an archbishop

Palaeocene (US **Paleocene**) of the first epoch of the Tertiary period

palaeography (US **paleography**) study of ancient writing
palaeographer (US *paleographer*)

palaeolithic (US **paleolithic**) earliest division of the Stone Age

palaeontology (US **paleontology**) study of fossils
palaeontologist (US *paleontologist*)

Palaeozoic (US **Paleozoic**) geological era

palatable agreeable or pleasant
palatability palatably

palate roof of the mouth; sense of taste
palatal

palatial of or like a palace

palatinate lord with sovereign power

palaver (*informal*) fuss

pale[1] lacking brightness or intensity
palely paleness

pale[2] wooden post used in fencing
paling

Paleocene (US) see **Palaeocene**

paleography (US) see **palaeography**

paleolithic (US) see **palaeolithic**

paleontology (US) see **palaeontology**

Paleozoic (US) see **Palaeozoic**

Palestine ancient Middle Eastern country
Palestinian

palette thin board used by artists for mixing colours
palette-knife

palindrome word or phrase that reads the same backwards as forwards
palindromic

palisade strong fence of stakes

pall[1] cloth covering for a coffin
pall-bearer

pall[2] to become tedious or boring

palladium soft silver-white metallic element

pallet[1] portable platform used in storing and transporting goods

pallet[2] straw-filled mattress

palliate to calm or relieve
palliating palliation palliative

pallid lacking colour; pale
pallidly pallor

palm[1] inner part of the hand

palm[2] kind of tropical tree or shrub
palm-honey palm-oil palmy

palmetto kind of tropical palm with fan-shaped leaves
palmettos

palmistry reading of a person's character or future by looking at the markings of his or her hands
palmist

palpable capable of being touched or felt; obvious
palpability palpably

palpate to examine by touch
palpation

palpitate to tremble; to beat quickly
palpitating palpitation

palsy paralysis; to paralyse
palsies palsied palsying

paltry worthless; insignificant
paltriness

pampas extensive plains of South America; tall grass
pampas-grass

pamper to treat too kindly; to spoil

pamphlet leaflet or booklet
pamphleteer

pan[1] round shallow cooking vessel; to wash earth while searching for gold
panned panning

pan[2] to follow a moving object with a camera
panned panning

panacea remedy for all diseases

panache verve or dash; flamboyant style

Panama country in Central America
Panamanian

pancake thin flat cake of batter

panchromatic sensitive to all colours

pancreas gland behind the stomach
pancreatic

panda large black and white bear-like mammal

pandemic affecting people over a wide area

pandemonium chaos

pander to gratify the desires of others

pane sheet of glass in a window

panegyric written expression or speech of elaborate praise

panel (to provide with a) flat section of a surface; group of people esp. jury; board of controls
panelist panelled (US *paneled*) *panelling* (US *paneling*) *panellist* (US *panelist*)

pang sudden sharp feeling

panic (to feel) sudden uncontrollable fear
panicked panicking panicky panic-stricken

pannier one of a pair of bags; large basket

panoply complete array
panoplies panoplied

panorama wide scenic view; survey
panoramic panoramically

pansy kind of garden plant
pansies

pant to breathe in short quick bursts

pantaloon old man in pantomime

pantaloons trousers

pantechnicon furniture removal van

pantheism belief that equates God with the universe or nature
pantheist pantheistic

panther leopard

panties women's or children's short knickers

pantihose tights

pantile roofing tile

pantograph electricity-collecting framework on a train, etc.; copying instrument

pantomime traditional Christmas musical and theatrical presentation for children

pantry room or cupboard where food is stored
pantries

pants underpants; knickers; (US) trousers

panzer (*German*) armoured unit

papacy office of the pope; system of government of the Roman Catholic Church
papacies

papal of the pope or papacy
papally

papaw or **papaya** see **pawpaw**

paper substance made from pulped wood, etc. used for writing, printing, etc.; newspaper; document
paperback paper-boy paper-clip paper-girl paper-knife paperweight paperwork

papier mâché pulped paper

papist (*derogatory*) Roman Catholic

papoose American Indian baby

paprika (seasoning from) sweet red pepper

Papua New Guinea country in SW Pacific
Papuan

papyrus ancient writing material; kind of tall aquatic plant

par average or standard; standard score for each hole on a golf-course

parable simple short story that illustrates a moral principle
parabolic or *parabolical*

parabola kind of curve
parabolic

paracetamol mild pain-killing drug

parachute device that slows down the speed of fall from a great height; to descend by parachute
parachuting parachutist

parade ordered march or assembly of troops; (to march in) procession; row of shops
parader parading

paradigm model

paradise blissful place
paradisiacal

paradox statement that seems absurd but may be true
paradoxes paradoxical paradoxically

paraffin (*Brit*) distillation of petroleum

paragliding sport similar to hang-gliding that uses a special parachute which allows a person to glide through the air

paragon excellent model; pattern

paragraph division of a piece of writing
paragraphic

Paraguay country in South America
Paraguayan

parakeet kind of small long-tailed parrot

parallax apparent change in the position of an object when it is viewed from different points

parallel at constantly the same distance from each other and never meeting; corresponding; parallel line; to make parallel
paralleled paralleling parallelism

parallelogram quadrilateral with opposite sides parallel and equal

paralyse (US **paralyze**) to cause to lose the ability to move or feel
paralysing (US *paralyzing*) *paralysis paralytic*

paramedical supplementing medical doctors' work
paramedic

parameter mathematical quantity that is constant in a specific case but varies in others; factor or guideline

paramilitary organized in a military manner but not part of the armed forces

paramount of the greatest importance

paranoia mental disorder with delusions of grandeur
paranoiac paranoid

paranormal beyond normal scientific explanation

parapet low wall on the edge of a platform

paraphernalia miscellaneous articles

paraphrase to express in other words
paraphrasing

paraplegia paralysis of the lower half of the body
paraplegic

parapsychology study of telepathy, clairvoyance, etc.
parapsychological

parasite animal, plant, or person living off another
parasitic parasitical

parasol sunshade

paratroops troops trained to be dropped by parachute
paratrooper

paratyphoid mild form of typhoid

parboil to boil briefly as the first part of a cooking process

parcel (to wrap up in a) package
parcelled (US *parceled) parcelling* (US *parceling)*

parch to make or become hot and dry
parches

parchment treated dried skin of an animal such as a sheep used for writing on
parchment-paper

pardon to excuse or forgive a mistake or offence; forgiveness
pardonable pardonably pardoner

pare to peel; to clip on the edge
paring

parent father or mother
parentage parental parentally parenthood

parenthesis additional explanatory, etc. phrase marked off from the rest of a sentence by brackets or commas
parentheses parenthetical parenthetically

parenthesize or **parenthesise** to place in parenthesis
parenthesizing or *parenthesising*

par excellence (*French*) to the highest degree; beyond comparison

pariah social outcast

parish part of a diocese with its own church
parishes parishioner

parity equality or equivalence of amount, rank, etc.
parities

park open land for recreation; to stop and leave a vehicle temporarily in a place
parking-meter parking-ticket parkland

parka kind of anorak

Parkinson's disease progressive nervous disease

Parkinson's law observation that work expands to fill the time available

parlance manner of speaking

parley discussion between leaders of opposing groups; (*of such leaders*) to discuss terms
parleys parleyed parleying

parliament (representatives in the) law-making assembly of a country
parliamentarian parliamentary

parlour (US **parlor**) sitting-room; room for specialized use

Parmesan kind of hard dry cheese

parochial of a parish; narrow in outlook
parochialism parochially

parody (to make a) comic imitation of someone's style or work
parodies parodic parodied parodist parodying

parole early release of a prisoner on condition of good behaviour

paroxysm sudden attack or outburst

parquet kind of wooden flooring
parqueted parquetry

parr young salmon

parricide murder or murderer of a parent of close relative
parricidal

parrot bird with bright plumage and an ability to mimic sounds

parry to ward off or evade; act of parrying
parries parried parrying

parse to describe the grammatical status of words
parsing

Parsee Zoroastrian descendant
Parsees

parsimonious extremely careful with money
parsimoniously parsimony

parsley kind of herb whose leaves are used in cooking

parsnip kind of plant with long white edible root

parson priest or clergyman
parsonage

part piece, portion, or subdivision; to divide
part-exchange part-owner part-song part-time part-timer

partake to have a share in; to receive
partaken partaking partook

parterre ornamental garden; area in a theatre between the orchestra and audience

parthenogenesis method of reproduction without fertilization
parthenogenetic

Parthian shot comment or gesture made while leaving

partial not total; not fair; fond of
partiality

partially not completely or fully
SEE PANEL

---

partially or partly?

Partially means 'not completely or fully': *facilities for the blind and partially sighted; The state of siege round the city has been partially lifted.*

Partly is used more frequently than *partially* and means 'not wholly; in part': *Performance is assessed partly by examination and partly by written course work; Partly because of the poor financial state of the economy and partly because of the weather, profits were down last year.*

---

participate to take part in
participant participating participation participator participatory

participle verbal form
participial

particle very small piece or amount; minor part of speech

particoloured variegated

particular individual; special; thorough or exact
particularity particularly

particularize or **particularise** to specify in detail
particularization or *particularisation*

parting separation or leaving; dividing line when combing hair

partisan or **partizan** loyal follower of a group; guerrilla
partisanship or *partizanship*

partition separation; thin wall or screen; to divide
partitioned partitioning

partitive referring to part of a whole

partly not wholly; in part
SEE PANEL at **partially**

partner one of a pair, as in sport
partnership

partook past tense of **partake**

partridge kind of Old World game-bird

parturient of childbirth
parturiency parturition

party social gathering; organized political group
parties party-wall

parvenu (*fem.* **parvenue**) upstart
parvenus (fem. *parvenues)*

PASCAL computer language

paschal of the Passover or Easter

pass to move onwards or proceed by; to hand over; to be accepted or successful; written permission; narrow gap in mountains
passes passable passbook passer-by passers-by passing passkey password past

passage passing; corridor; brief section of a book, etc.
passageway

passé (*French*) faded; out of date

passenger person travelling in a vehicle

passe-partout adhesive tape used in picture-framing; master-key

passerine (bird that is one of a group) of perching songbirds

passim (*Latin*) here and there; throughtout

passion deep feeling, esp. love
passionate passionately passion-flower

passive acted on by external forces; not resisting
passively passivity

Passover Jewish festival

passport official nationality and identity document carried by travellers abroad

past past participle of **pass**

pasta flour and water dough preparation shaped variously in spaghetti, macaroni, etc.

paste soft mixture; (to stick with an) adhesive
pasteboard paste-up pasting

pastel (crayon with) pale or light colour

pastern part of a horse's foot between the fetlock and the hoof

pasteurize or **pasteurise** to sterilize by heating briefly
pasteurization or *pasteurisation*
pasteurizing or *pasteurising*

pastiche work made up of different elements or that uses the style of an earlier work

pastille lozenge; aromatic substance

pastime activity to pass the time pleasantly

pastor clergyman responsible for a congregation
pastorate pastorship

pastoral of rural life; of a pastor or the spiritual care of a congregation

pastorale musical composition with a rural theme
pastoraler

pastry dough of flour and water, esp. baked
pastries

pasture (to feed on) grassland for grazing
pasturage pasturing

pasty[1] of or like dough; looking pale
pastier pastiest pastily pastiness

pasty[2] pastry filled with meat, vegetables, etc.
pasties

pat to tap softly with the hand; small lump of butter; right
patted patting

patch (to cover with a) piece of material for mending
patches patchwork patchy

patchouli kind of perfume from an Indian plant

pate head

pâté paste of spiced meat, fish, etc.

patella kneecap
patellae or *patellas patellar*

patent exclusive right to an invention; glossy leather; obvious
patency patentable patentee patently patentor

paternal of or like a father; related through the father
paternalism paternalistic paternally paternity

paternoster Lord's prayer in Latin

path track or way
pathway

pathetic arousing pity or sympathy; (*informal*) miserably inadequate
pathetically

pathogen agent that causes disease
pathogenic

pathology study of diseases
pathological pathologically pathologist

pathos quality of arousing compassion, sorrow, etc.

patience being tolerant and calm; card-game for 1 person

patient tolerant and calm; person receiving medical care
patiently patientness

patina surface appearance produced by age

patio paved terrace beside a house; open courtyard
patios

patisserie shop selling sweet pastries

patois dialect or jargon

patriarch male head of a family or tribe; head of Eastern Church
patriarchal patriarchate patriarchy patriarchies

patrician member of the nobility of ancient Rome

patricide murdering of one's own father
patricidal

patrimony inheritance from one's father or ancestors
patrimonies patrimonial

patriot person who is zealously devoted to his or her own country
patriotic patriotically patriotism

patrol to go round an area to maintain security; such a security check
patrolled patroller patrolling patrolman

patron (*fem*. **patroness**) person who supports a good cause; regular customer
patronage

patronize or **patronise** to act as a patron; to behave condescendingly towards
patronizer or *patroniser patronizing* or *patronisin**g patronizinglyorpatronisingly*

patronymic name derived from the name of the person's father or male ancestor

patter[1] to tap quickly and repeatedly; such tapping

patter[2] empty talk; sales talk

pattern repeated, esp. decorative, design; model; to model; to arrange with a pattern

patty small pie

paucity fewness or insufficiency

paunch belly, esp. when protruding
paunches paunchy

pauper poor person
pauperism

pauperize or **pauperise** to reduce to poverty
pauperization or *pauperisation*
pauperizing or *pauperising*

pause (to take a) temporary rest
pausing

pave to cover with a firm surface, esp. using flat stones or concrete
pavement paving paving-stone

pavilion building at a sports ground; summer-house

pavlova open meringue case filled with cream and fruit

paw clawed foot of an animal

pawl pivoted lever that permits motion in a single direction

pawn[1] to deposit an article as security for money borrowed
pawnbroker pawnshop

pawn[2] chess-piece of lowest value; person who is exploited by another

pawpaw, **papaw**, or **papaya** kind of (edible fruit of a) small North American deciduous tree

pay to give money in return for goods or services; salary or wages
paid payable pay-bed pay-claim pay-day payee payer paying payload paymaster payment pay-off

pea edible green seed of climbing plant
pea-green peashooter

peace ending or absence or war; calm
peaceable peaceably peaceful peacefully

peacefulness peacemaker peace-offering peace-pipe peacetime

peach juicy stoned fruit with a reddish-yellow skin
peaches peachy

peacock (*fem.* **peahen**) kind of bird with large fan-like tail
peafowl

peak sharp top of a mountain; projecting edge of a cap
peaked

peaky looking pale and sickly
peakier peakiest peakily peakiness

peal bells; to ring in peals

peanut kind of (oily edible seed of) tropical leguminous plant

pear kind of fleshy rounded fruit that narrows towards the stalk

pearl hard round mass found in an oyster and valued as a gem
pearly

peasant small landowner or farm labourer
peasantry

pease (*archaic*) pea
pease-pudding

peat decomposed vegetable matter used as a fertilizer or fuel
peatbog peaty

pebble small smooth roundish stone
pebbliness pebbly

pecan hickory tree with rough bark; smooth nut with edible kernel

peccadillo trifling fault
peccadilloes or *peccadillos*

peccary kind of pig-like American mammal
peccaries

peck[1] unit of dry measure

peck[2] to strike with the beak; nip or tap made with the beak

pectin substance used as a setting agent in jam
pectic pectinous

pectoral of the chest or breast
pectorally

peculate to embezzle or appropriate
peculating peculation

peculiar odd; special; exclusive (to)
peculiarity peculiarities peculiarly

pecuniary of money

pedagogue educator or teacher
pedagogic pedagogical pedagogically pedagogy

pedal (to operate by a) foot pedal
pedalled (US *pedaled*) *pedaller* (US *pedaler*) *pedalling* (US *pedaling*)

pedant person who insists on insignificant details and rules
pedantic pedantically pedantry

peddle to go from place to place selling goods; to sell drugs
peddler peddling pedlar

pederasty or **paederasty** sexual relations between men and boys
pederast

pedestal base supporting a column or statue

pedestrian person walking on foot; dull

pedestrianize or **pedestrianise** to convert a street into an area for pedestrians only
pedestrianization or *pedestrianisation pedestrianizing* or *pedestrianising*

pediatrics (US) see **paediatrics**

pediculosis infestation with lice

pedicure treatment of the feet

pedigree line of descent of an animal or person

pediment triangular gable of a 2-pitched roof

pedlar (US **peddler**) person who peddles

pedometer device that measures the distance covered by a walker

peduncle stalk bearing a flower
peduncular peduncular peduncular

peek to glance quickly; quick glance
peekaboo

peel (to remove the) skin or rind
peeling

peep[1] to look through an opening or from a hidden place; quick look
peeper peep-hole peep-show

peep[2] (to utter a) short shrill sound

peer[1] (*fem.* **peeress**) member of British nobility; someone's equal
peerage peerless

peer[2] to look at intently

peeve to irritate
peeved peeving

peevish irritable

peewit or **pewit** lapwing

peg small pin or clip; to fasten with a peg
pegboard pegged pegging pegleg

peignoir woman's dressing-gown

pejorative disparaging
pejoratively

Pekinese or **Pekingese** small short-legged Chinese dog

pekoe high-quality black tea

pelican kind of large waterbird with a long pouched bill

pellet small ball, bullet, or pill

pell-mell in a confused or disorderly way

pellucid very clear
pellucidity pellucidly

pelmet ornamental board above a window to hide the curtain rail

pelt[1] animal skin and fur

pelt[2] to throw missiles at; (*of rain*) to fall very hard

pelvis basin-shaped structure at the base of the trunk
pelvic

pen[1] instrument for writing or drawing with ink; to write or draw with a pen
pen-and-ink pen-friend penholder pen-name penned penning pen-pal pen-pushing

pen[2] (to confine in a) small enclosure
penned penning

penal of punishment
penally

penalize or **penalise** to impose a penalty on
penalization or *penalisation penalizing* or *penalising*

penalty punishment

penance something done to show repentance for sin

penchant strong inclination

pencil (to write or draw with an) implement containing a strip of graphite
pencilled (US *penciled*) *pencilling* (US *penciling*)

pendant hanging ornament

pendent hanging or overhanging

pending not yet settled; until

pendulous hanging downwards

pendulum hanging weight that swings, used esp. in clocks
pendulums

penetrate to pass through or into
penetrable penetrating penetration penetrative penetrator

penguin flightless short-legged Southern sea bird

penicillin antibiotic obtained from a mould

peninsula piece of land almost surrounded by water
peninsular

penis male organ of copulation and urination
penises

penitence expression of sorrow for doing wrong
penitent penitential penitentially

penitentiary (US) state prison
penitentiaries

penknife small pocket-knife
penknives

pennant flag that tapers to a point

penniless very poor; without money

pennon flag attached to the head of a knight's lance

Pennsylvania US state

penny bronze coin, 100 of which are worth £1 sterling
pence or *pennies penny-farthing penny-pincher penny-wise pennyworth*

penology study of punishment and management of prisons
penologist

pension[1] regular fixed sum of money paid to older people, etc.
pensionable pensioner

pension[2] small continental boarding-house; room and board

pensive deeply thoughtful
pensively pensiveness

pentagon polygon with 5 sides
pentagonal

Pentagon (US) military establishment and Defense Department

pentameter verse line of 5 metrical feet

Pentateuch first 5 books of the Old Testament

pentathlon athletic contest of 5 different events

Pentecost Christian festival of Whitsun; Jewish harvest festival
Pentecostal

penthouse flat on the top floor or roof of a tall building

pent-up repressed

penultimate next to last

penumbra area of partial darkness in a shadow
penumbrae

penurious very poor
penury

peony kind of plant with showy flowers
peonies

people human beings; to populate
peopled peopling

pep liveliness; to liven up
pepped pepping

pepper sharp hot powder for sprinkling on food; green, red, or yellow fruit; to sprinkle pepper over
pepper-and-salt peppercorn peppered peppering peppery

peppermint type of mint producing an aromatic oil; sweet made with this

pepsin stomach enzyme

peptic of digestion or the digestive juices

per for every; according to

peradventure (*archaic*) perhaps

perambulate (*formal*) to travel on foot
perambulating perambulation

perambulator (*formal*) pram

per annum (*Latin*) every year

per capita (*Latin*) for each person

perceive to become aware of
perceivable perceiver perceiving

per cent in each hundred
percentage

perceptible able to be perceived
perceptibility perceptibly
SEE PANEL

perceptible or perceptive?
Something that is *perceptible* can be seen or recognized: *In the distance, the island is just perceptible; There has been a perceptible change in his attitude towards her.*
A person, or someone's thoughts, may be described as *perceptive* if they are quick to notice and realize things: *one of the most perceptive statesmen of our time; a story full of perceptive insights.*

perception awareness or observation
perceptual perceptually

perceptive observant; discerning, sharp or shrewd
perceptively
SEE PANEL at **perceptible**

perch[1] place on which a bird rests; (*of a bird*) to rest; unit of measuring length
perches

perch[2] kind of small freshwater fish
perches

perchance (*archaic*) perhaps

percipient able to perceive
percipience

percolate to filter through slowly
percolating percolation percolator

percussion striking of a musical instrument; set of musical instruments such as xylophone and drum
percussionist percussive

perdition eternal damnation

peregrinate to travel or wander around a foreign country
peregrinating peregrination

peregrine kind of falcon

peremptory insisting on obedience; absolute
peremptorily peremptoriness
SEE PANEL

peremptory or perfunctory?
A person's manner or behaviour may be described as *peremptory* if it shows that they expect to be obeyed immediately: *He dismissed them with his usual peremptory nod.*
A *perfunctory* action is one that is done quickly, without any carefulness, interest, or thought: *He gave the letter a mere perfunctory glance.*

perennial (*of a plant*) growing for several years
perennially

perestroika (*Russian*) (in former USSR) policy of political and social restructuring

perfect faultless; complete; to make perfect
perfection perfectionism perfectionist perfectly

perfectible capable of becoming or being made perfect

perfidious treacherous or deceitful
perfidy

perforate to make holes in
perforating perforation perforator

perforce of necessity

perform to carry out; to enact a part
performable performance performer

perfume preparation of fragrant oils, etc.; sweet pleasant smell; to impart a perfume to
perfumer perfumery perfumeries perfuming

perfunctory done in a superficial routine manner
perfunctorily perfunctoriness
SEE PANEL at **peremptory**

pergola supporting framework for climbing plants

perhaps possibly

perianth outer part of a flower

pericardium membranous sac surrounding the heart

perigee point in the orbit of the moon, planet, or artificial satellite at which it is closest to the earth

perihelion point in the orbit of a planet or comet at which it is closest to the sun

peril danger
perilous perilously

perimeter outer boundary of a figure or an area

perineum part of the body between the anus and the external genital organs
perineums perineal

period portion or interval of time; school lesson; occurrence of menstruation
periodic periodically

periodical magazine published regularly

peripatetic going from place to place
peripatetically

peripheral of a periphery; of very little importance; device connected to a computer

periphery outer limits of a surface or area
peripheries

periphrasis roundabout way of expressing something
periphrases periphrastic

periscope optical instrument for viewing objects not in the direct line of sight
periscopic

perish to be destroyed; to die or decay
perishability perishable perishes perishing

peristalsis wavelike succession of muscular contractions

peristyle row of columns around a temple

peritoneum serous membrane lining the walls of the abdomen
peritoneums peritoneal

peritonitis inflammation of the peritoneum

periwig wig

periwinkle[1] kind of edible sea-snail

periwinkle[2] kind of evergreen trailing plant

perjure to give false evidence on oath
perjurer perjuring perjury perjuries

perk[1] incidental benefit; bonus

perk[2] to liven (up)
perky

perm (to give a) permanent wave to hair; permutation

permafrost ground that is permanently frozen

permanent lasting indefinitely; not expected to change
permanence or *permanency permanently*

permanganate salt containing manganese

permeable capable of being permeated, esp. by liquids
permeability permeably

permeate to fill every part of
permeating permeation

permissive liberal or tolerant, esp. regarding sexual or social matters
permissiveness

permit to allow; to consent to
permissible permissibly permission permitted permitting

permute to change the order of; to arrange in all possible ways
permutable permutation permuting

pernicious wicked or harmful
perniciously perniciousness

pernickety (*informal*) very fussy

peroration concluding; summing-up

peroxide oxide containing high proportion of oxygen; bleaching agent

perpendicular upright; style of architecture
perpendicularity

perpetrate to commit a crime
perpetrating perpetration perpetrator
SEE PANEL

perpetrate or perpetuate?
Someone *perpetrates* a crime when they commit it: *atrocities perpetrated in the Second World War; perpetrate fraud on a massive scale.*
Something is *perpetuated* when it is caused to last indefinitely: *The annual ceremony was intended to perpetuate the memory of those who died in the struggle; perpetuate a myth/tradition.*

perpetual never-ending
perpetually perpetuity perpetuities

perpetuate to cause to last indefinitely
perpetuating perpetuation perpetuator
SEE PANEL at **perpetrate**

perplex to confuse or complicate
perplexedly perplexingly perplexity perplexities

perquisite (*formal*) perk
SEE PANEL

perquisite or prerequisite?
Perquisite is a formal word for 'perk', an advantage or benefit given because of a job: *The post's perquisites include life insurance, medical insurance, and a company car.*
A *prerequisite* is something that must happen or exist for another thing to be possible: *Good exam results are a prerequisite of entry to the university; Informing the public of the importance of medical research is a prerequisite for increasing their financial support of it.*

per se (*Latin*) by itself

persecute to harass or cause to suffer
persecuting persecution persecutor

persevere to continue steadily
perseverance persevering

Persian Iranian language

persiflage friendly testing; banter

persimmon kind of tropical hardwood tree bearing orange-red fruits

persist to carry on steadfastly; to continue
persistence persistent

person human being
people or *persons*

persona individual's characteristics
personae or *personas*

personable attractive or pleasing
personableness personably

personage important person; character in a play, etc.

personal of a person; belonging to oneself; private
personally

personality sum of individual characteristics of a person; well-known person
personalities

personalize or **personalise** to mark as belonging to a particular person
personalization or *personalisation*
personalizing or *personalising*

personalty (*law*) personal property

persona non grata (*Latin*) unacceptable person
personae non gratae

personate to portray or represent
personating personation

personify to represent as having human characteristics; to typify
personification personified personifies personifying

personnel employees in an organization

perspective art of drawing 3 dimensions on a 2-dimensional surface; way of looking at different problems and giving them relative importance

Perspex (*trademark*) transparent acrylic plastic

perspicacious shrewd; quickly perceptive
perspicaciously perspicacity

perspicuous clearly expressed
perspicuity perspicuously

perspire to sweat
perspiration perspiring

persuade to urge successfully, esp. by reasoning; to convince *persuadable persuading persuasible persuasion persuasive*

pert impudent; lively

pertain to refer or relate to

pertinacious persistent
pertinacity

pertinent relevant
pertinence pertinently

perturb to trouble
perturbable perturbation

Peru country in South America
Peruvian

peruke long wig worn by men in the 17th and 18th centuries

peruse to read with close attention
perusal perusing

pervade to spread throughout
pervading pervasion pervasive pervasively

perverse deliberately opposing what is right or accepted; uncooperative
perversely perversity

pervert to lead into deviant ways; to distort; perverted person
perversion perversity

pervious permeable; receptive

peseta money unit of Spain

peso money unit of any of several South American countries
pesos

pessary device placed in the vagina; vaginal suppository
pessaries

pessimism inclination to expect the worst
pessimist pessimistic pessimistically

pest annoying person or thing; destructive or damaging animal or insect
pesticide pestiferous

pester to annoy constantly

pestilence very strong epidemic disease; plague

pestilent harmful or deadly; annoying

pestle club-shaped implement for pounding substances in a mortar

pet[1] domesticated animal; favourite; to pamper or fondle
petted petting

pet[2] fit of sulkiness
pettish

petal leaf-like part of flower-head
petalled (US *petaled*)

petard (*formerly*) explosive device; scheme

peter to fade (out) gradually

petersham thick corded ribbon

pethidine synthetic narcotic drug

petiole stalk of a leaf

petite small and trim

petit four small fancy cake or biscuit
petits fours

petition (to make a) formal appeal or request
petitioner

petrel kind of sea bird

petrify to change into stone; to paralyse with fear
petrifaction petrification petrified petrifies pertrifying

petrochemical substance obtained from petroleum

petrodollar unit of foreign exchange earned by a petroleum-exporting country

petrol refined petroleum used as a fuel

petroleum dark oily flammable liquid found underground

petrology study of rocks
petrologist

petticoat woman's underskirt

pettifog to quibble over insignificant details
pettifogged pettifoggery pettifogging

petty trivial; unimportant

pettier pettiest pettily pettiness

petulant bad-tempered and impatient
petulance petulantly

petunia kind of plant with brightly coloured funnel-shaped flowers

pew benchlike seat in a church

pewit see **peewit**

pewter alloy of tin, lead, etc.

phaeton light 4-wheeled horse-drawn carriage

phalanger kind of Australian marsupial mammal

phalanx compact body of people (pl. *phalanxes*); bone of the fingers or toes (pl. *phalanges*)

phallus (image of the) penis
phalli phallic phallicism

phantasm phantom
phantasmal

phantasmagoria or **fantasmagoria** shifting sequence of real or imagined figures
phantasmagoric or *fantasmagoric*

phantasy see **fantasy**

phantom spectre or ghost

Pharaoh title of ancient Egyptian kings

Pharisee member of ancient Jewish sect; self-righteous person
Pharisaic Pharisaical Pharisaism

pharmaceutical of drugs or pharmacy

pharmacology study of drugs
pharmacological pharmacologist

pharmacopoeia book describing drugs

pharmacy preparing and dispensing drugs
pharmacies pharmacist

pharynx part of the alimentary canal between the mouth and the oesophagus
pharynges pharyngeal pharyngitis

phase stage in a sequence or development
phasing

pheasant kind of long-tailed game-bird

phenobarbitone barbiturate used to treat insomnia and epilepsy

phenol carbolic acid
phenolic

phenomenal extraordinary
phenomenally

phenomenon observable fact or event; significant person or thing
phenomena phenomenalism

phial small container

philander to flirt with women
philanderer

philanthropy goodwill and practical generosity to one's fellow human beings
philanthropic philanthropically philanthropist

philately collecting postage stamps
philatelic philatelist

philharmonic fond of music

Philippines republic in SE Asia
Filipino Philippine

Philistine uncultured person; native of ancient country in SW Palestine

philology study (esp. historical aspects) of language
philological philologist

philosophize or **philosophise** to undertake philosophical reasoning
philosophizing or *philosophising*

philosophy study of existence, truth, etc, and right behaviour
philosophies philosopher philosophical philosophically

philtre (US **philter**) drink that allegedly arouses sexual desire

phlebitis inflammation of a vein
phlebitic

phlegm thick mucus secreted into the nose, etc.

phlegmatic unemotional
phlegmatically

phlogiston substance formerly thought to be the essence of fire

phlox kind of American plant

phobia illogical and abnormal fear
phobias phobic

phoenix mythical bird

phone (*informal*) short for **telephone**
phonecard phone-in

phoneme distinctive speech sound in a language
phonemic phonemics

phonetics study of production of human speech
phonetic phonetically phonetician

phoney or **phony** (*informal*) false
phonier phoniest phonily phoniness

phonic of sound
phonics

phonograph (early type of) gramophone

phonology study of the sound system of a language
phonological phonologically phonologist

phosphate salt of phosphoric acid

phosphoresce to give out light without emitting heat
phosphorescence phosphorescent phosphorescing

phosphorus non-metallic element that occurs as phosphates
phosphoric phosphorous

photo short for **photograph**
photos

photo- (*prefix*) light or photography
photoelectric photoengraving photogravure photojournalism photolithography photometer photometry photosetting

photocopy (to make a) photographic copy of a document, etc.
photocopied photocopiable photocopier photocopies photocopying

photofit system of reconstructing a facial likeness by assembling photographs of different features

photogenic appearing attractive in photographs

photograph image recorded by a camera
photographer photographic photographically photography photogravure

photon particle of electromagnetic radiation

Photostat (*trademark*) photocopying machine

photosynthesis (*in plants*) conversion of carbon dioxide and water into carbohydrates by absorbing sunlight
photosynthesize or *photosynthesise photosynthetic*

phrase group of words; expression; to express
phrasal phraseology phrasing

phrenetic see **frenetic**

phrenology study of the skull as a supposed method of indicating mental abilities
phrenologist

phut dull sound; wrong

phylactery either of 2 small boxes containing passages from Scripture worn by Jewish men
phylacteries

phylum major division of animals and plants
phyla

physical of the body; of material things
physically

physician doctor of medicine

physics science concerned with matter and energy
physicist

physiognomy person's facial features
physiognomies physiognomical physiognomist

physiology science concerned with the functions of living organisms
physiological physiologist

physiotherapy treatment of injury, etc. by massage and exercise
physiotherapist

physique person's general physical form and structure

pi letter of the Greek alphabet used to denote the ratio of the circumference of a circle to its diameter

pianissimo (*music*) very quietly

piano musical keyboard instrument; (*music*) softly
pianos pianist pianoforte

Pianola (*trademark*) kind of mechanical piano

piastre (US **piaster**) money unit in any of certain Middle Eastern countries

piazza open square
piazzas

pica unit of measuring typographical material

picador horseman in a bullfight

picaresque of a style of fiction describing the adventures of a rogue

piccalilli kind of pickled relish

piccolo small shrill flute
piccolos

pick[1] pointed tool for breaking rocks or hard ground
pickaxe (US *pickax*)

pick[2] to choose or select; to gather fruit
picker pick-me-up pick-up

pickaback see **piggyback**

picket pointed stake; strikers outside a place of work; to act as a protest (at)
picketed picketing

pickle solution of vinegar, etc. for preserving food; to preserve in a pickle
pickling

pickpocket person who steals from a person's pocket or bag

picnic (to take part in an) outing with an informal meal in the open air
picnicked picnicker picknicking

pico- (*prefix*) one million millionth

picot small decorative loop

picric of an acid used in dyeing, antiseptics, and explosives

pictograph or **pictogram** pictorial symbol or representation

picture painting or representation; mental image; to describe or imagine
pictorial picturing

picturesque pleasant; charming
picturesquely

pidgin language made up of elements from 2 or more languages, esp. used for business

pie baked dish of meat, fruit, etc. in pastry

piebald (horse) with patches of different colours, esp. black and white

piece part of; fragment; composition; coin; to join (together)
piecemeal piece-work piecing

pièce de résistance (*French*) most outstanding item or dish
pièces de résistance

pied of different colours

pied-à-terre (*French*) flat or other lodging for occasional use
pieds-à-terre

pier structure extending into the sea; support for an arch or bridge
pierhead

pierce to make a hole in something, esp. with a sharp instrument
piercing

pietisMm exaggerated piety
pietist pietistic

piety being pious

piffle (*informal*) nonsense

pig stout-bodied mammal with a long blunt snout; shaped mass of metal
piggery piggeries piggish piggy-bank pigheaded pig-iron piglet pigskin pigsty pigsties pigtail pigwash

pigeon bird of the dove family
pigeon-breasted pigeonhole pigeonholing pigeon-toed

piggery place where pigs are kept
piggeries

piggyback or **pickaback** ride on the back and shoulders of another person

pigment colouring substance
pigmentation

pigmy see **pygmy**

pike[1] kind of large freshwater fish

pike[2] medieval kind of spear
pikestaff

pilaff, **pilaw**, or **pilau** oriental dish of rice and meat, etc.

pilchard kind of small sea fish of the herring family

pile[1] heap; nuclear reactor; to gather into a pile
pile-up piling

pile[2] raised surface on a fabric

pile[3] column of steel, etc. driven into the ground as a support
pile-driver

piles haemorrhoids

pilfer to steal articles in small amounts
pilferage pilferer

pilgrim traveller to a sacred place
pilgrimage

pill small tablet of medicine; oral contraception
pillbox

pillage (to) plunder
pillager pillaging

pillar upright structure

pillion passenger seat behind the driver of a motor cycle, etc.

pillory (to place in a) wooden framework for locking the head and hands as a public punishment
pillories pilloried pillorying

pillow supporting cushion for the head
pillowcase pillowslip

pilot person qualified to control an aircraft in flight or to guide a ship; to act as a pilot; trial or experimental
pilotage piloted piloting pilot-light

pilule small pill
pilular

pimento allspice; Spanish sweet pepper
pimentos

pimp (to act as a) man who solicits for a prostitute or brothel

pimpernel primrose plant

pimple small inflamed swelling on the skin
pimply

pin short pointed piece of thin metal; to fasten with a pin
pinball pincushion pinhead pin-hole pin-money pinned pinning pinprick pinstripe pin-table pin-up

pinafore apron

pince-nez (*French*) eyeglasses held on the nose by a spring

pincers gripping tool

pinch to squeeze tightly between the finger and the thumb; such a squeeze
pinches pincher

pinchbeck alloy of copper and zinc used to imitate gold

pine[1] kind of evergreen tree
pine-cone

pine[2] to long for
pining

pineapple kind of (juicy yellow-fleshed fruit of a) tropical spiny-leaved plant

ping (to make a) short sharp resonant sound

ping-pong (*trademark*) table tennis

pinion[1] bird's wing

pinion[2] small cogwheel

pink[1] pale red colour

pink[2] kind of garden plant; very good condition

pink[3] to cut a serrated edge on
pinking shears

pink[4] (*of an engine*) to make a knocking sound

pinnace ship's tender

pinnacle highest point; high decorative pointed structure

pinnate like a feather

pinpoint to locate or determine precisely

pint measure of liquid capacity, one-eighth of a gallon
pint-sized

pinyin official romanized transcription of Chinese

pioneer explorer of new land; person who does something first; to be a pioneer
pioneered pioneering

pious devout and religious
piety piously

pip[1] small fruit seed

pip[2] spot on die, etc.; brief high tone, for example as a radio signal

pip[3] (*informal*) to defeat
pipped pipping

pipe tube for a gas or liquid to flow through; (to play a) wind instrument; object in which tobacco is smoked
pipeclay pipe-cleaner pipedream pipeline piper piping

pipette slender glass tube

pippin kind of eating apple

pipsqueak (*informal*) insignificant person

piquant having a sharp taste; stimulating
piquancy piquantly

pique (to cause to feel) resentment or wounded pride
piqued piquing

piqué strong ribbed fabric

piquet card-game for 2 players

piranha kind of ferocious tropical American fish

pirate sea-robber; to use, copy, etc. illegally
piracy piratical piratically pirating

pirouette (to perform a) rapid dancing spin
pirouetting

piscatorial of fishing

Pisces 12th sign of the zodiac

piscine of or like a fish

pistachio kind of (tree that bears a) hard-shelled nut
pistachios

piste skiing slope

pistil carpel
pistillate

pistol handgun

piston sliding disc or cylinder in an internal-combustion engine

pit hole in the ground; to mark with dents or hollows
pit-head pitman pitted pitting

pitch[1] dark tarry substance
pitches pitch-black pitchblende pitch-dark pitchy

pitch[2] to throw; to set up a tent; sports playing-field
pitches pitchfork

pitcher[1] large jug

pitcher[2] baseball player who throws the ball to the batter

piteous arousing or deserving pity

pitfall unforeseen difficulty

pith soft tissue in plant stems or under the rind of an orange, lemon, etc.; essence

pithy meaningful and concise
pithier pithiest pithily pithiness

pitiable arousing or deserving pity
pitiably

pitiful miserable; arousing or deserving pity or contempt
pitifully pitifulness

pitiless without pity; merciless
pitilessly pitilessness

piton metal spike used in mountaineering

pittance small amount of money

pitter-patter quick succession of light taps

pituitary small ductless organ at the base of the brain

pity (to feel) sympathy and sorrow for another person's suffering
pities pitied pitying

pivot (to turn on a) central rotating shaft
pivotal pivoted pivoting

pixel smallest element of the image on a computer screen

pixie or **pixy** small fairy
pixies

pizza baked Italian dish of dough covered with cheese, tomatoes, etc.
pizzas pizzeria

pizzicato (*music*) to be played by plucking

placard (to advertise by a) poster

placate to pacify
placability placable placating placatory

place (to set in a) particular point on a surface or in space
place-kick placement place-name placer place-setting placing

placebo inactive medicine-like substance given to satisfy a patient
placebos or *placeboes*

placenta organ providing nourishment to the foetus in mammals
placentae or *placentas*

placid calm
placidity placidly

plagiarize or **plagiarise** to take another person's ideas or words and pass them off as one's own
plagiarism plagiarist plagiarizing or *plagiarising plagiary*

plague deadly contagious disease; to harass
plaguer plaguing

plaice kind of edible flatfish

plaid woollen tartan cloth
plaided

plain simple; undecorated; clear or obvious; frank; flat area of ground
plainly plainness plain-spoken

plainsong church music for voices singing in unison

plaint protest

plaintiff person who brings a civil legal action

plaintive mournful
plaintively plaintiveness

plait to intertwine hair; plaited hair
plaited plaiting

plan detailed scheme or method; drawing of a building; to make a plan
planned planner planning

planchette small board on wheels with a pencil attached, used to trace messages in seances

plane[1] kind of tall tree having leaves with pointed lobes

plane[2] level (surface); aeroplane

plane[3] (to level with a) tool having a sharp metal blade used to smooth surfaces
planing

planet heavenly body that revolves around the sun

planetarium building with a domed ceiling on to which images of the stars and planets are projected
planetariums

plank long thick piece of wood

plankton microscopic organisms in water

plant living organism that grows with roots in the ground; to set in the soil to grow
plantation planter

Plantagenet family name of English royal house from 1154 to 1399

plantain[1] kind of tropical plant with a banana-like fruit

plantain[2] kind of short-stemmed plant with spikes of small flowers

plaque commemorative plate; filmy substance on teeth

plasma or **plasm** fluid in which blood or lymph are suspended
plasmatic plasmic

plaster (to coat with a) mixture of lime, sand and water, applied to walls; adhesive bandage
plasterboard plasterer

plastic (made of a) synthetic substance that can be moulded
plastically plasticity plasticky

Plasticine (*trademark*) soft modelling substance used by children

plate shallow dish for food; (to cover with a) coating, as of metal or glass
platelayer plate-rack plating

plateau broad flat area of raised ground
plateaux or *plateaus*

platen roller on a typewriter

platform flat raised structure or floor

platinum silvery precious metallic element

platitude obvious or trite remark
platitudinous

Platonic of Plato; free from sexual desire

platoon subdivision of a military group

platter large dish usually shallow and oval

platypus small Australasian aquatic mammal
platypuses or *platypus*

plausible apparently reasonable or valid
plausibility plausibly

play (to take part in a) game or recreation; to perform on a musical instrument; dramatic work performed on stage
play-acting playback playbill playboy player playfellow playful playfully playfulness playground playgroup playhouse playing playing-card playing-field playleader playmate play-off play-pen playroom playschool plaything playtime playwright

plaza open space or square
plazas

plea earnest appeal

plead to make a plea in a law-court; to beg
pleaded or *pled pleading*

pleasant agreeable or friendly
pleasantly pleasantry pleasantries

please to bring satisfaction to; used to express polite requests
pleasing

pleasure enjoyment; satisfaction
pleasurable pleasurableness pleasurably

pleat (to make a) flat fold in cloth
pleated pleatless

plebeian of the common people, esp. of ancient Rome; unrefined

plebiscite direct vote of the electorate on an issue

plectrum small piece of plastic, etc. for

plucking the strings on a musical instrument
plectra

pled past tense and past participle of **plead**

pledge (to give as a) solemn promise; (to give as a) security
pledging

Pleistocene epoch at the beginning of the Quaternary period

plenary absolute; attended by all members
plenarily

plenipotentiary (person) with full authority to transact, esp. government business
plenipotentiaries

plenitude abundance

plenty abundance; enough
plenteous plentiful plentifully plentifulness

pleonasm use of more words than is necessary
pleonastic

plethora excess

pleurisy inflammation of the membrane surrounding the lung and thorax lining
pleuritic

plexus network of nerves or veins
plexuses

pliable easily moulded or influenced
pliability pliably pliancy pliant

pliers gripping tool

plight[1] predicament

plight[2] to promise

plimsoll rubber-soled canvas shoe

Plimsoll line line on the hull of a ship showing the level to which it may be loaded

plinth supporting base of a column, etc.

Pliocene latest epoch of the Tertiary period

plod to walk with slow heavy steps; to work steadily
plodded plodder plodding

plonk[1] to drop heavily

plonk[2] (*informal*) cheap wine

plop (to fall with a) sound of something dropping into water without splashing
plopped plopping

plosion release of breath in the articulation of consonants

plot small piece of ground; story-line in a drama, etc.; (to plan a) conspiracy; (to make a) plan
plotted plotter plotting

plough (US **plow**) (to use an) implement with sharp blades to cut and turn over soil
ploughman (US *plowman*) *ploughshare* (US *plowshare*)

plover kind of wading bird

ploy tactic or ruse

pluck to pull the feathers off; to pull out; courage
plucky

plug stopper; device that makes electrical connections; to block with a plug
plugged plugging

plum kind of (tree that bears a) fleshy sweet fruit

plumage bird's covering of feathers

plumb lead weight used to measure the depth of water or to check that a wall is vertical
plumb-line

plumber person who installs and repairs pipes and fixtures for water and drainage

plumbing system of pipes and fixtures for water, drainage, etc.

plume large feather; to provide with plumes; (*of a bird*) to preen
pluming

plummet to drop down
plummeted plummeting

plump[1] chubby; rounded

plump[2] to drop heavily; abruptly

plunder to rob forcefully, esp. in wartime; such robbery or goods looted
plunderer

plunge to force into; to dive into
plunger plunging

pluperfect (*grammar*) verbal tense that expresses completion of an action before a past time

plural (*grammar*) referring to more than one person or thing
plurality plurally

pluralism development of different cultures by diverse groups in a society
pluralist pluralistic

pluralize or **pluralise** to make or become plural
pluralization or *pluralisation pluralizing* or *pluralising*

---

plurals

• Most English nouns are formed by adding -*s*: *bruise, bruises cat, cats galze, glazes pen, pens*

• Nouns ending in -*ch*, -*s*, -*sh*, -*ss*, or -*x* add -*es*: *church, churches bus, buses dish, dishes boss, bosses box, boxes*

• Nouns ending in -*y*
those ending in a consonant and -*y* change -*y* to -*ies*:
lady, ladies opportunity, opportunities
those ending in a vowel and -*y* simply add -*s*:
boy, boys day, days holiday, holidays

• Nouns ending in -*f* or -*fe* form the plural by replacing -*f* or -*fe* by -*ves*:
calf, calves half, halves shelf, shelves thief, thieves
Exceptions:
brief, briefs chief, chiefs dwarf, dwarfs or *dwarves handkerchief, handkerchiefs* or *handkerchieves hoof, hoofs roof, roofs safe, safes scarf, scarfs* or *scarves turf, turfs* or *turves wharf, wharfs* or *wharves*

• Nouns ending in -*o*
add -*es*: *potato, potatoes tomato, tomatoes*
add -*s*:
those ending in a vowel and -*o*:
kilo, kilos photo, photos piano, pianos radio, radios solo, solos zoo, zoos
some add -*es* or -*s*:
cargo, cargo(e)s flamingo, flamingo(e)s mango, mango(e)s manifesto, manifesto(e)s memento, memento(e)s motto, motto(e)s salvo, salvo(e)s volcano, volcano(e)s

• Some nouns have the same spelling for both singular and plural. Some of these refer to animals:
aircraft deer series sheep species

• A few nouns have irregular plurals:
child, children foot, feet goose, geese louse, lice man, men mouse, mice ox, oxen tooth, teeth woman, women

• Some words that come from foreign languages have special plurals. These include:
nouns ending in -*a* have a plural ending -*ae* (or -*as* or -*ae*):
formula, formulas or *formulae larva, larvae*
nouns ending in -*is* have a plural ending -*es*:
analysis, analyses axis, axes basis, bases crisis, crises
nouns ending in -*on* have plural ending -*a*:
criterion, criteria phenomenon, phenomena
nouns ending in -*um* have a plural ending -*ums* or -*a*:
memorandum, memorandums or *memoranda referendum, referendums* or *referenda*
nouns ending in -*us* have a plural ending -*i*:
nucleus, nuclei stimulus, stimuli

---

plus with the addition of; positive; bonus or advantage

plush fabric with a soft pile; lavish
plushy

Pluto planet farthest from the sun

plutocracy government by the wealthy
plutocracies plutocrat plutocratic

plutonium radioactive element formed in atomic reactors

pluvial of rain

ply[1] layer or thickness; strand in wool, rope, etc.
plywood

ply[2] to work at; to journey (between); to supply constantly
plied plies plying

pneumatic operated by compressed air
pneumatically pneumatics

pneumonia inflammation of the lungs
pneumonic

poach[1] to cook in a simmering liquid
poacher

poach[2] to take game, etc. illegally while trespassing
poacher

pock spot that erupts on the skin in smallpox; scar left by this
pock-marked

pocket (to put into a) small bag sewn into a garment
pocketbook pocketed pocketful pocketing pocket-knife pocket-knives pocket-money

pod long case of fruit or seed on a pea, bean, etc.
podded podding

podgy short and fat
podgier podgiest podgily podginess

podium small raised platform
podia or *podiums*

poem verse composition
poet poetaster poetess poetic poetical poetically poetry

po-faced (*informal*) with a solemn, humourless face

pogrom organized persecution

poignant sharply distressing; keen
poignancy poignantly

poinsettia kind of plant with large scarlet petal-like leaves

point dot; position; sharp tip; aim; to direct or indicate
point-blank pointer pointless pointsman point-to-point

pointillism artistic technique

poise composure; (to) balance
poising

poison (to give) deadly substance
poisoner poisonous

poke to thrust or jab
poking

poker[1] card-game

poker[2] metal rod used to stir a fire

poky cramped
pokier pokiest pokily pokiness

Poland country in Central Europe
Pole Polish

polar of the North or South Pole

polarity condition of having opposite forces, tendencies, or properties

polarize or **polarise** to (cause to) acquire polarity
polarization or *polarisation* *polarizing* or *polarising*

polder area of low land reclaimed from water, as in the Netherlands

pole[1] long thin rounded piece of wood or metal; measure of length
pole-jump pole-vault

pole[2] either of the ends of the earth's axis; either of the terminals of an electric cell

poleaxe (US **poleax**) (to strike with a) battleaxe
poleaxing

polecat kind of flesh-eating mammal

polemic controversial (argument)
polemical polemically polemicist

police civil force with the duty of maintaining public order; to control
policeman police-officer policewoman policing

policy[1] course of action
policies

policy[2] document setting out insurance contract

policies policyholder

polio short for **poliomyelitis**

poliomyelitis viral infection of the central nervous system that may result in paralysis

polish (substance used) to make smooth and shiny by rubbing
polishes polisher

Polish of Poland

politburo executive committee of Communist Party, esp. in former USSR

polite well-mannered; courteous
politely politeness politer politest

politic wise or shrewd

politicize or **politicise** to give a political tone to
politicization or *politicisation politicizing* or *politicising*

politics study or art of government
political politically politician

polity form of government
polities

polka lively Bohemian dance; to dance this
polkas polkaed polkaing

poll casting of votes at an election; survey of public opinion; to cast a vote

pollack or **pollock** kind of food-fish

pollard animal without its horns; tree with its branches cut off

pollen fine grains produced by the anther of a flower that fertilize the ovules

pollinate to put pollen on the stigma of a flower; to fertilize like this

pollute to make dirty; to contaminate
pollutant polluting pollution

polo game resembling hockey, played on horseback

polonaise (music for a ceremonial) Polish dance

polonium radioactive element

poltergeist noisy mischievous spirit

poly short for **polytechnic**

poly- (*prefix*) many

polyandry practice of being married to more that 1 husband at a time
polyandrous

polyanthus kind of hybrid primrose
polyanthuses

polychromatic multicoloured

polyester kind of synthetic material

polygamy practice of being married to more than 1 wife at a time
polygamous

polyglot (person) knowing many languages
polyglottal

polygon plane figure with many sides
polygonal

polygraph lie detector

polyhedron solid figure with many sides
polyhedrons or *polyhedra polyhedral*

polymath very learned person

polymer chemical compound of long chain molecules formed from simpler molecules
polymerization or *polymerisation*
polymerize or *polymerise*

polymorphous having many different forms
polymorphism

Polynesia group of Pacific islands
Polynesian

polynomial of 2 or more terms

polyp simple organism with a hollow cylindrical body; projecting growth of tissue

polyphony music with 2 or more relatively independent voice parts
polyphonic polyphonous

polystyrene synthetic thermoplastic material

polysyllable word consisting of more than 3 syllables
polysyllabic

polytechnic college offering courses in many subjects, esp. with practical emphasis

polytheism worship of more than 1 god
polytheistic

polythene light plastic material

polyunsaturated of a kind of animal or vegetable fat

polyurethane polymer used in foam, paint, varnish, etc.

polyvinyl chloride synthetic rubber substitute

pomade perfumed oil ointment for the hair

pomander bag or box containing aromatic substances, used to scent clothes

pomegranate kind of thick-skinned fruit with a juicy red pulp

pommel raised part on a saddle; knob at the top of a sword

pommy (*slang*) British person or immigrant in Australia or New Zealand
pommies

pomp splendour; ceremonial

pom-pom automatic cannon

pompon ornamental tuft

pompous self-important
pomposity pompously

ponce (*informal*) pimp; effeminate man; to move about effeminately

poncho kind of cloak
ponchos

pond pool of still water
pondweed

ponder to think about deeply
ponderable

ponderous cumbersome; dull

pong (*informal*) (to) stink

pontiff pope; bishop
pontifical

pontificate to speak in a dogmatic manner
pontificating

pontoon[1] kind of flat-bottomed boat; portable floating support for a bridge

pontoon[2] card-game

pony small horse
ponies ponytail pony-trekking

poodle breed of dog with curly hair

pooh expression of disgust
pooh-pooh

pool[1] small body of still water

pool[2] (to put into a) communal fund
pooled pooling

poop raised structure at the stern of a ship

poor having little money; unsatisfactory
poor-box poorhouse poorly

pop[1] (to cause to make an) explosive sound
popcorn pop-eyed popgun popped popping pop-up

pop[2] popular (music, etc.)

pope head of the Roman Catholic Church
popery popish

poplar slender tree

poplin strong cotton fabric

poppadom thin round crisp dough, eaten with Indian food

poppet term of affection

poppy kind of plant, esp. with red flowers
poppies

poppycock (*informal*) nonsense

populace (common) people

popular commonly liked; of the people
popularity popularly

popularize or **popularise** to make popular
popularization or *popularisation*
popularizing or *popularising*

populate to inhabit
populating population populous

porcelain high-quality translucent ceramic ware

porch enclosed covered entrance to a house
porches

porcine of pigs

porcupine kind of rodent with a body covering of sharp spines

pore[1] small opening in the skin

pore[2] (**pore over**) to study closely
poring

pork flesh of pigs used as food
porky

pornography books, photographs, etc. designed to arouse sexual excitement
pornographer pornographic

porous able to absorb liquids
porosity porously

porphyry igneous rock containing many large crystals set in a rock-mass
porphyries

porpoise kind of blunt-snouted sea mammal related to the whale

porridge dish made by heating and thickening oatmeal in milk or water

porringer small bowl from which porridge, soup, etc. are eaten

port[1] (town or city with a) harbour

port[2] left side of a ship or aircraft when facing forward
porthole

port[3] sweet fortified Portuguese wine

portable able to be carried easily
portability portably

portage transport of boats or goods overland between navigable bodies of water

portal large impressive entrance

portcullis iron grating at a castle gateway

portend to foreshadow
portent portentous

porter[1] doorman

porter[2] person who carries baggage at a railway station or hotel

porterhouse special cut of beefsteak

portfolio flat case for holding drawings, etc.; investor's securities; duties of a government minister
portfolios

portico covered entrance or walkway supported by pillars
porticoes or *porticos porticoed*

portion part or bit; helping of food; to divide

portly round and stout
portlier portliest portliness

portmanteau travelling trunk with 2 compartments; word made up of 2 words
portmanteaus or *portmanteaux*

portrait picture or description of a person
portraitist portraiture

portray to make a portrait; to describe
portrayal portrayed portraying

Portugal country in SW Europe
Portuguese

pose (to place in a) particular position; to pretend
poser poseur poseuse posing

posh (*informal*) smart

posit to postulate
posited positing

position (to put in a) particular place
positional

positive definite; explicit; absolute; type of electric charge; photographic image; greater than zero *positively positiveness*

positivism philosophical doctrine
positivist

positron positively charged particle like an electron

posse (US) body of men who may be called upon to keep order

possess to own; to take control of
possesses possession possessive possessively possessiveness possessor

possible capable of existing or being done
possibility possibilities possibly

post[1] length of wood, metal, etc. fixed into the ground; to fasten a notice to a board, etc.

post[2] place where a soldier is stationed; to station or appoint

post[3] system for delivering letters and parcels; to send by post
postage postal postbag postbox postcard postcode post-free postman postmark postmaster postmistress post-paid postwoman

post- (*prefix*) after
post-classical postwar

postdate to date a cheque, etc. with a date later than the actual one
postdating

poster placard or large notice

poste restante post that is intended for collection from a post office

posterior at the back or behind something; following

posterity future generations

postern back door or gate

postgraduate (of a) student pursuing advanced studies after a first degree

post-haste with great haste

posthumous received or published after someone's death; born after the death of the father
posthumously

postilion or **postillion** person who rides the near-side horse drawing a coach, esp. when there is no coachman

post meridiem (*Latin*) after noon

post-mortem examination of a body to determine the cause of death

postnatal happening after giving birth

postpone to delay until later
postponement postponing

postscript message added at the end of a letter after the signature

postulate to assume to be true
postulating postulation

posture manner in which one stands, sits, etc.; to assume a posture
posturer posturing

posy small bunch of flowers
posies

pot[1] rounded container used esp. for cooking; to put in a pot; to shorten
pot-bellied pot-belly pot-boiler pothole potholer potholing potted potting potting-shed

pot[2] (*slang*) cannabis; marijuana

potable drinkable

potash potassium carbonate

potassium light silvery metallic element

potato plant grown for its edible tubers
potatoes

poteen illicit Irish whiskey

potent powerful
potency potentate

potential possible but not yet realized
potentiality potentially

pother fuss or disturbance

potion drink

pot-pourri mixture of dried herbs and petals; medley of musical or literary items

potsherd broken fragment of pottery

potter[1] to occupy oneself aimlessly
potterer

potter[2] person who makes earthenware ornaments, etc.
pottery potteries

potty[1] (*informal*) crazy; silly
pottier pottiest pottiness

potty[2] chamber-pot for a child

pouch (to place in a) small flexible bag or container

pouffe or **pouf** large stuffed cushion used as a seat or footrest

poultice (to apply a) soft moist heated dressing to sores, etc.
poulticing

poultry domesticated birds kept for eggs or meat
poulterer poultryman

pounce to swoop down on suddenly
pouncing

pound[1] unit of weight, 16 ounces; unit of money in the UK and various other countries
poundage

pound[2] to crush

pound[3] enclosure for stray animals, or vehicles removed by the police

pour to (cause to) flow
pourer

pout to thrust out the lips
pouter

poverty state of being poor
poverty-stricken

powder fine loose dry particles; to cover with or reduce to powder
powder-puff powder-room powdery

power ability to do something; force or authority; to supply power to
powerboat powered powerful powerfully powerhouse powerless powerlessly powerlessness power-station

powwow meeting or talk

Powys Welsh county

practicable capable of being carried out
practicability practicably
SEE PANEL

---

practicable or practical?

Something that is *practicable* is capable of being carried out: *comply with all the legal responsibilities as soon as is reasonably practicable.*

Practical has a wide range of meanings: 'useful and realistic and likely to be successful': *offer practical suggestions to help solve the crisis;* 'concerned with action, rather than theory': *a practical guide to home economics.*

Someone can be described as *practical* if they are skilled at doing or making things or if they make down-to-earth decisions: *All that is needed here is some practical common sense.*

---

practical of action; not theoretical; sensible; skilled at doing or making things
practicality practicalities
SEE PANEL at **practicable**

practically in a practical way; nearly

practice regular repeated exercise; method or habit; professional business of law or medicine
practician practitioner
SEE PANEL

---

practice or practise?

Practice is a noun: *Practice makes perfect; a medical practice; the difference between what was supposed to happen and what happens in practice.*

Practise is a verb: *keep on practising the piano; practise medicine; practising Christians.* In American English, the verb is spelled *practice.*

---

practise (US **practice**) to carry out; to perform regularly to develop one's skill
practising (US *practicing*)
SEE PANEL at **practice**

praesidium see **presidium**

pragmatic concerned with practicalities; realistic
pragmatically pragmatism pragmatist

prairie area of level treeless grassland

praise to express a favourable opinion of; to extol God
praiseworthy praising

praline confection of nuts

pram 4-wheeled baby carriage

prance to move in a lively manner
prancing

prang (*informal*) (to have a) crash in a car, etc.

prank mischievous trick

prate to talk foolishly (about)
prater prating

prattle to talk in an idle or childish manner
prattler prattling

prawn edible 10-legged shellfish like a large shrimp

praxis practice, as opposed to theory
praxes or *praxises*

pray to speak to God; to entreat
prayed prayer praying

pre- (*prefix*) before
prearrange Precambrian precast precook predate pre-exist preheat prepack prepackage prerecord pre-school pre-select pre-set pre-shrunk prestressed pre-tax pre-war

preach to deliver a sermon
preacher preaching preaches preachy

preamble preliminary or introductory statement

prebendary title of the holder of a cathedral benefice

precarious risky; uncertain
precariously

precaution measure taken to avoid an undesirable event
precautionary

precede to go or come before
precedence
SEE PANEL

---

precede or proceed?

Precede means 'to go or come before': *The earthquake was preceded by several minor tremors; Apply by 30 September in the year preceding the intended date of entry; For further details see the preceding page.*

Something *proceeds* when it goes on, without stopping: *Unfortunately I am unable to proceed with this work; The discrepancy must be investigated before we proceed any further; to proceed at a slow pace along the track.* If you *proceed* to do something, you go on to do it after doing something else: *The officer proceeded to ask my name and address.*

---

precedent instance of something that may be used to justify something similar later

precentor clergyman responsible for choral services in cathedrals

precept rule or maxim
preceptive

precession turning about on the axis of a line that itself is the axis of a turning body

precinct (enclosed) area; (US) administrative district

precious loved; valuable; very fussy
preciously preciousness

precipice very steep rock face
precipitous

precipitant rash or hasty
precipitance precipitantly

precipitate to cause to happen too soon; to fling; to separate from a solution; to condense and fall as snow, rain, etc.; hasty
precipitable precipitately precipitating precipitation
SEE PANEL

---

precipitate or precipitous?

The adjective *precipitate* means 'hasty': *make a precipitate decision that is later regretted.*

Precipitous is used to describe a steep slope (*a precipitous cliff*) or a sudden change (*a precipitous drop in the price of shares*).

---

precipitous very steep; precipitate

precipitously precipitousness
SEE PANEL at **precipitate**

précis (to make a) summary
précised précising

precise exact; accurate; careful
precisely precision precisionism

preclude to make impossible; to exclude
precluding preclusion preclusive

precocious very advanced in development
precociously precocity

preconceive to form an idea beforehand
preconceiving preconception

precondition necessary condition

precursor predecessor; forerunner
precursory

predator predatory animal; person who exploits others

predatory preying on other animals for food
predatorily predatoriness

predecessor former holder of an office or position

predestine to ordain or determine in advance
predestination predestining

predetermine to arrange or decide beforehand
predeterminable predeterminate predetermination predetermining

predicament difficult situation

predicate (*grammar*) part of the sentence describing the subject; to declare
predicating predication predicative

predict to foretell
predictability predictable prediction predictive predictor

predilection preference

predispose to make inclined or susceptible (to)
predisposing predisposition

predominate to be greater in number, intensity, or power
predominance predominant predominantly predominating

pre-eminent outstanding
pre-eminence pre-eminently

pre-empt to render useless by acting in advance: to buy before the right to buy is given to others
pre-empting pre-emption pre-emptive

preen (*of a bird*) to clean its feathers with the beak

prefabricate to manufacture parts of a building for assembly on the site
prefabricating prefabrication

preface (to provide an) introductory statement
prefacing prefatory

prefect older secondary school pupil with authority; chief official of department in some countries
prefectorial prefecture

prefer to like better; to bring charges before a law-court
preferable preferably preference preferred preferring

preferential showing preference; biased
preferentially

preferment promotion to a higher office

prefigure to represent in advance; to foresee
prefiguration prefigurement prefiguring

prefix part of a word that goes in front of a word to change its meaning
prefixes

pregnant having a child or young developing in the womb; meaningful
pregnancy pregnancies pregnantly

prehensile adapted for grasping

prehistoric or **prehistorical** of the time before recorded history
prehistorically prehistory

prejudge to judge in advance, esp. without full information

prejudice opinion formed without full

information; bias; (to cause to have an) unreasonable dislike
prejudicial prejudicing

prelate bishop, abbot, etc. of high rank
prelacy prelacies prelatic

preliminary preparatory (item)
preliminaries preliminarily

prelude introductory music, action, etc.

premarital (*of sexual relations*) occurring before marriage

premature happening or done too early
prematurely prematurity

premeditate to consider carefully in advance
premeditating premeditation

premenstrual occurring before a menstrual period

premier prime minister; first in importance
premiership

première first performance of a film, play, etc.; to give a première of
premièred premièring

premise[1] to state by way of introduction
premising

premises building and land

premiss or **permise**[2] statement from which a conclusion may be drawn
premisses or *premises*

premium regular sum paid for insurance policy; bonus
premiums

premolar tooth growing between the molar and canine teeth

premonition uneasy feeling about something, esp. unpleasant, about to happen
premonitory

preoccupy to engage the total attention of
preoccupation preoccupied preoccupies preoccupying

preordain to ordain beforehand
preordination

prepare to make ready; to assemble
preparation preparatory preparedness preparer

prepay to pay for in advance
prepaid prepaying prepayment

preponderate to be greater than in amount, power, etc.
preponderance preponderantly preponderating

preposition word used with a noun or pronoun to show direction, time, etc.
prepositional

prepossess to prejudice in favour of a person or thing
prepossesses prepossession

prepossessing attractive

preposterous absurd or ridiculous
preposterously preposterousness

prepuce foreskin

Pre-Raphaelite of a group of English artists

prerequisite (something) required as a prior condition
SEE PANEL at **perquisite**

prerogative exclusive right or privilege, esp. because of rank

presage (to be a) sign of a future event
presaging

presbyopia failing of near sight in old age
presbyopic

presbyter elder or priest
presbytery

Presbyterian (of a) Protestant denomination governed by elders
Presbyterianism

presbytery eastern part of church chancel; residence of a Roman Catholic priest
presbyteries

prescience having knowledge of future events
prescient

prescribe to set down a rule; to recommend the use of medicine
prescribable prescribing prescriptive
SEE PANEL

prescribe or proscribe?
Doctors *prescribe* medicine or treatment when they recommend a particular medicine or course of treatment: *prescribe antibacterial eye drops to clear up the condition.* If an action is *prescribed*, it is stated in a style that it must be carried out: *follow the procedures prescribed by the relevant sections of the Local Authorities Acts.*

If something is *proscribed*, use of it is prohibited: *a list of proscribed organizations/drugs.*

prescription prescribing, esp. of medicine

presence being present; dignified bearing

present[1] existing now; (of the) time that is now
present-day presently

present[2] gift; to introduce or offer
presentable presentably presentation

presentiment premonition

preserve to keep safe; to protect from decay; fruit jam
preservable preservation preservative preserver preserving

preside to have authority or guidance over a meeting, discussion, etc.
presiding

president head of state of a republic; leader of a meeting, club, etc.
presidency presidential presidentship

presidium or **praesidium** permanent executive Communist committee

press to push steadily against; to force; newspapers, etc. collectively; machine for pressing
presses press-button press-gang press-stud press-up

pressure pressing force; urgent demands

pressurize or **pressurise** to increase the pressure on
pressurization or *pressurisation*
pressurized or *pressurised*

prestige good reputation gained from success, wealth, etc.
prestigious prestigiously

presto (*music*) quickly

presume to suppose; to take advantage of
presumable presumably presuming presumption presumptive

presumptuous bold; forward
presumptuously presumptuousness

presuppose to suppose in advance; to require necessarily
presupposing presupposition

pretence (US **pretense**) pretending; false show or claim

pretend to create a false appearance of
pretendedly pretender

pretension false claim; excuse

pretentious claiming to be important
pretentiously pretentiousness

preterite (US **preterit**) (*grammar*) past tense

preternatural abnormal; extraordinary
preternaturally

pretext false reason

prettify to make pretty
prettified prettifies prettifying

pretty attractive; quite
prettier prettiest prettily prettiness pretty-pretty

pretzel kind of crisp glazed salted biscuit

prevail to be superior; to occur widely
prevailing

prevalent occurring widely
prevalence prevalently

prevaricate to speak evasively or falsely intending to deceive *prevaricating prevarication prevaricator*

prevent to stop from happening or doing
preventable prevention preventive preventative

preview to view a film, play, etc. in advance of performance to the general public; such an advance view

previous coming before
previously previousness

prey animal hunted as food; to hunt or kill as prey
preyed preying

price sum of money for which something may be bought or sold; to put a price on
priceless pricelessness price-list pricey

prick to make a small mark or hole in with a sharp point; pricking

prickle sharp pointed spike on a plant; to feel a stinging sensation
prickling prickly

pride conceit; (to have a sense of) self-respect; group of lions
priding

priest (*fem.* **priestess**) clergyman
priesthood priestlike priestly

prig self-righteous person
priggery priggish priggishly

prim affectedly proper; prudish
primly primmer primmest primness

prima ballerina leading female ballet dancer
prima ballerinas

primacy state of being first
primacies

prima donna leading female operatic singer

primaeval see **primeval**

prima facie at first appearance

primal original; first

primary most important; first; first person; preliminary US election
primaries primarily

primate member of the order of mammals that includes human beings; archbishop

prime[1] most important

prime[2] to prepare for use
priming

primer[1] book for teaching children to read

primer[2] material used in priming a surface

primeval or **primaeval** of the first age of the world
primevally or *primaevally*

primitive of an early stage of development; unsophisticated
primitively primitivism primitivist

primogenitor ancestor

primogeniture being the first-born

primordial primeval; fundamental

primrose kind of plant with pale yellow flowers

primula group of plants that includes the cowslip and primrose

Primus (*trademark*) portable cooking stove

prince male member of a royal family, esp. son of the sovereign; ruler of a state
princedom princely

princeling petty or insignificant prince

princess female member of a royal family, esp. daughter of the sovereign; wife of a prince
princesses

principal chief; head of a school or other institution; sum of money on which interest is paid
principally
SEE PANEL

---

principal or principle?
The noun *principal* is used to refer to the headteacher of a school, the person in charge of a college, etc.: *Applications to enter the school*

should in the first instance be addressed to the Principal. Financially, a *principal* is a sum of money invested in a bank or lent to a person on which interest is paid: *keep the principal intact while spending the interest.*

A *principle* is a rule or standard, a basic truth, or a general law: *moral principles; the principles of scientific study; the guiding principle behind the legislation.*

---

principality state or land ruled by a prince
principalities

principle rule or standard, as of general behaviour; basic truth; general law
principled
SEE PANEL at **principal**

print to reproduce books, etc. by applying ink to paper, etc.
printable printer printing printing-press printout

prior[1] previous

prior[2] (*fem.* **prioress**) head of a priory

priority (thing taking) precedence
priorities prioritize or *prioritise*

priory religious house
priories

prise or **prize** to force open
prising or *prizing*

prism solid body whose sides are parallelograms and whose 2 ends are the same shape and size
prismatic

prison building in which criminals are confined
prisoner

prissy prim and fussy
prissier prissiest prissily prissiness

pristine undamaged; pure; of the earliest period

private of an individual, not public; confidential; soldier of the lowest rank
privacy privateer privately

privation loss of necessities
privative

privatize or **privatise** to assign to private ownership
privatization or *privatisation privatizing* or *privatising*

privet kind of shrub much used for hedges

privilege special right or advantage
privileged

privy knowing something secret
privily

prize[1] reward; to value highly
prize-fight prize-fighter prize-money prize-winner prizing

prize[2] see **prise**

pro[1] (*informal*) short for **professional**
pros

pro[2] in favour of
pros

pro- (*prefix*) in favour of
pro-life

proactive actively initiating changes

probable likely to happen or be true
probability probabilities probably

probate official process of proving that a will is valid

probation system in which offenders are supervised outside prison; trial period
probational probationally probationary probationer

probe to examine closely; slender surgical instrument
probing

probity integrity

problem something that is difficult to solve, understand, or deal with
problematic problematically

proboscis elephant's trunk; long tubular part of an invertebrate
proboscises

procedure (established) method
procedural procedurally

proceed to go on; to continue or advance
proceeding
SEE PANEL at **precede**

proceeds money or profit obtained

process series of actions; method; legal action; to treat or deal with
processes processor

procession line of people or vehicles moving forward in an orderly manner
processional

proclaim to announce publicly
proclamation proclamatory

proclivity inclination or tendency
proclivities

procrastinate to put off till later
procrastinating procrastination procrastinator

procreate to beget
procreating procreation procreator

proctor supervisor, as at certain universities
proctorial

procurator agent

procurator-fiscal Scottish law officer

procure to obtain; to provide a woman to act as a prostitute
procurable procural procuration procurement procurer procuress procuring

prod to poke
prodded prodder prodding

prodigal wasteful
prodigality prodigally

prodigious vast; amazing
prodigiously prodigiousness

prodigy unusual or exceptional person, esp. a child
prodigies

produce to bring into existence; to manufacture; something produced
producer producible producing production

product something produced; result of multiplying numbers

productive producing goods or services; fertile or fruitful
productively productivity

profane showing disrespect for holy things; secular; to treat profanely
profanation profanely profaning profanity profanities

profess to state openly; to pretend
professedly professes

profession something professed; occupation
professional professionalism professionally

professor highest-ranking academic in a university
professorial professoriate professorship

proffer to offer
proffered proffering

proficient skilled
proficiency proficiently

profile side view of a person's head; brief outline

profit gain or benefit, esp. financial; to gain a profit
profitability profitable profitably profited profiteer profiting profit-making profit-sharing

profiterole cream case of choux pastry

profligate recklessly extravagant; very immoral
profligacy

pro forma (*Latin*) as a matter of form; kind of invoice

profound very deep
profoundly profundity

profuse abundant; lavish
profusely profuseness profusion

progenitor ancestor or founder

progeny descendant or descendants
progenies

progesterone steroid sex hormone

prognosis forecast, as of the likely course
prognoses prognostic

prognosticate to predict
prognosticating prognostication

program set of instructions for a computer; to supply a computer with a program; (US) programme
programmer programming

programme (US **program**) plan or list of items or events; to plan as a programme
programmed (US *programed*)
programming (US *programing*)

progress (to) advance
progresses progression progressive

prohibit to forbid
prohibition prohibitionism prohibitionist prohibitive prohibitory

project to jut out; (to plan a) scheme
projection projectional projectionist projective projector

projectile object thrown forward; missile

prolapse sinking or falling down

prolegomena introductory remarks

proletariat working class
proletarian

proliferate to reproduce or grow rapidly
proliferating proliferation

prolific very fruitful
prolifically

prolix long-winded
prolixity

prologue (US **prolog**) introduction, as to a play

prolong to lengthen
prolongation

prom (*Brit informal*) promenade (concert); (US *informal*) formal high school or college dance

promenade paved walkway on the sea front

prominent conspicuous; distinguished; jutting-out
prominence prominently

promiscuous indulging in many casual sexual relationships
promiscuity promiscuously

promise (to give a) declaration assuring that one will do or not do something
promising

promissory containing or showing a promise

promontory headland
promontories

promote to raise in position or rank; to further or encourage
promoter promoting promotion promotional

prompt punctual; to help an actor remember the next words
prompter promptitude promptly

promulgate to declare openly
promulgating promulgation promulgator

prone lying face down; inclined to

prong sharp-pointed part of a fork

pronoun word used in place of noun
pronominal

pronounce to articulate; to declare officially
pronounceable pronouncement pronouncing pronunciation

proof evidence that shows something to be true; measure of the strength of alcoholic drink; trial printing impression
proofreader proofreading

prop[1] (to) support
propped propping

prop[2] object used on a stage or film set

propaganda information published to help or hinder the cause of a government or movement
propagandism propagandist

propagandize or **propagandise** to subject to propaganda
propagandizing propagandising

propagate to (cause to) reproduce
propagating propagation propagator

propane hydrocarbon gas found in petroleum and used as a fuel

propel to drive or move forwards
propelled propeller propelling

propellant something that propels

propellent capable of propelling

propensity natural tendency
propensities

proper suitable or right
properly properness

property something owned; land; quality or feature
properties

prophecy something prophesied; ability to prophesy
prophecies
SEE PANEL

---

prophecy or prophesy?
Prophecy is the noun; *prophesy* the verb: *a prophecy foretelling the end of the world; fulfil prophecies of the coming Messiah; prophesy that the government will fall by the autumn.*

---

prophesy to foretell (as if) by divine inspiration
prophesied prophesier prophesies prophesying prophetic prophetically
SEE PANEL at **prophecy**

prophet (*fem.* **prophetess**) person who prophesies

prophylaxis measure taken to prevent a disease
prophylactic prophylactically

propinquity nearness
propinquities

propitiate to appease
propitiating propitiation propitiator propitiatory

propitious favourable
propitiously propitiousness

proponent person who supports or puts forward a proposal

proportion part or ratio
proportional proportionality proportionally proportionate proportionately

propose to put forward for consideration; to make an offer of marriage
proposal proposer proposing

proposition proposal or statement; to suggest sexual intercourse to

propound to offer for consideration
propounder

proprietary belonging to a proprietor; produced and marketed under a trade name

proprietor (*fem.* **proprietress**) owner of a business
proprietorship

propriety correctness of behaviour or morals
proprieties

propulsion propelling
propulsive propulsory

pro rata in proportion

prorogue to terminate the meeting of parliament without dissolving it
prorogation prorogued proroguing

prosaic dull; ordinary
prosaically

proscenium front part of the stage
prosceniums or *proscenia*

proscribe to condemn; to outlaw
proscribing proscription proscriptive
SEE PANEL at **prescribe**

prose ordinary written or spoken language, not verse
prosy

prosecute to take legal action against
prosecuting prosecution prosecutor

proselyte convert

proselytize or **proselytise** to (try to) convert to a religion
proselytization or *proselytisation proselytizer* or *proselytiser proselytizing* or *proselytising*

prosody study of verse metre
prosodic prosodist

prospect view; expectation or possibility; to explore in search of
prospective prospector

prospectus formal statement describing a business undertaking or institution
prospectuses

prosper to flourish
prosperity

prosperous wealthy
prosperously prosperousness

prostate gland surrounding the neck of the bladder
SEE PANEL

prostate or prostrate?
The *prostate* gland is the gland situated around the neck of the bladder in male mammals: *go into hospital to have his prostate removed.*

The adjective *prostrate* means 'lying flat on the ground, face downward; overcome or devastated': *lie prostrate on the cold stone floor; be prostrate with grief.*

prostitute person who may be hired for sexual intercourse
prostitution

prostrate lying flat, esp. face downwards; to take up a prostrate or submissive position
prostrating prostration
SEE PANEL at **prostate**

protagonist main character in a play, etc.

protean able to assume different shapes

protect to defend; to help home industries
protection protectionism protectionist protective

protector (*fem.* **protectress**) person or thing that protects
protectorate

protégé (*fem.* **protégée**) a person under the protection of a patron
protégés (fem. *protégées*)

protein complex organic compound that is an essential constituent of all living cells
proteinaceous

protest (to make a) statement or expression of disapproval
protestation protester

Protestant member of any Christian group that accepts the principles of the Reformation
Protestantism

protocol formal procedure or etiquette

proton atomic particle with a positive electric charge

protoplasm complex of substances in a living cell
protoplasmic

prototype original model
prototypal

protozoan or **protozoon** minute single-celled animal
protozoa protozoal protozoic

protract to make longer
protraction protractor

protractor mathematical instrument for drawing and measuring angles

protrude to project
protruding protrusion protrusive

protuberant swelling
protuberance protuberantly

proud conceited or haughty; having self-respect
proudly

prove to provide proof of; to test the quality of
provable proven proving

provenance origin or source

Provençal Romance language of SE France

provender fodder

proverb short wise saying
proverbial proverbially

provide to supply
provider providing

providence God, considered as sustaining and guiding the creation; foresight or thrift
provident providential providentially

province administrative division of a country; area or sphere of an activity
provincial provincialism provincially

provision act of providing

provisional temporary or conditional
provisionally

Provisional of the terrorist wing of the Irish Republican Army

provisions food and drink

proviso condition or stipulation
provisos or *provisoes provisory*

provoke to anger; to stimulate
provocation provocative provocatively provoking

provost head of any of certain colleges; church dignitary; main magistrate of a Scottish burgh

prow bow of a ship or boat

prowess great skill or bravery

prowl to move about stealthily, esp. before attacking
prowler

proximity nearness
proximate

proximo of the next month

proxy (person with the) authority to vote or act on behalf of another
proxies

prude person who is excessively proper, esp. in sexual matters
prudery prudish

prudent wise or cautious
prudence prudential prudentially prudently

prune[1] dried plum

prune[2] to trim by cutting away parts of a tree or shrub
pruner pruning

prurient obscene or lustful
prurience

pruritus itching
pruritic

pry to investigate in an over-inquisitive manner
pried pries prying

psalm sacred song in the Bible
psalmist psalmodic psalmodist psalmody psalter

psaltery ancient stringed instrument
psalteries

psephology study of elections
psephological psephologist

pseudepigrapha writings ascribed to someone other than the real author

pseudo- (*prefix*) false
pseudo-intellectual

pseudonym name used by an author

psittacosis viral disease of parrots

psoriasis kind of skin disease
psoriatic

psyche human soul, spirit, or mind

psychedelic (*of drugs*) causing hallucinations; having vivid complex patterns

psychiatry study of mental disorders
psychiatric psychiatrist

psychic of the mind or soul; of powers that seem supernatural; responsive to such powers
psychical psychically

psychoanalyse (US **psychoanalyze**) to treat the mental disorders in a person
psychoanalysing (US *psychoanalyzing*) *psychoanalysis psychoanalyst psychoanalytic*

psychology study of the mind and mental processes
psychological psychologically psychologist

psychopath person with severe personality disorder
psychopathic psychopathy

psychopathology study of mental disorders
psychopathological

psychosis severe mental disorder
psychoses psychotic

psychosomatic of the mind and the body

psychotherapy treatment of disease by psychological methods
psychotherapeutic psychotherapist

ptarmigan grouse whose plumage turns white in winter

pterodactyl extinct flying reptile

ptomaine poisonous compound formed in decaying matter

pub (*informal*) public house

puberty stage at which a person's sexual maturity develops
pubescence pubescent

pubic of the lower part of the abdomen, at the front of the pelvis

public for people generally, not private; people in the community
public-spirited

publican person who keeps a public house

publication act of publishing

publicity notices, etc., to gain public attention

publicize or **publicise** to bring to public notice
publicist publicizing or *publicising*

publish to produce a book, etc. and sell and distribute to the public
publishable publisher publishes

puce brownish-purple

puck[1] hard rubber disc used in ice hockey

puck[2] mischievous spirit
puckish

pucker to gather into folds or wrinkles

pudding dessert, esp. cooked mixture of flour, milk, and eggs

puddle small pool of rainwater
puddly

puddling conversion of pig iron into wrought iron

pudendum external human genital organ, esp. of a female
pudenda

puerile childish; immature
puerility

puerperal of childbirth

puff short emission of air, smoke, etc.; to emit smoke, etc.; to pant; to swell
puff-adder puff-ball puffy

puffin kind of sea bird with a large brightly coloured bill

pug breed of dog with a short wrinkled nose
pug-nosed

pugilism boxing
pugilist pugilistic

pugnacious aggressive
pugnaciously pugnacity

puissance show-jumping competition; power

puissant powerful
puissance

puke (*slang*) (to) vomit
puking

pukka real or genuine

pulchritude (*formal*) beauty
pulchritudinous

pull to exert force on something so as to draw it to the source of the force; power or influence
puller pull-in pull-out

pullet young hen

pulley wheel with a grooved rim, used with a rope, etc. to lift heavy loads
pulleys

Pullman luxurious railway carriage

pullover knitted garment that is pulled on over the head

pulmonary of the lungs

pulp soft fleshy part of a fruit, etc.; soft shapeless mass
pulpwood pulpy

pulpit enclosed raised platform in a church, from which sermons are preached

pulsar celestial object that emits regular radiation pulses

pulsate to throb or vibrate
pulsating pulsation pulsator pulsatory

pulse[1] rhythmic throbbing of the arteries by the contractions of the heart; to throb rhythmically
pulse-rate pulsing

pulse[2] edible seeds growing in pods

pulverize or **pulverise** to reduce to powder
pulverization or *pulverisation pulverizing* or *pulverising*

puma large American mammal of the cat family

pumice light porous volcanic rock
pumice-stone

pummel to strike repeatedly with the fists
pummelled (US *pummeled*) *pummelling* (US *pummeling*)

pump[1] device for forcing liquid, air, etc. into or out of something; to transfer by using a pump

pump[2] kind of light shoe

pumpernickel dark slightly sour wholemeal rye bread

pumpkin kind of (plant with a) large round fruit having an orange rind

pun (to make a) play on words
punned punning

punch[1] to strike with the fist; blow with the fist
punches punchball punch-drunk punchline punch-up

punch[2] tool used to make a hole; to make such holes
punches

punch[3] mixed alcoholic drink

punctilious paying very close attention to detail
punctiliously punctiliousness

punctual arriving or happening at the agreed time
punctuality punctually

punctuate to interrupt; to add punctuation to
punctuating

punctuation marks such as a full stop and comma added to written material

puncture (to make a) small hole (in)
puncturing

pundit learn ed man or teacher

pungent sharp (to the taste)
pungency pungently

punish to cause to suffer for a crime
punishable punisher punishes punishment

punitive of punishment
punitively

Punjabi language spoken in the Punjab of NW India and Pakistan

punk of a style of music, fashion, or behaviour

punnet small basket in which strawberries, etc. are sold

punster person who is fond of making puns

punt[1] long narrow flat-bottomed boat, propelled by a pole; to propel such a boat with a pole

punt[2] to kick a ball after it has dropped

from the hands and before it hits the ground

punt[3] to gamble
punter

puny weak and small
punier puniest punily puniness

pup young dog

pupa chrysalis
pupae or *pupas pupal*

pupil[1] schoolchild taught by a teacher

pupil[2] opening in the centre of the iris
pupilar pupillary

puppet small doll moved by strings or one that fits over the hand
puppeteer puppetry

purblind nearly blind; obtuse

purchase to buy; something that is bought
purchasable purchaser purchasing

purdah keeping of Muslim and Hindu women in seclusion; screen used for this

pure free from other, esp. contaminating, materials
pure-blooded pure-bred purely purity

purée pulped and sieved fruit, vegetables, etc.

purgatory (*in Roman Catholic belief*) place after death where the soul is purified
purgatories purgatorial

purge to get rid of impurities in
purgative purging

purify to make pure
purification purified purifies purifying

purist person who stresses correct forms, esp. in language

puritan person with strict moral and religious principles
puritanical puritanically puritanism

purl (to make a) knitting stitch

purlieus surroundings; outskirts

purloin to steal
purloiner

purple colour made by mixing red and blue
purplish purply

purport to claim to be; meaning

purpose reason or intention for something; determination; to intend
purpose-built purposeful purposeless purposely purposing purposive

purr (to make a) low vibrating sound in the throat

purse small bag for money; to pucker the lips
purse-strings pursing

purser officer on a ship in charge of accounts

pursue to chase in order to catch; to carry on
pursuance pursuant pursued pursuer pursuing pursuit

purulent of or containing pus
purulence

purvey to provide food
purveyance purveyor

purview range or limit

pus yellowish fluid produced by inflammation

push to exert force on something so as to move it away from the source of the force; act of pushing
pushes push-bike push-button pushchair pusher pushing pushover push-start push-up pushy

pusillanimous timid; fearful
pusillanimity

puss (*informal*) cat
pussy

pustule small spot on the skin containing pus
pustular pustulate

put to place in a certain position; to throw

put-down putting put-up put-you-up

putative reputed to be
putatively

putrefy to decompose or not
putrefaction putrefied putrefies putrefying putrescence putrescent

putrid decomposed; foul
putridity putridly

putsch (*German*) revolutionary attempt or attack

putt to strike a golf ball lightly so that it rolls towards or into a hole
putter putting putting-green

putty stiff paste used to fix glass in windows

puzzle game designed to test one's skill; to perplex
puzzlement puzzler puzzling

pygmy or **pigmy** very short person, esp. of equatorial African tribe
pygmies or *pigmies*

pyjamas (US **pajamas**) loose lightweight jacket and trousers for sleeping in

pylon large tower-like structure that supports overhead power cables

pyorrhoea (US **pyorrhea**) discharge of pus

pyramid structure with flat square base with sloping sides that meet at a point
pyramidal

pyre pile of wood, etc. on which a corpse is cremated

Pyrenees mountain range between France and Spain

pyrethrum chrysanthemum-like plant

Pyrex (*trademark*) kind of glass that is resistant to heat

pyrotechnics art of making fireworks; (firework) display
pyrotechnic

Pyrrhic victory victory gained at an excessive cost

python large snake that crushes its prey

Q

Qatar state in East Arabia
Qatari

quack[1] (to make the) characteristic sound of a duck

quack[2] unqualified person who claims to have medical skill
quackery quackeries quackish

quad[1] short for **quadrangle**

quad[2] short for **quadruplet**

Quadragesima first Sunday in Lent

quadrangle 4-sided open area; 4-sided figure

quadrant one-quarter of (the circumference of a) circle; instrument for measuring angles

quadraphonics system of sound reproduction using 4 channels
quadraphonic quadraphonically

quadratic (*mathematics*) having terms of the second power

quadrennium period of 4 years
quadrenniums or *quadrennia quadrennial*

quadrilateral (figure) with 4 sides

quadrille old square dance

quadriplegia paralysis of both arms and legs
quadriplegic

quadruped animal with 4 feet

quadruple to multiply by 4; having 4 parts
quadrupling

quadruplet any of 4 offspring born at 1 birth

quadruplicate fourfold; to multiply by 4; set of 4 items

quaff to drink deeply

quagmire wet muddy ground; bog

quail[1] kind of game bird

quail[2] to flinch back in fear

quaint attractively old-fashioned
quaintly quaintness

quake to tremble or shake
quaking quaky

Quaker member of the society of Friends

qualify to make eligible for; to modify the meaning of
qualifiable qualification qualified qualifier qualifies qualifying

quality characteristic; (degree of) excellence
qualities qualitative

qualm sudden anxious feeling; sudden attack of nausea

quandary predicament
quandaries

quango autonomous body set up but not controlled by the government
quangos

quantify to express as a quantity
quantifiable quantification quantified quantifier quantifies quantifying

quantity (large) amount
quantities quantitative

quantum smallest indivisible unit of energy
quanta

quarantine (to impose) isolation in order to prevent disease spreading
quarantining

quark hypothetical elementary particle

quarrel (to have an) angry disagreement
quarrelled (US *quarreled*) *quarreller* (US

quarreler) quarrelling (US *quarreling*) *quarrelsome*

quarry[1] large open pit from which building materials are excavated; to extract from a quarry
quarries quarried quarrying

quarry[2] animal or person that is hunted
quarries

quart measure of liquid capacity

quarter one of 4 equal parts; coin worth 25 cents; to cut into quarters
quarterdeck quarter-final quarter-light quartermaster

quarterly occurring, published, etc. every 3 months

quarters accommodation or lodgings

quartet or **quartette** (musical composition for a) group of 4 singers or performers

quarto book or paper size

quartz mineral consisting of crystalline silica

quasar distant star-like celestial object that emits intense levels of energy

quash to subdue or nullify
quashes

quasi- (*prefix*) seemingly; so-called

Quasimodo first Sunday after Easter

quassia kind of (drug obtained from) tropical American tree

quaternary (set) of 4

Quaternary (of the) most recent period of geological time

quatrain poem with 4 lines

quaver to shake; musical note that lasts half the length of a crotchet

quay landing-place for loading and unloading ships
quays quayside

queasy feeling as if one is about to be sick
queasier queasiest queasily queasiness

queen female sovereign ruler; wife of a king

queer odd; faint or giddy; (*informal*) homosexual (person)
queerly queerness

quell to suppress

quench to satisfy one's thirst; to extinguish a fire
quenchable quencher quenches

querulous constantly complaining
querulously querulousness

query (to) question; to express doubt about
queries queried querying

quest (to) search

question expression designed to draw out information; matter under discussion; to interrogate
questionable questionably questioner questioning

questionnaire set of questions used in gathering statistics

quetzal kind of Central American bird; money unit of Guatemala

queue line of people, etc. waiting for something; to wait in a queue
queued queuing

quibble to object to minor matters; minor objection
quibbler quibbling

quiche open savoury tart

quick performed or happening in a short time; fast-moving
quick-fire quick-freeze quickie quickly quickness quickset quickstep quick-tempered quick-witted

quicken to make or become quicker
quickened quickening

quicklime lime

quicksand sucking mass of loose wet sand

quicksilver mercury

quid (*Brit slang*) pound sterling

quid pro quo something given in exchange for another

quiescent inactive
quiescence

quiet marked by the absence of noise; peaceful
quietism quietist quietly quietude

quieten to make or become quiet
quietened

quiff lock of hair brushed up

quill large feather, formerly used for writing

quilt thick padded bed-cover; to fill like a quilt

quin short for **quintuplet**

quince kind of tree bearing hard yellowish pear-shaped fruit used in making jam

quincentenary 500th anniversary
quincentenaries quincentennial

quincunx group of 5 items arranged in the same pattern as on dice
quincunxes quincuncial

quinine bitter drug

Quinquagesima Sunday before Lent

quinquennial occurring every 5 years

quinsy tonsillitis
quinsied

quintal unit of weight

quintessence perfect example; essence in purest form
quintessential quintessentially

quintet or **quintette** (musical composition for a) group of 5 singers or performers

quintuplet any of 5 offspring born at 1 birth

quip (to make a) witty sarcastic remark
quipped quipping

quire 24 sheets of writing-paper

quirk peculiarity

quisling traitor

quit to give up; to go away from
quitted or *quit quitter quitting*

quite completely; fairly

quits on even terms

quiver[1] case for arrows

quiver[2] (to) shake or tremble
quivery

quixotic impractically idealistic
quixotically

quiz series of questions to test knowledge; to question closely
quizzes quizzed quizzer quizzing

quizzical puzzled; teasing
quizzically

quoin solid outside angle of a building

quoit ring used in a game to toss at a peg

quorum minimum number needed to be present at a meeting before business can be transacted

quota fixed share or proportion; upper limit
quotas

quote to repeat a phrase or passage; to estimate costs
quotable quotation quoting

quotidian recurring daily

quotient result obtained when one quantity is divided by another

Qur'an see **Koran**

qwerty of the standard layout on English-language keyboards

R

rabbet groove in woodwork
rabbeted

rabbi Jewish leader or teacher
rabbis rabbinical

rabbit (to hunt) long-eared burrowing animal
rabbited rabbiting rabbit-warren rabbity

rabble disorderly crowd
rabble-rouser

rabid of rabies; fanatical

rabies acute viral infectious disease

raccoon see **racoon**

race[1] (to compete in a) contest
racecourse racegoer racehorse race-meeting racer racetrack racing racing-car

race[2] group of people with common characteristics; major division of mankind
race-riot racial racialism racialist racially racism racist

rack[1] framework for storing or displaying objects; to cause to suffer
rack-and-pinion racked

rack[2] (**rack and ruin**) destruction

racket[1] or **racquet** bat with interlaced strings used in tennis, etc.

racket[2] great noise; commotion; illegal enterprise
racketeer racketeering

rackets ball game similar to squash

rack-rent (to charge an) excessively high rent

raconteur person skilled in telling stories

racoon or **raccoon** kind of small flesh-eating animal

racy lively; slightly indecent
racier raciest racily raciness

radar system for detecting the position of an object by means of high-frequency radio waves

radial arranged like rays from a central point; kind of tyre
radially radial-ply

radiant sending out rays of light; glowing

radiate to send out light, heat, etc.; to display
radiating radiation

radiator appliance that radiates heat; cooling appliance in an internal-combustion engine

radical fundamental; wanting drastic political, etc. changes
radicalism radically

radicle part of a plant embryo that develops to form the main root

radio apparatus for receiving broadcast signals; to send a signal by radio
radios radioed radioing

radioactivity emission of particles upon disintegration of atomic nuclei
radioactive radioactivity

radiocarbon radioactive carbon; carbon 14

radiogram combined unit of radio and record-player

radiography production of X-rays or gamma-ray photographs
radiographer

radioisotope radioactive isotope

radiology study of X-rays or radioactivity in treatment of disease
radiologist

radiotelephone device that enables

telephone messages to be transmitted by radio waves
radiotelephony

radiotherapy treatment of cancer, etc. by means of X-rays and other forms of radiation
radiotherapist

radish kind of plant with edible crisp pungent root
radishes

radium kind of radioactive element

radius straight line from the centre of a circle to the circumference; outer shorter bone of the human forearm
radii or *radiuses*

raffia fibre from palm tree

raffle kind of lottery in which money is raised for charity; to sell in a raffle
raffler raffling

raft flat floating structure made of logs, used as a boat or platform
raftsman

rafter sloping roof beam

rag[1] piece of old cloth
rag-and-bone rag-bag ragged raggedly raggedness

rag[2] to play practical jokes on; practical joke; series of student stunts, etc.
ragged ragging

rag[3] piece of ragtime music

ragamuffin ragged unkempt person, esp. a child

rage (to express) violent anger; craze
raging

raglan (coat, etc.) having sleeves without shoulder seams

ragout rich meat stew

ragtime style of jazz music

ragwort kind of yellow-flowered plant

raid (to make a) sudden attack
raider

rail[1] horizontal bar of wood, etc.; either of the 2 lengths of steel that form a railway
railcar railcard railhead railing

rail[2] to complain bitterly

rail[3] kind of wading bird

raillery light-hearted ridicule
railleries

railroad (US) railway; to force through quickly in a law-making assembly

railway track consisting of 2 rails on which vehicles run
railwayman

raiment (*archaic*) clothing

rain drops of water that fall from the clouds
rainbow raincoat raindrop rainfall rainforest rainhat rainproof rainstorm rainwater rainy

raise to lift up; to rear
raising

raisin dried grape

raison d'être (*French*) reason for something's existence

raj period of British rule in India

raja or **rajah** Indian or Malay prince or chief; Hindu title

rake[1] (to use a) long-handled tool with a comb-like head
rake-off raking

rake[2] dissolute man
rakish

rake[3] (to) slope

rallentando (*music*) becoming slower

rally mass meeting; to come together
rallies rallied rallying

ram uncastrated male sheep; battering beam; to strike heavily against
rammed ramming ram-raid ramrod

Ramadan 9th month of the Muslim year, observed with fasting

ramble to stroll about; leisurely walk

rambler rambling

rambunctious (*informal*) boisterous

ramekin (cheese dish served in an) individual mould

ramification extended consequence

ramify to branch out
ramified ramifies ramifying

ramose having branches

ramp sloping way

rampage to rush about wildly; violent rushing about
rampageous rampaging

rampant spreading unrestrainedly

rampart broad embankment

ramshackle about to collapse; needing repair

ran past tense of **run**

ranch large North American cattle farm
ranches

rancid smelling or tasting like stale fat
rancidity

rancour (US **rancor**) deep resentment
rancorous

rand money unit of South Africa

random without plan or order
randomly

randy with a strong sexual lust
randier randiest randily randiness

ranee or **rani** Hindu queen or princess; wife of a raja

rang past tense of **ring**[2]

range extent or scope; line of things; to place in a row; to vary between limits
rangefinder ranger ranging

rank[1] position in a scale; status; to assign to a rank

rank[2] offensive, esp. to smell or taste; growing with
rankly rankness

rankle to cause continual irritation
rankling

ransack to plunder; to search very thoroughly

ransom amount of money demanded for the release of a captive; to pay this money and release from captivity

rant to talk in a very noisy manner

rap (to strike with a) sharp light blow
rapped rapping

rapacious greedy
rapaciously rapacity

rape[1] forcing a woman to have sexual intercourse against her will; to commit rape on
raping rapist

rape[2] kind of plant grown as fodder for livestock

rapid quick
rapidity rapidly

rapids part of a river where the current is very fast

rapier narrow 2-edged sword

rapine plunder or pillage

rapport sympathetic understanding

rapprochement (*French*) establishing or renewal of friendly relations

rapscallion rogue

rapt absorbed

rapture ecstasy
rapturous

rare[1] uncommon
rarely rarity

rare[2] lightly cooked

rarefied or **rarified** (*of air*) not dense; pure or exalted

raring enthusiastic

rascal villain or rogue
rascally

rase see **raze**

rash[1] eruption of red spots on the skin

rash[2] hasty; impetuous

rasher slice of bacon or ham

rasp (to scrape with a) coarse file or harsh grating sound

raspberry kind of (shrub bearing) edible purplish-red fruit
raspberries

Rastafarian religious movement among black West Indians
Rasta Rastafarianism

rat mouse-like rodent; to betray one's friends, etc.
rat-catcher ratted ratting ratty

ratafia kind of almond-flavoured biscuit

ratan see **rattan**

ratatouille vegetable casserole

ratchet device with toothed wheel

rate charge or amount in relation to a unit; local authority tax; to consider the value of
rateable or *ratable rate-cap rate-capping ratepayer rating*

rather slightly; preferably

ratify to confirm officially
ratification ratified ratifier ratifies

rating ranking; non-commissioned sailor

ratio relation between 2 numbers or amounts
ratios

ratiocinate to reason logically
ratiocination

ration (to limit to a) fixed amount

rational using reason; sensible
rationality rationally

rationale reasoned basis

rationalism theory that reason is the source of knowledge, rather than perception of experience
rationalist rationalistic

rationalize or **rationalise** to justify; to make more efficient
rationalization or *rationalisation*
rationalizing or *rationalising*

rattan or **ratan** kind of climbing-plant with tough stems, used for wickerwork

rattle (to make a) series of short sharp sounds; toy that rattles
rattlesnake rattletrap rattling rattly

raucous harsh and loud
raucously raucousness

ravage to damage extensively
ravaging
SEE PANEL

---

ravage or ravish?
A place that has been *ravaged* has been extensively damaged: *a country ravaged by decades of civil war; The area has been ravaged by the worst storms in living memory.*
Ravish means 'to delight': *completely ravished by her smile; You look absolutely ravishing in that dress!; the ravishing scenery of Scotland.* *Ravish* also means 'to rape': *a film about a man's ravished daughter and the family's revenge.*

---

rave to talk wildly; wildly exciting event
rave-up raving

ravel to entangle; to disentangle
ravelled (US *raveled*) *ravelling* (US *raveling*)

raven large bird of the crow family

ravenous starving
ravenously ravenousness

ravine deep narrow valley

ravioli small pasta cases containing meat, etc.

ravish to delight; to rape
ravishing
SEE PANEL at ravage

raw uncooked; not processed; inexperienced
rawhide rawly rawness

ray[1] thin beam of light; trace

ray[2] kind of large flat-fish

rayon fabric made from cellulose

raze or **rase** to demolish completely and make level with the ground
razing or *rasing*

razor hair-shaving instrument

razzmatazz or **razzle-dazzle** (*informal*) boisterous showy activity

re concerning; (*music*) 2nd note in a major scale

re- (*prefix*) again; back
reactivate readdress readjust reappear reappoint reappraisal rearrange rebuild recapture recommence reconsider redevelop redirect rediscover redo re-echo re-elect re-emergence re-examine refuel re-heat rehouse reinvent reissue rekindle re-lay relive remarry remortgage reorganize reorientate replay reprint re-route re-run reshuffle resit resole respray restart retake rethink retrain retrial reunite reusable or *reuseable reuse rewind rewire reword rewrite*

reach to arrive at; to extend; distance
reaches reachable reach-me-down

react to act in response to something
reaction reactionary reactionaries reactive reactor

read to be able to understand written words
readability readable reader readership reading reading-room read-out

ready prepared for use
readier readiest readily readiness ready-made ready-to-wear

reagent substance that takes part in a chemical reaction

real existing; true; natural
reality really real-time

realism awareness and acceptance of things as they are; artistic and literary style
realist realistic realistically

realize or **realise** to understand or grasp; to turn into a fact; to convert into money
realizable or *realisable realization* or *realisation realizing* or *realising*

realm kingdom; sphere or field

realty property in buildings and land

ream 500 sheets of paper

reap to cut or harvest a crop
reapable reaper

rear[1] back (part)
rearguard rearmost rearward rearwards

rear[2] to care for; (*of a horse*) to rise on its hind legs

rearm to provide with better weapons
rearmament

reason cause or explanation; to think or persuade logically

reasonable sensible; fair
reasonableness reasonably

reassure to restore confidence to
reassurance reassuring

rebate reduction or refund of money

rebel to oppose authority; person who rebels
rebelled rebelling rebellion rebellious rebelliously

rebirth second birth; revival; spiritual renewal

reboot to restart a computer

rebound to spring back; instance of this

rebuff to reject or refuse bluntly; instance of this

rebuke to reprimand; reprimanding
rebuking

rebus kind of picture puzzle
rebuses

rebut to prove to be false
rebuttal rebutted rebutting

recalcitrant stubbornly defiant of authority
recalcitrance recalcitrantly

recall to remember; to call back

recant to withdraw a belief

recap (*informal*) short for **recapitulate**
recapped recapping

recapitulate to state again the main points of
recapitulating recapitulation recapitulatory

recce[1] (*informal*) short for **reconnaissance**
recces

recce[2] (*informal*) short for **reconnoitre**
recced or *recceed recceing*

recede to withdraw; to slope backwards
receding

receipt written acknowledgement of receiving payment

receive to accept; to welcome visitors
receivable receiver receiving

recent not long ago; modern or new
recently

receptacle container

reception receiving; formal party or welcome
receptionist

receptive open to new ideas or suggestions
receptively receptiveness or *receptivity*

recess part of a wall that is set back; interval
recesses

recession decline in economic activity

recessional musical piece at the end of a service when clergy and choir withdraw

recessive tending to recede

recherché exotic or affected

recidivist person who returns to crime
recidivism

recipe set of cooking instructions

recipient person who receives

reciprocal given and received in return; mutual
reciprocality reciprocally

reciprocate to give and receive in return or mutually
reciprocating reciprocation reciprocity

recital musical performance; detailed account

recite to repeat from memory; to speak aloud
recitation reciting

reckless marked by a lack of care
recklessly recklessness

reckon to calculate; to think
reckoner reckoning

reclaim to gain possession of again; to make land available for human use
reclamation

recline to put in a resting position
reclining

recluse person who lives in seclusion
reclusive

recognizance or **recognisance** bond given to a court to do something
recognizant or *recognisant*

recognize or **recognise** to identify; to realize or acknowledge
recognition recognizable or *recognisable recognizably* or *recognisably recognizing* or *recognising*

recoil to spring back; to withdraw

recollect to remember
recollection recollective

recommend to advise; to speak favourably about
recommendable recommendation recommendatory

recompense (to) reward
recompensing

reconcile to bring to being on friendly terms again; to cause to accept
reconcilable reconciler reconciliation reconciliatory reconciling

recondite little known or obscure

recondition to restore to working order

reconnaissance preliminary survey of an area

reconnoitre (US **reconnoiter**) to make a preliminary survey of
reconnoitred (US *reconnoitered*)
reconnoitrer (US *reconnoiterer*)
reconnoitring (US *reconnoitering*)

reconstitute to restore to its former state, esp. by adding water
reconstituting reconstitution

reconstruct to build again; to re-create an event
reconstruction

record flat disc on which sound is recorded; written account; best performance; to copy sound; to set down in writing
recorded recorder recording record-player

recount to relate or narrate

re-count to count again; second count

recoup to recover what has been lost

recourse source of help

recover to return to a healthy condition
recoverable recovery
SEE PANEL

---

recover or re-cover?
The verb *recover* (without the hyphen) means 'to become well again, after an illness or injury': *She never really recovered after the shock of her husband's death,* or 'to get back something that has been lost or stolen': *The police eventually recovered all the missing diamonds.*

Re-cover (with the hyphen) means 'to cover again': *We decided to re-cover the dining-room chairs.*

---

re-cover to cover again
SEE PANEL at **recover**

re-create to create again
re-creation re-creator

recreation relaxation; leisure activity
recreational

recrimination counter accusation
recriminatory

recrudesce (*of something unpleasant*) to break out again
recrudescence

recruit (to enlist a) new soldier, member, or supporter
recruitable recruiter recruitment

rectangle parallelogram with 4 right angles
rectangular

rectify to put right
rectifiable rectification rectified rectifier rectifies rectifying

rectilinear in or of a straight line

rectitude correctness

recto right-hand page of a book
rectos

rector clergyman; head of any of certain colleges
rectorial rectory rectories

rectum last section of the intestine of a vertebrate
rectums or *recta rectal*

recumbent lying down
recumbence

recuperate to regain one's health
recuperating recuperation recuperative

recur to happen again; to come back to the mind
recurred recurrence recurrent recurring

recusant person who refuses to submit to authority
recusance or *recusancy*

recycle to process into a useful product
recyclable recycling

red of the colour of blood
red-blooded redbreast redbrick redcoat redcurrant redden redder reddest reddish reddy red-handed redhead red-hot redly redness red-water redwing redwood

redeem to recover something by payment; to make amends for; to save from the consequence of sin
redeemer redemption redemptive

redeploy to send to a new position
redeployed redeploying redeployment

redolent smelling strongly of
redolence

redouble to intensify
redoubling

redoubtable formidable
redoubtably

redound to lead to

redress to rectify; reparation
redresses

reduce to lessen; to bring into a particular condition
reducible reducing reduction reductionism

redundant unnecessary; no longer needed
redundancy redundancies redundantly

reduplicate to make or become double; to repeat
reduplicating reduplication reduplicative

reed tall grass-like plant; vibrating part in wind instruments
reedy

reef[1] ridge or rock close to the surface of the sea

reef[2] part of a ship's sail
reef-knot

reefer[1] double-breasted jacket

reefer[2] marijuana cigarette

reek (to give off a) strong unpleasant odour

reel[1] cylindrical device on to which tape, etc. may be wound; winding device attached to a fishing-rod; to wind on a reel
reeler reel-to-reel

reel[2] to whirl about; to sway

reel[3] lively Scottish dance

re-entry act of re-entering, esp. the return of a spacecraft into the earth's atmosphere

refectory dining-hall
refectories

refer to speak about; to direct; to consult
referable reference referential referral referred referring

referee official who supervises the playing of a game such as football; person bearing witness to someone's character; to act as a referee
refereed refereeing

referendum direct vote by electorate on a political issue
referendums or *referenda*

refill to fill again; replacement

refine to purify; to make more distinguished
refinement refinery refineries refining

refit to renew the fittings of a ship; instance of this
refitted refitting

reflate to introduce a controlled increase in a country's money supply
reflating reflation

reflect to throw back light, etc.; to ponder
reflection or *reflexion reflective reflector*

reflex automatic response; occurring automatically; turned back
reflexology

reflexive (*grammar*) (*of a word*) referring to the agent or subject

reform to change for the better; improvement
reformation reformatory reformatories reformer

Reformation 16th-century religious movement that resulted in the establishment of Protestant churches
Reformed

refraction bending or deflection of a ray of light
refract refractive refractor

refractory obstinate
refractorily refractoriness

refrain[1] to keep back

refrain[2] regularly repeated lines of a song

refresh to restore the vitality of
refresher refreshes refreshing refreshment

refrigerate to make or keep cold or cool
refrigerant refrigerating refrigeration refrigerator

refuge shelter

refugee person who flees for safety to a foreign country

refulgence (*formal*) brilliance; radiance
refulgent

refund to return money that has been paid; money refunded

refurbish to renovate
refurbishes refurbishment

refuse[1] to say one is unwilling
refusal refusing

refuse[2] waste or rubbish

refute to prove that something is wrong
refutable refutation refuting

regain to recover possession of

regal of or fitting for a king or queen
regally

regale to give delight to
regalement regaling

regalia ceremonial insignia or clothes

regard to look closely at; to consider; respect

regarding concerning

regardless careless; despite everything

regatta series of races for yachts or boats
regattas

regenerate to give new life; to renew
regenerating regeneration regenerative regenerator

regent person appointed to fulfil the duties of king or queen
regency regencies

reggae West Indian popular music

regicide killing of a king

regime system of government

regimen systematic course such as a diet

regiment army unit; to control strictly
regimental regimentation

region (administrative) area or district
regional regionally

register list or record; to enter in a register
registrable registration registry registries

registrar official keeper of records; hospital doctor

regnant reigning

regress to return to a former condition
regresses regression regressive regressor

regret to be very sorry for; feeling of sorrow and remorse

regretful feeling regret
regretfully regretfulness regretted regretting
SEE PANEL

---

regretful or regrettable ?
A person is *regretful* if they feel sorrow for something: *feel regretful for being so rude.*

You describe something as *regrettable* if you think it should not have happened or you are sorry that it happened: *the most regrettable incident in which a soldier's gun accidentally went off, fatally wounding the soldier.*

---

regrettable causing regret
regrettably
SEE PANEL at **regretful**

regular usual or normal; occurring at fixed points of time
regularity regularly

regularize or **regularise** to make or become regular
regularizing or *regularising*

regulate to adjust; to control by rules
regulating regulation regulator

regurgitate to bring back food to the mouth
regurgitating regurgitation

rehabilitate to restore to a state of good behaviour
rehabilitating rehabilitation

rehash (*informal*) to present in a different form without substantial change

rehearse to practise a play, concert, etc.
rehearsal rehearsing

reign monarch's rule; to exercise rule as a monarch

reimburse to repay
reimbursable reimbursement reimbursing

rein long strap attached to a bridle, used to guide a horse; to control with a rein

reincarnate to bring into a new body after death
reincarnating reincarnation reincarnationist

reindeer kind of large northern deer

reinforce to make stronger
reinforcement reinforcing

reinstate to restore to a former position or rank
reinstatement reinstating

reiterate to say or do again repeatedly
reiterating reiteration reiterative

reject to refuse to accept; to discard
rejecter or *rejector rejection*

rejig (*informal*) to rearrange
rejigged rejigger rejigging

rejoice to feel great joy
rejoicer rejoicing

rejoin[1] to join again

rejoin[2] to reply
rejoinder

rejuvenate to cause to feel young again
rejuvenating rejuvenation rejuvenator

rejuvenescence feeling young again

relapse to fall back into a previous, esp. worse condition; such a condition

relate to tell or narrate; to connect
relatable relatedness relater relating

relation connection; relative
relationship

relative measured in relation to something else; person related to another; (*grammar*) referring to a preceding noun or clause
relatively relativity

relax to make or become less tense
relaxant relaxation relaxer relaxes

relay people who relieve others; electrical triggering device; to supply with relays
relayed relaying

release to set free; to make widely known; something made widely known
releasing

relegate to transfer to a lower position
relegating relegation

relent to become less harsh

relentless not relenting
relentlessly

relevant connected with the matter in hand
relevance or *relevancy relevantly*

reliable dependable
reliability reliably

reliance confidence or trust
reliant

relic something surviving from an earlier time

relief lessening of pain or worry; worker who takes over from another; carving in which the design stands out from its background
relief-painting

relieve to lessen pain or worry; to take over from another person
relieving

religion belief in and worship of a god
religiosity religious religiously

relinquish to give up or surrender
relinquisher relinquishes relinquishment

reliquary container for sacred relics
reliquaries

relish to enjoy; savoury sauce; delight
relishes

relocate to move to a new location
relocating relocation

reluctant unwilling; disinclined
reluctance reluctantly

rely to depend on; to trust
reliable reliance relied relies relying

remain to continue to be; to be left
remainder remains

remand to return to custody

remark (to) comment or notice

remarkable noteworthy
remarkably

remedy cure; to rectify
remedies remediable remediably remedial remedied remedying

remember to keep in the memory; to bring to mind
rememberer remembrance

remind to cause to remember
reminder

reminisce to talk about old times
reminiscence reminiscent reminiscing

remiss negligent

remission period of time when an illness is less severe; reduction in the length of a prison sentence; excusing or pardon
remissible
SEE PANEL

---

remission or remittance?

Remission is a period of time when an illness is less severe: *The cancer is at present in remission but may reappear at any time.* If a prisoner gets *remission*, the length of the prison sentence which they are serving is reduced: *With remission for good behaviour, the men are likely to be released a year early.*

A *remittance* is an amount of money that is sent to someone as payment; *Return the application form with your remittance as soon as possible; No bookings can be accepted unless accompanied by your remittance.*

---

remit to send money; to refer; to excuse; to become less intense
remittal remitted remitting

remittance sending of money as payment
SEE PANEL at **remission**

remittent (*of a fever*) returning at intervals

remnant remaining part

remonstrate to argue in protest
remonstrance remonstrating remonstation remonstrative remonstrator

remorse deep regret
remorseful remorsefully remorsefulness remorseless remorselessly remorselessness

remote distant
remotely remoteness remoter remotest

remould (US **remold**) to refashion the mould of a tyre; remoulded tyre

remove to take away or off; to move to a new location
removable removal removing

remunerate to pay for work, etc.
remunerating remuneration remunerative remunerator

renaissance revival or rebirth

Renaissance 14th–16th century revival of arts and literature

renal of kidneys

renascent being reborn
renascence

rend to tear
rent

render to present; to cause to become
rendering rendition

rendezvous arranged meeting; to meet at a specified time or place
rendezvoused rendezvousing

renegade traitor

renege to go back on one's promise
reneging

renew to make new; to extend
renewable renewal

rennet substance used to curdle milk

renounce to give up; to disown
renounceable renouncing renunciation

renovate to restore to good condition
renovating renovation renovator

renown fame
renowned

rent[1] regular payment for the use of something
rentable rent-a-car rental renter

rent[2] past tense and past participle of **rend;** slit or tear

rep[1] short for **representative**

rep[2] short for **repertory company**

repair[1] to mend; state or condition
repairable

repair[2] (*formal*) to go to a place

reparable capable of being made good

reparation making amends

repartee (skill in making) quick and witty replies

repast (*formal*) meal

repatriate to send a person back to his or her country of origin
repatriating repatriation

repay to pay back
repaid repayable repaying repayment

repeal to revoke a law
repealable repealer

repeat to do or say again
repetition repetitious repetitive repetitively

repel to force back; to be disgusting to
repelled repellent repeller repelling

repent to feel regret; to turn from sin
repentance repentant

repercussion effect or consequence

repertoire dramas, etc. that a company or actor is prepared to perform

repertory repertoire
repertories

replace to put back in its place; to take the place of
replaceable replacement replacer replacing

replenish to fill again
replenisher replenishes replenishment

replete filled (with)
repleteness or *repletion*

replica exact copy
replicas

reply (to) answer
replies replied replier replying

report (to given an) account, statement, or description
reportable reportedly reporter

reportage (style of) reporting news

repose (to) rest; composure
reposing

repository storage place
repositories

repossess to take back possession of
repossesses repossession

reprehend to criticize

reprehensible deserving blame
reprehensibly

represent to act on behalf of; to describe; to stand for
representation representative

repress to hold back
represses repressible repression repressive repressor

reprieve to postpone or cancel a punishment
reprieving

reprimand to rebuke formally; formal rebuke

reprisal act of retaliation

reproach (to) blame or rebuke
reproaches reproachable reproachful

reprobate immoral (person); to condemn
reprobation

reproduce to produce a copy of; to produce young or offspring
reproducer reproducible reproducing reproduction reproductive

reprography process or reproducing graphic material
reprographic

reproof rebuke; censuring

reprove to rebuke or censure
reproval reprover reproving

reptile cold-blooded air-breathing vertebrate animal
reptilian

republic form of government in which the people or their elected representatives possess the supreme power
republican Republican republicanism

repudiate to reject or disclaim
repudiation repudiator

repugnant disgusting
repugnance repugnantly

repulse to drive back
repulsing repulsion

repulsive disgusting
repulsively

reputable having a good reputation
reputably

reputation overall opinion of a person

repute to consider to be
reputedly reputing

request to ask for; thing asked for

requiem Mass celebrated for the dead

require to need or demand
requirement requiring

requisite essential (requirement)

requisition (to make a) formal demand

requite to repay in a suitable manner
requital requiting

reredos screen behind an altar
reredoses

rescind to repeal or cancel
rescindable rescission

rescue to free from danger; instance of rescuing
rescuable rescuer rescuing

research (to undertake a) careful study
researches researcher

resemble to be like
resemblance resembling

resent to feel indignant or bitter
resentful resentment

reservation reserving; booking; qualification

reserve to set aside for later or special use; auxiliary military force; land set aside for animals
reservable

reserved set aside; quiet in manner
reservedly

reservoir lake for storage of water

reside (*formal*) to live in
residing

residence place in which one resides; home
residency residencies resident residential residentially

residue something remaining after a part has been taken
residual residuary

resign to give up
resignation resignedly resigner

resilient able to recover its original form; able to withstand shock, illness, etc. well
resilience or *resiliency*

resin (to treat with a) gum-like plant secretion
resined resining resinous

resist to withstand; to fight against

resistance resistant resister resistible resistibly

resistor electrical component in a circuit that provides opposition to a flow of current

resolute determined; steadfast
resolutely resoluteness resolution

resolve to decide firmly; to pass by voting; to separate into parts
resolvable resolving

resonant echoing
resonance

resonate to reverberate
resonating resonator

resort to turn to; holiday centre

resound to reverberate

resource means of help or support; supply

resourceful ingenious; skilful
resourcefully resourcefulness

respect (to hold in) high regard; aspect or detail
respectful respectfully respectfulness

respectable decent, worthy, or acceptable
respectability respectably

respective relating to each separately
respectively

respire to breathe
respiration respirator respiratory respiring

respite rest or delay

resplendent splendid
resplendence or *resplendency resplendently*

respond to answer; to react
respondent

response responding; reply
responsive responsively

responsible answerable (to); important; trustworthy
responsibility responsibilities responsibly

rest[1] to stop work, etc.; to lie down; relaxation; support
rest-cure rest-day rest-home rest-room

rest[2] to remain; remainder

restaurant commercial establishment where meals are bought and eaten
restaurateur

restful peaceful; soothing
restfully restfulness
SEE PANEL

---

restful, restive, or restless?
Something that is *restful* makes you feel calm and relaxed: *two weeks' restful holiday; the restful sound of waves on the seashore.*

A person becomes *restive* when they become impatient or resist control: *The audience became restive as the beginning of the performance was delayed still further; The shareholders became increasingly restive and mutinous.*

A person becomes *restless* when they become anxious, bored, or dissatisfied: *He spent a restless night, tossing and turning as he worried about the problems of the day; I become restless if I stay in the same job for too long.*

---

restitution returning something to its owner; compensation

restive impatient; unmanageable; uneasy
restively restiveness
SEE PANEL at **restful**

restless agitated; fidgety
restlessly restlessness
SEE PANEL at **restful**

restore to return (to its original condition); to bring back
restorable restoration restorative restorer restoring

restrain to hold back forcefully
restraint

restrict to confine or regulate
restriction restrictionist restrictive

result (to occur as an) outcome; answer to a calculation
resultant

resume to start again; to occupy again
resuming resumption resumptive

résumé summary
résumés

resurgent rising again
resurgence

resurrect to bring back to life or into use
resurrection

resuscitate to revive
resusciating resuscitation resuscitator

retail (of or associated with the) sale of goods to the general public
retailer

retain to continue to keep
retainable retainer retention retentive

retaliate to return like for like; to gain revenge
retaliating retaliation retaliative retaliatory

retard to slow down
retardation retarded

retch to try to vomit
retches

reticent unwilling to say much
reticence reticently

reticulate to divide into a network
reticulating reticulation

retina sensory membrane at the back of the eye
retinas or *retinae retinal*

retinue group of attendants accompanying an important person

retire to give up one's work; to withdraw to a quieter place; to go to bed
retirement retiring

retort[1] to utter sharply as a response; sharp response

retort[2] vessel used in distilling

retouch to make minor changes to
retouches

retrace to go back over one's steps, etc.
retraceable retracing

retract to withdraw; to draw in
retractable retractile retraction

retread to replace and remould the tread of a worn tyre; worn tyre that has been retreaded
retreaded retreading

retreat to withdraw; (period of) rest and meditation

retrench to reduce costs
retrenches retrenchment

retribution deserved punishment
retributive

retrieve to get back again; to bring back
retrievable retrieval retriever retrieving

retroactive affecting the past
retroactively

retrograde going backwards; declining

retrogress to move backwards; to decline
retrogresses retrogression retrogressive

retro-rocket rocket engine, fired esp. to slow down the aircraft or spacecraft

retrospect survey of the past
retrospection retrospective retrospectively

retroussé (*of a nose*) turned up

retsina resin-flavoured Greek wine

return to go or come back; to take back; profit or proceeds
returnable returner

reunion meeting again after a separation

Reuters news agency

rev (*informal*) motor revolution; to increase the number of revolutions
revved revving

revamp to revise, making only minor changes

reveal to make known; to uncover
revealing revelation

reveille morning bugle call

revel to delight in; to indulge in merrymaking
revelled (US *reveled*) *reveller* (US *reveler*) *revelling* (US *reveling*) *revelry revelries*

revenge retaliatory act; vengeance; to avenge
revengeful revenging

revenue income, esp. government income from taxes

reverberate to re-echo; resound
reverberant reverberating reverberation reverberator

revere to respect deeply; to be in awe of
reverence reverent revering

Reverend title of respect for a member of the clergy

reverie day-dream(ing)

revers turned-back front of a garment

reverse to put or move in the opposite way or direction; opposite
reversal reversely reversing

reversible capable of being reversed
reversibility

revert to return to a former condition, owner, etc.
reversion

review to examine again; (to undertake a) survey or critical report of a book, etc.
reviewer

revile to use abusive language towards
revilement reviling

revise to consider and amend; to study for an examination
revisable reviser revising revision

revitalize or **revitalise** to give new life to
revitalization or *revitalisation revitalizing* or *revitalising*

revive to return to life, consciousness, activity, etc.
revival revivalism revivalist reviving

revivify to revive
revivified revivifies revivifying

revoke to withdraw or cancel
revocable revocation revoking

revolt to rebel; to disgust
revolting

revolution overthrow of a government, etc.; single rotation
revolutionary revolutionaries

revolutionize or **revolutionise** to change fundamentally
revolutionizing or *revolutionising*

revolve to turn on an axis
revolving

revolver pistol that allows several shots to be fired in succession without reloading

revue kind of light-hearted entertainment

revulsion sudden strong loathing

reward (to give) something offered in return for a service or good deed
rewarding

rhapsodize or **rhapsodise** to be wildly enthusiastic about
rhapsodizing or *rhapsodising*

rhapsody composition showing strong feeling
rhapsodies rhapsodic

rhea kind of South American bird similar to the ostrich

rheostat variable resistor for adjusting an electric current

rhesus South Asian macaque monkey

rhesus factor blood protein present in red blood cells of some people

rhetoric art of effective use of language
rhetorical rhetorically

rheumatism disease causing pain in the joints or muscles
rheumatic rheumatically rheumatoid

rhinal of the nose

rhino (*informal*) short for **rhinoceros**
rhinos

rhinoceros massive thick-skinned mammal with 1 or 2 horns on the snout
rhinoceroses

rhizome thick horizontal underground stem

rhodium hard white metallic element

rhododendron kind of evergreen shrub with large clusters of showy flowers

rhombus diamond-shaped figure
rhombuses or *rhombi* *rhomboid*

rhubarb kind of garden plant with long edible stalks

rhyme (to form a) correspondence in the sound of words
rhyming

rhymester inferior poet

rhythm pattern of recurring beats or emphases in music or speech
rhythmic *rhythmical* *rhythmically*

rial money unit of Iran, Oman, or Saudi Arabia

rib any of the thin curved bones that protect the heart, lungs, etc.; (*informal*) to tease
ribbed *ribbing*

ribald marked by coarse or obscene humour
ribaldry

ribbon narrow strip of fine fabric, etc.

riboflavin vitamin of the vitamin B complex

rice kind of grass whose grains are used as food

rich wealthy
richly *richness*

riches wealth

Richter scale scale for measuring the intensity of an earthquake

rick[1] large stack of hay, etc.

rick[2] (to) wrench or sprain

rickets deficiency disease of young children

rickettsia micro-organism causing typhus
rickettsiae or *rickettsias*

rickety shaky
ricketiness

rickshaw 2-wheeled carriage pulled by people

ricochet (*esp. of a bullet*) to rebound off a surface
ricocheted or *ricochetted* *ricocheting* or *ricochetting*

rid to free of
riddance *ridded* or *rid* *ridding*

ridden past participle of **ride;** overwhelmed by

riddle[1] puzzle or question

riddle[2] to make full of holes; (to) sieve
riddled *riddler* *riddling*

ride to sit on a horse, bicycle, etc. and control its movements; to be carried by a bus, etc.
ridable *ridden* *riding* *rode*

rider person who rides; something that qualifies
riderless

ridge raised strip, esp. of land
ridge-piece *ridge-pole* *ridge-tile* *ridgeway* *ridgy*

ridicule to make fun of; derision
ridiculing

ridiculous absurd
ridiculously *ridiculousness*

Riesling kind of dry white wine

rife abundant

riffle to look casually through
riffling

riff-raff rabble

rifle[1] firearm with a long grooved barrel
rifleman

rifle[2] to search and steal from a house, etc.
rifler *rifling*

rift gap or break

rig[1] to fit a ship with sails, etc.; to clothe; special machinery
rigged *rigger* *rigging*

rig[2] to manipulate dishonestly
rigged rigger rigging

right correct or proper; opposite of left; having conservative political views; to return to an upright position; just entitlement
right-angled rightful rightfully rightfulness right-handed rightist rightly right-minded rightness rightward rightwards right-winger

righteous virtuous
righteously righteousness

rigid strict; stiff
rigidity rigidly

rigmarole long absurd procedure

rigor mortis (*Latin*) stiffening of muscles after death

rigour (US **rigor**) strictness or harshness
rigorous rigorously

rile to annoy
riling

rill small stream

rim (to produce an) outer edge of a circular object
rimless rimmed rimming

rime (to cover with a) frost
riming rimy

rind hard outer layer of skin or peel

ring[1] circular band of metal worn on a finger; enclosed area where circus acts are performed; to surround
ringed ring-binder ring-fence ringing ringleader ringlet ringmaster ring-pull ringside

ring[2] to (cause to) sound like a bell
rang ringing rung

ringworm fungal disease of the skin or nails

rink expanse of ice for skating on

rinse to wash lightly to remove soap; solution used for tinting the hair
rinser rinsing

riot (to take part in a) wild disturbance
rioted rioter rioting riotous

rip (to) tear; to rush on
rip-cord rip-off ripped ripping rip-roaring

riparian of a river bank

ripe mature; ready to be eaten or used
ripely ripeness riper ripest

ripen to make or become ripe
ripening

riposte quick reply; quick thrusting return in fencing

ripple (to make a) slight wave
rippling

rise to increase; to go upwards; to get up; instance of rising
risen riser rising rose

risible tending to laugh; ridiculous
risibility

rising rebellion

risk (to expose to the) possibility of loss, injury, or damage
riskier riskiest riskily riskiness risky

risotto Italian rice dish
risottos

risqué slightly improper

rissole small fried cake of minced meat, etc.

rite formal act, as in a religious ceremony

ritual (of a) formal act, as in a religious ceremony
ritualism ritualist ritualistic ritualistically ritually

rival person or group that competes with another; to compete with as a rival
rivalled (US *rivaled*) *rivalling* (US *rivaling*) *rivalry rivalries*

riven (*archaic*) split

river large natural stream of flowing water
river-bank river-mouth riverside

Riviera Mediterranean coastal region

rivet (to fasten with a) short metal pin; to attract and hold the attention of
riveted riveter riveting

rivulet small stream

riyal money unit of Qatar or Yemen Arab Republic

roach kind of small freshwater fish
roaches or *roach*

road open surfaced way for vehicles
roadblock road-hog roadholding road-map roadshow roadside roadster roadway roadworks roadworthy

roam to wander aimlessly

roan (*esp. of horses*) having a reddish-brown coat mixed with grey

roar (to utter a) long deep cry
roaring

roast to cook by dry heat, esp. in an oven

rob to steal from
robbed robber robbery robberies robbing

robe (to put on a) long loose gown
robing

robin small bird with a red breast

robot machine that performs tasks automatically, esp. in the manner of human beings
robotics

robust strong
robustly robustness

roc enormous mythical bird

rock[1] solid part of the earth's crust; hard mass
rockery rockeries rock-garden rock-plant rocky

rock[2] to move from side to side
rock-and-roll rocker rocking-chair rocking-horse

rocket self-propelling device, esp. used to launch a spacecraft; to increase or move very fast
rocketed rocketing rocketry

rococo elaborate style of architecture and decoration

rod straight thin pole

rode past tense of **ride**

rodent gnawing animal

rodeo performance of skills of cowboys; cattle round-up
rodeos

rodomontade bragging talk

roe[1] eggs of fish

roe[2] kind of small deer
roebuck

Rogation Sunday Sunday before Ascension Day

roger used in radio communication to indicate that the message has been received and understood

rogue dishonest person; scoundrel
roguery rogueries roguish roguishly

roister to engage in noisy revelry

role actor's part; function
role-play role-playing

roll to move by turning over and over; small rounded cake of bread
roll-call roll-neck roll-off roll-on rollover

roller-coaster fair-railway with very sharp curves and steep slopes

roller-skate (to move on a) boot with 4 small wheels attached to the sole
roller-skater roller-skating

rollick to behave boisterously

rollmop rolled and pickled herring fillet

roly-poly kind of suet pastry filled with jam, etc.
roly-polies

roman (*of letters*) not slanted

romance atmosphere of something captivating; love affair; to compose or tell strongly imaginative stories
romancer romancing romantic romantically romanticism romanticist

Romania or **Rumania** country in SE Europe
Romanian or *Rumanian*

romanticize or **romanticise** to give a romantic character to
romanticizing or *romanticising*

Romany gypsy; language of gypsies
Romanies

romp to play about boisterously
romper

rondeau poem with only 2 rhymes
rondeaux

rondo musical composition with a recurring theme
rondos

Roneo (*trademark*) duplicating machine
Roneos

rood crucifix; measure of land area, one-quarter of an acre

roof (to put on the) cover of a building
roofs roof-garden roof-rack roof-top

rook[1] large black crow; (*informal*) to swindle
rookery rookeries

rook[2] chess piece shaped like a castle

room enclosed area in a building; space
room-mate roomy

roost (to settle on a) bird's perch
rooster

root[1] part of a plant that holds it in the ground and absorbs food; source; to send down roots into the ground
rootless

root[2] to burrow; to search for
rooter

root[3] to cheer for
rooter

rope (to fasten with a) strong thick cord
rope-dancer rope-ladder rope-walk ropey or *ropy roping*

Roquefort (*trademark*) kind of strong flavoured French cheese

rosaceous of or belonging to the rose family

rosary string of beads used in saying and counting prayers
rosaries

rose[1] past tense of **rise**

rose[2] kind of garden shrub with a thorny stem and showy flowers
rosebud rose-bush rose-coloured rose-water rosewood rosy

rosé pink wine

rosemary kind of evergreen shrub with aromatic leaves used as a herb in cooking

rosette decoration made of material to resemble a rose

rosin resin produced from distilling turpentine

roster list of names showing the order of duties

rostrum stage for public speaking
rostrums or *rostra*

rot (to) decay
rotted rotter rotting

rota list of names showing the order of duties
rotas

rotary turning

rotate to turn on an axis
rotatable rotating rotation rotator rotatory

rote mechanical use of the memory to learn

rotisserie rotating spit on which food is cooked; restaurant

rotor rotating part of a machine

rotten decayed; (*informal*) unpleasant
rottenly rottenness

rotund rounded; plump
rotundity rotundly

rotunda round building, esp. with a dome

rouble money unit of the Soviet Union

rouge (to apply) red cosmetic
rouging

rough not even; not gentle; violent; coarse
roughage rough-and-ready rough-and-tumble roughcast rough-dry rough-hew roughneck roughshod

roughen to make or become rough

roulette gambling game

round (to make) circular; (one in a) set; stage in a tournament; on all sides of
roundhead round-shouldered roundsman round-up

roundabout merry-go-round; road junction at which traffic moves in a circle

rounders team game played with a bat and ball

rouse to wake up; provoke
rousing

rout[1] to defeat decisively

rout[2] to find by searching

route (to send by a) course taken to get to a destination
routeing routemarch

routine usual procedure

rove to wander
rover roving

row[1] arrangement or line

row[2] to propel a boat with oars
rowed rower rowing

row[3] (to) quarrel

rowan kind of small tree of the rose family

rowdy noisy and disorderly
rowdier rowdiest rowdily rowdiness rowdyism

rowel revolving spiked disc at the end of a spur

rowlock device for holding an oar in place on a boat

royal of, belonging to, or suitable for a king or queen
royalist royally

royalty state of being royal; royal people, payment made to the writer of a book or performer of a record
royalties

rub to move something backwards and forwards over a surface, applying pressure
rub-a-dub rubbed rubbing

rubber[1] elastic substance from certain plants; pencil eraser
rubberneck rubbery

rubber[2] match of 3 games of bridge, whist, etc.

rubberize or **rubberise** to coat or impregnate with rubber
rubberizing or *rubberising*

rubbish worthless matter
rubbishy

rubble fragments of broken bricks and stones

rubella German measles

rubicund rosy

rubric heading

ruby deep-red precious stone
rubies

ruche gathered lace trimming
ruching

ruck to crease

rucksack large bag carried on the back

ruction noisy disturbance

rudder device for steering a ship or aircraft
rudderless

ruddy red; having a healthy complexion
ruddier ruddiest ruddily ruddiness

rude not polite; primative
rudely rudeness ruder rudest

rudiment basic principle
rudimentary

rue[1] to regret
rued rueful ruefully ruefulness rueing or *ruing*

rue[2] kind of aromatic shrub with bitter leaves

ruff broad frill around the neck; band of feathers or hair round the neck of a bird or animal

ruffian violent lawless person
ruffianism

ruffle to disturb the smoothness of; ruff
ruffling

rug floor covering

rugby form of football in which the ball may be handled and kicked

rugged uneven; jagged

ruin state of collapse; destroyed building; to bring to ruin
ruination ruinous ruinously ruinousness

rule principle; authority; to govern or control; to draw a straight line
ruler ruling

rum[1] spirit made from sugar-cane

rum[2] (*informal*) odd

Rumania see **Romania**

rumba dance originating in Cuba

rumble (to make a) deep resonant sound
rumbler rumbling

rumbustious boisterous

ruminant (of an) animal that chews the cud

ruminate to chew the cud; to consider
ruminating rumination ruminative ruminator

rummage to search (through)
rummaging

rummy card-game in which players try to gain combinations of cards

rumour (US **rumor**) information which may not be true that is passed on verbally

rump buttocks of an animal

rumple to crease
rumpling rumply

rumpus commotion

run to move quickly; to flow; enclosure for animals; point in cricket, etc.
ran runabout runaway run-down runner runner-up running run-of-the-mill run-up

rune letter in ancient Germanic alphabet
runic

rung[1] past participle of **ring**[2]

rung[2] crosspiece of a ladder

runnel small stream

runny flowing
runnier runniest

runt smallest animal in a litter

runway hard level surfaced strip for aircraft to land and take off

rupee money unit of India, Pakistan, or Sri Lanka

rupture (to) break or burst
rupturing

rural of the country
SEE PANEL

---

rural or rustic?
Both adjectives mean 'of the country', but there are differences. *Rural* is used to contrast with *urban*: *rural schools; health care in rural areas; rural communities.*

Rustic has the connotation of simple or unsophisticated: *the authentic rustic charm of a village pub.*

---

ruse trick

rush[1] to move forward quickly; sudden forceful movement
rushes rusher rush-hour

rush[2] tall grass-like plant growing near water
rushes rushlight rushy

rusk kind of light biscuit

russet yellowish-brown; kind of apple

Russia country in North Asia and East Europe
Russian

rust reddish-brown coating forming on iron, etc. when exposed to air and moisture; to affect with rust; to deteriorate through lack of use
rustless rust-proof rusty

rustic rural; roughly made; unrefined
rusticity
SEE PANEL at **rural**

rusticate to settle in the country
rusticating

rustle (to make a) light crisp sound; (US) to steal cattle or horses
rustler rustling

rut[1] (to mark with a) narrow furrow in the ground
rutted rutting

rut[2] annual period of sexual excitement of male animals

ruthless showing no mercy or compassion
ruthlessly ruthlessness

Rwanda country in Central Africa
Rwandan

rye kind of grass used as fodder and in making flour

S

Sabbatarian person who adheres strictly to religious observance on the Sabbath

Sabbath day of worship and rest, Saturday in Judaism and Sunday in Christianity

sabbatical period of leave, as granted to university staff

sable kind of small ferret-like animal valued for its dark-brown fur

sabot wooden shoe

sabotage (to commit) deliberate destruction of machinery, equipment, etc.
sabotaging saboteur

sabre (US **saber**) sword with curved blade
sabre-toothed (US *saber-toothed*)

sac bag-like part in an animal or plant

saccharin sweet substance used as a substitute for sugar

saccharine sugar

sacerdotal of priests
sacerdotalism

sachet small sealed packet containing shampoo, etc.

sack[1] large bag made of coarse cloth, etc.; (*informal*) to dismiss from employment
sackcloth sackful sacking sack-race

sack[2] to plunder
sacker

sackbut medieval trombone

sacrament formal religious act considered as a sign of inner spiritual reality
sacramental sacramentalism

sacred dedicated to a god; holy

sacrifice (to make an) offering to a god; to give up for the sake of something else
sacrificial sacrificing

sacrilege violation of something sacred
sacrilegious

sacristan church official in charge of the contents of a church

sacristy room attached to a church where sacred vessels, etc., are kept
sacristies

sacrosanct very sacred
sacrosanctity

sad unhappy; regrettable
sadder saddest sadly sadness

sadden to make or become sad

saddle leather seat on the back of a horse; bicycle seat; to put a saddle on; to burden
saddleback saddle-bag saddler saddlery saddleries saddle-sore saddling

Sadducee member of ancient Jewish group that denied the resurrection of the dead

sadhu Indian holy man

sadism delight in inflicting pain on others
sadist sadistic sadistically

safari long journey or hunting expedition
safaris

safe giving protection; free from danger; container for the safe storage of valuables
safe-conduct safeguard safekeeping safely safeness safer safest

safety state of being safe
safety-belt safety-catch safety-pin safety-valve

saffron orange colouring and flavouring

sag to droop; to hang unevenly
sagged sagging saggy

saga long detailed old story

sagacious wise
sagaciously sagacity

sage[1] wise person

sage[2] kind of plant with grey-green leaves used for flavouring in cooking

Sagittarius 9th sign of the zodiac

sago starchy cereal
sagos

said past tense and past participle of **say**

sail sheet of strong material secured to catch the wind on a ship; to travel on the water
sailcloth sailing-boat sailing-ship sailplane

sailor member of a ship's crew

saint holy person
sainted sainthood saintlike saintliness saintly

sake[1] benefit or purpose

sake[2] Japanese fermented liquor

salaam oriental greeting

salacious appealing to sexual desire
salaciously salaciousness

salad cold dish of lettuce, tomatoes, etc.
salad-dressing

salamander kind of amphibian resembling a lizard

salami highly seasoned (garlic) sausage

salary (esp. monthly) payment for regular professional work
salaries salaried

sale act of selling; selling of goods at reduced prices
saleable or *salable saleroom salesman salesmanship salesperson saleswoman*

salicylic acid acid whose derivatives are used in the manufacture of pain-relieving drugs

salient conspicuous; prominent
saliently

saline of or containing salt
salinity

saliva fluid secreted by glands in the mouth
salivary

salivate to produce saliva, esp. excessively
salivating salivation

sallow of a sickly yellow colour
sallowish

sally to rush forward; act of this
sallies sallied sallying

salmagundi seasoned salad dish; miscellany

salmon kind of large fish with orange-pink flesh

salmonella bacterium causing food poisoning
salmonellae or *salmonellas*

salon large reception area; hairdresser's premises

saloon standard design of car; public room

salsify herb grown for its fleshy-white root
salsifies

salt white powder or solid used as a flavouring or preservative; chemical compound formed by the action of an acid on a metal; to season with salt
salt-cellar saltier saltiest saltiness salt-mine salty

saltpetre (US **saltpeter**) potassium nitrate

salubrious favourable to health
salubriously salubrity
SEE PANEL

---

salubrious or salutary?

A place that is *salubrious* is healthy and pleasant
or respectable: *live in a salubrious neighbourhood/part of the city.*

A *salutary* experience is one that is intended to have, or has, a good effect, even though it may seem unpleasant at the time: *The international crisis is a salutary reminder of just how fragile world peace still is.*

---

salutary intending to cause an improvement
salutarily
SEE PANEL at **salubrious**

salute (to greet with a) gesture of respect
salutation saluting

salvage saving a ship or its cargo from loss at sea; to save from loss
salvageable salvager salvaging

Salvadorean of El Salvador

salvation deliverance from power and punishment of sin

salve (to apply a) healing ointment; to soothe
salving

salver tray, esp. of silver

salvia kind of herb or shrub of the mint family

salvo discharge of guns; outburst
salvos or *salvoes*

sal volatile ammonium carbonate used as smelling salts

samarium silvery metallic element

same identical; being previously mentioned
sameness

Samoa group of islands in South Pacific
Samoan

samosa triangular spicy meat or vegetable pasty

samovar Russian metal urn for making tea

sampan small flat-bottomed boat used in the Far East

sample (to take a) small representative part
sampling

sampler piece of embroidery that shows many different stitches

samurai (member of) former Japanese warrior caste

sanatorium establishment for convalescents and the chronically ill
sanatoriums or *sanatoria*

sanctify to make holy
sanctification sanctified sanctifies sanctifying

sanctimonious pretending to be holy; self-righteous
sanctimoniously sanctimony

sanction (to give an) authorization; coercive measure taken against a country

sanctity holiness

sanctuary holy place; refuge
sanctuaries

sanctum holy place; room giving total privacy
sanctums or *sancta*

sand fine particles of rock; beach; to smooth with sandpaper
sandbag sandbank sandblast sandboy sandcastle sand-dune sander sandpaper sandpiper sandpit sandstone sandstorm sandy

sandal light shoe held on to the foot by straps, thongs, etc.
sandalled (US *sandaled*)

sandalwood hard sweet-smelling light-coloured wood

sandwich 2 or more slices of bread with a filling; to insert between 2 things
sandwiches sandwich-board

sane not mad; reasonable
sanely saner sanest

sang past tense of **sing**

sang-froid (*French*) composure

sanguinary (*formal*) accompanied by or liking bloodshed

sanguine optimistic; ruddy
sanguinely sanguineness

sanitary free from germs; concerned with good health

sanitation (methods of) improving of sanitary conditions

sanity state of being sane

sank past tense of **sink**

sanserif typeface without serifs

Sanskrit ancient Indian language

Santa Claus Father Christmas

sap[1] watery solution that circulates in a plant; to drain
sapped sapping sappy sapwood

sap[2] (to dig a) trench to approach the enemy
sapped sapper sapping

sapient wise
sapience

sapling young tree

saponify to undergo a process in which an ester is decomposed into an acid or alcohol
saponification saponified saponifies saponifying

sapphire transparent blue precious stone

saraband stately Spanish dance

Saracen Muslim at the time of the Crusades

Sarawak state of Malaysia
Sarawakian

sarcasm mocking ironic language
sarcastic sarcastically

sarcophagus stone coffin
sarcophagi or *sarcophaguses*

sardine young pilchard

Sardinia island in the Mediterranean
Sardinian

sardonic scornfully mocking
sardonically

sari traditional dress of Hindu women
saris

sarong national garment of Malaya; long garment worn by men or women of Malaysia and the Pacific islands

sarsaparilla (dried root of a) tropical American trailing lily plant

sartorial of tailoring

sash[1] brightly coloured band of cloth
sashes

sash[2] frame containing panes on a window
sashes sash-cord sash-window

Sassenach (*Scottish derogatory*) English person

sat past tense and past participle of **sit**

Satan the Devil
satanic Satanism Satanist

satchel bag with shoulder strap for carrying school books

sate to satisfy fully
sating

sateen glossy linen or cotton fabric

satellite celestial body orbiting a planet; man-made device orbiting a celestial body

satiate to satisfy to excess
satiable satiably satiating satiety

satin fabric of silk with a glossy surface

satinwood kind of (smooth yellowish-brown wood of an) Indian tree

satire piece of writing in which people or things are ridiculed
satirical satirically satirist

satirize or **satirise** to ridicule by satire
satirization or *satirisation satirizing* or *satirising*

satisfaction state of being satisfied

satisfactory satisfying needs; acceptable
satisfactorily

satisfy to make contented; to provide enough for; to convince
satisfied satisfies satisfying

satsuma sweet seedless kind of orange

saturate to soak thoroughly; to fill totally
saturating saturation

Saturday 7th day of the week

Saturn the planet 6th from the sun

saturnine gloomy

satyr Greek god of the woods; lecherous man
satyric

sauce liquid preparation served with some foods
saucepan saucy

saucer small round dish on which a cup is set

Saudi Arabia kingdom in SW Asia
Saudi Arabian

sauerkraut pickled and shredded cabbage

sauna Finnish form of steam bath

saunter to walk in a leisurely manner

saurian of a lizard

sausage minced meat, etc. stuffed into a tube-shaped casing
sausage-dog sausage-meat sausage-roll

sauté to fry in a small amount of fat
sautéd sautéing

savage wild; fierce; to attack wildly
savagely savageness savagery savaging

savanna or **savannah** expanse of open grassland

savant (*fem.* **savante**) person of learning
savants (fem. *savantes*)

save to rescue; to put aside for future use
saver saving

saveloy kind of smoked sausage

saviour (US **savior**) person who rescues others from danger, etc.

savoir-faire (*French*) skill in doing the right thing in a certain situation

savory kind of aromatic plant

savour (US **savor**) (to have a) certain taste or smell; to enjoy

savoury (US **savory**) (of) food having a salty or spicy taste
savouries (US *savories*)

savoy kind of cabbage with a compact head

saw[1] past tense of **see**[1]

saw[2] tool with a sharp-toothed blade
sawdust sawed sawfish sawing sawmill sawn sawn-off

saw[3] wise saying

sawyer person who saws timber

saxifrage kind of rock-plant

Saxon member of the Germanic people that invaded England in the 5th century

saxophone kind of woodwind instrument
saxophonist

say to speak or utter
said saying says

scab dried crust that forms over a healing wound; (*informal*) blackleg
scabby scabious

scabbard sheath for a sword, dagger, etc.

scabies contagious skin infection

scabious plant with cluster of small flowers at the end of a long stalk

scabrous roughened; indecent

scaffold temporary structure around a building being built or repaired; execution platform
scaffolding

scalawag (US) see **scallywag**

scald to burn with hot liquid; to heat almost to boiling-point; injury from scalding

scale[1] thin hard plate covering a fish or reptile; coating of chalk or dirt; to remove scale from
scaling scaly

scale[2] one of the pans of a balance

scale[3] graduated series of marks for measuring; set of musical notes; to climb
scaling

scallop kind of shellfish; (to ornament with a) decorative curve
scalloped scalloping

scallywag (US **scalawag**) (*informal*) rascal

scalp (to cut off the) skin and tissue on top of the head

scalpel surgeon's knife

scam (*informal*) swindle

scamp rascal

scamper to run about playfully

scampi large prawns

scan to read through quickly; to examine closely
scanned scanner scanning

scandal malicious gossip; (discredit produced by) outrageous behaviour
scandalmonger scandalous scandalously

scandalize or **scandalise** to shock or offend
scandalizing or *scandalising*

Scandinavia Norway, Sweden, Iceland, and Denmark
Scandinavian

scansion (analysis of) metrical pattern of verse

scant barely sufficient

scanty inadequate; meagre
scantier scantiest scantily scantiness

scapegoat person made to carry the blame for others' faults

scapegrace unprincipled rascal

scapula shoulder-blade

scar[1] mark left after an injury has healed; to form a scar
scarred scarring

scar[2] craggy part of a mountain

scarab ancient Egyptian amulet in the form of a beetle

scarce rare; not abundant
scarcely scarcity

scare to fill with fear; sudden attack of fear
scarecrow scaremonger scaremongery scaring scary

scarf piece of cloth worn round the neck, etc. for warmth or decoration
scarves or *scarfs*

scarify to make small cuts in; to break up and loosen soil, etc.
scarification scarified scarifier scarifies scarifying

scarlatina scarlet fever

scarlet bright red

scarp steep slope

scarper (*slang*) to run away

scat[1] (*informal*) to leave quickly
scatted scatting

scat[2] (to perform a) kind of jazz singing
scatted scatting

scathing severely critical

scatology study of excrement; interest in obscenities
scatological

scatter to throw about or send in different directions
scatter-brained

scatty (*informal*) unable to concentrate
scattier scattiest scattily scattiness

scavenge to search for usable objects among rubbish; (*of animals*) to feed on decaying food
scavenger scavenging

scenario outline of a film or play; account of projected course of events
scenarios

scene place where something happens; view or landscape; division of an act in a play *scene-shifter scenic scenically*

scenery attractive natural landscape; backdrops on a theatre stage
sceneries

scent pleasant smell; perfume; to detect by smelling

sceptic (US **skeptic**) person who doubts
sceptical (US *skeptical*) *sceptically* (US *skeptically*) *scepticism* (US *skepticism*)

sceptre (US **scepter**) ceremonial staff carried by a monarch or an emblem of authority

schadenfreude (*German*) enjoyment of others' misfortunes

schedule (to draw up a) plan showing times or method
scheduling

schema plan or scheme
schemata schematic

scheme plan or arrangement; (to) plot
schematize or *schematise schemer scheming*

scherzo lively musical composition or passage
scherzos or *scherzi*

schilling money unit of Austria

schism division into opposed groups
schismatic schismatically

schist metamorphic rock

schizoid of schizophrenia; person suffering from schizophrenia

schizophrenia mental disorder, esp. causing personality confusion
schizophrenic

schmaltz sentimentalism
schmaltzy

schnapps kind of strong gin

schnitzel thin slice of veal

scholar schoolchild; learned person
scholarly scholarship scholastic scholastically scholasticism

school[1] institution where children are taught; to teach or discipline
schoolboy schoolchild schoolchildren school-days schoolgirl school-leaver schoolmaster schoolmistress schoolroom schoolteacher

school[2] group of fish

schooner kind of sailing ship

sciatic of the hip or hip-bone
sciatica

science systematic study, esp. dealing with the material and physical universe
scientific scientifically scientist

scientology religious and psychotherapeutic movement

sci-fi (*informal*) science fiction

scimitar sword with a curved blade

scintilla tract

scintillate to sparkle
scintillating scintillation

scion shoot of a plant

scissors cutting implement with 2 crossing blades

sclerosis (disease marked by a) hardening of tissue
sclerotic

scoff[1] to mock
scoffer

scoff[2] (*slang*) to eat greedily
scoffer

scold to find fault with
scolder scolding

sconce[1] wall bracket for holding a candle or light

sconce[2] fortification

scone small light cake

scoop (to take up with a) long-handled implement with a round bowl; news reported in a newspaper before its competitors
scooped scooper scooping

scoot (*informal*) to go away quickly

scooter light motor cycle; child's toy vehicle

scope opportunity for action, range of influence, etc.

scorch to burn so as to discolour; mark caused by such burning
scorches scorcher

score record of points made by different players or teams in a game; to gain points in a game; to cut a notch; set of 20; written copy of a musical composition
scoreboard score-card scoreline score-sheet scorer scoring

scorn (to show) open contempt
scornful scornfully scornfulness

Scorpio 8th sign of the zodiac

scorpion eight-legged animal belonging to the same class as spiders, with a poisonous sting in its tail

scotch to put an end to
scotcher

Scotch Scotch whisky

scot-free without punishment or injury

Scotland country in the northern part of Great Britain
Scot Scots Scotsman Scotswoman Scottish

scoundrel villain

scour[1] to clean by rubbing hard
scourer

scour[2] to move quickly over an area, searching for something

scourge (to) whip; to torment
scourging

scout (person sent) to gain information; member of worldwide movement of boys that teaches character, etc.
scoutmaster

scowl (to make an) angry frown

scrabble to grope for
scrabbling

scrag bony part, esp. of an animal's neck

scraggy long and thin; rugged
scraggier scraggiest scraggily scragginess

scramble to move or climb quickly; to cook eggs by stirring in the pan; to make a message unintelligible
scrambler scrambling

scrap[1] fragment; waste material; to throw away
scrapbook scrapped scrapping

scrap[2] (*informal*) (to) fight or quarrel
scrapped scrapping

scrape to move a rough object across a surface, esp. to clean or smooth
scraper scraping

scrappy disjointed
scrappier scrappiest scrappily scrappiness

scratch to mark a surface with a sharp instrument; mark made by scratching; to scrape with the fingernails to relieve itching
scratches scratchcard scratchy

scrawl to write or draw carelessly or quickly

scrawny lean and bony
scrawnier scrawniest scrawnily scrawniness

scream (to utter a) long piercing cry of pain, fear, etc.

scree loose stones or fragments of rock on the side of a mountain

screech (to utter a) harsh shrill cry
screeches screech-owl

screed long speech or piece of writing; layer of cement, etc. on a floor

screen light movable frame; surface on to which images, etc. are projected; to shelter
screenplay

screw tapering threaded metal rod used to fasten things together; to twist
screwdriver

screwy (*informal*) eccentric or odd

scribble to write quickly and carelessly
scribbler scribbling

scribe professional copier of documents
scribal

scrimmage rough struggle

scrimp to be very frugal

scrip certificate

script handwriting; written text
scriptwriter

Scriptures sacred writings
scriptural

scrofula tuberculosis of lymph glands

scroll rolled paper document; decorative design

scrolling presentation of material on a VDU screen in which the text appears to move up the screen

Scrooge miserly person

scrotum pouch of skin containing testicles in mammals
scrota or *scrotums*

scrounge (*informal*) to obtain by cadging
scrounger scrounging

scrub[1] (vegetation or land covered with) bushes and stunted trees, etc.
scrubby

scrub[2] to rub with a stiff brush in order to clean something
scrubbed scrubbing

scruff back of the neck

scruffy dirty in appearance; untidy
scruffier scruffiest scruffily scruffiness

scrum of **scrummage** play in rugby in which teams bunch together to try to gain possession of the ball
scrum-half

scrumptious (*informal*) delicious
scrumptiously

scrunch to crunch or crumple
scrunches

scruple hesitation because of consideration of moral principles

scrupulous very precise; principled
scrupulously scrupulousness

scrutinize or **scrutinise** to examine in detail
scrutineer scrutinizer or *scrutiniser*
scrutinizing or *scrutinising scrutiny*

scuba aqualung
scubas

scud (*of clouds*) to move along quickly
scudded scudding

scuff to scrape or drag one's feet so that one's shoes become worn

scuffle (to take part in a) rough confused struggle
scuffling

scull (to propel with a) short-handled oar used by a single rower
sculler

scullery room for washing dishes, etc.
sculleries

sculpt to sculpture

sculpture art of carving stone, etc. into objects; to carve in this way
sculptor sculptress sculptural sculpturing

scum layer of dirty matter on the surface of a liquid
scumminess scummy

scupper[1] opening in the side of a ship to drain water

scupper[2] (*informal*) to ruin

scurf small flakes of dead dry skin from the scalp
scurfy

scurrilous insulting and coarse
scurrility scurrilously

scurry (to) hurry
scurries scurried scurrying

scurvy disease caused by lack of vitamin C

scut short tail of a deer or rabbit

scuttle[1] box, etc. for coal by a fireside

scuttle[2] to hurry about
scuttling

scuttle[3] small opening in a ship; to sink a ship by making holes in its hull, etc.

scythe (to cut with an) implement with a long curved blade
scything

sea body of salt water
sea-animal seabed sea bird seaboard seaborne sea breeze seafarer seafaring sea fish seafood sea front seagoing seagreen seagull sea horse seakale sea legs sea level sea lion seaman seamanlike seamanship seaplane seaport seascape sea shell seashore seasick seasickness seaside sea urchin seaway seaweed seaworthy

seal[1] kind of sea mammal with flippers
sealer sealing sealskin

seal[2] piece of wax used to keep a parcel closed; to close tightly
sealing-wax

seam line formed where 2 pieces of material are sewn together; layer of coal, etc.
seamless seamstress

seamy sordid
seamier seamiest seamily seaminess

seance or **séance** meeting at which spiritualists try to communicate with the dead

sear to burn or scorch

search to look for; to examine thoroughly; act of searching
searches searcher searchlight search-party search-warrant

season one of the 4 periods of the year; to flavour food
seasoning season-ticket

seasonable expected at a certain time; normal
seasonableness seasonably
SEE PANEL

seasonable or seasonal?
Seasonable means 'expected at a certain time; normal': *seasonable November winds.*

Seasonal is used much more frequently than *seasonable*. A *seasonal* job is one that is available only at a particular time of the year: *seasonal employment such as selling ice-creams in the summer.* A *seasonal* change is one that takes place at a particular time of the year: *Allowing for seasonal factors, unemployment dropped slightly last month.*

seasonal happening at a particular time of the year
seasonally
SEE PANEL at **seasonable**

seat chair, stool, etc.; to cause to sit; location for something
seat-belt

sebaceous of or secreting fat

sebum fatty secretion of the sebaceous glands

secant trigonometric function

secateurs pair of pruning shears

secede to withdraw from membership of
seceder seceding secession secessionist

seclude to keep away from
secluded secluding seclusion

second[1] next after first
second-guess second-hand second-rate secondly

second[2] 60th part of a minute

second[3] to support
seconder

second[4] to release an official, etc. temporarily to another department, etc.
secondment

secondary of lesser importance
secondarily

secret (something) kept hidden from the knowledge of other people
secrecy secretive secretively secretiveness secretly

secretariat (government) administrative department

secretary person who deals with correspondence, filing, etc. in an office; head of government department
secretaries secretarial secretaryship

secrete[1] (*of a gland*) to produce and release fluid
secreting secretion secretor secretory

secrete[2] to put in a hidden place
secreting secretion

sect exclusive religious group

sectarian of a sect; narrow-minded and intolerant
sectarianism

section part of division; cross-section
sectional sectionalism sectionalize or *sectionalise sectionally*

sector division or part; part of a circle between 2 radii

secular not spiritual; worldly

secularize or **secularise** to make secular
secularization or *secularisation secularizing* or *secularising*

secure (to make) safe; to obtain
securely securing security securities

sedan (US) saloon car; enclosed chair carried on 2 poles

sedate[1] calm and composed
sedately sedateness

sedate[2] to give a sedative to
sedating sedation

sedative (drug) having a calming effect

sedentary marked by the need to spend a lot of time sitting down
sedentarily sedentariness

sedge kind of tufted marsh plant
sedgy

sediment matter that settles at the bottom of a liquid
sedimentary sedimentation

sedition incitement to defy the State
seditious

seduce to persuade someone to disobey or to have sexual intercourse with one
seducer seducing seduction seductive

sedulous persevering steadily
sedulity

see[1] to (be able to) perceive with the eyes; to understand or experience
seeing see-through

see[2] office or diocese of a bishop

seed part of a plant, etc. that is capable of germination to produce a new plant, etc.
seed-bed seed-cake seedless seed-pearl seed-potato seedsman

seedling young plant growing from a seed

seedy containing seeds; squalid; unwell
seedier seediest seedily seediness

seek to try to find
sought

seem to appear (to be)
seemingly

seemly fitting or proper
seemliness

seen past participle of **see**[1]

seep to ooze out to leak slowly
seepage

seer person who predicts future events

seersucker fabric of cotton, linen, etc. with a crinkled surface

see-saw plank balanced in the middle to allow up and down movement

seethe to boil; to be extremely angry
seething

segment part or piece that has been separated or cut off
segmental segmentary segmentation

segregate to separate different groups
segregating segregation segregationist

seine large fishing-net

seismic of or caused by earthquakes

seismograph instrument for measuring and recording earthquakes

seismology study of earthquakes
seismological seismologist

seize take hold of forcefully; to become jammed
seizing seizure

seldom rarely

select to choose; chosen
selection selective selectively selectivity selectness selector

selenium non-metallic solid element

self individual's own character, etc.
selves selfless selflessness

self- (*prefix*) of, to, etc. oneself
self-addressed self-assembly self-assertive self-assured self-catering self-centred (US *self-centered*) *self-confident self-conscious self-contained self-control self-defeating self-defence* (US *self-defense*) *self-denial self-determination self-discipline self-drive self-effacing self-employed self-esteem self-explanatory self-government self-help self-important self-indulgent self-interest self-made self-pity self-portrait self-raising self-respect self-righteous self-sacrifice self-satisfied self-seeking self-service self-styled self-sufficient self-supporting self-taught self-willed*

selfish caring only about one's own interests
selfishly selfishness

selfless not caring for oneself
selflessly selflessness

selfsame the very same

sell to transfer in exchange for money
sell-by seller sell-off sell-out sold

Sellotape (*trademark*) kind of transparent adhesive tape

selvage or **selvedge** edge of cloth

semantics study of meaning in language
semantic

semaphore (to send messages by a) signalling system
semaphoring

semblance appearance; show

semen whitish fluid produced in the male genital glands

semester academic term lasting half a year, as in the US or Germany

semi- (*prefix*) half; partly or partially
semi-aquatic semibreve semicircle semicircular semifinal semifinalist semi-official semiprecious semi-professional semiquaver semi-skilled semi-solid semitone semi-trailer semi-transparent

semicolon punctuation mark; see colon[2]

semiconductor substance that has conducting properties between that of a conductor and insulator

semi-detached joined to another building by a common wall

seminal of seeds or semen; important; basic

seminar (student's) discussion group

seminary training college for priests
seminaries

semiotics study of signs and symbols

Semite member of a group of people that includes Jews and Arabs
Semitic

semolina hard grains of wheat used in puddings, etc.

senate upper assembly in legislative body of some countries; governing body of some universities
senator senatorial

send to cause to be taken or conveyed
sender send-off send-up sent

Senegal country in West Africa
Senegalese

senile showing bodily or mental weakness because of old age
senility

seniority older; higher in rank

senna kind of tropical plant, the dried leaves of which are used as laxative

sensation perception through the senses; (something causing) excitement
sensational sensationalism sensationalist sensationally

sense power of sight, touch, etc.; to notice; meaning
senseless sensing

sensibility capacity to feel or perceive
sensibilities

sensible marked by good sense or reason
sensibleness sensibly
SEE PANEL

---

sensible of sensitive?
Someone who is *sensible* makes wise decisions based on good sense or reason rather than feelings: *It would be sensible to take an umbrella in case it rains; Lucy is growing up into a sensible young woman.*

Someone who is *sensitive* is easily offended by other people's comments: *be very sensitive to any form of criticism.* To be *sensitive* to others' feelings or problems means that you understand them and are kind to them: *He was a sensitive, supporting colleague who always listened sympathetically.* A *sensitive* subject is one that arouses strong feelings or opinions: *Euthanasia is a sensitive issue. Sensitive* skin reacts harshly to chemicals: *Highly perfumed products may irritate sensitive skin.*

---

sensitive capable of sensing; easily offended; delicate
sensitively sensitivity
SEE PANEL at **sensible**

sensitize or **sensitise** to make sensitive
sensitizer or *sensitiser sensitizing* or *sensitising*

sensor responsive device

sensory of the senses

sensual of or indulging the senses, esp. bodily
sensualism sensualist sensuality sensually
SEE PANEL

---

sensual or sensuous?
Something that is *sensual* relates to the senses and the body, and suggests particularly physical or sexual satisfaction: *her rich, sensual lips; the sensual pleasures of eating and drinking.*

Something that is *sensuous* appeals to the senses, in contrast to the mind: *the sheer sensuous pleasure of driving this car.*

---

sensuous of, perceived by, or derived from the senses
SEE PANEL at **sensual**

sent past tense and past participle of **send**

sentence self-contained group of words; (to impose a) judgement
sentencing

sententious seeming wise, but dull
sententiously sententiousness

sentient capable of feeling things
sentience

sentiment thought or (excessive) emotion

sentimental marked by (excessive) emotion
sentimentalism sentimentalist sentimentality sentimentally

sentimentalize or **sentimentalise** to make sentimental
sentimentalization or *sentimentalisation sentimentalizing* or *sentimentalising*

sentinel person who keeps guard

sentry soldier who keeps guard
sentries sentry-box sentry-go

sepal part of the calyx of a flower

separable able to be separated
separability separably

separate to move apart; not connected; divided
separating separation separatist separator

sepia brown pigment used as ink

sepsis infection of the body by pus-forming bacteria

September 9th month of the year

septet (piece of music composed for a) group of 7 performers

septic of sepsis or the decomposition of living matter

septicaemia (US **septicemia**) blood-poisoning

septuagenarian (person) aged between 70 and 79 years

Septuagesima 3rd Sunday before Lent

Septuagint Greek version of the Old Testament

sepulchre (US **sepulcher**) tomb
sepulchral sepulchrally

sequel something that follows; consequence
sequence sequent sequential

sequester to set apart; to sequestrate
sequestered sequestering

sequestrate to confiscate temporarily until debts have been paid
sequestrating sequestration sequestrator

sequin small disc of shiny metal used as a decoration

sequoia giant Californian coniferous tree

seraglio harem; Turkish palace
seraglios

seraph angel
seraphim or *seraphs seraphic*

Serbia republic in SE Europe, formerly part of Yugoslavia
Serbian

serenade (to play) (romantic) music
serenading

serendipity faculty of making fortunate discoveries by chance

serene calm; peaceful
serenely serener serenest serenity

serf feudal agricultural labourer
serfdom

serge strong twilled fabric

sergeant rank in the army or police force
sergeant-major

serial (story) presented or performed in several parts; of a series
serially

serialize or **serialise** to present or publish in a serial
serialization or *serialisation serializing* or *serialising*

series group of related things in succession

serif short line at the extremity of a stroke of a letter

serious solemn; sincere; crucial
seriously seriousness

serjeant sergeant

sermon religious or moral talk

sermonize or **sermonise** to preach a moral or religious talk
sermonizing or *sermonising*

serous of or like serum
serosity

serpent large snake
serpentine

serrated with a notched or toothed edge
serration

serried compactly arranged

serum watery part of blood (that contains certain antibodies)
sera or *serums*

servant employee who performs household duties

serve to work for; to attend to customers; to function as; to be a member of the armed forces
server serving

service help; (to undertake an) overhaul of a vehicle or appliance; one of the armed forces
serviceable serviceman servicewoman

serviette table napkin

servile like a slave
servilely servility

servitude slavery

servo-motor power-assisted motor

sesame kind of tropical plant with small edible seeds

session meeting of a law-court, parliament, etc.

set[1] to put or present; to apply; to adjust; group of similar things; television or radio receiver; stage scenery
setback set-square setting set-to set-up

set[2] see **sett**

sett badger's burrow

settee long seat with a back and arms

setter breed of long-haired dog

settle[1] to put in a fixed position; to make or become calm; to pay a bill, etc.
settlement settler settling

settle[2] long wooden seat with a back and arms

seven number 7
seventeen seventeenth seventh seventieth seventy seventies

sever to divide
severance

several some; different
severally

severe harsh; extreme
severely severer severest severity severities

sew to join by means of stitches made with a needle and thread
sewed sewer sewing sewing-machine sewn

sewage waste matter, esp. excrement, carried away in drains

sewer drain or pipe to carry away sewage
sewerage

sex male or female; physical desires resulting from difference in sex
sexist sexless sexual sexuality sexy

sexagenarian (person) aged between 60 and 69 years

Sexagesima second Sunday before Lent

sexology study of sexual behaviour in humans
sexological sexologist

sextant navigation instrument

sextet (piece of music composed for a) group of 6 performers

sexton church caretaker

sextuple 6 times

sextuplet any of 6 offspring born at 1 birth

Seychelles group of islands in the Indian Ocean
Seychellois

shabby dirty; broken-down; mean
shabbier shabbiest shabbily shabbiness

shack rough hut

shackle (to confine with a) metal ring put round a person's ankle
shackling

shad kind of fish of the herring family

shade partial darkness produced by the blocking out of light; to protect from the heat or light of the sun; darker colour
shadeless shading

shadow dark image caused by something cutting off rays of light; to watch and follow someone closely
shadow-box shadowy

shady giving shade; dark; disreputable
shadier shadiest shadily shadiness

shaft long handle of a spear, etc.; rotating rod that transmits power or motion

shag mass of hair or other covering; coarse tobacco

shaggy covered with rough hair
shaggier shaggiest shaggily shagginess

shagreen rough hide of a shark or ray used as an abrasive

shah title of the former sovereign of Iran

shake to move up and down quickly
shakeable or *shakable* *shake-down* *shaken* *shaker* *shake-up* *shaking* *shook*

shaky unsteady or uncertain
shakier *shakiest* *shakily* *shakiness*

shale dark finely laminated rock
shaly

shall auxiliary verb used to form future tense and to express determination, obligation, etc.
shan't *should*

shallot kind of plant resembling an onion

shallow not deep
shallower *shallowest* *shallowly* *shallowness*

shalom (*Hebrew*) Jewish greeting or farewell

sham hypocrisy; (to) counterfeit
shammed *shamming*

shamble to walk unsteadily, dragging the feet
shambling

shambles place of great confusion or destruction

shame feeling caused by awareness of guilt, failure, etc.; to cause to feel shame
shamefaced *shameful* *shamefully* *shamefulness* *shameless* *shamelessly* *shamelessness* *shaming*

shammy (*informal*) chamois (leather)

shampoo (to clean or wash one's hair using a) preparation of soap
shampoos *shampooed* *shampooing*

shamrock plant whose leaves have 3 leaflets, emblem of Ireland

shandy drink consisting of beer mixed with lemonade or ginger beer

shanghai to kidnap and compel to join a ship's crew
shanghaied *shanghaiing*

shank part of the leg between the knee and ankle; stem or main shaft of a key, nail, spoon, etc.

shan't (*informal*) shall not

shantung kind of heavy silk fabric

shanty[1] rough hut; shack
shanties *shantytown*

shanty[2] or **chanty** sailor's song
shanties or *chanties*

shape outward form or figure; to make or form
shapable or *shapeable* *shapeless* *shapelessly* *shapelessness* *shapely* *shaping*

shard fragment of something brittle

share[1] to divide; part or portion; part of the capital or stock of a business company
shareholder *shareware* *sharing*

share[2] cutting blade of a plough

shark[1] kind of ferocious predatory fish
sharkskin

shark[2] person who extorts money from others

sharp having a fine cutting edge or point; perceptive; acute; (*of a musical note*) higher by a semitone
sharpen *sharpener* *sharp-set* *sharpshooter* *sharp-tongued*

shatter to break in many pieces

shave to remove hair, esp. from the face, with a razor
shaven *shaver* *shaving* *shaving-brush* *shaving-cream* *shaving-soap* *shaving-stick*

shawl piece of material worn round a woman's shoulders or a baby

she subject pronoun referring to a female person or animal

sheaf bundle of corn, etc. tied together
sheaves

shear to cut or clip hair or fleece from sheep, etc.
shearer *shearing* *sheared* or *shorn*

shears cutting instrument resembling a large pair of scissors

sheath case or covering

sheathe to insert into a sheath
sheathing

shed[1] small building; workshop

shed[2] to allow to flow or fall
shedding

she'd (*informal*) she would; she had

sheen lustre; shine

sheep kind of grass-eating animal that has a thick woolly fleece
sheep-dip sheepdog sheepfold sheepish sheep-run sheepskin

sheepshank kind of knot

sheer[1] perpendicular; very steep; utter

sheer[2] to change direction

sheet large piece of cotton, etc. used esp. as a bed-covering

sheikh Arab chief; Arab religious leader
sheikhdom

sheldrake (*fem.* **shelduck**) kind of water bird

shelf narrow board attached horizontally to a wall
shelves shelf-life

shell (to remove the) protective hard casing of an egg or nut; (to fire a) metal case containing explosives
shellfire shellfish shellproof shell-shock

she'll (*informal*) she will

shellac (to varnish with a) yellowish resin
shellacked shellacking

shelter (to provide) protection or safety

shelve[1] to put on a shelf; to postpone
shelving

shelve[2] to slope gradually
shelving

shepherd (*fem.* **shepherdess**) person who looks after sheep

sherbet flavoured effervescent powder

sheriff (US) chief law-enforcing officer in a county; (*Brit*) chief executive officer of the Crown in a county

Sherpa member of a Tibetan people living on the southern slopes of the Himalayas

sherry fortified Spanish wine
sherries

she's (*informal*) she is; she has

Shetland Islands islands off the north coast of Scotland

shibboleth phrase or custom that distinguishes members of a particular group

shield strong piece of body armour carried on the arm; to protect

shift to move position; to remove with difficulty; group of workers working at a particular period

shiftless lacking ambition or initiative

shifty deceitful; devious
shiftier shiftiest shiftily shiftiness

shilling former British coin; unit of money in some African countries such as Kenya, Tanzania, and Uganda

shilly-shally to be indecisive
shilly-shallied shilly-shallies shilly-shallying

shimmer (to shine with a) wavering light

shin front part of the lower leg; to climb up with the hands or arms and legs
shin-bone shinned shinning

shindig (*informal*) noisy party

shine to emit a steady light; to be outstanding
shined or *shone shining*

shingle[1] wood tile; woman's short haircut; to cut the hair short
shingling

shingle[2] small pebble on the beach
shingly

shingles viral disease producing inflammation and blisters on the skin

Shinto animistic religion of Japan
Shintoism Shintoist

shiny polished; bright
shinier shiniest shinily shininess

ship (to transport by a) large sea-going vessel
shipboard shipbuilder shipbuilding shipload shipmaster shipmate shipment shipowner shipped shipper shipping shipping-agent shipping-office shipshape shipwreck shipwright shipyard

shire county

shirk to avoid or evade
shirker

shirt garment worn on the upper part of the body, usually with a collar and sleeves
shirting shirt-sleeve shirt-tail

shirty (*slang*) bad-tempered
shirtier shirtiest shirtily shirtiness

Shiva see **Siva**

shiver[1] (to) tremble
shiverer shivery

shiver[2] to break into tiny pieces; tiny piece

shoal[1] body of shallow water

shoal[2] large group of fish

shock[1] to experience a sudden disturbance in one's mind or feelings
shockable shocker shocking shockproof

shock[2] pile of sheaves

shock[3] thick mass of hair

shoddy of poor quality; fabric of inferior quality
shoddier shoddiest shoddily shoddiness

shoe (to provide with) one of a pair of coverings for the foot; to fix horseshoes on to a horse
shod shoeblack shoehorn shoeing shoelace shoemaker shoemaking shoestring shoe-tree

shone past tense and past participle of **shine**

shoo to drive away by shouting, 'Shoo'
shooed shooing

shook past tense of **shake**

shoot to hit or wound with a bullet, etc.; to move very quickly; to aim at a goal; new growth on a plant
shooter shooting shot

shop building where goods are sold to the public; to go to a shop to buy goods
shopkeeper shoplifter shopped shopper shopping shop-soiled shoptalk shopwalker

shore[1] land adjoining the sea, a river, etc.
shoreline shoreward shorewards

shore[2] (to support with a) wooden beam
shoring

shorn past participle of **shear**

short not long; insufficient; curt; (*of pastry*) crumbly
shortage shortbread shortcake shortcrust shortfall shorthand short-handed short-lived shortly short-sighted short-tempered short-term

short-change to give less than the correct change to a person
short-changed short-changing

shortcoming deficiency

shorten to make or become short

shot[1] past tense and past participle of **shoot**; firing a gun; photograph; attempt to strike a ball into a goal; hypodermic injection
shotgun

shot[2] (*of textiles*) having changing and contrasting colouring effects

should past tense of **shall**, used to express obligation, etc.
shouldn't

shoulder part of the body where the arm joins the trunk; to bear the burden of

shout (to give a) loud cry
shouter

shove (to give a) violent push
shover shoving

shovel tool for scooping loose material; to lift or scoop with a shovel
shovelful shovelled (US *shoveled*) *shoveller* (US *shoveler*) *shovelling* (US *shoveling*)

show to make or be clear or visible; to exhibit or display; public exhibition or entertainment
showcase showdown showed showgirl showing showjumping showman showmanship shown show-off show-piece showroom show-stopper

shower brief fall of rain; device that sprays water on to a person's body; to present in abundance
showerproof showery

showy ostentatious
showier showiest showily showiness

shrank past tense of **shrink**

shrapnel artillery shell containing a number of bullets, etc. that explode before impact

shred (to cut or tear into a) long narrow strip
shredded shredder shredding

shrew kind of long-snouted mammal resembling a mouse; bad-tempered woman
shrewish

shrewd astute; wise
shrewdly shrewdness

shriek (to give a) shrill cry

shrike kind of predatory songbird

shrill sharp and high-pitched
shriller shrillest shrillness shrilly

shrimp kind of small edible shellfish

shrine holy place such as an altar or temple

shrink to make or become smaller, esp. from wetness; to recoil (from)
shrank or *shrunk shrinkage shrinking shrink-wrap shrunk* or *shrunken*

shrivel to dry up and become wrinkled
shrivelled (US *shriveled*) *shrivelling* (US *shriveling*)

shroud garment or cloth used to wrap a dead body; (to) cover

Shrove Tuesday Tuesday before Ash Wednesday
Shrovetide

shrub woody plant smaller than a tree
shrubbery shrubberies shrubbiness shrubby

shrug to raise and drop the shoulders to express ignorance, doubt, etc.
shrugged shrugging

shrunk past tense or past participle of **shrink**

shrunken past participle of **shrink**

shudder (to) tremble from horror, fear, etc.

shuffle to move along without lifting the feet clearly from the ground; to mix up the order of playing-cards
shuffler shuffling

shun to avoid
shunned shunning

shunt to move trains from one track to another
shunter

shush to demand silence by calling, 'Shush'

shut to cover an opening; to close
shutdown shut-eye shut-in shut-off shutting

shutter movable outside window cover; camera device that opens and closes the lens aperture

shuttle weaving device for passing the weft thread between the warp threads; to move backwards and forwards
shuttlecock shuttling

shy[1] withdrawn and timid; to draw back
shied shies shyer shyest shying shyly shyness

shy² to throw
shied shies shyer shying

Siamese cat short-haired cat with a slender body

Siamese twin 1 of 2 babies born joined together at some point

sibilant having a hissing sound
sibilance

sibling brother or sister

sic (*Latin*) thus

Sicily largest island in the Mditerranean
Sicilian

sick likely to vomit; ill
sickbay sickbed sick-leave sicklier sickliest sickliness sickly sickness sick-pay sickroom

sicken to make or become sick or disgusted
sickening

sickle implement with a curved blade for cutting grass

side surface or part; aspect; to support
side-arms side-car side-dish side-door side-effect sidekick sidelight sideline sidelines sidelong side-piece side-road side-saddle sideshow sidesman side-splitting sidestep side-street sidestroke sidetrack sidewalk sidewards sideways siding

sideboard piece of dining-room furniture with drawers and shelves for keeping china in

sideburns or **sideboards** hair growing down either side of the face to below the ears

sidereal of the stars

siding railway track off a main line into which trains are shunted

sidle to approach furtively
sidling

siege surrounding of a city, etc. to force it to surrender

sienna natural earth containing iron oxides

sierra range of mountains with jagged peaks

Sierra Leone country in West Africa
Sierra Leonean

siesta short afternoon sleep or rest
siestas

sieve (to pass through a) device for separating finer particles from the coarser
sieving

sift to sieve; to examine in detail
sifter

sigh (to give a) long audible breath

sight power of seeing; something seen; device that helps to aim
sightless sight-screen sightseeing sightseer

sight-read to perform music without previous preparation
sight-reader sight-reading

sign symbol or gesture; notice; to write one's signature on
signboard signpost

signal sign; device that gives warning; to communicate by signals; notable
signal-box signalled (US *signaled*) *signaller* (US *signaler*) *signalling* (US *signaling*) *signally signalman*

signalize or **signalise** to distinguish
signalizing or *signalising*

signatory person who signs a document
signatories

signature person's name as written by that person

signet person's seal

significant important; having meaning
significance significantly

signify to mean; to matter
signification significative signified signifier signifies signifying

Sikh member of a religion of India
Sikhism

silage green fodder for livestock

silence (to cause an) absence of noise or sound
silencer silencing

silent marked by an absence of noise or sound

silhouette black outline of a person in profile; to cause to appear in a silhouette
silhouetted silhouetting

silica hard white mineral
silicate

silicon non-metallic element that is abundant in the earth's crust
SEE PANEL

silicon or silicone?
Silicon is a non-metallic element that occurs abundantly in the earth's crust. It is a major constituent of nearly all rock-forming minerals. A *silicon* chip is a tiny piece of *silicon* that has minute electric circuits on it.
Silicone is a *silicon* compound that is used for example in oils, paints, and cosmetic surgery: *silicone rubber.*

silicone polymeric organic silicon compound used as oils, resins, etc.
SEE PANEL at **silicon**

silicosis disease of the lungs

silk fine soft fibre produced by silkworms
silken silk-screen silkworm silky

sill shelf along the bottom of a window, etc.

sillabub or **syllabub** cold dessert of curdled milk or cream mixed with wine

silly absurd or foolish
sillier silliest silliness

silo structure in which silage is stored
silos

silt (to fill with) mud or clay sediment

silvan see **sylvan**

silver (to coat or plate with a) shining greyish-white metal; articles made of silver
silverfish silversmith silvery

silviculture study of development and care of forests
silvicultural silviculturist

simian of an ape or monkey

similar resembling or like
similarity similarities similarly

simile figure of speech that draws a comparison

similitude likeness

simmer to cook just at boiling-point

simnel rich fruit cake

simoom or **simoon** hot dry wind in Asian or African desert

simper to smile in a foolish self-conscious way
simperingly

simple easy; plain; humble; unsophisticated
simple-minded simpleness simpler simplest simplicity simplistic simply

simpleton silly or ignorant person

simplify to make easier
simplification simplified simplifies simplifying

simulate to pretend
simulating simulation simulative simulator

simultaneous taking place or functioning at the same time
simultaneity or *simultaneousness simultaneously*

sin (to commit an) offence against God's law
sinful sinfully sinfulness sinless sinlessly sinlessness sinned sinner sinning

since from a former time until now; as

sincere genuine; honest
sincerely sincereness sincerity

sine trigonometric function

sinecure paid employment requiring minimal work

sine qua non (*Latin*) essential requirement

sinew tendon
sinewy

sing to utter musical sounds
sang singer singsong sung

Singapore country in SE Asia
Singaporean

singe to burn superficially
singeing

single only 1; unmarried; (ticket) for outward, not return journey; to choose deliberately
single-breasted single-decker single-handed single-lens single-minded singleness single-stick singleton singling singly

singlet sleeveless vest

singular unusual or extraordinary; (*grammar*) referring to 1 person or thing
singularity singularities singularize or *singularise singularly*

Sinhalese member of the predominant people living in Sri Lanka; Indic language of this people

sinister threatening evil; (*heraldry*) on the left side from the bearer's point of view

sink (to cause) to go down below the surface of water; to appear to go down below the horizon; fixed basin in a kitchen
sank sinkable sinker sunk sunken

Sinn Fein Irish republican political movement

sinology study of Chinese history, language, etc.
sinological sinologist sinologue

sinter chalky deposit formed by hot springs

sinuous full of curves
sinuosity sinuosities sinuously

sinus cavity in a bone, esp. connecting with the nostrils
sinuses sinusitis

Sioux North American Indian
Siouan

sip to drink a liquid by taking small mouthfuls; small mouthful
sipped sipping

siphon or **syphon** bent tube for transferring liquid from one container to another; to draw off through a siphon

sir polite term of address to a man

Sir title of address of a knight or a baronet

sire (to be the) male parent of
siring

siren device producing a loud high-pitched warning signal

sirloin cut of beef from the upper part of the loin

sirocco hot dusty wind from Libyan deserts
siroccos

sisal kind of plant whose leaves are used for making rope

sissy see **cissy**

sister daughter of the same parents; senior nurse; nun
sisterhood sister-in-law sisters-in-law sisterly

sit to rest on a seat; to take an examination; to be in session
sat sitcom sit-down sit-in sitter sitting sitting-room

sitar kind of Indian stringed instrument

site (to provide with an) area of ground with a particular use
siting

situate to place
situated

situation position or location; job; circumstances

Siva or **Shiva** Hindu god of destruction

six number 6
sixfold sixteen sixteenth sixth sixthly sixtieth sixty sixties

size[1] set of measurements; to order according to size
sizeable or *sizable sizing*

size[2] (to cover with a) glue-like solution
sizing

sizzle (to make the) hissing sound of frying
sizzling

skate[1] (boot fitted with a) metal blade for gliding over ice
skateboard skater skating

skate[2] kind of edible flat-fish

skedaddle (*informal*) to go away quickly
skedaddling

skein long coil of yarn

skeleton hard bony framework of an animal body
skeletal

skeptic (US) see **sceptic**

sketch rough quickly drawn plan, etc.; short comic play; to make a sketch of
sketchbook sketcher

sketchy superficial
sketchier sketchiest sketchily sketchiness

skew oblique
skew-whiff

skewbald (horse) having patches of different colours

skewer (to pierce with a) long pin for meat

ski 1 of a pair of long narrow strips of wood used for gliding over snow
skis skied or *ski'd skier skies skiing*

skid to slide sideways while out of control
skidded skidding skidpan

skiff small light boat

skill ability to do something well
skilful (US *skillful*) *skilfully* (US *skillfully*) *skilled*

skillet small saucepan

skim to remove floating material from the surface of; to glide lightly over
skimmed skimmer skimming

skimp to work quickly and carelessly; to be very sparing
skimpy

skin (to remove the tissue forming the) outer covering of a body, fruit, etc.
skin-deep skin-diver skin-diving skinflint skinhead skinned skinning skin-tight

skinny very thin
skinnier skinniest skinnily skinniness

skint (*Brit*) having no money

skip[1] to move with short quick jumps
skipped skipping skipping-rope

skip[2] large container for rubbish

skipper captain

skirmish (to take part in a) minor fight in war
skirmishes skirmisher

skirt girl's or woman's garment hanging from the waist; to go along the border of
skirting-board

skit brief satirical sketch

skittish lively
skittishly skittishness

skittle 1 of a set of wooden pins that are to be bowled over in the game of skittles

skive (*informal*) to shirk one's work
skiver skiving

skivvy (*Brit derogatory*) drudge
skivvies

skua kind of predatory sea bird

skulduggery trickery

skulk to move stealthily
skulker

skull bony skeleton of the head
skullcap

skunk animal that gives off an unpleasant smell when attacked

sky upper atmosphere; to hit a ball high into the air
skies skied sky-blue skydiving sky-high skying skyjack skylark skylight skyline skyscraper skyward skywards

slab thick flat piece of something solid such as rock

slack[1] not tight or tense; not busy; to be lazy
slacker slackly slackness

slack[2] small pieces of coal left after coal has been screened

slacken to make or become slack

slacks trousers for causal wear

slag waste remaining after smelting of metals

slain past participle of **slay**

slake to satisfy or quench; to cause lime, etc. to disintegrate by treating with water
slaking

slalom ski-race down a zigzag course

slam to close a door noisily
slammed slamming

slander (to utter a) false defamatory statement
slanderer slanderous slanderously

slang highly informal language; language of a particular group; to abuse verbally
slanging-match slangy

slant (to) slope; to present in a biased way

slap (to strike with a) sharp blow of the open hand
slapped slapping slap-up

slapdash careless

slap-happy casual; carefree

slapstick comedy with horseplay and farcical action

slash (to cut with a) violent long cut
slashes slasher

slat narrow thin strip of wood, etc.
slatted

slate (roofing-tile made of) smooth fine rock; to criticize very strongly
slater slating slaty

slattern dirty untidy woman
slatternly

slaughter killing of animals for food; to kill animals for food
slaughterer slaughter-house

Slav (member of a people) living in East Europe or Soviet Asia
Slavonic

slave person who is owned by and forced to work for another
slave-driver slaver slavery slaving slavish

slaver to dribble saliva

slay to kill
slain slayer slaying slew

sleazy disreputable
sleaze sleazier sleaziest sleazily sleaziness

sledge or **sled** (to ride on a) vehicle with runners that travels over snow
sledging

sledgehammer large heavy long-handled hammer

sleek smooth and shiny
sleekly sleekness

sleep (to be in a state of) natural suspension of consciousness
sleeping sleeping-bag sleeping-car sleeping-pill sleepless sleeplessly sleeplessness sleepwalker sleepwalking sleepy sleepyhead slept

sleeper person or animal that sleeps; beam that supports railway track; railway sleeping carriage

sleet mixture of snow and rain
sleety

sleeve part of a garment covering the arm; cover for a gramophone record
sleeved sleeveless

sleigh sledge

sleight (**sleight of hand**) skill and dexterity in performing tricks

slender slim or thin

slept past tense and past participle of **sleep**

sleuth (*informal*) detective
sleuth-hound

slew[1] past tense of **slay**

slew[2] to turn, twist, or swing about

slice thin flat piece cut from something; to cut into slices
slicer slicing

slick smooth; suave; film of oil in water

slide to move over smoothly; chute; photographic transparency
slid slider sliding

slight small or slight; not significant; (to) insult
slightingly slightly slightness

slim slender; small; to make oneself thinner by dieting
slimly slimmed slimmer slimmest slimming slimness

slime runny mud or other sticky substance
slimy

sling looped supporting bandage; loop of leather used in throwing stones; to throw with a sling
slingback slinger slinging slung

slink to move (away) stealthily
slinky slunk

slip[1] to lose one's balance and slide over; to move smoothly; mistake; petticoat
slipknot slip-on slipped slipping slippy slip-road slipshod slipstream slip-up slipway

slip[2] small piece of paper; plant cutting; young thin person

slip[3] mixture of clay and water used in pottery

slipper light shoe worn in the house
slippered

slippery tending to cause slipping
slipperiness

slit (to make a) long narrow cut
slit slitting

slither to slide unsteadily
slithery

sliver splinter

slob (*slang*) stupid person

slobber to dribble saliva, etc. from the mouth

sloe (fruit of the) blackthorn

slog to work hard; to hit hard
slogged slogger slogging

slogan phrase used in advertising a product, etc.

sloop single-masted sailing vessel

slop to spill over
slopped slopping

slope (to) slant; hill
sloping

sloppy untidy or messy; excessively sentimental
sloppier sloppiest sloppily sloppiness

slops human waste food fed to animals; liquid household waste

slosh (*informal*) to hit; to pour or throw carelessly

sloshed (*slang*) drunk

slot (to insert in a) narrow groove or opening
slot-machine slotted slotting

sloth kind of slow-moving mammal; laziness
slothful slothfully slothfulness

slouch to sit or stand in a weary drooping position

slough[1] muddy place; dejected state

slough[2] (to cast off) dead skin or tissue

Slovak member of a Salvonic people of East Czechoslovakia

Slovenia republic of former Yugoslavia

slovenly unclean and untidy
slovenliness

slow not quick; dull or sluggish; showing an earlier time
slowcoach slower slowest slowly slowness slow-worm

sludge soft thick mud

slug[1] slimy snail-like creature

slug[2] kind of bullet

slug[3] to hit very hard
slugged slugging

sluggard lazy person

sluggish lacking energy; slow
sluggishly sluggishness

sluice (device controlling flow in a) channel that carries away surplus water; to draw out by a sluice
sluicing

slum (to live in an) area of dirty dilapidated housing; unpleasant dirty house
slummed slumming slummy

slumber (*literary*) (to) sleep
slumberer slumbrous or *slumberous*

slump to fall suddenly and heavily; decline in business activity

slung past tense and past participle of **sling**

slunk past tense and past participle of **slink**

slur to utter words, etc. indistinctly; to cast scorn on
slurred slurring

slurp to drink or eat noisily

slurry watery mixture of clay, mud, etc.

slush melting snow; sentiment
slushy

slut dirty or promiscuous woman
sluttish

sly crafty or deceitful
slyer slyest slyly slyness

smack[1] (to have a) slight smell or flavour

smack[2] to strike with the open hand; striking with the hand; to open the lips noisily

smack[3] small inshore fishing vessel

small not large or great; not important; humble; narrow part of the back
smaller smallest smallholding small-minded smallness small-scale small-time

smallpox contagious viral disease with pustules that leave scars

smarm to smear grease on the hair

smarmy too flattering

smart neat; fashionable; to cause a stinging pain; clever
smarten smartly smartness

smash to break into pieces; to hit or strike hard; to defeat; act of smashing
smashes smash-and-grab smasher smashing smash-up

smattering slight knowledge

smear to spread over with oil, etc.; mark made by this; to try to discredit

smell power of perceiving through the nose; to perceive in this way; (to emit an) odour
smelled or *smelt smelling-salts*

smelly having an unpleasant smell
smellier smelliest smellily smelliness

smelt[1] past tense and past participle of **smell**

smelt[2] to extract a metal from an ore
smelter smeltery smelteries

smelt[3] kind of small edible freshwater fish

smile (to show an) amused or happy facial expression
smiling

smirch to make dirty; stain
smirches

smirk (to give a) scornful smile
smirker

smite to strike heavily
smiter smiting smitten smote

smith worker in metals
smithy

smithereens tiny pieces

smock long loose garment with gathered upper part
smocking

smog mixture of smoke and fog
smoggy

smoke visible gas produced from burning; to breathe in and out the fumes of burning tobacco
smokable or *smokeable smoke-filled smokeless smoker smokescreen smokestack smokier smokiest smokiness smoking smoky*

smooch to kiss or caress
smoocher

smooth (to make) even; not rough
smooth-spoken smooth-tongued

smorgasbord Scandinavian buffet

smote past tense of **smite**

smother to stifle or suffocate

smoulder (US **smolder**) to burn slowly without flames

smudge (to make a) dirty mark
smudgily smudginess smudging smudgy

smug very self-satisfied
smugger smuggest smugly smugness

smuggle to import or export illegally
smuggler smuggling

smut dirt; something obscene

smutty dirty
smuttier smuttiest smuttily smuttiness

snack quick light meal

snaffle[1] simple jointed bridle bit

snaffle[2] (*informal*) to steal
snaffling

snag difficulty; (to catch on a) sharp projection
snagged snagging

snail kind of mollusc having a spiral shell

snake (to move like a) long-bodied legless reptile
snaking snaky

snap to make a cracking noise; to break; to speak angrily; (to take a) photograph; sudden spell of cold weather
snapped snapper snapping snappish snappy snapshot

snapdragon kind of plant with spikes of showy flowers

snare (to catch in a) device for trapping animals
snarer snaring

snarl[1] to growl, baring the teeth; act of snarling

snarl[2] (to) tangle
snarl-up

snatch to seize suddenly; brief part of a conversation, etc.
snatches snatcher snatchy

snazzy (*informal*) fashionably attractive
snazzier snazziest snazzily snazziness

sneak to move stealthily; to tell tales; person who sneaks
sneaky

sneaker soft canvas shoe

sneer to show contempt; contemptuous expression

sneeze (to make a) sudden involuntary expulsion of air from the nose and mouth
sneezer sneezing

snick (to cut a) small notch; (to hit a ball with a) light glancing blow

snide discrediting in an underhand manner
snidely snideness

sniff to draw air audibly up the nose
sniffer

sniffle to breathe relatively loudly through the nose, as when one has a cold
sniffler sniffling

snigger (US **snicker**) (to give a) quiet mocking laugh

snip (to cut with a) small quick stroke of the scissors, etc.
snipped snipping

snipe to fire from a concealed position; kind of game bird living in marshy areas
sniper sniping

snippet small piece

snitch (*informal*) to steal; to inform on someone
snitches

snivel to cry in an unhappy manner
snivelled (US *sniveled*) *sniveller* (US *sniveler*) *snivelling* (US *sniveling*)

snob person who looks down on those of a lower social position
snobbery snobbish snobby

snog (*slang*) to kiss and cuddle
snogger snogging

snood net formerly worn at the back of the head by women to keep the hair in place

snooker game played on a billiard table
snookered

snoop to pry
snooper

snooty (*informal*) haughty or snobbish
snootier snootiest snootily snootiness

snooze (*informal*) (to have a) short light sleep
snoozer snoozing

snore (to make a) snorting noise in one's sleep
snorer snoring

snorkel device allowing swimmers to breathe while underwater; to use a snorkel
snorkeled snorkeling

snort to force air noisily out through the nostrils
snorter snorty

snout long projecting nose and mouth of an animal

snow ice crystals falling from the sky in white flakes
snowball snow-blind snowbound snowcapped snow-clad snow-covered snowdrift snowdrop snowfall snowfield snowflake snowline snowman snowmobile snowplough (US *snowplow*) *snowshoe snowstorm snow-white snowy*

snub to insult contemptuously; (*of noses*) short and slightly turned up
snubbed snubbing snub-nosed

snuff[1] powdered tobacco for sniffing up the nostrils
snuffbox

snuff[2] to extinguish the flame of a candle
snuffer

snuffle to breathe noisily
snuffling

snug comfortably warm
snugger snuggery snuggeries snuggest snugly snugness

snuggle to nestle cosily
snuggling

so to such an extent; extremely; in order (that); with the result (that); therefore
so-and-so so-called so-so

soak to make or become saturated

soap substance used to remove dirt
soapbox soapsuds soapy

soar to rise or fly upwards

sob to weep while catching the breath; act of sobbing
sobbed sobbing

sober not drunk; serious; subdued
soberly sobriety

sobriquet or **soubriquet** nickname

soccer Association football

sociable friendly
sociability or *sociableness* *sociably*
SEE PANEL

sociable or social?
Someone who is *sociable* is friendly, companionable, and enjoys talking to others: *Helen likes going to parties – she's an outgoing, sociable personality; I'm sorry I'm not feeling very sociable tonight – do you mind if I make tracks for home now?*

Social means 'of society' or 'concerned with leisure activities in which you meet and spend time with other people': *The government's social policy; social studies; He had an active social life that centred on the bowling club; organize social events for new students.*

social (preferring) living in groups; of society
socialite *socially*
SEE PANEL at **sociable**

socialism political and economic theory in which the means of production are owned by the community collectively
socialist

socialize or **socialise** to behave in a sociable way
socializing or *socialising*

society social community; association or club
societies

socio- (*prefix*) social
socio-economic

sociology study of society and of behaviour of social groups
sociological *sociologist*

sock[1] cloth covering for the foot

sock[2] (*informal*) (to) punch

socket device into which an electric plug is fitted to complete a circuit

sod turf

soda compound of sodium

sodden wet through

sodium silver-white metallic element

sodomy anal sexual intercourse
sodomite

sofa long seat with a back and arms

soft not hard; not loud or glaring; easily moulded; (*of drink*) non-alcoholic
soft-boiled *soft-core* *softer* *softest* *soft-hearted* *softly* *softness* *soft-pedal* *soft-spoken* *software* *softwood* *softy*

soften to make or become soft
softener

soggy moist; saturated
soggier *soggiest* *soggily* *sogginess*

soh 5th note in a major scale

soil[1] earth or ground; land

soil[2] to make dirty

soirée evening party

sojourn to stay temporarily; temporary stay

solace source of comfort

solar of the sun

solarium room exposed to the sun
solaria or *solariums*

sold past tense and past participle of **sell**

solder (to join with a) meltable alloy
soldering-iron

soldier (to serve as a) member of an army

sole[1] underpart of the foot or shoe; to fit with a (new) sole
soling

sole[2] being the only one
solely

sole[3] kind of edible flat-fish

solecism mistake in speech, writing, or behaviour

solemn serious; very formal
solemnity *solemnities* *solemnly* *solemness* or *solemnness*

solemnize or **solemnise** to celebrate

formally; to perform the marriage ceremony
solemnization or *solemnisation*
solemnizing or *solemnising*

solenoid coil of wire that becomes magnetic when an electric current passes through it

sol-fa use of syllables or names for the notes of the major scale

solicit to request; to accost, offering sexual relations
solicitation

solicitor kind of lawyer; legal officer of a city or state

solicitous eager to help
solicitousness solicitude

solid not hollow; (substance that is) neither liquid nor gas; firm
solidity solidly solid-state

solidarity unity of interests

solidify to make solid
solidification solidified solidifier solidifies solidifying

solidus short oblique stroke /
solidi

soliloquize or **soliloquise** to utter a soliloquy
soliloquizing or *soliloquising*

soliloquy speech to oneself
soliloquies soliloquist

solitaire board-game played by 1 player; diamond set by itself in a ring

solitary (preferring to be) alone; single
solitarily solitariness solitude

solo composition for 1 performer
solos soloist

solstice time when sun is furthest away from the equator

soluble that can be solved or dissolved
solubility solubly

solution answer to a problem; mixture of a solid and a liquid

solve to find an answer to a problem
solvable solving

solvent able to pay one's debts; able to dissolve another substance
solvency

Somalia country in NE Africa
Somali

somatic of the body

sombre (US **somber**) dismal
sombrely (US *somberly*) *sombreness* (US *somberness*) *sombrous*

sombrero wide-brimmed hat, worn esp. in Mexico
sombreros

some any; several; certain unspecified
somebody somehow someone something sometime sometimes somewhat somewhere
SEE PANEL

---

sometime, some time, or sometimes?

Sometime means 'at an unknown or unstated time in the past or future': *Shall we meet up sometime soon?* When used in this way, *sometime* is occasionally written as two words. *Some time* also means 'a period of time': *Please give me some time to think through all the issues. Sometime* is also used in front of a title of a person's job or position to note the fact that they held such a post at some time in the past but do so no longer: *Lord Richard Brooke, sometime President of the local Youth Development Council.*

Sometimes means 'happening on some occasions but not all the time': *Sometimes I get awful headaches; Sometimes I travel by bus into work, sometimes I drive.*

---

somersault (to make a) forward roll in which a person turns head over heels

somnambulism sleep-walking
somnambulist

somnolent sleepy
somnolence somnolently

son male child of parents
son-in-law sons-in-law sonless sonship

sonar echo sounder

sonata musical composition for 1 or 2 instruments
sonatas

song musical composition with words to be sung
songbird songbook songster songstress

sonic of sound

sonnet poem of 14 lines with a particular rhyming scheme

sonorous producing (a resonant) sound
sonority or *sonorousness sonorously*

soon in short time
sooner soonest

soot black powder from a fire and deposited in a chimney
sooty

soothe to calm; to relieve a pain
soothing soothingly

soothsayer prophet

sop piece of food dipped in a liquid

sophism misleading argument
sophist sophistic sophistry sophistries

sophisticated refined; high-class; elaborate or complex
sophistication

soporific inducing sleep

sopping saturated

soppy wet; (*informal*) foolishy sentimental
soppier soppiest soppily soppiness

soprano (singer with or music for the) highest singing voice of women or boys
sopranos

sorbet kind of water-ice

sorcery magic or witchcraft
sorceries sorcerer sorceress

sordid dirty; evil
sordidly sordidness

sore painful or painfully sensitive part of the body
sorely soreness sorer sorest

sorghum tropical cereal grass

sorrel[1] (horse of) reddish-brown colour

sorrel[2] kind of herb with sharp-tasting leaves

sorrow (to feel) grief or regret
sorrowful sorrowfully sorrowfulness

sorry feeling regret or sorrow; miserable
sorrier sorriest sorrily sorriness

sort group or kind with similar characteristics; to separate into different groups
sortable sorter

sortie sudden emergence of troops; mission by a single aircraft

SOS internationally recognized distress signal
SOSs

sot habitual drunkard
sottish

sotto voce (*Italian*) in an undertone

soubriquet see **sobriquet**

soufflé light dish made with beaten egg whites, etc.

sought past tense and past participle of **seek**
sought-after

soul spiritual part of a human being; innermost part; person
soul-destroying soulful soulfully soulfulness soulless soullessly soullessness soul-searching

sound[1] noise
soundless soundproof soundtrack

sound[2] healthy; undamaged; whole; deep
soundly

sound[3] to measure the depth of water; (to) probe
sounding

sound[4] narrow channel of water

soup[1] liquid food made from meat, vegetables, etc.

soup[2] (**soup up**) to increase the power of

soupçon slight amount

sour having an acid or vinegary taste; bad-tempered
sourish sourly sourness

source point of origin; starting-point of a river

souse to steep in liquid; to pickle
sousing

soutane priest's cassock

south one of the 4 compass points, opposite of north
South Africa South African South America South American southbound south-east southeaster south-easterly south-eastern southerly southern southerner southernmost southwards south-west south-westerly south-western

souvenir something that serves as a reminder of a person or place

sou'wester kind of waterproof hat

sovereign king or queen; supreme; former British gold coin worth 1 pound
sovereignty

soviet elected council in the former USSR

Soviet of the former Soviet Union

sow[1] to plant seed
sowed sower sowing sown

sow[2] female adult pig

soy soya bean

soya bean king of protein-rich bean

spa (resort with) spring of mineral water

space boundless expanse in which objects are located; area beyond earth's atmosphere; distance between objects; to place with spaces between
spacecraft spaceman spacer spaceship spacesuit space-time spacing spatial

spacious having a lot of room
spaciously spaciousness

spade[1] tool for digging and lifting soil
spadeful spadework

spade[2] black symbol on a playing-card; playing-card suit

spaghetti pasta in the form of long thin strings

Spain country in SW Europe
Spaniard Spanish

span[1] distance or space between 2 points, esp. supports of a bridge or arch; period of time; to reach across
spanned spanning

span[2] past tense of **spin**

spangle (to decorate with a) small glittering ornamental disc
spangling

spaniel dog with large drooping ears

spank to smack the buttocks hard

spanking remarkable; brisk

spanner tool for gripping and turning a nut

spar[1] strong pole such as a mast on a vessel

spar[2] to box lightly
sparred sparring sparring-match sparring-partner

spar[3] kind of non-metallic mineral

spare to manage to give or afford; to refrain from using, hurting, or punishing; additional; duplicate
sparely spareness sparing sparingly spare-rib

spark small burning particle thrown out from a fire; flash of light produced electrically; trace; to produce a spark
sparking-plug or *spark-plug*

sparkle to reflect flashes of light
sparkler sparkling

sparrow kind of small songbird
sparrowhawk

sparse thinly scattered
sparsely sparseness sparser sparsest

spartan austere or strict

spasm involuntary muscular contraction

spasmodic occurring in sudden short spells
spasmodically

spastic person suffering from spastic paralysis

spat[1] past tense and past participle of **spit**[1]

spat[2] young oyster

spate sudden flow

spatial of space
spatially

spatter to splash or scatter in drops

spatula implement with a wide flexible blade
spatulas

spavin bony enlargement of the hock of a horse

spawn (to produce) eggs of fish, frogs, etc.

spay to remove the ovaries of a female animal
spayed spaying

speak to utter or talk; to show
speakeasy speaker speaking spoke spoken

spear (to hit or pierce with a) sharp-pointed weapon
spearhead

spearmint mint plant used for flavouring

special not common; individual or exceptional

specialist person who specializes in a skill or area of knowledge
specialism

speciality or **specialty** special interest, skill, etc.
specialities or *specialties*

specialize or **specialise** to work or be interested in a particular skill or area of knowledge
specialization or *specialisation specializing* or *specialising*

specie coin money

species (biological) group

specific exact; particular
specifically

specify to mention or refer to
specifically specification specified specifies specifying

specimen individual (typical) item

specious apparently correct, but really false
speciously speciousness

speck small spot
specked

speckle (to mark with a) small spot
speckled speckling

spectacle public display or entertainment

spectacles pair of lenses in a frame to correct vision

spectacular very impressive
spectacularly

spectator onlooker or observer

spectre (US **specter**) ghost; unpleasant image
spectral

spectroscope instrument for examining light spectra
spectroscopic spectroscopist spectroscopy

spectrum series of different colours produced when light is dispersed by a prism
spectra spectral

speculate to conjecture; to risk money in the hope of gaining profit
speculating speculation speculative speculator

speech faculty of speaking; public talk
speech-day speechless speechlessly speechlessness

speed rate at which something moves; rapidity; to move quickly
sped speedboat speeding speed-trap speed-up speedway

speedometer instrument for measuring the speed at which a vehicle travels

speedwell kind of plant with blue or white flowers

speedy fast
speedier speediest speedily speediness

speleology study of (exploring) caves
speleological speleologist

spell[1] to say or write the letters of a word or words in the correct way
spelled or *spelt speller spelling*

spell[2] period of time; duty

spell[3] words used as a magic formula
spellbound

spend to pay out money; to use up or pass time
spender spending spendthrift spent

sperm male reproductive cell; semen

spermatozoon generative cell in semen
spermatozoa spermatozoic

spew to vomit

sphagnum peat moss; bog moss
sphagnums or *sphagna sphagnous*

sphere round ball or globe; area or range of knowledge, activities, etc.
spherical spheroid

sphinx ancient Egyptian statue with a lion's body and a human head
sphinxes

spice substance used as a flavouring; to flavour with spices
spicier spiciest spicily spiciness spicing spicy

spick (**spick and span**) clean and tidy

spider 8-legged creature that spins threads of silk
spidery

spiel glib persuasive talk

spigot plug to stop the hole of a cask

spike[1] sharp point; sharply pointed object such as a nail
spiky

spike[2] ear of grain; elongated cluster of flowers

spill[1] to (allow to) fall over; overflow
spilled or *spilt spilling spillway*

spill[2] taper for lighting a candle, etc.

spillikin thin rod or straw used in the game of spillikins

spin to draw out and twist into a thread; to turn round and round fast; short ride in a car, etc.
spin-drier or *spin-dryer spinner spinning spinning-jenny spinning-top spinning-wheel spin-off spun* or *span*

spina bifida congenital condition in which the meninges of the spine protrude

spinach kind of plant with green edible leaves

spindle rod on which a thread is spun; shaft
spindly

spindrift sea spray

spine backbone; spike on a leaf or stem; bound edge of a book
spinal spineless spiny

spinet harpsichord

spinnaker large triangular sail on a yacht

spinney small wood
spinneys

spinster unmarried woman
spinsterhood spinsterish

spiral winding round and round at an increasing distance from the centre; to move in this way
spiralled (US *spiraled*) *spiralling* (US *spiraling*)

spire tall pointed structure on a church

spirit animating part of human beings; ghost; enthusiasm; alcohol *spirited spiritless spirit-level spiritual spiritualism spiritualist spirituality spiritually*

spiritualize or **spiritualise** to render in a spiritual manner
spiritualizing or *spiritualising*

spirituous containing alcohol

spit[1] to eject saliva from the mouth; (*of rain*) to fall lightly
spat spitter spitting

spit[2] thin metal spike pushed into meat for roasting; long narrow projecting strip of land

spite maliciousness; defiance; to annoy out of spite
spiteful spitefully spitefulness spiting

spittle saliva

spittoon container for spit

spiv (*slang*) flashy person who makes a living from dishonest dealing
spivvish

splash to make wet with drops of water
splashdown

splatter to scatter in small drops

splay to spread out
splayed splaying

spleen body organ that produces lymph cells and breaks down red blood corpuscles

splendid brilliant; excellent
splendidly splendour (US *splendor*)

splenetic of the spleen; irritable

splice to join by weaving strands or overlapping
splicer splicing

splint rigid support to keep a broken limb in position

splinter sharp thin fragment of wood, etc.; to break into splinters
splintery

split to break or divide into parts; act of splitting; division or part
split-level splitting split-up

splodge or **splotch** (to form a) large irregular spot
splodgy or *splotchy*

splurge (*informal*) to show ostentatiously; ostentatious show
splurging

splutter to speak unclearly (and with spitting sounds); to spit out saliva, etc.

Spode kind of china or porcelain

spoil to damage the value, usefulness, etc. of; to pamper
spoilage spoiled or *spoilt spoilsport*

spoiler device on an aircraft or car

spoils plunder; benefits

spoke[1] past tense of **speak**

spoke[2] rod connecting the hub and rib of a wheel

spoken past participle of **speak**

spokeshave 2-handled smoothing plane

spokesman (*fem.* **spokeswoman)** representative speaker
spokesperson

spoliate to plunder
spoliating spoliation spoliatory

spondee metrical foot consisting of 2 long syllables
spondaic

sponge kind of sea animal with a very porous body; skeleton of this, used for washing; to live at another person's expense
sponge-bag sponge-cake sponger sponging spongy

sponsor person who supports or promotes a project
sponsorship

spontaneous produced naturally and without external influence
spontaneity spontaneously

spoof (*informal*) light parody

spook (*informal*) ghost
spooky

spool device on to which film, tape, etc. can be wound

spoon utensil with a small shallow round bowl on a handle
spoon-fed spoonful spoonfuls

spoonerism unintentional transposition of initial sounds of words

spoor track of a wild animal

sporadic occurring irregularly
sporadically

spore tiny reproductive cell produced by fungi, ferns, etc.

sporran fur pouch worn in front of a kilt

sport game with physical activity, played for entertainment or exercise; to wear or show
sporting sportingly sportive sportively sports sports car sportsground sports jacket sportsman sportsmanship sportswear sportswoman sporty

spot small mark; drop; pimple; to mark with spots
spotless spotlessly spotlessness spot-on spotted spotter spotting spotty

spotlight light that gives a powerful focused beam

spouse husband or wife

spout projecting tube or pipe; to discharge or eject

sprain (to injure by) wrenching a joint

sprang past tense of **spring**

sprat small or young herring

sprawl to lie or sit with one's limbs spread out inelegantly

spray[1] (to disperse) fine particles of a liquid
sprayer spray-gun

spray[2] single slender branch or shoot

spread to unfold or extend; to apply

spreadsheet computer program that allows manipulation of data in table form

spree lively unrestrained time

sprig small shoot or twig

sprightly lively
sprightlier sprightliest sprightliness

spring to rise quickly and suddenly; (device that has the capacity) to return quickly to its earlier form; season between winter and summer
sprang springboard spring-clean springier springing springtime springy sprung

springbok kind of swift African antelope

sprinkle to scatter lightly in drops
sprinkler sprinkling

sprint to run a short distance at full speed
sprinter

sprit light spar

sprite elf or fairy

sprocket tooth on a wheel rim that interlocks with the links of a chain

sprout to push out new shoots or leaves; new shoot or leaf; Brussels sprout

spruce[1] (to make oneself) neat and tidy
sprucely spruceness sprucing

spruce[2] kind of coniferous tree

sprung past participle of **spring**

spry active; nimble
spryer spryest spryly spryness

spud (*informal*) potato; kind of spade

spume foam or surf

spun past tense and past participle of **spin**

spunk courage; fungus

spur pointed device worn on a horserider's heel to urge on a horse; stimulus; projecting ridge; to urge on
spurred spurring

spurious not genuine
spuriously spuriousness

spurn to reject contemptuously

spurt to gush out in a jet; instance of this; (to make a) sudden increased effort

sputnik (Soviet) satellite

sputter to splutter

sputum saliva, mucus, etc. coughed up
sputa

spy person employed to discover secret information about a rival country or institution; to catch sight of
spies spied spyglass spyhole spying

squab young pigeon; thick cushion for a car, etc.

squabble (to) quarrel over petty matters
squabbled squabbler squabbling

squad small group of people working together as a team

squadron unit of an air force, cavalry or navy

squalid dirty and neglected
squalidly squalor

squall[1] violent burst of wind
squally

squall[2] to cry very noisily
squaller

squander to waste extravagantly
squanderer

square figure with 4 equal sides and 4 right angles; to multiply a number by itself; result of this; even
squarely squareness squarer squarest

squash[1] to crush or squeeze; crushed fruit drink; state of being squashed; game played with rackets in an enclosed court
squashes squashy

squash[2] kind of plant of the cucumber family

squat to sit on one's heels; to occupy property illegally; dumpy
squatted squatter squatting

squaw North American Indian woman

squawk (to utter a) harsh noisy cry
squawker

squeak (to utter a) short shrill cry; (*informal*) escape
squeaker squeaky

squeal (to utter a) long shrill cry; (*informal*) to act as an informer
squealer

squeamish easily shocked or nauseated

squeegee implement with rubber blades used for sweeping water off a surface

squeeze to press tightly; to force through a narrow space; act of squeezing
squeezable squeezer squeezing

squelch (to make a) sucking sound as when removing an object from thick wet mud
squelches

squib small hissing firework; short witty satirical attack

squid kind of sea animal with 10 legs

squiggle (to draw a) short twisting line
squiggling squiggly

squint to have the eyes looking in different directions; defect in which the eyes are like this
squinter

squire main landowner
squirearchy squirearchies squiring

squirm (to) wriggle

squirrel kind of small tree-climbing rodent with a bushy tail

squirt (to force out liquid in a) thin jet
squirter

Sri Lanka country in South Asia
Sri Lankan

stab to pierce or wound with a sharp pointed instrument; instance of stabbing; attempt
stabbed stabber stabbing

stabilize or **stabilise** to make stable
stabilization or *stabilisation stabilizer* or *stabiliser stabilizing* or *stabilising*

stable[1] steady or firm
stability

stable[2] shelter for horses; to put in a stable
stabling

staccato (*music*) performed in a sharp disconnected way

stack (to put in an) ordered pile; (*informal*) large quantity

stadium large sportsground or arena
stadiums or *stadia*

staff personnel or workers (pl. *staffs*); pole (pl. *staffs* or *staves*); musical stave (pl. *staves*)

stag male deer; (*of a party*) for men only

stage raised platform in a theatre; step or period of development; to perform a play
stagecoach stage-manage stage-manager staging stage-struck

stagger to walk unsteadily; to surprise greatly; to arrange in alternating times or positions
staggerer

stagnant (*of water*) not flowing; inactive
stagnancy

stagnate to become stagnant
stagnating stagnation

staid sedate and restrained

stain to discolour, dye, or blemish; mark caused by staining
stainless

stair one of a series of indoor steps from one floor to another
staircase stairway stairwell

stake pointed piece of metal or wood used as a marker or support; to mark or support with a stake; money risked on the outcome of a race, etc.; to risk money
staking

stalactite icicle-like deposit of limestone hanging from the roof of a cave
SEE PANEL

---

stalactite or stalagmite?

A *stalactite* is a deposit of limestone that hangs from the roof of a cave; a *stalagmite* rises from the floor of a cave

A useful mnemonic to help remember the difference is to think of the *c* of *stalactite* as standing for ceiling and the *g* of *stalagmite* as standing for ground.

---

stalagmite pillar-like deposit of limestone rising from the floor of a cave
SEE PANEL at **stalactite**

stale not fresh; dull
saleness staler stalest

stalemate (to bring to a) deadlock or a position in chess in which the king can move only into check
stalemating

stalk[1] main stem of a plant

stalk[2] to pursue or approach stealthily; to walk stiffly
stalker stalking-horse

stall booth from which business is transacted; compartment in a stable for an animal; seat in the ground floor of a theatre; (*of an engine*) to stop unintentionally
stallage stalled stall-holder stalling

stallion uncastrated male horse

stalwart strong; dependable

stamen male part of a flower
stamens

stamina enduring strength

stammer to speak with involuntary hesitations
stammerer stammeringly

stamp printed piece of paper to be stuck on letters to show postage has been paid; to bring the foot down heavily; to print

stampede sudden rush of panicking horses or other large group; to rush in this way
stampeding

stance manner of standing or thinking

stanch or **staunch** to stop the flow of blood, etc.
stanches or *staunches*

stanchion vertical support

stand to take up and remain in an upright position; to endure; table for displaying goods; stall
standby stand-in standing stand-offish standpipe stood

standard flag; principle; level of quality, etc. by which things may be evaluated; accepted or conventional
standard-bearer

standardize or **standardise** to make or become standard
standardization or *standardisation standardizing* or *standardising*

standpoint point of view

standstill stoppage or halt

stank past tense of **stink**

stanza verse of a poem
stanzas

staple[1] (to secure with a) piece of wire bent into a square U-shape
stapler stapling

staple[2] main (food, etc.)

star heavenly body seen as a point of light at night; famous person; to mark with a star; to perform a leading role in
stardom starfish stargazer stargazing starless starlet starlight starlit starred starring starry starry-eyed star-spangled star-studded

starboard right side of a ship or aircraft when facing forward

starch carbohydrate found in potatoes, bread, etc.; form of this used as a stiffener
starches starchiness starchy

stare to look at fixedly; such a look
staring

stark bare; utter; completely
starkly stark-naked starkness

starling kind of common social bird

start to begin; to make a sudden startled movement; beginning; lead
starter starting-point starting-post

startle to make surprised or shocked
startling

starve (to cause) to die from lack of food
starvation starving

stash to store away for future use
stashed stashes

state condition; to express or utter; civil government; political community
stateless statement state-of-the-art stateroom stating

stately dignified
statelier stateliest stateliness

statement something stated

statesman widely respected political leader
statesmanlike statesmanship

static not moving or changing; atmospherics causing electrical interference

station stopping-place for trains; local office of police; rank; to locate
station-master

stationary not moving
SEE PANEL

---

stationary or stationery?

Something that is *stationary* is not moving: *The van ploughed into the back of a stationary lorry; Do not use the toilet while the train is stationary; a stationary target.*

Stationery refers to writing materials, such as paper, pens, and envelopes: *The company specializes in supplying office stationery.*

---

stationer person who sells stationery

stationery writing materials
SEE PANEL at **stationary**

statistics study of collecting, analysing, etc. data; presentation of such data
statistical statistically statistician

statuary (of) statues

statue carved or moulded figure of a person or animal
statuesque

statuette small statue

stature person's height; greatness

status person's rank or standing

status quo existing state of affairs

statute written law of a country
statute-book

statutory required by statute
statutorily

staunch[1] loyal; dependable

staunch[2] see **stanch**

stave 1 of a set of curved pieces that form the side of a barrel; group of 5 parallel lines used in musical notation; to crush or be crushed; to ward (off)
staved or *stove* *staving*

stay[1] to remain; to reside temporarily; period of staying
stay-at-home *stayed* *stayer* *staying*

stay[2] supporting rope, wire, etc.

stead place; benefit

steadfast determined
steadfastly *steadfastness*

steady (to make) stable
steadier *steadiest* *steadily* *steadiness*

steak thick slice of meat or fish
steakhouse

steal to take the property of someone else illegally or without permission; to move stealthily
stealing *stole* *stolen*

stealth moving furtively to avoid being noticed
stealthily *stealthiness* *stealthy*

steam vapour into which boiling water turns; to cook by this
steamboat *steam-engine* *steamer* *steamroller* *steamship* *steamy*

stearic acid waxy acid used in making candles, etc.

steed (*poetic*) horse

steel hard alloy of iron and carbon; to make hard or unfeeling
steel-plated *steelworks* *steely*

steelyard portable balance

steenbok kind of small African antelope

steep[1] sloping sharply; (*informal*) unreasonable
steeply *steepness*

steep[2] to soak in liquid; to saturate

steepen to make or become steep or steeper

steeple tall spire on a church
steeplechase *steeplejack*

steer[1] to guide the course of a vehicle
steerage *steerer* *steering-wheel* *steersman*

steer[2] bullock

stegosaurus plant-eating dinosaur

stein earthenware beer mug with a hinged lid

stele upright decorated slab or column
stelae or *steles*

stellar of stars

stem[1] stalk of plant; main part of a word; to arise (from)
stemmed *stemming*

stem[2] to stop the flow of
stemmed *stemming*

stench very strong and unpleasant smell
stenches

stencil thin sheet of metal, card, etc. with a design cut out; piece of waxed paper on which words have been cut by a typewriter; to produce a copy or design using a stencil
stencilled (US *stenciled*) *stencilling* (US *stenciling*)

Sten gun light sub-machine-gun

stenographer shorthand typist
stenography

stentorian extremely loud

step surface for the foot when going up and down; to move the foot by raising and setting it down; point of advance
stepladder stepped stepping stepping-stone step-up

step- (*prefix*) related by remarriage
stepbrother stepchild stepdaughter stepfather stepmother step-parent stepsister stepson

steppe vast expanse of treeless plain

stereo stereophonic sound; stereophonic record-player
stereos

stereophonic using 2 channels for sound reproduction, etc.
stereophonically stereophony

stereoscope optical instrument with 2 eyepieces that give slightly different views
stereoscopic

stereotype something that is fixed and unchanging; to make a stereotype of
stereotyped stereotyping

sterile unable to produce offspring; barren
sterility

sterilize or **sterilise** to make sterile
sterilization or *sterilisation sterilizing* or *sterilising*

sterling (of) British money; first class

stern[1] severe or strict
sterner sternest sternly sternness

stern[2] rear end of a ship or boat

sternum breastbone

steroid any of a group of organic compounds including various hormones

stertorous snoring loudly

stet (instruction) to retain a word, etc. that has been deleted
stetted stetting

stethoscope instrument for listening to sounds produced in the chest, etc.

stetson man's felt hat with a broad brim

stevedore person who is employed to load and unload ships

stew to cook by simmering for a long time; dish of food prepared in this way

steward (*fem.* **stewardess**) person who attends to passengers on an aircraft or ship; manager
stewardship

stick[1] long narrow piece of wood
stick-insect

stick[2] to attach by using an adhesive, etc.; to push with a pointed instrument; to become fixed
sticker sticking-point stick-in-the-mud stick-on stick-up sticky stuck

stickleback kind or small fish with spines along its back

stickler person who insists on accuracy in tiny details

stiff rigid; not flexible; formal; difficult
stiff-necked

stiffen to make or become stiff
stiffener stiffening

stifle to suffocate; to suppress
stifling

stigma mark of shame (pl. *stigmas*); part of a flower that receives the pollen (pl. *stigmas*); mark resembling wound received by Christ at the crucifixion (pl. *stigmata*)

stigmatize or **stigmatise** to describe contemptuously
stigmatizing or *stigmatising*

stile arrangement of steps for climbing over a wall or fence

stiletto small tapering dagger; tapering heel on a woman's shoe

still[1] not moving; not effervescent; to make still; nevertheless; even
stillness

still[2] distilling apparatus

stillborn (*of a child*) dead at birth

stilt 1 of a pair of long poles with footrests, on which a person may walk above the ground

stilted unnatural; stiff
stiltedly stiltedness

Stilton kind of rich English cheese

stimulant drug that stimulates the body
SEE PANEL

---

stimulant or stimulus?

Both *stimulant* and *stimulus* are used to describe something that stimulates activity. A *stimulant* is usually applied to drugs, alcohol, etc.: *Caffeine is a mild stimulant; He was disqualified from the competition for taking banned stimulants.*

A *stimulus* is a more general word used to describe something that encourages activity: *The reduction in taxes may give a substantial stimulus to the country's ailing economy; new teaching methods that act as a stimulus to a child's creative imagination.*

---

stimulate to arouse or excite
stimulating stimulation stimulative stimulator

stimulus something that stimulates; incentive
stimuli
SEE PANEL at **stimulant**

sting to inflict a wound or to inject poison; act of stinging; organ that stings
stinger stingless stingray stung

stingy mean and miserly
stingier stingiest stingily stinginess

stink (to emit a) strong offensive smell
stank or *stunk stinker stinking stinkwood*

stint to restrict to a small amount; allotted amount of work
stinter

stipend salary paid to a clergyman
stipendiary stipendiaries

stipple to draw, paint, etc. with dots or flecks
stippler stippling

stipulate to state or require as a condition
stipulating stipulation

stir to move slightly; to mix with a turning movement; commotion
stirred stirrer stirring

stirrup support for a horserider's foot

stitch (to make a) complete loop made by a needle and thread; sudden sharp pain in the side
stitches stitcher

stoat weasel-like animal with a black-tipped tail

stock (to) supply or store; farm animals; money lent to a government; liquid in which meat, etc. has simmered
stockbreeder stockbroker stockfish stockholder stock-in-trade stockist stockjobber stock-still stocktaking stockyard

stockade defensive wall of vertical posts

stocking close-fitting covering for a woman's leg and foot
stockinged

stockpile (to acquire an) accumulation of goods
stockpiling

stocks (*formerly*) wooden framework in which criminals' feet, etc. were locked as a punishment

stocky (*of a person*) solidly built
stockier stockiest stockily stockiness

stodge (*informal*) heavy filling food

stodgy (*informal*) (*of food*) heavy and filling, very dull
stodgier stodgiest stodgily stodginess

stoic showing no signs of feeling pain or pleasure
stoical stoically

stoke to add fuel to and tend a fire
stokehold stokehole stoker stoking

stole[1] past tense of **steal**

stole[2] long strip of fur worn by women around the shoulders; long narrow band worn by some clergymen

stolen past participle of **steal**

stolid showing little feeling
stolidity stolidly

stoma tiny hole in the surface of a leaf
stomata

stomach bag-like part of the body into which food passes after it has been swallowed; abdomen; to tolerate
stomach-ache stomach-pump

stomp to tread heavily

stone small piece of rock; to throw stones at; (to remove the) hard covering round the seed of some plants; unit of weight, 14 pounds
stone-cold stonecutter stone-deaf stone-fruit stoneless stonemason stoneware stonework stonier stoniest stonily stoniness stoning stony stony-broke stony-hearted

stonechat kind of Eurasian songbird

stonecrop kind of plant with fleshy leaves

stonewall to bat defensively in cricket; to obstruct parliamentary business

stood past tense and past participle of **stand**

stooge subservient person; assistant

stool seat without a back or arms; discharge from the bowels

stoop to bend forwards; to condescend

stop to bring or come to a halt; to prevent; to block or suppress; state of being stopped; place where buses, etc., stop
stopcock stop-go stopover stoppage stopped stopper stopping stop-press stopwatch

stopgap temporary substitute

storage (space available for) storing something

store to keep for future use; supply; shop; storage place
storehouse storekeeper storeroom storing

storey (US **story**) floor or level of a building
storeys (US *stories*)

stork kind of large long-legged wading bird

storm burst of violent weather; (to) attack violently
stormbound stormier stormiest stormily storminess stormproof storm-tossed storm-trooper stormwater stormy

story account of events; (US) storey
stories storied story-book story-line storyteller

stout sturdy; rather fat; kind of strong beer
stout-hearted stoutly stoutness

stove[1] cooking or heating apparatus

stove[2] past tense and past participle of **stave**

stow to pack away
stowage stowaway

strabismus squint
strabismic

straddle to stand or sit with 1 leg either side of
straddling

strafe to fire upon troops from the air
strafing

straggle to grow wildly; to tag behind or wander away
straggler straggling straggly

straight (part that is) not curved; correct or honest; directly
straightaway straight-faced straightforward straightness

straighten to make straight

strain[1] to tighten; to exert oneself to the limit; to filter; stress
strainer

strain[2] line of ancestry

strait narrow channel between 2 areas of water; difficult position
straiten strait-jacket strait-laced

strand[1] to run aground; to abandon; shore or beach

strand[2] one of a set of threads that is twisted with others to form a rope

strange peculiar; unfamiliar
strangely strangeness stranger strangest

strangle to choke by squeezing the throat
stranglehold strangler strangling

strangulate to constrict an organ such that it can no longer function as a passage
strangulating strangulation

strap (to secure with a) long strip of leather or other flexible material
strapped strapping

strapping tall and robust

stratagem cunning trick
SEE PANEL

---

stratagem or strategy?

A *stratagem* is a plan or trick, especially one that is cunningly designed to deceive people: *apply every possible stratagem to secure the take-over.*

Strategy is the art of planning operations or campaigns: *military strategy,* and is also used to refer to a general plan, especially one that is long-term: *develop the company's marketing strategy.*

---

strategy art of planning operations or campaigns
strategies strategic strategical strategically strategics strategist
SEE PANEL at **stratagem**

strathspey Scottish dance

stratify to form into strata
stratification stratified stratifies stratifying

stratosphere upper layer of the atmosphere
stratospheric

stratum horizontal layer of rock in the earth's crust; layer or class
strata

stratus low layer of cloud
strati

straw stalks of threshed grain; narrow drinking tube

strawberry kind of (plant bearing) juicy red fruit
strawberries

stray to wander away; lost domestic animal; occasional
strayed strayer straying

streak (to mark with a) long thin mark of colour; trace; to move quickly; to run naked through a public place
streaked streaker streakier streakiest streakiness streaky

stream small river; (to move in a) steady flow; to group according to ability

streamer long narrow flag or ribbon

streamline to impart a more efficient shape or design to
streamlined streamlining

street road in a town

streetwise (*informal*) experienced in modern city life

strength state or quality of being strong

strengthen to make stronger
strengthener

strenuous needing a lot of effort
strenuously strenuousness

streptococcus kind of bacteria occurring in a chain-like formation
streptococci streptococcal

stress emphasis; to emphasize; tension
stresses stressful

stretch to make wider or longer by pulling; to extend; continuous expanse
stretches stretchable stretchy

stretcher sheet of canvas between 2 poles, used to carry a patient to hospital

strew to scatter
strewed strewing strewn

stria tiny groove or ridge
striated striation

stricken afflicted

strict demanding obedience; severe; precise
strictly strictness

stricture criticism; constriction of a bodily passage

stride long step; to walk in long steps
stridden striding strode

strident harsh and loud
stridence or *stridency stridently*

strife conflict or discord

strike to hit; to inflict a blow; to produce a sound; to stop work because of a grievance; stoppage of work because of a grievance
strikebreaker striker striking stroke struck

Strine (*informal*) Australian English

string thin length of cord; tightly stretched wire on a musical instrument; to provide with strings
stringy strung

stringent strict; rigorous
stringency stringently

strip[1] to remove the covering of
stripped stripper stripping strip-search strip-tease

strip[2] long narrow piece

stripe band of a different colour, texture, etc.
striped stripy

stripling lad; adolescent boy

strive to make a great effort; to fight
striven striver striving strove

stroboscope instrument that produces an intense flashing light

strode past tense of **stride**

stroganoff rich dish of sliced beef in a sour cream sauce

stroke[1] to pass the hand gently over
stroking

stroke[2] blow or movement; striking of a ball; sudden attack, esp. causing paralysis

stroll (to go for a) leisurely walk

strong having strength or power; robust, not fragile; alcoholic
strong-arm strongbox stronghold strong-minded strongroom

strontium soft silvery-white metallic element

strop (to use a) leather strap for sharpening razors
stropped stropping

stroppy (*informal*) quarrelsome and awkward
stroppier stroppiest

strove past tense of **strive**

struck past tense and past participle of **strike**

structure construction, arrangement, or framework; building
structural structuralism structurally

strudel pastry consisting of a thin sheet of baked and filled dough

struggle to make great efforts; great effort or fight
struggler struggling

strum to play a guitar, etc. by sweeping the fingers lightly over the strings
strummed strummer strumming

strung past tense and past participle of **string**

strut to walk about in a pompous stiff manner; supporting part of a framework
strutted strutter strutting

strychnine highly poisonous substance

stub short remaining piece of a cigarette, etc.; to hit against a hard surface
stubbed stubbing

stubble short bristly growth of hair; ends of cereal stalks after harvesting
stubbly

stubborn obstinate
stubbornly stubbornness

stubby short and broad
stubbier stubbiest stubbily stubbiness

stucco (to cover with a) kind of wall plaster
stuccoes or *stuccos stuccoed stuccoing stuccowork*

stuck past tense and past participle of **stick**
stuck-up

stud[1] number of horses, etc. kept for breeding

stud[2] kind of fastener; nail, etc. with a large head on the sole of a boot; to provide with a stud
studded studding

student person who studies
studentship

studio room in which radio or television programmes are made; workroom of an artist or photographer
studios

studious hard-working
studiously studiousness

study to use the mind in order to gain knowledge of; to examine closely; room for studying
studies studied studying

stuff to pack tightly; material or substance
stuffing

stuffy lacking fresh air; dull
stuffier stuffiest stuffily stuffiness

stultify to make futile or ridiculous
stultification stultified stultifier stultifies stultifying

stumble to trip while walking or running
stumbler stumbling stumbling-block

stump remaining part of a tree-trunk after the tree has been felled; 1 of 3 upright posts of a wicket in cricket; (*informal*) to baffle
stumpy

stun to overwhelm; to make unconscious
stunned stunner stunning

stung past tense and past participle of **sting**

stunk past participle of **stink**

stunt[1] to prevent the growth of

stunt[2] unusual risky feat

stupefy to make senseless; to bewilder
stupefaction stupefied stupefies stupefying

stupendous tremendous; astounding
stupendously stupendousness

stupid foolish; unthinking; dazed
stupidity stupidly

stupor drowsy dazed condition, caused by drink, drugs, etc.

sturdy strong and robust
sturdier sturdiest sturdily sturdiness

sturgeon kind of large edible fish valued for its roe

stutter (to) stammer
stutterer

sty[1] enclosure for pigs
sties

sty[2] or **stye** inflamed swelling on the edge of an eyelid
sties or *styes*

style manner; form or appearance; elegance; to shape
styling stylish stylist stylistic stylistically

stylize or **stylise** to give a conventional style to
stylization or *stylisation stylizing* or *stylising*

stylus needle-like piece that follows the groove of a gramophone record
styluses or *styli*

stymie to obstruct or thwart; obstruction
stymies stymied stymieing

styptic (something) that stops bleeding

suable or **sueable** that can be sued

suave very agreeable and sophisticated in manner
suavely suaver suavest suavity

sub[1] (*informal*) submarine

sub[2] (*informal*) (to act as a) substitute
subbed subbing

sub[3] (*informal*) subscription

sub- (*prefix*) below; subordinate
subcommittee subheading sub-plot subsection subspecies substratum subsystem subzero

subaltern commissioned army officer below a captain

subatomic of particles smaller than atoms

subconscious of mental activities of which one is not aware
subconsciously subconsciousness
SEE PANEL

---

subconscious or unconscious?

A *subconscious* thought, feeling, or action is one that exists or is influenced by the *subconscious,* the part of your mind that can have an effect on your behaviour and actions without your being aware of it: *a subconscious urge to punish himself.*

A person who is *unconscious* is not conscious: *He was knocked unconscious by a blow on the head.* If you are *unconscious* of something, you are unaware of it: *The children played amidst the earthquake ruins, happily unconscious of the danger they were in.* if something is *unconscious* it is unintentional: *The unconscious smiles of a baby's early days.*

In psychology, both words as nouns relate to the part of the mind that you are not usually aware of and that can have an effect on your behaviour. *Subconscious* is the more frequently used in general language: *Memories of the trauma surrounding their divorce had been driven deep into his subconscious.*

---

subcontinent large land mass that is part of a continent

subcontract (to let out or accept under a) contract with a person, company, etc. not party to the original contract
subcontractor

subculture culture within a national culture

subcutaneous under the skin

subdivide to divide into smaller parts
subdivision

subdue to control or overcome; to make less intense
subduing

sub-edit to prepare (newspaper copy) for printing or publication
sub-editor sub-editorial

subfusc dark formal clothing worn at some universities

subhuman less than human

subject branch of study; topic being discussed; word or phrase in a sentence about which something is said; to conquer; to cause to undergo
subjection

subjective not objective; personal
subjectively subjectivism subjectivist subjectivity

subjoin (*formal*) to append

sub judice (*Latin*) under judicial consideration

subjugate to bring under control; to conquer
subjugating subjugation subjugator

subjunctive (*grammar*) (*of a word*) used to express condition, possibility, wish, etc.

sublet to let the property that one is oneself renting to someone else
subletting

sub-lieutenant junior commissioned naval officer

sublimate to direct energy or emotion into a socially more acceptable form; to sublime
sublimating sublimation

sublime of the most noble value; inspiring awe; to cause to pass from solid to vapour (and to solid again)
sublimely sublimer sublimest sublimity

subliminal directed at the subconscious
subliminally

sub-machine-gun automatic or semi-automatic portable rapid-firing gun

submarine vessel, esp. a warship, designed to travel under water

submerge to place under water; to sink
submergence submerging submersible submersion

submissive willing to submit
submissively submissiveness

submit to yield; to present for consideration
submission submitted submitting

subnormal less than normal

subordinate (person or thing that is) lower in rank or significance
subordinating subordination

suborn to induce a person by bribery
subornation

subpoena (to serve with an) order requiring a person to appear in court
subpoenas subpoenaed subpoenaing

subroutine sequence of computer instructions that can be repeated

subscribe to pay money regularly to an organization providing a magazine, etc.
subscriber subscribing subscription

subsequent following
subsequently

subservient servile; submissive
subservience subserviently

sub-set (*maths*) set whose elements are contained within a larger set

subside to sink; to become less intense
subsidence subsiding

subsidiarity principle that political decisions should be made at the lowest, most local level

subsidiary auxiliary; subordinate; subsidiary person or thing
subsidiaries

subsidize or **subsidise** to provide with a subsidy
subsidization or *subsidisation subsidizing* or *subsidising*

subsidy money paid by a government, as to an industry in financial difficulty
subsidies

subsist to succeed in living on
subsistence

subsoil layer of soil below the surface layer

subsonic less than the speed of sound
subsonically

substance (solid) matter; essential part
substantial substantiality substantially

substandard below the normal or required standard

substantiate to prove to be true
substantiating substantiation

substantive (*grammar*) noun; existing (independently)

substitute (to put a) person or thing in the place of another
substituting substitution

subsume to incorporate into a group
subsuming subsumption

subtenant person who rents from a tenant

subtend (*geometry*) to be opposite to

subterfuge cunning trick

subterranean under the surface of the earth

subtitle subordinate title; written translation of a foreign dialogue on a film

subtle not easily detectable or incomprehensible
subtler subtlest subtlety subtleties subtly

subtotal total of part of a series of figures

subtract to take away one number or quantity from another
subtraction

subtropical near the tropical zone

suburb residential district on the outskirts of a city or town
suburban suburbanite suburbanization or *suburbanisation suburbanize* or *suburbanise suburbanizing* or *suburbanising suburbia*

subvention grant or subsidy

subvert to undermine the authority of
subversion subversive subversively subversiveness

subway underground passage for pedestrians; (US) underground railway

succeed to achieve an aim; to inherit; to follow
succession successor

success achievement of an aim

successful achieving the intended aim
successfully
SEE PANEL

---

successful or successive?
A person who is *successful* has achieved fame, riches, or power; something that is *successful* has achieved what it intended to: *At 30, she had become one of the company's most successful business executives; a successful attempt to conquer Everest; an immensely successful film that broke all box-office records.*

Successive means following on immediately after another: *the team's sixth successive victory; The country is still suffering from the failure of successive governments to invest in manufacturing industry.*

---

successive consecutive
successively
SEE PANEL at **successful**

succinct expressed concisely
succinctly

succour (US **succor**) (to give) assistance or relief at a time of need

succubus female demon believed to have intercourse with sleeping men
succubi

succulent juicy; having thick fleshy leaves
succulence succulently

succumb to give way to; to die

such of the same or that kind; so great or intense; mentioned before
suchlike

suck to draw a liquid into the mouth
sucker suction

suckle to feed by taking milk at the breast
suckling

sucrose natural sugar

Sudan country in NE Africa
Sudanese

sudden quickly and unexpectedly
suddenly suddenness

suds bubbles on soapy water

sue to bring a legal action against
suable or *sueable sued suing*

suede leather with a soft napped surface

suet hard animal fat used in cooking
suety

suffer to experience pain, etc.; (*formal*) to tolerate
sufferable sufferance sufferer suffering

suffice to be adequate for
sufficing

sufficient adequate
sufficiency sufficiently

suffix part of a word that goes at the end of a word to change its meaning
suffixes

suffocate to kill or choke by depriving of oxygen
suffocating suffocation

suffragan (assistant) bishop

suffrage right to vote

suffragette (*historical*) woman who advocates women's right to vote

suffuse to spread through or over
suffusing *suffusion*

Sufi Muslim mystic

sugar sweet substance obtained from sucrose; to add sugar to
sugar-beet *sugar-bowl* *sugar-cane* *sugar-coated* *sugary*

suggest to present for consideration; to evoke
suggestibility *suggestible* *suggestion*

suggestive evocative
suggestively *suggestiveness*

suicide (person who commits the) deliberate killing of oneself
suicidal

sui generis (*Latin*) of its own kind; unique

suit set of outer clothes; set of playing-cards; legal case; to be appropriate for
suiting *suitor*
SEE PANEL

---

suit or suite?
A *suit* is a set of outer clothes: *wear a smart pin-stripe suit;* a set of playing-cards, or a legal case: *file a multi-million pound libel suit.*
A *suite* is a set of rooms: *stay in the hotel's honeymoon suite,* a matching set of furniture: *buy a new three-piece suite for the sitting-room; a bathroom suite,* or a musical composition: *a ballet suite.*

---

suitable appropriate or fitting
suitability or *suitableness* *suitably*

suitcase portable travelling case for clothes

suite set of rooms; matching set of furniture; musical composition
SEE PANEL at **suit**

sulfate (US) see **sulphate**

sulfide (US) see **sulphide**

sulfur (US) see **sulphur**

sulk to be silent and resentful, because one is in a bad mood
sulky

sullen gloomy; morose
sullenly *sullenness*

sully to tarnish or stain
sullied *sullies* *sullying*

sulphate (US **sulfate**) salt or ester of sulphuric acid

sulphide (US **sulfide**) binary compound of sulphur and an electropositive element

sulphur (US **sulfur**) yellow non-metallic element
sulphuric (US *sulfuric*) *sulphurous* (US *sulfurous*)

sultan (*fem.* **sultana**) Muslim ruler
sultanate

sultana seedless raisin

sultry unpleasantly humid
sultrier *sultriest* *sultrily* *sultriness*

sum total amount; simple arithmetical problem; to summarize
summation *summed* *summing*

Sumatra island in West Indonesia
Sumatran

summarize or **summarise** to be or make a summary of
summarizing or *summarising*

summary concise statement of facts; concise; performed without delay
summaries

summer season between spring and autumn
summer-house *summer-time* *summery*

summit top of a mountain; meeting of heads of governments

summon to order to come
SEE PANEL

---

summon or summons?
If you *summon* a person, you order them to come to you: *be summoned to the manager's office; to summon* up courage means to make a

great effort to be courageous: *I eventually summoned up the courage to ask her to marry me.*

A *summons* is an order to appear in a court of law: *He had been served with a summons to appear in the High Court.* If a person is *summonsed*, they are ordered officially to appear in a court of law: *I was summonsed to appear before the magistrates' court.*

summons (to) order to appear in court
summonses
SEE PANEL at **summon**

sump hole into which liquid waste drains; oil reservoir in an internal combustion engine

sumptuary regulating expenditure

sumptuous lavish; extravagant
sumptuously sumptuousness

sun star, around which the earth and other planets revolve
sunbathe sunbeam sunbed sunblind sunblock sun-bonnet sunburn sunburnt or *sunburned sundial sundown sunfish sunflower sunglasses sun-god sun-hat sunlamp sunless sunlight sunlit sunrise sunset sunshade sunshine sunspot sunstroke sun-tan sun-trap sun-up*

sundae ice-cream with fruit, nuts, etc.
sundaes

Sunday 1st day of the week

sundries various small items

sundry various

sung past participle of **sing**

sunk past participle of **sink**

sunken hollow; sunk

sunny having a lot of sunshine; bright
sunnier sunniest sunnily sunniness

sup to eat supper
supped supper supping

super (*informal*) excellent

super- (*prefix*) beyond; greater than usual
superabundant

superannuate to retire on a pension
superannuable superannuating superannuation

superb magnificent
superbly

supercargo person on a merchant ship who supervises the commercial concerns of the voyage
supercargoes

supercharger device supplying air to an internal-combustion engine

supercilious arrogantly disdainful
superciliously superciliousness

superconductivity loss of electrical resistance by certain metals at temperatures close to absolute zero

superego division of the mind that is only partly conscious
superegos

superficial of or restricted to the surface
superficiality superficially

superficies surface

superfluous more than is required
superfluity superfluously

superglue extremely strong glue

superhuman with exceptional human ability or strength

superimpose to place on top of something else
superimposing superimposition

superintend to direct or supervise
superintendence superintendent

superior (person who is) higher in rank or worth
superiority

superlative of the highest quality or degree; (*grammar*) (form of an) adjective or adverb expressing the highest degree of comparison

superman (*fem.* **superwoman**) person with superhuman powers

supermarket large self-service shop

supernatural of phenomena beyond the natural laws
supernaturally

supernova star that explodes, becoming temporarily very bright
supernovae

supernumerary exceeding the usual number; extra assistant
supernumeraries

superpower extremely powerful nation

superscribe to write on top of
superscribing superscription

supersede to take the place of
superseding supersedure supersession

supersonic greater than the speed of sound
supersonically

superstition belief in magic, chance, sorcery, etc.
superstitious superstitiously

superstore very large supermarket

superstructure part of a building above the foundation; part of a ship above the main deck

supertanker very large tanker

supertax income tax payable by people with higher incomes

supervene to happen as an interruption to a process
supervenient supervening supervention

supervise to be in charge of or direct work or workers
supervising supervision supervisor supervisory

supine lying on the back; lethargic
supinely

supper evening meal or snack
supperless

supplant to take the place of
supplanter

supple bending easily; flexible
suppleness suppler supplest supplely or *supply*

supplement (to make an) addition
supplementary supplementation

suppliant entreating

supplicate to humbly request
supplicant supplicating supplication

supply to provide with; something supplied; store
supplies supplied supplier supplying

support to bear the weight of; to give aid to; to back; structure that supports
supportable supporter supportive

suppose to believe to be true; to necessitate
supposable supposed supposedly supposing supposition

suppositious hypothetical
suppositiously suppositiousness

supposititious spurious

suppository medicated substance to be put into the vagina or rectum where it melts
suppositories

suppress to prohibit or restrain
suppresses suppressible suppression suppressive suppressor

suppuration formation of pus

supranational involving more than one nation

supreme highest (in authority, etc.)
supremacy supremely

supremo (*informal*) person with overall authority
supremos

surcharge (to make an) additional charge
surcharging

surcoat loose outer coat

surd (*maths*) irrational root

sure certain or confident
sure-fire sure-footed surely sureness surer surest

surety guarantee or security
sureties

surf white foam made by waves breaking
surfboard surfer surfing surf-riding

surface external or top of something; to rise to the surface
surfacing

surfeit excess (of); to supply excessively

surge to move forward like waves; to increase in intensity; surging movement
surger surging

surgeon doctor who specializes in surgery
surgical surgically

surgery treatment of diseases by operations; place where a doctor or dentist treats patients
surgeries

Surinam country in NE South America

surly bad-tempered
surlier surliest surlily surliness

surmise (to) guess
surmising

surmount to overcome
surmountable

surname family name

surpass to be better than
surpassable surpasses

surplice loose white ecclesiastical gown

surplus amount in excess of what is required

surprise to amaze suddenly; to startle; something unexpected
surprised surprising surprisingly

surrealism modern movement in art and literature
surrealist surrealistic

surrender to yield control over; to give (oneself) up

surreptitious performed secretly or stealthily
surreptitiously surreptitiousness

surrogate substitute or deputy

surround to enclose on all sides; border
surroundings

surtax graduated additional income tax

surveillance close watch

survey to view; to examine or inspect; to measure and plot land; view; examination or report
surveying surveyor

survive to continue to live (through)
survival surviving survivor

sus (*informal*) suspicion of loitering

susceptible easily affected by
susceptibility susceptibilities susceptibly

suspect to have doubts about; to consider likely; to believe to be guilty of a crime

suspend to hang; to postpone; to stay immobile in a liquid or air
suspender suspensory

suspense feeling of tense waiting
SEE PANEL

---

suspense or suspension?
Suspense is the feeling of tense waiting for something that is going to happen or be revealed: *Don't keep me in suspense – tell me whether you passed or not!*
Suspension is the postponement or delay of something, or the temporary removal of a person from a position or job: *the suspension of all flights because of bad weather; Smith faces a two-month suspension following the incident on the pitch.* The *suspension* on a vehicle is the system of springs and shock absorbers, etc., that supports the upper part of the vehicle and which reduces the effects of bumps in the road.

---

suspension postponement or delay; temporary removal of a person from a position or job; system of springs and shock absorbers, etc.
SEE PANEL at **suspense**

suspicion doubt; feeling that something is likely
suspicious suspiciously suspiciousness

suss (*informal*) to detect; to work (out)
sussed sussing

sustain to maintain; to support; to undergo
sustainable sustenance

suttee custom of a Hindu woman burning herself to death on her husband's funeral pyre

suture surgical stitch or stitches sewn to close a wound
sutural suturally

suzerain nation exercising dominion over another state
suzerainty

svelte attractive and slender

swab (to clean with a) wad of absorbent material
swabbed swabber swabbing

swaddle to wrap a baby in long narrow strips of cloth
swaddling

swag (*informal*) goods obtained illegally; loot

swagger to walk or behave arrogantly
swaggerer swaggeringly

Swahili language of East Africa

swallow[1] to send food, etc. down the throat into the stomach

swallow[2] forked-tailed migratory insect-eating bird
swallow-tail

swam past tense of **swim**

swami Hindu religious teacher

swamp waterlogged land; to flood with water
swampy

swan kind of large long-necked water bird; (*informal*) to wander aimlessly (about)
swanned swannery swanning
swansdown swansong swan-upping

swank (*informal*) to show off
swanky

swap or **swop** (*informal*) to exchange
swapped or *swopped swapper* or *swopper*
swapping or *swopping*

sward (stretch of) turf

swarm[1] group or great cluster of bees, etc.; to move together in great numbers

swarm[2] to climb (up)

swarthy dark-complexioned
swarthier swarthiest swarthily swarthiness

swashbuckler swaggering adventurer
swashbuckling

swastika cross-shaped symbol, adopted by the Nazi Party

swat to hit flies, etc. with a flat implement
swatted swatter swatting

swatch sample piece of cloth
swatches

swath line of cut grass

swathe to bind or wrap
swathing

sway to (cause to) swing gently from side to side; (to) influence

Swaziland country in southern Africa
Swazi

swear to promise or assert on oath or emphatically; to use bad language
swearer swearing swear-word swore sworn

sweat (to exude) moisture passed out of the body through pores
sweat-band sweated sweatshirt sweatshop sweaty

sweater pullover

swede kind of large yellow turnip

Sweden country in NW Europe
Swede Swedish

sweep to clean or clear away with a brush; to move or pass quickly *sweepback sweeper sweeping sweep-out sweep-up swept*

sweeping wide-ranging; without reservation

sweepstake kind of gambling

sweet tasting of or like sugar; fresh; piece of confectionery; dessert
sweet-and-sour sweetbread sweet-brier sweetcorn sweeten sweetener sweetheart sweetie sweetmeat

swell to expand; to bulge
swelled swelling swollen

swelter to suffer from too much heat

swept past tense and past participle of **sweep**
swept-back swept-wing

swerve to turn suddenly from a course; swerving movement
swerving

swift fast; kind of long-winged bird that has a fast darting flight

swig (*informal*) (to) gulp (of) a drink
swigged swigging

swill to wash out; waste food and liquid

swim to move the body through water; to have a dizzy feeling
swam swimmer swimming swimming-bath swimming-costume swimming-pool swimmingly swim-suit swum

swindle to cheat
swindler swindling

swine pig; contemptible person
swineherd swinish

swing to move to and fro, hanging freely; child's suspended seat that swings
swing-boat swing-door swinging swing-wing swung

swingeing drastic; severe

swipe (*informal*) to hit hard; to steal
swiper swiping

swirl (to) turn in a whirling movement
swirly

swish to move with a whistling sound
swishes swishy

switch (to turn on or off using a) device that operates an electric current; to shift
switches switchback switchboard switch-over

Switzerland country in West Europe
Swiss

swivel to turn on a pivot that allows the moving part to rotate freely
swivelled (US *swiveled*) *swivelling* (US *swiveling*)

swizz (*slang*) swindle
swizzes

swizzle alcoholic drink

swollen past participle of **swell**
swollen-headed

swoon (to) faint

swoop (to come down in a) fast attacking movement

swop see **swap**

sword weapon with long blade
sword-dance swordfish swordplay swordsman swordsmanship swordstick

swore past tense of **swear**

sworn past participle of **swear**

swot (*Brit informal*) to study hard for an examination; person who swots
swotted swotter swotting

swum past participle of **swim**

swung past tense and past participle of **swing**

sycamore kind of large maple tree

sycophant flatterer
sycophancy sycophantic

syllabify to divide into syllables
syllabification syllabified syllabifies syllabifying

syllable unit of a word that contains a vowel

syllabub see **sillabub**

syllabus outline of a course of study
syllabuses or *syllabi*

syllogism form of deductive reasoning
syllogistic *syllogize* or *syllogise*

sylph slender graceful girl; female fairy
sylphlike

sylvan or **silvan** of woods

symbiosis close relationship between individuals of different organisms
symbiotic

symbol sign that represents something
symbolic *symbolical* *symbolically* *symbolism*

symbolize or **symbolise** to serve as a symbol of
symbolization or *symbolisation* *symbolizing* or *symbolising*

symmetry balance or correspondence between parts of a system
symmetrical *symmetrically* *symmetrize* or *symmetrise*

sympathetic marked by sympathy
sympathetically

sympathize or **sympathise** to show or feel sympathy
sympathizer or *sympathiser* *sympathizing* or *sympathising*

sympathy ability to share another person's feelings; feeling of compassion
sympathies

symphony musical composition for an orchestra
symphonies *symphonic* *symphonically*

symposium conference
symposia or *symposiums*

symptom sign, esp. of a disease
symptomatic

synaeresis (*grammar*) contraction of 2 vowels
synaereses

synagogue place of Jewish worship
synagogal

synchromesh system for changing gear

synchronize or **synchronise** to (cause to) occur at the same time
synchronism *synchronistic* *synchronization* or *synchronisation* *synchronizing* or *synchronising* *synchronous* *synchronously*

syncopate (*music*) to modify the beat
syncopating *syncopation*

syncope fainting; (*grammar*) dropping of a sound

syncretism combination of different systems of belief
syncretist

syndic business agent of a university, etc.

syndicalism theory that workers should control the means of production
syndical *syndicalist*

syndicate association of business partners, enterprises, etc. for the simultaneous publication of an article in several newspapers
syndicating *syndication*

syndrome combination of symptoms that indicate a disease

synecdoche figure of speech in which a part is substituted for the whole or vice versa

synergy combined action in which the effect of two or more things is greater than the sum of the individual effects of each one
synergies

synod church council
synodal *synodic*

synonym word with a very similar meaning to another
synonymous *synonymy*

synopsis brief outline or statement
synopses *synoptic*

synovia transparent viscous lubricating fluid secreted by a joint or tendon membrane
synovial *synovitis*

syntax arrangement of words in larger units
syntactic syntactically

synthesis combination of parts to form a whole
syntheses

synthesize or **synthesise** to make by synthesis
synthesization or *synthesisation synthesizer* or *synthesiser synthesizing* or *synthesising*

synthetic artificially made
synthetically

syphilis kind of contagious venereal disease
syphilitic syphiloid

syphon see **siphon**

syringa mock orange, kind of garden shrub

Syria country in West Asia
Syriac Syrian

syringe (to use a) device for injecting or withdrawing liquids
syringing

syrup thick sweet liquid
syrupy

system combination of related parts; ordered scheme
systematic systematically systemic

systematize or **systematise** to arrange in a system
systematization or *systematisation*
systematizing or *systematising*

systole contraction of the heart
systolic

syzygy configuration in which the sun, moon, and earth lie in a straight line
syzygies

T

tab (to provide with a) small flap or tag
tabbed tabbing

tabard short sleeveless jacket

tabby striped domestic cat
tabbies

tabernacle (*Bible*) portable sacred sanctuary of the ancient Israelites; place of worship

table flat-topped piece of furniture; orderly arrangement of data; to present for discussion
tablecloth tableland table-mat tablespoon tablespoonful tablespoonfuls tabletop tabling

tableau scene, esp. represented by a group of silent motionless people
tableaux

table d'hôte meal in a restaurant with little or no choice and at a fixed price

tablet small flat slab; small compressed piece; pill

tabloid popular newspaper with a relatively small page size

taboo (something) forbidden by social or religious custom

tabor kind of small drum

tabulate to arrange in table form
tabular tabulating tabulation tabulator

tachograph device that records the speed and duration of a journey in a vehicle

tachometer device for measuring speed

tacit understood but not stated explicitly
tacitly

taciturn not talkative
taciturnity

tack (to fasten with a) small nail; to sew with a long loose stitch; to sail a zigzag course

tackle arrangement of ropes and pulleys for lifting things; to deal with; to try and take the ball from
tackling

tacky slightly sticky
tackier tackiest tackily tackiness

tact skill in dealing with people without causing offence
tactful tactfully tactfulness tactless tactlessly tactlessness

tactic plan for achieving an aim
tactical tactically

tactics skilful strategy, as of manoeuvring forces in battle
tactician

tactile of the sense of touch
tactility

tadpole larva of a frog or toad

taffeta crisp shiny plain-woven fabric

taffrail rail at the stern of a ship

tag[1] (to fit with a) label; common saying
tagged tagging

tag[2] children's chasing game

Tagalog member of a people of the Philippines; their language

tagliatelle narrow strips of pasta

Tahiti island in the South Pacific
Tahitian

t'ai chi Chinese martial art and system of exercises

tail movable part that extends from the back of an animal; to follow closely
tail-back tailboard tailgate tailless tail-light tailpiece tailpipe tailplane tailspin tailwind

tailor person who makes men's clothes; to adjust or adapt
tailor-made

taint to spoil, pollute, or contaminate; trace of something that taints

Taiwan island in SE Asia
Taiwanese

Tajikistan country in Central Asia

take to hold or seize; to obtain; to carry; to steal
take-away take-home take-off take-over take-up taking took

talc smooth soft mineral
talcum

tale story; lie or gossip
tale-bearer

talent natural ability or skill
talented

talisman charm or amulet
talismans talismanic

talk to speak; conversation or lecture
talkback talker talking-to

talkative given to talking a lot
talkatively talkativeness

tall of greater than the average height
taller tallest tallness

tallboy high chest of drawers

tallow animal fat used for making candles, soap, etc.

tally account of expenditure; to agree or correspond
tallies tallied tallying

tally-ho huntsman's cry
tally-hos

Talmud compilation of Jewish law and tradition

talon sharp claw of a bird of prey

tamarind kind of (fruit of a) tropical evergreen tree

tamarisk kind of Mediterranean tree and shrub

tambour kind of drum; rolling front of a desk

tambourine small shallow drum with loose metallic discs round the edge

tame not wild; (to bring) under human control
tameable or *tamable tamely tameness tamest taming*

Tamil language of South India and Sri Lanka; Tamil-speaking person

tam-o'-shanter Scottish woollen or cloth cap

tamp to force down

tamper to interfere

tampion plug for a muzzle of a gun

tampon plug of absorbent material used to stop bleeding, etc.

tan to turn animal skin into leather; to turn brown from exposure to the sun; yellowish-brown
tanned tanner tannery tanneries tanning

tandem bicycle for 2 riders, one sitting behind the other

tandoori food cooked over charcoal in a clay oven

tang strong taste or flavour
tangy

tangent straight line that touches a curve but does not intersect it; different course
tangency tangential tangentially

tangerine kind of small orange-like fruit

tangible that can be touched; actual or real
tangibility tangibly

tangle (to (cause to) become in a) confused mass or state
tangling tangly

tango (to perform a) slow Latin American dance
tangos tangoed tangoing

tank large container for liquids or gases; heavily armoured military vehicle
tankage tanker tankful

tankard large single-handed drinking vessel

tanner person who tans hides

tannin compound obtained from tree-bark, etc.

Tannoy (*trademark*) kind of public-address system

tansy kind of aromatic plant
tansies

tantalize or **tantalise** to torment by offering something desirable but not within reach, etc.
tantalizer or *tantaliser tantalizing* or *tantalising tantalizingly* or *tantalisingly*

tantalum hard greyish-white metallic element

tantamount equivalent (to)

tantrum fit of rage
tantrums

Tanzania country in East Africa
Tanzanian

Taoism Chinese philosophy and religion
Tao Taoist

tap[1] to strike gently
tap-dance tapped tapping

tap[2] valve for controlling the flow of a gas or liquid; to draw from; to connect a listening device to in order to gain secret information
tapped tapper tapping taproom taproot tap-water

tape long narrow strip of material; long narrow strip of plastic with a coating that can be magnetized, used to record sound, video, etc. signals; to record on to magnetic tape
tape-measure tape-recorder tape-recording tapeworm taping

taper to become narrower towards one end
tapering

tapestry heavy woven fabric, often used as a wall hanging
tapestries

tapioca starchy food obtained from cassava

tapir pig-like mammal of tropical Asia and America

tappet projection in a machine that causes a movement

tar (to coat with a) dark sticky substance obtained from wood, coal, etc.
tarred tarring tarry

taramasalata pale pink paste made from fish roe

tarantella lively Italian folk dance

tarantula kind of large hairy spider
tarantulas or *tarantulae*

tarboosh red hat resembling a fez

tardy slow or late
tardier tardiest tardily tardiness

tare[1] kind of vetch

tare[2] weight of a container when empty

target object or aim, esp. for shooting at; to make a target of
targeted targeting

tariff tax on goods imported or exported; list of prices

Tarmac (*trademark*) road-surfacing material

tarn small mountain lake

tarnish to (cause to) lose brightness
tarnishes

tarot any of a set of playing-cards used in fortune-telling

tarpaulin piece of heavy waterproof canvas

tarragon kind of plant with aromatic leaves that are used in seasoning

tarry to linger
tarried tarrier tarries tarrying

tarsus 7 small bones of the instep
tarsi tarsal

tart[1] pastry pie with fruit filling; (*slang*) prostitute; sexually promiscuous girl or woman; to smarten (up) in a showy way

tart[2] acid; cutting
tartly tartness

tartan (*Scottish*) cloth with a pattern of coloured stripes crossing at right angles

tartar[1] substance that forms a hard deposit on the teeth; substance deposited inside wine casks
tartaric

tartar[2] fearsome or exacting person

tartrazine yellow soluble powder used as an artificial colouring

task piece of work; duty
taskmaster taskmistress

Tasmania island south of Australia
Tasmanian

Tass main news agency of the former Soviet Union

tassel bunch of hanging threads used as a decoration
tasselled (US *tasseled*)

taste sense by which flavour is perceived; to recognize or have the flavour of; ability to appreciate aesthetically fine matters
taste-bud tasteful tastefully tastefulness tasteless tastelessly tastelessness taster tastier tastiest tastily tastiness tasting tasty

tat to make by tatting
tatted

tattered old and ragged

tatters old ragged clothing

tatting (work of making a) kind of delicate lace

tattle (to) gossip
tattler tattling

tattoo[1] drum or call signalling soldiers back to their quarters; outdoor military display
tattoos

tattoo[2] to mark the skin by pricking and staining with indelible colours; design that has been tattooed
tattoos tattooed tattooer tattooing tattooist

tatty shabby
tattier tattiest tattily tattiness

taught past tense and past participle of **teach**

taunt to tease in a provocative way
taunter tauntingly

Taurus 2nd sign of the zodiac

taut tightly stretched; tense
tautly tautness

tauten to make or become taut

tautology needless repetition of words
tautological tautologous

tavern public house

tawdry showy and cheap
tawdrily tawdriness

tawny brownish-orange

tax sum of money levied by a government on income, etc.; to levy a tax on; to make demands of
taxes taxable taxation tax-deductible tax-free taxpayer

taxi car that may be hired with a driver; (*of an aircraft*) to move along the ground
taxis or *taxies taxied taxies taxiing taximeter*

taxidermy art of preparing, stuffing, and mounting the skins of animals
taxidermist

tea drink made from the dried leaves of an Asian evergreen shrub; late-afternoon or early-evening meal
tea-bag tea-break teacake tea-chest tea-cloth tea-cosy teacup tea-leaf teapot tea-room tea-set tea-shop teaspoon teaspoonful teaspoonfuls teatime tea-towel

teach to give instruction to
taught teachability teachable teacher teaches teaching

teach-in intensive teaching session with instruction and discussion

teak kind of (large tropical tree with a) hard wood used to make furniture

teal kind of small freshwater duck

team group of people organized to work or play together
team-mate teamster teamwork

tear[1] drop of liquid coming from the eye
tear-drop tearful tear-gas tear-jerker

tear[2] to pull apart forcefully; to rip; to make a hole in something
tearable tearaway tore torn

tease to make fun of; to annoy; to untangle with a comb; to raise the nap on
teaser teasing

teasel, **teazel**, or **teazle** kind of plant with prickly flower-heads, formerly used for teasing cloth

teat nipple

technetium silver-grey metallic element

technical of or concerned with industrial or applied sciences
technicality technicalities technically
SEE PANEL

---

technical or technological?

Technical refers to the special practical knowledge of industrial or applied sciences, such as communications or engineering: *The delay is because of a technical problem; offer technical support; The post requires a technical qualification. Technical* also refers to the specialist terms used to describe a particular subject: *a dictionary of the technical words used in microbiology*

Technological refers to the application of science to industry and commerce: *technological changes that have enabled many individuals to buy their own personal computer; the implications of the latest technological developments.*

---

technician skilled scientific or industrial worker

Technicolor (*trademark*) process of colour photography in the cinema

technique method of doing something skilfully

technocracy government by technical experts
technocracies technocrat technocratic

technology application of science to industry and commerce
technologies technological technologically technologist
SEE PANEL at **technical**

tectonics study of construction or building; branch of geology
tectonic tectonically

ted to spread grass for drying
tedded tedder tedding

teddy bear stuffed toy bear

Teddy boy British youth in 1950s

tedious long and dull
tediously tediousness

tedium dullness or boredom

tee level area from which the ball is driven in golf; to place the ball on a tee
teed teeing

teem[1] to have abundantly

teem[2] (*of rain*) to fall heavily

teenage of a person in his or her teens
teenaged teenager

teens years of one's age from 13 to 19

teeny (*informal*) very small
teenier teeniest teeny-weeny

teeny-bopper young teenage girl who enthusiastically follows latest fashions, etc.

teeter to move unsteadily

teeth pl. of **tooth**

teethe to develop one's first teeth
teething

teetotal abstaining from alcoholic drink
teetotalism teetotaller (US *teetotaler*)

tele- (*prefix*) by telephone or television
tele-ad telebanking telecommute teleconference telecottage telemarketing telemessage telesales teleshopping teleworker teleworking

telecast to televise

telecommunications communications by television, telephone, radio, etc.

telegram communication sent by telegraph

telegraph system or device for sending messages by electric current along a wire
telegrapher telegraphese telegraphic telegraphy

telekinesis apparent change in the movement of an object by mental effort
telekinetic

telemark skiing turn

telemeter electrical measuring device that transmits the result to a distant point
telemetric telemetry

teleology study of aims and the ultimate good
teleological teleologist

telepathy communication from one mind to another without the use of known senses
telepathic telepathically telepathist

telephone (to use an) electrical device for speaking and listening to someone at a distance
telephonic telephoning telephonist telephony

telephoto of a lens that produces a magnified image of a distant object
telephotographic telephotography

teleprinter device similar to a typewriter that receives or transmits messages by telegraph

Teleprompter (*trademark*) device that displays a script in front of a speaker on television

telescope optical instrument used to view distant objects; to become shorter or crushed
telescopic telescoping telescopy

teletext computerized television information service

televise to broadcast or transmit by television
televising

television system that transmits images and sound over a distance; apparatus that receives these

telex communication service that uses teleprinters; (to send a) message by telex

tell to inform or relate; to order; to distinguish; to court
teller telling tell-tale told

tellurian (inhabitant) of the earth

temerity boldness
SEE PANEL

---

temerity or timidity?

Temerity means 'boldness' or 'presumption': *I'm amazed that he had the temerity to question my teaching style – after all I've been a lecturer for over ten years now.*

Timidity refers to a person's shyness and lack of courage and self-confidence: *the timidity of a child on their first day at school.*

---

temp temporary employee; to work as a temp

temper mood; angry state; to harden a metal; to moderate
temperable temperer

temperament person's character and disposition
temperamental temperamentally

temperance restrained behaviour; abstinence from alcoholic drink

temperate moderate
temperately temperateness

temperature level of heat

tempest violent storm

tempestuous violent; stormy
tempestuously tempestuousness

template or **templet** pattern or gauge used as a guide in cutting, shaping, etc.

temple[1] building dedicated to the worship of a god

temple[2] flat area on either side of the forehead

tempo speed or pace, esp. the speed at which music is to be played
tempos or *tempi*

temporal of time; secular or earthly
temporality

temporary lasting only for a limited time
temporarily temporariness

temporize or **temporise** to use delaying tactics
temporization or *temporisation temporizer* or *temporiser temporizing* or *temporising*

tempt to entice or attempt to persuade to do something
temptation tempter temptress

ten number 10
tenfold tenner tenth tenthly

tenable that can be upheld or defended
tenability or *tenableness tenably*

tenacious holding firmly
tenaciously tenacity or *tenaciousness*

tenant person who rents land or property
tenancy tenantless tenantry

tench kind of freshwater fish
tenches or *tench*

tend[1] to look after

tend[2] to be inclined to

tendency inclination; general trend
tendencies

tendentious having an intentional bias

tender[1] not tough; delicate or sensitive; loving
tenderfoot tender-hearted tenderize or *tenderise tenderizer* or *tenderiser tenderloin*

tender[2] to present or offer; (*formal*) offer

tender[3] small boat serving a ship; vehicle supplying fuel and water for a steam locomotive

tendon band of fibrous tissue that joins a muscle to a bone

tendril thread-like part by which a climbing plant clings to a support

tenement dwelling house; (flat in a) large building

Tenerife Spanish island in the Atlantic

tenet belief or dogma

Tennessee US state

tennis ball-game for 2 or 4 people who hit a bal with rackets over a net
tennis-ball tennis-court tennis-racket

tenon projecting end of a piece of wood that fits into a mortise joint

tenor (singer with or music for a) male voice between alto and baritone; general drift or course

tenpin bowling bowling game in which a ball is rolled at 10 skittles

tense[1] tightly stretched; to make or become tense
tensely tenseness tenser tensest tensile tensing

tense[2] (*grammar*) verb form expressing time distinctions

tension (degree of) tenseness; mental or emotional strain

tent collapsible shelter supported by poles

tentacle long flexible part on an octopus, etc. used for feeling or grasping
tentacled tentacular

tentative provisional
tentatively tentativeness

tenter frame on which cloth is dried and stretched
tenterhook

tenuous slight; delicate

tenuously *tenuousness* or *tenuity*

tenure holding of property, an office, etc.

tepee wigwam

tepid slightly warm
tepidly *tepidness* or *tepidity*

tera- (*prefix*) 10^{12}

tercentenary 300th anniversary
tercentenaries *tercentennial*

tergiversate to equivocate; to become disloyal
tergiversation *tergiversator*

term expression; period of time; division of academic year
term-time

termagant brawling woman

terminable able to be terminated
terminably

terminal at the end; (*of a disease*) ending in death; terminus; airport building
terminally

terminate to bring or come to an end
terminating *termination* *terminative* *terminator*

terminology technical expressions in a particular subject
terminologies *terminological*

terminus station at the end of a railway or bus route
termini or *terminuses*

termite kind of wood-eating insect

tern kind or water bird with a forked tail

terrace level area of ground; row of houses; tier around sportsground
terraced

terracotta (object made of) unglazed brownish-red fired clay

terra firma firm ground; dry land

terrain area of land, considered from its physical features

terrapin water tortoise

terrazzo floor of smoothed marble chips set in concrete
terrazzos

terrestrial of land or the earth

terrible (*informal*) very bad; extreme; terrifying
terribleness *terribly*
SEE PANEL

---

terrible or terrific?
Something is *terrible* if it is very bad: *suffer terrible injuries; have a terrible headache. Terrible* is also used to emphasize, usually with disapproval, how great something is: *a terrible waste of money*

Something is *terrific* if it is very good: *have a terrific time on holiday. Terrific* is also used to emphasize, usually with approval, how great something is: *There's a terrific amount of information available on the internet.*

---

terrier breed of small dog

terrific (*informal*) very good; intense
terrifically
SEE PANEL at **terrible**

terrify to fill with terror
terrified *terrifies* *terrifying*

terrine (food, esp. pâté, cooked in an) earthenware baking dish

territory land; region of a country
territories *territorial* *territorially*

terror great fear; (*informal*) troublesome person
terror-stricken or *terror-struck*

terrorism use of violence and intimidation to achieve esp. political goals
terrorist

terrorize or **terrorise** to fill with terror; to force with threats, etc.
terrorization or *terrorisation* *terrorizer* or *terroriser* *terrorizing* or *terrorising*

terry absorbent fabric with uncut loops on its pile

terse brief; concise
tersely *terseness* *terser* *tersest*

tertiary third in degree or order

Tertiary geological period

Terylene (*trademark*) synthetic polyester fibre

tessellate to decorate with mosaics
tessellation

tessera small square tile used in mosaics
tesserae tesseral

test to examine; to try (out)
test-tube

testament will; main division of the Bible
testamental testamentary

testate having made a valid will
testacy testator testatrix

testicle either of the 2 sperm-producing male reproductive glands
testicular

testify to give evidence; to serve as evidence of
testification testified testifier testifies testifying

testimonial written reference

testimony statement, declaration, or evidence
testimonies

testis testicle
testes

testy irritable
testier testiest testily testiness

tetanus disease resulting in stiffening of the muscles

tetchy touchy
tetchier tetchiest tetchily tetchiness

tête-à-tête private conversation between 2 people

tether (to tie with a) chain or rope that restricts the movement of an animal

tetrahedron solid with 4 faces
tetrahedrons or *tetrahedra*

Teutonic Germanic

text written matter, as opposed to illustrations
textbook textual

textile woven or knitted cloth

texture surface characteristics of something as perceived by touch or sight; special quality
textural textured

Thailand country in Asia
Thai

thalidomide sedative drug found to cause malformation of foetuses

thallium white poisonous metallic element

than word used in comparisons

thank to express gratitude to
thankful thankfully thankfulness thankless thanklessly thanklessness thank-offering thanksgiving

that person or thing referred to; opposite of **this**; used to introduce a clause
that'll that's

thatch (to cover a roof with) straw and other plant material
thatches thatcher

thaw to melt; period when ice and snow melt

the definite article

theatre (US **theater**) place where plays are performed publicly; hospital room where surgical operations are carried out
theatrical theatrically theatricals

thee (*archaic*) object form of **thou**

theft stealing

their possessive form of **they**
theirs

theism belief in the existence of one god
theist theistic theistical

them object form of **they**
themselves

theme topic; main musical melody
thematic thematically

then at that time; next

thence from that place; from that time
thenceforth thenceforward

theocracy government by a deity or priests
theocracies theocratic

theodolite surveying instrument for measuring angles
theodolitic

theology study of God and religious truth
theologian theological theologically

theorem proposition shown by reasoning to be true

theorize or **theorise** to form a theory
theorizing or *theorising*

theory set of explanatory ideas; principles of a subject
theories theoretical theoretically theorist

theosophy religious and philosophical system emphasizing mystical intuitive insight
theosophical theosophist

therapeutic treating a disease; curative
therapeutically therapeutics

therapy treatment of a disease
therapies therapist

there in or to that place; used to introduce a sentence
thereabouts thereafter thereby there'd therein there'll thereof thereon there's thereto theretofore thereunder thereupon therewith

therefore for that reason

therm unit of heat
thermal

thermionic of a device, esp. a valve, in which electrons are emitted at high temperatures

thermo- (*prefix*) of heat
thermoelectric thermoplastic

thermocouple instrument used to measure temperature, consisting of a pair of wires of different metals joined at both ends

thermodynamics study of heat and its relationship with other forms of energy
thermodynamically

thermometer instrument used to measure temperature
thermometric thermometry

thermonuclear of nuclear reactions that occur only at very high temperatures

Thermos (*trademark*) vacuum flask

thermostat device that automatically controls the temperature

thesaurus dictionary consisting of words arranged systematically according to meaning; dictionary of synonyms
thesauri or *thesauruses*

these pl. of **this**

thesis long essay or dissertation; statement presented with supporting reasons
theses

thespian of drama or the theatre

they people or things mentioned; people in general
they'd they'll they're they've

thiamine vitamin forming part of the vitamin B complex

thick not thin; dense; (*informal*) stupid
thick-headed thickly thickness thickest thick-skinned thick-witted

thicken to make or become thick
thickener thickening

thicket dense growth of shrubs, trees, etc.

thief person who steals
thieves thievish

thieve to steal
thievery thieving

thigh part of the leg between the hip and knee
thigh-bone

thimble small protective cap worn on the end of the finger when sewing
thimbleful thimblerig

thin narrow; slender; not thick; to make or become thin
thinly thinned thinner thinness thinnest thinning thin-skinned

thine (*archaic*) (the one or ones) belonging to thee

thing object, event, or circumstance

thingamabob, **thingumabob**, **thingamajig**, **thingumajig**, **thingamy** or **thingummy** (*informal*) person or thing whose name is unknown or forgotten

think to consider; to have as an opinion
thinkable thinker thinking thinking-cap think-tank thought

third coming next after second
thirdly third-rate

thirst (to feel a) great longing for a drink
thirstier thirstiest thirstily thirstiness thirsty

thirteen number 13
thirteenth

thirty number 30
thirties thirtieth

this person or thing that is near; opposite of **that**; to such an extent
this'll

thistle kind of prickly plant
thistledown thistly

thither (*archaic*) in that direction

thole peg or pin in the gunwale of a boat to serve as a rowlock
thole-pin

thong thin strip of leather

thorax part of the body between the neck and abdomen
thoraxes or *thoraces thoracic*

thorium silvery-white radioactive metallic element

thorn sharp-pointed prickle on a plant
thornier thorniest thornily thorniness thorny

thorough careful; complete
thoroughly thoroughness

thoroughbred (animal) of pure stock

thoroughfare road or public way

thoroughgoing very thorough

those pl. of **that**

thou (*archaic*) you
thee thine thy

though although; however

thought past tense and past participle of **think**; result or act of thinking
thoughtful thoughtfully thoughtfulness thoughtless thoughtlessly thoughtlessness thought-provoking

thousand number 1000
thousandth

thrall slave; bondage
thraldom

thrash to give repeated blows to; to defeat; act of thrashing
thrashes thrasher thrashing
SEE PANEL

---

thrash or thresh?

If you *thrash* an animal or a person, you hit them repeatedly: *to thrash a horse with a whip.* If one team *thrashes* another, they defeat them significantly: *United thrashed the home team in the Cup 5–0.* To *thrash out* a matter or problem is to discuss it thoroughly or decide on it after much discussion: *A new deal between managers and unions is still being thrashed out.*

Thresh means to beat out grain from the stalks of ripe cereal plants: *a threshing machine.*

---

thread strand of material, esp. cotton; to pass a thread through a needle
threadbare threader threadlike threadworm

threat intention to injure or punish; sign of something unpleasant

threaten to be or express a threat to
threatener threateningly

three number 3
three-dimensional threefold three-legged three-piece three-ply three-point three-quarter three-quarters threescore threesome

thresh to beat out grain from the stalks of ripe cereal plants
thresher threshes threshing threshing-floor threshing-machine
SEE PANEL at **thrash**

threshold piece of wood or stone below a doorway; beginning

threw past tense of **throw**

thrice three times

thrift cautious management of money
thriftier thriftiest thriftily thriftiness thriftless thriftlessly thrifty

thrill (to (cause to) feel a) sudden sensation of pleasurable excitement
thriller thrilling thrillingly

thrips kind of small sucking insect

thrive to prosper
thrived or *throve thriven thriving*

throat front of the neck; passage in the neck through which food passes
throatier throatiest throatily throatiness throaty

throb to beat, esp. intensely; intense beat
throbbed throbbing

throes convulsions; tumultuous process

thrombosis formation of a clot in a blood-vessel
thromboses

throne ceremonial seat of a sovereign or a bishop

throng (to) crowd

throstle song thrush

throttle device that controls the flow of fuel, etc. to an engine; to kill or injure by squeezing the throat
throttler throttling

through into one side and out the other; from the beginning to the end (of); by manner of
throughout throughput throughway

throve past tense of **thrive**

throw to send forcefully through the air, to shape on a potter's wheel
threw throwaway throwback throw-in throwing thrown

thrum to strum
thrummed thrumming

thrush[1] kind of songbird

thrush[2] infection of the mucous membrane of the mouth

thrust (to give a) violent push
thruster

thud (to fall or strike with a) dull heavy noise
thudded thudding

thug tough violent man, esp. a criminal
thuggery thuggish

thumb short thick finger that is at an angle to the other fingers; to turn pages with the thumb
thumb-index thumbnail thumb-print thumbscrew thumb-through

thump (to strike with a) heavy solid blow

thumping (*informal*) very great

thunder loud noise following a flash of lightning; to sound with or like thunder
thunderbolt thunderclap thundercloud thundering thunderous thunderstorm thunderstruck thundery

thurible censer

Thursday 5th day of the week

thus in this way; therefore

thwack (to) hit with a sharp blow

thwart to prevent; to frustrate

thy (*archaic*) possessive form of **thou**
thyself

thyme kind of small shrub whose dried leaves are used as a herb in cooking
thymy

thymol white crystalline compound used as an antiseptic, etc.

thyroid of a gland at the base of the neck

tiara woman's headband; pope's crown
tiaraed

Tibet administrative region in West China
Tibetan

tibia shin-bone
tibiae or *tibias*

tic spasmodic muscle twitching

tick[1] (*of a clock, etc.*) (to make a) regular light clicking sound; (to place the) mark √ beside an item that has been checked or is correct, etc.
ticker ticker-tape tick-tock

tick[2] small parasitic creature

tick[3] covering of a pillow, mattress, etc.
ticking

tick[4] (*informal*) credit

ticket printed card showing that the holder has certain rights, for example to travel; label; to issue tickets to
ticketed ticketing ticket-office

tickle to touch lightly, so as to cause laughter
tickled tickler tickling ticklish ticklishness

tiddler (*informal*) small fish; small child

tiddly (*informal*) very small; slightly drunk

tiddlywinks game in which players try to flick small counters into a cup

tide regular rise and fall of the level of the sea; to help a person live through a difficult period
tidal tidemark tidewater tideway tiding

tidings news

tidy (to make) neat and orderly
tidied tidier tidies tidiest tidily tidiness tidying tidy-up

tie to fasten or attach; piece of cloth worn round the neck; (to make an) equal score
ties tie-break tie-breaker tie-clip tied tie-dye tie-dyed tie-dyeing tie-in tie-on tie-pin tie-up tying

tier one of a set of rows or levels in a series

tiff slight quarrel

tiger (*fem.* **tigress**) large tawny animal of the cat family with black stripes

tight fully stretched; packed closely; not loose
tighter tightest tight-fisted tight-lipped tightly tightness

tighten to make or become tighter

tightrope rope that is stretched taut, on which acrobats perform

tights close-fitting one-piece garment worn over the body from the waist to the feet

tilde mark ˜ used in Spanish

tile (to cover with a) thin slab of baked clay, linoleum, etc.
tiling

till[1] until

till[2] to cultivate and work land for raising crops
tillage tiller

till[3] cash register; container for money in a shop

tiller lever used to turn the rudder of a boat

tilt to (cause to) slope at an angle

tilth land that has been tilled

timber wood that is suitable for carpentry or building
timbered timbering

timbre distinctive quality or tone of sound

time period during or point at which something happens; continuous passage of existence; point in time shown in

hours, minutes, and seconds; to measure the duration of
timeable time-and-motion time-consuming timed time-honoured (US *time-honored*) *timekeeper time-keeping time-lag timeless timelessly timelessness timelier timeliest time-limit timeliness timely timepiece timer time-saving time-scale timeserver time-sharing time-sheet time-signal time-switch timing*

timetable chart showing times of arrival and departure of trains or buses; (to) schedule
timetabling

timid shy; lacking courage and self-confidence
timidity timidly
SEE PANEL at **temerity**

timorous timid
timorously timorousness

timpano kettledrum
timpani timpanist

tin (to cover with a) soft silvery-white metal; (to preserve in a) container made of tin-plate
tinfoil tinned tinning tin-opener tin-plate tinpot tinsmith tinware

tincture alcoholic solution of a drug, for medical use; (to give a) slight trace (of)
tincturing

tinder dry substance that catches fire easily
tinder-box tindery

tine prong of a fork; branch of a deer's antler

ting (to make a) high ringing sound
ting-a-ling tinging

tinge (to give a) slight colouring or trace
tingeing

tingle (to feel a) prickling or thrilling sensation
tingling tingly

tinker travelling mender of pots and pans; to meddle or mend in a clumsy manner

tinkle (to make a) high ringing sound
tinkling

tinny of tin; having a light ringing sound
tinnier tinniest tinnily tinniness

tinsel decorative thread of foil that gives a sparkling effect
tinselled (US *tinseled*)

tint (to give a) shade of colour

tintinnabulation ringing of bells

tiny very small
tinier tiniest tinily tininess

tip[1] end of something; to mark the end of
tipped tipping tiptop

tip[2] to tilt or overturn
tipped tipping tip-up

tip[3] to hit or touch lightly
tipped tipping

tip[4] (to give a) sum of money for service; piece of advice or information
tip-off tipped tipping tipster

tippet woman's cape

tipple to drink small amounts of alcohol habitually
tippler tippling

tipsy slightly drunk
tipsier tipsiest tipsily tipsiness

tiptoe (to walk on the) ends of the toes
tiptoed tiptoeing

tirade long angry speech or denunciation

tire[1] to make or become weary
tired tiredness tireless tirelessly tirelessness tiresome tiring

tire[2] (US) see **tyre**

tiro or **tyro** novice
tiros or *tyros*

tissue thin paper handkerchief; fine cloth; mass of cells or fibres that make up a structure in the body
tissued tissue-paper

tit[1] kind of small songbird

tit[2] (**tit for tat**) equivalent given in retaliation

titanic enormous

titanium grey metallic element

titbit tasty morsel; interesting item of gossip, etc.

tithe tenth part of income, produce, etc., given to the church

titillate to excite or arouse pleasurably
titillating titillation

titivate to smarten up
titivating titivation

title name of a book, etc.; word that shows rank or status; proof of ownership or right
titled title-deed title-holder title-page title-role titular

titmouse tit; see **tit**[1]
titmice

titration process of measuring the concentration of a solution
titrate titrating

titter (to) snigger

tittle-tattle (to) gossip
tittle-tattler tittle-tattling

titular in name only

tizzy (*informal*) state of confused excitement
tizzies

to in the direction of; as far as; before the hour of

toad amphibian animal related to the frog
toad-in-the-hole

toadstool fungus with a cap and a slender stalk, often poisonous

toady person who flatters someone in order to gain favour; to act in this way
toadies toadied toadying toadyism

toast to make bread crisp and brown by heating; toasted bread; (to) drink to someone's health, etc.
toaster toastmaster toastmistress toast-rack

tobacco plant, the leaves of which are used to make cigarettes, cigars, etc.
tobaccos tobacconist

Tobago island in the West Indies
Tobagonian

toboggan (to ride on a) long low platform or runners, used to slide down an icy or snowy slope
tobogganer tobogganing

toccata musical composition marked by a rapid free style

tocsin alarm signal or bell

today on this day; at the present time

toddle to walk in short unsteady steps
toddler toddling

toddy hot drink made with whisky
toddies

to-do (*informal*) fuss
to-dos

toe (to touch with) one of the 5 digits of the foot
toecap toed toe-hold toeing toenail

toffee kind of sweet made from sugar and butter
toffee-apple toffee-nosed

tog[1] (*informal*) to dress up

tog[2] unit for measuring thermal insulation

toga loose outer garment worn by citizens of ancient Rome

together with each other; into contact
togetherness

toggle kind of peg that is attached to a loop to act as a fastening

Togo country in West Africa
Togolese

togs (*informal*) clothes

toil (to engage in) long hard work
toiler toilsome

toilet (room containing) fixture for receiving and disposing of urine and

faeces; act of washing and preparing oneself
toilet-paper toilet-roll toiletry toiletries

token sign or mark; nominal
tokenism

told past tense and past participle of **tell**

tolerate to allow or endure
tolerable tolerably tolerance tolerant tolerantly tolerating toleration

toll[1] (*of a bell*) to (cause to) ring slowly and regularly
tolled tolling

toll[2] tax levied for the use of a road, bridge, etc.
tollbooth toll-bridge toll-gate toll-house toll-road

toluene flammable hydrocarbon used as a solvent

tom male of animals, esp. the cat
tom-cat

tomahawk North American Indian fighting axe

tomato kind of (plant with) red fleshy fruit
tomatoes

tomb place for burying a corpse

tombola kind of lottery

tomboy girl who behaves in a manner thought typical of a boy

tome large book; volume

tomfool fool
tomfoolery tomfooleries

tommy British private soldier
tommies

tommyrot (*informal*) nonsense

tomorrow day after today

tomtit kind of small bird; blue-tit

tom-tom small drum beaten with the hands

ton unit of weight

tone (quality of) sound; shade of colour; musical interval of 2 semitones; to give a tone to
tonal tonality tonalities toned tone-deaf toneless tonelessly toner toning

Tonga country in the Pacific
Tongan

tongs instrument consisting of a pair of joined arms used for gripping things

tongue movable organ in the mouth; power of speech; language; to touch with the tongue
tongued tongue-in-cheek tongueing tongue-tied tongue-twister

tonic medicine, etc. that improves bodily health; stimulant
tonically

tonight evening or night of the present day

tonnage measurement in tons

tonne unit of weight, metric ton, 1000 kilograms

tonsil 1 of a pair of 2 masses of tissue at the back of the throat
tonsillar tonsillectomy tonsillitis

tonsure shaving of a man's head; shaved part of the head

too excessively; as well

took past tense of **take**

tool implement, esp. one that is held in the hand
tool-box toolmaker

toot (to give a) short hoot on a horn, etc.

tooth hard bony structure in the mouth used for biting, chewing, etc.
teeth toothache toothbrush toothcomb toothed toothless toothpaste toothpick toothsome

toothy having prominent teeth
toothier toothiest toothily toothiness

tootle to toot softly; soft toot
tootler tootling

top[1] highest part of something; to cover; to exceed
topcoat top-flight top-heavy topless top-level topmost top-notch topped topping topsail topside topsoil top-up

top[2] child's spinning toy

topaz semiprecious stone, esp. yellow

tope to drink alcoholic drink in large quantities
toper toping

topi or **topee** lightweight hat
topis or *topees*

topiary art of trimming trees and shrubs into decorative shapes

topic subject or theme

topical of current interest; of topics
topicality topically

topography study of the surface features of a region
topographies topographical

topology branch of mathematics

topper (*informal*) top hat

topping garnish or food decoration; (*slang*) excellent

topple to tip over

topsy-turvy upside down; in a confused state
topsy-turvily topsy-turvydom

toque woman's small round brimless hat

tor high rocky hill

Torah 5 books of Moses; Jewish religious writings and teachings

torch portable electric light powered by batteries
torches torchlight

tore past tense of **tear**[2]

toreador bullfighter

torment (to afflict with) great pain
tormentor

torn past participle of **tear**[2]

tornado violent whirling destructive wind
tornadoes

torpedo (to attack with a) large cigar-shaped missile
torpedoes torpedoed torpedoing

torpid inactive; slow and dull
torpidity torpidly torpor

torque rotating force

torrent violently rushing stream; violent flow
torrential

torrid extremely hot
torridity or *torridness torridly*

torsion twisting

torso trunk of the human body; something mutilated
torsos or *torsi*

tort civil wrong for which the wronged person may claim damages

tortilla a kind of thin pancake made from unleavened maize bread

tortoise slow-moving reptile with a hard dome-shaped shell
tortoiseshell

tortuous winding; intricate
tortuously tortuousness or *tortuosity*

torture to inflict intense pain on, esp. to obtain information from; infliction of such pain
tortured torturer torturing

Tory Conservative
Tories Toryism

toss to throw; to move about restlessly; tossing action
tosses toss-up

tot[1] young child; small alcoholic drink

tot[2] to add (up)
totted totting totting-up

total whole amount; whole or complete; to add up the total
totality totalled (US *totaled*) *totalling* (US *totaling*) *totally*

totalitarian of a dictatorial one-party state
totalitarianism

totalizator, **totalisator**, or **tote** betting device

totalize or **totalise** to add up
totalizer or *totaliser* *totalizing* or *totalising*

totem object, etc. used to symbolize a family or tribe
totemism totem-pole

totter to move unsteadily; to sway as if about to collapse
totterer tottery

toucan kind of tropical fruit-eating bird with a large coloured bill

touch to feel or handle; to come into contact with; to move emotionally; sense of feeling
touches touchable touchdown touched touching touch-lines touch-paper touchstone touch-type touch-typing touch-typist touch-wood

touché used to acknowledge that one's opponent has made a valid point

touchy easily offended
touchier touchiest touchily touchiness

tough difficult to tear, cut, or chew; determined; strong
tough toughest toughly tough-minded toughness

toughen to make or become tough
toughener

toupee hairpiece covering a bald place

tour (to make a) journey in which several visits are made
tourer touring touring-car

tour de force (*French*) feat of strength or skill
tours de force

tourist person who travels for pleasure
tourism touristy

tournament series of sporting games

tourniquet bandage or device to stop the flow of blood

tousle to tangle or ruffle hair
tousling

tout to sell information or tickets; to seek customers or business

tow to pull or drag with a rope, etc.
towable towage tow-bar tow-path tow-rope

towards or **toward** in the direction of

towel absorbent cloth for drying or wiping after washing; to use a towel
towelled (US *toweled*) *towelling* (US *toweling*)

tower tall structure; to rise to a great height
tower-block towering

town densely populated area larger than a village but smaller than a city
townscape townsfolk township townsman townspeople townswoman

toxaemia (US **toxemia**) blood-poisoning

toxic poisonous
toxically toxicant toxicity toxicological toxicologist toxicology toxin

toy object designed to be played with; to treat or handle casually
toys toyed toying toy-shop

trace[1] mark left by something; slight indication; to follow the course of; to copy the outline of through thin paper
traceable tracer tracing tracing-paper

trace[2] either of the 2 straps that attach a vehicle to a horse

tracery decorative stone openwork
traceries

trachea windpipe
tracheae tracheal tracheate tracheotomy

trachoma contagious conjunctivitis of the eye

track trail or series of marks made by the passage of a person, animal, etc.; rough path; to follow the track of
tracker track-laying trackless

tract[1] large area of land; system in the body

tract[2] religious pamphlet

tractable easily controlled or handled
tractably tractableness or *tractability*

traction (power used in) pulling
tractional tractive

tractor powerful vehicle used to pull farm machinery

trade (to engage in) buying and selling goods; business
tradable or *tradeable trade-in trademark trader tradesman tradespeople tradeswoman trade union* or *trades union trade-unionism trade-unionist trading trading-stamp*

tradition passing down of belief, custom, etc. from one generation to another; belief, custom, etc. passed down in this way
traditional traditionalism traditionalist traditionally

traduce to defame
traducement traducer traducing

traffic flow of vehicles; to trade in illegal goods
trafficator trafficked trafficker trafficking traffic-light

tragedy calamity or disaster; kind of drama
tragedies tragedian tragedienne tragic tragically tragicomedy

trail (to follow a) mark or track left by a person or thing; to drag
trail-blazer trail-blazing trailer

train connected line of a railway engine and coaches or wagons; to teach a particular skill to
train-bearer trainee trainer training

traipse to walk heavily
traipsing

trait individual feature

traitor (*fem.* **traitress**) person who acts disloyally or commits treason
traitorous traitorously

trajectory curved path followed by an object such as a missile moving through space
trajectories

tram passenger vehicle that runs on rails set in the road
tramcar tramline tramway

trammel to prevent movement; to entangle
trammelled (US *trammeled*) *trammelling* (US *trammeling*)

tramp person who travels about and lives roughly; to walk heavily; cargo vessel with no regular route
trampish

trample to walk roughly (on); to act insensitively towards
trampler trampling

trampoline strong sheet of canvas, etc. set in springs, used for jumping on

trance sleepy or hypnotic state

tranny (*informal*) transistor radio
trannies

tranquil calm; peaceful
tranquillity tranquilly

tranquillize or **tranquillise** (US **tranquilize**) to make tranquil; to relieve the anxieties of
tranquillized or *tranquillised* (US *tranquilized*) *tranquillizer* or *tranquilliser* (US *tranquilizer*) *tranquillizing* or *tranquillising* (US *tranquilizing*)

trans- (*prefix*) across; changed

transact to conduct business
transaction transactional transactor

transalpine beyond the Alps, esp. from Italy

transatlantic across the Atlantic

transceiver combined radio transmitter and receiver

transcend to go beyond the limits of; to surpass
transcendence or *transcendency*
transcendent transcendental
transcendentalism transcendentalist
transcendentally

transcontinental across a continent

transcribe to copy in writing
transcribing transcript transcription

transept part of a cross-shaped church that is at right angles to the nave

transfer to move from one place to another; to convey the ownership of to another person; to move a design from one surface to another; design moved in this way
transferable transferee transference
transferral transferred transferrer
transferring

transfiguration change in the appearance, esp. of Jesus

transfix to hold motionless with emotion; to pierce through
transfixion

transform to change the form, nature, etc. of
transformable transformation transformer

transfuse to transfer blood from one person to another; to permeate
transfusible transfusing transfusion

transgress to sin; to go beyond a limit
transgresses transgressible transgression
transgressive transgressor

tranship see **trans-ship**

transient lasting only a short time
transience transiency transiently

transistor semiconductor device; portable radio having transistors

transistorize or **transistorise** to equip with transistors
transistorization or *transistorisation*
transistorizing or *transistorising*

transit passage or transport of goods or people

transition development from one condition, stage, etc., to another
transitional transitionally

transitive (*of verbs*) having a direct object

transitory lasting only a short time
transitorily transitoriness

translate to express in another language
translatable translating translation
translator

transliterate to represent in the letters of a different alphabet
transliterating transliteration transliterator

translucent allowing the passage of diffused light
translucence or *translucency translucently*

transmit to send a signal, etc., to transfer or pass on
transmissible or *transmittable transmission*
transmitted transmitter transmitting

transmogrify (*informal*) to change into an odd or grotesque form
transmogrification transmogrified
transmogrifier transmogrifying

transmute to change the form or substance of
transmutability transmutable
transmutation transmuting

transom horizontal piece across or over a window, door, etc.

transparency being transparent; photographic slide
transparencies transparence

transparent allowing the uninterrupted passage of light; obvious
transparently

transpire to become known; (*informal*) to occur; to give off a water vapour
transpiration transpiratory transpiring

transplant to transfer to another person or place; something transplanted
transplantable transplantation

transport to convey from one place to another; means of transporting
transportable transportation transporter

transpose (to change the) position of; to put music in a different key
transposable transposal transposing transposition

transsexual person with an overwhelming desire to be indentified with the opposite sex
transsexualism

trans-ship or **tranship** to transfer from one ship or vehicle to another
trans-shipment or *transhipment trans-shipped* or *transhipped trans-shipping* or *transhipping*

transubstantiation doctrine of the Eucharist that the bread and wine become the body and blood of Christ

transverse lying across
transversal transversely
SEE PANEL

---

transverse or traverse?
Transverse is an adjective that means 'lying across; at right angles': *a transverse section; The transverse architrave goes across the top of a door or window opening.*
Traverse is a verb used in formal contexts to mean 'to go across': *to traverse great expanses of land in search of the missing jewels.*

---

transvestite person who wears clothes associated with the opposite sex
transvestism

trap device for catching animals; device or ruse to trick a person; to catch in a trap; light 2-wheeled carriage
trapdoor trapped trapper trapping

trapeze bar attached to ropes that is used by acrobats

trapezium (*Brit*) quadrilateral with only 2 sides parallel
trapeziums or *trapezia*

trapezoid (US **trapezium**)
trapezoidal

trappings decorations or accessories

trash nonsense; rubbish
trashy

trattoria Italian restaurant
trattorias or *trattoriae*

trauma powerful and deep shock
traumas or *traumata traumatic traumatically traumatism traumatize* or *traumatise*

travail (*literary*) exertion; to work very hard
travailed travailing

travel to make a journey; to move
travelled (US *traveled*) *traveller* (US *traveler*) *travelling* (US *traveling*) *travelogue*

traverse to cross
traversable traversal traverser traversing
SEE PANEL at **transverse**

travesty (to make a) mocking imitation
travesties travestied travestying

trawl large net that is dragged along the bottom of the sea to catch fish; to catch fish in such a net

trawler boat used in trawling

tray open receptacle with a low rim for carrying articles

treacherous betraying; dangerous
treacherously

treachery act of betraying; disloyalty
treacheries

treacle dark thick sticky syrup
treacly

tread to step or walk; to crush; external surface of a tyre
treading treadmill trod trodden

treadle foot-operated lever that drives a machine; to work a treadle
treadling

treason betrayal of one's country
treasonable treasonably

treasure very valuable object; wealth; to value highly
treasured treasure-hunt treasure-trove treasuring treasury treasuries

treasurer person who looks after the funds of a society, etc.
treasureship

treat to deal with or act towards; to care for medically; entertainment paid for by others
treatable treater treatment

treatise long formal written exposition

treaty formal agreement between countries
treaties

treble 3 times as great; to multiply by 3; (having the) highest musical pitch
trebling trebly
SEE PANEL

---

treble or triple?
Both *treble* and *triple* can be used as a verb meaning 'to multiply by three': *Fees will treble/triple in the New Year.* If one thing is *treble/triple* the size or amount of another, it is three times as great: *The accident rate increased dramatically to treble/triple the average.*

Only *treble* is used to describe the highest musical pitch: *a solitary treble voice singing the solo of 'Once in Royal David's City'; treble recorders; treble clef.*

Triple also means 'having three parts': *a triple somersault; the triple jump.*

---

tree large perennial woody plant with a trunk and branches
treeless treetop tree-trunk

trefoil leaf having 3 leaflets

trek (to make a) long difficult journey
trekked trekker trekking

trellis lattice structure, as used to support climbing plants
trellised trellis-work

tremble to shake or quiver; trembling movement
trembler trembling trembly

tremendous great; (*informal*) very good
tremendously tremendousness

tremolo trembling musical effect
tremolos

tremor trembling; shaking

tremulous trembling; fearful
tremulously tremulousness

trench deep ditch used in military defence
trenches

trenchant sharp; effective
trenchancy trenchantly

trend (to show a) general tendency
trendier trendiest trendily trendiness trendsetter trendsetting trendy

trephine instrument for cutting out a circular piece, esp. bone from the skull

trepidation great anxiety and fear

trespass to go on the property or land of someone else unlawfully; (*archaic*) to sin; act of trespassing
trespasses trespasser

tress lock of hair

trestle braced supporting wooden framework

trews close-fitting (tartan) trousers

tri- (*prefix*) 3; 3 times

triad group of 3

trial legal examination to determine a person's guilt or innocence; test

triangle 3-sided geometric figure; triangular percussion instrument
triangular triangularity triangulate triangulation

Triassic geological period

triathlon athletic contest of 3 different events

tribe very large social group
tribal tribalism tribally tribesman tribeswoman

tribulation intense distress

tribunal court of justice or arbitration

tribune¹ person who defends individual's rights

tribune² raised platform

tributary stream or river that flows into a larger one
tributaries

tribute something given or said as an expression of thanks, respect, etc.

trice moment

triceps muscle in the upper arm that has 3 points of attachment
tricepses or *triceps*

trick cunning or mischievous action; to deceive or cheat; cards played in 1 round of a card-game
trickery trickier trickiest trickily trickiness trickster tricky

trickle (to flow in a) thin slow stream
trickling

tricolour (US **tricolor**) flag with 3 colours; French flag

tricycle 3-wheeled cycle
tricyclist

trident 3-pronged spear

tried past tense and past participle of **try**

triennial occurring every 3 years; lasting 3 years
triennially

triennium period of 3 years
trienniums or *triennia*

trier person who tries

trifle something of little value; dessert made with sponge, jelly, custard, etc.; to deal carelessly (with)
trifler trifling

trifoliate having 3 leaflets

triforium gallery above an aisle of a church
triforia

trigger lever that releases the firing mechanism on a gun; to set (off)
trigger-happy

trigonometry branch of mathematics that studies triangles and angles
trigonometric trigonometrical

trilby man's soft felt hat
trilbies

trill (to sound or play with a) rapid alternation of 2 musical notes

trillion indefinitely large number; (*Brit*) million million million; (US) million million

trilogy group of 3 related works
trilogies

trim neat and tidy; to clip; (physical) condition
trimly trimmed trimmer trimming trimness

trimaran vessel having 3 hulls side by side

Trinidad island in the West Indies
Trinidadian

trinitrotoluene explosive, TNT

Trinity (*Christianity*) unity of Father, Son, and Holy Spirit in 1 Godhead; summer term at some universities
Trinitarian Trinitarianism

trinket small trifling ornament

trio group of 3 instruments, players, etc.
trios

trip to (cause to) stumble; journey; (*informal*) experience resulting from drug-taking
tripped tripper tripping

tripartite having 3 parts
tripartition

tripe part of an animal's stomach lining used as food; (*informal*) nonsense

triple having 3 parts; (to make or become) 3 times as great
tripling triply
SEE PANEL at **treble**

triplet any of 3 offspring born at 1 birth

triplicate having 3 parts; being 1 of 3 identical copies; to make 3 identical copies of
triplicating

tripod 3-legged stand

tripos honours degree examination at Cambridge University

triptych picture or carving on 3 panels

trisect to divide into 3 (equal) parts
trisection

trismus lockjaw

Tristan da Cunha islands in the South Atlantic

trite hackneyed
tritely triteness

tritium radioactive isotope of hydrogen

triumph (to win a) victory or success
triumphal triumphant triumphantly

triumvir member of a ruling commission of 3 people
triumvirs or *triumviri triumvirate*

trivalent having a valency of 3
trivalency

trivet stand for cooking-vessels over a fire

trivia unimportant matters or details

trivial unimportant
triviality trivially

trivialize or **trivalise** to make or become trivial
trivialization or *trivialisation trivializing* or *trivialising*

trochee metrical foot of 1 long and 1 short syllable
trochaic

trod past tense of **tread**

trodden past participle of **tread**

troglodyte cave-dweller
troglodytic

troika Russian vehicle drawn by 3 horses abreast

Trojan horse something intended to undermine from within

troll[1] supernatural creature in Scandinavian folklore

troll[2] to fish by drawing a baited line through water from a moving boat; (*informal*) to wander

trolley basket on wheels for carrying goods; small truck; small table on castors
trolleys trolley-bus

trollop promiscuous or slovenly woman

trombone kind of brass musical instrument
trombonist

troop military unit; (to move as a) large group
trooper troopship

trophy prize; memento of a success
trophies

tropic either of the 2 parallel lines of latitude, north (**tropic of Cancer**) and south (**tropic of Capricorn**) of the equator
tropical tropically

tropics region between the 2 tropics

tropism tendency of a plant to grow in a curved direction because of a stimulus

troposphere lowest atmospheric layer

trot (*of horses*) (to move at a) speed that is faster than a walk but slower than a canter
trotted trotter trotting

troth (*archaic*) promise of loyalty in marriage

Trotskyism political, social, etc. principles advocated by Leon Trotsky
Trotskyist

trotter foot of an animal, esp. a pig, used as food

troubadour medieval lyric poet

trouble (cause of) difficulty; to cause trouble; (to make an) effort
troublemaker troubleshooter troublesome trouble-spot troubling

trough long narrow open container for animal food; area of low atmospheric pressure

trounce to beat
trouncing

troupe group of actors, acrobats, etc.
trouper

trousers 2-legged garment covering the body from the waist to the ankles
trouser-suit

trousseau bride's outfit of clothes, linen, etc.
trousseaus or *trousseaux*

trout kind of freshwater fish valued as food and game

trowel small garden tool with a curved blade; hand tool with a flat blade for spreading mortar

troy British system of units of weight for precious metals

truant child who stays away from school without permission
truancy truancies

truce agreement to stop fighting temporarily

truck[1] railway wagon; (*chiefly* US) lorry
trucker trucking

truck[2] dealings

truckle to yield weakly
truckling

truculent aggressive and defiant
truculence or *truculency truculently*

trudge to walk heavily or wearily
trudging

true not false; real; exact; faithful; accurate alignment
true-blue trueness truer truest true-love true-to-life truly

truffle kind of edible fungus

trug gardener's long shallow basket

truism obvious truth
truistic

trump playing-card of a higher value than others
trump-card

trumpery (something that is) cheap or worthless

trumpet (to blow a) kind of valved brass musical instrument
trumpeted trumpeter trumpeting

truncate to shorten by cutting
truncated truncating

truncheon short club carried by policemen

trundle to move heavily along on wheels
trundling

trunk main stem of a tree; large strong box with a hinged lid; human body excluding head and limbs; elephant's snout; (US) car boot

trunks man's swimming-costume or shorts

trunnion 1 of a pair of projections attached to opposite sides of a mounting or container enabling something to rotate

truss to tie or fasten (up); supporting framework of a bridge or roof; bundle of hay or straw
trusses

trust (to have a) firm belief or confidence; responsibility
trustable trustee trusteeship trustful trustfully trustily trustiness trusting trustingly trustworthily trustworthiness trustworthy trusty

truth quality of being true; something that is true

truthful telling the truth; accurate
truthfully truthfulness

try (to) attempt; to examine or test; to investigate in a law-court; (*rugby*) touching-down of the ball behind the opponent's goal-line
tries tried trier trying try-on try-out

try-sail small fore-and-aft sail

tryst (*poetic*) secret meeting of lovers

tsar or **czar** (until 1917) emperor of Russia

tsarina wife of a tsar

tsetse kind of African fly that transmits diseases

T-shirt collarless short-sleeved shirt

T-square instrument for drawing horizontal lines, etc.

tub open flat-bottomed container; small container for ice-cream, etc.

tuba kind of large, valved low-pitched brass musical instrument

tubby short and fat
tubbier tubbiest tubbily tubbiness

tube hollow cylinder; (*Brit*) London underground railway
tubed tubeless tubing tubular

tuber fleshy underground stem of a plant
tuberous

tubercle small rounded projection
tubercular

tuberculosis infectious disease affecting the lungs and marked by swellings on the body
tubercular tuberculous

tuck to fold into place; to cover comfortably in bed; stitched fold in material; (*informal*) food
tuck-box tuck-in tuck-shop

Tudor English royal house from 1485 to 1603

Tuesday 3rd day of the week

tuffet low seat

tuft bunch of grass, hair, etc.
tufted tufty

tug to pull hard; powerful boat for towing ships
tugboat tugged tugger tugging tug-of-war tugs-of-war

tuition instruction or teaching
tuitional

tulip kind of bulbous plant with large bell-shaped flowers

tulle fine net fabric of silk, etc. used for veils and dresses

tumble to fall awkwardly; to roll over
tumbledown tumble-drier or *tumble-dryer tumbling*

tumbler drinking glass with no handle or stem; acrobat

tumbrel or **tumbril** cart

tumefaction swelling

tumescent swollen
tumescence

tumid swollen; bombastic
tumidity tumidly

tummy (*informal*) stomach
tummies tummy-ache

tumour (US **tumor**) abnormal swelling

tumult loud commotion; violent agitation
tumultuous tumultuously tumultuousness

tumulus ancient grave; barrow
tumuli

tun large cask; measure of capacity

tuna[1] or **tunny** kind of fish used for food and game
tuna-fish

tuna[2] kind of prickly pear

tundra vast arctic treeless plain

tune melody; (to put into) standard pitch; to adjust a radio or television set to receive a signal; to adjust an engine to give the best performance
tuneable or *tunable tuneful tunefully tunefulness tuneless tuner tune-up tuning tuning-fork*

tungsten hard greyish metallic element

tunic jacket worn as part of a uniform; hip-length or knee-length garment

Tunisia country in North Africa
Tunisian

tunnel (to dig an) underground passageway

tunnelled (US *tunneled*) *tunnelling* (US *tunneling*)

tunny see **tuna**

tup male sheep

turban long cloth worn round the head, worn by Muslims and Sikhs; woman's brimless hat
turbaned

turbid muddy; confused
turbidity or *turbidness* *turbidly*
SEE PANEL

---

turbid, turbulent, or turgid?
Turbid means 'muddy': *the stream's turbid waters*, and, by extension, 'confused': *an emotionally turbid response.*

Turbulent means 'stormy; agitated': *a turbulent sea*; and, by extension, 'having a great deal of disorder and confusion': *He's been through four turbulent marriages; a turbulent period of history.*

Turgid is used to describe a thick mass of mud, water, etc.: *the river's dark, turgid waters;* and, by extension, language that is elaborate, pompous, and difficult to understand; *have to plough through all this dull, turgid prose.* In technical language, *turgid* also means 'swollen': a *turgid* cell is one that is swollen and stiff, having taken in water.

---

turbine machine or engine driven by a wheel that is turned by a flow of water or gas

turbo- (*prefix*) consisting of or driven by a turbine
turbocharger *turbo-jet* *turbo-prop*

turbot kind of large edible flat-fish

turbulent stormy; agitated
turbulence *turbulently*
SEE PANEL at **turbid**

tureen large, deep rounded dish used for serving soup, etc.

turf (to cover with a) thick growth of grass and its roots; horse-racing
turfs or *turves*

turgid muddy; pompous; swollen
turgidity or *turgidness* *turgidly*
SEE PANEL at **turbid**

turkey kind of large bird farmed for its meat
turkeys

Turkey country in West Asia and Europe
Turk *Turkish*

Turkmenistan republic of Central Asia

turmeric kind of plant used as a condiment and as a yellow colouring agent

turmoil disorder; tumult

turn to (cause to) move round; to change position or direction; to shape on a lathe; turning action; opportunity or right to do something
turnabout *turncoat* *turner* *turning* *turning-circle* *turning-point* *turn-off* *turn-on* *turn-out* *turnover* *turnpike* *turn-round* *turnstile* *turntable* *turn-up*

turnip kind of plant with a large white edible roots this root, eaten as a vegetable

turpentine oily liquid used as a solvent, paint thinner, etc.

turpitude depravity

turquoise greenish-blue (gemstone)

turret small defensive projecting tower; rotating structure on warships, in which guns are mounted
turreted

turtle sea-reptile with a hard shell and paddle-like flippers
turtle-dove *turtle-neck* *turtle-necked*

tusk large pointed tooth projecting from the mouth of an elephant, etc.
tusked

tussle (to) struggle
tussling

tussock clump of grass, etc.

tutelage guardianship; instruction

tutor private teacher; university teacher; to act as a tutor to
tutorial tutorially tutorship

tutti-frutti ice-cream containing a mixture of chopped or candied fruits

tutu very short projecting skirt worn by a ballet dancer

tu-whit tu-whoo cry of an owl

tuxedo (US) dinner-jacket
tuxedos or *tuxedoes*

twaddle nonsense

twang (to (cause to) make the) sharp sound of a taut wire being plucked

tweak to pinch and twist; tweaking movement

tweed thick woollen cloth
tweedy

tweeds clothes made of tweed

tweet (to) chirp

tweeter loudspeaker used for the reproduction of high-frequency sounds

tweezers pincer-like instrument

twelve number 12
twelfth twelve-plus

twenty number 20
twenties twentieth

twerp or **twirp** (*informal*) silly person

twice 2 times

twiddle to twist lightly; to play with idly
twiddling

twig[1] small branch or shoot of a tree
twiggy

twig[2] (*Brit informal*) to understand
twigged twigging

twilight soft dim light between sunset and full darkness
twilit

twill kind of strong cloth with a ridged appearance
twilled

twin either of the 2 offspring born at the same birth; similar or related; to pair
twinned twinning twin-set

twine string or thread
twiner twining

twinge sudden sharp pain

twinkle (to shine with a) flickering or sparkling light; instant
twinkler twinkling

twirl to twist quickly; twirling action
twirler

twirp see **twerp**

twist to wind strands together to form a thread; to wind; twisting (movement)
twister twisty

twit[1] to tease
twitted twitting twitty

twit[2] (*informal*) silly person

twitch (to move or pull with a) sudden jerky movement

twitter (*of birds*) to chirp; (*of people*) to talk away excitedly

two number 2
two-dimensional two-edged two-faced twofold two-handed two-piece two-ply two-seater two-sided twosome two-step two-time two-timing two-way

tycoon powerful wealthy businessman

tyke objectionable fellow; small child

tympanum eardrum
tympana or *tympanums*

Tynwald governing assembly of the Isle of Man

type class or group that share similar characteristics; to write with or use a typewriter; set of blocks used in printing
typeface typescript typeset typesetter typesetting typing typist

typecast to cast an actor continually in the same role
typecasting

typewriter machine with a keyboard for

reproducing letters and figures resembling printed ones
typewrite typewriting typewritten typewrote

typhoid infectious disease caused esp. by drinking infected water

typhoon tropical cyclone

typhus infectious disease with fever, skin rash, etc.

typical having the main characteristics of
typically

typify to be typical of; to characterize or symbolize
typification typified typifies typifying

typography art or practice of composing type for printing; style of type
typographer typographic typographical typographically

tyrannize or **tyrannise** to rule over oppressively and unjustly
tyrannizing or *tyrannising*

tyrannosaur or **tyrannosaurus** kind of large flesh-eating dinosaur

tyrant oppressive and unjust ruler
tyrannical tyrannically tyrannous tyranny tyrannies

tyre (US **tire**) rubber rings set round a wheel

tyro see **tiro**

U

ubiquitous being everywhere at the same time
ubiquitously ubiquity

U-boat German submarine

udder bag-like milk-secreting gland of animals

Uganda country in East Africa
Ugandan

ugli kind of large juicy citrus fruit
uglis or *uglies*

ugly unpleasant to look at; menacing
uglier ugliest uglily ugliness

Ukraine country in SW Asia, formerly a republic in the Soviet Union
Ukrainian

ukulele small 4-stringed guitar

ulcer open sore on the skin or mucous membrane
ulcerous

ulcerate to make or become affected with an ulcer
ulcerating ulceration ulcerative

ullage amount by which a container is less than full

ulna inner and longer of 2 bones on the human forearm
ulnae or *ulnas ulnar*

Ulster Northern Ireland; province in Eire
Ulsterman Ulsterwoman

ulterior lying beyond what is revealed

ultimate final; fundamental
ultimately

ultimatum final demand
ultimatums or *ultimata*

ultimo of the previous month

ultra- (*prefix*) beyond; extreme
ultra-conservative ultra-high ultramodern

ultramarine deep-blue

ultramontane of peoples or countries beyond the Alps

ultrasonic (*of sound waves*) having a frequency higher than is audible to the human ear
ultrasonically ultrasonics

ultraviolet (*of radiation*) having a wavelength between the violet end of the spectrum and X-rays

ululate to wail
ululant ululating ululation

umbel flattened flower-cluster in which the stalks spring from the same point

umber natural brown pigment

umbilical of the navel; of the cord or structure that connects a foetus to the placenta in the womb

umbra area of total shadow
umbrae or *umbras*

umbrage feeling of resentment

umbrella portable device that gives protection from the weather

umlaut mark placed over a vowel in some Germanic languages ¨

umpire referee in a sport; judge; to act as a referee in
umpiring

umpteen (*informal*) many
umpteenth

un- (*prefix*) not; showing reversal of an action or state
unabated unable unabridged unacceptable unaccompanied unaccustomed unafraid unaided unambiguous unambitious unannounced

unappealing unappetizing or unappetising unapproachable unarmed unasked unattainable unattended unauthorized or unauthorised unavoidable unbearable unbeatable unbeaten unbiased or unbiassed unbind unblock unbolt unbreakable unbridled unbuckle unburden unbutton unceasing unchanging uncharacteristic uncharitable uncharted unchecked unclaimed unclassified unclean uncomfortable uncommitted uncommunicative unconcerned unconfirmed uncongenial unconnected unconstitutional uncontrollable unconventional unconvincing uncooked uncooperative uncoordinated uncritical uncrossed uncut undamaged undated undecided undefined undemocratic undeserved undetected undeterred undeveloped undisclosed undiscriminating undisputed undistinguished undivided undock undomesticated undoubted undoubtedly undrinkable unearned uneconomic uneducated unemployable unending unethical uneventful unexciting unexplained unexploded unexpurgated unfair unfaithful unfashionable unfasten unfavourable (US unfavorable) unfinished unforeseen unforgettable unforgivable unformed unfreeze unfriendly unfruitful unfulfilled unfurnished ungovernable ungrammatical ungrateful unharmed unhealthy unheated unheeded unhelpful unhook unhurried unhurt unhygienic unidentified unimaginable unimaginative unimportant unimpressed uninhabited uninhibited uninitiated uninspired uninsured unintelligible unintentional uninteresting uninterrupted uninvited unjust unjustifiable unkind unladened unleavened unlimited unlined unlisted unload unlucky unmanageable unmarked unmarried unmoved unnamed unnatural unnecessarily unnecessary unnoticed unobserved unobtainable unofficial unopen unopposed unorthodox unpaid unpalatable unpatriotic unplanned unpleasant unpopular unpredictable unprepared unpretentious unpriced unproductive unprofessional unprofitable unpromising unprompted unpronounceable unprovoked unpublished unpunished unreadable unreal unrealistic unreality unrealized or unrealised unrecognizable or unrecognisable unrecorded unregistered unrelated unreliable unrepeatable unrepresentative unresolved unrestrained unrestricted unrewarding unsafe unsaid unsaleable or unsalable unsalaried unsatisfactory unscheduled unscientific unscramble unscrew unscripted unselfconscious unselfish unshakeable or unshakable unshaven unshockable unsigned unskilled unsliced unsmoked unsold unsolicited unsolved unsophisticated unsound unspecified unspectacular unspoilt unspoken unstable unsteady unsterilized or unsterilised unstressed unstuck unsuccessful unsuitable unsuited unsupervised unsupported unsure unsurpassed unsuspecting unswayed unsweetened unswerving unsympathetic untamed untapped untenable untested untidy untiring untraceable unrained untreated untried untrue untrustworthy untruthful unusable or unuseable unused unvoiced unwaged unwanted unwashed unwavering unwelcome unwell unwise unworkable unworthy

unabashed not embarrassed or disconcerted

unaccountable that cannot be explained; not responsible
unaccountability unaccountably

unadopted (*of a road*) not maintained by a local authority

unaffected not affected; genuine

unanimous agreeing; marked by complete agreement
unanimity unanimously

unanswerable that cannot be refuted

unassuming modest

unattached independent; not committed, engaged, or married

unaware not aware
unawares

unbalanced not balanced; deranged

unbecoming unattractive; not proper

unbeknown or **unbeknownst** without the knowledge of

unbelievable astonishing
unbelievably

unbeliever person who does not believe esp. in a particular religion
unbelief unbelieving

unbend to straighten; to release from restraints; to relax
unbending unbent

unborn not yet born

unbroken complete; continuous; (*of a horse*) not yet tamed; (*of a record*) not improved on

uncalled-for unnecessary; unwarranted

uncanny mysterious; extraordinary
uncannily

unceremonious not polite; rude
unceremoniously

uncertain not certain; not to be relied on
uncertainty

uncle brother of one's father or mother; aunt's husband

uncommon remarkable

unconditional absolute; unqualified
unconditionally

unconscionable unprincipled; excessive

unconscious not aware; not conscious; unconscious mind
unconsciously unconsciousness
SEE PANEL at **subconscious**

uncork to remove the cork from

uncouple to detach
uncoupling

uncouth awkward; boorish

uncover to remove the cover from; to disclose

unction anointing with oil as a religious rite

unctuous marked by smug pretence
unctuously unctuousness

undaunted not discouraged

undeniable obviously true
undeniably

under below; less than

under- (*prefix*) below; subordinate; less than; insufficiently
under-age underbid undercharge undermanned undermentioned undernourished underproduction underseal understaffed

underachieve to fail to achieve the expected result
underachievement underachiever underachieving

underarm thrown or bowled with the arm kept below the shoulder

undercarriage landing gear of an aircraft

underclothes underwear
underclothing

undercoat layer of paint applied before the final coat; to apply an undercoat to

undercover acting or performed secretly

undercurrent current below the surface; underlying influence, etc.

undercut to charge a lower price than a competitor; beef tenderloin
undercutting

underdeveloped not fully developed, esp. economically

underdog person who is disadvantaged or expected to lose a competition

underdone not fully cooked

underestimate to make too low an estimate of
underestimating underestimation

underexpose to expose photographic film for too short a time
underexposing underexposure

underfeed to feed with too little food
underfed

underfelt thick felt laid under a carpet to provide insulation

underfoot on the ground; under one's feet

undergarment garment worn under another

undergo to experience; to be subjected to
undergoing undergone underwent

undergraduate person studying for a first degree

underground beneath the earth's surface; secretly or secret; underground railway

undergrowth dense mass of shrubs, bushes, etc. growing beneath trees

underhand sly

underlay to place under; material placed under a carpet
underlaid underlaying

underlie to be or lie under; to form the basis of
underlain underlay underlying

underline to draw a line under; to emphasize
underlining

underling subordinate

undermine to tunnel under; to weaken
underminer undermining

underneath below or beneath

underpants men's pants

underpass passage or tunnel for a road under another road or a railway

underpay to pay someone insufficient money
underpaid underpaying underpayment

underpin to strengthen or support from beneath
underpinned underpinning

underprivileged deprived of some of the fundamental rights of society

underproof containing less alcohol than proof spirit contains

underrate to underestimate
underrated underrating

undersea beneath the surface of the sea

under-secretary assistant secretary; high-ranking civil servant
under-secretaries

undersell to sell at a lower price than
underselling undersold

under-sexed with less than normal sexual potency or desire; lacking sexual desire or urge

undershoot to land short of a runway
undershot

underside bottom surface

undersigned people who have signed their names at the foot of a document

undersized of less than the usual size

underskirt petticoat

understand to realize the meaning of; to have a thorough knowledge of; to believe; to sympathize
understandable understandably understanding understood

understate to state in very restrained terms

understudy (to act as a) substitute for someone, esp. a performer in a play
understudies

undertake to take a task upon oneself; to promise
undertaken undertaking undertook

undertaker person whose business is to prepare the dead for burial and to arrange funerals

under-the-counter sold or done illicitly

undertone hushed tone of voice; undercurrent of feeling

undertow current below the surface of the water that moves in the opposite direction to the surface movement

undervalue to put too low a value on
undervaluation undervalued undervaluing

underwater beneath the surface of water, esp. the sea

underwear garments worn next to the skin under other clothing

underweight weighing less than is normal or healthy

underwent past tense of **undergo**

underwhelm (*informal*) to fail to impress

underworld criminal society; (*mythology*) dwelling-place of the dead

underwrite to accept for insurance; to accept responsibility or liability for
underwriter underwriting underwritten underwrote

undesirable objectionable or unwanted (person or thing)
undesirably

undies (*informal*) women's underwear

undo to untie or unfasten; to ruin; to reverse the effect of
undid undoing undone

undreamed or **undreamt** not conceived (of)

undress to remove the clothes of; state of having too few clothes on; ordinary dress, not ceremonial uniform

undue too much; improper
unduly

undulate to have a wavy appearance or movement
undulating undulation undulator undulatory

undying eternal

unearth to dig up; to disclose

unearthly mysterious; ghostly; (*informal*) unreasonable

uneasy awkward
uneasily uneasiness

unemployed (people who are) out of work; not being used
unemployment

unequal not equal; not able to meet the requirements that are necessary for
unequally

unequivocal clear
unequivocally

unerring faultless
unerringly

unexceptionable that cannot be objected to
unexceptionably
SEE PANEL

---

unexceptionable or unexceptional?
Unexceptionable means 'that cannot be objected to': *The speech was unexceptionable, but it didn't contain anything new or exciting.*
Unexceptional means 'ordinary or usual; of average quality': *It was a predictable, unexceptional film.*

---

unexceptional ordinary or usual
SEE PANEL at **unexceptionable**

unfailing constant

unfamiliar not well-known; not well acquainted
unfamiliarity

unfeeling not sympathetic; callous

unfit unsuitable; incapable; unwell; to make unfit
unfitted unfitting

unflagging tireless
unflaggingly

unflappable imperturbable

unflinching bold
unflinchingly

unfold to open out; to disclose gradually

unfortunate unlucky; regrettable; unfortunate person
unfortunately

unfounded not based on fact

unfrequented not often visited

unfrock to deprive of the right to serve as a priest

unfurl to spread out

ungainly lacking grace; clumsy
ungainliness

unget-at-able inaccessible

ungodly not reverent; evil; (*informal*) outrageous
ungodliness

unguarded imprudent; not protected

unguent ointment

ungula hoof
ungulae

ungulate mammal with hooves

unhappy not happy; inappropriate
unhappier unhappiest unhappily unhappiness

unheard not heard

unheard-of unprecedented

unhinge to remove from its hinges; to make unbalanced
unhinging

unholy not holy; evil; (*informal*) outrageous

unhoped-for not expected

unhorse to throw from a horse
unhorsing

uni- (*prefix*) one

unicellular consisting of a single cell
unicellularity

unicorn imaginary creature with a single long straight horn

unidirectional operating in only 1 direction

uniform identifying clothing worn by members of a particular group; unchanging
uniformed uniformity uniformly

unify to make uniform
unification unified unifier unifies unifying

unilateral by or affecting one side only
unilateralism unilateralist unilaterally

unimpeachable completely trustworthy
unimpeachably

uninterested having no interest in; bored
SEE PANEL at **disinterested**

union uniting; group of workers formed to advance members' interests
unionism unionist

unionize or **unionise** to (cause to) organize a trade union
unionization or *unionisation*

un-ionized or **un-ionised** not ionized

uniparous producing a single egg or offspring at birth

unique being the only one of its kind
uniquely uniqueness

unisex of or for people of both sexes

unison agreement; identity of musical pitch

unit single person, thing, or group; standard measurement; part having a particular function
unitary

Unitarian (member of the) Christian Church that rejects the doctrine of the Trinity
Unitarianism

unite to join; to become one
united United Arab Emirates United Kingdom United States of America uniting unity

universal of or affecting all; existing everywhere
universality universally

universalize or **universalise** to make universal
universalization or *universalisation*

universe all things that exist; everyone

university higher educational institution for teaching and research
universities

unkempt untidy or dishevelled

unknown not known (person, thing, etc.)

unlearn to discard or try to forget something already learned
unlearned or *unlearnt*

unleash to release from a leash or other restraint

unless if not

unlike different (from)

unlikely not probable
unlikelihood

unlooked-for not expected

unloose or **unloosen** to release
unloosing

unman to deprive of courage, etc.; to castrate
unmanned *unmanning*

unmanly weak; effeminate
unmanliness

unmanned operated without a crew

unmask to remove the mask from; to show the true character of

unmentionable not fit to be mentioned
unmentionably

unmistakable obvious
unmistakably

unmitigated absolute

unnerve to cause to lose courage
unnerving

unnumbered countless; not having a number

unobtrusive not very easily noticed
unobtrusively *unobtrusiveness*

unpack to remove the contents from a container

unparalleled having no equal

unparliamentary against parliamentary practice

unpick to undo the stitches from

unplaced not among the first 3 in a competition

unplug to disconnect from an electric circuit
unplugged *unplugging*

unprecedented having no precedent

unprincipled having no moral principles

unprintable unsuitable to be printed

unputdownable (*informal*) (*of a book*) being compulsive reading

unqualified not having qualifications; absolute

unquestionable without doubt; certain
unquestionably

unquestioning without showing any hesitation
unquestioningly

unquiet agitated; uneasy

unquote used to mark the end of a quotation

unravel to disentangle; to explain
unravelled (US *unraveled*) *unravelling* (US *unraveling*)

unreasonable not governed by reason; excessive
unreasonably

unreasoning not influenced by reason

unrelenting not weakening in determination, etc.
unrelentingly

unremitting constant

unrequited not returned

unreserved unqualified; frank
unreservedly

unrest agitation

unrivalled (US **unrivaled**) matchless

unroll to open out

unruffled calm

unruly difficult to control
unrulier unruliest unruliness

unsavoury (US **unsavory**) nasty

unscathed not injured in any way

unscrupulous having no moral scruples
unscrupulously

unseat to throw from a saddle; to remove from office

unseemly improper
unseemliness

unseen invisible; passage of writing for translation to be undertaken without previous preparation

unsettle to disturb; to make changeable
unsettled unsettling

unsightly ugly

unsociable not enjoying social activity
unsociability unsociably
SEE PANEL

---

unsociable or unsocial?
Someone who is *unsociable* dislikes or avoids the company of others: *After the meeting, I joined the others in the pub, not wishing to appear unsociable.*

Unsocial usually occurs in the expression *work unsocial hours,* that is working at night, early in the morning and at weekends: *You must be prepared to work unsocial hours.*

---

unsocial not social; not within normal working hours
unsocially
SEE PANEL at **unsociable**

unspeakable that cannot be described in words
unspeakably

unspotted blameless

unstop to remove an obstruction or stopper from
unstoppable unstopped unstopping

unsung not celebrated in song or poetry

unswerving constant
unswervingly

unthinkable incredible
unthinkably

unthinking inconsiderate
unthinkingly

unthought-of not imagined

until up to the time that

untimely happening before the natural time

unto (*archaic*) to

untold vast; not told

untouchable not able to be touched; member of the lowest Hindu caste in India

untoward unfortunate

untruth falsehood

unusual strange
unusually

unutterable too intense or great to be described in words
unutterably

unveil to remove a veil from; to reveal

unwarranted not justified

unwieldy awkward to handle
unwieldily unwieldiness

unwind to unroll; to relax
unwinding unwound

unwitting not intended; not aware
unwittingly

unwrap to take off the wrapping from
unwrapped unwrapping

unwritten not written down formally

unzip to open using a zip
unzipped unzipping

up from a lower to a higher position, level, etc.; to an upright position; to act suddenly; to increase
up-and-coming up-and-over up-and-up up-country uphill up-market upped upping upstairs upstream up-train upward upwards

up-beat unaccented beat in a musical bar

upbraid to reproach

upbringing education and training

update to bring up to date
updater updating

upend to set on end

upgrade to raise to a higher grade or quality
upgrader upgrading

upheaval violent disturbance

uphold to support or maintain
upheld upholding

upholster to fit a soft covering, springs, etc. to a chair
upholsterer upholstery

upkeep maintenance of something in good condition; money needed for this

upland area of high land

uplift to raise, esp. morally or spiritually; such a raising

upon on

upper higher; part of a shoe or boot above the sole

uppermost or **upmost** in the highest or most prominent position

uppish or **uppity** (*informal*) self-assertive; supercilious
uppishly uppishness or *uppityness*

upright vertical; honest; honourable; vertical support

uprising rebellion

uproar commotion

uproarious noisy; very funny
uproariously

uproot to remove by pulling up by the roots; to displace

upset to turn over; to disturb; disturbance
upsetting

upshot outcome or conclusion

upside down turned over completely; in confusion

upstage at the back of the stage; to draw attention to oneself away from someone else
upstaging

upstanding honourable; standing up

upstart person who has risen suddenly to a powerful position

upsurge sudden rise

upswing upward movement; noticeable increase

uptake taking in; (*informal*) understanding

uptight (*informal*) nervously very tense

upturn to turn over; upward turn; improvement

uranium radioactive silvery white metal

Uranus 7th planet from the sun

urban of or resembling a city or town
SEE PANEL

---

urban or urbane?

Urban means 'of or resembling a city or town': *the urban population; urban development; the Urban District Council.*

Urbane means 'sophisticated or suave': *When you met him, he came across as a well-mannered, confident, and urbane young man.*

---

urbane sophisticated; suave
urbanely urbanity urbanities
SEE PANEL at **urban**

urbanize or **urbanise** to make more urban
urbanization or *urbanisation urbanizing* or *urbanising*

urchin mischievous scruffy boy

Urdu official language of Pakistan, also spoken in India

ureter tube that conveys urine from the kidney to the bladder
ureteral *ureteric*

urethra canal through which urine is discharged from the bladder
urethrae *urethritis*

urge to drive on; to plead; strong drive
urging

urgent requiring immediate action
urgency *urgently*

urinal room containing a fixture used by men for urination

urinate to discharge urine
urinating *urination*

urine waste liquid secreted by the kidney and discharged from the body
uric *urinary*

urn large metal container for making tea, etc.; decorative vase for the ashes of a dead person

ursine of bears

Uruguay country in South America
Uruguayan

us object form of **we**

usage established way that words are used

use to put into action or service; to apply or consume; to exploit
usable or *useable* *user* *user-friendly* *using*

used already used; accustomed (to); having done or experienced something regularly in the past

useful able to be used practically; commendable
usefully *usefulness*

useless having no practical use; weak; futile
uselessly *uselessness*

usher (*fem.* **usherette**) official who shows people to their seats, to direct; to introduce

usual normal or customary
usually *usualness*

usurer person who practises usury

usurp to seize without authority
usurpation *usurper*

usury lending of money at an exorbitant rate of interest
usurious

utensil implement or tool

uterus womb
uteri or *uteruses* *uterine*

utilitarian designed for practical use
utilitarianism

utility usefulness; public service
utilities

utilize or **utilise** to put to practical use
utilizable or *utilisable* *utilization* or *utilisation* *utilizer* or *utiliser* *utilizing* or *utilising*

utmost or **uttermost** (at the) furthest or greatest point or degree

utopia imaginary perfect place or society
utopian

utter[1] to express
utterance

utter[2] absolute
utterly

U-turn complete reversal

uvula fleshy flap of tissue that hangs down at the back of the roof of the mouth
uvulae or *uvulas* *uvular*

uxorious excessively fond of or dependent on one's wife
uxoriously *uxoriousness*

Uzbekistan country in Central Asia

V

vac (*informal*) short for **vacation**

vacant empty; marked by a lack of thought
vacancy vacancies
SEE PANEL

vacant or vacuous?
Something that is *vacant* is not being used: *a vacant seat; vacant rooms*; a job is *vacant* if no-one is doing it and people can apply for it: *several vacant positions*; someone who has a *vacant* expression looks as if they are not thinking about anything: *a vacant look on his face.*

If you describe a comment as *vacuous*, you mean that it does not show intelligent thought: *He muttered the usual vacuous remarks about the team losing again.*

vacate to make vacant; to give up the possession of
vacating

vacation vacating; holiday

vaccinate to inoculate with a vaccine
vaccinating vaccination vaccinator

vaccine preparation designed to produce immunity to a disease

vacillate to fluctuate in one's opinions; to waver
vacillating vacillation vacillator

vacuous empty; stupid
vacuity vacuities vacuously
SEE PANEL at **vacant**

vacuum space that contains no matter
vacuum or *vacua vacuum-packed*

vade-mecum handbook for ready reference
vade-mecums

vagabond tramp or wanderer

vagary erratic idea or movement
vagaries

vagina passage from the vulva to the womb in female mammals
vaginae or *vaginas vaginal vaginitis*

vagrant tramp; wandering or erratic
vagrancy vagrantly

vague not clear; imprecise
vaguely vagueness vaguer vaguest

vain excessively proud of one's appearance; futile
vainly
SEE PANEL

vain, vane, or vein?
Someone who is *vain* is excessively proud of their appearance, achievements, etc.: *He is very vain about his clothes.* A *vain* attempt, or something done *in vain* is futile: *We tried to find the missing dog, but our search was in vain; We do want you to know that your daughter did not die in vain.*

A *vane* is a flat blade that moves round an axis and is pushed by water or the wind: *the vane on a propeller; a weather vane.*

The *veins* are the thin-walled blood-vessels; a *vein* is also a layer of a mineral in a rock (*a vein of iron ore*); when you write or speak in a particular *vein* what is expressed is in that mood: *In a lighter vein, let us move on to the touches of irony in the play.*

vainglory boastfulness
vainglorious

valance short draping along the edge of a bed, canopy, etc.

vale (*chiefly poetic*) valley

valediction saying goodbye
valedictory

valency degree of combining power of an element
valencies

valentine card sent to one's lover on 14 February; person to whom this card is sent

valerian kind of perennial plant with a medicinal root

valet manservant who takes care of a man's clothes, etc.

valetudinarian person with a weak constitution; hypochondriac

valiant courageous
valiantly

valid legally effective; justifiable
validity validly

validate to make valid; to confirm
validating validation

valise small travelling case

valley hollow in the earth's surface, esp. between hills or mountains
valleys

valour (US **valor**) courage
valorous

valuable (something) having a great monetary value

value (to estimate the) amount of money thought to be equivalent to something; (to estimate the) importance (of); to esteem
valuation valuator value-added valued valueless valuer valuing

valve device for controlling the flow of a liquid or gas

vamp to renovate; to improvise; front part of the upper of a shoe

vampire blood-drinking corpse believed to rise from its grave at night
vampiric vampirism

van covered motor vehicle or railway wagon for transporting goods

vandal person who deliberately destroys property
vandalism

vandalize or **vandalise** to damage or destroy as a vandal
vandalizing or *vandalising*

vane flat blade moved round an axis, as on a propeller
SEE PANEL at **vain**

vanguard front advancing part of an army; forward part

vanilla (kind of tropical plant providing a) flavouring
vanillic

vanish to disappear
vanisher vanishes

vanity being vain
vanities

vanquish to defeat
vanquishable vanquisher vanquishes

vantage point providing an advantageous position

vapid dull
vapidity vapidly

vaporize or **vaporise** to turn into vapour
vaporization or *vaporisation vaporizer* or *vaporiser vaporizing* or *vaporising*

vapour (US **vapor**) particles of fog, smoke, etc. in the air; gaseous form of a liquid
vaporous vapoury (US *vapory*)

variable liable to vary
variability variably

variation (extent of) varying

varicoloured (US **varicolored**) having many colours

varicose (*of veins*) swollen and tortuous

variegated having patches, etc. of different colours
variegation variegator

variety quality of being different; range of different kinds; group
varieties

various several; different

varnish (to cover with a) solution that gives a shiny coating
varnishes varnisher

vary to change
variance variant variation varied varies varying

vascular of vessels that conduct a liquid in an organism

vase ornamental vessel

vasectomy surgical operation to remove part of each of the ducts that convey sperm from the testicle
vasectomies

Vaseline (*trademark*) kind of petroleum jelly

vassal tenant in feudal society
vassalage

vast very great
vastly vastness

vat large container for holding liquids

Vatican pope's palace in Rome

vaudeville variety entertainment

vault[1] arched roof; underground storage room
vaulted vaulting

vault[2] to leap (over); act of vaulting
vaulter

vaunt to show boastfully

veal flesh of calf as food

vector (*maths*) quantity that has magnitude and direction; carrier of a disease

Veda ancient Hindu sacred writings

veer to change direction

vegan strict vegetarian

vegetable plant with a part used as food; this part

vegetarian person who has a diet that excludes meat
vegetarianism

vegetate to grow like a plant; to lead an inactive monotonous life
vegetating

vegetation plant life; vegetating

veggie (*informal*) vegetarian; vegetable

vehement intense; energetic
vehemence vehemently

vehicle means of conveying passengers or goods, esp. one fitted with wheels
vehicular

veil light fabric worn by a woman to hide or protect the face or head; something that conceals; to cover with a veil

vein thin-walled blood-vessel; streak of colour
veined veiny venation
SEE PANEL at **vain**

Velcro (*trademark*) fastening device consisting of 2 strips of nylon fabric

vellum fine parchment

velocipede early kind of bicycle

velocity speed
velocities

velour fabric having a velvet-like finish

velvet fabric of silk, cotton, etc. with a soft thick pile

velveteen cotton cloth similar to velvet

venal marked by bribery or corruption
venality venally
SEE PANEL

---

venal or venial?

Venal is used to describe a person who is prepared to accept bribes for acting dishonestly or corruptly, or a system marked by bribery or corruption: *the country's venal financial system.*

Venial is used to describe a sin that is not considered very serious and is therefore easily forgiven. In Roman Catholic theology a *venial* sin is one that does not wholly deprive the soul of divine grace, as opposed to a mortal sin, which does.

vend to sell
vendible vending-machine vendor or *vender*

vendetta private feud between families
vendettas vendettist

veneer (to cover with a) thin layer of wood; superficial appearance

venerable worthy of respect
venerability

venerate to respect deeply
venerating veneration venerator

venereal (*of disease*) transmitted by sexual intercourse

venetian blind window blind consisting of adjustable horizontal slats

Venezuela country in South America
Venezuelan

vengeance taking revenge
vengeful vengefully vengefulness

venial easily forgiven
veniality venially
SEE PANEL at **venal**

venison flesh of a deer used as food

Venn diagram representation of relations between sets in set theory

venom poison; spite or malice
venomous venomously venomousness

venous of the veins

vent[1] opening that allows fumes, etc. to escape; to express

vent[2] slit in the back of a jacket or other garment

ventilate to allow fresh air to circulate freely in
ventilating ventilation ventilator

ventral abdominal; front
ventrally

ventricle small cavity in the heart or brain

ventriloquism art of producing vocal sounds in such a way that they seem to come from a different source
ventriloquial ventriloquist

venture to risk; risky undertaking
venturer venturesome venturing venturous

venue place for a meeting

Venus[1] planet 2nd from the sun

Venus[2] Roman goddess of love

veracious truthful
veraciously veracity

veranda or **verandah** open roofed gallery attached to the outside of a house

verb word expressing performance of an action, etc.

verbal in words; spoken; of verbs
verbally

verbalize or **verbalise** to express in words
verbalizing or *verbalising*

verbatim word for word

verbena kind of American plant with fragrant flowers

verbiage excessive use of words

verbose using an excess of words
verbosely verboseness verbosity

verdant green
verdancy verdantly

verdict decision, esp. one reached by a jury

verdigris green pigment on copper

verdure green vegetation
verdured verdurous

verge edge; grassy border; to be near to
verging

verger church official

verify to prove to be true
verifiable verification verified verifier verifies verifying

verily (*archaic*) in truth

verisimilitude appearance of truth

veritable true
veritably

verity truth; true statement
verities

vermicelli long threads of pasta

vermicide substance used to kill worms

vermiculite kind of mica

vermiform similar to a worm

vermilion brilliant red

vermin small animals that are harmful
verminous

vermouth wine flavoured with aromatic herbs

vernacular commonly spoken language of a people or area

vernal of spring

vernier measuring instrument consisting of a graduated scale that runs parallel to a larger graduated scale

veronica speedwell

verruca wart on the foot or hand
verrucae or *verrucas*

versatile able to be used in many different ways
versatilely versatility

verse group of lines in a poem or song; poetry

versed having a knowledge of

versify to turn into verse
versification versified versifier versifies versifying

version account or description from a particular point of view

verso left-hand page of a book
versos

versus against

vertebra one of the small bony segments that form the backbone
vertebrae or *vertebras vertebral*

vertebrate (animal) having a backbone

vertex highest point; point of a triangle, etc.
vertices

vertical upright
vertically

vertigo feeling of dizziness
vertigos vertiginous vertiginously

verve liveliness

very to a high degree; actual

vesicle small sac containing fluid; cavity
vesicular

vespers service of evening worship

vespiary nest of wasps
vespiaries

vessel container for liquids; ship or boat

vest (*Brit*) undergarment for the upper part of the body; (US) waistcoat; to give rights to

vestal chaste or pure

vestibule small entrance hall

vestige trace
vestigial

vestment ceremonial robe, esp. as worn by a priest

vestry room in church where vestments are kept or meetings are held
vestries

vet to assess or examine thoroughly; (*informal*) short for **veterinary surgeon**
vetted vetting

vetch climbing or twisting plant of the bean family

veteran person with long, esp. military, experience; experienced; very old (car)

veterinary of a branch of medicine concerned with the health and treatment on animals

veto authority to forbid; act of forbidding; to forbid
vetoes vetoed vetoing

vex to annoy
vexation vexatious vexer vexes

via by way of

viable practicable; able to exist independently
viability viably

viaduct bridge carrying a road or railway across a valley

vial small container; phial

vibes (*informal*) vibrations; feeling that is sensed

vibraphone kind of musical instrument resembling a xylophone

vibrate to move backwards and forwards rapidly; to resound
vibrant vibrating vibration vibrator

vibrato fast slight fluctuation in musical pitch
vibratos

vicar clergyman
vicarage

vicarious experienced by imagining the feeling of another person
vicariously vicariousness

vice[1] (form of) wickedness

vice[2] (US **vise**) tool with 2 jaws for gripping an object

vice- (*prefix*) deputy
vice-president vice-regent

viceroy (*fem*. **vicereine**) representative governor of a colony, province, etc.
viceroys viceregal viceroyalty viceroyship

vice versa the other way round

vicinity neighbourhood
vicinities

vicious cruel or wicked
viciously viciousness
SEE PANEL

---

vicious or viscous?

A *vicious* person is cruel or wicked; a *vicious* comment is cruel and spiteful; *a vicious criminal; a vicious attack on his reputation.* A *vicious circle* is a problematic situation that creates new problems leading back to the original situation: *the vicious circle of debt.*

A *viscous* liquid is one that is thick and sticky: *viscous* oil.

---

vicissitude change in the conditions of one's life

victim person or thing that suffers harm or is tricked

victimize or **victimise** to make a victim of
victimization or *victimisation victimizing* or *victimising*

victor conqueror

victoria kind of large sweet plum

Victorian of or characteristic of the reign of Queen Victoria

victory success or winning
victories victorious victoriously

victual to supply with victuals
victualled (US *victualed*) *victualler* (US *victualer*) *victualling* (US *victualing*)

victuals provisions; food

vide (*Latin*) see

video recording of sound and vision on magnetic tape
videos videotape

vie to contend
vied vier vies vying

Vietnam country in SE Asia
Vietnamese

view to watch or inspect; seeing; scene; opinion
viewdata viewer viewfinder viewpoint

vigil time of staying awake to watch and pray

vigilant alert
vigilance vigilantly

vigilante self-appointed protector of public order in a neighbourhood
vigilantes

vignette illustration with shaded edges
vignettist

vigour (US **vigor**) strength or energy
vigorous vigorously

Viking Norse warrior of the 8th to 11th centuries

vile shameful; unpleasant
vilely vileness viler vilest

vilify to defame
vilification vilified vilifier vilifies vilifying

villa large country house; seaside house
villas

village group of houses in a country area, smaller than a town
villager

villain scoundrel
villainous villainously villainy

villein serf
villeinage

vinaigrette small bottle of smelling-salts; salad-dressing

vindicate to clear of guilt; to uphold
vindicating vindication vindicator

vindictive seeking revenge
vindictively vindictiveness

vine kind of climbing plant that bears grapes; climbing or trailing plant
vinery vineries vineyard

vinegar sour liquid used for flavouring and preserving

viniculture viticulture

vintage produce of grapes; kind of wine; class; old (car)

vintner wine merchant

vinyl kind of plastic

viol kind of medieval bowed stringed instrument

viola[1] kind of stringed instrument larger and lower in pitch than a violin

viola[2] violet plant

violate to break a law; to disturb; to rape
violable violating violation violator

violent forceful
violence violently

violet kind of plant with sweet-scented bluish-purple flowers

violin kind of stringed musical instrument played with a bow
violinist

viper venomous snake

virago ill-tempered woman
viragos or *viragoes*

viral of a virus

virgin person who has not had sexual intercourse; undefiled; untouched
virginal virginity

virginal early type of keyboard musical instrument

Virgo 6th sign of the zodiac

virile having the characteristics of an adult male
virility

virology study of viruses
virological

virtual in effect though not in fact
virtuality virtually

virtue goodness; chastity; advantageous quality
virtuous virtuously

virtuoso person who excels in the skills of an art, esp. the performance of music
virtuosos or *virtuosi virtuosity*

virulent developing quickly; deadly
virulence virulently

virus tiny organism that causes a disease; (*informal*) disease caused by this
viruses viral

visa endorsement in a passport allowing entrance to a particular country; to provide with a visa
visas visaed visaing

visage (*literary*) face

vis-à-vis (*French*) in relation to; opposite

viscera internal organs of the body
visceral

viscid sticky
viscidity viscidly

viscose viscous cellulose, used in the manufacture of rayon, etc.

viscount (*fem.* **viscountess)** person with the rank of nobility below an earl and above a baron
viscountcy viscountship

viscous thick and sticky
viscosity
SEE PANEL at **vicious**

vise (US) see **vice**[2]

Vishnu preserver god in Hinduism

visible capable of being seen
visibility visibly

vision power of seeing; vivid mental image; foresight
visionary visionaries

visit to go to see; act of visiting
visitant visitation visited visiting visitor

visor or **vizor** protective part of a helmet or the peak of a cap; sun-shield in a car

vista view
vistas

visual of or associated with seeing
visually

visualize or **visualise** to form a mental image of
visualization or *visualisation visualizing* or *visualising*

vital of or concerned with living; essential
vitally

vitality liveliness; vigour or energy
vitalities

vitalize or **vitalise** to make vital; to put (new) life into
vitalization or *vitalisation vitalizing* or *vitalising*

vitamin organic compound essential for healthy life and growth

vitiate to make imperfect; to render ineffective
vitiating vitiation vitiator

viticulture (study of) cultivation of grapevines
viticultural viticulturist

vitreous of or made of glass
vitreosity or *vitreousness vitreously*

vitrify to change into glass or a glassy substance
vitrifiable vitrification vitrified vitrifies vitrifying

vitriol sulphuric acid
vitriolic

vituperate to speak in a harsh condemning manner (about)
vituperating vituperation vituperative

viva (voce) oral examination; to examine by viva
vivas viva voces vivaed vivaing

vivace (*music*) quickly; lively

vivacious lively
vivaciously vivacity

vivarium place where animals are kept under natural conditions
vivaria or *vivariums*

vivid (*of a colour*) bright; strong or lively
vividly vividness

vivify to make vivid; to animate
vivification vivified vivifies vivifying

viviparous producing live young that develop within the mother's body
viviparously viviparousness or *viviparity*

vivisect to perform vivisection (on)
vivisector

vivisection operations on or experiments with live animals, esp. for scientific purposes
vivisectional vivisectionist

vixen female fox
vixenish

vizier high-ranking officer in various Muslim countries

viz. namely

vizor see **visor**

V-neck garment with a V-shaped neck

vocable word

vocabulary (alphabetical) list of words; set of words that are used
vocabularies

vocal of or produced by the voice
vocally

vocalism vocal singing technique

vocalist singer

vocalize or **vocalise** to utter or sing
vocalization or *vocalisation* *vocalizer* or *vocaliser* *vocalizing* or *vocalising*

vocation (sense of calling that one is to follow a) particular profession
vocational

vocative (*grammar*) case used to express the person addressed

vociferate to cry out loudly
vociferating *vociferation*

vociferous expressing one's views in a 'noisy insistent manner
vociferously *vociferousness*

vodka spirit distilled from potatoes, rye, etc.

vogue popular fashion
voguish

voice sound produced from the mouth in speaking or singing; to express one's opinion, etc.
voice-box *voiceless* *voice-over* *voice-print* *voicer* *voicing*

void empty (space); not legally valid

voile fine soft semi-transparent fabric

Volapük artificial international language

volatile (*of a liquid*) evaporating quickly; fickle, lively, or unstable
volatility

volatilize or **volatilise** to (cause to) evaporate
volatilizable or *volatilisable* *volatilization* or *volatilisation* *volatilizing* or *volatilising*

vol-au-vent light pastry case with a savoury filling

volcano opening in the earth's crust from which lava, steam, etc. may be forced out
volcanoes or *volcanos* *volcanic*

vole kind of small rodent

volition use of one's own will in making a decision
volitional *volitive*

volley simultaneous discharge of guns; to return a ball before it touches the ground
volleys *volleyed* *volleying*

volleyball team-game in which a ball is volleyed by hand over a net

volt basic metric unit of electric potential
voltage *voltmeter*

volte-face sudden reversal of attitude

voluble talking quickly and readily
volubility *volubly*

volume book, esp. one of a series; amount of space; loudness of sound
volumetric

voluminous having great volume; full
voluminously *voluminousness* or *voluminosity*

voluntary of one's own free choice; organ solo
voluntaries *voluntarily* *voluntariness*

volunteer to offer (oneself) freely; person who volunteers

voluptuous causing pleasure to the senses
voluptuary *voluptuaries* *voluptuously*

volute spiral
voluted

vomit to eject stomach contents through the mouth; matter that is vomited
vomited *vomiter* *vomiting* *vomitory*

voodoo magical practices of West African origin
voodooism

voracious eager or greedy
voraciousness voracity

vortex whirling mass of air, water, etc.
vortexes or *vortices vertical vorticity*

votary devotee or advocate
votaries

vote to express one's choice or opinion formally; formal expression of voting
votable or *voteable voter voting*

votive performed or dedicated in the fulfilling of a vow

vouch to give personal assurance of
vouches

voucher document, receipt, or coupon

vouchsafe (*formal*) to grant, esp. graciously or condescendingly
vouchsafing

vow (to make a) solemn promise

vowel speech sound or letter of the alphabet that is not a consonant

voyage (to make a) long journey by sea or into space
voyager voyaging

voyeur person who derives pleasure from watching the sexual activities of others
voyeurism

Vulcan Roman god of fire

vulcanize or **vulcanise** to treat rubber to increase its elasticity, strength, etc.
vulcanization or *vulcanisation vulcanizing* or *vulcanising*

vulgar showing a lack of good taste; obscene
vulgarity vulgarly

vulgarism coarse or obscene expression

vulgarize or **vulgarise** to make popular or vulgar
vulgarization or *vulgarisation vulgarizing* or *vulgarising*

Vulgate Latin version of the Bible

vulnerable capable of being hurt or wounded
vulnerability vulnerably

vulpine of or like a fox

vulture large bird of prey that eats the flesh of dead animals

vulva external parts of the female genital organs
vulvas or *vulvae*

wad (to form into or stuff with a) small compact mass; roll of banknotes
wadded wadding

waddle to walk with short swaying steps
waddler waddling

wade to walk through water or mud
wader wading wading bird

wadi bed of a stream in North Africa of SW Asia that is dry except in the rainy season
wadis

wafer very thin crisp biscuit

waffle[1] (to express in) vague wordy talk
waffle waffling

waffle[2] crisp indented cake of batter
waffle-iron

waft to move in a light drifting manner through the air or water

wag[1] to move from side to side or up and down
wagged wagging

wag[2] jocular person
waggery waggish

wage payment for work, esp. paid weekly; to engage in war
wages waged wage-earner wageless waging

wager (to make a) bet

waggle (to) wag
waggler waggling waggly

wagon or **waggon** open railway goods truck; 4-wheeled vehicle used for carrying heavy loads
wagoner or *waggoner wagonette* or *waggonette wagonless* or *waggonless*

wagtail kind of small bird with a tail that moves up and down

waif homeless child; helpless person

wail (to utter a) long high-pitched cry

wainscot (to line with) panelled woodwork on an inside wall
wainscoted wainscoting

waist narrow part of the body between the ribs and hips
waistband waistbelt waistcoat waist-deep waist-high waistline

wait to remain, expecting; to delay; to serve at table
waiter waiting-list waiting-room waitress

waive to refrain from insisting on or applying
waiver waiving
SEE PANEL

---

waive or wave?

To *waive* a right or a rule means that someone does not insist on applying or enforcing it: *waive the right to appeal; waive charges/requirements; waive the fee in cases of financial hardship.*

As a verb *wave* means 'to move the hand from side to side': *She turned and waved goodbye; The police officer waved the traffic on; wave flags at the President.*

---

wake[1] to rouse or become roused from sleep; to make or become conscious of; vigil by a corpse before burial; annual holiday in northern England
wakeful wakefully wakefulness waking woke woken

wake[2] track or trail left by something moving

waken to wake
wakened wakening

wale raised mark left on the skin by a heavy blow or slash of a whip, etc.

Wales principality in the west of Great Britain

walk to move on foot; journey of foot; calling or occupation
walkabout walker walking walking-stick walk-in walk-on walk-out walk-over walkway

walkie-talkie compact portable 2-way radio set

wall (to protect, etc. with a) solid vertical construction of stone, brick, etc.
wallboard wallflower wall-painting wallpaper wall-to-wall

wallaby kind of small kangaroo
wallabies

wallah (*slang*) man, esp. with certain responsibilities

wallet small folding case for banknotes, credit cards, etc.

wall-eye eye with a whitish iris
wall-eyed

wallop (*informal*) to strike hard; hard blow
walloped walloping

wallow to roll about in water or mud; to indulge excessively in
wallower wallowing

walnut kind of (edible nut of a) tree

walrus large arctic sea mammal with tusks
walruses

waltz (to dance a) ballroom dance in triple time
waltzes waltzer

wan pale; weak
wanly wanner wanness wannest

wand slender rod, as used by magicians

wander to travel about aimlessly; to meander
wanderer
SEE PANEL

---

wander or wonder?

If someone *wanders* in a place, they walk about in it aimlessly: *spend the afternoon wandering around the old part of the city; wander off into the woods for a walk*. If your thoughts *wander*, you stop concentrating on what you should be thinking about and start thinking about other matters.

If you *wonder* about something, you want to know more about it: *I wonder how they're getting on in Norway*; if you *wonder* at something you feel surprise and amazement at it: *After seeing the play you'll leave the theatre, wondering again at the greatness of life.*

---

wanderlust great desire to travel

wane (*of the moon*) to show a decreasing area of illumination; to decrease in power, etc.
waney or *wany waning*

wangle (*informal*) to use deception, manipulation, etc. to obtain
wangler wangling

wankel engine kind of rotary internal-combustion engine

want (to) desire; (to) need; to lack

wanton irresponsible; immoral
wantonly wantonness

wapiti kind of large American deer

war (to engage in) armed fighting between countries
war-cry war-dance war-game war-god warhead warhorse warlike warlord warmonger warpaint warpath warred warring warship wartime

warble to sound or sing in a trilling manner
warbler warbling

ward room in a hospital; administrative division of a town, etc.; child under the protection of a guardian or court; to fend (off)

warden person who is responsible for something

warder (*fem.* **wardress**) prison guard

wardrobe large cupboard for clothes; collection of clothes or costumes

wardroom mess-room for commissioned officers in a warship

ware goods, esp. of a kind that is mentioned
wares warehouse warehouseman

warfare (form of) fighting

warlock man who practises black magic

warm not hot or cold; having a moderate heat; friendly; generous; to make warm
warm-blooded warmer warmest warm-hearted warmish warmly warmth warm-up

warn to advise, esp. of future possible dangers
warner warning

warp to twist out of shape; to distort; lengthways yarn in a loom
warpage warper

warrant authorization or justification; to justify; to assure
warrantable warrantee warranter warrant-officer warrantor

warranty guarantee or assurance; warrant
warranties

warren area of ground having an interconnected series of rabbit burrows

warrior fighter

wart small hard growth on the skin caused by a virus

wary cautious or watchful
warier wariest warily wariness

was singular of past tense of **be**
wasn't

wash to clean with water; washing; thin coating of paint; rushing movement of waves behind a moving ship
washes washable wash-basin washboard wash-down washerman washerwoman wash-house washing-machine washing-up wash-out washroom washstand

washer washing-machine; flat ring for sealing a joint or used with a bolt or nut

washy pale or weak
washier washiest washily washiness

wasp kind of social stinging insect
waspish waspishly waspishness

wassailing (*archaic*) making merry
wassailer

waste to use carelessly and inefficiently; rejected becuase no longer needed; waste material; to weaken
wastable or *wasteable wastage wasteful wastefully wastefulness wasteland waste-paper waster wasting*

wastrel worthless person

watch to look at; to pay close attention to; to guard; small device that indicates the time, worn on the wrist
watches watch-chain watchdog watcher watchful watchfully watchfulness watchmaker watchman watch-tower watchword

water colourless odourless tasteless liquid that is a compound of oxygen and hydrogen; to sprinkle with water
waterage water-bed waterbird water-biscuit water-bottle water-cannon water-closet water-colour (US *water-color*) *watercourse watercress waterfall waterfowl waterfront water-heater waterhen water-hole water-ice watering-can watering-place waterish waterjump water-level water-lily water-line waterlogged water-main watermark water-melon water-mill water-pistol water-power waterproof water-rat water-rate watershed waterside water-skiing water-softener waterspout water-table watertight water-tower waterway water-wings waterworks watery*

watt basic metric unit of electric power
wattage

wattle structure of rods interwoven with twigs, used in building

wave to move the hand from side to side as a greeting; moving ridge of water on

the sea; curve; vibration conveying sound or light
waveband wavelength wavier waviest wavily waviness waving wavy
SEE PANEL at **waive**

waver to hesitate or fluctuate
waverer

wax[1] smooth fatty substance produced by bees
waxes waxen waxiness waxwork waxy

wax[2] (*of the moon*) to show an increasing area of illumination; to increase in power, etc.
waxes

way course, method, or direction; road or path
way-out wayside

wayfarer traveller on foot
wayfaring

waylay to approach; to intercept unexpectedly
waylaid waylayer waylaying

wayward capricious; uncontrollable
waywardly waywardness

we subject pronoun referring to the person who is speaking or writing and others

weak not strong; fragile; diluted
weak-kneed weakling weakly weak-minded weakness

weaken to make or become weak

weal raised mark on the skin produced by a blow

wealth large amount of money or riches; abundance
wealthier wealthiest wealthily wealthiness wealthy

wean to get a baby used to taking food other than its mother's milk

weapon object used in fighting
weaponed weaponless weaponry

wear to have as clothing on the body; damage by ordinary use
wearable wearer wore worn

weary (to make or become) tired
wearied wearier wearies weariest wearily weariness wearisome wearying

weasel kind of flesh-eating mammal with reddish-brown fur

weather conditions of the atmosphere as regards sunshine, rain and wind; to make or become dry, discoloured, etc. through exposure to the air; to survive a storm, etc.
weather-beaten weatherboard weatherboarding weatherbound weathercock weatherman weatherproof weather-vane weather-wise
SEE PANEL

---

weather, wether, or whether?

The *weather* is the atmospheric conditions as regards sunshine, rain, and wind: *What's the weather like?; listen to the weather forecast; The mountain rescue team have to work in all weathers.*

A *wether* is a castrated male sheep.

Whether is used to introduce an alternative or an indirect question: *I don't know whether it is right or not; They asked whether they might stay longer.*

---

weave to make a fabric by interlacing threads
weaver weaverbird weaving wove woven

web network of fine threads spun by a spider; membrane joining toes of some water birds
webbed web-footed web-toed

webbing strong strip of woven fabric

wed to marry
wedded or *wed wedding wedding-cake wedding-day wedding-ring*

we'd (*informal*) we had; we would

wedge (to fasten with a) tapering block of wood, etc.
wedging

Wedgwood (*trademark*) kind of fine ceramic ware

wedlock married state

Wednesday 4th day of the week

wee very small

weed troublesome wild plant
weedkiller

weeds widow's black mourning clothes

weedy containing weeds; very thin
weedier weediest weedily weediness

week period of 7 days
weekday weekend weekender weekly

weeny (*informal*) very small
weenier weeniest

weep to shed tears
weeping weepy wept

weevil kind of small beetle that is a pest to grain, fruit, etc.

weft crossways yarn in a loom

weigh to measure the weight of; to consider carefully; to raise anchor
weighbridge weigh-in

weight measure of heaviness; burden; influence or importance
weightier weightiest weightily weightiness weightless weightlessly weightlessness weightlifting weighty

weir low dam built across a river to raise the water-level or to regulate the flow of the river

weird strange; eerie; odd
weirdly weirdness

welch see **welsh**

welcome to greet in a friendly manner; received with pleasure
welcomer welcoming

weld to join pieces of metal by heat and hammering
welder

welfare good health, happiness and prosperity

well[1] in a good way; favourably; in good health
well-adjusted well-advised well-appointed well-being well-born well-bred well-disposed well-doer well-done well-established well-heeled well-informed well-known well-meaning well-off well-preserved well-read well-spoken well-timed well-to-do well-tried well-versed well-wisher

well[2] hole or shaft bored into the earth to reach a supply of water, oil, gas, etc.; source
wellspring

we'll (*informal*) we will

wellington waterproof boot of rubber, etc. that reaches almost to the knee

wellnigh almost

well-worn worn by much use; hackneyed

welsh or **welch** to evade paying a debt; to break one's promise
welsher or *welcher*

Welsh (language) of Wales
Welshman Welshwoman

Welsh rarebit or **rabbit** melted cheese on toast

welt strip of leather joining sole and upper of shoe; seam or edge on a garment; weal

welter to toss; turmoil

welterweight boxing weight

wen small cyst

wench (*old-fashioned* or *humorous*) young woman
wenches

wend (**wend one's way**) to proceed

went past tense of **go**

wept past tense and past participle of **weep**

were plural of past tense of **be**
weren't

we're (*informal*) we are

werewolf person who supposedly turns into a wolf at night
werewolves

west one of the four compass points; direction of sunset; opposite of east
westbound westerly westerner westernmost West Indian West Indies westward westwards

western of or in the west; film about cowboys, etc. in the western USA in the time of early development

westernize or **westernise** to influence with qualities associated with the West
westernization or *westernisation westernizing* or *westernising*

Westminster British parliament

wet moistened or covered with water; rainy; to make wet
wetlands wetly wetness wetsuit wetted wetter wettest wetting

wether castrated male sheep
SEE PANEL at **weather**

we've (*informal*) we have

whack (to strike with a) heavy blow

whale (to hunt a) very large sea mammal valued esp. for blubber
whalebone whaler whaling

wham (to strike with a) forceful heavy blow
whammed whamming

whammy (*informal*) unpleasant effect
whammies

wharf platform at a harbour or river where ships dock and load and unload
wharves or *wharfs wharfage wharfinger*

what used to ask about the identity, nature, etc. of a person or thing
what-d'you-call-it whatever what's whatsit whatsoever

wheat kind of cereal grass, from whose grain flour is made
wheaten wheatgerm wheatmeal

wheedle to obtain by flattery
wheedler wheedling

wheel circular frame that turns on an axle; to turn on an axis
wheelbarrow wheelbase wheelchair wheelie wheelwright

wheeler-dealer person who engages in tough business dealing or bargaining
wheeler-dealing

wheeze (to breathe with a) whistling chesty sound
wheezer wheezily wheeziness wheezing wheezy

whelk kind of large edible marine snail

whelp young of certain animals, esp. a dog; pup; to give birth to whelp

when at what time; at the time at which
whenever whensoever

whence from what place

where to, at, or in what place
whereas whereby wherefore whereon wheresoever whereupon wherever wherewithal

whereabouts in what general area; general location

wherry kind of boat
wherries wherryman

whet to sharpen by rubbing against a stone; to stimulate one's appetite
whetstone whetted whetting

whether used to introduce an alternative
SEE PANEL at **weather**

whey watery part of milk that separates from the curds

which what (person or thing); and that
whichever

whiff light puff of air; brief smell; to smell

whiffle to give out a light whistling sound; to vacillate
whiffler whiffling

while (short) period of time; during the

time that; effort; although; to spend time pleasantly
whiling whilst

whim sudden passing fanciful idea

whimper (to utter a) low whining sound
whimperer

whimsical fanciful
whimsicality whimsicalness

whimsy or **whimsey** whim
whimsies

whin furze

whine (to utter a) long plaintive cry; to complain
whiner whining whiny

whinge (*informal*) to complain constantly

whinny (to utter a) low gentle neighing sound
whinnies whinnied whinnying

whip instrument with a lash used for flogging; to flog with this; to beat eggs, cream, etc.
whipcord whiplash whipped whipping whippy whip-round

whippersnapper young insignificant pretentious person

whippet breed of dog similar to a greyhound

whippoorwill North American nightjar

whirl to swing or spin round fast
whirlpool whirlwind whirlybird

whirligig spinning toy; top

whirr (to make a) vibrating or buzzing noise

whisk instrument for beating eggs, cream, etc.; to beat with a whisk; to brush lightly from; to move quickly and lightly

whisker long hair growing near the mouth of a cat, etc.

whiskers (*informal*) moustache

whiskey whisky made in Ireland or the USA
whiskeys

whisky spirit distilled from fermented rye, barley, etc.
whiskies

whisper (to utter in a) soft voice, not vibrating the vocal cords
whisperer

whist card-game for 2 pairs of players

whistle (to make a) shrill piercing noise; device that produces a whistling noise
whistle-blower whistler whistle-stop whistling

whit smallest bit

Whit Whitsun

white colour of newly-fallen snow
whitecap white-collar whitefish whitefly whitely whiteness white-out whiter whitest whitewood whiting whitish or *whiteish*

whitebait young herring, etc. as food

Whitehall British government and its central administration

whiten to make or become white
whitener whitening

whitewash mixture of lime, chalk, water, etc. used to whiten walls; deceptive actions or statements to hide faults

whither (*chiefly formal*) to what place; to what purpose
whithersoever

whiting[1] kind of marine food fish

whiting[2] washed and ground white chalk

whitlow pus-producing inflammation of a finger or toe near the nail

Whitsun 7th Sunday after Easter; Whit Sunday
Whitsuntide

whittle to cut off thin strips from wood
whittling

whiz (to make a) loud buzzing sound; to move very fast
whizzes whiz-kid whizzed whizzing

who what person or people
whoever whosoever

who'd (*informal*) who had; who would

whodunit (*informal*) detective novel or play

whole not broken; complete; sound; unit; thing that is complete in itself
wholefood wholegrain wholehearted wholemeal wholeness wholewheat wholly

wholesale selling of goods in large quantities to a retailer for further selling; extensive
wholesaler

wholesome beneficial for health or moral or physical well-being
wholesomely wholesomeness

who'll (*informal*) who will

whom object form of **who**
whomever whomsoever

whoop (top utter a) loud excited cry; (to make a) crowing cough
whooping-cough

whop (*informal*) to beat, strike, or defeat
whopped whopping

whopper (*informal*) (something) very big; outrageous lie

whore (to act as a) prostitute
whoredom whore-hose whoremonger whoring

whorl coiled form or shape; ring of leaves or petals round a stem or central point
whorled

whortleberry bilberry
whortleberries

who's (*informal*) who is; who has

whose of whom; of which

why for what reason; reason
whys

wick twisted fibres in a candle

wicked bad or evil

wicker interlaced twigs
wickerwork

wicket (*cricket*) set of 3 stumps at which the batsman stands; small gate
wicket-gate wicket-keeper

wide extending a long way from side to side
wide-angle wide-eyed widely wideness wider wide-ranging widest width

widen to make or become wide
widener

widespread extensive; widely distributed

widgeon or **wigeon** kind of duck

widget (*informal*) device or gadget

widow woman whose husband has died, esp. one who has not remarried
widowed widowhood

widower man whose wife has died, esp. one who has not remarried

width measurement from one side to another; wideness

wield to handle a tool; to exercise authority, etc.

wife married woman in relation to her husband
wives wifely

wig artificial covering of hair
wigged wigless

wigeon see **widgeon**

wiggle to move from side to side jerkily
wiggling

wigwam North American Indian hut

wild not tame; savage; uncontrolled; stormy
wildfire wildfowl wildlife

wildcat wild cat; (*of a strike*) called spontaneously; hot-tempered person

wildebeest gnu

wilderness wild uncultivated area of land

wile deceitful trick; to deceive
wiling

wilful (US **willful**) intentional; stubborn
wilfully (US *willfully*) *wilfulness* (US *willfulness*)

will[1] auxiliary verb used to express the future, firm intention, etc.
would

will[2] mental faculty directing wishes, etc.; determination; to determine; written statement concerning disposal of property after death
will-power

willing ready or inclined
willingly willingness

will-o'-the-wisp light sometimes seen over marshy ground at night

willow kind of tree, often growing near streams and rivers, that bears catkins
willowy

willy-nilly haphazardly; performed without choice

wilt to droop or become limp
wilting

wily sly
wilier wiliest wilily wiliness

wimp (*informal*) feeble person
wimpish

wimple cloth covering worn over the head and round the neck and chin, worn by some nuns

win to come first in a competition; to gain a victory; to succeed
winner winning won

wince to shrink back slightly, from pain
wincer wincing

winceyette light cotton fabric

winch (to pull up with a) hoisting machine
winches

Winchester disk hermetically sealed metal computer disk

wind[1] movement of air; air breathed; gas in the stomach or intestines
windbag wind-blown windbreak windcheater windchill windfall windflower windless windmill windpipe windscreen wind-sock windsurfing windswept windward

wind[2] to turn; to coil; to tighten (up)
winder wound

windlass hoisting device consisting of a rope of chain wound round a drum

window opening in a wall, to provide light and air
window-box window-dressing window-frame window-pane window-seat window-shopping window-sill

windy blowing with a strong wind; wordy
windier windiest windily windiness

wine alcoholic drink made from fermented grapejuice
winebottle wineglass wineless winepress wineskin wine-tasting winy

wing limb of a bird or insect used in flight; projecting support or an aeroplane; to fly
winged winger wingless wing-nut

wink to close and open one eye deliberately; to shine intermittently
winker

winkle to prise out; see **periwinkle**[1]
winkling

winner person or thing that wins

winning victory or success; attractive
winningly winningness

winnow to separate chaff from grain

winsome attractive; charming
winsomely winsomeness

winter season between autumn and spring
wintergreen wintry or *wintery*

wipe to clean or dry by rubbing with a cloth
wipe-down wipe-out wiper wiping

wire thin flexible piece of metal; to install an electrical circuit in
wirable wire-haired wireworm wiring wiry

wireless (*old-fashioned*) radio set

wiry made of or like wire; thin and strong
wirier wiriest wirily wiriness

Wisconsin US state

wisdom knowledge and discernment

wise having knowledge and discernment; prudent
wiseacre wisecrack wisely wiser wisest

wish (to) desire
wishes wishbone wishful wishfully wishfulness

wishy-washy not substantial; watery

wisp thin streak or twist of hair; small bundle of hay
wispy

wisteria kind of climbing plant with showy flowers

wistful yearning sadly for something
wistfully wistfulness

wit ability to make ingeniously funny comments

witch person, esp. a woman, who practises magic or sorcery
witchcraft witch-doctor witchery witch-hunt

witch-elm see **wych-elm**

witch-hazel kind of (astringent medicinal solution made from the bark of a) shrub with decorative yellow flowers

with by means of; having

withdraw to take back; to remove; to retreat
withdrawal withdrawing withdrawn withdrew

withe or **withy** strong flexible twig, esp. of willow
withes or *withies*

wither to become dry and shrivelled
withering

withers highest part of the back of a horse

withhold to hold back; to keep back
withheld withholding

within inside; not more than

without not having

withstand to resist
withstander withstanding withstood

withy see **withe**

witless foolish

witness person who gives evidence in a law-court; to see first hand
witnesses witness-box witnesser

wits ability to think and act quickly; balanced mental well-being

witticism witty comment

witting intentional
wittingly

witty ingeniously funny

wizard sorcerer; skilled person
wizardly wizardry

wizen to make or become shrivelled
wizened

woad plant whose leaves yield a blue dye

wobble to move unsteadily
wobbler wobbliness wobbling wobbly

wodge (*informal*) bulky mass

woe great misery
woebegone woeful woefully woefulness

wok large Chinese bowl-shaped cooking pot

woke past tense of **wake**[1]

woken past participle of **wake**[1]

wold area of open rolling country

wolf wild flesh-eating dog-like animal; to eat greedily
wolves wolfed wolfhound wolfing wolfish

wolfram tungsten
wolframite

woman adult female human
women womanhood womanish womankind womanless womanlike womanliness womanly womenfolk

womanize or **womanise** to seek the company of women, esp. for sexual purposes
womanizer or *womaniser womanizing* or *womanising*

womb hollow organ of female mammals in which a foetus develops

wombat kind of Australian plant-eating burrowing marsupial mammal

won past tense and past participle of **win**

wonder feeling of surprise and awe; something marvellous; to feel wonder; to desire to know
wonderer wonderland wonderment wonder-struck wonder-working wondrous
SEE PANEL at **wander**

wonderful causing wonder; very good
wonderfully

wondrous (*poetic*) wonderful
wondrously wondrousness

wonky (*slang*) unsteady; crooked
wonkier wonkiest

wont accustomed
wonted

won't (*informal*) will not

woo to try to gain the affection or favour of
wooed wooer wooing

wood hard fibrous substance of which trees are made; group of trees, esp. one smaller than a forest
woodblock wood-carving woodcock woodcraft woodcut woodcutter wooded wooden woodland woodman wood-nymph woodpecker woodpile woodruff woodshed woodwork woodworm woody

woodbine honeysuckle

woodlouse kind of small wingless creature living in decaying wood, etc.
woodlice

woodwind wind orchestral instruments such as the oboe and clarinet

woof[1] weft

woof[2] (to make the) growling sound of a dog

woofer loudspeaker used for the reproduction of low-frequency sounds

wool fine soft hair from the fleece of sheep, goats, etc.
woollen (US *woolen*) *woolpack woolsack wool-sorter*

woolly of or made of wool; woolly sweater; vague
woollies woollier woolliest woollily woolliness

word meaningful unit of sounds or letters; comment or message; promise; to express in words
word-blind word-for-word wording wordless word-perfect wordplay

wordy having too many words
wordier wordiest wordily wordiness

wore past tense of **wear**

work effort (used to perform an activity); job; result of a process; to perform an activity; to function or operate
workable workaday workaholic work-basket workbench workbook workday worked worker workforce workhouse working-class workload workman workmanlike workmanship workmate workout workpiece workroom worksheet workshop workshy workstation work-table worktop work-to-rule

world earth, with all its inhabitants; human race
world-beater worldling world-shaking world-weary worldwide

worldly of this world; material, not spiritual
worldlier worldliest worldliness worldly-minded worldly-wise

worm long small invertebrate animal; to move very slowly
wormcast worm-eaten wormhole wormy

wormwood kind of plant with a bitter taste; bitterness

worn past participle of **wear**
worn-out

worry (to make or become) troubled or anxious; trouble or anxiety; (*of a dog*) to shake or tear at something with the teeth
worries worried worrier worrisome worrying

worse bad or ill to a greater degree
worse-off

worsen to make or become worse
worsened worsening

worship (to take part in an) act of reverence offered to a deity; to adore; title used to address an official such as a mayor or magistrate
worshipful worshipfully worshipped (US *worshiped*) *worshipper* (US *worshiper*) *worshipping* (US *worshiping*)

worst bad or ill to the greatest degree; to defeat

worsted kind of fine woollen yarn or cloth

worth having a value (of); deserving of
worthless worthlessly worthlessness

worthwhile worth the time or effort spent

worthy deserving or honourable; worthy person
worthier worthiest worthily worthiness

would past tense of **will**[1] used to express a condition
would-be wouldn't

wound[1] to injure the body; injury

wound[2] past tense and past participle of **wind**[2]

wove past tense of **weave**

woven past participle of **weave**

wrack seaweed or other marine vegetation

wraith apparition or ghost

wrangle to argue noisily; noisy argument
wrangler wrangling

wrap to fold paper, cloth, etc. round something; shawl or cloak
wrapped wrapper wrapping wrapround

wrasse kind of brightly coloured marine fish

wrath great anger
wrathful

wreak to inflict or cause

wreath ring of flowers, etc. as a sign of respect; coil of smoke, etc.
wreaths

wreathe to form into a wreath
wreathing

wreck to damage severely; severely damaged remains, esp. of a ship at sea
wreckage wrecker wrecking

wren kind of small brown songbird

wrench (to give a) sharp pull or twist; kind of spanner, esp. one with adjustable jaws
wrenches

wrest to pull sharply; to obtain forcefully

wrestle (to) struggle; to engage in wrestling
wrestler

wrestling unarmed hand-to-hand combat

wretch unfortunate person
wretches

wretched unfortunate; miserable
wretchedly wretchedness

wriggle to move with quick short twisting and turning actions
wriggler wriggling

wring to twist and squeeze tightly, esp. to force out water
wringer wringing wrung

wrinkle (to form a) slight ridge in a surface such as skin
wrinkling wrinkly

wrist joint between the hand and the forearm
wristband wristlet wrist-watch

writ formal legal document

write to form letters, words, etc. on paper, esp. with a pen or pencil
writable or *writeable write-down write-off writer write-up writing writing-desk writing-paper written wrote*

writhe to twist (part of) the body in pain
writher writhing

wrong not right, correct, or true; unjust action; to do a wrong to
wrongdoer wrongdoing wrong-foot wrongful wrongfully wrongfulness wrong-headed wrongly wrongness

wrought (*archaic*) past tense and past participle of **work**; formed; shaped by hammering

wrung past tense and past participle of **wring**

wry twisted; ironically humorous
wryer wryest wryly wryness

wryneck kind of bird related to a woodpecker

wych-elm or **witch-elm** kind of elm tree

wych-hazel see **witch-hazel**

Wyoming US state

xanthine (derivative of) yellow compound found in animal or plant tissue

xebec small Mediterranean 3-masted boat

xenon noble gas used in photography

xenophobia fear or hatred of foreigners
xenophobe xenophobic

xerography dry electrostatic process used in photocopying
xerographic

xerox to produce photocopies on a Xerox
xeroxed xeroxing

Xerox (*trademark*) kind of xerographic photocopying process
Xeroxes

Xmas (*informal*) short for **Christmas**

X-ray photograph or examination by a form of electromagnetic radiation that can penetrate solids; to treat, photograph, or examine by means of X-rays
X-rays X-rayed X-raying

xylem plant tissue that conveys water and salts

xylene colourless toxic flammable liquid obtained from wood tar, coal tar, etc.

xylography art of making wood engravings
xylograph xylographic

xylophone percussion instrument consisting of a series of wooden bars that are struck with 2 hammers
xylophonist

y and i

When a suffix is added to a word that ends in *-y*, the *-y* becomes an *-i* if the preceding letter is a consonant:

body, bodies carry, carries early, earliest easy, easily happy, happier hurry, hurried try, tried

Exceptions:

- words where a suffix beginning with an *-i* (e.g. *-ing*) is added:

baby, babyish try, trying

- individual words:

day, daily pay, paid say, said

Usage varies on the following:

dry, drier or *dryer drily* or *dryly fly, flyer* or *flier*

yacht small sailing-boat
yachting yachtsman yachtsmanship yachtswoman

Yahweh see **Jehovah**

yak large long-haired ox of central Asia

Yale (*trademark*) kind of lock with a revolving barrel

yam kind of (edible starch tuber of a) tropical climbing plant; sweet potato

yammer (*informal*) to whimper or grumble; yammering sound

Yangtze longest river in China

yank (*informal*) (to pull with a) short sharp jerk

yap (*of a dog*) (to make a) quick sharp bark; (*informal*) (to) jabber
yapped yapper yapping

yard[1] unit of length, 3 feet; long spar on a mast to support a sail
yardage yard-arm yardstick

yard[2] piece of enclosed ground

yarmulke Jewish skullcap

yarn (spun) thread, ready for use in knitting, weaving, etc.

yarrow kind of plant with clusters of white flowers

yashmak veil worn over the face by Muslim women

yaw to deviate from a (straight) course

yawl 2-masted sailing vessel

yawn to open the mouth wide and breathe, as when sleepy; act of yawning

ye (*archaic*) you

yea (*archaic*) yes; indeed

year time taken by the earth to go once round the sun; 12 months
yearbook yearling yearlong yearly

yearn to long for deeply
yearner yearning

yeast substance that causes fermentation, used in making bread and in brewing beer
yeasty

yell (to utter a) piercing loud cry

yellow colour of butter; to make or become yellow
yellow-hammer yellowish yellowness yellow-wood yellowy

yelp (to utter a) quick sharp cry
yelper

Yemen country in the Middle East
Yemeni

yen[1] money unit of Japan

yen[2] (*informal*) to have a yearning
yenned yenning

yeoman farmer who cultivates his own land; petty officer
yeomen yeomanry

yes used to express agreement or approval
yes-man

yesterday (on the) day before today; recent time

yesteryear (*poetic*) recent past

yet up to this time; still; nevertheless

yeti abominable snowman

yew kind of (wood of) evergreen tree with needle-like leaves

Yiddish language spoken by Jews
Yiddisher

yield to produce; result or amount produced; to give way; to surrender

yob (*slang*) loutish youth

yodel to sing with frequent changes from an ordinary to a high-pitched voice; yodelling cry
yodelled (US *yodeled*) *yodeller* (US *yodeler*) *yodelling* (US *yodeling*)

yoga Hindu spiritual philosophy; exercises designed to attain tranquillity and control
yogi yogic yogism

yoghurt or **yogurt** semi-solid food prepared from fermented milk

yoke wooden frame attached across the necks of oxen so that they can work together; to fasten a yoke on to; burden
yoking

yokel simple country person

yolk round yellow part of an egg

Yom Kippur (*Judaism*) Day of Atonement

yonder over there

yore time long past

you subject and object pronoun referring to the person or people addressed; referring to people generally

you'd (*informal*) you would; you had

you'll (*informal*) you will

young being in an early period of development
younger youngest youngish youngster

your possessive form of **you**
yours yourself yourselves

you're (*informal*) you are

youth quality of being young; young man; young people
youthful youthfully youthfulness

you've (*informal*) you have

yowl (to) wail

yo-yo toy consisting of a reel that can be spun up and down
yo-yos

ytterbium metallic element

yttrium metallic element

yuan money unit of China

yucca kind of plant of the lily family with spikes of white flowers

Yugoslavia former country in Europe
Yugoslav Yugoslavian

yule (*chiefly archaic*) Christmas
yule-log yuletide

yuppie or **yuppy** (*informal*) young urban professional person
yuppies

Z

zabaglione Italian dessert of egg yolks, sugar and Marsala wine

Zaïre country in Central Africa
Zaïrean

Zambia country in Central Africa
Zambian

zany crazily foolish; buffoon
zanies zanier zaniest zanily zaniness

zap (*slang*) to hit, kill, or destroy; to change television channels
zapped zapper zapping

zeal great enthusiasm or eagerness
zealot zealotry zealous zealously zealousness

zebra wild animal of the horse family with a black-and-white hide

zebu humped domesticated ox

Zen Japanese school of Buddhism

zenith highest point; point in the sky directly above the observer
zenithal

zephyr soft breeze

zeppelin large cigar-shaped airship

zero symbol 0; nought; nothing
zeros or *zeroes zero-rated*

zest stimulating excitement or enjoyment; peel of a citrus fruit
zestful zestfully zestfulness zesty

zeugma used of a word with 2 or more words of which it is strictly appropriate to only 1
zeugmas zeugmatic

zigzag line or course marked by sharp turns in alternate directions; to follow a zigzag course
zigzagged zigzagging

zilch (*slang*) nothing

zillion (*informal*) large unspecified number

Zimbabwe country in SE Africa
Zimbabwean

zinc brittle bluish-white metallic element; to treat with zinc
zinced or *zincked zincic zincing* or *zincking zincous*

zinnia kind of plant with brightly coloured flowers

Zion Jewish people; Jewish homeland; heaven
Zionism Zionist

zip fastening device consisting of 2 toothed edges and a sliding interlocking tab
zip-bag zip-fastener zipped zipping zippy zip-up

zirconium greyish-white metallic element
zircon

zither kind of stringed instrument played by plucking

zloty money unit of Poland
zlotys

zodiac zone of the sky divided into 12 equal parts
zodiacal

zombie corpse that has been revived by a supernatural spirit
zombies

zone area or district; to arrange or divide into zones
zonal zoning

zonked (*slang*) exhausted; drunk

zoo place where animals are kept
zoos

zooid independent animal body

zoology study of animals
zoological zoologist

zoom to move fast, esp. with a humming or buzzing sound

zoophyte animal resembling a plant

Zoroastrianism religion founded by the Persian prophet
Zoroaster

zucchetto skullcap worn by Roman Catholic Church ecclesiastics
zucchettos

zucchini courgette

Zulu member of a Bantu people of Natal

zugote cell resulting from fertilization

zymotic of or causing fermentation